Trustee Handbook

SEVENTH EDITION

Trustee Handbook

A GUIDE TO LABOR-MANAGEMENT EMPLOYEE BENEFIT PLANS

Claude L. Kordus
Editor and Contributor

International Foundation
EDUCATION – BENEFITS • COMPENSATION

The opinions expressed in this book are those of the authors.
The International Foundation of Employee Benefit Plans disclaims responsibility for views expressed and statements made in books published by the Foundation.

Edited by:
Claude L. Kordus, M.A., J.D. and SPHR
Patricia A. Bonner, Ph.D., GBA

Copies of this book may be obtained from:
Publications Department
International Foundation of Employee Benefit Plans
18700 W. Bluemound Road
Brookfield, WI 53045

Payment must accompany order.

Call (888) 334-3327, option 4, for price information or see www.ifebp.org/bookstore.
Published in 2011 by the International Foundation of Employee Benefit Plans, Inc.

Library of Congress Control Number: 2011937276
ISBN 978-0-89154-677-3
Printed in the United States of America

1M/911

Table of Contents

Health and Welfare Benefits

Pension and Retirement Benefits

Accounting and Auditing

Investment Management

Plan Administration and Communication

Supplemental Handbook Content at www.ifebp.org/Handbook7 (password protected)

About the Author

Claude L. Kordus
Editor and Contributor

Editing the seventh edition of the *Trustee Handbook* is a homecoming of sorts for Claude L. Kordus. As a young partner in a benefits consulting firm, Mr. Kordus saw a need for trustees to have a reference to help them understand the key issues facing multiemployer trustees. He developed the idea for and wrote much of the first three handbook editions. Mr. Kordus spent 34 years with Hewitt Associates (now Aon/Hewitt), the largest human resource consulting firm in the United States. A partner, region manager and 20-year member of the Hewitt's executive committee, he consulted to such major firms as S.C. Johnson and Johnson Controls. Among the Taft-Hartley multiemployer plans that benefited from his expertise were the Building Trades Pension Plan for Milwaukee and Vicinity, the Ornamental Iron Workers Pension Fund of Chicago and the Glass Bottle Blowers Retirement Medical Plan. Mr. Kordus was raised in Milwaukee and earned B.S., M.A. and J.D. degrees from Marquette University. He has completed a number of executive programs and is a lifetime member of Stanford Business School Alumni Association. Mr. Kordus has also been designated as a Senior Professional in Human Resources.

Foreword

One of the most troublesome realizations of a newly appointed and seated trustee of an employee benefit plan subject to ERISA (as well as the Internal Revenue Code, the Taft-Hartley Act and other federal laws) is the enormity of the task he or she has accepted. Suddenly, the business manager of the local union, or employer chapter manager, the carpenter or meat cutter, the trucking executive or painting contractor has become an active, managing director of a multimillion dollar insurance-type business.

Immediately, newly appointed trustees must learn and use a completely foreign vocabulary. The terms *COB, subrogation, recertification, concurrent review, TMJ* and *TPA* are some of the terms used in managing a welfare plan. Pension trustee counterparts must understand *QDROs, joint and survivor annuities, equities and convertibles, GICs and BICs, inverse interest curves* and *risk/reward trade-off, disintermediation and arbitrage, early retirement subsidies* and *actuarial equivalences.* The new trustee's left- and right-hand allies become fund counsel, the enrolled actuary, the administrative manager, the investment manager and the investment consultant as well as the International Foundation with its extensive publications and educational programs.

To meet the great need for authoritative information, the International Foundation of Employee Benefit Plans in 1970 published the first edition of the *Trustee Handbook.* Less than 300 pages in length, referencing only three major federal statutes and a dozen landmark court decisions, the book was an attempt to help new and experienced trustees to bridge the gap from labor or management representative to plan fiduciary. Since that time, the handbook has been updated five times, the most recent being the sixth edition in 2006.

Just as the last edition was being published, Congress passed a significant new piece of legislation affecting pension plans—the Pension Protection Act 2006. Of course, more recently there has been the Patient Protection and Affordable Care Act (PPACA), its amendments and associated regulations impacting health and welfare plans. A seventh edition was in fact, due.

Since Marc Gertner, my long-time friend and professional associate, was unable to serve as editor for this edition, I was approached to serve as editor and principle contributor. This is an enormous work covering the entire gamut of Taft-Hartley pension and welfare plans. It goes from plan organization through design, funding, delivery and communication of benefits. It covers legal, actuarial, accounting, investment and administrative issues. A new chapter has been added concerning apprenticeship and training funds.

I am appreciative to the many contributors to this important reference. Those who have written articles are enumerated in the table of contents and at the outset of each article, as well as profiled in the contributor's section. I am particularly appreciative to the members of the ad hoc editorial committee for this update. These leaders in the field of multiemployer plans have provided the following to the editor and foundation staff:

- Help in selecting topics
- Help in selecting authors
- Reviews of copy in area(s) of expertise
- Communication with the editor and author(s) concerning content and style changes
- Help in marketing the new handbook at International Foundation meetings.

The *Trustee Handbook* would not be a quality publication without the great contribution of time and talent from this group of experts who are among the top specialists in the field:

Name	Affiliation	Specialty
Lawrence R. Beebe	Bond Beebe	Accounting
Joseph A. Brislin	Timber Operators Council, Inc. (retired)	Law
William K. Ecklund	Felhaber, Larson, Fenlon & Vogt, P.A.	Law
R. Scott Gregory	R. Scott Gregory, Inc.	Actuarial Sciences
Sandy Lincoln	BMO Asset Management, N.A.	Investments
Jackson A. Loos	Rael & Letson	Welfare Plans
Regina C. Reardon	Healthcare Strategies, Inc.	Administration
Peter M. Rosene	Felhaber, Larson, Fenlon & Vogt, P.A.	Law

I am particularly grateful to Patricia Bonner, Associate Director of Publications at the Foundation, whose professional editing and organization made this text possible, and kept it on time. Thanks also to other Foundation staff who have worked behind the scenes providing expertise in editing, design and proofreading. Persons of special note who contributed in these ways are Suzanne Aschoff, Michael Krieger, Rebecca Martin, Rachel Ver-Duin and Christine Vogel. Finally, I must thank Michael Wilson, Chief Executive Officer; Beth Harwood, Vice President, Educational Programs and Content Management; and Dee Birschel, Senior Director, Information Services and Publications for their active and thoughtful support for this project.

Claude L. Kordus

Preface

The lifeblood of the International Foundation is, without question, its volunteers. Trustees, administrators, attorneys and others who work in the complex field of Taft-Hartley fund oversight contribute their experiences and insights to help others in the field.

For more than three decades, the *Trustee Handbook* has reflected the experience and knowledge of Foundation volunteers. More than 50 multiemployer trustees, administrators and advisors have contributed to this book as authors and reviewers. Additionally, the book exemplifies the Foundation's mission to provide leading, objective and relevant information for employee benefit leaders.

This seventh edition, which has been painstakingly edited to be the most comprehensive, concise and helpful version to date, could not have been done without Claude Kordus. Claude has volunteered for the Foundation since 1960, serving in a wide range of capacities. He has firsthand experience with the implementation of ERISA and many of the momentous changes that occurred in the benefits field over the last half-century. We are indeed, fortunate to have Claude serving as the editor of this time-tested publication.

I am certain this book will be an important reference for every trustee and administrator making informed decisions on the management of a multiemployer benefit plan.

Michael Wilson

Michael Wilson
CEO, International Foundation

Contributors*

Rory Judd Albert is the co-chairman of Proskauer Rose LLP's labor and employment law department, as well as the head of its employee benefits and executive compensation law group. He provides leadership and guidance to almost 165 labor relations, employment and employee benefits law attorneys of the firm. Mr. Albert serves as legal counsel for boards of trustees of more than 60 multiemployer plans. Elected one of the "top 40" employee benefit law attorneys in the country, he is a member of the American College of Employee Benefits Counsel. Mr. Albert obtained his juris doctor degree from Columbia Law School and received his B.S. degree in business management from the Massachusetts Institute of Technology.

Daniel Aronowitz is president of Ullico Casualty Company. He has been instrumental in the return of Ullico Casualty as a leading provider of specialty property and casualty insurance risk solutions for labor unions and organized employers. Ullico Casualty is a key insurer for its affinity market, offering fiduciary and other professional liability programs, creative captive and loss-sensitive workers' compensation, and commercial lines solutions. Prior to joining Ullico, Mr. Aronowitz was a partner at Shaw Pittman in Washington, D.C. and a nationally renowned directors' and officers' insurance lawyer. He is a graduate of Ohio State University and Vanderbilt University School of Law.

Kathryn L. Bakich is senior vice president and national health care compliance practice leader for The Segal Company in Washington, D.C. Ms. Bakich has more than 20 years of experience specializing in research and analysis of federal laws and regulations affecting health coverage. She is a member of the Health Technical Issues Taskforce of the American Benefits Council (ABC) and the Employers Council on Flexible Compensation (ECFC) Flex Advisory Council. She is the author of the *Employers' Guide to HIPAA Privacy Requirements* published by Thompson Publishing Group and is a member of the International Foundation's Government Liaison Committee. Ms. Bakich received her J.D. degree from the University of Missouri in Columbia.

Mark Bartmann is a real estate investment associate based in the Chicago office of R.V. Kuhns & Associates, Inc. His current responsibilities include performing due diligence analysis on private equity real estate managers, underwriting real estate investments and creating performance measurement reports for clients. Prior to joining RVK, Mr. Bartmann worked as a project manager and financial analyst for Ridge Property Trust where he developed financial analysis models, performed due diligence on various real estate investments and assisted in property management activities. Mr. Bartmann graduated from the University of Wisconsin-Madison with a bachelor of business administration degree, majoring in real estate and finance.

Lawrence R. Beebe* is a partner with the accounting firm of Bond Beebe, based in the Washington, D.C. metropolitan area. He has over 40 years of experience as an accountant and auditor, specializing in labor and em-

*Denotes members of the ad hoc editorial committee

ployee benefit plans. Mr. Beebe is currently the chair of the International Foundation's Financial Review Committee and an advisory member of its Board of Directors. He previously chaired the Accountants and Continuing Education Committees and was a member of the Educational Program Committee. Mr. Beebe's book *Payroll Auditing: A Guide for Multiemployer Plans* was published by the International Foundation in 2008. He received a B.S. degree in accounting from the University of Maryland and an M.S. degree from Central Michigan University.

Sean M. Brandle is vice president and leader of the national pharmacy benefits practice for The Segal Company. Mr. Brandle's current focus is the evaluation of PBM services, prescription plan design strategies and overall PBM performance measure development. He provides national guidance to Segal consultants regarding all aspects of prescription drug benefit plans. Prior to joining The Segal Company, Mr. Brandle served as a financial director at a major PBM organization and an underwriting manager for an insurance company with responsibilities for risk assessment, rate setting and creation of custom risk-sharing arrangements for group life, medical and prescription drug plans. He received a B.A. degree in economics with business emphasis from Montclair State University.

Steven A. Brannon is a consulting actuary with McGinn Actuaries Ltd. He has worked for both regional and national actuarial consulting firms as an actuary and benefits consultant. His experience covers local, statewide and regional multiemployer programs. Mr. Brannon has served as consultant to several of the largest multiemployer plans in the United States. He is skilled in all phases of multiemployer health and welfare and pension programs, with an emphasis on creative design, innovative cost strategies and clear communications. Mr. Brannon is a fellow of the Society of Actuaries and an enrolled actuary. He graduated from Pomona College with a B.A. degree in mathematics and holds a master's degree in mathematics from California State University.

Joseph A. Brislin* has served as a management trustee of the CIC–TOC and TOC–IAM Woodworkers Pension and Health and Welfare Funds. He was general counsel for TOC and an attorney with the law firm of Dezendorf, Spears, Lubersky & Campbell. Mr. Brislin has served as the president of the Joint Council of Presidents of the Western Pension Conference. An active supporter of the International Foundation, he has served on a myriad of committees. Mr. Brislin is a Past President and a member of the Strategic Initiative Steering Committee. He is the author of *Multiemployer Plans: A Guide for New Trustees* and a contributing author of four other Foundation publications. Mr. Brislin received his J.D. degree from the University of Oregon School of Law.

Bennett E. Choice is an attorney in the employee benefits department of Reinhart Boerner Van Deuren s.c., a law firm based in Milwaukee, Wisconsin. He advises Taft-Hartley trustees on issues involving the design and operation of health and welfare, defined benefit pension, 401(k) and other defined contribution plans. Mr. Choice also counsels trustees on their fiduciary obligations. He is a co-author of the *HIPAA Privacy Compliance Manual for Health Plans.* Mr. Choice obtained his bachelor of business administration degree from the University of Iowa. He is a graduate (with high honors) of the University of Iowa College of Law.

Terry A. Dennison is a senior partner and U.S. director of consulting with Mercer. In this capacity he is responsible for developing and disseminating the intellectual capital and consulting processes supporting Mercer IC's Investment Consulting business. During his 38-year career, Mr. Dennison has had the opportunity to develop a broad and deep knowledge of all aspects of investment management. His investment consulting clients include a number of large private and public sector clients. As of June 30, 2011, he served as the lead consultant to clients with assets totaling over $50 billion. Mr. Dennison holds an M.B.A. degree in finance, investments and banking from the University of Wisconsin–Madison and is a certified public accountant.

Ted L. Disabato is managing director of Disabato Advisers, LLC in Chicago, Illinois. Prior to establishing Disabato Advisers, he spent more than ten years as senior vice president of Kidder Peabody & Co., where he managed Kidder's national investment consulting practice and administered the firm's retirement plans. Previously, he was chief investment officer for Clark Consulting, an NYSE-listed national benefits consulting firm, and has been the primary investment consultant for many nationally recognized corporate, Taft-Hartley, foundation and endowment, health care, and public funds. Mr. Disabato is also a member of the Research Committee of the Profit Sharing/401(k) Council of America. He received a master's degree in finance from the Wharton School and a B.S. degree in chemical engineering from the University of Illinois.

William K. Ecklund is a shareholder of the law firm of Felhaber, Larson, Fenlon & Vogt, P.A., where he specializes in the areas of employee benefits and nonprofits and trade associations. The firm represents many multiemployer plans. Mr. Ecklund is also general counsel to the National Finishing Contractors Association and to the Sheet Metal and Air Conditioning Contractors' National Association. He has written articles and spoken before many groups on ERISA and employee benefit-related matters. Mr. Ecklund is the founder and first chair of the Employee Benefits Section of the Minnesota State Bar Association, a fellow of the American College of Employee Benefits Counsel and a former chair of the International Foundation's Attorneys Committee. He received his juris doctorate from the University of Minnesota Law School.

William J. Einhorn* serves as administrator of the Teamsters Health and Welfare and Pension Trust Funds of Philadelphia and Vicinity, and is the president of a third-party administration firm servicing 12 other Taft-Hartley trust funds. He has particular expertise in benefit administration, claims automation, benefit cost containment, data analysis, plan design and management reporting. Prior to joining the funds on a full-time basis, Mr. Einhorn actively practiced law, specializing in labor relations and ERISA. He received his J.D. and B.A. degrees from Temple University in Philadelphia. Mr. Einhorn has served as chair of the Foundation's Health Care Management and Coalition Committee and its Administrators Committee, as well as a member of the Foundation's Financial Review, Accountants and Educational Programs Committees. He presently serves as a voting member of the Foundation's Board of Directors and member of its Committee on Training and Education.

Vivian C. Folk is a partner with Shumaker, Loop & Kendrick, Toledo, Ohio. Active in employee benefits for more than 30 years, her law practice is devoted primarily to serving as counsel to employee benefit plans, fiduciary responsibility and prohibited transaction issues. Ms. Folk has spoken extensively in these fields. She is co-author of *The Annotated Fiduciary* (3rd ed.); and contributing author to the last three editions of the *Trustee Handbook* and multiple editions of the *IF Textbook for Plan Trustees, Administrators and Advisors.* Ms. Folk has served as an arbitrator for the AAA Multiemployer Pension Plan Amendments Act Panel. She received her law degree from Case Western University Law School, where she was executive editor of the *Law Review.*

Ken Friedman is a consulting actuary with the New York office of Milliman. He has more than 30 years of pension and employee benefit consulting experience and provides advice in the design and implementation of comprehensive pension and welfare plans to both domestic and international companies; not-for-profit organizations; governmental employers; and multiemployer pension funds. Services to his clients include defined benefit plan funding and expense valuations, retiree medical expense valuations, experience studies, modeling of projected plan liabilities and costs, assisting bargaining parties during collective bargaining negotiations, plan terminations and mergers. Mr. Friedman has a B.A. degree in mathematics from the University of Pennsylvania.

Jeffrey R. Fuller is a director with Reinhart Boerner Van Deuren s.c., in Milwaukee. He has authored several articles in legal, tax and employee benefit journals dealing with employee benefits and compensation arrangements. Mr. Fuller serves as counsel for several national and regional Taft-Hartley multiemployer pension and welfare plans, and for a number of corporate retirement plans. He has served on the International Foundation's Board of Directors and several committees, and presently serves as general counsel to the Foundation.

R. Scott Gregory,* FSA, EA, is president of R. Scott Gregory, Inc. (RSGI), an actuarial and consulting firm in Annapolis, Maryland. Prior to establishing RSGI, he was a senior actuary at PriceWaterhouse and a principal with Mercer. Mr. Gregory has served a range of plan sponsors including multiemployer plans. He has assisted with the design, creation, installation, costing, administration and communication of retirement plans. Mr. Gregory has calculated withdrawal liability amounts and testified in legal proceedings. He is a frequent speaker at International Foundation events. Mr. Gregory has chaired the Actuaries and Consultants Committee and is currently an Advisory Director and a member of the Professionals Committee.

Carrie J. Grove, a partner in the Employee Benefits Group of Seyfarth Shaw in Los Angeles, has over 12 years' experience as an ERISA attorney. Her practice focuses on large multiemployer pension and benefit plans. Ms. Grove routinely reviews private equity and hedge fund limited partnership agreements and related documentation, and negotiates side letters containing provisions that afford greater protection to the ERISA plans she represents. Ms. Grove also has experience with advising employers on the topics of withdrawal liability, COBRA, health care reform and domestic partner issues. She received her law degree magna cum laude from the University of California Hastings College of the Law.

Lonie Hassel is principal at Groom Law Group, an employee benefits law firm in Washington, D.C. She joined the firm after eight years of practice at the Pension Benefit Guaranty Corporation (PBGC). At Groom Law Group, Ms. Hassel advises ERISA-covered pension and welfare plans and public employee plans on fiduciary issues and defends and prosecutes individual and class actions involving fiduciary breach and benefit claims. She also represents clients on employee benefit issues arising in bankruptcy and in mergers and acquisitions. Ms. Hassel negotiates agreements with PBGC relating to plan terminations, PBGC premiums and multiemployer plan issues. She received her J.D. degree from the University of Virginia School of Law.

Michael I. Helmer is a vice president and consulting actuary with The Segal Company's Minneapolis office where he consults with clients on design, funding and reserve strategies for health and welfare plans and funding requirements for pension plans. He joined The Segal Company as a health actuary in their Chicago office. Prior to joining Segal, Mr. Helmer provided actuarial consulting services to the national health and welfare programs and pension plans of a large religious denomination. He is an enrolled actuary and a member of the American Academy of Actuaries. Mr. Helmer received a B.A. degree in mathematics from Rutgers University in New Brunswick, New Jersey.

Jill S. Herbold is a consulting actuary with the Indianapolis Health Practice for Milliman. She has developed an expertise in the analysis of the financial risks associated with financing and delivery of health care services. Ms. Herbold routinely works with self-funded groups, multiemployer funds, insurance companies and managed care organizations. Her experience includes self-funded financial projections, benefit plan design, reserve reviews and opinions, retiree medical evaluations, and provider contract evaluations. An honors graduate of the University of Illinois–Urbana, Ms. Herbold is a fellow of the Society of Actuaries and a member of the American Academy of Actuaries.

Edward A. Kaplan is senior vice president and national health practice leader in New York for The Segal Company. He has worked with managed care programs since 1986, with special emphasis on pricing and plan design strategies for managed medical, dental and prescription drug programs. Mr. Kaplan created the Segal Health Plan Trend Cost Survey in 1996, now a standard in the industry. Prior to joining The Segal Company, he served as an associate manager of underwriting for a major insurance carrier and health consultant for a major consulting firm. Mr. Kaplan received a B.A. degree in economics from Rutgers University. He is a member of several pharmacy benefit industry advisory boards.

Richard T. Kennedy is a member of the Employment Law and Employee Benefits Group at the Pittsburgh law firm of Meyer, Unkovic & Scott LLP. He has legal, consulting and administrative experience in all aspects of employee benefits. Mr. Kennedy's practice focuses on the representation of multiemployer pension and welfare plans. Besides his law firm practice, Mr. Kennedy's background includes positions with the U.S. Department of Labor, an international management consulting firm and a major manufacturing corporation. He is a graduate of the University of Pittsburgh School of Law and received a bachelor's degree and master's degree from Ball State University.

Travis J. Ketterman is a partner with the Chicago law firm of Whitfield McGann & Ketterman. His practice is devoted to representing labor organizations and multiemployer trust funds in federal court litigation. In fall 2008, his first book, *Collecting Employer Contributions: The ERISA Litigation Guide,* was published by the International Foundation of Employee Benefit Plans. Mr. Ketterman has also published numerous articles in various bar journals, all involving the federal practice of law. Mr. Ketterman graduated from Marquette University with a triple major in political science, philosophy and criminology and received his juris doctor degree from Loyola University Chicago School of Law.

Dainius A. (Dan) Krivinskas is a consultant and director of real estate consulting with R.V. Kuhns & Associates, Inc. Located in the firm's Chicago office, he has 12 years' experience with governmental organizations in real estate, private equity, mergers and acquisitions. Mr. Krivinskas started his career with the United Nations Development Program and the Government of Lithuania, focusing on transition economics. He has extensive relationships with corporations, endowments and public pension programs. His experience includes developing investment policy statements, structuring pooled fund and joint venture investments, conducting manager searches, and reviewing client portfolios. A licensed attorney, Mr. Krivinskas earned his A.B. degree in economics and public policy from Duke University and a J.D. degree from the University of Michigan.

Scott Krouse is a consultant with R.V. Kuhns & Associates, Inc. and is located in the firm's Chicago office. He joined RVK from RBC Capital Markets where he was the vice president of investor relations. his previous experience includes working for Courtland Partners, Ltd. as a consultant and with National City Bank as a business analyst and audit supervisor. Mr. Krouse has advised public and Taft-Hartley pension funds on real estate investment allocations, due diligence, portfolio modeling, pooled funds analysis and private real estate joint ventures. His responsibilities at RVK include meeting with real estate managers and working with real estate clients, as well as general consulting. He assists on the real estate needs of general consulting clients. Mr. Krouse has a B.S. degree in finance from Pennsylvania State University and an M.B.A. degree from the Weatherhead School of Management at Case Western Reserve University.

David C. Lee is a partner in the accounting firm of Berdon LLP, with more than 30 years' experience in public accounting. He specializes in providing accounting services to employee benefit funds and labor organizations. Mr. Lee served on the task force that changed reporting rules for New York City municipal benefit funds and on the Employee Benefits Committee of the American Institute of Certified Public Accountants. He has published in the *Employee Benefits Journal,* and he regularly teaches continuing professional education courses to attorneys and accountants. A former member of the International Foundation's Accountants Committee, Mr. Lee has spoken and moderated at Foundation conferences. He received his education from Pace University.

Sandy Lincoln* is chief market strategist for BMO Asset Management, North America and is located in Milwaukee, Wisconsin. His prior employment includes chief investment officer of Kemper Financial Services and Kemper Corporation, president of William M. Mercer's Investment Consulting Services subsidiary and a member of the Mercer Board of Directors. Mr. Lincoln has been quoted in the *Wall Street Journal* and *Investors Business Daily* and has been a featured guest on CNBC, CNN and Bloomberg News. He contributed to papers regarding asset allocation, S&P inclusion effect and performance measurement time horizon. Mr. Lincoln holds an undergraduate degree from Valparaiso University and an M.B.A. degree from Loyola University.

Jackson A. Loos* is chief consulting officer with Rael & Letson, an actuarial and consulting firm in Colorado, Washington and California. He has been a health, welfare and pension consultant for over 30 years. Mr. Loos is a graduate of Wesleyan University and also has completed postgraduate curricula at Wayne State University and San Francisco City College. He has served as commissioner on the Health Service System for the city and county of San Francisco and was a member of the mayor's task force on family policy. Mr. Loos has been a member of the International Foundation's Health Care Services Committee, the Public Employees Committee, the Educational Program Committee, and the Actuaries/Consultants Committee, serving as chair for four years.

Edward R. Mackiewicz, a partner with the law firm of Steptoe & Johnson LLP, practices primarily in the employee benefits area, representing clients before ERISA agencies and advising them on pending legislation. Prior to joining Steptoe & Johnson, Mr. Mackiewicz served as general counsel of the Pension Benefit Guaranty Corporation. He also served as the multiemployer plan representative on the Secretary of Labor's ERISA Advisory Council in 1991 and 1992. Mr. Mackiewicz received a B.A. degree from Yale University and a J.D. degree from Columbia University Law School. He co-authored a text on *Pension Plan Terminations,* published by BNA Books.

Jeffrey D. Mamorsky is a shareholder and chairman of the employee benefits group of Greenberg Traurig LLP. He serves as employee benefits counsel to major multiemployer pension and welfare funds among others. Mr. Mamorsky participated in the drafting of ERISA and subsequently authored a two-volume treatise, *Employee Benefits Law,* which has been cited as authority by the U.S. Supreme Court and other federal and state courts. He is also the editor of the *Employee Benefits Handbook,* author of *Health Care Benefits Law* and founder and editor in chief of the *Journal of Compensation and Benefits.* Mr. Mamorsky received a J.D. degree from New York Law School and an LL.M. degree, in taxation from New York University School of Law. He is a charter fellow of The American College of Employee Benefits Counsel.

Roman Nemtsov is a consultant in the Chicago office of R.V. Kuhns & Associates, Inc. He has six years' experience in private and public equity real estate. Mr. Nemtsov assists in the review and negotiation of private equity real estate and infrastructure transactions. He also has experience developing investment policy statements, conducting manager searches and reviewing client portfolios. As a former member of the performance management team for Courtland Partners, Ltd., Mr. Nemtsov monitored performance of public and Taft-Hartley pension funds. His prior experience includes financial analysis and internal auditing positions with MeadWestvaco Corp. Mr. Nemtsov earned a B.S. degree in business administration with a concentration in finance from Wright State University.

Philip R. O'Brien is a shareholder in Reinhart Boerner Van Deuren's Taft-Hartley group of the Employee Benefits Practice Area. He serves Taft-Hartley health and pension fund clients across the country with a particular focus on ERISA contribution delinquency protection, contract enforcement, and subrogation and reimbursement issues. An experienced author and speaker, Mr. O'Brien has frequently presented to professional, business and plan management audiences on the most relevant and topical issues impacting employee benefits. He earned his law degree and his undergraduate degree magna cum laude from Marquette University. Since 2005, Mr. O'Brien has consistently been selected as one of Wisconsin's Super Lawyers in the field of employee benefits.

Paul J. Ondrasik Jr. is a partner in the law firm of Steptoe & Johnson, LLP, working primarily in the employee benefits plan field, with particular emphasis on ERISA litigation and fiduciary responsibility matters. Mr. Ondrasik has received a first ranking in the area of national ERISA litigation in *Chambers USA 2011, America's Leading Business Lawyers.* He is a graduate of Princeton University and the University of Virginia School of Law and is a charter fellow of the American College of Employee Benefits Counsel. Mr. Ondrasik has served the International Foundation as an Advisory Director and as a member of its Government Liaison, Educational Programs and Attorneys Committees.

Timothy J. Parsons is special counsel at Pendleton, Friedberg, Wilson and Hennessey P.C. A nationally recognized ERISA expert, he represents private and governmental multiemployer and single employer benefit plans. Mr. Parsons has particular expertise representing fiduciaries and administrators of collectively bargained plans in contested regulatory matters and federal court litigation. He is a frequent speaker and prolific author. A charter fellow of the American College of Employee Benefits Counsel, Mr. Parsons has served as chair of the Foundation's Benefit Communications Committee and on both the Attorneys Committee and the Educational Program Committee. He has also served as co-chair of several committees of the Employee Benefits Committee of the Section of Labor and Employment Law of the American Bar Association. He is the current co-chair of the Ethics Subcommittee.

Regina C. Reardon* is president of Healthcare Strategies, Inc., a third-party employee benefits administration and consulting firm that provides services to Taft-Hartley health and welfare, pension, prepaid legal and other trust funds. Prior to founding Healthcare Strategies, Inc., Ms. Reardon was engaged in the private practice of law, specializing in labor, employment practices and employee benefits law. She continues in the practice of employment and employee benefits law on a limited basis. Ms. Reardon received a juris doctor degree from Widener University School of Law. She currently serves as a member of the Administrators Committee and as a Voting Director on the International Foundation's Board of Directors.

Julian M. Regan is a senior consultant who joined The Marco Consulting Group (MCG) as part of the firm's expanding commitment to public and jointly trusteed benefit plans. He has provided leadership, overseen investments and managed risk for some of the nation's largest institutional investors. Prior to joining MCG, Mr. Regan was executive director, New York State Deferred Compensation Board. He also served as a chief divisional risk officer for Fidelity Institutional Retirement Services Company and as assistant general manager and budget director, Massachusetts Bay Transportation Authority. In 2005, he was appointed to the IRS Advisory Committee on Tax Exempt and Government Entities. Mr. Regan received his M.B.A. degree from Suffolk University.

Peter M. Rosene* is a partner of the law firm Felhaber, Larson, Fenlon & Vogt. He has served as primary attorney for many of the firm's multiemployer fringe benefit fund clients. Mr. Rosene advises on all aspects of federal fiduciary law, federal health care compliance, pension plan design/compliance issues and vendor contracting. He is a frequent national speaker on employee benefit and fiduciary law topics, primarily with the International Foundation. Mr. Rosene teaches the pension design segment of the Essentials of Multiemployer Plans at the International Foundation's headquarters each year and is a member of its Professionals Committee. He graduated from William Mitchell College of Law with a J.D. degree.

Neal S. Schelberg is a partner in the law firm of Proskauer Rose LLP. He practices exclusively in the employee benefits area and provides legal counsel to single employer and multiemployer pension and welfare funds and their plan sponsors. Mr. Schelberg is a fellow of the American College of Employee Benefits Counsel and has been recognized as a leading employee benefits lawyer by such organizations as U.S. Legal 500, *National Law Journal* and Euromoney Legal Group Guide to the World's Leading Labour and Employment Lawyers. Mr. Schelberg writes and speaks frequently on employee benefit law topics. He has taught employee benefit courses at Fordham University Law School and New York University. Mr. Schelberg is a graduate of the Hofstra University School of Law and the Georgetown University Law Center.

Paul M. Secunda is an associate professor of law at the Marquette University Law School, where he teaches employee benefits law, labor and employment law, and education law. Mr. Secunda writes, researches and lectures on public and private pension and welfare plan issues. Recent work has included a constitutional analysis of public pension litigation, an analysis of the current state of multiemployer benefit plans, and a proposal concerning the intersection of remedial and preemption provisions under ERISA. He is a member of the American Law Institute, past chair of the Association of American Law School's Section on Employee Benefits and Executive Compensation, and a chapter co-editor of the American Bar Association's *Employee Benefits Law Treatise.*

Barry S. Slevin, president of the law firm of Slevin & Hart, P.C., specializes in employee benefits law and related litigation. He represents many pension, health, annuity, 401(k), severance and legal benefit plans, and is advisor to a number of labor organizations and companies. Mr. Slevin has testified before Congress on employee benefit matters, speaks often before a number of groups and has published numerous articles in the field of employee benefits. He was formerly special counsel with PBGC. Mr. Slevin is a charter fellow of the American College of Employee Benefits Counsel and has been recognized as a Super Lawyer for Employee Benefits/ERISA law in the publication *Washington, D.C. Super Lawyers* for 2007 through 2010.

Patrick C. Stines is a partner at BST, a multidisciplinary public accounting firm with a specialty in providing accounting and auditing services to multiemployer employee benefit funds. He has over 12 years of public accounting experience working exclusively with Taft-Hartley plans and labor unions. Mr. Stines's clients include some of the largest local unions in the New York region. His experience includes development of internal control policies, cost-allocation studies, Department of Labor examinations and compliance payroll audits. He has co-authored articles concerning financial reporting featured in *Benefits Magazine* published by the International Foundation. Mr. Stines graduated from the State University of New York at Old Westbury with a bachelor of science degree.

William H. Tobin is a shareholder of Reinhart Boerner Van Deuren s.c. in Milwaukee, Wisconsin. His practice focuses on advising trustees of Taft-Hartley multiemployer pension and health and welfare plans throughout the country on all aspects of employee benefits. Mr. Tobin regularly speaks and writes on retirement and health and welfare issues. He has spoken at the International Foundation's Annual Conference. Mr. Tobin is a past director of the Wisconsin Retirement Plan Professionals, Ltd., serves on the board of the Milwaukee Bar Association's Employee Benefits Section and is a member of the Wisconsin Bar Association. He received his bachelor of arts degree from Middlebury College and his law degree cum laude from Boston University School of Law.

Michael A. Van Sertima, CPA, is a partner with Gould, Kobrick & Schlapp, P.C. of New York City. He specializes in performing financial statement, operational and internal control audits of employee benefit plans and labor organizations. Mr. Van Sertima earned bachelor of science and master of science degrees in accounting and business management from the City University of New York. He is an adjunct lecturer in accounting and auditing at the City University of New York and is a member of the American Institute of Certified Public Accountants and the New York State Society of Certified Public Accountants. Mr. Van Sertima is an International Foundation speaker and author.

Joseph A. Vater Jr. is a partner with the law firm of Meyer, Unkovic & Scott LLP in Pittsburgh, Pennsylvania. In addition to serving as legal counsel to multiemployer funds in Western Pennsylvania, he represents national funds in collection and other litigation. Mr. Vater has more than 30 years' experience in the multiemployer field representing health and welfare funds, apprenticeship plans and defined benefit and defined contribution funds. He has a J.D. degree from the University of Pittsburgh School of Law. Mr. Vater is a frequent speaker on multiemployer plan issues and has published articles on collection and insurance issues for the International Foundation.

Russell J. Walker is a vice president and principal with the Consulting Division of Wilshire Associates, an investment consulting and analytics firm based in Santa Monica, California. Mr. Walker joined Wilshire in 1988 and currently conducts investment research within Wilshire Consulting. His specialties include portfolio risk analysis, performance attribution and performance measurement. Prior to his investment research work, Mr. Walker served as a consulting team liaison for Wilshire Consulting's Performance Measurement Group. His duties included heading quality assurance for Wilshire Analytics, as well as client service and support for several Wilshire Analytics software applications. Mr. Walker earned a B.A. degree from the University of Pittsburgh.

Ralph M. Weinberg is a principal and consulting actuary with Milliman. He co-heads the employee benefits practice in the Chicago office of Milliman. Mr. Weinberg joined the firm in 1993. He has more than 30 years of experience in the design, funding, communication and administration of retirement plans, working with corporate and multiemployer plan sponsors. Mr. Weinberg is a frequent speaker for trade organizations and for plan participants of client plans. He served three terms as an Advisory Director of the International Foundation and chaired various Foundation committees.

Mitchell Whitehead is a partner in the Los Angeles office of Seyfarth Shaw, with over 25 years' experience advising clients with respect to ERISA and fiduciary issues. His practice is focused on the representation of large governmental retirement systems, multiemployer pension, and health and welfare funds. He received his law degree from Loyola University School of Law and a bachelor's degree from the University of California at Riverside.

Arthur L. Wilmes is the managing principal of the Indianapolis Health Insurance and Clinical Management Practice for Milliman USA. Mr. Wilmes's major area of expertise is individual and group health insurance and disability income, including strategic planning, new product development, financial projections, and benefit plan design and funding. He currently consults to a number of multiemployer funds and association plans. Mr. Wilmes is a fellow of the Society of Actuaries and a member of the American Academy of Actuaries. An honors graduate of Ball State University, he is an active speaker and participant in various regional and national professional meetings.

Daniel L. Wolak is the president of The Union Labor Life Insurance Company (ULL). He joined ULL in 2007 as the vice president and chief actuary, a position held until 2010. Mr. Wolak has been in the group insurance field for over 30 years, previously in positions as the senior vice president of group reinsurance at General Re Life Corporation and the vice president and group actuary of American United Life Insurance Company. He is a fellow, Society of Actuaries and previously served as the chairperson for the Society of Actuaries (SOA) Health Section Council. Mr. Wolak earned both his bachelor and master of science degrees in statistics from Purdue University in West Lafayette, Indiana.

Sheree Yoder currently serves as director of institutional portfolio management, overseeing institutional portfolio managers throughout the M&I national footprint. She serves on the Trust Investment Committee and the Risk Management Committee of M&I Investment Management Corp. Ms. Yoder's investment industry experience includes director of investment consulting, institutional portfolio manager, fixed income portfolio manager and manager of performance measurement services. She earned a bachelor of arts degree from Messiah College, a general banking diploma from the American Institute of Banking and holds the FINRA Series 65 license.

Chapter 1

Effective Trusteeship and Decision Making

Claude L. Kordus

A challenge facing any new employee benefit plan trustee is that there is no logical starting point. There are stories of new jointly managed benefit plan trustees who have become so overwhelmed by their first board of trustees meeting that they wanted to resign. They may have had to review the annual actuarial report, analyze an investment manager's performance and hear appeals on claim denials before they fully comprehend the benefits provided by the plan. These trustees have a legal responsibility to act in accordance with plan documents and laws that they are still struggling to fully understand.

What follows in the next 56 chapters is an overview of the important role trustees have in the management and oversight of jointly managed multiemployer benefit plans. More than 50 respected experts in different aspects of the multiemployer benefit industry have collaborated to provide background information and advice to help both new and experienced trustees fulfill their responsibilities with the utmost care and prudence. No other single work brings together such a wealth of knowledge, experience and expertise. A question-and-answer format is used to help the reader quickly find the specific text that will provide insight on the issue of interest.

One cannot overstate the importance that legal matters have for trustees and others who have responsibility for a multiemployer benefit plan. Nevertheless, a concern solely for carrying out duties in a legally correct way does not guarantee effective or efficient plan management. Within the limits of the legal framework, there are many alternatives that must be considered. Attention must be given to not only making legally correct decisions, but also to making choices that are the best for the interests of the participants and their families. How does one judge whether the best decisions are being made? Some of the ultimate questions to ask:

- Are the needs of participants and other beneficiaries best served?
- Does the decision lead to the best cost/benefit relationship for the plan?
- Is the long-term financial solvency of the plan fully protected?
- Are the current and potential economic fluctuations of the industry fully recognized?
- Will participants be able to understand the reasons and results of a decision?
- Is the decision of the highest ethical quality, so that full disclosure is possible?
- Does the decision lead to administrative procedures that assure a fast and appropriate response to participant concerns?

By what process are best decisions made? The decision-making process, a key element in what is called *management,* has been the subject of much analysis, research and debate. (For the purpose of this discussion, *management* is used in the broad sense as directing organizational affairs *not* management versus labor as used in the collective bargaining setting. Here, management applies equally to the officers of a corporation and the officers of a union.) In this chapter, key elements of effective decision making are set forward.

Plan Objectives

Good decisions start with a clear understanding of the objectives related to the decision being made.

Welfare Benefits

In the design of health and welfare benefits, trustees must consider priorities for limited dollars:

- Where should the emphasis be in spending available dollars?
  - Medical benefits?
  - Drug benefits?
  - Mental health and addiction benefits?
  - Disability benefits?
  - Rehabilitation benefits?
  - Death benefits?
  - Dental benefits?
  - Vision benefits?
- Should greater concern be shown for active or retired participants?
- Should full-time workers receive more benefits than part-time workers?
- Should spouses and dependents receive the same benefits as workers?
- Should the needs of younger or older workers be emphasized (e.g., maternity benefits and dependent coverage versus a Medicare wraparound and long-term care)?
- Should benefits that most plan participants use (e.g., prescription drugs, physical examinations, office visits) be emphasized, or those that cost the most (e.g., orthodontics, organ transplants)?
- Should catastrophic protection or "something for everyone" be emphasized?
- Should in-hospital or out-of-hospital benefits be emphasized?
- Should benefit design encourage the best possible medical delivery system?
- What are the implications of the Patient Protection and Affordable Care Act as amended (ACA)?

Pension and Retirement Benefits

In the design of pension benefits:

- Should retirement income or ancillary benefits be emphasized?
- When should participants be able to retire with full benefits?
- At what age should participants be allowed to retire with a reduced benefit?
- When should participants be forced to retire (if at all)?
- How many hours of work in a year should entitle participants to full-benefit accrual?
- Should retired persons drawing a pension be allowed to work and receive a paycheck? Should they be allowed to work full-time, part-time or only when demand warrants?
- What are the implications of the Pension Protection Act (PPA) and all of its progeny?

Investing Fund Assets

Each plan should have an investment policy statement that addresses these types of issues:

- What rate of return should be expected?
- How much risk should be taken?
- How should rate of return be measured?
- What actual rate of return will trigger a review of alternative options?
- To what extent should principal be protected?
- Should alternative investments be part of the plan portfolio?
- How should assets be allocated among investment options?

Every major decision faced by plan trustees can begin with questions concerning plan objectives. Of course, there will not always be initial total agreement. If, however, basic policy issues are thrashed out, it does save time and possibly professional fees later on. Having clearly written objectives limits the alternatives that must be reviewed by legal counsel, priced by the fund actuary, etc. More importantly, better decisions result because they are made on a solid foundation of principles rather than on a piecemeal basis.

The Decision Process

Effective decision making begins with a clear understanding of the broad objectives trustees have established for a plan. It follows with an orderly process that takes into account all relevant aspects of a problem. For benefit plans, this process can be outlined as follows:

Define Objectives

- What do we want to do?
- What are the measurable limits for an acceptable solution?

Determine Alternatives

- How have other plans reacted to these issues?
- What other solutions fulfill the objectives?

Establish Costs

- Based upon established funding assumptions and methods, what will the alternatives cost?

Trustee Checklist

The following questions are provided to stimulate the thinking of trustees concerning basic effectiveness:

- Does the board of trustees review the issue of trustee responsibility and liability from time to time with legal counsel?
- Does the board of trustees hold discussions from time to time concerning the implications of legislation such as ERISA, PPA, ACA and all of their progeny?
- Do trustees understand the major tools available to help them do their job: financial statements, actuarial reports, annual audits, insurance experience statements, investment performance appraisals, etc.?
- Do trustees ask questions of advisors when not clear about the content of oral or written presentations?
- Do any trustees reduce the effectiveness of trustee meetings by overemphasizing the unimportant, monopolizing the discussion or failing to pursue areas of uncertainty?
- Do trustees begin the process of making major decisions by establishing clear objectives?
- Does the board of trustees review alternatives for meeting the objectives of the plan or is it "sold" specific packaged responses?
- Do trustees attend meetings faithfully?
- Do trustees read minutes in a timely fashion?
- Do trustees read material sent by the administrator and advisors in preparation for meetings?
- Do trustees really have the time to serve as a trustee?
- Can trustees take off the bargaining hat, as much as possible, and put on the hat of a trustee when dealing with benefit plan matters?
- Are trustee decisions "right" for plan participants and their families, and totally without regard to any personal interest?

Select the Best Alternative

- Based upon the objectives and the costs of various alternatives, what is the best alternative available?

Implement the Decision

Having decided upon a course of action, what steps need to be taken to get the selected alternative in operation? These steps will often encompass:

- Drafting documents and getting additional approval when required
- Preparing disclosure and communication materials for participants
- Preparing reports for government
- Establishing administrative procedures and systems to carry out the decision
- Making arrangements with plan personnel or external service providers
- Establishing standards to evaluate success
- Monitoring results to identify areas needing modification and for insight in future decisions.

Decision Tools

Trustees can view their role as a craft. The craft of trusteeship requires the effective use of certain tools:

- Meeting minutes
- Monthly or quarterly financial statements
- Regular reports of the administrator on plan operations
- Annual audits
- Actuarial valuation reports
- Special studies by administrators, attorneys, consultants, actuaries, investment counsel, etc.

Trustees must ask themselves whether they are using these tools intelligently. Some specific questions that trustees can ask to respond to this question are:

- Do I read fund material sent to me prior to meetings?
- Do I review minutes and other materials sent to me while the information is still fresh in my mind?
- Do I know how to interpret the financial statements and annual audits?
- If I am a pension trustee, do I understand the actuarial reports?

Concerning the last two questions, trustees must be able to understand the material presented by plan professionals. This handbook will help if perused from cover to cover. Trustees should never believe that it's below their dignity to ask for an explanation or clarification. Any professional that cannot describe his area of responsibility in language that reasonably informed trustees can understand is not worth having around.

Adequate Advice

Trustees must often depend on the advice of professionals: administrators, attorneys, accountants, actuaries, benefit consultants, investment consultants, etc. No single trustee or even a board of trustees will ever be an expert in all of these fields. The role of these advisors will become clearer as the various sections of this handbook are reviewed. For now, it is sufficient to say trustees should be familiar with a few key issues concerning the selection of professional help. The following questions apply to the selection of any firm that a board of trustees might use:

- What is the reputation of the firm regionally or nationally? Within the community?
- What is the background and capability of the specific persons who will serve the trust?
- What are the fees that will be charged?
- Can the firm demonstrate objectivity?
- Does the firm understand the multiemployer benefits field?

These seem like simple questions, but some of them are not asked by trustees when seeking professionals. An example is the question concerning the specific individuals who will serve a plan. A firm with an excellent reputation will underperform if the help provided a particular board of trustees comes from a mediocre person. It is important to meet those who will serve a plan. Moreover, it is important to get a commitment that the quality will be maintained even if there are personnel changes. For more information on the selection of professional advisors, a good starting place in this book is Chapters 6 and 7.

Some trustees expect the "experts" to tell them the "right choice" in the decision process. There are times when this approach may be appropriate—particularly when the issue is clearly legal compliance. However, the typical problem faced by a board of trustees has a number of reasonable alternatives. The best choice is the one that fulfills trustee objectives in the best interests of plan participants. In addition, trustees cannot avoid their fiduciary responsibility by looking to others to make decisions. Under the Employee Retirement Income Security Act of 1974 (ERISA), trustees are expected to make the key decisions where discretion is involved. Chapter 5 outlines trustee fiduciary responsibilities under ERISA.

The professionals serving multiemployer benefit plans have spent a substantial part or all of their working life in a specialized field using language that sounds like gibberish to the average person. Trustees must understand what these advisors are saying not only for good decisions to emerge, but also to protect trustees as plan fiduciaries. Not understanding a term in an advisor's report may make the advisor's effort a costly and worthless exercise. Even worse, trustee misunderstanding of a term may lead to a totally incorrect conclusion.

Trustees of multiemployer benefit plans must become familiar with many technical terms, even though it seems difficult. The advice by a writer on general language skills is appropriate:

> *Don't try to find excuses for a poor vocabulary (I'm too dumb, I'm too busy, I've got other things on my mind). A poor vocabulary can't be excused in this day and age. It can only be explained. And the explanation can be summed up in one word: laziness. If you want a good vocabulary, you can have it. But don't expect it to come without effort; you've got to go after it.*

Ethics

The most important quality for effective trusteeship is ethics. Many of the difficulties that trustees and benefit plans have gotten into that have led to litigation stem from basic human frailties—greed, pride and favoritism for friends or persons who can do something for the trustee. No amount of reading or going to seminars can overcome these basic problems.

Conclusion

Multiemployer benefit plan trustees do not "run" a plan in an operational sense. Trustees delegate day-to-day operations to others. Trustees, however, do have a legal responsibility for giving a plan direction—setting objectives and policies, planning, and monitoring to ensure their guidance is being followed. Trustees can only do their job if they use the tools at their disposal effectively and understand what is being said by their advisors.

Endnote

1. Lucile Payne, *The Lively art of Writing* (Chicago: Follett Publishing Company 1965), pages 133 and 134.

More Information

The International Foundation of Employee Benefit Plans sponsors an Annual Conference as well as many individual seminars, workshops and online courses that specifically target the needs and interests of benefit plan trustees and administrators. In addition, the Foundation provides books, magazines, research reports and other materials that can also support both new and experienced trustees. Visit ifebp.org for information on current educational programs and ifebp/bookstore for books. The professionals working with a plan can often recommend particular events and publications.

Two Foundation books of special note are:

- *The Benefits and Compensation Glossary.* A person who wants to know the meaning of a standard word goes to a general dictionary. A trustee who wants to know the meaning of a technical term can use various references. This comprehensive glossary of benefits and compensation terms, published by the International Foundation, puts the many terms and legislation associated with the benefits field in one book with easy-to-comprehend explanations.
- *Multiemployer Plans: A Guide for New Trustees.* Authored by Joseph A. Brislin, an attorney and trustee to several multiemployer plans, this book should be at the top of every new trustee's reading list. Using plain language that trustees will find reassuring, the author reviews the fiduciary duties and responsibilities assumed by a new trustee. Actual questions from trustees are part of each chapter—along with easy-to-understand answers. A collection of checklists identifies the plan documents that new trustees should be familiar with, questions to ask when communicating with professional advisors and much more.

One of the best ways to learn is simply to attend all board of trustee meetings. Ask questions and participate in the discussion of key issues. Over time, trustees who do these things will have the knowledge to do the best job possible in protecting the interests of those who depend on them for their economic security.

Chapter 2

Jointly Managed Multiemployer Benefit Plans: A Historical Perspective

*Claude L. Kordus**

The Early Years (1880-1930)

The history of multiemployer benefit plans in the United States is closely tied to the history of the nation's unions. Prior to the American Revolution, crafts and guilds—the entities that gave birth to unions—formed benevolent societies in a few towns for masters, journeymen and apprentices to help members injured in accidents, as well as widows and minor children. Benevolent societies were a financial safety net that paid sick benefits, gave money to indigent members, occasionally loaned money and provided "strong boxes" for savings.

Benefit plans sponsored by unions and employers began to emerge after the Civil War. The nation's first union-sponsored benefit fund was established by the Cigar Makers Union in 1867.[1] Just a few years later, in 1875, the American Express Company implemented the nation's first employer-provided retirement plan—its benefits were available only to disabled workers over the age of 60 with 20 years of service. The company's general manager had to recommend an employee's retirement, which was subject to approval by an executive committee of the board of directors. The first formal benefit plan to be funded jointly by employer and employee contributions was a pension plan established by the Baltimore and Ohio Railroad in 1880.[2]

Early benefit programs were primarily pension plans in the railroad, banking and public utilities industries. As manufacturing companies began to form near the turn of the 20th century, these businesses saw the competitive advantage of providing employees with pension plans and quickly established their own plans.

A clarification of the federal tax treatment of pension plan costs for employers in the early 1920s helped spur growth of employer-sponsored plans. While it had been common practice to allow businesses to deduct "ordinary and necessary business expenses" if they were "reasonable," the Internal Revenue Act of 1921 confirmed a federal tax deduction for pension plans by employers was acceptable.

By 1930, most large companies provided pensions and more than three-fourths were entirely employer financed. In industries without pension plans, some trade unions had begun to set up plans financed by member contributions.[3] Union plans covered 20% of union members.[4,5] Government regulation of these plans was almost nonexistent. Nearly all pension plans could be modified or terminated at any time. An employer could also withhold or terminate the pension of an individual employee at any time. *Vesting*, an employee's guaranteed right to a future benefit, did not exist.[6]

In contrast to pension plans, health and welfare plans were just barely getting started. It was not until 1929 that the first known employer-sponsored health plan for employees emerged. It was an agreement negotiated with Baylor Hospital in Texas to provide health care to Dallas County public school teachers.

The 1930s—The Great Depression

During the 1930s, the immediate financial concerns of the Great Depression outweighed employer interest in providing workers with a secure retirement or any other benefits.

---

*Some of the historical content of this chapter through 2006 is based on a chapter written by Wayne Wendling for the 6th Edition of the *Trustees Handbook: A Practical Guide to Labor-Management Employee Plans* published in 2006 by the International Foundation of Employee Benefit Plans.

However, the widespread suffering caused by the Depression prompted support for a national old-age insurance system. The Social Security Act of 1935 created the Social Security retirement income program for the elderly that exists today—financed by taxes collected from workers and their employees versus government funds.

Did the Depression or the introduction of Social Security retirement benefits result in many privately sponsored plans being terminated? One study suggests this was not the case. Of businesses with pension plans at some time during the preceding decade, 80% were still in existence in the spring of 1939. About half (53%) of the plans terminated were due to the introduction of Social Security; the remainder were reported to have been discontinued due to the Depression. The most significant change in employer-sponsored plans was a reduction in benefits and employer contributions.[7] Employers that were now paying half of the cost of an employee's Social Security benefits could hardly be expected also to pay the entire cost of what was now viewed as an employee's supplementary pension.[8]

The Wagner Act of 1935

Another event during the same decade, however, set the groundwork for employees to demand more benefits from employers. The Wagner Act of 1935—commonly referred to as the *National Labor Relations Act*—gave employees the right to organize and bargain collectively. The act prohibited unfair labor practices by employers. Among its provisions, the Wagner Act required employers to collectively bargain with employee representatives over wages, hours of employment and other conditions of employment. In the years following the Wagner Act, union participation increased from four million in 1935 to 16 million in 1948. The number of collective bargaining agreements also rose.[9] Labor was gaining the power to negotiate higher wages and increased benefits from their employers that would have implications in several decades to follow.

The 1940s—World War II

A combination of factors—a new tax policy, war restrictions on wage increases and more regulatory decisions concerning collective bargaining—spurred the resurgence and expansion of benefit programs in the years after the Depression. First was a change in the Internal Revenue Code. When the Internal Revenue Service (IRS) confirmed in 1926 that employers could deduct their contributions to private pension plans for employees, it also provided that income earned in these trusts would not be taxable until it was actually distributed to beneficiaries. Many pension plan trusts were created that provided benefits only to key employees and corporate officers. The trusts became a way for a select group of high-income persons to avoid taxes.

To halt this practice, Congress imposed certain conditions for "qualified" pension trusts in 1942.[10] For example, a certain percentage of employees that are not highly compensated must be covered by the plan. In addition, a "qualified" plan also cannot discriminate in favor of officers, shareholders or other highly compensated employees by making larger contributions on their behalf or providing them with better benefits. Only if these conditions are met are employers allowed to deduct contributions to the plans and can earnings on contributions be tax-free until an employee reaches retirement and starts receiving benefits.

Federal wage ceilings imposed during World War II also encouraged the reemergence of employer-sponsored plans in the U.S. Freezing wages was an effort to keep inflation from getting out of hand during the global conflict, but another form of compensation—employee benefits—was exempted. As a result, employers that needed to attract and retain workers resorted to offering a growing range of fringe benefits such as pensions, medical insurance, paid holidays and vacations, and even child care.[11,12]

The Taft-Hartley Act of 1947

As union participation grew in the years just before and during the war, a sentiment emerged among employers that the Wagner Act of 1935 gave unions an unfair advantage. Congress responded by enacting the Taft-Hartley Act of 1947 to provide more balance between employers and unions. While the Wagner Act had prohibited unfair labor practices by employers, the new Taft-Hartley legislation prohibited unfair labor practices by unions (e.g., featherbedding, refusing to bargain in good faith and closed shops) and gave employers certain bargaining rights.

Not all legislation and regulatory acts at the end of the war, however, favored employers over the unions. National Labor Relations Board (NLRB) decisions were paving the way for benefit negotiations to be part of the collective bargaining process. In a landmark 1949 decision involving the *Inland Steel Co.,* NLRB declared that pensions and insurance benefits were mandatory subjects in collective bargaining.

Prior to the passage of the Taft-Hartley Act, only a few multiemployer benefit plans existed. Embedded within the extensive text of the Taft-Hartley Act is an exception to a general rule that bans employers from giving money or anything else of value to persons or unions representing employees. The act allowed employers to contribute to jointly administered labor-management trust funds for the sole and exclusive benefit of employees, their families and dependents. It was no longer illegal for employers to contribute to a multiemployer benefit plan if:

- Payments are held in a trust.
- The basis for payments is in a written agreement with the employer.
- The basis for payments is in a written agreement.
- Labor and management have equal representation in administering the fund.
- There is an annual audit.
- The fund is separate from other monies, and is used solely to provide pension and welfare benefits.
- The agreement provides for employers and employees to agree upon an impartial umpire for disputes (if agreement cannot be reached, neutral parties are authorized to break deadlocks).

The wider spectrum of considerations affecting all employee benefit plans—such as fiduciary responsibility, funding, reporting and disclosure—were not addressed at the federal level until several years later.

The initial jointly administered multiemployer plans—often referred to as *Taft-Hartley plans*—primarily offered health and pension benefits. Over time, the purposes of these plans have grown to include educational scholarships, child-care centers, legal services and financial assistance for housing—all added through amendments in the late 1950s, late 1960s, early 1970 and 1990. Exhibit 1 summarizes the purposes for which Taft-Hartley plans may now be established.

Exhibit 1

Purposes of Taft-Hartley Plans

- Accident Insurance
- Child-Care Centers
- Disability/Sickness Insurance
- Educational Scholarships
- Financial Assistance for Housing
- Life Insurance
- Medical/Hospital Care
- Occupational Illness/Injury
- Pension
- Pooled Vacation/Holiday/Severance

The Importance of Taft-Hartley Jointly Managed Plans

Taft-Hartley plans have become a small but essential subset of the benefits community. They are a response to the unique needs of union workers who have made a commitment to a craft or industry, as opposed to making a commitment to a specific employer. For an example of these workers, consider those in the building and construction trades. Workers move from one employer to another depending on who has a project that can use them. In addition, projects and the ability to find work are sensitive to economic cycles and seasonal demand.

Taft-Hartley multiemployer plans accommodate these workers. Those employees who move from one employer to another are able to take their credits for service and benefit eligibility with them. In addition to this portability, Taft-Hartley plans may offer other features such as an "hours bank" that allows workers to set aside extra work hours during peak work periods that they can use to maintain benefit eligibility during economic downturns. Among the other industries that have workers who benefit from multiemployer plans are arts and entertainment, hospitality, retail, transportation, health care, mining and communication. (Exhibit 2 provides a look at the proportion of workers presently participating in multiemployer benefit plans insured by the Pension Benefit Guaranty Corporation (PBGC).)

Jointly managed multiemployer plans also have advantages for employers. These plans foster a flexible, trained workforce committed to a craft or industry. The stable benefit costs help employers compete for skilled workers in their industry. Because operation and administration of the plans is centralized, employers have access to benefit experts to assist in plan design and cost management. There are also advantages to small employers such as the economies of scale for benefit administration and risk pooling that might otherwise be available only to large employers.

The 1950s and 1960s—Benefit Growth and Public Outrage

By the end of 1950, private pension plans covered more than one-quarter of U.S. workers in industry and commerce. Although service requirements for plans varied from one to 30 years, most employees were able to retire after 15 or more years of service. Almost all plans had established the age of 65 as an age requirement for "normal" retirement, while early retirement was commonly available at the

Exhibit 2

PBGC—Insured Multiemployer Plan Participants by Industry 2008

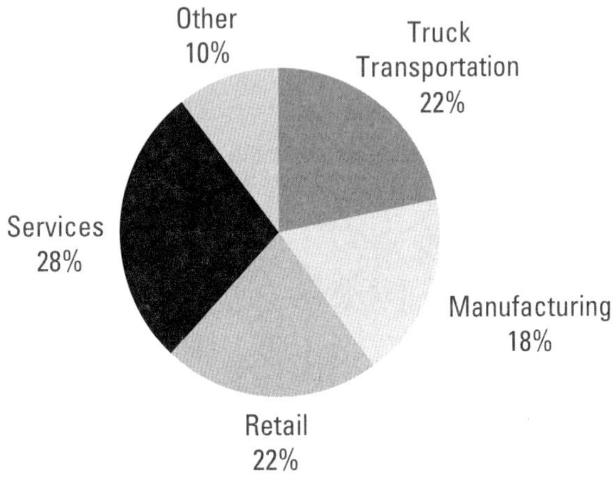

Source: The Pension Insurance Data Book 2009. (The Pension Benefit Guaranty Corporation): 104.

age of 55. Interestingly, more than 40% of those who wanted to retire early had to obtain company approval first.[13]

While there were a number of pension plan failures over the years in various industries, a pivotal event occurred in the 1960s that would ultimately lead to new federal legislation governing all private sector benefit plans—both multiemployer and single employer plans. The year was 1963 and the event was the collapse of the Studebaker Company—the nation's oldest major auto manufacturer. When Studebaker closed its factory doors in South Bend, Indiana, its pension fund was so poorly funded that 4,500 workers under the age of 60 with an average of 23 years' service received a lump-sum payment equal to only about 15% of their benefits.[14] As the Studebaker situation unfolded, stories of workers with years of experience losing pensions at other companies were also being reported by the media. Both the public and politicians became outraged.

The Employee Retirement Income Security Act of 1974 (ERISA)

Though it would take a decade after the Studebaker debacle to do so, Congress enacted ERISA in 1974. Still considered the most significant legislation in pension history, ERISA created new requirements for all private sector defined benefit (DB) pension plans regarding funding, vesting, reporting, fiduciary duties and financial disclosure. The statute ensures that:

- Workers are not subjected to unreasonable age-and-service requirements before they are eligible for participation in an employer-sponsored pension plan.
- Individuals who work for a specified minimum period while covered by a pension plan must receive at least some pension at retirement through vesting, benefit accrual and break-in-service provisions.
- Spouses of retired beneficiaries are protected through joint and survivor provisions.
- Pension promises are adequately funded by establishing minimum standards.
- Money set aside to meet pension promises is invested as a prudent man would invest.
- Within limits, promises made by DB plans are guaranteed in the event of plan termination through plan termination insurance.

ERISA established the Pension Benefit Guaranty Corporation (PBGC) as the federal insurance program protecting workers who lost their promised retirement benefits. Employers would pay an insurance premium to PBGC that would be used to provide financial assistance when needed.

It is important to understand that despite the word "retirement" in its name and that the discussion thus far has focused on pension plans, ERISA also regulated welfare (including health) plans. The legislation requires both pension and welfare plans to:

- Provide participants with information regarding plan features and funding
- Establish a grievance-and-appeals process for claim disputes.

ERISA also established fiduciary duties for trustees and others who manage and control assets for both types of plans. Trustees became personally liable for failures to fulfill their fiduciary responsibilities in the operation of a plan. In addition, the legislation gives participants the right to sue for benefits and breaches of fiduciary duty.

1980 Through Today

The Multiemployer Pension Plan Amendments Act of 1980 (MPPAA)

In the late 1970s, PBGC studied the financial situation of multiemployer plans and advised Congress that potential liabilities from the termination of these plans could reach more than $4 billion within ten years. It also reported that the size of premiums needed to fund the insurance program would be unacceptably high and could encourage additional multiemployer plan terminations.

Exhibit 3

PBGC Maximum Guaranteed Benefits (1980-2010)

Annual Date of Plan Insolvency	Maximum Monthly Benefit Formula	Monthly Guarantee (30 years of service)*	Maximum Guarantee (30 years of service)*
September 27, 1980 to December 21, 2000	The participant's years of service multiplied by the sum of: 100% of the first $5 of the monthly benefit accrual rate plus 75% of the next $15 of the monthly accrual rate	$487.50	$5,850.00
On or after December 22, 2000**	The participant's years of service multiplied by the sum of: 100% of the first $11 of the monthly benefit accrual rate plus 75% of the next $33 of the monthly accrual rate	$1,072.50	$12,870.00

* The formula presumes that the workers' monthly benefits are calculated by multiplying the monthly benefit accrual rate (a plan-specified dollar amount) times years of service. If the monthly benefit accrual rate prior to December 22, 2000, was less than $20 per year of service or if the accrual rate after December 21, 2000 is less than $44 per year of service then the maximum benefit guarantee for a participant with 30 years of service will be lower than the amounts shown. Note that there is no cap on applicable years of service; 30 years was selected for illustrative purposes only.

**The increased guarantee does not apply to multiemployer plans that received financial aid from PBGC between December 22, 1999 and December 21, 2000. The original, lower monthly benefit guarantee continues to apply to participants in these plans.

Source: The Pension Insurance Data Book 2009. (The Pension Benefit Guaranty Corporation): 111.

PBGC submitted a number of recommendations to Congress for revising the program. These recommendations were designed to financially strengthen multiemployer plans, and to give substantial PBGC insurance protection at reasonable premium levels. Congress acted on these recommendations and, on September 26, 1980, the Multiemployer Pension Plan Amendments Act of 1980 (MPPAA) became law.

The framers of ERISA originally envisioned that PBGC would operate the same for single employer and multiemployer DB plans. There was, however, an assumption that because multiemployer plans depend on the performance of a number of employers these plans would be more stable and less likely to terminate than single employer plans. If the financial fortunes of one employer declined, other employers serving the industry or region would hire the workers of this employer. Since there seemed to be less risk that a multiemployer plan would experience financial difficulties, the premium rate paid by multiemployer plans to PBGC was one-half the rate of single employer plans.

ERISA also allowed employers contributing to multiemployer DB pension plans to withdraw from a plan with no further financial obligation as long as the plan they withdrew from continued for another five years. When a plan was terminated, only those employers still contributing and those who had contributed during the previous five years would be responsible for a pro-rated share of the plan's unfunded liabilities. It became evident, however, that such withdrawals threatened the financial stability of even healthy multiemployer plans.

Exhibit 4

PBGC's Historic Premium Rates—Multiemployer Program

For Plan Years Beginning	Premium Rate (per participant)
September 2, 1974-August 31, 1979	$0.50
September 1, 1979-September 26, 1980	$0.50 for plan years beginning in September 1979, growing gradually to $1 for plan years beginning September 1, 1980 to September 26, 1980
September 27, 1980-September 26, 1984	$1.40
September 27, 1984-September 26, 1986	$1.80
September 27, 1986-September 26, 1988	$2.20
September 27, 1988-September 26, 2005	$2.60
2006-2007	$8.00
2008-2010	$9.00

Source: The Pension Insurance Data Book 2009. (The Pension Benefit Guaranty Corporation): 112.

MPPAA required employers withdrawing from a multiemployer plan to pay a pro-rata share of the plan's projected unfunded liabilities. In addition, the amendments:

- Changed the definition of *multiemployer plan* to include all collectively bargained plans to which more than one employer contributed
- Strengthened the funding requirements for multiemployer plans in general
- Raised insurance premiums paid by plans
- Reduced the benefit guarantees to plan participants
- Established mandatory requirements for financially weak plans to reorganize
- Changed the trigger for PBGC intervention from plan termination to plan insolvency.

PBGC considers a plan insolvent when plan assets are not sufficient to pay benefits expected to become payable over the next three years. If a multiemployer plan is unable to pay benefits when due, PBGC loans the plan the funds needed to make benefit payments at the "guaranteed" level and to cover reasonable administrative expenses. Only basic benefits—not supplemental benefits—are insured. The PBGC loan must be repaid if the plan's financial condition improves.

The level of multiemployer DB plan benefits insured by PBGC assuming a worker has 30 years of service is presented in Exhibit 3, and the premium arrangement for the same plans is described in Exhibit 4. Beginning in 2007, the PBGC insurance premium is adjusted annually based on changes in the national average wage index (as defined in Section 209(k)(1) of the Social Security Act). The premium rate will not decline even if the national average wage index declines. The adjusted premium rate is rounded to the nearest multiple of $1.

In 1980 there were more than 90,000 single employer DB plans and 2,244 multiemployer DB plans covered under the PBGC insurance program. As of 2009, the latest year for which numbers are available, the number of single employer DB plans was 27,647 whereas the number of multiemployer DB plans stood at 1,495.[15] Exhibit 5 shows the steady decline in the number of multiemployer DB pension plans since 1980. Though the 30% decline is substantial, it has not been nearly as severe as the 70% decline in single employer plans during the same period.

Daniel McGinn has attributed the decline in multiemployer DB plans to MPPAA.[16] The withdrawal liability provision—designed to ensure that employers withdrawing from a plan did not "put" accumulated liabilities on remaining employers—actually discouraged new employers from participating in the plans. Others say ERISA requirements such as vesting and minimum benefit standards may have increased the cost of DB plans leading to the decline.

It is probably fair to say ERISA and MPPAA hastened

Exhibit 5

PBGC-Insured Multiemployer Plans (1980-2009)

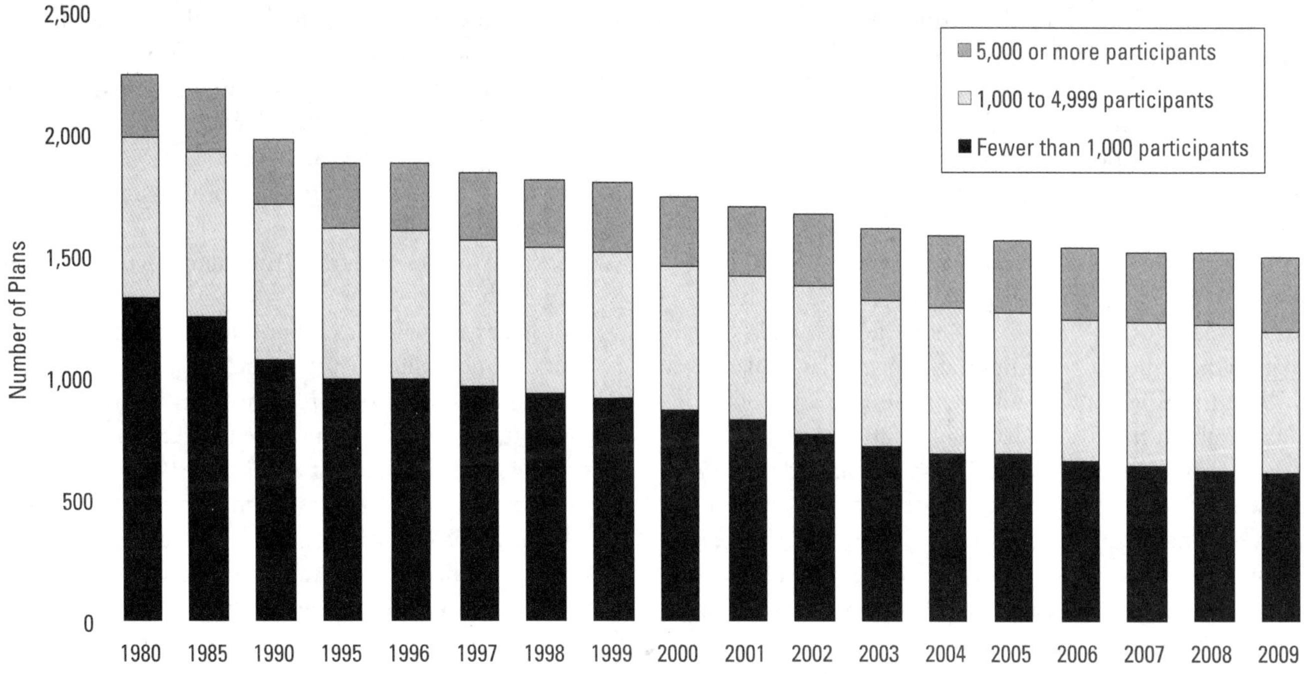

Source: The Pension Insurance Data Book 2009. (The Pension Benefit Guaranty Corporation): 102.

Exhibit 6

PBGC-Insured Multiemployer Plan Participants (1980-2007)

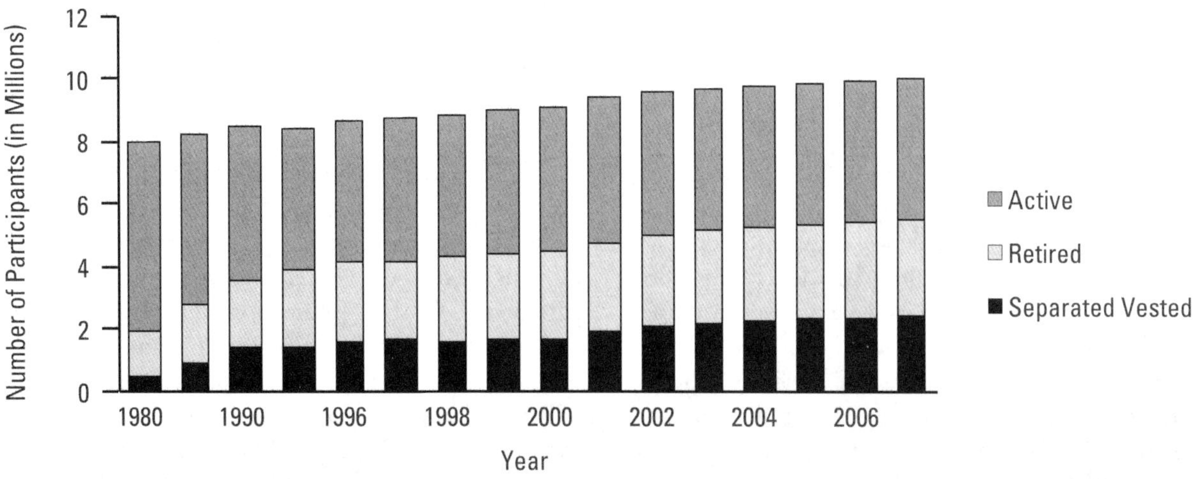

Source: The Pension Insurance Data Book 2009. (The Pension Benefit Guaranty Corporation): 102.

the termination of DB pension plans but other factors were also in play. The federal government's favorable tax treatment of defined contribution (DC) plans offered employers an alternative means to provide employees with retirement benefits free of the future liability connected to DB plans. Structural shifts in the U.S. economy may be another reason. Employment in industries that historically have had jointly managed plans such as manufacturing have been in decline while smaller, service-oriented businesses that do not participate in collective bargaining have increased.

According to PBGC data, the proportion of multiemployer DB plans with more than 10,000 participants has almost doubled from 11% to 20% between 1980 and 2009. The growth in the relative importance of the large plans is less about the growth of the underlying unions and regions, and more about the consolidation of locals and plans.[17]

In almost every year since Congress enacted ERISA, there has been a significant legislative initiative affecting employee benefits. As weaknesses in ERISA and the need for other benefit protections have become known, new laws and regulations have been imposed. In the past decade, areas of particular concern have been:

- **The aging population in multiemployer plans.** The population of multiemployer plans continues to grow older with benefits to an increasing number of vested and retired participants funded by a declining number of active workers. As illustrated in Exhibit 6, the ratio of active to vested/retired plan participants has been declining for more than two decades.
- **Underfunded pension plans.** In 2007—the most recent year for which numbers are available—92.3% of PBGC-insured multiemployer plans were underfunded. Plan liabilities exceeded assets by nearly 195 billion.[18] Declining stock prices and interest rates combined with the aging plan population are key contributors to this troubling statistic.
- **Chronic PBGC deficits.** From 1982 to 2002, contributions to the PBGC's insurance program for multiemployer plans yielded a surplus. Since then, it has had a deficit. In 2009, the deficit was $869 million. The deficit of the single employer insurance program was even more serious at $21.1 billion.[19]
- **Increasing health care costs.** In 2008, U.S. health care spending was about $7,681 per resident and accounted for 16.2% of the nation's gross domestic product (GDP); this is among the highest of all industrialized countries. Total health care expenditures grew at an annual rate of 4.4% in 2008, a slower rate than recent years, yet still outpacing inflation and the growth in national income.[20]

The Pension Protection Act of 2006 (PPA '06)

In an effort to enhance and protect both privately funded retirement savings plans—including both single and multiemployer defined benefit plans—Congress passed the Pension Protection Act in 2006. Considered the most sweeping pension legislation since ERISA, PPA '06:

- Establishes new minimum funding standards for pension plans
- Sets forth rules governing the valuation of plan assets and liabilities
- Provides special rules for at-risk plans including certification and notice requirements
- Establishes additional requirements for annual plan reports to the U.S. Department of Labor (DOL)
- Allows the Secretary of the Treasury to waive minimum funding standards in the event of temporary hardship or if a standard would be adverse to the interests of plan participants as a whole
- Provides multiple exemptions to prohibited transaction rules.

The legislation requires multiemployer plan actuaries to submit a report that assigns a zone status reflecting the funding situation of the plan. The status of a plan may be red (critical), orange (seriously endangered), yellow (endangered) or green (none of the above). If the plan is certified as "nongreen" for any year, then plan trustees must adopt either a funding improvement plan or a rehabilitation plan (depending on the plan's zone status). If a plan is classified as "seriously endangered" or "critical," the plan must notify the DOL, PBGC, plan beneficiaries, unions and employers that it has received this designation. A plan must be prepared and implemented to improve the financial status of the plan. More information on these designations and the action required of plans is provided in Chapters 27 and 28.

The market downturn of 2008/2009 combined with the recession amplified the financial troubles experienced by multiemployer pension plans and made it even more difficult to comply with the funding rules of PPA '06. As part of the Worker, Retiree, and Employer Recovery Act of 2008 (WRERA), Congress gave plans emergency relief from the legislation approved just two years prior. Through WRERA, Congress temporarily eased some PPA rules that were to become effective in 2009—giving the pension plans time to recover. Viewing 2008 and 2009 as historic investment aberrations, Congress acted again in June of 2010. The Pension Relief Act of 2010 offered additional short-term options to help pension plans cope with the funding challenges exacerbated by market conditions.

In the spring of 2011, the Segal Company released its survey of about 230 calendar-year multiemployer plans that indicated two-thirds of calendar-year plans were in the green zone as of January 1, 2011. For comparison, only a little more than half of plans were in this zone one year earlier. In 2009, the proportion was just over one-third.[21] Though the impact of recent economic events will continue to be felt for years to come, it appears plans are beginning to recover.

The Patient Protection and Affordable Care Act of 2010 as Amended (ACA)

The other great change in the benefits environment is, of course, the Patient Protection and Affordable Care Act of 2010 as amended, titled the Affordable Care Act (ACA). As this book goes to press, many questions remain regarding the implications of this law to be phased in through 2018. Once the changes affecting multiemployer plans are clearer, more information will be posted at the supplemental website for this Handbook (ifebp.org/Handbook7).

ACA covers most plans, but there are some exceptions: among these are standalone dental and vision plans, and most health flexible spending accounts. The legislation creates an important distinction whether a plan is grandfathered or not. *Grandfathered plans* are defined as plans in place before ACA's enactment and do not have to incorporate a significant number of the ACA requirements. To remain grandfathered, plan sponsors may not substantially reduce benefits or increase costs to participants. The decision whether to be grandfathered is complex. Importantly, if a plan follows all the requirements for grandfathering, the plan must provide a disclosure of this fact to participants.

The following provisions apply to both grandfathered and nongrandfathered plans for plan years beginning on or after September 23, 2010:

- Coverage of dependent children to age 26—grandfathered plans are exempt until 2014 if a child has access to other coverage.
- Elimination of preexisting condition exclusions for children up to age 19—after 2014, this rule applies to all individuals.
- Elimination of annual limits on dollar value of essential benefits—phased in between 2010 and 2014
- Elimination of lifetime limits
- Elimination of rescissions (cancellation or discontinuance of coverage) that are retroactive unless there is fraud or an intentional misrepresentation of material fact prohibited by the terms of the plan or coverage.

Additional mandates apply only to nongrandfathered plans:

- Where a plan incorporates a primary care physician, a network pediatrician can be designated as a primary care physician for a child, and a female participant or beneficiary does not need a referral to see an in-network obstetrical or gynecological specialist.
- A plan may not require more restrictive requirements or benefit limitations for out-of-network emergency services than are required for in-network emergency services. Plans are to provide a notice of these rights.
- A plan must provide coverage for certain preventive care benefits.
- For nongrandfathered fully insured plans, discrimination is prohibited for both participation and benefits in favor of highly compensated individuals.
- Standards are set for internal claims and appeals processes. Plans must institute processes according to ERISA claims and appeals requirements, as well as additional requirements.

Other challenges will arise. For example, many high-cost jointly managed plans will be subject to a "cadillac tax" in 2018 unless Congress or the courts intervene.

Conclusion

Today's multiemployer health and welfare plans have a history that extends back 250 years, if not further. It is a rich history of providing (1) a financial safety net and savings opportunities for members, and (2) a stable workforce that helped multiemployer industries grow and succeed. In the three decades since passage of ERISA and MPPAA that was intended to strengthen worker benefit protections, the number of multiemployer benefit plans has decreased because of mergers and insolvencies. This history ends in a flurry of economic distress, negative demographic trends and increased interest in DC plans that depend on individual savings and management of retirement assets. Will an improved economic climate and new government regulations help turn things around? Only time will tell.

Endnotes

1. Weinstein, Harriet and William J. Wiatrowski. "Multiemployer Pension Plans," *Compensation and Working Conditions* (Spring 1999): 19.
2. Seburn, Patrick W. "Evolution of Employer-Provided Defined Benefit Pension." *Monthly Labor Review* (Bureau of Labor Statistics, December 1991): 16.
3. Ibid: 17.
4. Latimer, Murray W. *Industrial Pension Systems in the United States and Canada,* v1 (New York, Industrial Relations Counselors, 1932)

5. American Council of Life Insurance. *1987 Pension Facts* (Washington, DC: American Council of Life Insurance, 1987): 33.
6. Seburn, Patrick W. "Evolution of Employer-Provided Defined Benefit Pension," *Monthly Labor Review* (Bureau of Labor Statistics, December 1991): 17.
7. National Industrial Conference Board. "Company Pension Plans and the Social Security Act," *Studies in Personnel Policy,* n16 (New York, 1939) cited in "Effect of Social Security Act on Company Pension," *Monthly Labor Review* (March 1940): 643.
8. "Effect of Social Security Act on Company Pensions," *Monthly Labor Review* (March 1940): 644.
9. Taylor, Benjamin J. and Fred Whitney. *Labor Relations Law,* 5th Ed. (Englewood Cliffs, NJ, Prentice-Hall, Inc., 1987): 163, 195.
10. Dearing, Charles L. *Industrial Pension* (Washington, DC, The Brookings Institution, 1954): 286.
11. Schumann, Richard E. "Compensation from World War II through the Great Society," *Compensation and Working Conditions* (Bureau of Labor Statistic, Fall 2001). www.bls.gov/opub/cwc/cm20030124ar04p1.htm.
12. Kaiser Permanente. "A Total History of Health: Wartime Shipyard Child Care Centers Set Standards for Future. (September 29, 2010). www.kaiserpermanentehistory.org/latest/wartime-shipyard-child-care-centers-set-standards-for-future/.
13. Seburn, Patrick W. "Evolution of Employer-Provided Defined Benefit Pension," *Monthly Labor Review* (Bureau of Labor Statistics, December 1991): 20.
14. "At Last: Pension Reform," *Time* (August 26, 1974). www.time.com/time/magazine/article/0,9171,944964,00.html#ixzz1WFKLKOen.
15. Pension Benefit Guaranty Corporation. *Pension Insurance Data Book,* 2009 Edition.
16. Daniel F. McGinn. *Multiemployer Retirement Plans: Handbook for the 21st Century* (Brookfield, WI: International Foundation of Employee Benefit Plans, 2004, xiv).
17. Pension Benefit Guaranty Corporation. *Pension Insurance Data Book,* 2009 Edition.
18. Ibid.
19. Ibid.
20. Kaiser Family Foundation. "U.S. Health Care Costs." www.kaiseredu.org/Issue-Modules/US-Health-Care-Costs/Background-Brief.aspx.
21. Segal Company. *Survey of Calendar Year Plans 2011 Zone Status.* (Spring 2011).

Chapter 3

Future Directions and Challenges

Paul M. Secunda

Many multiemployer benefit plans are experiencing difficulties today. Although they once represented one of the great triumphs in labor relations—providing pension, welfare and health benefits to unionized workers—these plans are now challenged by a series of financial, demographic, legislative and judicial developments. The health of multiemployer plans is extremely important; there are still some ten million participants nationwide in nearly 1,500 plans. Many of these workers are in industries such as trucking, entertainment, construction and retail—industries where employees frequently move between jobs in the same industry.

Three principal challenges face multiemployer plans in the coming years. First, there is the financial challenge, which is closely connected to demographic issues. Like almost all retirement plan investments, the value of multiemployer plan investment portfolios was negatively impacted by the 2007-2009 global recession. The assumption that employer contributions for current employees will support older workers in their retirement has aggravated the financial situation of multiemployer plans. The number of active employees covered under multiemployer plans is at a low point—the proportion of U.S. workers that are private-sector union members recently fell to 6.9%. This declining union workforce must fund an increasing number of retirees.

The Pension Protection Act of 2006 (PPA) attempted to address some of the structural issues faced by multiemployer plans. The unstable economic environment that followed led President Obama to sign the Pension Relief Act of 2010 (PRA) to also provide funding relief to multiemployer pension plans. PRA provisions reduce required employer contributions and extend the period for recovering investment losses experienced by multiemployer plans. On the other hand, more recent legislation to financially strengthen multiemployer plans such as the Create Jobs and Save Benefits Act of 2010 died in Senate committee. At present, the Pension Benefit Guaranty Corporation (PBGC) that provides insurance for insolvent multiemployer plans has insufficient funds to cover insured benefits. The PBGC multiemployer plan program has run a deficit every year since 2003.

One could argue that many of these pension problems were caused by the Employee Retirement Income Security Act of 1974 (ERISA)—its funding mechanisms, vesting schemes and the way the PBGC insurance scheme it created operates. Nevertheless, it is unlikely the next few years will see substantial change in ERISA provisions, including how PBGC is funded. Trustees will likely continue to make decisions within this same legal environment.

Second, and in addition to the financial issues, legislative and political challenges exist. So far, in this chapter, only pension challenges have been broached. New health insurance challenges for multiemployer plans must also be addressed. Multiemployer health benefits are perceived as too generous, called "Cadillac" plans and targeted for a new 40% excise tax in 2018 under comprehensive health care reform legislation passed in 2010. Although the federal Patient Protection and Affordable Care Act of 2010 as amended (ACA) will face numerous constitutional and policy challenges in the coming years that may result in the 2018 Cadillac tax and other provisions being struck down, this chapter proceeds with the assumption that these parts of health care reform are here to stay for the foreseeable future. This means multiemployer plan trustees must consider new ACA terminology such as *grandfathered plans, minimum essential benefits* and *health benefit exchanges.*

Finally, multiemployer plans face significant judicial challenges. Recent court decisions have made plan governance even more difficult. A case in point concerns the appropriate standard of review when a plan denies a claimed benefit to a participant or beneficiary. The U.S. Supreme Court's recent decision in *Metropolitan Life v. Glenn* was supposed to provide more predictability and uniformity in benefits processing when plan administrators have a conflict of interest deciding a benefit claim. Instead, the *Glenn* case, which has now been adopted in the multiemployer context, leaves much of the same confusion.

All of this is problematic for plan trustees—they need to know the scope of their fiduciary obligations when dealing with claim issues so they do not unintentionally breach their responsibilities to plan participants and beneficiaries. Of course, judicial interpretation problems are not limited to denial of benefit issues, but this example gives some indication of the complexity of judiciary issues.

In all, multiemployer plans face a challenging future based on financial, legislative and judicial challenges. The hope is that by addressing these challenges through reform and system modifications, these historically important plans will continue to provide needed employee benefits.

Challenge #1: The Financial and Demographic Challenge to Multiemployer Plans

Multiemployer plan underfunding is not a new issue or challenge. Congress amended ERISA in 1980 to try to address the problem of underfunding. The Multiemployer Pension Plan Amendments Act of 1980 (MPPAA) was enacted to protect the financial stability of these plans. MPPAA's introduction of *withdrawal liability*—a liability triggered when an employer partially or completely withdraws from a multiemployer pension plan—did not, however, eliminate all funding challenges (including those based on asset declines in such plans). Although withdrawal liability was supposed to keep employers in multiemployer arrangements by basing their liability on their share of a plan's unfunded vested benefits, this provision alone has not kept certain multiemployer pension plans from terminating.

Whether based on overall declines in plan assets, the impact of withdrawal liability provisions or decline in union membership, conflicting evidence exists concerning the extent of the underfunding problem for multiemployer plans. Moody's Investor Service estimated the total unfunded liability for 126 of the nation's largest multiemployer pension plans at over $165 billion in 2008. The National Coordinating Committee for Multiemployer Plans found in a 2009 survey that the funding levels of four out of every five of the plans reviewed were "endangered" or in "critical" condition. The Government Accountability Office (GAO) reported recently that the proportion of multiemployer plans less than 80% funded rose from 23% of plans in 2008 to 68% plans in 2009.

On the other hand, commentators point out that while it is true most multiemployer pension plans are to some degree underfunded and treading carefully to deal with the challenges of tough economic times, actual plan insolvency threatens only about 10% of all such plans. Although this is certainly a serious concern, these same numbers suggest that 90% of multiemployer pensions are not in danger of insolvency. More plans are underfunded generally, but only a small percentage are in danger of becoming insolvent.

Not surprisingly, the primary culprits that led to the underfunding problem are the global recession of 2007-2009 and dwindling union economic power. Some investments made by multiemployer trustees during this period have not turned out well. Of course, multiemployer plans are not alone in this regard—for instance, public pension plans also have endured significant losses in value during the recent recession. There is new evidence that with the recovery of global and domestic markets, a good number of multiemployer pension plans are starting to recover financially. For instance, The Segal Company Winter 2011 Survey of the firm's 370 client plans found more than half of those surveyed (53%) were in good financial health, a significant increase from 38% in 2009.

There are important structural issues as well. There are fewer new employee participants in multiemployer plans; at the same time, there is a larger aging workforce that needs to be paid out of these funds. The growth of multiemployer plans has been stalled by a lack of growth in union representation and the resultant lack of union economic power to bargain pension benefits for members. Finally, PGBC—as many predicted when it was first established—has been unable to keep up with the number of newly terminated multiemployer pension plans. This is so even though the recent PBGC-guaranteed maximum monthly benefit is relatively low at $1,320 per participant (this works out to $12,870 per year for 30 years of employment). Part of the problem is that PBGC already owes some $2.3 billion in future assistance to distressed plans.

Employee Contributions and Defined Contribution Plans

Many reforms potentially could cure some of these funding issues. For instance, like their public pension plan counterparts, current participants of multiemployer plans might directly contribute to their pension plans. Most multiemployer pension plans are defined benefit plans that put the risk of plan funding squarely on employers. Defined benefit plans also require compliance with complicated and time-consuming benefit vesting schedules. Multiemployer pension plans could also adopt a defined contribution plan paradigm similar to that of single employer plans. Once an employer contributes to a defined contribution plan, the employer's responsibility for funding ends.

It is very likely both increased employee contributions and a shift to the defined contribution model would lead to strong union and employee objections. There is a belief among unions and union members that pensions are a form of deferred compensation; members accept lower salaries in order to have retirement benefits later. The argument continues that members should not have to accept a further reduction in salary through increased contributions.

Unions and their members also maintain that they should not have all the responsibility of investing their retirement money so that they have enough to retire in the future. Indeed, recent experience in the single employer plan environment with 401(k) plans suggests employees are far less ready for retirement under the defined contribution plan model. Generally, these employees do not have enough money saved for a successful retirement. Some attribute this state of affairs to a lack of financial sophistication.

Permit Cutting of Vested Benefits if Deemed Necessary

George Kraw, an attorney who specializes in the representation of multiemployer plans in California and a former member of PBGC's Advisory Committee, has put forth other alternatives for curing multiemployer funding issues.

Kraw's first suggested reform is to let plans cut vested benefits if plan trustees consider it necessary and plan sponsors (i.e., the employer and union) agree. Currently, PPA allows multiemployer plans to cut some vested benefits for plan participants if the plan's underfunded status becomes "critical." Kraw suggests extending this power to plans not yet critically underfunded, but headed in that direction. The thought is that underfunded plans should have the ability to restructure vested benefits—making it possible for individual multiemployer plans and the industries that sponsor them to survive. It is also generally easier for multiemployer plans to act if insolvency is not around the corner.

Given the sanctity of vested benefits in the law and in the minds of workers, such a drastic move would likely be vetoed by union trustees to protect the interests of individual union members. In any event, such a step should be taken only if the long-term prospects for a plan are dubious—with immediate and aggressive action needed to keep the industry from shedding jobs. As discussed above, many plans are now recovering financially and do not currently need such strong medicine.

Cap or Eliminate Withdrawal Liability to Incentivize Employers to Join Plans

A second possibility would be to cap or eliminate withdrawal liability to allow more employers to join multiemployer plans. The idea here is that employers are going it alone or not at all, because they are concerned about joining a multiemployer pension plan and then incurring large withdrawal liability if they leave the plan. The suggestion would be for a multiemployer plan to encourage more employer members by either capping the possible amount of withdrawal liability or doing away with it altogether. Kraw argues that even though withdrawal liability is supposed to motivate employers, unions and participants to find solutions to plan funding issues, the reality is that withdrawal liability has interfered with collective bargaining and kept new employers from joining.

The problem with this proposal from a legal perspective is that such voluntary steps would be unlawful under MPPAA. From a policy perspective, there is much debate over what impact withdrawal liability has on both the entry into and the exit out of plans. Contrary to Kraw, other pension plan commentators maintain that withdrawal liability is less a barrier to entry of employers into a multiemployer plan than it is a barrier to the exit of those currently in the plan.

In any event, another problem with amending MPPAA is that almost all multiemployer pension plans are defined benefit plans. The PBGC needs the withdrawal liability money, so it would likely oppose such a plan. Even if MPPAA could be amended in this way, a cap may create a moral hazard problem and further increase PBGC's potential future liabilities. PBGC premiums for insurance coverage are based on actuarial assumptions, and the current ability to assess withdrawal liability is most likely built into these assumptions.

Allow Plans Flexibility to Reduce Investment Assumption Rates and Permit Hedging

Another reform would allow plans greater flexibility to reduce investment assumption rates below current levels and to "immunize" or *hedge* part or all of their assets and liabilities. Currently, most plans assume between 6% and 8% rates of return on their investments. Plans are unwilling to reduce these now unrealistic rates because they would increase their plan liabilities by doing so. Moreover, the lower the assumed rate of investment return, the more assets the plan must have on hand to pay current obligations to retirees.

Kraw argues that pension plans should be able to reduce their rate-of-return assumptions freely. At the same time, plans should be allowed to change some portion of vested benefits into contingent benefits. Kraw also says that plans should be able to *immunize* portions of their investment portfolio by investing in assets that will increase or decrease in direct relationship with an increase or decrease in plan liabilities.

Critics argue that such an approach will lead to lower investment returns. These lower investment returns, however, might be more consistent with the "new normal" for investment returns of 4-5% rather than 6-8%. By balancing liability-driven investment with fixed income securities, much of the same risk-return profile on investments can be maintained. The larger problem with this idea may be undermining workers' vested benefit status. As discussed above, such strong measures should be taken only if there is more evidence plans as a whole are struggling financially.

Create a Chapter 11-Type Bankruptcy Procedure for Severely Distressed Plans

Kraw's fourth and final proposed reform would create a Chapter 11-type bankruptcy procedure for severely distressed plans. This reform would be in addition to the already proposed plans to expand PBGC's authority to partition multiemployer plans to save viable parts. A bankruptcy procedure would permit financial issues to be handled in a more orderly fashion and on a case-by-case basis. Kraw suggests special bankruptcy rules for multiemployer plans that still have significant financial holdings but whose financial obligations greatly exceed assets.

The objection from unions and employees to this method of dividing up pension liabilities among stakeholders is the same objection they have for nonbenefit issues involving other terms and conditions of employment. These procedures often lead to benefits and even whole collective bargaining agreements being terminated. This idea would have to be a last resort—one where the very survival of the employer and/or industry is at stake. Short of that, it is unlikely unions will sign off on such a proposal.

* * *

Many multiemployer plans may need to be restructured to some degree. Creative, out-of-the-box thinking is needed. Whether the reform proposals discussed above will be voluntarily implemented or result from legislation depends on how distressed multiemployer pension plans become, and whether the state of affairs negatively impacts industry and workers' jobs. With the current financial state of affairs for multiemployer plans slowly starting to stabilize, perhaps many of these more drastic proposals can be shelved for the time being.

Challenge #2: The Legislative Challenge to Multiemployer Health and Welfare Plans

Multiemployer plans face numerous challenges as a result of the 2010 health care reform legislation: (1) an excise tax on benefits that exceed a threshold amount, (2) the idea of *grandfathered plans,* (3) the meaning of *minimum essential coverage* and (4) the nature of *health benefit exchanges.*

The Cadillac Tax

Multiemployer health plans were at the center of one of the political storms surrounding passage of ACA. Some observers will remember that a last-minute compromise—not taxing "Cadillac" health care plans until 2018—permitted the legislation to finally get support of the labor movement. A number of these high-cost plans are multiemployer health plans that unions successfully bargained for on behalf of their members over the years.

A 40% excise tax will be imposed starting in 2018 on the value of these employer-sponsored health care plans exceeding a threshold amount of $10,200 for individuals and $27,500 for family coverage. For multiemployer plans, the $27,500 threshold applies to the average of individual and family premiums. To be clear, this is just the starting number for determining the thresholds for taxing excess benefits—other factors will be taken into account to further adjust this number. Prior to ACA, health coverage has not been taxed; indeed, it has been a highly tax-favored employee benefit.

Because of the way various adjustments to these thresholds will be made under ACA, an employer or employers with a workforce that is more expensive to insure due to age and gender characteristics should not be put at a disadvantage. Nevertheless, multiemployer health plans tend to provide generous coverage, and many plans will have to modify their coverage or be forced to pay the 40% excise tax on excess benefits if the Cadillac provision still exists in 2018.

Grandfathered Plans

Under ACA, persons may keep individual and group health plans that were in effect upon enactment of the legislation in March 2010. These *grandfathered plans* are exempt from many, but not all, of the health care market reforms that started to take place in 2010. Just because a preexisting group plan is a grandfathered plan does not mean the plan does not have to comply with some provisions of the new law concerning annual limits, preexisting health condition exclusions and extension of dependent coverage to the age of 26.

Group health coverage subject to a collective bargaining agreement (CBA) ratified before the enactment of ACA is not covered by the law's market reforms until the CBA terminates. If a CBA is modified to comply with the new health care requirements, the CBA is considered to have remained in effect and will not be treated as terminated.

Multiemployer plans may be concerned that grandfathered status might inadvertently be lost based on a change in the employer contribution rate to a plan. The U.S. Department of Labor's Employee Benefit Security Administration (EBSA) has issued a FAQ concerning the implementation of ACA. EBSA addresses concerns that multiemployer plans do not always know whether (or when) a contributing employer changes its contribution rate as a percentage of the coverage cost. Many plans wanted to know what steps to take to communicate with employers regarding employer contributions toward coverage. EBSA's answer was that if multiemployer plans and contributing employers follow steps similar to those outlined in the next paragraph, the same relief will apply to the multiemployer plan unless or until the multiemployer plan knows that the contribution rate has changed.

The Department indicates that until the issuance of final regulations, insured group health plans that have been grandfathered and have a change in an employer contribution rate will retain their grandfathered status if the employer and issuer take the following two steps:

1. Upon renewal, the issuer requires the plan sponsor to make a representation regarding its contribution rate for the plan year covered by the renewal, as well as its contribution rate on March 23, 2010 (if the issuer does not already have it).
2. The issuer's policies, certificates or contracts of insurance disclose in a prominent and effective manner that plan sponsors are required to notify the issuer if the contribution rate changes at any point during the plan year.

In short, multiemployer health plans should be able to keep their grandfathered status by following these provisions until the issuance of final regulations on this topic.

Minimum Essential Coverage

The essential health benefits package offered by qualified health benefit plans in the exchanges (see below) must include specific categories of benefits, meet certain cost-sharing standards and provide particular levels of coverage. Multiemployer plans must similarly meet such new requirements. Minimum benefits include ambulatory patient services, emergency services, hospitalization, maternity and newborn care, mental health and substance abuse disorder services, prescription drugs, rehabilitative services and devices, laboratory services, preventive and wellness services, and pediatric services (including oral and vision care).

Self-insured plans are not "health plans" for this purpose, and thus will not have to comply with the requirements of the essential health benefits package. This might lead even more multiemployer health plans to take the self-insured route—with or without the help of stop-loss insurance and the use of fairly low attachment points.

A self-insured plan with stop-loss coverage pays up to a certain amount of a claim, say $50,000. The stop-loss insurance coverage then kicks in and pays the rest. Although at lower claim levels this begins to look like a fully insured health plan, federal appellate courts continue to treat these plans as self-insured for employee benefit law purposes. All of this might not matter much in the end, since a large majority of multiemployer health plans are either partially or wholly self-funded already.

Health Benefit Exchanges

By 2014, state-based American Health Benefit Exchanges and Small Business Health Options Program (SHOP) Exchanges will be established. Through these programs, individuals as well as small businesses with up to 100 employees can purchase qualified health coverage. States may also form regional exchanges or allow more than one exchange to operate in the state as long as each exchange serves a distinct geographic area. These exchanges will be administered by a governmental agency or a nonprofit organization.

Although health benefit exchanges do not directly affect multiemployer health plans, their presence may exacerbate some of the disturbing financial difficulties these plans are facing. For example, smaller employers may decide that instead of joining a multiemployer plan or providing health coverage, they will let employees get their health coverage through these exchanges.

Here is where a cap on or elimination of withdrawal liability may provide employees an incentive to join multiemployer health plans. MPPAA's withdrawal liability provisions that apply to pension plans do not apply to multiemployer health and welfare plans. The current practice among a smaller number of plans is to impose withdrawal liability by contractual agreement. Therefore, an expanded role for the voluntary cap/waiver idea could work in this context.

* * *

Comprehensive health care reform under ACA will have divergent impacts on multiemployer health plans. The discussion above highlights some of the more significant issues that plan trustees might face in the coming years. Of course, restating what was said initially, all of this new regulation hinges on the legislation being deemed constitutional by the U.S. Supreme Court.

Challenge #3: The Judicial Challenge to Multiemployer Plans

All is not well in the land of judicial interpretation of ERISA and Taft-Hartley Section 302(c)(5). The problem stems from the sometimes vague and expansive language used in both laws. The U.S. Supreme Court and lower federal courts have struggled over numerous and important issues concerning both single and multiemployer health and welfare and pension plans. The length of this chapter does not permit going into all the detail in all the areas where the law continues to shift as successive courts interpret those laws. Nevertheless, some insight can be gained by considering just one complicated area: the standard of review when a multiemployer plan denies a claim benefit.

Denial of Benefit Claims Under Section 502(a)(1)(B) of ERISA

ERISA Section 502(a)(1)(B) claims are instituted to recover benefits, to enforce rights under benefit plans or to clarify rights to future benefits. Claims for benefits are by far the most common claims brought under ERISA. Such suits may be filed against plans by participants or beneficiaries for the value of denied benefits or rights. Consider a plan participant denied payment for a particular heart procedure; the participant may file a claim against the plan for recovery of the value of that heart procedure. Significantly, however, other forms of relief, including compensatory and punitive damages, are not available under Section 502(a)(1)(B).

Before filing a Section 502(a)(1)(B) claim in state or federal court, plan participants must exhaust their plan's internal claims procedures. When a claim is denied, participants must file an appeal with the plan administrator and wait for another adverse determination before the claim may be pursued in state or federal court. The claims issue for the courts becomes under what standard of review courts should review a plan administrator's benefit determinations.

In 1989, the U.S. Supreme Court in *Firestone Tire & Rubber Company v. Bruch* directed that the benefit decision be reviewed under a very deferential arbitrary and capricious standard if the plan vests the administrator with discretion to make such decisions. This standard becomes less deferential when a conflict of interest exists, as when a plan determines both whether a qualified claim exists and whether to cover the claim. Because most multiemployer health plans are self-funded, these plans are often found to have a conflict of interest. Under the more recent 2009 *Metropolitan Life v. Glenn* Supreme Court case, if it is determined that the plan administrator is operating under a conflict of interest in making the claim determination, the court must take that conflict of interest into account in deciding whether to defer to the plan administrator's decision to deny the claim.

In 2010, the federal appellate court for New York, Connecticut and Vermont (the Second Circuit Court of Appeals) decided multiemployer plans are inherently conflicted when making benefit decisions. Going forward, federal trial courts deciding multiemployer plan denial-of-benefit cases will need to scrutinize conflict more seriously when deciding whether a claim was properly denied.

The court reasoned that the structure of these plans, in which employers also help evaluate the claims they will ultimately have to pay, represents the type of conflict addressed in the Supreme Court's *Glenn* decision. In other words, because multiemployer plans are administered by trustee boards made up of an equal number of labor and employer representatives, the plans suffer from board members with conflicting loyalties.

Although trustees have fiduciary interests that weigh in favor of participants and beneficiaries of the plan, they also tend to have interests that favor the employer over these employees. Mostly importantly, by rejecting claims they reduce future employer contributions to the plan. The court rejected the plan's contention that it was not conflicted because it was composed of equal members from management and labor, though it did agree the presence of labor representatives should be considered in deciding how much weight to give to the conflict of interest some management representatives have.

All of this is not to say that plan trustees cannot deny a claim if the benefit is simply not provided by a plan. Given this new conflicted legal standard (and it will be necessary to see if other federal appellate courts agree), plan trustees and their advisors need to do double diligence when denying claims and make sure there is substantial evidence for the claim decision. A good paper trail full of necessary findings and all the proverbial ducks in a row will be essential. For instance, if a participant has a report from a treating physician, make sure the report is considered along with any other employer-provided or independent medical examinations.

Thorough action on the part of plan decision makers will make it less likely a federal court will find a plan decision to be "arbitrary and capricious" and overturn it. It is also important to realize that although the Second Circuit raised the level for benefit denials in the states over which it has authority, it will actually be up to individual federal trial courts in New York, Connecticut and Vermont to decide how much weight a conflict of interest should be given. The weight accorded to any conflict should vary in direct proportion to the likelihood that the conflict affected the benefits decision.

Certain best practices do exist to lessen the potential conflict, including: (1) walling off claims administrators from those interested in firm finances; and/or (2) imposing management checks that penalize inaccurate decision making irrespective of whom the inaccuracy benefits.

Finally, and to make matters even more complicated, the Ninth Circuit—covering California, Oregon, Washington, Arizona, Nevada, Montana, Idaho, Hawaii and Alaska—has come to the opposite conclusion in a 2008 case called *Anderson*.

This discussion shows just how convoluted multiemployer health plan legal issues can become. We might not have a final answer to how to approach this denial-of-benefit issue until the U.S. Supreme Court steps in. In the meantime, trustees should be on the lookout for claim denials that do not seem to add up or are not supported by the evidence.

Conclusion

This chapter has sought to give Taft-Hartley trustees a taste of the future challenges that face their respective multiemployer plans. It also has sought to highlight some possible future reforms to overcome financial, legislative and judicial challenges that might face multiemployer plans in the future. The outlook right now for multiemployer plans in 2011 may look challenging to some and more hopeful for others, but this chapter has sought to show how various legislative, judicial and internal reforms may help Taft-Hartley plans become more sustainable going forward. The hope is that some recalibration and restructuring of multiemployer plans today will lead to more secure beneficiaries in the future.

Chapter 4

DOL and IRS: ERISA Enforcement Responsibilities

Bennett E. Choice

The Employee Retirement Income Security Act of 1974 (ERISA) governs the establishment and administration of employee benefit plans. Responsibility for ERISA is divided among the Department of Labor (DOL), the Department of the Treasury (Treasury) and the Pension Benefit Guaranty Corporation (PBGC).

When Congress first passed ERISA, the statute created bureaucratic confusion because DOL and the Treasury had overlapping authority. Reorganization Plan No. 4 of 1978 helped eliminate much of the administrative overlap. DOL was given responsibility for:

- Disclosure
- Reporting
- Fiduciary obligations
- Prohibited transaction exemptions
- Plan investment rule interpretations.

The Internal Revenue Service (IRS)—an agency within the Treasury—was directed to enforce ERISA's vesting, minimum participation and funding requirements.

Established under ERISA, PBGC is responsible for insuring pension benefits provided by defined benefit pension plans. Sponsors of defined benefit plans pay premiums to PBGC annually. In return, PBGC guarantees that plan participants will receive the benefits promised by their plan—up to a maximum established by law—if a plan experiences financial difficulties. PBGC is responsible for overseeing this insurance program as well as for processing terminations of defined benefit pension plans and overseeing multiemployer pension plan withdrawal liability.

This chapter provides an overview of ERISA enforcement responsibilities and the organizational structure of DOL and IRS

What Is the Role of the Department of Labor?

DOL administers and enforces more than 180 federal laws, including significant portions of ERISA. The Department has principal jurisdiction over ERISA Title I that requires those managing and/or controlling benefit plans and/or plan assets to:

- Manage plans for the exclusive benefit of participants and beneficiaries
- Carry out their duties in a prudent manner
- Comply with plan documents
- Refrain from conflict-of-interest transactions expressly prohibited by ERISA
- Use plan assets to pay plan benefits and appropriate plan expenses
- Fund benefits in accordance with ERISA and plan rules.

ERISA Title I also requires plan fiduciaries to report and disclose information to participants, beneficiaries and DOL. The reporting and disclosure provisions of ERISA require plans to provide the following types of information to participants:

- Summary plan description
- Summary annual report
- COBRA notice and HIPAA certificates (health plans)
- Form 5500 (upon request)
- Plan document (upon request)
- Blackout notice (for participant-directed plans)
- 404(c) disclosure (optional for participant-directed plans)
- Notice of benefit reductions (for pension and health plans)
- Various notices required by the Patient Protection and Affordable Care Act as amended (ACA).

In addition, ERISA's reporting and disclosure requirements obligate plan sponsors to file an annual report (Form 5500) with DOL.

Employee Benefits Security Administration

DOL established the Employee Benefits Security Administration (EBSA) to enforce ERISA provisions. (Prior to February 2003, EBSA was known as the Pension and Welfare Benefits Administration.) Any individual or organization may request an advisory opinion or information letter from EBSA regarding the interpretation or application of ERISA provisions that are within DOL jurisdiction.

Administrators, employers, trustees, service providers and other plan fiduciaries most frequently encounter EBSA when (1) requesting an interpretive ruling regarding ERISA, (2) requesting a prohibited transaction exemption or (3) their plan is undergoing a process that is part of the EBSA enforcement program.

In fiscal year 2010, EBSA closed 3,112 civil investigations. Nearly 74% of those investigations resulted in correction of violations under ERISA. In addition, criminal investigations led to the indictment of 96 individuals during that year.

Audits

EBSA conducts audits of employee benefit plans to ensure plans are in compliance with Parts 1 and 4 of ERISA Title I. These parts of the law deal with establishing a plan and trust, fiduciary duties, investment of plan assets, reporting and disclosure, prohibited transactions and bonding.

Sometimes the agency conducts random plan audits. It is more likely, however, that a specific event or factor will trigger an audit. For example, EBSA may initiate an audit based on a complaint from a plan participant. A plan may also be selected for an audit if a plan's Form 5500 indicates the plan does not maintain a fidelity bond or a plan reports unusual investment activity. EBSA also may audit a plan as the result of a referral from another governmental agency, such as IRS, PBGC or Securities and Exchange Commission.

Certain EBSA initiatives intended to facilitate ERISA compliance can also trigger an audit. To safeguard employee contributions to 401(k) plans, EBSA investigates situations in which employers improperly delay depositing employee contributions into a plan's trust.

With respect to EBSA audit procedure, the agency sends a letter notifying the plan that there will be an audit. The letter requests certain information for review prior to an on-site visit by the agency. The requested information typically includes past Form 5500 returns, plan documents, participant disclosures and related plan records. During the on-site visit, an EBSA investigator usually interviews trustees as well as other plan officials and employees. The investigator may request and review additional plan documents. ERISA gives EBSA the power to *subpoena* (order the provision of) records as part of the investigation.

After completing an audit, plan trustees are typically notified of the investigator's conclusions. If the investigator determines a fiduciary *breach* (violation of the law) has occurred, the plan is typically required to correct the breach. In addition, civil and/or criminal penalties may be imposed. DOL also has the authority to remove a fiduciary that caused a breach.

Other Investigations

To monitor and enforce compliance with ERISA, EBSA also investigates plan service providers such as third-party administrators, insurance brokers, investment providers, accountants, actuarial consulting firms, etc.

Penalties

ERISA authorizes DOL to assess civil penalties against *parties in interest*—generally, plan sponsors, trustees, other fiduciaries and certain related parties—that engage in prohibited transactions with employee benefit plans. A *prohibited transaction* is generally an act involving a conflict of interest between what is best for a plan and what might benefit individuals and organizations that have a relationship with a plan. DOL penalties start at 5% and may increase to 100% of the amount involved in the transaction. A similar provision in the Internal Revenue Code (IRC) imposes an excise tax against *disqualified persons*—generally, the same as parties in interest—who engage in prohibited transactions. ERISA requires DOL to assess a mandatory civil penalty equal to 20% of the amount recovered when a fiduciary breach results in either a settlement agreement or a court order against a fiduciary. In addition, ERISA provides that a plan fiduciary is personally liable to restore any plan losses or profits made as a result of a fiduciary breach.

Voluntary Compliance Programs

EBSA has established two compliance programs to help plan fiduciaries voluntarily correct certain ERISA violations:

1. The **Delinquent Filer Voluntary Compliance Program** allows plan administrators to pay reduced civil penalties for voluntarily complying with annual reporting requirements (typically filing overdue Form 5500 returns).

2. The **Voluntary Fiduciary Correction Program** permits plan administrators to identify and correct 19 specific transactions, including prohibited purchases, sales and exchanges; improper loans and delinquent participant contributions.

A plan sponsor can use these programs to voluntarily correct a defect and avoid penalties that are more serious.

What Is the Role of the Internal Revenue Service?

IRS has primary responsibility for enforcing ERISA vesting, minimum participation and funding requirements. IRS also determines whether a retirement plan is *tax-qualified,* which means the plan receives favorable tax treatment.

IRS has both a national office and regional offices. The IRS Restructuring and Reform Act of 1998 prompted the most comprehensive reorganization of IRS in nearly 50 years. IRS now has four major operating divisions, one of which is the Tax Exempt and Government Entities Division (TE/GE Division). Under the TE/GE Division, the Office of Employee Plans and Exempt Organizations oversees the Employee Plans Examination Program, which is responsible for ERISA enforcement and tax qualification determinations.

Audits

Plan sponsors, administrators and service providers most often encounter IRS enforcement agents through plan audits. These audits typically involve potential prohibited transactions or tax-qualification issues. An IRS audit may result from an independent investigation by IRS or a referral from another agency, such as DOL. Audits are also conducted on a random basis. Exhibit 1 identifies some of the common problems that IRS finds when auditing a multiemployer benefit plan.

Rulings

IRS issues notices, announcements, revenue procedures and so forth to promote uniform application of tax laws. IRS also issues private letter rulings that apply tax laws to specific taxpayer situations and revenue rulings that provide interpretations of tax laws for taxpayers in general.

IRS decides whether prohibited transactions have occurred with respect to retirement plans. If a prohibited transaction occurs, the party who engaged in the transaction must correct the transaction, file a Form 5330 with IRS and pay an excise tax. This tax equals 15% of the value of the transaction for each year it existed.

Exhibit 1

Preparing for an IRS Audit

IRS has published a guide to help multiemployer benefit plans prepare for an IRS audit. In this guide, IRS lists several recurring issues it has encountered during examinations:

- Plans fail to make required distributions to participants who have reached the age of 70½ as required under IRC Section 401(a)(9). Plan administrators should be more proactive with respect to monitoring required minimum distribution requirements.
- Plans fail to meet IRC's "definitely determinable" benefit requirements (primarily an issue for defined benefit plans).
- Required actuarial adjustments or interest-adjusted back payments are not paid to participants whose retirement benefits first began after the "normal retirement date" stipulated in the plan.
- Errors are made when participant benefits are calculated, often because (1) benefit provisions in the plan are misapplied, (2) applicable law is not understood, (3) faulty participant data is used and/or provided by an employer and (4) combinations of all the above.
- Vesting is miscalculated due to use of an incorrect vesting schedule or due to errors when calculating a participant's vesting percentage.
- Plans subject to IRC Section 412 minimum funding requirements fail to receive the necessary contribution amounts within the required time period.
- Plan language has been unclear or has not met IRC Section 401(a). In addition, plan documents are inconsistent with language in other written agreements. Administrators should ensure plan language meets IRC requirements and agrees with all other written agreements.
- Plans sometimes fail to follow or do not have participation agreements for each participating employer. A plan may fail to be a definite written program under the law if it does not define its eligibility and participation requirements in the plan document, collective bargaining agreement or participation agreement.
- Plans have used pension funds for purposes other than the benefit of plan participants or the trust. Common errors include using trust assets for personal purposes, improper allocation of expenses between trusts, improper transfer of assets between related trusts and paying inappropriate plan expenses.

Tax Status

IRS also determines the tax-qualified status of retirement plans. As state previously, tax-qualified plans receive favorable federal tax treatment—employers are able to deduct their plan contributions when reporting their annual income, earnings on contributions accumulate tax-free until distributed and employees are not taxed on their retirement benefits until they receive them. A plan must satisfy numerous requirements to maintain its tax-qualified status. For example, a plan must be in writing. There are other requirements that relate to the timing and amount of contributions and distributions.

Plans are disqualified for many reasons:

- Administration that is not in accordance with the plan's written terms
- Violation of nondiscrimination rules
- Accepting employer contributions in excess of specified limits
- Excluding eligible employees from plan accruals
- Failure to begin making pension payments in the year after a participant reaches the age of 70½.

Plan disqualification has devastating tax consequences for participants, a trust and sponsoring employer. These consequences may include employers losing prior deductions, participants being taxed immediately on vested amounts and the trust becoming taxable. This would require the affected parties to file amended returns for all the years affected by the disqualification.

Given the severe consequences of plan disqualification, IRS has established the Employee Plans Compliance Resolution System (EPCRS) as an alternative to disqualification. EPCRS includes three correction programs that enable retirement plan sponsors that have experienced compliance violations to preserve the tax-qualified status of their plans. Under EPCRS, a sponsor can avoid plan disqualification if it corrects defects in a prescribed manner:

1. **The Self-Correction Program (SCP)** is available for correcting nonegregious operational failures, and does not require any fee or filing with IRS. Under SCP, a sponsor can self-correct a defect on its own without IRS involvement.
2. **The Voluntary Correction Program (VCP)** makes it possible to correct several failures (including egregious failures), but requires paying a fee and filing with IRS.
3. **The Correction on Audit Program (CAP)** is used to correct failures discovered by IRS during an audit. Under CAP, the sponsor must pay a penalty to IRS and correct the defect. The amount paid depends on the nature, extent and severity of the failure.

EPCRS is beneficial to plan sponsors because it provides an alternative to disqualification. The system is also beneficial to IRS because it encourages plan sponsors to correct defects.

What Other Laws Apply to Multiemployer Benefit Plans?

While ERISA is the primary law that applies to multiemployer benefit plans, other state and federal laws apply. Besides the IRC, there is the Taft-Hartley Act, the Health Insurance Portability and Accountability Act (HIPAA), the Family and Medical Leave Act (FMLA), ACA and a host of others. IRS or DOL administers some of these laws; others are enforced by agencies such as Health and Human Services or Equal Employment Opportunity Commission (EEOC).

It is important to understand that while IRS or DOL will have the most significant oversight of employee benefit plans, fiduciaries may have contact with other agencies. For example, the Office of Civil Rights (OCR) is responsible for enforcing HIPAA privacy obligations for health plans that became effective in recent years. Fiduciaries are already witnessing complaints that are leading to contact with OCR. Because EEOC is responsible for enforcing workplace discrimination laws, health plans are also dealing with EEOC on issues such as retiree health eligibility rules and coverage of fertility treatment.

For plans that directly administer their programs, state and federal labor laws and other elements of employment law may also apply.

Chapter 5

Fiduciary Responsibility Under ERISA

*Jeffrey Fuller**

A hallmark of the Employee Retirement Income Security Act of 1974 (ERISA) is the attempt by Congress to identify who are employee benefit plan fiduciaries and to describe the duties of these fiduciaries. It is important for trustees of multiemployer benefit plans to understand how ERISA's fiduciary rules apply to them. It is equally important for trustees to understand how these rules apply to other fiduciaries such as the individuals and entities that trustees appoint for help with plan management. Each trustee has a fiduciary duty to monitor other fiduciaries to ensure that they are complying with ERISA.

Sections 403 and 404 of ERISA provide broad rules governing all aspects of fiduciary activity. ERISA Sections 406 and 407 identify specific types of transactions that fiduciaries are not allowed to engage in with "parties in interest unless there is an individual or class exemption." These *prohibited transaction rules* supplement the general fiduciary duty rules.

Fiduciaries that *breach* (violate) one or more of these fiduciary rules may be subjected to a variety of punishments including civil penalties, excise taxes and making up for any losses experienced by the plan. Under a *co-fiduciary liability* rule, there are certain situations in which fiduciaries may also be responsible for a breach by other fiduciaries. Whether the liability results from a fiduciary's own breach or co-fiduciary liability, the fiduciary is *personally liable* for the breach and may not use plan assets to offset this liability.

Who Is a Plan Fiduciary?

In general, a *fiduciary* is a person in a position of trust. For the purposes of a benefit plan covered by ERISA, a fiduciary is a person or entity that performs certain functions for a plan. Some persons become a fiduciary merely by holding a certain plan position. Plan trustees, for example, are automatically fiduciaries.

ERISA requires the documents governing a benefit plan to identify a *named fiduciary* by (1) a name, title or position or (2) a procedure described in the documents. For almost all multiemployer plans, the named fiduciary is the board of trustees.

Under ERISA, named fiduciaries have the ultimate fiduciary responsibility for a plan. Named fiduciaries have powers that other plan fiduciaries do not have—for example, the power to appoint an investment manager and to make final benefit claims determinations. In fact, the person responsible for final claims determination must be a named fiduciary.

ERISA also provides for other fiduciaries, sometimes referred to as *general fiduciaries.* These fiduciaries include anyone who:

- Exercises any discretion or control over the management of a plan or plan assets, including the disposition of plan assets;
- Provides investment advice to the plan for a fee or other compensation; or
- Has any discretionary responsibility in administering the plan.[1]

*The author wishes to acknowledge Stephen M. Saxon and Jon Bourgault for their previous contribution on this topic in the prior edition of this Handbook, which provided the foundation for this update.

Professional service providers such as accountants, actuaries and legal counsel that limit their involvement to merely performing their normal professional functions are not ordinarily considered fiduciaries.[2] However, if these persons exceed their professional functions, they can be considered fiduciaries. Be aware that those fitting these criteria have fiduciary responsibility regardless of whether they expressly agree to be a fiduciary. In some cases, it is possible to be a fiduciary without even knowing it!

Are Investment Managers and Advisors Fiduciaries?

Yes, investment managers are clearly fiduciaries because they control plan assets. On the other hand, whether an investment advisor is a fiduciary depends on the specifics of the relationship between the advisor and the plan. ERISA considers investment advisors providing advice to a plan for a fee or other compensation to have a fiduciary responsibility to the plan. Both the Department of Labor (DOL) and the courts have concluded this compensation may be direct or indirect. Even if the advisor is paid by a third party instead of the plan, the advisor is still considered a plan fiduciary.[3] DOL defines *investment advisors* as those who

- Provide advice individualized to the plan on (1) the value of securities or other property or (2) whether a plan should invest in securities or other property; and
- Provide this advice (1) on a regular basis and (2) pursuant to a mutual understanding that the advice will serve as the primary basis for an investment decision.

When someone provides investment recommendations to a plan just once or twice (versus regularly), it is not necessarily considered "advice" for the purposes of ERISA. For example, information provided at a general marketing presentation is not provided on a "regular basis." The information is also not "individualized." Under these circumstances, the party making the presentation would not be considered an advisor with fiduciary responsibility. Recent proposed rules by DOL in 29 CFR 2610 seek to expand the scope of fiduciary status to persons or entities giving advice and valuations unless they advise that they are not impartial advisors. If adopted, these rules could substantially expand the scope of fiduciary status.

What Is Co-Fiduciary Liability?

Fiduciaries are not only liable for their individual activities, but also for certain types of breaches by other fiduciaries. A fiduciary is liable for the actions of another fiduciary if the first fiduciary (1) knowingly participates in or conceals a breach by the other, (2) enables the second fiduciary to commit a breach or (3) has knowledge of a breach and fails to make reasonable efforts to remedy the breach.[4]

Fiduciaries are generally not liable for the fiduciary breaches of others that were committed either before they became, or after they ceased being, a fiduciary.[5] However, a fiduciary may be held liable if they learn of a predecessor's breach and fail to take reasonable actions to remedy it. Reasonable steps may include examining and voiding the prior actions of a predecessor if the actions violated ERISA.

DOL has indicated that when a fiduciary is aware only that a breach of fiduciary duty *might* have taken place, the fiduciary need not take steps to further investigate the potential breach. The fiduciary's duty may be satisfied by notifying plan trustees of what information is known regarding the potential violation. In these situations, the fiduciary is also not required to implement special procedures for the sole purpose of evaluating whether a given transaction constituted a breach.

Those not deemed fiduciaries are not liable for participating in a fiduciary's breach even if they were aware the activities constituted a violation. This does not mean a nonfiduciary always escapes liability. If the breach involves a prohibited transaction under Section 406(a) of ERISA and the nonfiduciary was the *party in interest* involved in the transaction, the nonfiduciary party in interest could be compelled to rescind the transaction.[6]

Can Fiduciary Responsibility Be Transferred to Others?

ERISA specifies the ways in which *named fiduciaries* can allocate and delegate fiduciary authority. Named fiduciaries can transfer their broad plan responsibility, and thus liability, using these three methods:

1. Allocate responsibilities among themselves
2. Designate others to carry out responsibilities on their behalf
3. Appoint an investment manager to manage some or all of a plan's assets.

If named fiduciaries do not allocate or delegate their responsibilities, or do not allocate and delegate within the guidelines established by ERISA, each is jointly and *severally* (separately) responsible with the other named fiduciaries for controlling and managing the operation and administration of a plan. Delegation and allocation are explained in much greater detail in Chapters 6 and 7.

What Are a Fiduciary's Responsibilities?

ERISA has five general guidelines concerning the conduct of plan fiduciaries. Fiduciaries are required to:

1. Act solely in the interest of plan participants and beneficiaries
2. Hold and deal with plan assets for the exclusive purpose of paying benefits and defraying reasonable costs of plan administration
3. Act prudently
4. Diversify plan investments
5. Act in accordance with plan documents, but only to the extent that the plan documents are consistent with ERISA.

Sole Interest

When fulfilling their fiduciary duties, fiduciaries must act "solely in the interest" of plan participants and beneficiaries.[7] Fiduciaries must have complete loyalty to these persons and exclude the interests of all other parties including themselves. ERISA, as well as decisions of the courts and the federal government, all indicate this standard is the central responsibility of fiduciaries. Drawing on this standard of conduct, here are some examples of what would be considered a breach of fiduciary duty:

- Trustees try retroactively to cancel accrued benefits of participants working for employers that have withdrawn from a plan.
- A person who is a trustee for two benefit plans consistently favors the interests of one plan over the other in business dealings.

Sometimes fiduciaries must make decisions that treat participants differently with respect to the amount, type and timing of benefit payments. A breach does not occur simply because only participants with smaller vested benefits may receive a lump-sum distribution. Further distinctions among participants concerning benefit distributions, however, are more troublesome. Courts have viewed these attempts in varying ways. Trustees should seek the advice of legal counsel in such situations.

Exclusive Purpose of Assets

ERISA requires plan assets be held for the *exclusive purpose* of providing benefits to participants and beneficiaries.[8] To a large extent, this provision overlaps with the ERISA requirement that fiduciaries act solely in the interest of the plan, its participants and beneficiaries. The exclusive purpose rule, however, applies only to providing plan benefits and paying administrative expenses.

Paying Benefits. Violations of this standard are using plan assets for:

- Personal interests or the interests of anyone other than the plan and its participants and beneficiaries
- Paying benefits to persons who are not eligible for plan benefits.

A particularly interesting issue concerning the exclusive purpose rule is socially responsible investments. Plan participants receive economic benefit from these investments, but nonparticipants also benefit. The DOL position is that fiduciaries cannot sacrifice investment performance to achieve a social policy goal. However, if two or more investments are economically equal for a plan, plan fiduciaries may consider the noneconomic factors in choosing between these investment options. This is consistent with a general rule that it is okay for others to receive benefits from plan investments as long as the principal goal is the financial well-being of the plan.

Defraying Reasonable Costs of Administration. When determining whether a fiduciary act is "defraying reasonable costs of plan administration," two factors are considered:

1. Plan assets are only to be used to pay expenses properly charged to the plan. Plan documents often identify the expenses that may be paid out of plan assets.
2. Even when expenses may be paid, assets may only be used to pay those that are reasonable in amount.

Though a plan may permit the use of plan assets to pay administrative expenses, not all expenses qualify as administrative expenses under ERISA.[9] One example is the cost of services connected with the establishment, design and termination of a plan. Ordinarily these costs are considered business activities of a plan sponsor, *not* plan administrative expenses. As a result, these expenses cannot be paid from plan assets. Nevertheless, DOL recognizes that a board of trustees—versus a union or employer sponsors—is typically responsible for making multiemployer plan design decisions. If multiemployer plan documents state plan trustees are acting in a fiduciary capacity when they make design decisions, the cost of the actions may be paid from plan assets.[10]

When it is permissible to pay an expense using plan assets, fiduciaries must also determine whether the expense amount is "reasonable." In most situations, reasonableness is assessed by comparing the expense amount with the scope and quality of services received. The amount committed to administrative expenses relative to the total value of plan assets may indicate a breach has occurred.

Prudence

ERISA states plan fiduciary duties must be fulfilled:

"with the care, skill, prudence and diligence under the circumstances then prevailing that a prudent man acting in a like capacity and familiar with such matters would use in the conduct of an enterprise of a like character and with like aims." [11]

In other words, a trustee must act in the same manner as a person of ordinary intelligence who is familiar with the matter being considered. Trustees with more knowledge or skill than a person of ordinary intelligence, however, are expected to use all that they possess.

This provision establishes an extremely high standard for plan fiduciaries. In fact, it has been asked whether a fiduciary must act as a "prudent expert." The courts have generally responded "no," but they do emphasize the importance of expertise in satisfying the prudence standard. The test of prudence is an objective one, based upon a court's review of a fiduciary's conduct, as measured against a similarly situated "prudent person." One court has stated that in an ERISA prudence case, the court is to inquire "whether the individual [fiduciaries], at the time they engaged in the challenged transactions, employed the appropriate methods to investigate the merits of the investment."[12] There is some flexibility as to the meaning of prudence in different situations. Procedural prudence and engaging an expert knowledgeable about a transaction as described for investment prudence below are key concepts in determining whether a fiduciary acted prudently.

Investment Prudence. When managing plan assets, DOL requires fiduciaries to have either the expertise necessary to analyze investment opportunities or to seek outside experts for assistance. DOL also says a fiduciary is prudent for the purpose of investing plan assets if the fiduciary has (1) given appropriate consideration to the facts and circumstances the fiduciary knows or should know are relevant to the particular investment or investment course of action, and (2) has acted accordingly given the scope of the fiduciary's investment duties.[13, 14]

A *paper trail* or record supporting fiduciary decisions is important. Fiduciaries who carefully document the procedures they follow may be found to have acted prudently, even if the loan, investment or conduct at issue goes sour. On the other hand, fiduciaries who reach the right result, by good fortune or Ouija board, but not through any reasoned process—are liable for prudence violations.[15] Prudence is measured as of the time of the decision or action, not in hindsight or with the benefit of a crystal ball.

Fiduciaries may not claim a transaction was over their head. "A pure heart and an empty head are not enough" under ERISA.[16] Fiduciaries that do not have the knowledge required for a particular issue may be required to obtain expert advice and assistance.

In DOL's view, "appropriate consideration" of an investment includes (but is not limited to) fiduciary determination that the investment will further the purposes of the plan. Fiduciaries must take into consideration the

- Risk of loss and the opportunity for gain (or other return) associated with the investment
- Composition of the portfolio with regard to diversification
- Liquidity and current return of the portfolio relative to the anticipated cash flow requirements of the plan
- Projected return of the portfolio relative to the funding objectives of the plan. [17]

Noninvestment Prudence. The prudence requirement does not apply just to plan investments. Fiduciaries must exercise prudence in all of their duties. One area that has attracted particular attention from the courts is the prudent selection and monitoring of plan service providers. Plan fiduciaries must determine whether the service to be provided (1) is necessary and (2) will benefit plan participants and beneficiaries. If the answer to both is "yes," the plan fiduciary must prudently select the service provider. This involves inquiring into the qualifications of candidates and following accepted industry procedures for selection of the provider.

A fiduciary who selects a service provider also has a fiduciary responsibility to monitor the performance of the provider at reasonable intervals to ensure the provider (1) is in compliance with the law and the terms of the plan, and (2) satisfies the needs of the plan. A formal periodic review, day-to-day contact and evaluation, or another process that is appropriate given the circumstances may satisfy this review requirement.[18] Courts have also recognized that a prudent fiduciary should be guided by generally accepted standards in conducting such review.

Diversification

To minimize the risk of large losses that might result from a concentration of plan investments in one type of asset, ERISA requires fiduciaries to invest in diversified assets unless it is "clearly prudent" not to do so.[19] If plan fiduciaries fail to diversify plan assets, they must (1) show the prudence of each nondiversified investment and (2) demonstrate the plan was not exposed to any significant risk of large losses because of the failure to diversify.

In ERISA, Congress did not specify fixed percentages for compliance with the investment diversification requirement, but it did provide a list of factors that fiduciaries should consider when investing assets that includes the following:

- The purposes of the plan
- The amount of plan assets
- Financial and industrial conditions
- Types of investment (e.g., mortgages, bonds or stock)
- Distribution as to geographic location
- Distribution as to industries
- Dates of maturity.[20]

Plan assets are often placed in pooled investment vehicles such as mutual funds. In these situations, the diversification requirement is met if the assets in the investment pool are diversified. Similarly, a plan may invest all of its assets in insurance contracts as long as the insurance company's investments are diversified.

Accordance With Plan Documents

The last of the general fiduciary duties is the requirement that a plan fiduciary act in accordance with the "documents and instruments governing the plan" to the extent they are consistent with provisions of ERISA.[21] Congress did not specify precisely which "documents and instruments" it is referring. Surely, the document establishing a plan qualifies as one of these documents. The trust agreement is another obvious governing document. The courts and DOL have identified a wide variety of other documents they view as governing a plan for certain purposes. Among these materials are collective bargaining agreements, investment management agreements, investment guidelines and summary plan descriptions.

While fiduciaries are responsible for acting in accordance with plan documents, fiduciaries also have a duty to determine whether their plan requires any actions that may violate ERISA. Clearly, compliance with plan terms that are illegal under ERISA is a fiduciary breach. Generally, a fiduciary does not violate Section 404(a)(1)(D) merely by incorrectly interpreting plan documents. An action to enforce the incorrect interpretation, however, may be a breach.

What Are Prohibited Transactions?

ERISA's prohibited transactions rules were created to prevent those with a close relationship to an employee benefit plan from benefiting from the relationship.

Per Se Prohibitions

ERISA Section 406(a) establishes a number of *per se prohibitions* that prevent fiduciaries from causing plans to engage in transactions with parties in interest unless the transaction qualifies under an exemption, which is discussed below. To understand these rules, it is essential to know a plan's parties in interest. Among those deemed *parties in interest* are fiduciaries, service providers, employer sponsors and their owners (including certain relatives of fiduciaries, service providers and employer sponsors and owners). Select parties associated with a plan's assets also are considered parties in interest. A complete list of parties in interest, under ERISA, is provided in Exhibit 1.

Unless there is an exemption, the following transactions between a plan and a party in interest are absolutely prohibited under ERISA Section 406(a):

- **A sale or exchange of property.** For example, the sale of stock or real estate by a plan sponsor to a benefit plan is prohibited. Similarly, the sale of a bond to the plan in a principal transaction by a broker who provides other services to the plan would be prohibited.
- **A loan or other extension of credit.** A plan sponsor is not allowed to lend money to a plan for daily securities transactions. A plan purchasing a bond issued by a service provider or plan sponsor is prohibited. Even an extension of time to pay an obligation to the plan by a party in interest can be viewed as a prohibited extension of credit.
- **The provision of services, goods or facilities.** A prohibited transaction occurs when a plan renews its contract with an investment manager. Once the manager begins to provide services, it becomes a "party in interest." Thus, any contract renewal is the provision of services by a party in interest and must qualify as an exemption to permit the transaction.
- **The transfer of plan assets to or for the use or benefit of a party in interest.** An example of this type of prohibited activity is a fiduciary convincing a plan to purchase a plan sponsor's stock from an unrelated third party to help a plan sponsor block a takeover.

The above transactions are prohibited whether direct or indirect. The transaction is *indirect* when a third party provides the benefit. For example, an agreement for a plan to sell a plan asset to a third party who has agreed to then sell the asset to a party in interest is an indirect prohibited transaction.

A fiduciary authorizing a prohibited transaction and the party in interest are both liable for the prohibited transaction. The fiduciary is liable for plan losses and the party in interest is liable for excise taxes or civil penalties. The transaction may also be rescinded and any of the fiduciary's profits surrendered. It should be noted that even if a prohibited transaction benefits the plan, it is still prohibited under these per se rules.

Exhibit 1

Parties in Interest

Section 3(14) of ERISA identifies each of the following as a benefit plan "party in interest:"

(A) Any fiduciary (including, but not limited to, any administrator, officer, trustee or custodian), counsel, or employee of such employee benefit plan;

(B) A person providing services to such plan;

(C) An employer any of whose employees are covered by such plan;

(D) An employee organization any of whose members are covered by such plan;

(E) An owner, direct or indirect, of 50% or more of—

- (i) The combined voting power of all classes of stock entitled to vote or the total value of all shares of stock of a corporation;
- (ii) The capital interest or profits interest of a partnership; or
- (iii) The beneficial interest of a trust or unincorporated enterprise which is an employer or an employee organization described in subparagraph (C) or (D);

(F) A relative of any individual described in subparagraph (A), (B), (C) or (E);[22]

(G) A corporation, partnership, or trust or estate of which (or in which) 50% or more of—

- (i) The combined voting power of all classes of stock entitled to vote or the total value of shares of all classes of stock of such corporation;
- (ii) The capital interest or profits interest of such partnership; or
- (iii) The beneficial interest of such trust or estate, is owned directly or indirectly by persons described in subparagraph (A), (B), (C), (D) or (E);

(H) An employee, officer, director (or a person having powers or responsibilities similar to those of officers or directors) or a 10% or more shareholder directly or indirectly of a person described in (B), (C), (D), (E) or (G), or of the employee benefit plan;

(I) A 10% or more (directly or indirectly in capital or profits) partner or joint venturer of a person described in subparagraphs (B), (C), (D), (E) or (G).

This ERISA provision is interpreted and applied in a literal manner. For example, Section 3(14)(G) requires a 50% ownership interest. Ownership of up to 49.9% will not cause party-in-interest status under this section. In addition, when calculating the ownership percentages, the interests held by a group trust, bank collective investment fund or insurance company separate account are attributed to the plan participating in the trust, fund or account, but *not* the managing trustee, bank or insurance company.

Fiduciary Self-Dealing and Conflicts of Interest

Section 406(b) of ERISA prohibits self-dealing and conflicts of interest involving plan fiduciaries Distinct from the prohibited transaction rules of Section 406(a), the prohibitions of Section 406(b) are not interpreted as literally. Determining whether a violation exists typically requires analysis of all surrounding facts and circumstances. Hence, fiduciaries must use an additional level of care to avoid Section 406(b) breaches.

Self-Dealing. ERISA Section 406(b)(1) says fiduciaries may not deal with plan assets in their "own interest" or for their "own account." This means fiduciaries may not cause a plan to participate in any transaction in which they have an interest that could affect their fiduciary judgment. Deciding whether a violation may occur requires a determination of whether the fiduciary's "own interest" will affect the fiduciary's judgment. The courts agree that a fiduciary receiving an incidental benefit is not self-dealing.

Fiduciary fees and fee structures often raise concerns of self-dealing. A service provider who is also a fiduciary should have no discretion with respect to the amount or timing of its fee payments. DOL has indicated that certain performance fee arrangements may result in fiduciary self-dealing. For example, it is self-dealing if a fiduciary's decisions to sell assets, and which assets to sell, directly affect the timing and amount of a performance fee.

DOL has also indicated fiduciaries may not hire themselves or their affiliates to provide services to a plan unless (1) the fiduciary charges no additional fee, or (2) the fee is limited to the recovery of "direct expenses" in providing the service. The *direct expenses* exception allows fiduciaries to be reimbursed for certain costs if they maintain records sufficient to show the cost would not have been incurred had it not been for the provision of services to the plan.

Fiduciary Conflict of Interest. The next part of ERISA, Section 406(b)(2), forbids fiduciaries from representing or acting on behalf of a party with interests contrary to those of the plan in transactions involving plan assets. A conflict of interest clearly exists when a fiduciary is a participant on both sides of a transaction. Consider a sale of property from a plan sponsor to the plan. A person representing the sponsor who is also a plan fiduciary may not represent both the sponsor *and* the plan during sale negotiations.

When there is a conflict of interest, a fiduciary can take a number of steps to avoid a breach of duty. The fiduciary facing the conflict can:

- Avoid any participation in the discussion of the matter—physically leaving the room during the discussion and voting may be appropriate
- Abstain from voting
- Request the appointment of an independent decision maker
- Request the minutes of the meeting document that the fiduciary did not discuss the matter with any other trustees, has not participated in the discussion of the issue, and has not attempted to exert any influence on other trustees regarding the issue.

DOL has also ruled that if a fiduciary who has recused himself or herself "has material information" concerning a matter "that would be necessary in order for other plan fiduciaries to make an appropriate and prudent decision," the recused fiduciary has a duty under ERISA Section 404 to provide that information to the deciding fiduciaries.[23]

Kickbacks. ERISA Section 406(b)(3) prohibits fiduciaries from receiving any consideration for their personal account in connection with plan asset transactions. This rule clearly prohibits traditional kickbacks. It also prohibits benefits that are less obvious. For example, a plan sponsor that invests plan assets with an investment manager may not receive a discount from that manager for other services provided to the plan sponsor rather than the plan.

Kickbacks are such a serious violation of fiduciary duty that DOL rarely grants exemptions. For the same reason, however, the Department and the courts have narrowly interpreted what is meant by "in connection with" plan asset transactions. For example, Section 406(b)(3) is not violated when a plan sponsor, rather than the plan itself, pays the trustee's fee. As a result, a fiduciary receiving a payment from a third party has the opportunity to show the payments were for services other than a transaction involving plan assets. Similarly, the payment of 12b-1 or shareholder servicing fees from a mutual fund to a service provider, including a fiduciary, will not necessarily involve a violation of Section 406(b)(3) where the payment has been disclosed to the plan's fiduciary and the service provider has not caused the plan to invest in the mutual fund paying the fees.[24]

Employer Securities and Real Property

ERISA Sections 406(a)(2) and 407 prohibit plans from holding "employer securities" or "employer real property" unless they are "qualifying" assets. Some explanation of terms will be helpful here:

- ***Employer securities***—stocks, bonds and so forth issued by a plan sponsor or affiliate[25]
- ***Employer real property***—land and buildings owned by or leased to the plan sponsor or an affiliate
- ***Qualifying employer securities***—stock, marketable obligations and certain limited partnership interests if, immediately following the acquisition, no more than 25% of the stock is held by the plan and at least 50% of the outstanding stock is held by persons independent of the issues. Qualifying real property must be dispersed geographically and be suitable for more than one use. If the plan is not an individual account plan, no more than 10% of the plan assets are invested in employer securities and employer real property.

In addition, a plan may not purchase employer securities or real property from a party in interest, such as the employer, absent an exemption.

Exemptive relief is provided by ERISA Section 408(e) for a plan's purchase or sale of qualifying employer securities or qualifying employer real property if (1) no commission is charged, (2) the compensation is adequate and (3) the 10% limit applicable to nonindividual account plans is observed.

What Are the Exceptions to Prohibited Transactions?

Aware of the broad scope of transactions prohibited under ERISA, a number of exceptions are included in the statute. These exceptions are for transactions that Congress considered common in the marketplace and not posing a threat of abuse. For additional flexibility, Congress also gave DOL the authority to grant administrative exemptions provided the exemption would (1) be administratively feasible; (2) be in the interests of the plan, plan participants and plan beneficiaries; and (3) protect the rights of these same persons. Over the years, DOL has granted exemptions for individual transactions as well as a wide range of transaction classes. Summarized below are some of the more important statutory exceptions and administrative class exemptions.

Provision of Services by a Party in Interest. Section 408(b)(2) ERISA provides an exemption from the prohibited transaction provisions of ERISA for the retention of parties in interest to provide services to a plan if, among other things, the services are provided pursuant to a reasonable arrangement. In the legislative history for ERISA, Congress noted that one hallmark of a reasonable arrangement is a plan's ability to terminate the contract or arrangement on relatively short notice if the contract or arrangement had become disadvantageous to the plan. This presumes that appropriate plan fiduciaries will be reviewing the arrangement to determine if it has begun to operate to the plan's detriment A party in interest may provide (and be paid for) services to a plan if (1) the services are necessary for plan operation, (2) the services are supplied under a reasonable arrangement (which includes the plan's right to terminate without penalty on reasonably short notice) and (3) the plan pays no more than reasonable compensation.[26] This exemption does not provide relief for self-dealing. For instance, a fiduciary cannot cause the plan to pay itself additional fees.

It is important to be aware that the payment of service fees may not always involve a direct transfer of funds from a plan to a party in interest. Consider a trust company that may receive part of its compensation in the form of fees paid by mutual fund companies.[27] Similarly, a bank may receive a portion of its compensation by retaining the "float" earned on funds in a general transfer account.[28] Compensation methods such as these are proper if they are disclosed to the appropriate fiduciary and the fiduciary includes the compensation as part of the overall cost to the plan for receiving the services from the party in interest. Recently, DOL issued expanded disclosure requirements, and failure to comply will preclude application of this exemption.

Interest-Free Loans. Another exemption allows a party in interest to make an interest-free, unsecured loan to (or guarantee the debt of) a benefit plan.[29] The loan proceeds may be used only for (1) payment of the ordinary operating expenses of the plan (including benefit payments) or (2) purposes incidental to the operation of the plan. Importantly, effective April 7, 2007, if an interest-free loan made for purposes incidental to the operation of the plan is for a period longer than 60 days, the loan agreement must be in writing and include all the material terms of the loan.

Qualified Professional Asset Managers (QPAMs). A *QPAM* is a bank, insurer or registered investment advisor that meets minimum capital requirements. The QPAM exemption permits most party-in-interest transactions that would otherwise be prohibited if, among other conditions, the assets involved in the transaction are managed by a QPAM.[30] Again, this exemption provides no relief for self-dealing violations nor does it cover transactions between a fund and the QPAM or those who have appointment authority over the QPAM.

Securities Lending. If certain conditions are met, plans are allowed to lend securities to banks and broker-dealers (both foreign and national) who are parties in interest. Payment of compensation to "lending fiduciaries" for their services in lending plan securities is also allowed. [31]

Short-Term Investments. Plans may invest in bankers' acceptances, commercial paper, repurchase agreements and certificates of deposit that might otherwise be prohibited as party-in-interest transactions. There are specific conditions for each type of investment.[32]

Investments in a Bank Collective Fund or Insurance Company Pooled Separate Account. If certain conditions are met, plans may purchase units in a bank collective fund or pooled separate account maintained by a party-in-interest bank or insurance company.[33] DOL has confirmed this exemption covers the prohibitions of both Section 406(a) and 406(b).[34]

Transactions by a Bank Collective Fund or Pooled Separate Account. If a plan invests in an insurance company pooled separate account or bank collective fund, the account or collective fund is deemed to hold plan assets. Thus, in order to engage in transactions with parties in interest with respect to any investing plan, the account or fund must comply with PTE 90-1 (pooled separate accounts) or PTE 91-38 (bank collective fund). These class exemptions do not exempt self-dealing violations by the managers of the account or fund.

Broker-Dealer Exemption. Under this exemption, (1) a fiduciary broker may execute securities transactions for the plan, (2) certain agency cross transactions may also be executed if the broker does not have discretion on both sides, (3) securities may be bought or sold in principal transactions between a plan and a party-in-interest broker, bank or reporting dealer and (4) certain market-making and underwriting transactions between plans and fiduciary broker-dealers are authorized. This class exemption does not exempt self-dealing violations.[35]

Insurance Agents, Consultants and Mutual Fund Underwriters. If certain conditions are met, fiduciary salespersons representing these entities are allowed to provide investment advice to plans and receive commissions on plan transactions. It also authorizes sales of insurance or mutual fund shares to plans by party-in-interest insurers or underwriters.[36]

What Are the Penalties if a Fiduciary Duty Is Breached?

When fiduciaries violate their responsibilities under ERISA, they are personally liable to make good any losses suffered by the plan because of the breach; plan assets *cannot* be used to pay for a fiduciary's liability. Fiduciaries must also give their plan any profits that they made through the use of plan assets in violation of their fiduciary duties. Fiduciaries may also be removed from their position as a fiduciary and prevented from serving as a fiduciary for any other plan.

Fiduciaries may also be sued by DOL, plan participants and beneficiaries, and other plan fiduciaries. If any of these parties win their legal suit, they may be awarded attorney fees and court costs. When DOL is involved in a lawsuit, fiduciaries may also be assessed a civil penalty equal to 20% of the amount recovered on behalf of the plan.

If a fiduciary violation involves a prohibited transaction, additional penalties apply. In the case of a qualified pension plan, the party in interest involved in the transaction (which includes the fiduciary in the case of fiduciary self-dealing) is liable for an excise tax equal to 15% of the transaction amount for each taxable year in which the transaction remains uncorrected. A failure to correct a transaction in response to a request from IRS can increase the excise tax to 100% of the amount involved. Similar civil penalties are imposed by DOL in the case of welfare plans and pension plans not subject to the qualification rules in the Internal Revenue Code.

Can Plan Fiduciaries Purchase Insurance to Reduce Their Liability?

ERISA declares void and against public policy any plan provision that attempts to relieve a fiduciary from personal liability for a breach. This is not to say fiduciaries cannot take steps to protect themselves from liability. Plan assets may be used to purchase fiduciary liability insurance as long as the policy provides recourse against a fiduciary in breach. In such cases, the fiduciary typically purchases a nonrecourse rider with his or her own assets.

If plan documents allow and no fiduciary breach is involved, plan assets can be used to *indemnify* (reimburse) the fiduciary. For example, a fiduciary can be reimbursed by a plan for court costs, attorney fees and other expenses incurred in successfully defending a suit for fiduciary breach. In addition, if the entity that appointed the fiduciary is not otherwise prohibited from doing so, the fiduciary may also obtain indemnity from this appointing entity.

Conclusion

In concluding, remember the five fiduciary requirements to:

1. Act solely in the interest of plan participants and beneficiaries
2. Hold and deal with plan assets for the exclusive purpose of paying benefits and defraying reasonable costs of plan administration
3. Act prudently
4. Diversify plan investments
5. Act in accordance with plan documents, but only to the extent that the plan documents are consistent with ERISA.

Compliance demands great attention and skill. With the help of legal counsel, most trustees are to be commended for fulfilling these duties.

Endnotes

1. ERISA §3(21)(A).
2. *Pappas v. Buck Consultants, Inc.*, 923 F.2d 531, 535-37 (7th Cir. 1991) (actuary not a fiduciary; not liable under ERISA for plan's underfunding due to improper recommendations); *Painters of Philadelphia District Council v. Price Waterhouse*, 879 F.2d 1146 (3d Cir. 1989)(accountants); *see also* 29 C.F.R. §2509.75-5.
3. ERISA §3(21)(A)(ii).
4. ERISA §405(a).
5. ERISA §409(b).
6. ERISA §3(14) defines *party in interest.*
7. ERISA §404(a)(1).
8. ERISA §403(c)(1) and §404(a).
9. ERISA §404(a)(1)(A)(ii).
10. Field Assistance Bulletin 2002-2 (November 4, 2002).
11. ERISA §404(a)(1)(B).
12. *Donovan v. Mazzola*, 716 F.2d 1226, 1231-32 (9th Cir. 1983), *cert. denied*, 464 U.S. 1040 (1984). *See also Donovan v. Cunningham*, 716 F.2d 1455, 1467 (5th Cir. 1983), *cert. denied*, 467 U.S. 1251 (1984); *Katsaros v. Cody*, 744 F.2d 270 (2d Cir.), *cert. denied*, 469 U.S. 1072 (1984).
13. DOL Regs. 29 CFR §2550.404a-1(b)(1).
14. *Brock v. Robbins*, 830 F.2d 640, 648 (7th Cir. 1987).
15. *Brock v. Robbins*, 830 F.2d 640, 648 (7th) Cir. 1987).
16. *Donovan v. Cunningham*, 716 F.2d 1455, 1467 (5th Cir. 1983) *cert. denied*, 467 U.S. 1251 (1984).
17. *Howard v. Shay*, 100 F.3d 1484 (9th Cir. 1996).
18. DOL Regs. 29 CFR §2550.404a-1(b)(2).
19. DOL Regs. 29 CFR §2509.75-9.
20. ERISA §404(a)(1)(C).

21. H.R. Rep 93-1280, 93d Cong., 2d Sess. p. 304.
22. ERISA §3(15) defines *relative* as "a spouse, ancestor, lineal descendant, or spouse of a lineal descendant."
23. Information Letter to William Lindsay issued on February 23, 2005.
24. DOL Advisory Opinions 97-15A and 97-16A (May 22, 1997).
25. ERISA §407(d)(1), (2).
26. ERISA §408(b)(2).
27. DOL Advisory Opinion 2003-09A (June 25, 2003).
28. DOL Field Assistance Bulletin 2002-3 (November 5, 2002).
29. PTE 80-26 (as amended, April 7, 2006).
30. PTE 84-14.
31. PTE 2006-16 (amending and replacing PTE 81-6 and 82-63, October 31, 2006).
32. PTE 81-8.
33. ERISA §408(b)(8).
34. DOL Adv. Opinion 96-15A (Aug. 7, 1996).
35. PTE 75-1 (as amended, February 3, 2006).
36. PTE 84-24 (as amended, February 3, 2006).

Chapter 6

Allocation and Delegation of Fiduciary Responsibility

William H. Tobin

The operation and administration of a multiemployer benefit plan involves many duties and responsibilities—monitoring and adjusting plan design, collecting contributions, investing plan assets, making benefit payments and much more. If a trustee had to do all of these functions personally, he or she would have to possess the skills and knowledge of an administrator, attorney, actuary, accountant and investment advisor. No such person exists.

Most multiemployer plan trustees do not have the expertise necessary to manage a plan without the assistance of qualified experts. As fiduciaries, trustees who try to manage a plan without this assistance risk a *breach* (violation) of their fiduciary duties. Consequently, a primary function of benefit plan trustees is the allocation and delegation of their fiduciary responsibilities to others who have the abilities to fulfill these duties to the extent permitted by law and plan documents. Trustees are still responsible for monitoring those to whom they have delegated fiduciary duties.

This chapter reviews the legal guidelines that apply to the delegation of responsibility by benefit plan fiduciaries. The extent to which the law allows delegation is examined along with the effect of such delegation on fiduciary liability.

How Do Fiduciaries Transfer Their Responsibilities?

ERISA provides three methods by which named trustees of a benefit plan can transfer fiduciary responsibilities to others. The *named fiduciaries* of a multiemployer plan are typically a plan's board of trustees. These trustees are permitted to:

- Allocate responsibilities among themselves
- Designate others to carry out fiduciary responsibilities on their behalf
- Appoint an investment manager to manage some or all of their plan's assets.

It is essential to note that trustees can do these things only if a plan's governing documents allow the action and provide procedures for doing so. If the delegation or allocation is in accordance with plan documents and with ERISA as described below, fiduciaries are relieved of their liability for the acts or omissions of the parties given the responsibility.[1] Of course, the named fiduciary delegating responsibility remains responsible for the prudent selection and monitoring of those to whom responsibility is transferred.

Be aware that there is one major exception with respect to fiduciary responsibility—ERISA's *co-fiduciary rules.* These rules say fiduciaries are liable for the breach of other fiduciaries under certain circumstances. Fiduciaries are liable if they actively participate in or conceal a breach. They are also liable if they make it possible for the breach to occur as a result of their own breach, or fail to take reasonable steps to correct a breach.[2] A more complete explanation of co-fiduciary liability is provided in Chapter 5.

Allocation Among Named Fiduciaries

ERISA permits named fiduciaries to *allocate* (distribute) fiduciary responsibilities among themselves—as when specific named trustees are given the responsibility (and the liability) for particular activities. An example of allocation would be the appointment of an audit or delinquency committee consisting of two individual trustees charged with monitoring employer contribution collections. Another committee might be created to consider claims appeals.

Tip for Trustees

Under some circumstances, such as investments in mutual funds, fiduciary responsibility for plan assets does not transfer to investment managers. With your advisors, carefully review documentation concerning the investment arrangement to assess who has fiduciary responsibility for these assets.

Delegation to Others

ERISA also allows named fiduciaries to delegate their fiduciary responsibilities to parties other than named fiduciaries.[3] While this chapter focuses on delegation that involves the transfer of fiduciary duties, it is useful for trustees to know that ERISA also permits the delegation of some plan executive and discretionary functions that does not involve the transfer of fiduciary responsibility.

Appointment of Investment Manager

ERISA requires one or more trustees to hold all benefit plan assets in trust.[4] These trustees have exclusive authority and discretion to manage and control those assets. ERISA permits named fiduciaries to delegate this authority to an "investment manager." Under ERISA, these managers are any fiduciaries that:

- Have the power to manage, acquire or dispose of any plan assets
- Are (1) registered as an investment advisor under the Investment Advisors Act of 1940, (2) a bank or (3) a qualified insurance company
- Have acknowledged their fiduciary status in writing.[5]

Unless trustees delegate the responsibility for a plan's investment portfolio to an investment manager—and the manager provides a written statement accepting the responsibility—the responsibility for the investment of plan assets remains with the trustees.[6] In general, trustees also retain responsibility for any plan assets placed in mutual funds. Trustees must carefully review all documents that detail the arrangement to assess who has fiduciary responsibility.

What Are the ERISA Guidelines for Transferring Fiduciary Responsibilities?

The same broad ERISA standards that govern fiduciary conduct apply to the delegation and allocation of fiduciary responsibility. Fiduciaries are not liable for an act or omission of a person to whom they delegate or allocate responsibility if, in transferring the responsibility, the fiduciary acts:

- Prudently in accordance with ERISA
- Solely in the interest of the plan, plan participants and plan beneficiaries
- In accordance with plan documents.

Plan documents are a focal point in determining when and how fiduciaries can allocate and delegate duties. A plan document must authorize the transfer of responsibilities and contain a procedure for how it happens. Fiduciaries must act in accordance with all procedures. If both of these requirements are not met, a court may determine fiduciaries have breached their fiduciary duty. In fact, if a named fiduciary fails to comply with plan requirements in delegating responsibility, the fiduciary has not transferred fiduciary responsibility.

Selection

ERISA supplies limited guidance on the prudent selection of service providers when fiduciary responsibility is delegated. It is clear from Department of Labor (DOL) regulations and court decisions that trustees are expected to establish objective selection procedures. Part of the process must be an assessment of the potential providers' qualifications, the quality of their services and whether provider fees are appropriate for the service promised. The specifics of the selection process depend on the circumstances, including the type of benefit plan and the services to be provided. Documentation of the selection process is often key to demonstrating prudence.

Monitoring

Named fiduciaries have a responsibility to monitor the performance of fiduciaries that they have selected to carry out fiduciary duties. Named fiduciaries also have a duty to withdraw transferred responsibilities when it becomes clear the duties are not being properly fulfilled.

Prudent monitoring includes periodic review of the designated fiduciaries. This requirement may be satisfied through any one of the following:

- Normal periodic review (which may be by all the named fiduciaries who have participated in the delegation or a specially designated review committee)
- Day-to-day contact and evaluation
- Other ways considered appropriate given the circumstances.

Since effective review may result in terminating a provider's services, trustees should work with their consultants to assess the ability to promptly terminate the arrangement (within the limits of the circumstances).

Training and Information

In addition to appointing and monitoring those who have been assigned fiduciary duties, court decisions also suggest that there is a responsibility to train and inform them.

Is Any Documentation Required When Transferring Fiduciary Responsibilities?

It is important to create a "paper trail" or record supporting fiduciary decisions to delegate or allocate responsibilities. If there is an audit by DOL or the Internal Revenue Service (IRS)—or a lawsuit—named fiduciaries are likely to be required to demonstrate that the transfer of duties was appropriate. Fiduciaries should document the process they followed in selecting, retaining and monitoring providers, including the basis for the decision, the factors reviewed and the care given to the decision. This will provide an "institutional memory" of the decision.

Fiduciaries that delegate or allocate responsibility should clarify the nature of the delegation. For example, if fiduciaries delegate responsibility to a service provider, the fiduciaries should require the provider to identify in writing the services that it is providing as a fiduciary or co-fiduciary.

Fiduciaries should document that all fiduciary obligations are assigned to specific parties (either in plan documents or by action of the plan sponsor or a fiduciary), and that each party is performing all obligations delegated to that party.

Under What Circumstances Are Fiduciaries Liable for the Breach of Another?

When named fiduciaries allocate or delegate responsibility in accordance with plan provisions and procedures, the named fiduciaries usually are not liable for the acts or omissions of those to whom they delegate fiduciary responsibility. They can, however, be considered liable to the extent that they did not exercise prudence with respect to (1) the allocation or delegation, (2) the continuation of the allocation or delegation, or (3) the establishment or implementation of the delegation procedures.

If responsibilities have not been appropriately allocated or delegated, each named fiduciary is jointly and *severally* (separately) responsible. Consider a plan administration committee that appoints a fiduciary to make claims determinations, where the committee has the fiduciary duty to perform that activity. A trustee on this committee may be responsible for a breach by the appointed fiduciary even if the trustee never actually participates in the claims process.

Decisions From the Courts

Liability for Investment Losses

In *Schetter v. Prudential-Bache Securities, Inc.*, 695 F. Supp. 1077 (E.D. Cal. 1988), a plan lost money when a plan account was mishandled by a broker and the brokerage house that employed the broker. Because the broker gave investment advice to plan trustees, the trustees argued the actions of the broker and the broker's employer were a breach of fiduciary duty. Nevertheless, the court stated that the only way to delegate the fiduciary responsibility for investments was through the appointment of an investment manager. The court found that the broker was not an investment manager because the broker had not acknowledged his status in writing.

Prudent Selection When Transferring Responsibility

Whitfield v. Cohen, 682 F. Supp. 188 (S.D.N.Y. 1988), provides an example of what a court expects of trustees when choosing a person or firm for the delegation of fiduciary responsibility for plan investment management. In this case, the court held that evaluation of a firm's ability to manage plan assets "fell far short of the careful inquiry required of a trustee." The plan trustees failed to determine the investment experience of the firm or any of its employees, the educational credentials of any of the firm's employees, whether the firm was registered as an investment advisor, the identity of other clients of the firm in order to obtain references, the nature of the investments to be made by the firm on behalf of the plan and the fees to be paid to the firm.

Prudent Monitoring When Transferring Responsibility

In *Mazur v. Gaudet*, 14 EBC 2844 (E.D. La. 1992), the court determined that individual members of a plan's board of trustees were subject to co-fiduciary liability for failing to properly monitor the actions of a co-trustee to whom investment authority had been allocated. Because of the board members' lack of oversight and their failure to review independently the investment actions of the co-trustee (who was solely responsible for investing the assets), the co-trustee embezzled $2.6 million.

Further, ERISA's general co-fiduciary rules apply. Even when a fiduciary has allocated a responsibility to another fiduciary, he or she will still be liable if:

- His or her failure to act prudently enables the other fiduciary to commit a breach
- He or she has knowledge of the other fiduciary's breach and fails to make reasonable efforts to remedy the breach
- He or she conceals the other fiduciary's breach.

What Actions Help Ensure the Prudent Transfer of Fiduciary Responsibilities?

Unfortunately, there are no clear, concise rules that can be followed to guarantee a fiduciary is fully insulated from liability. A fiduciary of an employee benefit plan should be comforted, however, knowing that (1) the law recognizes fiduciaries need help in carrying out fiduciary responsibilities and (2) it provides protection from the acts or omissions of those delegated the responsibility if selection and retention were prudent.

There are some general rules fiduciaries can follow to demonstrate prudence in selecting persons and firms to provide assistance. Plan records should always document the

- Process followed in selecting the person or firm
- Information regarding those solicited
- Experience of the candidates
- Basis for selection.

In many cases, this may require that the fiduciaries undertake a formal competitive bidding process.

After retaining a service provider, fiduciaries must establish techniques and procedures to ensure that the provider performs tasks properly. A written record should also provide evidence of prudence in the retention process.

Operation and administration of an employee benefit plan can be divided into four major categories: (1) recordkeeping, (2) collections, (3) providing benefits and (4) investments. For each of these functions, additional tips follow that can help fiduciaries prudently carry out their responsibilities.

Recordkeeping

The employee benefit records that need to be maintained are numerous and diverse. There are the financial records that account for all payments to and from a plan, as well as all plan assets and liabilities. These records provide the basis for the plan's financial statements. The reports and disclosures required by ERISA can also be included as recordkeeping. Additional documentation is needed to track a person's entitlement to plan benefits.

Recordkeeping for employee benefit plans is generally delegated to two types of professionals: administrators and accountants. The administrators may be salaried persons employed by the plan or an independent firm that contracts with the plan to provide administrative services.

To verify that an administrator is adequately performing recordkeeping duties assigned, fiduciaries can request the following:

- Have an auditor review and comment on the adequacy of the administrator's financial recordkeeping systems and procedures. This assessment is often performed in conjunction with the auditor's preparation of the management letter to the board of trustees.
- Have the auditor or actuary review recordkeeping systems for establishing benefit eligibility. In pension plans, the auditor or actuary annually reviews the systems for keeping track of the vesting and benefit credits each plan participant earns.

Trustees can also delegate the filing of government reports to either a plan administrator or accountant. Responsibility for compliance with ERISA's disclosure requirements such as a summary annual report and summary plan description might be assigned to an administrative manager. When delegating tasks, fiduciaries should still verify that reports and disclosures are timely and comply with applicable laws and regulations.

Decisions From the Courts

Training and Monitoring When Transferring Responsibility

In *American Fed. of Unions Local 102 Health and Welfare Fund v. Equitable Life Assur. Soc. of the U.S.*, 841 F.2d 658 (5th Cir. 1988), an insurance agent appointed by plan trustees as administrator for a health plan was found to have breached his fiduciary duty. Efforts to hold the insurance company responsible failed. The court held the plan trustees responsible for not having trained the agent.

Courts have also entertained claims that the duty to monitor includes a duty to supply the delegate with information. In *Sprint Corporation ERISA Litigation*, 2004 WL 1179371, *21 (D. Kan. 2004), the court declined to dismiss the case and allowed discovery to proceed in part because of a failure to monitor a delegate and inform him or her of critical information pertaining to employer stock. The failure was considered a breach of duties by the named fiduciary.

Collections

Multiemployer plan fiduciaries must collect all monies owed to a plan by participating employers. To ensure that contributions are being paid, trustees should consider these actions if they are not already in place.

- Adopt delinquency rules and procedures that provide for:
  - Notices from administrative personnel when an employer's plan contributions are delinquent
  - Assessment of interest and liquidated damages against delinquent employers
  - Referral of collection to legal counsel on a timely basis.
- Retain an accounting or other firm to audit the payroll records of participating employers to confirm that employers make all contributions to the plan as required by the employer's collective bargaining agreement; they should also review materials for communication effectiveness.

Providing Benefits

This broad area includes benefit plan design, plan funding and the payment of benefits. The design and funding of benefits is one of the most technical aspects of plan operations and as such, unquestionably requires professional assistance from a benefit consulting/actuarial firm(s).

As a practical matter, it is difficult for fiduciaries to monitor the technical adequacy of these firms' performance. At a minimum, trustees should insist upon timely, written reports and make certain the substance of these reports is understandable. Trustees for pension plans may wish to have legal counsel confirm that the funding status of the plan complies with all legal requirements.

Payment of benefits is usually a task delegated to an administrative manager. To ensure that benefits are being paid in accordance with a plan's written rules, trustees can have a benefit consultant or auditor audit the claim payments.

Investment

This is probably the area of most concern to the average trustee. Responsibility for investing millions of dollars can be overwhelming. An investment consultant can counsel the trustees. Specifically, a consultant can assist in the creation and maintenance of investment guidelines and objectives, as well as the selection and retention of investment managers. A named fiduciary may even appoint a delegate to handle all trustee responsibilities related to the investment of plan assets.

A properly drafted agreement is essential when allocating fiduciary responsibilities to an investment manager. The agreement with the investment manager should document the basis for the relationship and address such issues as:

- Acknowledgment of fiduciary status
- The scope of the engagement
- Style of management
- Applicable benchmarks
- Reporting obligations
- Fees
- ERISA qualifications
- Compliance with bonding requirements
- Proxy voting reports
- Any other representations or warranties required of the manager.

Remember, proxy voting responsibility accompanies the investment in publicly traded securities. The duty to monitor an investment manager includes the duty to monitor the manager's proxy voting (or the proxy voting service if such is retained). An agreement should require a manager or service to provide proxy reports.

Decisions From the Courts

Documenting Transfers

In *In re Unisys Savings Plan Litigation*, 74 F.3d 420 (3rd Cir. 1996), the court denied summary judgment in favor of plan fiduciaries because they had failed to adequately document their investigation into certain insurance contracts before investing. Three years later, after a ten-day bench trial and another appeal, the court found sufficient evidence that the fiduciaries had conducted a prudent investigation prior to investment. Although the plan fiduciaries eventually won, the failure to adequately document their investigation resulted in three years of litigation and legal fees.

Court cases also make clear that fiduciaries should ensure that the appropriate party performs all duties. For example, in *Bass v. Prudential Insurance Co.*, 14 EBC 1837 (D. Kan. 1991), an employer claimed it had no duty to notify a participant that his benefit claim had been denied. The employer believed it had delegated that responsibility to its insurer, Prudential. However, the court determined that the plan documents specifically assigned this duty to the employer. Thus, the employer breached its fiduciary duty by failing to notify the claimant.

For each investment manager, trustees should establish, in concert with the investment manager, a written statement of investment objectives and guidelines. Trustees should also consider periodic meetings with each manager to compare the manager's performance against these objectives and guidelines, as well as the performance of other investment managers. An investment consultant can be very useful in this process.

Conclusion

Regardless of whether a function that a trustee assigns to another party is fiduciary or not, ERISA requires the trustee to prudently select the person or firm that will take on the responsibility. When the function is ongoing in nature, the trustee must prudently monitor performance of the task.

Trustees are advised to create a written record that documents the rationale for assigning the duty to another, how the provider was chosen to do the task and the trustees' review of the provider's performance.

With a reasonable amount of common sense and effort, trustees can satisfy ERISA's requirements for transferring fiduciary responsibilities and rest assured they fully satisfy the requirements of the law.

Endnotes

1. ERISA §405(c)(2).
2. ERISA §405.
3. ERISA §405(c).
4. ERISA §403(a).
5. ERISA §3(38).
6. *McManus & Pellouchoud, Inc. Employees' Profit Sharing Trust v. L.F. Rothschild,* 1989 U.S. Dist. LEXIS 10098 (N.D. Ill. 1989).

Chapter 7

Utilizing Professional Advisors in Fulfilling Fiduciary Responsibility

*Paul J. Ondrasik Jr. and Edward R. Mackiewicz**

Professional advisors to employee benefit plans are much like spouses—you can't live with them, and you can't live without them. This age-old adage is even truer today. The administration of a modern employee benefit plan is more complex and time-consuming than ever before. Plan assets have grown greatly, and increasingly sophisticated investment options are available. Providing adequate medical coverage to plan participants in the face of increasing costs and competing demands for dollars is a daunting task. The legal and regulatory environment in which plans operate seems to change on an almost daily basis and can be confusing even to the regulators.

It is not surprising multiemployer plan trustees have turned to professional advisors for assistance with plan operations. Virtually all trustees have full-time jobs and other responsibilities also demanding their attention. Service as a trustee is secondary to what trustees do for a living. No matter how hard trustees work or how bright they are, it is difficult to bring to their trustee responsibilities the same degree of expertise they must have in their regular jobs.

In turning to professionals for assistance, however, trustees cannot forget one overriding fact: The ultimate responsibility (and liability) for plan administration largely remains on their shoulders. It is *their* plan. *They*, not their advisors, are responsible for plan success.

This chapter explores the relationship trustees have with professional advisors, from both a legal and a practical perspective. At the outset, there is a brief overview of the general legal standards that govern this area; particular focus is given to the fiduciary issues connected with selecting and monitoring experts to assist trustees in doing their work. The next section identifies the common members of a plan's professional advisor "team" and briefly describes the types of services typically expected from each member. Some practical aids and guides will help fiduciaries in hiring and using professional advisors.

What Basic Fiduciary Standards Apply When Employing Professional Advisors?

The Employee Retirement Income Security Act of 1974 (ERISA) places the ultimate responsibility for the operation and administration of a plan on the board of trustees.[1] In performing this role, trustees must adhere to ERISA's general fiduciary rules and avoid prohibited transactions.[2] In essence, trustees must act:

- With "undivided loyalty" to the interests of plan participants and beneficiaries
- With the "care, skill, prudence, and diligence" of a prudent person (or, as discussed below, a prudent expert)
- In accordance with plan documents except where they are inconsistent with ERISA.

Trustees must also not engage in self-dealing with plan assets or enter into plan transactions with "parties in interest" unless an exemption is applicable.[3] Generally, *parties in interest* are persons or entities with which the plan's trustees, employers or union have a close relationship.[4] All of these duties are explained in greater depth in Chapters 5 and 6 of this handbook.

*The authors gratefully acknowledge the assistance of Edward Thomas Veal, senior counsel in the firm's Chicago office, in preparing the update of this chapter.

The Department of Labor (DOL) and many courts view ERISA's requirement that fiduciaries be prudent as a "prudent expert" standard. This is a good way to think about prudence. If a fiduciary decision is challenged in court, the fiduciary can expect to face testimony from acknowledged experts detailing what they would have done under similar circumstances.

It is also important to bear in mind that prudence is primarily a matter of *procedure* rather than *outcome.* Consider two fiduciaries confronted by the same issue. One fiduciary is able to demonstrate he or she sought advice and followed a prudent decision-making process. The liability exposure for this fiduciary is far less than that of a fiduciary acting without adequate advice (or who neglected to document that advice). This is true even if both fiduciaries make the same decision and get the same results.

ERISA permits, and in many ways encourages, trustees to use professional advisors for help in carrying out fiduciary responsibilities. With some duties, a professional advisor is almost a necessity. This is particularly true when (1) important decisions are made about matters on which trustees lack expertise or (2) a potential conflict of interest exists.

Getting expert advice is not, however, a flu shot against liability; trustees cannot hire a team of well-credentialed advisors and then go fishing. Three areas are of particular concern:

1. In recent years, the Employee Benefits Security Administration (EBSA) has paid increasing attention to the fees that plans pay for professional services:
   a. The Form 5500 annual report now requires extensive information about service providers' direct and indirect compensation.[5]
   b. Recent regulations state arrangements between retirement plans and investment advisors (and some other service providers) are not "reasonable" unless the advisor furnishes the plan with disclosures to help plan fiduciaries evaluate the reasonableness of its fees.[6] ERISA does not permit arrangements considered unreasonable.
   c. In addition, plan participants or DOL can bring lawsuits against plan trustees who overpay for services and force these trustees to reimburse the plan for any overages. Suits alleging excessive fees have become a major issue for 401(k) plans.[7] EBSA has published an overview of the key issues, "Understanding Retirement Plan Fees and Expenses," on its website.[8]
2. As discussed at greater length below, fiduciaries have an obligation to prudently select advisors and monitor their performance. Not doing so risks liability for mistakes.[9]
3. Fiduciaries may not select (or take part in the selection of) an advisor with whom they have a personal or business relationship that might affect their judgment.[10] It would be improper, for example, for a fiduciary to name a firm owned by a close relative as a plan investment manager, unless the choice was made by other trustees with no input into the decision-making process from the related fiduciary.

Professional advisors should be a source of assistance and comfort to trustees fulfilling their fiduciary responsibilities. They should *not* be a source of potential liability. Therefore, it is essential that trustees have a basic understanding of their legal duties and responsibilities in this area.

What Are the Benefits of Using Professional Advisors?

The relationship between professional advisors and a multiemployer plan board of trustees can be one of two types under ERISA.

Delegation

In the first type of relationship, an advisor is "delegated" a share of fiduciary responsibilities held by trustees. In effect, the share of fiduciary responsibility is transferred to the advisor. Be aware that when fiduciaries delegate, they retain the responsibility to prudently select the advisor and monitor the advisor's activities. Trustees also retain their co-fiduciary liability. If, for instance, a trustee learns there has been a breach of duty by an advisor, the trustee must take reasonable steps to correct it or he or she is in breach of duty. More information about the first option and the transfer of liability when delegating fiduciary responsibility is provided in Chapter 6.

Nondelegation

Alternatively, trustees may use input from advisors as a basis for decisions that the trustees make on their own. This is the more typical way trustees use professional advisors other than investment managers. There is *no* transfer of fiduciary responsibility to the advisor. The trustees remain fully responsible for the performance of their fiduciary duties with respect to the matter for which assistance is given. If the trustees reach decisions that the ERISA agencies or the courts find to be imprudent or improper, they, not the professional advisors, will be liable.

Consultation with qualified professionals—particularly in areas where trustees cannot reasonably be expected to possess specialized knowledge—helps trustees:

- Make decisions that are more likely to have positive results and not attract challenge
- Demonstrate the process followed in arriving at a challenged decision was prudent, even if the consequences may not have been what was expected or hoped for
- Counter any later claim that they acted without (1) considering factors that would be important to experts faced with the same decision or (2) understanding their fiduciary duties in the situation.[11]

Trustees should make sure they understand the bases for an advisor's opinion and question any points that seem doubtful or unclear.[12] Advice on any important decision should also be in writing.

What Rules Govern the Delegation of Fiduciary Responsibilities to an Advisor?

ERISA permits trustees to delegate fiduciary duties to others provided certain requirements are satisfied:[13]

- Plan documents must allow the delegation of the responsibility and set forth a procedure for delegation. Usually, the procedure is stated in very general terms that make compliance easy. The presence of this language is essential.
- Trustees must follow the procedure set forth in plan documents.
- The delegation must be designed and operated in a manner that will lead to the choice of an advisor who is qualified to carry out the delegated responsibilities.
- After the advisor is selected, the advisor's performance must be regularly monitored to ensure it meets the needs of the plan and complies with all laws and regulations.

Two further requirements must be satisfied when delegating responsibility to an investment manager:[14]

1. The investment manager must be registered under the Investment Advisers Act of 1940, or must be either a national bank or an insurance company qualified to do business under the laws of more than one state.
2. The investment manager must acknowledge in writing that it is an ERISA fiduciary with respect to the plan.

If all the applicable conditions are not met, a delegation does not relieve fiduciaries of their liability. The advisor's decisions are considered, in effect, trustee decisions.

What Procedures Must Be Followed When Selecting a Professional Advisor?

The key to selecting and monitoring advisors is to view them as what they are: plan assets that should provide a return at least equal to the plan's outlay for their professional services. Hiring an advisor is a major investment decision that should be made with the same care. Trustees who follow clearly defined procedures demonstrate they did not approach their decision in a haphazard fashion—their process was reasonable, responsible and thoughtful.

Selection Procedures

ERISA offers little concrete guidance on just what should be part of the selection process, and DOL regulations offer only generalities.[15] It is clear that trustees should set up an objective procedure to gather the information needed to assess a provider's qualifications, the level and quality of the provider's services, and the reasonableness of the provider's service fees.

While the specifics of the process depend on the type of benefit plan and the services to be provided, there are some key considerations and steps included in virtually every selection process:[16]

- **Determine what services the plan needs.** A steadily expanding range of benefit and legal complexities has created the need for professional services that were at one time rare (e.g., specialized 401(k) plan consultants and investment education providers). Review a plan's team of advisors periodically to make sure there are no gaps or overlaps.
- **Identify appropriate candidates.** A later section of this chapter discusses the resources available to find high-quality candidates for open positions.
- **Solicit bids and proposals from candidates.** In many cases, a formal request for proposal (RFP) is circulated to potential candidates. The RFP should provide relevant information about the plan and be identical for all candidates. The information requested in the RFP should include:
  - The candidate's experience with plans of a similar kind, size and complexity
  - The identity, experience and qualifications of the persons who will directly provide services to the plan
  - The financial condition of the candidate
  - The manner in which services will be provided
  - Proposed fees, including a specific description of what services the fees cover and the circumstances under which additional charges will be incurred

– Whether and under what circumstances the provider will receive "float," "soft dollar" or other compensation from third parties for services provided to the plan[17]
– Any enforcement, malpractice or similar actions that have been brought against the provider
– Client references (and be sure to *check all references*).

- **Verify that candidates satisfy mandatory licensing requirements.** While it is rare for professionals to lie about whether they are admitted to the bar, are licensed as CPAs or are registered under the Investment Advisers Act, it does happen. Check whether state or federal authorities have reported any enforcement actions against the candidates.
- **Conduct interviews.** Remember, an interview is useful only if those conducting the interview are thoroughly prepared. Scrutinize RFP responses for gaps, evasions and other weak spots. Quiz the candidates on these issues.
- **Compare qualifications and fees.** A reasoned decision considers all of the information obtained. Bear in mind there is no obligation to accept the lowest bid. The goal is the greatest value for a plan's money.[18]
- **Make a written record of the selection process.** Include reasons for the selection decision.
- **Review the successful candidate's proposed contract or engagement letter.** Make sure it is fully understood before signing.

What Procedures Must Be Followed When Monitoring Professional Advisors?

The monitoring process is equally undefined by ERISA. DOL also offers little other than stating in a regulation:

> . . . *"at reasonable intervals" performance should be "reviewed . . . in such manner as may be reasonably expected to ensure that [the party's] performance has been in compliance with the terms of the plan and statutory standards, and satisfies the needs of the plan. No single procedure will be appropriate in all cases. . . ."*[19]

These rather vague statements suggest reviews on a regular schedule and that trustees should establish written standards for evaluating advisor performance.

For investment managers, as discussed in the next section, DOL has provided more detail concerning what it regards as adequate procedures. For other advisors, both the frequency of the review and the matters addressed will vary with the type of services performed. Here are some general guidelines:[20]

- **Regularly review and evaluate *every* professional advisor.** Investment managers are not the only ones who should have to submit to performance appraisals. Just because an advisor is currently used does not entitle the advisor to the job in the future. The frequency and method of review, of course, will vary with a plan and the circumstances. It is usually a good idea to conduct a review (1) at least every two or three years, (2) after any major change in plan circumstances and (3) any time there is a significant change in firm representatives.
- **Read all advisor reports.** Consider whether the reports convey useful information in an understandable manner. Or are they filled with boilerplate and jargon? How do they compare to what the advisor promised during the selection process?
- **Compare promises to performance.** Is the plan receiving all of the services identified in the RFP? Are there any problems with timeliness, responsiveness or excessive personnel turnover? How do the service fees compare with expectations when the provider was hired?
- **Pay attention to comments and complaints—especially from plan participants.** Ultimately, participants are the provider's real clients. If they are unhappy with a service, something is wrong.
- **Ask for regular updates to the information furnished by advisors when they were hired.** For instance, a plan's board of trustees or administrator should be notified of significant structural changes (e.g., a merger, acquisition or spin-off that affects the personnel serving the account) as well as any enforcement actions.
- **Consider whether advisors are keeping up-to-date with change.** Nothing in the employee benefit field remains static. Plan trustees depend on professional advisors to remain updated on changes in the legal, regulatory and business environment. Does the service provider show awareness of developments that affect its services? Does the provider take the initiative to recommend steps to meet emerging needs?

What Guidance Is There for Selecting and Monitoring Investment Managers?

Consent judgments by DOL in benefit plan litigation are more concrete as to what this ERISA enforcement agency considers appropriate when selecting and monitoring investment managers for multiemployer plans.[21] These consent judgments set forth detailed rules that DOL insisted trustees follow. These procedures are not legal requirements that all trustees must follow; indeed, some of the requirements may not be appropriate or realistic for all plans. These guidelines, however, typically provide trustees with a useful checklist against which to compare their own selection and monitoring procedures. Obviously, the more closely trustees conform to what DOL has approved for other plans, the less likely it is that DOL or some other party will be able to mount a successful fiduciary challenge against them.

On a general level, consent judgments emphasize the importance of establishing formal procedures for investment manager selection and review. The detailed and sophisticated data that trustees consider with respect to investment management underscores the importance of using professional advisors such as investment consultants and performance monitoring firms. The fact that investments are the source of the greatest potential fiduciary liability magnifies the need for professionals.

With that background, let us look at what consent judgments reveal. With respect to the selection of investment managers, the judgments emphasize the collection and evaluation of relevant information concerning a candidate's experience, capabilities and practices, including:

- Whether the candidate meets the basic ERISA requirements for serving as an investment manager (i.e., is a bank, licensed insurance company or registered investment advisor)[22]
- The business structure and affiliations of the candidate
- The financial condition and capitalization of the candidate
- A description of the investment style proposed by the candidate
- A description of the investment process to be followed by the candidate
- The identity, experience and qualification of the specific professionals who will be handling the plan's portfolio
- Whether any relevant litigation or enforcement actions have been initiated within a reasonably relevant time period against (1) the candidate, (2) the candidate's officers or directors, or (3) the candidate's investment professionals who will have responsibility for the plan's portfolio
- A description of the experience and performance record of the candidate and its investment professionals—over an appropriate period of time—including experience managing other tax-exempt or employee benefit plan assets
- Whether the candidate has or would propose to use the services of an affiliated broker/dealer and, if so, the types of transactions for which such broker/dealers would be used and the financial arrangement the candidate would have with these affiliates
- The procedures the candidate would use to comply with ERISA's prohibited transaction restrictions, including whether the candidate is a Qualified Professional Asset Manager
- Whether the candidate has the fidelity bond required by ERISA
- Whether the candidate has fiduciary liability or other insurance that would protect the interests of the plan in the event of a breach of fiduciary duty
- The candidate's proposed fee structure
- References from other clients of the candidate
- The total value of assets that the candidate currently manages
- The candidate's policy with respect to the voting of proxies
- Any other appropriate and relevant information.

Verify this information with reliable independent sources. Specifically, ask DOL and the Securities and Exchange Commission whether there have been any enforcement actions against the candidate, the candidate's officers and directors, or any of the candidate's investment professionals who will have responsibility for the plan's portfolio.

The monitoring procedures set forth in the consent judgments are equally detailed. They require the review and evaluation of similarly sophisticated investment information:

- A review, at least quarterly, of an investment manager's portfolio for compliance with the plan's investment guidelines
- At least a quarterly review of the basis on which assets under the investment manager's control are valued
- A quarterly computation of the rate of return for the investment manager on an overall basis, by asset class and, where investments are in more than one industry, by sector
- A comparison, at least quarterly, of the investment results of the investment manager with appropriate indexes or benchmarks
- At least an annual review of the investment manager's practices regarding brokerage and trading, including those regarding—
  - brokerage costs
  - use of soft dollars

  - quality of securities execution
  - portfolio turnover.
- At least quarterly verification of the investment manager's fee computation
- A review, at least annually, of the investment manager's proxy voting policies and performance
- At least one meeting a year with the investment manager to review the manager's investment performance and any significant changes in corporate or capital structure, investment style, brokerage affiliation or practices, investment process and professional staff
- The development and at least an annual review of procedures for communicating information regarding both plan investments and the investment manager to plan trustees, staff and service providers (including but not limited to the plan's attorneys, actuaries and custodial trustees)
- At least an annual review of a plan's cash management, short-term investment procedures and performance, as well as the overall performance of the plan's custodial trustee(s).

Each investment manager's contract should have a mechanism for terminating services as soon as prudently possible if the performance is unsatisfactory or inconsistent with plan guidelines.

What Are Some Recommendations for Dealing With Plan Advisors?

When dealing with professional advisors, it is important to keep one point in mind: There is *no substitute* for good judgment and common sense. While outside advice based on an advisor's expertise and experience with similar plans can be helpful, trustees have knowledge of their industry and local conditions that is important, too. Trustees must seek the guidance of professionals—applying the input of the advisor to what they (the trustees) already know. Trustees should:

- Question advisors, on the record, concerning the development of their recommendations.
- Get recommendations in writing on all major or controversial issues.
- Where appropriate, obtain "second opinions" from experts with different perspectives.
- Evaluate all recommendations in light of their personal knowledge of the facts and circumstances of the issue at hand and the local industry.

No matter how qualified an advisor may be, it is the *trustees'* plan and the *trustees* bear the ultimate fiduciary responsibility for its successful operation.

Who Are These Professional Advisors?

As the variety of negotiated benefits continues to expand, many professional advisors have expanded their areas of expertise. New advisors have emerged to fill new plan needs. An example of this evolution is the negotiated 401(k) plan that did not exist only a few years ago. The establishment of these defined contribution plans gave rise to the immediate need for professionals who can provide advice on how to:

- Evaluate a broad range of investment alternatives
- Select an appropriate package of investment vehicles from which plan participants can choose
- Monitor the ongoing performance of each of the investment vehicles offered.

In addition, many 401(k) plans need help educating participants regarding basic investment principles or offering individualized investment advisory services. All of these activities have led to the engagement of new advisors.

The evolution of legislative, judicial and regulatory interpretations and mandates also requires expanded areas of professional expertise. The universe of "professional advisors to multiemployer plan trustees" is not a static community.

As the scope of multiemployer plans continues to grow and mature and the environment in which these plans evolves, trustees may find professional expertise useful or essential in other areas. The remainder of the answer to this question provides a brief description of professional services commonly used by multiemployer plans now. This list is not comprehensive. There are professionals in other disciplines now serving a few funds that may be universally used in the coming years. The fact that these professionals are not specifically included here does not mean that the services they offer are not worthwhile.

Administrator

There are two basic approaches to multiemployer plan administration: (1) self-administration and (2) administration through contract by a third-party administrator (TPA).

Plan employees manage *self-administered plans.* Often, a family of plans—health and welfare, pension, vacation and 401(k)—established by a set of collective bargaining agreements will jointly employ a staff to administer all of the plans. The scope of staff responsibilities varies. Some health and welfare plans, for example, process claims in-house while others turn to insurance companies, preferred provider organizations (PPOs) or health maintenance organizations (HMOs) for this part of plan administration. Similarly, staffs of some pension plans review domestic relations orders while others delegate this task to outside counsel. Plan staff or an actuary may calculate pension plan benefits.

Third-party administrators are independent companies hired by plan trustees to do administrative functions. Multiemployer plans began contracting with TPAs well before "outsourcing" became a popular trend among single employer plans. As with an in-house staff, the scope of a TPA's services varies from plan to plan.

One can debate the relative merits of these two approaches to administration, but the question is usually moot. A fund is unlikely to switch from one approach to the other unless an event occurs that compels trustees to consider the possibility. Such events include the retirement of an employee-administrator or a serious dispute with a TPA.

Neither internal nor external administration has proven decisively superior to the other. The advantage of self-administration is a dedicated staff providing focus and consistency. A TPA, on the other hand, can offer more knowledge of how other funds handle common problems. With a TPA, also, there is less danger that the sudden loss or absence of one or two key employees will disrupt operations. Trustees will also be concerned about the costs of the two options. When *all* costs are considered, one approach should cost about the same as the other.

Regardless of how a plan's administration is structured, it is the job of the administrator to:

- Maintain plan eligibility rolls
- Receive employer contributions
- Keep records of employees' covered work
- Verify eligibility for benefits
- Pay benefits
- Maintain other records of the fund.

The administrator of a 401(k) or other individual account plan must also:

- Allocate contributions to participant accounts
- Keep track of the individual account balances
- Carefully follow participant investment elections (if the plan allows participants to direct investments).

The bank, insurance company or mutual fund family in which plan participants are able to invest will often administer individual accounts at little or no direct cost; the accounts can also be separated and outsourced to a TPA. Plan trustees who outsource to a TPA, count on higher quality service in return for higher fees. Unless a plan is very small, in-house recordkeeping for an individual account plan is almost always a bad idea.

Auditor

Multiemployer plans engage accountants to perform two distinct types of audits. The first is the annual financial audit required by ERISA and submitted with the plan's annual report on Form 5500. An independent qualified public accountant must perform this audit.[23]

Payroll audits represent the second service provided by accountants. Such audits make certain participating employers are making all their contributions to a plan in accordance with collective bargaining agreements.[24] In order to secure a favorable ERISA audit opinion on internal controls, the standard practice is to audit every employer periodically. Most plans increase audit frequency for delinquent employers. There are also instances in which trustees suspect an employer is not contributing for all covered employment, which leads to an ad hoc audit.

While this does not have to be the case, most plans secure the services of one accounting firm to perform both the annual audit and payroll audits. In some geographical areas, all or a number of building trade benefit plans have a cooperative agreement retaining one firm for their audits. The trustees of these plans recognize that a contractor delinquent on contributions for employees to one plan is likely to be delinquent on obligations to other plans as well. Consolidating payroll audits spreads the expense over several funds and reduces costs for each fund.

Benefits Consultant and Actuary

A plan actuary and a plan pension or benefits consultant are often employees of the same firm or even the same person. While this sometimes creates confusion as to the services they provide, these roles are separate and distinct.

In simplest terms, the actuary's job is to forecast a plan's future financial needs. ERISA requires every pension plan to engage an enrolled actuary to annually value plan assets and liabilities.[25] The results of the valuation determine:

- The employer contributions required under ERISA's minimum funding standards
- The value of unfunded vested benefits upon which withdrawal liability is based
- Whether a plan is in the "red zone" or "yellow zone" and thus, required to improve its funding beyond the level produced by the minimum funding rules
- Whether a plan is subject to the restrictions for moderately or seriously underfunded plans, such as limitations on lump-sum distributions when plan funding falls below 80%.

The actuary can also help the plan administrator with unusual or problematic benefit calculations.

A benefits consultant, on the other hand, advises trustees on matters of plan design and operation. The consultant helps answer questions such as:

- Given the resources the actuary estimates are available, what level of benefits can a plan support? What optional forms of distribution should be offered?
- What benefit suspension rules should a plan adopt?
- How can a health plan control costs?
- Do communications with participants provide necessary information in an intelligible fashion?
- If a plan is experiencing funding shortfalls, which alternatives for coping with the situation are best?

Every plan faces issues that do not fall within the specific expertise of any one professional advisor. The consultant is a kind of utility infielder to assist in handling them.

Almost all medium- or large-sized actuarial firms serve as consultants. These firms may also offer TPA services, communication material preparation, investment manager selection and monitoring, staff training and the like. There are no legal obstacles to combining all three functions, but trustees should be aware these roles require very different skills. Getting two or three of these functions from a single provider can (but does not always) save money. Separating them may yield performance that is more satisfactory. While only an enrolled actuary can prepare an ERISA valuation, many TPAs and insurance companies compete for administration of plans. Many law and accounting firms have some expertise in benefits consulting.

Regardless of how trustees fill a plan's benefits consultant slot, it is important to keep in mind that all professional advisors from time to time will be able to provide valuable advice on plan design and related issues. Benefits consulting is not an insulated function that can be carried out only by the person designated for this specific role.

Legal Counsel

Many multiemployer plans retain a single attorney to serve as counsel for the entire board of trustees. Many other plans employ co-counsels—one selected by the employer trustees and the other by the labor trustees. ERISA does not bar this practice, nor has DOL or any court ever expressed disapproval. There are, however, a few special considerations:

- Each fund counsel has an obligation to represent and advise all of the trustees, not just the side that appointed him or her. Like trustees, fund attorneys have fiduciary obligations to the plan as a whole rather than to the employers or the union.
- Legal work must be divided between co-counsels in a way that avoids service duplication.
- The combined legal fees of the co-counsels must be comparable to the costs the fund would have incurred had the trustees chosen a single fund counsel.

In some cases, an attorney representing the union or management association affiliated with a plan is also fund counsel or co-counsel. This dual role is permitted, though it requires a high degree of objectivity on the lawyer's part. Some law firms, as a matter of policy, refuse to represent a multiemployer benefit plan if their clients include employers, the employer association or the union connected to the plan; other firms split the work among several separate departments.

Investment Manager

It is noted above that ERISA permits a board of trustees to delegate fiduciary responsibility for the investment of fund assets to one or more *investment managers.* To take on this role, an advisor must be a national bank, an insurance company licensed to do business in more than one state or a registrant under the Investment Advisers Act of 1940. It must also acknowledge in writing its status as an ERISA fiduciary.[26]

Trustees may retain an advisor that does not qualify as an investment manager under this definition; however, trustees cannot delegate their fiduciary responsibility for investment to this advisor. Trustees may also be exposed to liability for this advisor's actions.

A further consideration is whether an investment manager meets DOL criteria for a "qualified professional asset manager" (QPAM).[27] A QPAM may engage in a number of transactions with a plan that ordinarily would be prohibited by ERISA. This flexibility is often not needed but may be important if the manager performs other services for the plan or if the assets under its management include derivatives.

Investment Consultant

An *investment consultant* assists trustees in choosing and monitoring investment managers. The growth of this specialty reflects the increasing complexity of fund investment strategies. Today, many plans use a number of managers with each manager responsible for a specific class or subclass of assets. What portion of a plan investment portfolio each manager should handle is a major question. The evaluation of manager performance is no longer simply a matter of comparing last quarter's returns to the S&P 500 or some other handy benchmark. Few trustees have the background to decide prudently what fraction of plan assets should be allocated to, say, "emerging markets" or to pick a manager for that segment.

Investment consultants help plan trustees do these tasks by offering a wide range of services such as:

- Investment manager searches
- Asset allocation studies to assess the probable long-term impact of different strategies on investment performance

- Investment performance reports that compare the results of a plan's investment managers to those of similar managers, benchmark indexes and the managers' stated investment strategies
- Evaluation of custodian performance
- Proxy voting (which DOL regards as a fiduciary responsibility).

Originally, these services were offered only to pension plans, but a growing number of larger health and welfare plans are turning to investment consultants to help improve the yield on their fund reserves as well.

401(k) Consultant

The popularity of 401(k) plans—a type of defined contribution plans—has spawned the new specialty of *401(k) consulting,* which combines elements of benefits and investment consulting. Trustees seek the aid of 401(k) consultants for some or all of the following:

- Construction and periodic review of a "menu" of investment options
- Evaluation and monitoring of investment-related fees
- Selection of a plan recordkeeper
- Preparation of communications to participants, including educational material on investments and retirement planning
- "Nondiscrimination" testing of elective deferrals, when necessary[28]
- Procedures for ensuring the timely remittance of participant deferrals to the plan trust fund[29]
- Compliance with DOL fee disclosure and other legal requirements.

Plan investment choices and participant communications are of special importance if trustees want to limit their liability for participant investment decisions.[30] There is some debate as to the scope of these protections in light of DOL positions. However, few trustees are willing to give up these potential protections. Though it does require scrupulous attention to detail, compliance is not particularly difficult.

Other advisors can handle much of the work of the 401(k) consultant. Whether specialized 401(k) consulting is useful and economical depends on a plan's size and complexity, as well as the capabilities of a plan's legal counsel, accountant, etc.

Investment Education or Advice for Participants

401(k) and other individual account plans that give participants the ability to direct how their dollars are invested may engage professionals to provide individual employees with investment advice. Recent legislation attempted to encourage these arrangements by relaxing prohibited transaction rules that made it difficult to compensate advisors for these services.[31] DOL has subsequently furnished some generalized guidance on selecting and monitoring these advisors. The guidelines apply regardless of whether the advisor takes advantage of the statutory prohibited transaction exemption.[32]

It makes sense that this guidance parallels that of choosing plan investment managers—an advisor to participants offers the same kinds of service an investment manager provides a plan as a whole with some exceptions. "Retail" investment advice requires an appreciation of the way in which age, economic circumstances and tolerance for risk affect individual investment needs.

Investment education, as distinguished from advice keyed to individual circumstances, varies widely, from pamphlets explaining the elements of diversification and dollar averaging through seminars. What makes sense for a plan depends largely on the participant population. Materials geared to a young, low-paid, unsophisticated audience are of little use to an older, more affluent group, and vice versa.

Do All Plans Need Each of These Professional Advisors?

The easy answer to this question is "no." There are only three positions required by law: (1) a plan administrator (either in-house or a TPA), (2) an independent public accountant to perform the ERISA-mandated annual audit and (3) for defined benefit pension plans, an enrolled actuary to certify the annual valuation. Beyond these roles, in theory, trustees can handle plan design and operation matters without professional advice. Many health and welfare funds, for instance, do not have an investment manager—they pay out contributions as quickly as they receive them and have little cash to manage in the long term. On the other hand, benefit consultants provide benefit design services hard to replicate through trustee input.

What about an attorney? While trustees can hire counsel ad hoc, as legal issues arise, this approach entails serious risks. New laws, regulations and court decisions continually change the rules that plans must follow. Trustees who overlook or misunderstand new requirements could face potentially disastrous consequences. Most trustees believe legal counsel to advise them of their legal rights and obligations is imperative.

Trustees of any plan that invests significant assets is wise to engage an investment manager rather than rely on trustee personal financial expertise. The need for the next layer—an investment consultant—increases as plan assets grow and more sophisticated investment strategies are used. The point at which hiring an investment consultant becomes a necessity is hard to pinpoint, but it is probably earlier than many trustees think.

Trustees of a start-up 401(k) plan are strongly encouraged to seek the aid of a 401(k) consultant. Even though trustees may have personal experience with a 401(k) plan and regard themselves as reasonably familiar with how these plans work, "a little learning is a dangerous thing." Most trustees do not know a great deal about the full range of available 401(k) investment options, trusteeship arrangements, plan recordkeeping, the requirements of ERISA Section 404(c), etc. Then there is the reality that the rules governing 401(k) plans are subject to change—the recent expansion of required disclosures for service providers' direct and indirect compensation arrangements provides one noteworthy example. All of these considerations argue against simply relying on a plan's investment provider for advice.

Every plan from time to time needs the advice of other professional consultants on design and related issues. Whether a plan should formalize that role depends upon plan size, complexity and other circumstances. The Pension Protection Act of 2006 led to many changes in the rules governing multiemployer pension plans. Only a very bold board of trustees would try to cope with these changes without the almost continuous guidance of a qualified consultant. A similar wave of change is about to strike health plans as they adjust to the implementation of the Patient Protection and Affordable Care Act of 2010.

The best way to think about the value of professional services is to contemplate a fiduciary challenge to trustee actions. In what position will trustees and their plan find themselves if they do not employ a particular type of advisor? What plan losses, legal turmoil or administrative upheaval might be avoided with the advisor's assistance?

As noted earlier in this chapter, and as discussed more fully elsewhere in this handbook, courts generally judge trustee performance against a "prudent expert" standard. Trustees are expected to discharge their fiduciary responsibilities in the same manner as a professional. Trustees, therefore, must assess their own capabilities and experience, and ask whether they could satisfy this standard. How much exposure will they and their plan face if they do not seek advice?

How Do Plans Find Good Advisors?

Of these two questions, the first is easier to answer. Plan trustees with a fund of any substantial size really do not have to look for professional advisors. Want-to-be advisors will find them. Trustees can expect to accumulate a long list of individuals and firms that are more than eager to provide whatever professional service a plan wants.

Still, trustees may not always have on file an adequate list of candidates for a particular task, nor will trustees want to consider only those that have solicited plan business. Where do trustees turn for other candidates?

Trustees sometimes do not realize they can easily access a wealth of information. By virtue of their position, labor trustees of multiemployer funds will have corresponding trustees on multiemployer funds elsewhere in the country. For example, the union trustees of the Paperhangers Health and Welfare Fund of Hahira, Georgia can easily get in touch with the union trustees of the Paperhangers Health and Welfare Funds in Jacksonville or Atlanta, as well as other cities in their region. Plan trustees can also communicate with trustees from other trades or unions. The trustees of a retail food fund might make inquiries of trustees from a building trades or service employees plan. Likewise, employer trustees can contact their counterparts through their employer association. From these connections, trustees can learn which advisors are used by other plans and gather information concerning the quality, user satisfaction and cost of these providers.

The scope of a search does not have to be limited by geography. The fact that a given service provider does not have an office in a plan's immediate vicinity does not mean the provider cannot be considered. Many attorneys, accountants, consultants, actuaries and TPAs serve funds over a wide geographic area. Others might be interested in establishing an office in a new city if a substantial plan located there used their services.

Another excellent source of information is a plan's other professional advisors. It is very likely most of these advisors serve more than one plan and have worked with advisors that have expertise in other disciplines. When looking for candidates, it always makes sense to ask current advisors who they work with for other plans and, who they believe would provide good services.

Cost and Quality

Balanced against the benefits of expert advice are the costs of the advice. The cost of professional services varies widely by discipline and geography. Substantial differences in compensation also exist within a discipline and locale. Naturally, the aim of trustees is to get the highest quality service *in relation to a plan's needs* at the lowest feasible price.

The italicized phrase is important. A 100-member health and welfare plan does not have the same needs as a 10,000-member national pension fund. The smaller plan should not be paying for the same level of expertise. Small plans tend to look to small or midsized local practitioners while larger plans seek out firms with national reputations. If a plan is "too small" for its service providers, it will pay premium prices and be lost among the firm's bigger clients. If a plan is "too large," its fees may be low, but the provider will have difficulty providing the services needed by the plan.

Of course, firms of similar size may be very dissimilar in the quality of their work. In some fields, relatively objective indicators are available to assess providers. The Society of Actuaries, for instance, awards the titles of "associate" and "fellow" based on rigorous examinations. Many law, consulting and accounting firms produce newsletters for clients; reading these communications will at least provide some idea of whether their personnel are able to explain complex concepts in a way that can be understood. Investment managers have track records, though trustees must always keep in mind that past performance is no guarantee of future results.

References furnished by candidates can be invaluable but do be aware of their limitations. Most notably, a client's satisfaction with an advisor often depends largely on the particular personnel with whom it works. Plan trustees may wind up dealing with a completely different team, especially with a large firm.

Evaluating the proposed fees of an advisor can be confusing. In an ideal world, quality and price would go hand in hand—the task of plan trustees would be a simple comparison of one to the other. In reality, bids include a variety of factors and many are beyond trustee knowledge. A high bidder may not be very interested in a plan's business. Another high bidder may believe that it has an inside track with a plan and therefore does not have to compete vigorously to get a client. Sometimes a high bidder is unaware that its fees are out of line with the marketplace. On the other hand, the bidder may merely have an exceptional reputation and see no need to offer discounts to anyone.

Low bidders are sometimes mediocre and able to gain clients only by offering their services cheaply, but this is not always the case. A high-quality firm may have underutilized personnel because of new hires or the loss of a major client. The firm regards a plan's business as especially desirable—perhaps it has a long-run strategy of expanding its multiemployer practice.

One other risk trustees face is the "lowball" bidder that deliberately quotes fees it expects to exceed. The bidder hopes the plan will passively pay up later. There is no need to view every unusually low bid with suspicion, but trustees should try to understand the *why* behind each candidate's fee structure.

A final point: Trustees are under no obligation to "take or leave" what is offered. It is proper to negotiate with candidates when dissatisfied with responses to an RFP.

The unfortunate truth is that there are no surefire formulas for identifying the best service provider at the best price. Inevitably, trustees make some less-than-ideal choices. As with other fiduciary duties, the best way to approach it is to have a well-designed selection process, adhere to it carefully and document the reasons for the decisions.

Endnotes

1. ERISA §402(a) designates the board of a multiemployer plan as its "named fiduciary."
2. ERISA §404(a) and §406.
3. ERISA §408.
4. ERISA §3(14).
5. The additional information requirements for Form 5500, Schedule C were described in a *Federal Register* notice issued jointly by DOL, the Internal Revenue Service and the Pension Benefit Guaranty Corporation. 72 Fed. Reg. 64731 (Nov. 16, 2007). Two sets of followup questions and answers are at www.dol.gov/ebsa/faqs/faq_scheduleC.html and www.dol.gov/ebsa/faqs/faq-sch-C-supplement.html.
6. DOL Regs. 29 CFR, §2550.408b-2(c), 75 Fed. Reg. 41600 (July 16, 2010). DOL is considering similar rules for arrangements between welfare plans and their advisors.
7. *Tibble v. Edison International*, 49 Emp. Ben. Cas. (BNA) 1725 (C.D. Cal. July 8, 2010); *Dole v. Formica*, 14 Emp. Ben. Cas. (BNA) 1397 (N.D. Ohio 1991); *Whitfield v. Tomasso*, 9 Emp. Ben. Case. (BNA) 2438 (E.D.N.Y, 1988).
8. www.dol.gov/ebsa/publications/undrstndgrtrmnt.html.
9. *Martin v. Harline*, 15 Empl. Ben. Cas. (BNA) 1138 (D. Utah 1992); *Field Assistance Bulletin* 2002-3. www.dol.gov/ebsa/regs/fab_2002-3.html.
10. DOL Regs. 29 CFR, §2550.408b-2(e).
11. *Katsaros v. Cody*, 568 F. Supp. 360 (E.D.N.Y. 1983), aff'd as modified, 744 F. Supp. 270 (2d Cir.), cert. denied, 409 U.S. 1072 (1984); *Donovan v. Bierwirth*, 680 F.2d 263 (2d Cir. 1982).
12. For a case in which the court was particularly stringent in demanding that fiduciaries evaluate expert advice, *Howard v. Shay*, 100 F.3d 1484 (9th Cir. 1996), cert. denied sub. nom. Shay v. Howard, 520 U.S. 1237 (1997).
13. ERISA §405(c)(2).
14. ERISA §3(38) and §405(d)(1).
15. DOL Regs. 29 CFR §2550.404a-1(b)(1)
16. "Tips for Selecting and Monitoring Service Providers for Your Employee Benefit Plan" (www.dol.gov/ebsa/newsroom/fs052505.html) and "Meeting Your Fiduciary Responsibilities" (www.dol.gov/ebsa/publications/fiduciaryresponsibility.html).
17. *Field Assistance Bulletin* No. 2002-3 (www.dol.gov/ebsa/regs/fab_2002-3.html); "Statement on Policies Concerning Soft Dollar and Directed Commission Arrangements," ERISA Technical Release No. 86-1 (May 22, 1986).
18. "Understanding Retirement Plan Fees and Expenses" (www.dol.gov/ebsa/publications/undrstndgrtrmnt.html) and "401k Plan Fee Disclosure Form" (www.dol.gov/ebsa/pdf/401kfefm.pdf).
19. DOL Regs. 29 CFR §2509.75-8, Q&A-FR-17.

20. "Understanding Retirement Plan Fees and Expenses" (www.dol.gov/ebsa/publications/undrstndgrtrmnt.html) and "401k Plan Fee Disclosure Form" (www.dol.gov/ebsa/pdf/401kfefm.pdf).
21. Consent judgments in *Arizona State Carpenters Pension Trust Fund v. Miller,* No. Civ. 89-0693 (D. Ariz., 11/1/94) and *In re Masters, Mates & Pilots Pension Plan and IRAP Litigation,* Lead File No. 85 Civ. 9545 (VLB) (S.D.N.Y., 12/15/92).
22. ERISA §3(38).
23. ERISA §103; DOL Regs. 29 CFR, §2520.103-1*ff.*
24. Lawrence Beebe and Philip Vivirito, *Payroll Auditing: A Guide for Multiemployer Plans* (International Foundation of Employee Benefit Plans, 2008).
25. An *enrolled actuary* is a professional who has satisfied the requirements for enrollment prescribed by the Joint Board for the Enrollment of Actuaries, a federal agency jointly managed by IRS, DOL and the Pension Benefit Guaranty Corporation. Enrolled actuaries qualify for that status by passing examinations administered by the Joint Board for the Enrollment of Actuaries, which is staffed and supervised by IRS, DOL and the Pension Benefit Guaranty Corporation.
26. ERISA §3(38). In some cases, an investment advisor registered under state law rather than the 1940 Act may qualify as an investment manager.
27. ERISA Prohibited Transaction Class Exemption 84-14, 49 Fed. Reg. 9494 (March 13, 1984); corrected, 50 Fed. Reg. 41430 (Oct. 10, 1985); amended, 75 Fed. Reg. 38837 (July 6, 2010).
28. IRC §401(k)(3) and 401(m)(2). Nondiscrimination testing is most often an issue for plans that cover employees of the plan or the union rather than being limited to a collective bargaining unit.
29. DOL Regs. 29 CFR §2510.3-102. Tardy deposits can result in the imposition of excise taxes under I.R.C. §4975.
30. ERISA §404(c); DOL Regs. 29 CFR §2550.404(c)-1*ff.*
31. Pension Protection Act of 2006, Pub. L. No. 109-280, §601; ERISA, §408(b)(14); IRC, §4975(b)(17).
32. *Field Assistance Bulletin* No. 2007-1, See also"Tips for Selecting and Monitoring Service Providers for Your Employee Benefit Plan" (www.dol.gov/ebsa/newsroom/fs052505.html) and "Meeting Your Fiduciary Responsibilities" (www.dol.gov/ebsa/publications/fiduciaryresponsibility.html).

Chapter 8

The Appointment, Monitoring and Removal of Trustees

Philip R. O'Brien

Although much has been written over the years on fiduciary responsibility under the Employee Retirement Income Security Act of 1974 (ERISA), very little has focused on the fiduciary aspects of the appointment, monitoring and removal of multiemployer benefit plan trustees. Many trustees and service providers do not even realize that their roles have fiduciary considerations.

The appointment and removal of trustees for multiemployer benefit plans is always addressed in the trust declaration governing a plan's operation. Frequently, all that is said on this vital topic is that a union (or its equivalent) has the power to appoint and remove labor trustees, and an employer association (or its equivalent) has the same powers with regard to employer trustees.

Because the people representing employer and labor organizations appoint trustees, these people and their organizations exercise "discretionary authority or control respecting management."[1] Under ERISA Section 3(21)(A), these people and organizations are considered plan fiduciaries who must comply with ERISA rules and plan documents.[2] The responsibility (and liability) of these fiduciaries, however, is limited to the selection, monitoring and removal of their named fiduciaries.

Are There Any Limits on Appointments of Trustees?

For the most part, employer and labor associations may pick anyone they want to be trustees, subject to their fiduciary duties under ERISA Section 404(a). One of the very few restrictions imposed is that neither side can have any role in the appointment of trustees on the other side of the table.[3] Of course, people who have been convicted of certain types of crimes are not eligible to serve as fiduciaries or to act in certain other capacities with respect to a plan.[4]

Neither ERISA nor the Taft-Hartley Act places a specific limit on the length of time a fiduciary may serve. In the past, many trust agreements had no limits on trustee length of service other than a statement that trustee served until death, disability, retirement or removal by the appointing plan sponsor. In recent years, the courts have increased the scrutiny on trustee appointments. Courts have held that lifetime appointments without removal rights at the will of the appointing party violate both the Taft-Hartley Act and ERISA. Department of Labor Advisory Opinion 85-41A (December 5, 1985) supports the court decisions stating:

> *". . . the Department is generally of the view that a lifetime term of appointment for a pension fund trustee would be inconsistent with ERISA's fiduciary responsibility provisions."*

Limited terms, such as for a specified number of years, that are reasonable under the facts and circumstances of the plan are generally consistent with ERISA.

What Should Trustees Be Told to Expect When Asked to Serve as a Trustee?

Every person chosen to serve as a trustee is extremely busy, but appointment to serve as a trustee is a great honor that most individuals are reluctant to decline. People who fully appreciate the fiduciary responsibility placed upon their shoulders cannot and should not accept an appointment unless they are willing and able to spend the time and energy necessary to be an effective trustee. This means there must be a commitment to:

- Read all materials submitted to trustees in preparation for each meeting
- Ask questions at meetings until they are satisfied they understand the information presented sufficiently to make a decision
- Be willing to challenge the advice of qualified professionals, but ultimately to accept sound advice—even if it is contrary to preconceived ideas the trustees hold
- Place the interests of the plan, its participants and beneficiaries above any personal interest they may have when making decisions related to the plan.

Potential trustees should be informed of the extensive liabilities and ethical responsibilities they will have and be encouraged to consider their duties seriously before they accept the role of trustee. A person who is already overburdened by union or business activities should think twice before accepting an offer to serve as a trustee.

The duties of potential trustees should be stated in a document titled "Acceptance of Trusteeship." Samples of these forms are provided in the appendixes to this chapter. It is best practice for both health and pension plans to have each person appointed as a trustee review and sign such an agreement. With the passage of HIPAA Privacy Regulations, it is particularly important that potential health plan trustees be keenly aware of their duty to protect the confidentiality of plan participants' health information.

What Is the Fiduciary Responsibility of Those Who Appoint Trustees?

Just as guidance on the appointment of trustees is very limited, guidance on the monitoring and removal of named trustees is also scarce. DOL indicates the performance of fiduciaries (which includes trustees) should be reviewed by the appointing fiduciaries at regular intervals. The review should be in a manner that reasonably ensures a fiduciary's performance (1) complies with the terms of the plan and statutory standards, and (2) satisfies the needs of the plan. The procedure adopted may vary based on the nature of the plan, and other facts and circumstances relevant to the choice of the procedure.[5] These instructions do not differentiate between the responsibility to review the performance of trustees and the responsibility of trustees to monitor the performance of those to whom trustees delegate fiduciary duties.

Decisions From the Courts

Appointment and Removal of Trustees

In *Teamsters Local No. 145 v. Kuba,* 631 F. Supp. 1063 (D. Conn. 1986), the local union attempted to replace union representatives on the board of trustees of a health services and insurance plan. The trust agreement governing the plan provided for governance by a four-person board of trustees, two to be appointed by the local union and two to be appointed by the contributing employers. The trust agreement originally provided that trustees would serve until death, disability, resignation or removal. On June 15, 1985, the trustees voted to amend the trust agreement to provide that each trustee would continue to serve until death, incapacity or removal for "proper and just cause only." The court held that the "for proper and just cause" amendment provided sufficient potential for abuse to make it a violation of Taft-Hartley Section 302.

In *Mobile, Alabama-Pensacola, Florida Building and Construction Trades Council v. Daugherty,* 684 F. Supp. 270 (S.D. Ala. 1988), rival factions of a local union were involved in a dispute. One faction sought the removal of the trustees of the union's pension and welfare plans following the election of new trustees. Initially, the employer association and the building trades council had the power to appoint and to remove trustees of these plans. Later, the respective trust agreements were amended to provide that trustees would serve until death, incapacity, resignation or removal for misfeasance, malfeasance or nonfeasance in the execution of the trust pursuant to an elaborate procedure set forth in the agreement. The court concluded that lifetime appointment, absent the other stated events (e.g., incapacity, resignation or removal for cause), is contrary to ERISA.

Common law and ERISA provide insight into the issue. In most jurisdictions, if an owner-employer exercises prudence and due care in selecting and engaging an independent contractor, the owner-employer is not liable for the acts or omissions of the independent contractor. The test for the hirer is prudence and due care in the selection process, not the ultimate conduct. The same is true when labor and management select plan trustees.

Closer to home for multiemployer benefit plan fiduciaries is an ERISA analogy. If a plan document allows it, plan trustees may designate investment managers to manage plan assets. Trustees are generally not liable for the acts or omissions of these investment managers if the trustees exercise prudence in:

- Selecting the investment manager
- Developing investment guidelines for the manager to follow
- Monitoring the performance of the manager.[6]

Similarly, those who appoint trustees—labor and employer associations—have no liability for trustee appointments if they exercise prudence in:

- Selecting the trustees
- Creating the scope and sphere of trustee conduct
- Monitoring the performance of the trustees.

Courts have held liable those who appoint trustees and failed to monitor prudently the performance of their appointees or failed to take action when they discovered improper performance. Additionally, at least one case (*Liss v. Smith* summarized in Decisions From the Courts below) suggests trustees may have a duty to monitor and prevent the improper conduct of appointees.

Sponsors of multiemployer benefit plans are well advised to review and, to the extent necessary, revise the steps and procedures they currently employ in the appointment, monitoring and removal of trustees.

Decisions From the Courts

Liability for Trustees' Appointments

Liss v. Smith, 991 F. Supp. 278 (S.D. N.Y. 1998) dealt with trustees who engaged in repeated and significant fiduciary violations. The court held that the power to appoint and remove trustees carries with it a duty to monitor their performance and to take action upon discovery of improper performance. The court determined the appointing fiduciary failed to monitor appointees and to remove nonperforming fiduciaries. The fiduciary was held liable for the appointee's breaches.

In *Howell v. Motorola*, 337 F. Supp. 2d 1079, at 1095-1099 (N.D. Ill. 2004), the court found that those with the power to appoint, retain and remove plan fiduciaries have a duty to monitor such fiduciaries and may even have a duty to prevent wrongful conduct. The court rejected the argument that those with appointment power were simply required to appoint persons with the appropriate level of education, knowledge and experience.

What Guidelines Exist Regarding the Removal of Trustees?

The group or entity that has the authority to appoint fiduciaries also has the authority to remove fiduciaries. Of course, the removal must be consistent with the policies of the appointing labor or employer association. Federal courts also have the authority to order the removal of a fiduciary under ERISA Section 409(a) in breach of fiduciary duty lawsuits.

When fiduciaries of an employee benefit plan resign or are removed, the reasons may need to be disclosed—at least to the other fiduciaries. This is particularly important if the information is material to the person's service as a fiduciary, the plan, or other fiduciaries are not aware of the information and need to know it for their own protection.[7] In one legal dispute, a federal appeals court discussed that the resignation of a fiduciary was subject to the fiduciary standard of care in ERISA Section 404(a) and must be in accordance with the procedures and requirements stated in plan documents.[8]

Conclusion

Often those who appoint trustees do not understand that their roles entail fiduciary responsibility and liability. These individuals need to be informed through discussion with counsel and personal reading such as this handbook.

Endnotes

1. ERISA §3(21)(A).
2. ERISA §404(a); DOL Regs. §2509.75-8, D-4.
3. *Quad City Builders Association, Inc. v. Tri City Bricklayers Union No. 7, AFL-CIO*, 431 F. 2d 999 (8th Cir. 1970).
4. ERISA §411(a).
5. DOL Regs. §2509.75-8, FR-17.
6. ERISA §405(d)(1) and (2).
7. *Glaziers & Glassworkers Union Local No. 252 Annuity Fund*, 93 F.3d 1171 (3rd Cir. 1996); *see also, Ream v. Frey*, 107 F. 3d 147 (3d Cir. 1997) (a trustee has a fiduciary duty to disclose its reasons for resignation if the resignation and subsequent appointment of a successor trustee could result in potential harm to the beneficiaries of the trust).
8. *Ream v. Frey*, 107 F. 3d 147 (3d Cir. 1997).

Consent Forms

[PENSION FUND NAME]

ACCEPTANCE OF TRUSTEESHIP

The undersigned, having been duly designated as an/a [Employer][Union] Trustee of the ________________________ ____________Fund effective as of ________________ [date], does hereby accept the trust imposed upon all the terms and conditions set forth in the Trust Agreement, a copy of which has been delivered to the undersigned, and the undersigned agrees to perform his duties as required by said Trust Agreement.

I understand that section 411(a) of the Employee Retirement Income Security Act of 1974 (ERISA) provides that no person who has been convicted of or has been imprisoned as a result of a conviction of robbery, bribery, extortion, embezzlement, fraud, grand larceny, burglary, arson, a felony violation of Federal or State law involving substances defined in section 102(6) of the Comprehensive Drug Abuse Prevention and Control Act of 1970, murder, rape, kidnapping, perjury, assault with intent to kill, any crime described in section 9(a)(1) of the Investment Company Act of 1940, a violation of any provision of ERISA or section 302 of the Labor-Management Relations Act of 1947, a violation of section 63 of Title 18, United States Code, a violation of sections 874, 1027, 1503, 1505, 1506, 1510, 1951 or 1954 of Title 18, United States Code, a violation of the Labor-Management Reporting and Disclosure Act of 1959, any felony involving abuse or misuse of a position or employment in a labor organization or an employee benefit plan to seek or obtain an illegal gain at the expense of the members of the labor organization or the beneficiaries of the employee benefit plan, or a conspiracy to commit or attempt to commit any such crimes, or a crime in which any of the foregoing crimes is an element, shall be permitted to serve as an administrator, fiduciary, officer, trustee, custodian, counsel, agent, employee, representative, advisor or consultant to any employee benefit plan or in any capacity involving decision making authority or custody or control of the assets of any employee benefit plan during or for 13 years after such conviction or after the end of such imprisonment, whichever is later, unless the sentencing court on motion of the person convicted sets a lesser period of at least three years after the end of such conviction or imprisonment, whichever is later, or unless prior to the end of the period, citizenship rights revoked as a result of such conviction have been fully restored or if the offense is a Federal offense, the sentencing judge or, if the offense is a State or local offense, the United States district court for the district in which the offense was committed, approves of service in one of the aforementioned capacities with respect to the Plan. I certify that I have not been convicted or imprisoned on account of the aforementioned offenses and that my acceptance herein is not contrary to the provisions of section 411(a) of the Employee Retirement Income Security Act of 1974.

Dated as of this ____________, 2____.

____
Sign Name

____
Print/Type Name

[HEALTH AND WELFARE FUND NAME]

ACCEPTANCE OF TRUSTEESHIP

The undersigned, having been duly designated as an/a [Employer] [Union] Trustee of the ______________________ ______________________ Fund ("Fund"), effective as of ________________ [date], does hereby accept the trust imposed upon all the terms and conditions set forth in the Trust Agreement, a copy of which has been delivered to the undersigned, and the undersigned agrees to perform his duties as required by said Trust Agreement.

I understand that section 411(a) of the Employee Retirement Income Security Act of 1974 (ERISA) provides that no person who has been convicted of or has been imprisoned as a result of a conviction of robbery, bribery, extortion, embezzlement, fraud, grand larceny, burglary, arson, a felony violation of Federal or State law involving substances defined in section 102(6) of the Comprehensive Drug Abuse Prevention and Control Act of 1970, murder, rape, kidnapping, perjury, assault with intent to kill, any crime described in section 9(a)(1) of the Investment Company Act of 1940, a violation of any provision of ERISA or section 302 of the Labor-Management Relations Act of 1947, a violation of section 63 of Title 18, United States Code, a violation of sections 874, 1027, 1503, 1505, 1506, 1510, 1951 or 1954 of Title 18, United States Code, a violation of the Labor-Management Reporting and Disclosure Act of 1959, any felony involving abuse or misuse of a position or employment in a labor organization or an employee benefit plan to seek or obtain an illegal gain at the expense of the members of the labor organization or the beneficiaries of the employee benefit plan, or a conspiracy to commit or attempt to commit any such crimes, or a crime in which any of the foregoing crimes is an element, shall be permitted to serve as an administrator, fiduciary, officer, trustee, custodian, counsel, agent, employee, representative, advisor or consultant to any employee benefit plan or in any capacity involving decision making authority or custody or control of the assets of any employee benefit plan during or for 13 years after such conviction or after the end of such imprisonment, whichever is later, unless the sentencing court on motion of the person convicted sets a lesser period of at least three years after the end of such conviction or imprisonment, whichever is later, or unless prior to the end of the period, citizenship rights revoked as a result of such conviction have been fully restored or if the offense is a Federal offense, the sentencing judge or, if the offense is a State or local offense, the United States district court for the district in which the offense was committed, approves of service in one of the aforementioned capacities with respect to the Fund. I certify that I have not been convicted or imprisoned on account of the aforementioned offenses and that my acceptance herein is not contrary to the provisions of section 411(a) of the Employee Retirement Income Security Act of 1974.

I understand that I may receive health information regarding individuals covered by the Plan that is confidential and protected under privacy regulations issued pursuant to the Health Insurance Portability and Accountability Act of 1996 ("HIPAA Privacy Regulations"). I understand that the HIPAA Privacy Regulations protect the confidentiality of "protected health information" ("PHI"), which is any health or medical information regarding individuals covered by the Plan that is individually identifiable. I hereby agree that I will not at any time—either during my association with the Plan or after my association ends—disclose PHI to any person or entity, or use such PHI, except as is required and permitted in the course of my Plan administration duties and responsibilities as a Trustee, as set forth in the Plan's privacy policies and procedures and the Plan document or as permitted or required under the HIPAA Privacy Regulations. I understand that this obligation extends to any PHI that I may acquire during the course of my term as a Trustee of the Plan.

I understand that unauthorized use or disclosure of PHI will result in disciplinary action in accordance with the Plan's disciplinary procedure and the potential imposition of civil and criminal penalties under applicable federal and state law.

I understand that this confidentiality obligation with respect to PHI will survive the end of my association with the Plan. I agree to return or destroy the PHI I receive, or to maintain the confidentiality of the PHI I receive, and not to use or disclose such PHI after my term as Trustee ends.

Dated as of this _____ of _____________, 2____.

____
Sign Name

____
Print/Type Name

Chapter 9

Trustee Meetings

Timothy J. Parsons

To properly fulfill their responsibilities, trustees must understand how to conduct plan meetings appropriately and efficiently. Trustees must also maintain a record of decisions and the processes they use to make these decisions. This chapter discusses both the legal and practical aspects of how trustees conduct plan business. Practical considerations are:

- Effective service to plan participants and beneficiaries
- Effective use of plan assets
- Avoidance of possible personal liability.

One of the first lessons new trustees learn is that plan documents and federal law concerning trustee conduct govern much of what they can and cannot do.[1] Trustees must understand these documents and have a thorough knowledge of their fiduciary duties under the Employee Retirement Income Security Act of 1974 (ERISA). Only then can trustees contribute to effective decision making during trustee meetings.

Trustees should meet at least quarterly or as required by the terms of plan documents.[2] Some trust agreements provide that trustees can act without a meeting, if they do so by unanimous written consent.

Procedural or plan documents should give guidelines on providing notices of regular meetings and of specially called meetings. The documents should also identify who creates the agenda, the timing of agenda distribution and how to modify the agenda.

What Policies Are Needed for Trustee Meetings?

Attendance

If a policy does not already exist, plan trustees should consider adopting a policy statement that addresses these issues:

- Who should attend meetings?
- Must trustees attend in person?
- What constitutes a quorum for conducting business?
- Will proxies or alternate trustees be recognized?
- Who else can attend meetings?
  - Plan participants (active and/or retired)?
  - Nontrustee representatives of unions and employers?
  - Service providers?

An example of an attendance policy for a multiemployer plan is provided in Exhibit 1.

Attorney-Client Privilege

When legal advice is given, particularly on current or anticipated litigation, meetings should be limited to fiduciaries in an executive session (i.e., the clients). Discussion should not be disclosed in regular meeting minutes. Minutes or a summary of the meeting should be prepared and retained by the attorney. When a plan does not have a staff of employees, outside advisors may be considered "functional employees" covered by the attorney-client privilege.

Voting

Plan documents should specify the procedure for voting. It is common to include provisions prohibiting proxy voting. Another common provision is a requirement that official action requires a majority vote of trustees present at a meeting for which proper notice was given and there is a quorum. Some plan documents require that advance notice be given when certain types of actions will be discussed at a meeting.

What Happens If a Quorum Is Not Present?

A plan's trust agreement usually specifies what constitutes a *quorum*—the number of trustees who must attend a meet-

Exhibit 1

Attendance Policy for Trustee Board and Committee Meetings

1. Meetings of the board of trustees and meetings of committees of the board of trustees are private business meetings, not public meetings.
2. Attendance at meetings of the board of trustees is generally limited to only the members of the board of trustees, the plan administrative staff and the trustees' professional advisors.
3. The business matters discussed at meetings of the board of trustees generally involve discussion of confidential financial, claim and legal issues. Therefore, plan participants and representatives of signatory employers may not attend the meetings as observers.
4. Service providers such as investment managers, performance monitors and auditors should attend only the portion of a meeting that is necessary for discussion of particular issues.
5. Upon advance written request submitted to the fund administrator identifying interest in a particular issue or subject, a participant may receive permission to attend a specific meeting of the board of trustees. The participant may attend only the portion of the meeting that involves discussion of that issue or subject. When permitted to attend a meeting, participants are in the status of an observer. Unless specifically requested to do so by the chair of the board of trustees, participants may not ask questions, participate in discussion or vote on any matter.
6. Participants may not attend meetings of committees of the board of trustees, except for meetings of the claim appeals committee. To attend this committee meeting, a participant must make an advance request for a personal appearance concerning his or her own appeal. If a personal appearance is permitted by the plan administrator, the participant's attendance shall be limited to the time necessary for making a personal presentation of the appeal and for answering any questions that committee members and/or the trustee advisors may have.
7. The board of trustees, through the chairs of the board and of each committee, reserves the right to reject any or all requests for attendance at meetings of the board of trustees or committees.
8. The board of trustees may amend or rescind this policy statement at any time.

ing in order to conduct plan business. Some plans define a *quorum* as a minimum number of trustees with equal representation by labor and management. Assume a board of trustees consists of eight members with four persons appointed by employers and four by labor. The required quorum might consist of at least four trustees present in person, provided there are at least two employer trustees and two labor trustees present. If a quorum is not present, a meeting may still proceed, but any action taken is subject to approval by the absent trustees.

What Happens When Labor and Management Are Not Represented Equally at a Meeting?

Taft-Hartley's "equal representation" for labor and management has generally been interpreted to require that both sides have equal voting power even if there are not equal numbers of trustees present. In other words, each side should have "equal voting power" on any proposed action.[3] For example, assume a quorum is present at a meeting but there are four employer trustees and two labor trustees present. Each employer trustee could cast a vote with a weight of one while each labor trustee could cast a vote with a weight of two.

An alternative procedure is *unit voting*. Labor and management trustees divide into their separate groups and decide how to vote. Each group casts a single vote determined by a majority vote of the individual trustees within the group. Official action occurs only if both groups vote the same. The Department of Labor (DOL) has ruled that a unit-voting procedure such as this is not in violation of ERISA.[4]

What Are Some of the Obstacles to Effective Meetings?

Psychological Barriers

Nitpicking. There is a type of trustee who has a compulsion to dig into the smallest details of every report and issue. This trustee seems not to be able to establish priorities because of his or her need to know everything about the plan. Often, the decision involves expertise normally not possessed by this trustee. This particular type of trustee spends an unreasonable amount of time in meetings, and perhaps outside of meetings, reviewing relatively minor matters.

Trustees who see this tendency in themselves should try to establish priorities as to where their attention should be placed. They should attempt to be comfortable with the delegation of authority that has occurred until there are clear signs there may be a problem.

Power seeking. Men and women who have achieved roles of authority within their union or industry are not shrinking violets. They have sought power and achieved it. The desire to achieve is a normal human tendency, but a person who cannot control the use of power is more of a hindrance than a help.

Some trustees attempt and are successful in dominating meetings and the decision-making process. Such behavior reduces the effectiveness of a plan's board of trustees. The behavior is also contrary to the spirit of the Taft-Hartley Act in that it reduces bipartisan efforts. No one person has all the answers to the problems that face a board of trustees. The input of the varied persons on the board usually leads to the best possible decision.

Possible embarrassment. Some trustees find it difficult to admit that they lack knowledge on an issue and will not ask questions of plan professionals. Of all of the behavioral habits discussed here, this is perhaps the most common—and the most harmful to the effective operation of a board of trustees. No trustee should expect to immediately understand all the concepts, technical aspects or terminology of the various professionals who counsel the board.

It would be helpful to the operations of many trusts if trustees could feel freer to discuss what they do not know as well as what they do know. Trustees should remember that often their question is the same question other trustees have.

Conflicting Duties

Work responsibilities. Most plan trustees are busy people. Labor trustees are usually occupied by activities of a local, regional or national union organization. Management trustees are often directing a business or trade association. Too often, the persons who take on the responsibility of trusteeship do not realize beforehand the amount of work involved in being a trustee. Sometimes the best trustees are those who do not have key roles in their organizations but have roles that are less demanding.

Collective bargaining. Many people who are not involved in multiemployer benefit plans have condemned them as impossible to operate. Most often, such persons point to the fact that trustees appointed half by labor and half by management will act with total disregard for their labor and management backgrounds.

All trustees are human beings—each is the sum total of his or her background and experience. In this context, a person who has served 25 years in the union movement or as management cannot easily walk into trustee meeting and forget these roots—nor is that desirable. The great strength trustees bring to the multiemployer trustee table is the knowledge of the industry and the people in it. The overwhelming majority of trustees are able to separate their collective bargaining agreement duties and responsibilities from their trustee duties and responsibilities.

Legal counsel or another advisor may have to intervene on occasion—reminding trustees that they have dual roles and must keep their priorities in the correct order. During trustee meetings, the responsibility of trustees is to act in the sole interest of the plan and its participants.

What Should Trustees Do When There Is a Conflict of Interest?

From time to time, individual trustees encounter situations where their personal or business interests may be in conflict with their fiduciary responsibility to act "solely in the interest" of plan participants and beneficiaries. Participation in discussion or taking action might be a prohibited transaction under the rules of the ERISA.[5] In these types of situations, DOL regulations provide that a trustee can avoid prohibited transaction issues by "removing him or herself from all consideration" of the particular issue or transaction and "by not otherwise exercising" any fiduciary authority, control or responsibility.[6] A full discussion of potential conflicts and prohibited transactions is provided in Chapter 5.

DOL has pointed out, however, that if a plan trustee who has recused himself or herself "has material information" concerning a particular transaction "that would be necessary in order for other plan fiduciaries to make an appropriate and prudent decision," then the recused fiduciary's duties under ERISA Section 404 "would require informing the deciding fiduciaries" of that information.[7]

It may be useful for a board to consider a policy that states that, at the start of any meeting, trustees review the agenda and immediately declare any potential or actual conflict of interest with respect to any of the anticipated items of business.

May a Board of Trustees Ask a Committee to Handle Some of Its Responsibilities?

Earlier in this handbook (Chapters 5 and 6), the authority of trustees to allocate and delegate fiduciary duty to others is discussed in substantial detail. For the purposes of this chapter, it is safe to say that multiemployer trustees are usually permitted to transfer duties to individual fiduciaries or committees consisting of board members if the transfers are (1) provided for in plan documents and (2) not contrary to any law or regulation governing multiemployer benefit plans.[8] To avoid fiduciary liability, appointing trustees must prudently appoint and monitor the activities of their appointees on a regular basis to be certain the transferred functions are performed properly.

It is a good idea for officers of the board of trustees to attend committee meetings. Officers that are not designated members of committees, however, should attend only in an ex officio or observer capacity for purposes of obtaining information and participating in discussion. They should not vote.

Committee Reports

If a committee is asked to make a decision on a particular issue, the committee should report its decision to the full board of trustees, preferably in the form of approved minutes from its meeting(s).

Committees may be asked to study a certain issue or make a recommendation to the full board of trustees. For example, they may advise the board regarding individual benefit claim appeals or the termination of an investment manager. In these situations, the committee should report its recommendations with reasons to the full board of trustees for consideration and possible action.

A committee may also be asked to monitor or oversee certain service providers. In these situations, the committee should provide a report to the full board of trustees on its activities, with any recommendations considered necessary. The full board can accept the report and take action on the recommendations.

What Guidelines Exist Concerning Meeting Minutes?

Minutes are a brief written summary of what occurred at a meeting, not a detailed log of everything said by each person on every topic. The report should be a complete and accurate record of (1) persons present, (2) presentations made, (3) opinions presented, (4) discussions held and (5) votes taken.

Approved minutes are primary evidence of the business transacted and decisions made during a meeting. Other evidence such as trustee testimony or an advisor report used by trustees may be part of the record. To avoid possible uncertainty or later dispute, it is good practice (when possible) to have all trustees sign the minutes to acknowledge their approval. An alternative is to have the minutes of a meeting prepared and distributed prior to the next meeting, then reviewed and approved as one of the first items of business at that next meeting.[9]

Tape Recordings

Tape recordings are not required. If plan policy allows taping, use of the tape should be limited to being an aid in preparing written minutes. After the written minutes have been prepared and approved, the recordings should be immediately destroyed. Tapes are subject to discovery and can be used as evidence in litigation—particularly when there are issues concerning trustee intent or motivation.

Disclosure of Minutes

ERISA gives plan participants and beneficiaries the right to submit a written request for copies of plan documents under which a plan is established and operates, in addition to specific reports (e.g., the latest Form 5500, the annual report and any terminal report).[10] Plan fiduciaries have 30 days to respond or they may be subject to civil penalties, other relief the court "deems proper," and possible attorney fees and costs.[11]

Are minutes included in these documents? Two DOL Advisory Opinions indicate that minutes of trustees meetings do not have to be produced unless the minutes are an instrument under which the plan was established or operated—for example, the minutes of a meeting that established a benefits claim procedure.[12]

Endnotes

1. ERISA §404(a)(l)(D).
2. Consent Order with Eighth District Electrical Workers Pension Fund, entered on April 4, 2002, in *Chao v. Legino,* (D.Oreg.), at part II H.
3. *Associated Contractors of Essex County, Inc., v. LIUNA,* 559 F.2d 222 (3d Cir. 1977).
4. DOL Advisory Opinion 92-11A (March 31, 1992).
5. ERISA §§404(a)(1) and 406(b)(1-3).
6. DOL Regs. 29 CFR §2550.408b-2(e).
7. Information Letter to William Lindsay issued on February 23, 2005.
8. ERISA §§403(b)(2) and 405(c)(l).
9. See, generally, W. M. Fletcher, Cyclopedia on the Law of Private Corporations (Perm. Ed.) at §3:23.
10. ERISA §104(b)(4).
11. ERISA §§502(a)(l)(A) and 502(c)(2) for civil penalties; ERISA §502(g)(l) for attorney fees and costs.
12. DOL Advisory Opinions 82-21A (April 21,1982) and 82-33A (July 21, 1982).

Chapter 10

Trustee Action When Trustees Don't Agree on a Decision

Vivian C. Folk

From time to time, plan trustees disagree on what action to take. This is often healthy. Additional dialogue, debate and compromise can lead to good decision making. Occasionally, however, an economic motive, bargaining or other hidden agenda threatens to derail a prudent decision-making process. Strong views may yield a deadlock in the administration of plan affairs. In rare circumstances, trustee compliance with ERISA or another law is at issue.

At the risk of oversimplification, when deciding how to react to a dispute, trustees must determine what the dispute involves. Is it a "discretionary" issue with numerous appropriate results? Discretionary decisions are "fence sitters"—different results are possible without violating the law. For example, trustees may disagree on which of two well-qualified individuals to hire. If plan documents and the trust agreement give trustees broad discretion in making plan decisions, courts do not interfere with the trustee judgment. The only exceptions are when decisions are "arbitrary or capricious" or an "abuse of discretion."[1]

On the other hand, is the dispute a legal issue that limits what is an acceptable action on the part of trustees? Department of Labor (DOL) regulations provide this example:

> *An employee benefit plan is considering the construction of a building to house the administration of the plan. One trustee has proposed that the building be constructed on a cost-plus basis by a particular contractor without competitive bidding. When the trustee was questioned by another trustee as to the basis of choice of the contract, the impact of the building on the plan's administrative costs, whether a cost-plus contract would yield a better price to the plan than a fixed price basis and why a negotiated contract would be better than letting the contract for competitive bidding, no satisfactory answers were provided.*[2]

In these circumstances, a possible violation of law is the issue. A dissenting trustee's actions and reactions should be much different when the dispute concerns whether an action violates a law. The dissenting trustee must be concerned with co-fiduciary liability.

What Is Co-Fiduciary Liability?

Under ERISA Section 405(a), a fiduciary is responsible for another fiduciary's breach if the first fiduciary:

- Participates knowingly in another's breach or duty, or knowingly attempts to conceal the other's breach *(participation violation)*
- Fails to fulfill his or her specific fiduciary responsibilities under ERISA, making it possible for another fiduciary to commit a breach *(enablement violation)*
- Knows there has been a breach by another fiduciary and does not make reasonable efforts under the circumstances to remedy the breach *(guilty knowledge violation).*[3]

Co-fiduciary liability is generally based on whether a trustee addresses a decision directly, or attempts to run and hide from the decision-making process. Inaction will result in co-fiduciary liability.[4] By contrast, DOL says:

> *If, having taken all reasonable and legal steps to prevent the imprudent action, the minority trustees have not succeeded, they will not incur liability for the action of the majority.*[5]

In short, neither the courts nor DOL tolerate a co-fiduciary's abdication of responsibility through inaction or otherwise.

How Must Trustee Decision Making Be Documented?

When a question arises as to whether a trustee decision was legal or appropriate, meeting minutes are consulted to determine the details of the decision and the rationale for the decision. Trustees who disagree with a decision should make certain their dissenting votes and reasons are reflected in the minutes. DOL has made this clear in regulations:

> *[T]rustees should take great care to document adequately all meetings where actions are taken with respect to management and control of plan assets. Written minutes of all actions taken should be kept, describing the action taken, and stating how each trustee voted on each matter. If. . . trustees object to a proposed action on the grounds of possible violation of the fiduciary responsibility provisions of the Act [ERISA], the trustees so objecting should insist that their objections and the responses to such objections be included in the record of the meeting.*[6]

Dissenting trustees should insist that the minutes provide a "full and complete" record of the trustee meeting. The minutes should:

- Reflect the date, time and place the meeting was called to order
- State who was present for the meeting (e.g., the specific trustees, administrative manager, certified public accountant, investment manager, consultant and counsel)
- State whether there was a quorum to conduct all business coming before the board of trustees
- Reflect each and every topic discussed at the meeting
- Answer who, what, when, where and why with regard to each and every topic discussed to establish that the decision was made after a thorough decision-making process consistent with ERISA's standard of prudence. Examples of these questions are:
  - Who gave the report on investments?
  - What course of action did the investment manager recommend?
  - What questions did trustees ask the investment manager concerning the manager's recommendation?
  - Why did trustees decide to adopt the investment manager's recommendation?
- State motions with completeness and accuracy.

If minutes are inadequate, incomplete or inaccurate, dissenting trustees should note their proposed changes and additions in writing and communicate them. This helps protect the trustees if there are subsequent legal proceedings.

How Is a Deadlock Handled?

Every plan trust agreement should contain provisions on dealing with a deadlock consistent with the Taft-Hartley Act. Trustees should consult those provisions.

Administrative Issues

Section 302 of the Taft-Hartley Act contains guidelines for resolving disputes when there is a deadlock in the administration of a plan. If plan labor and management groups deadlock, the act says the two groups must agree on an "impartial umpire" to *arbitrate* (decide) the dispute. If the two groups fail to agree on selection of an umpire within a reasonable length of time, either group may petition the District Court of the United States where the plan has its principal office to appoint an impartial umpire.[7]

Even if a deadlock is appropriate for arbitration, trustees are encouraged to resolve the dispute without an arbitrator. Trustees have a better understanding of the management and administration of a plan than an "outside" arbitrator. More importantly, the hard feelings that may remain from a hard-fought arbitration can affect trustee relations and plan management for years to follow. Disputes are best resolved by trustees themselves.

Not every deadlocked dispute is subject to arbitration with an impartial party—only those suits involving a plan's "administration." The term *administration* is only day-to-day practical questions—generally, the discretionary decisions referred to earlier.[8] The term has been interpreted to exclude any legal disputes and issues.[9] Because of this latter interpretation, issues regarding breach of fiduciary responsibility under ERISA are outside the Taft-Hartley Act's arbitration provision.

Legal Issues

Generally, fiduciary violations and other legal issues must be determined by the courts or in another forum. Using the example recited earlier in this chapter on awarding a contract without competitive bidding, DOL provided the following guidance:

Q: Several of the trustees have argued that letting such a contract would be a violation of their general fiduciary responsibilities. Despite their arguments, a majority of the trustees appear to be ready to vote to construct the building as proposed. What should the minority trustees do to protect themselves from liability under section 409(a) of the Act and section 405(b)(1)(A) of the Act?

A: Here, where a majority of trustees appear ready to take action which would clearly be contrary to the prudence requirements of section 404(a)(1)(B) of the Act, it is incumbent on the minority trustees to take all reasonable and legal steps to prevent the action. Such steps might include preparations to obtain an injunction from a Federal District court under section 502(a)(3) of the Act, to notify the Labor Department, or to publicize the vote if the decision is to proceed as proposed.[10]

The courts agree with DOL that trustees must occasionally challenge fiduciary conduct in a judicial proceeding.[11]

Can Disputes Be Given to the Labor-Management Associations to Resolve?

Action by plan trustees is generally subject to review under ERISA's fiduciary responsibility provisions. In contrast, labor-management sponsors are permitted to make business decisions that might not meet fiduciary standards if the trustees had made the decisions.[12] Trustees may not hand over their fiduciary responsibility to plan sponsors. However, trustees may look to the sponsors for resolution—through bargaining—of issues trustees are unable to resolve. Trustees can then follow the written resolution between the labor and management associations on the matter, as long as the resolution complies with ERISA and other applicable law.[13]

Can a Trustee Avoid Liability Through Resignation?

There is some temptation, when faced with actions with which we do not agree, simply to walk away from the situation. DOL has suggested that trustees usually cannot avoid liability by resignation:

Mere resignation, however, without taking steps to prevent the imprudent action, will not suffice to avoid liability for the minority trustees once they have knowledge that the imprudent action is under consideration.[14]

In fact, resignation might be considered inconsistent with the trustee duty to remedy the breach:

It should be noted that, where a trustee believes that a trustee has already committed a breach, resignation by the trustee as a protest against such breach will not generally be considered sufficient to discharge the trustee's positive duty under section 405(a)(3) to make reasonable efforts under the circumstances to remedy the breach.[15]

In short, resigning may create additional liability.

When a trustee resigns with no successor, an additional breach of fiduciary responsibility may result. Having accepted the appointment as trustee, a trustee cannot simply walk away without adequate provision for a successor and management of plan affairs.[16]

Conclusion

Much of the satisfaction of serving as a trustee comes from the lively dialogue, debate and give-and-take among fellow trustees. In most circumstances, this same dialogue, debate and give-and-take eventually leads to good decision making and the prompt resolution of a trustee dispute.

In rare circumstances, however, a deadlock results. If a dissenting trustee honestly believes that the majority of trustees are taking an action that violates their fiduciary responsibilities, inaction and/or "flight" are inappropriate and dangerous responses. At a minimum, a trustee must make certain that his or her actions and dissent to the action of other fiduciaries are recorded in the minutes or otherwise. In extreme circumstances, a trustee may be required to institute an action for declaratory or injunctive relief.

Endnotes

1. *Firestone Tire and Rubber Co. v. Bruch*, 489 U.S. 101, 109 S. Ct. 948, 103 L. Ed. 2d 80 (1989).
2. 29 C.F.R. §2509.75-5, FR-10.
3. 29 U.S.C. §1105.
4. *Free v. Briody*, 732 F.2d 1331 (7th Cir. 1984). See also *Tittle v. Enron Corp. (In re Enron Corp. Sec. Derivative & ERISA Litig.)*, 284 F.Supp. 2d 511, 2003 U.S. Dist. LEXIS 17492, 31 Employee Benefits Case. (BNA) 2281 (S.D. Tex. 2003) (co-fiduciaries' failure to inform plan fiduciaries about employer's actual financial status and/or failure to monitor fiduciaries); *Kling v. Fid. Mgmt. trust Co.*, 323 F.Supp. 2d 132, 2004 U.S. Dist. LEXIS 12634, 33 Employee Benefits Case. (BNA) 1035 (D. Mass. 2004) (directed trustee may be liable for failing to disclose material information to plan fiduciaries and participants regarding imprudence of investing in company stock).
5. 29 C.F.R §2509.75-5, FR-10.
6. 29 C.F.R §2509.75-5, FR-10.
7. 29 U.S.C. §186(c)(5).

8. In *Employee Trustees of the Eighth District Electrical Pension Fund v. Employer Trustees of the Eighth District Electrical Pension Fund,* 959 F.2d 176 (10th Cir. 1992), plan trustees deadlocked on whether the pension fund should establish an annuity plan in addition to the defined contribution plan. The court found appointment of an umpire appropriate as the deadlock involved ordinary administration within trustee discretion. Determining whether issues are administrative involves determining the extent of trustee authority under the trust agreement and otherwise, and discretion under the trust agreement. The court concluded that the dispute before it was administrative because it did not involve amending the trust agreement or interpreting the collective bargaining agreement. See also *Sandman v. Local Union No. 141 Sheet Metal Workers International Association,* 564 F. Supp. 895 (S.D. Ohio 1982) (dispute over standard for allowance of apprentices arbitrable); *Donaldson v. Archiable,* 1982 U.S. Dist. LEXIS 14317 (S.D. Ohio, W.D. 1982) (dispute over increase in weekly supplemental unemployment compensation benefits arbitrable); *Enix v. Burrell,* 572 F. Supp. 1364 (S.D. Ohio, W.D. 1983) (parties dispute over the amount of certain pension funds due retirees was not an "extraordinary" matter which should be left to collective bargaining, but, rather, was committed to the "day-to-day management" of the trustees); *Yale Citrin v. Christopher Erikson, et al.,* 918 F. Supp 792 (S.D.N.Y. 1996) (dispute over commencement of apprenticeship classes was administrative issue for umpire); and *Mahoney v. Fischer,* 277 F.2d 5 (2nd Cir. 1960) (question was whether present or former broker could be paid $600 for services).
9. *Bath v. Pixler,* 283 F. Supp. 632, at 635 (D.C. Colo. 1968) ("The dispute among the trustees is a legal controversy, not a dispute over the practical administration of the trust"); *Ader v. Hughes,* 570 F.2d 303 (10th Cir. 1978) (decision whether to amend the trust agreement was not a matter of "plan administration"; *Bueno v. Gill,* 237 F. Supp. 2d 447, 2002 U.S. Dist. EXIS 22206, 29 EBC (BNA) 1932 (S.D. N.Y. 2002) (issues are not arbitrable where they are outside the trustees' power, absent amendment of the plan's trust agreement); *McMahan, et al. v. George H. Cornelius, et al,* 756 F. Supp. 1156 (S.D. Indiana 1991) (dispute as to whether assets should be distributed to participants or returned to employer upon plan termination was not a deadlock on administration; the disposal of surplus funds was an extraordinary matter requiring resolution of numerous legal and factual matters); *Botto v. Friedberg,* 568 F. Supp. 1253 (E.D. N.Y. 1982) (disputed pension increase was not a matter of trust fund administration subject to arbitration as decision not appropriate by trustees in the absence of an agreement on this subject by the collective bargaining parties); *Jackson v. Smith,* 927 F.2d 544 (11th Cir. 1991) (dispute over increase in pension benefits was not arbitrable under Taft-Hartley Act as it was not an administrative matter under the plan); and *Arlen Hodges, et al v. Rudy Holzer, et al.,* 707 F. Supp 232 (M.D. La. 1988) (merger decision was determined to be "extraordinary," rather than a matter of plan administration).
10. 29 C.F.R. §2509.75-5, FR-10.
11. *Cf. Modern Woodcrafts, Inc. v. Hawley,* 534 F. Supp. 1000 (D. Conn. 1982). See also *Weiler v. Lapkoff,* 2002 U.S. Dist. LEXIS 23485, 29 Employee Benefits Case. (BNA) 2219 (N.D. Ill. Dec. 5, 2002) (trustees have standing to sue original plan's trustees for failing to credit split-off plan with demutualization compensation).
12. It should be noted that there is some authority that trustees act as settlors when they amend plans and are not subject to ERISA's fiduciary responsibility provisions. *Walling vs. Brady,* 125 F.3d 114 (3d Cir. 1997) and *Gard vs. Blankenburg,* 33 Fed. Appx. 722 (6th Cir. 2002). But compare *Abbott vs. Pipefitters Local Union No. 522,* 94 F.3d 236 (6th Cir. 1997), cert. denied 519 U.S. 1111 (U.S. 1997) (where trustees required one local union to pay higher contributions than other participating locals, court ruled that trustees had not actually modified or amended the plan, but, rather, taken administrative action which should be evaluated under ERISA's fiduciary standards); *Hartline v. Sheet Metal Workers' National Pension Fund,* 134 F. Supp. 2d 1 (D.C. 2000) (trustees' establishment of varying contribution rates was deemed settlor activity under the circumstances presented). In short, trustees proceed at their risk in assuming a court will treat their plan modifications or amendments as settlor activity not subject to fiduciary standards. Even if the trustees' action is settlor activity, their implementation thereof will be evaluated under ERISA fiduciary standards.
13. ERISA §404(a)(1)(D) requires fiduciaries to discharge their "duties with respect to a plan solely in the interest of the participants and beneficiaries and . . . in accordance with the documents and instruments governing the plan insofar as such documents and instruments are consistent with provisions of this title and title IV." (emphasis added) 29 U.S.C. §1104(a)(1)(D).
14. 29 C.F.R. §2509.75-5, FR-10.
15. 29 C.F.R. §2509.75-5, FR-10.
16. See, e.g., *Freund, et al. v. Marshall & Ilsley Bank, et al. and Marshall v. R.W. DeKeyser, et al.,* 485 F.Supp. 629 (W.D. Wisc. 1979); *Usery v. Conser,* et al. No. C77-61, sub nom *Marshall v. Conser, et al.* (N.D. Oh. March 2, 1977); *Lane v. Marshall,* Civ. Action No. 779-0868, F. Supp. (N.D. Cal. 1979).

Chapter 11

Fiduciary Liability Insurance: A Benefit Consultant Perspective

Jeffrey D. Mamorsky

Trustees increasingly realize the liability attached to a multiemployer benefit plan. In addition to the plan's liability, individual fiduciaries face potential personal liability. The risk that trustees may have to dip into their individual pockets to defend a lawsuit, pay damages or cover civil penalties connected with their service to a plan has increased with events such as these:

- The Sarbanes-Oxley Act of 2002 (SOX) has imposed white-collar criminal penalties on trustees who fail to establish internal control procedures to ensure benefit plan operation conforms to plan documents and applicable law.
- The Internal Revenue Service (IRS) has established a Multiemployer Plans Examination Program that imposes monetary sanctions on trustees for failure to adopt "self-audit" control procedures under the Employee Plans Compliance Resolution System (EPCRS).
- The Department of Labor (DOL) has heightened its oversight of ERISA compliance with the Voluntary Fiduciary Correction Program (VFCP), and increased fiduciary and plan expense audits that can result in personal liability and ERISA civil penalties.
- Scandals in the financial and investment community—combined with poor funding of pension plans—have spawned participant and government litigation.

The purpose of this chapter is to sift through the insurance maze. An overview is provided of the basic types of insurance coverage available to multiemployer plans and trustees. One of these types, fiduciary liability coverage, is discussed in detail with an explanation of what may and may not be covered. Recommendations also are made on how multiemployer plan trustees can reduce liability risk and, where this is not possible, use an insurance program to protect both their plan and personal assets.

What Types of Liability Insurance Should Plans Have?

The insurance coverage needed to protect a multiemployer employee benefit plan and its trustees includes (1) bonding insurance, (2) fiduciary liability insurance, (3) employee benefits liability insurance and (4) IRS liability insurance.

Fidelity Bonding

A *fidelity bond* involves a contract with an insurance company or other issuer agreeing to reimburse a benefit plan for losses resulting from dishonest acts (e.g., theft and fraud) by persons who handle plan assets. ERISA requires all plan trustees and employees who handle plan funds to be bonded. Some carriers expand coverage to any other person who handles plan assets regardless of whether or not ERISA requires they be bonded—for example, the employees of banks and insurance companies who are typically exempt from ERISA bonding requirements. Employees of a nonfiduciary service provider are covered if they embezzle plan assets. Broader coverage is also available that covers other persons and activities such as third-party computer fraud, wire fraud and forgery.

Under ERISA, each person must be bonded for 10% of the total amount of assets "handled"—subject to a minimum bond of $1,000 and a maximum bond of $500,000. The maximum can be higher in some circumstances; for example, the maximum increases to $1,000,000 if plan assets are invested in securities of any sponsor or contributing employer, unless these investments are a mutual find, index fund or other investment "pool." For plans with assets in the tens of millions or more, trustees should consider whether a $500,000 or $1,000,000 limit of liability is sufficient. ERISA does not allow a deductible for the required $500,000 or $1,000,000 limit of liability.

An exception to the bonding requirement, however, exists for corporate trustees and insurance companies that have a combined capital and surplus of at least $1 million if:

- The only assets from which benefits are paid are the general assets of the employer or a union, or
- DOL finds other bonding arrangements or the overall condition of the plan are adequate to protect participants.

Plans can comply with the bonding requirement by purchasing a fiduciary dishonesty policy that pays for losses from fraudulent or dishonest acts committed by persons that ERISA requires be bonded. These persons include plan employees, trustees, administrators, and other fiduciaries or persons who handle plan funds.

Fiduciary Liability Insurance

Even though benefit plan trustees make a concerted effort to carry out their fiduciary duties, the drafters of ERISA recognized that (1) lawsuits may still occur and (2) it is unreasonable to expect fiduciaries to dip into their own pockets to cover defense costs every time someone decides to file a lawsuit. Fiduciary liability insurance protects benefit plans and plan fiduciaries from losses caused by the unintended acts or omissions of fiduciaries that cause a plan to lose assets. Note that while fidelity bonds are mandatory and cover intentional wrongdoings, fiduciary liability insurance covers unintentional acts and coverage is discretionary. Fiduciary liability policies generally:

1. Pay for the cost of defending a plan and plan trustees when there are accusations of fiduciary *breaches* (violations)
2. *Indemnify* (compensate) trustees and the plan for monetary liabilities that result from a legal settlement or judgment.

Employee Benefits Liability Insurance

While fiduciary liability insurance covers claims alleging breach of fiduciary duties under ERISA, employee benefits liability insurance covers claims involving administrative errors—for example, a failure on the part of plan personnel to name a beneficiary on a life insurance policy. There are several confusing aspects involved in coordinating these two forms of liability coverage. Most—although not all—insurers automatically cover employee benefits liability exposure as part of a fiduciary liability policy or add it as an *endorsement*. On the other hand, employee benefits liability policies do not cover fiduciary liability exposures.

IRS Liability Insurance

Under the Closing Agreement Program (CAP), IRS may impose monetary penalties on trustees for failing to operate a retirement plan in accordance with IRS qualification requirements. Penalties can also be imposed for not following the terms of plan documents even if plan operation complies with IRS qualification requirements. Trustees are required to establish self-audit internal control procedures to qualify for self-correction and mitigate the amount of IRS monetary sanctions. Ideally, self-audits should be conducted by an independent legal counsel to preserve the confidentiality of the attorney-client privilege that may not be available to fund legal counsel as a result of the fiduciary exception to the attorney-client privilege.

CAP monetary sanctions are not covered under a standard fiduciary or employee benefits liability policy since sanctions are civil penalties; civil penalties are generally excluded from coverage under these policies. The standard fiduciary liability policy also does not cover the costs of correcting disqualifying defects for which a plan fiduciary is responsible. In both instances, trustees may be personally liable. If CAP coverage is provided through a fiduciary liability insurance policy, the coverage is a nominal amount of no more than $100,000. Trustees should check current CAP coverage and consider purchasing a separate *IRS fiduciary liability insurance* product to protect the plan and board of trustees for any liability that arises because of a failure to operate the plan in accordance with Internal Revenue Code (IRC) qualification requirements.

Some carriers offer enhanced CAP coverage as well as coverage for the cost of corrections required by IRS as the result of an audit. This enhanced protection is conditioned upon the completion of a Fiduciary Audit® Operational Review evaluating a plan's administrative procedures to determine compliance with the IRC qualification requirements. In addition, the audit identifies operational defects that require correction. This evaluation involves the completion of a questionnaire and a "pre-IRS audit." A Fiduciary Audit® Annual Report is then prepared by independent counsel recommending corrections of operational defects, if any, and improvements to the plan's internal control procedures.

Who Is Insured by a Fiduciary Liability Policy?

The "insured" protected by a fiduciary liability policy are the benefit plan and specific persons affiliated with the plan.

The Plan

All fiduciary liability insurance policies include the benefit plan as an insured. Such coverage is critical because ERISA specifically provides that an "employee benefit plan may sue or be sued as an entity."[1] In most suits filed under ERISA, it is a common practice to sue not only the trustees, but also the plan itself.

In some cases, one policy may cover more than one plan if the various plans (pension, welfare, vacation, etc.) have the same trustees or involve essentially the same contributing employers or union.

Although this arrangement may result in some premium savings compared with insuring each plan separately, it is important to remember that whatever limit of liability is selected applies to all plans combined and not to each plan individually. Consequently, if there is a major claim against one of the plans resulting in substantial defense and/or settlement costs, it may leave the other plans with little protection left for the remainder of the policy period. Most carriers do not permit restoration of the liability limit during the policy period, even with the payment of an additional premium.

Another problem with multiple fund coverage is that when a carrier experiences a significant loss on behalf of any one of the plans, the policy may be canceled—leaving all the plans with no coverage. This approach is not recommended.

Trustees

Past, present and future trustees are protected from claims filed during the insurance policy period. It is usually not necessary to include the specific name of each trustee in the policy schedule for coverage to be in effect for each trustee. Consequently, new trustees are automatically covered if board changes occur during the policy period.

The initial application form, however, usually asks for the names of the present trustees and sometimes the names of all trustees who have served the preceding five or six years. This information may become a factor when a carrier is determining whether to underwrite coverage, especially if any of the trustees have been involved in prior litigation or wrongdoing.

Employees

In addition to trustees, fund employees are also typically insured under a fiduciary liability policy. If a plan has salaried personnel, such employees are protected if named in the suit.

Tip for Trustees

The best protection against trustee liability is not a liability insurance policy—it is actually trustee actions that reduce the risk of litigation in the first place. These actions include:

- Hiring competent professional advisors
- Delegating investment responsibility to a professional investment manager or managers—providing managers with a clear statement of the plan's investment objectives and carefully monitoring manager performance
- Delegating fiduciary responsibilities to appropriate trustee committees
- Maintaining an effective delinquency control program for contributions
- Carefully monitoring trustee expenses
- Authorizing legal counsel and/or a plan consultant to undertake periodic compliance audits to assure that the fund is in full compliance with new federal laws and regulations.
- Participating in ongoing trustee education such as attending International Foundation meetings and utilizing the Foundation's vast library resources

Although it may be comforting to have fiduciary liability insurance, trustees must ultimately rely on their own behavior to protect themselves and their plan.

Who Purchases Fiduciary Liability Insurance?

ERISA does not allow a benefit plan to:

- Excuse a fiduciary from liability for a breach of duty or use plan assets to pay such a liability—even if the breach was unintentional and in good faith
- Pay for the defense of trustees who breach their duties to their plan.

ERISA, however, does allow trustees to purchase fiduciary liability insurance with plan assets to cover losses resulting from acts or omissions of fiduciaries. For a plan to do so, the insurance policy must have a *recourse provision.* Such a policy statement gives the insurance carrier the right to seek reimbursement directly from fiduciaries for costs incurred by the carrier if the fiduciaries are found to have *breached* (violated) a fiduciary duty to the insured plan.[2] The recourse provision requirement stems from congressional concern that trustees would otherwise have no incentive to take reasonable care in the performance of their fiduciary duties.

Waiver-of-Recourse Provision

Insurance carriers quickly realized it might be difficult to market fiduciary liability insurance policies with the recourse provision—they feared trustees might view the policies as providing very little protection if the carrier could turn around under certain conditions and seek recovery directly from the trustees. Carriers also reasoned that, if they selected funds carefully, there would be no need for the recourse provision. The probability of trustees being found guilty of a fiduciary breach would be relatively low and, as a result, there would be little need to exercise the recourse provision anyway.

With these considerations in mind, most carriers permit benefit plans to buy a *waiver-of-recourse provision* that provides the insurance company will not try to recover from a trustee any payments the insurance company makes to cover trustee liability. This provision is either a part of the basic policy or an *endorsement* (addition) to it. The charge for the waiver is extremely reasonable, usually no more than $100-$200 a year for each trustee or other insured party. This extra charge cannot be paid out of plan assets; each trustee must pay for it individually, or it may be paid by a trustee's employer, the employer association or the labor organization on the trustee's behalf.

What Does Fiduciary Liability Insurance Cover?

A *primary insuring clause* at the beginning of a fiduciary liability policy states the carrier's basic intent regarding what actions and losses will be covered. Typically, the clause states that the carrier will cover damages, settlements, judgments and defense costs up to the policy limit of liability for any claim providing the claim meets these three criteria:

1. The claimant alleges the insured has committed a "wrongful act."
2. The claimant seeks monetary damages.
3. The claimant filed during the policy period (typically, one year).

Usually, the clause also states the carrier has an obligation to defend the insured even though the allegations may be "groundless, false, or fraudulent."

Defense costs are usually included in the limit of liability; they involve the costs of investigating, defending and settling claims. These items include attorney fees, adjuster services, court costs, bonds and related expenses required as part of the claim settlement process. Policies usually do not cover fines and penalties imposed by law, taxes and punitive damages.

Wrongful Acts

Key to determining what is covered by a fiduciary liability policy is understanding what the insurance carrier considers a *wrongful act*—generally defined as "any alleged or actual breach of fiduciary duty committed by the insured in the discharge of their fiduciary duties." Some policies extend this language to include "any alleged or actual errors, omissions or negligence on the part of the insured in the administration of the fund." This additional language provides coverage for mistakes in the day-to-day operations of the fund such as recordkeeping, collection of delinquencies, providing information to participants, eligibility determination, etc., even if there is no charge a fiduciary breach has occurred.

It is important to keep in mind that outside organizations are not insured; these policies cover only plan and trustee liability for the acts of these outside entities. Accordingly, make sure that outside organizations such as a contract administrator maintain their own separate professional liability for their activities.

Damages

Carriers generally take the position that for a claim to be covered, the claimant must be seeking some type of monetary settlement that will result in a loss of plan assets if paid by the plan. Several types of claims do not generally meet this definition: (1) benefit claims and (2) nonpecuniary claims.

Benefit claims are participant disputes over eligibility, benefit amounts, type of benefit payable, interpretation of plan provisions, etc. Normally, participants do not seek damages with these claims. The claimants merely seek payment of a benefit and if they win, the plan simply pays the amount it was legally obligated to pay in the first place.

Requests by a claimant for damages and/or attorney fees included in a benefit claim are covered. For example, a claimant contends he was entitled to but not offered health insurance under the Consolidated Omnibus Budget Reconciliation Act of 1985 (COBRA) and as a result he had to sell his home, close out his savings accounts and borrow against his pension plan to pay his medical expenses. The claimant may seek not only reimbursement of his medical expenses, but compensatory damages for the other monetary losses sustained. In this case, most policies would cover compensatory damages.

Claims for nonpecuniary relief are also excluded from coverage. This would include actions under Section 502 of ERISA, which specifically authorize participants, beneficiaries, DOL and fiduciaries to take civil action to enforce or clarify a participant's rights or to obtain equitable relief for an ERISA violation. These actions include requests to the court and court orders that do not involve monetary relief. An example would be a situation where DOL prohibits trustees from making certain real estate investments considered imprudent.

Claims Made

The third critical element is whether a claim is covered. Fiduciary liability policies are usually *claims-made policies*—claims are covered regardless of when the alleged wrongful act occurred. In effect, trustees have retroactive coverage, a comforting thought for trustees who may be relatively new and may not be fully aware of earlier fiduciary decisions.

What Other Provisions Are Frequently Included in a Fiduciary Liability Policy?

Restrictions on Prior Acts Coverage

A carrier's application or renewal form usually asks trustees if they are aware of any potential claim situations. Failure to answer this question honestly and accurately may result in loss of coverage if a claim is later filed and the carrier can demonstrate trustees knew, or should have known, the claim would be filed. As a result, a plan's legal counsel (not the administrative manager or insurance broker) in consultation with trustees should answer this question.

Claims-Made Extension Clause

Sometimes, after a policy period has begun, an insured becomes aware of a wrongful act that could later lead to a claim. A *claims-made extension clause* addresses this possibility and requires the insured to notify the carrier of the wrongful act. If a claim is later made related to the wrongful act, coverage is automatically extended as if the claim were first made during the policy period, even though the policy may no longer be in effect (i.e., canceled or not renewed).

Tip for Trustees

Check with your plan legal counsel to see if there are any coverage restrictions on prior wrongful acts attached to your policy. If there are, explore the cost of eliminating these restrictions.

Retroactive Effective Date

The schedule attached to a policy or an endorsement to a policy may specify a *retroactive effective date*. If a wrongful act occurred before this date, the policy provides no coverage. This retroactive date is often the same as the starting date of the policy. For coverage prior to this date, a plan may have to pay an extra charge. An endorsement may also exclude claims arising out of prior or pending litigation.

All-Risk Insurance

As long as a claim meets the broad definition of a wrongful act and seeks damages, *all-risk insurance* protection obligates the carrier to provide coverage unless there is specific wording in the policy itself excluding the specific claim. When wording in an all-risk policy is vague, the courts generally favor the insured. That is why it is important periodically to review specific exclusions under a policy with a plan's broker and legal counsel.

Nonaccumulation Provisions

A fiduciary liability policy usually includes a *nonaccumulation clause* that states what happens if a series of claims made during the policy period result from a single wrongful act, error or omission. The clause establishes the limit of coverage that applies. As an example, assume a pension plan terminates, and plan trustees are sued separately for denial of benefits by three different beneficiaries in the three years that follow. One claim is filed in each of these years. Under a nonaccumulation clause, the policy limits that apply in the year of the first claim represent the total limit available to pay and defend all three claims—regardless of the fact that claims were made in the two years that followed.

Deductible Provisions

Fiduciary liability policies normally state a deductible applies to the carrier's full cost of the claim—regardless of whether it is for damages or the expense of defending the insured. Most policies also include an *antistacking clause* in their deductible provisions. These clauses state the policy deductible applies per wrongful act rather than to each separate claim. Assuming the same $10,000 deductible used in the previous illustration, the insured would pay no more than $10,000 in total even if multiple claims arise out of the same wrongful act.

Recourse Provisions

One unusual aspect of fiduciary liability policies is that carriers have a *right of recourse*—the "right" to recover money paid on the behalf of trustees who breach their fiduciary duties to their plan. Mandated by ERISA, this provision means—despite the insurance policy—a trustee's personal assets are still at risk for all losses caused by the trustee. This is a distinct departure from other professional liability insurance where recourse is barred. The logic for ERISA employee benefit plans is apparent—fiduciaries should bear the consequences of their wrongful acts that harmed plan beneficiaries when the liability insurance coverage was purchased using plan assets.

As stated previously in this chapter—despite the required recourse provisions just explained—most fiduciary liability policies offer a *waiver-of-recourse provision* that states the insurance company will not make an effort to recover from a trustee any payments made by the insurance company that are the trustee's liability. The insurance company charges an additional premium for this provision that trustees themselves, trustee employers, the employer association or labor organization can pay. It is usually a good idea to purchase this endorsement, especially since the cost is generally $100 per covered fiduciary.

Exhibit 1

Government Fines and Penalties

Federal agencies are relying more heavily on fines, penalties and excise taxes as the principal sanctions for enforcement. Examples of such fines or penalties are:

- IRS CAP monetary sanctions for failure to operate a pension fund or 401(k) plan in accordance with the Code's qualification requirements
- $100 a day for failing to provide required information to a participant within 30 days after the request is made
- $1,000 a day for late or incomplete filing of a Form 5500 (unless revised Form 5500 is filed within 45 days)
- 100% excise tax penalty on the amount involved in any prohibited transaction (some insurers specifically cover the 5% penalty for "inadvertent" violation of Section 406 of ERISA)
- $100 to $2,500 a day for COBRA violations under certain conditions
- Double damages for certain violations of the "Medicare as secondary payer" rules.

What Else Might Not Be Covered by Fiduciary Liability Insurance?

Certain exposures may not be specifically excluded under fiduciary liability policies; nevertheless, many insurers would refuse to provide coverage for claims produced by these exposures. For example, although not all of the policies contain an exclusion for claims involving libel/slander, it is obviously not the purpose of fiduciary liability policy to cover such claims.

Exclusions that are specified in policies may result from: (1) definitions of terms, (2) specific *enumeration* (listing) in the basic policy or (3) endorsements attached to the basic policy. Regardless of how and where they are presented, exclusions can have a significant impact on the scope of coverage and require careful examination of a policy.

Exclusions by Definition

Some exclusions are expressed via policy definitions. For instance, *loss* in a fiduciary policy is usually defined *not* to include:

- Routine benefit claims unless the claimant seeks compensatory damages and/or the trustees are held personally liable
- Nonpecuniary claims based on ERISA Section 502 (e.g., a DOL injunction)
- Civil or criminal fines or penalties (for some examples of current civil penalties, see Exhibit 1)
- Punitive or exemplary damages
- The two-thirds portion of any treble damage award (e.g., civil RICO claims)
- The portion of any compensatory award that is enhanced or multiplied in any way (though certain policies specify that the "multiplier" exclusion does not apply to the award of attorney fees under ERISA).
- Defense costs in any proceeding, audit or investigation by a governmental agency such as DOL or IRS.

Exclusions by Enumeration

The exclusions most often listed in a fiduciary liability policy are set forth below.

Contractual liability. Fiduciary liability policies often do not provide coverage for situations where an insured benefit plan must indemnify or hold a third party "harmless" in conjunction with the operation of the plan. For instance, assume a CPA firm requests trustees hold harmless the firm if sued because of the auditing services it performs for the plan. Also suppose that the CPA certifies that the plan's financial statements have been prepared according to generally accepted accounting principles and fairly represent the plan's true financial condition. Six months later, the plan is declared insolvent by the Pension Benefit Guaranty Corporation (PBGC). The plan participants sue the CPA firm, which in turn seeks indemnification by the trustees of the plan.

Contractual liability exclusions eliminate coverage for hold harmless agreements of this type because outside service providers should maintain their own professional liability coverage. If trustees must indemnify another entity, the underwriter should be advised prior to policy inception. This allows the insurer time to evaluate the exposure and assess an appropriate additional premium if the underwriter is willing to cover such an agreement.

Benefits payable to a beneficiary. The most common claims against benefit plans and trustees are for money owed participants. For instance, a participant sues because he thinks his medical claim was wrongly denied or a retiree claims her pension payment was miscalculated. Fiduciary liability policies do not pay these types of contractual obligations between a plan and plan beneficiaries. However, the policy may pay for any legal defense costs associated with the claim.

Bankruptcy of bank/broker. Under this exclusion, liability coverage is not available if plan trustees fail to evaluate adequately the solvency and financial strength of a bank or broker. The rationale is that banks and brokers usually carry their own separate liability coverage, and a claimant would ordinarily have direct recourse against the broker or bank.

Bodily injury, property damage, libel and slander. Coverage of claims alleging bodily injury, property damage, libel and slander are beyond the scope of fiduciary liability insurance because normally they fall within the purview of commercial general liability insurance.

Known circumstances surrounding a claim. On nearly all policies, insurers state they will not cover a claim if those insured by the policy were aware prior to the start of the policy period that circumstances or events might lead to a claim. Such claims fall more properly within the purview of the prior insurer. In an extreme case where the insured withheld information, the insurer may cancel the policy. More likely, the insurer will continue coverage with a modified policy and higher premium reflecting the information revealed.

Claims reported to prior insurers. Most fiduciary liability policies contain an exclusion for claims (and circumstances surrounding these claims) that have been reported to another insurer.

Discrimination. The majority of policies restrict coverage where fiduciaries are charged with discrimination. Some policies exclude coverage only when discrimination is based on race, creed, age or gender, but others eliminate coverage for any discrimination. The former exclusion is clearly preferable and should include defense cost coverage for allegations of discrimination.

Dishonesty. Insuring individuals for liability that results from intentional illegal activity is not permitted as a matter of public policy. However, nearly all policies do provide defense coverage if it is eventually proven in court or other proceedings (e.g., DOL determination) that the insured did not commit the alleged dishonest act. Even when a policy does not include this exception, an insurer's duty to defend is generally considered broader than its duty to indemnify and, in practice, insurers typically provide coverage of defense costs as long as dishonest acts are alleged yet not proven. Finally, it is important to note that the policies provide defense coverage against allegations of dishonesty only in civil claims as opposed to criminal court cases.

Failure to collect contributions owed to an employee benefit plan. The majority of policies do not cover claims stemming from fiduciary failure to collect contributions owed to a benefit plan because the collection of plan contributions from employers and/or employees is within the control of insureds. Thus, the policies will not cover such claims because insurers do not intend to provide what would in effect be "financial guarantee insurance."

Failure to purchase/maintain insurance or bonds. As noted earlier, ERISA requires surety bonds be purchased to protect the assets of pension and welfare plans if a claim arises from a failure to comply with such regulations. Again, avoidance of such claims is clearly within the control of the insured.

Failure to fund in accordance with ERISA. Virtually all policies contain this exclusion because it is contrary to public policy to provide insurance coverage for intentional violations of federal law. Of course, defense coverage is provided for allegations of such failures.

Other insurance. This provision states that if a loss is covered under another valid insurance policy, the issuer of this contract will not cover the claim nor will it provide coverage in excess of that provided by the other policy. The purpose of this clause is to avoid covering claims typically covered by other types of insurance.

Personal profit. Carriers will not cover the liability of fiduciaries who receive a personal financial benefit to which they were not legally entitled. For instance, a trustee purchases stock for the plan and at the same time buys some of the same stock for his or her personal portfolio—accepting a sharply discounted commission on the personal purchase. Most fiduciary liability policies do not apply this exclusion unless the claim of personal profit is factually established. It is important, therefore, to be sure policies do contain this exception language and to negotiate with underwriters for its inclusion in the event that it does not.

Workers' compensation, unemployment insurance, Social Security and disability benefits. It is extremely rare for a fiduciary liability policy to cover obligations stemming from workers' compensation, unemployment insurance and disability laws. Remember, the purpose of fiduciary liability insurance is to cover only those duties that arise in conjunction with ERISA-covered employee benefit programs. Nevertheless, since workers' compensation, unemployment insurance and disability plans are closely related to plans falling within the scope of ERISA, many insurers will, by endorsement, provide coverage for a nominal premium. It is prudent to broaden coverage in this manner if an underwriter makes this endorsement available.

Willful or reckless violation of any statute, rule or law. This represents a troublesome exclusion. It is not uncommon for a suit to allege that trustees have not only breached a fiduciary duty but that the violation of law is "willful or reckless." It is not clear in some policies whether the mere allegation of "willful or reckless" conduct is sufficient for a carrier to exclude defense costs or whether defense costs will be covered until the guilt or innocence of the trustees has been determined by the court. Legal counsel should clarify this matter with the carrier.

Co-fiduciary liability policies also contain specific language excluding coverage that addresses co-fiduciary liability—not just for deliberate or intentional fiduciary violations under ERISA, but also where the insured had knowledge of violations and failed to take appropriate action. For a full explanation of co-fiduciary responsibility under ERISA, see Chapter 5.

* * *

Other exclusions are:

- Liability of any insured to any other insured
- The rendering or failure to render services contracted for with any service provider
- Any professional services (e.g., legal, accounting, actuarial, investment counseling, fund managing) rendered or that should have been rendered by an insured or third party
- Any wrongful act alleged by the Pension Benefit Guaranty Corporation (PBGC), or any person or entity against whom PBGC has asserted any claim or demand
- Defects and potential defects in the operation of a plan that were identified in a Fiduciary Audit® Operational Review conducted at the insured's request for the purpose of obtaining enhanced IRS liability insurance coverage.

Exclusions by Amendatory Endorsements and/or Riders

Not all exclusions are in the basic policy; some may be attached to the basic policy as endorsements or riders. Here are some examples.

Real estate investments. DOL has made no secret of the fact that it has targeted Taft-Hartley funds for continuing investigations regarding real estate investments.[3] Accordingly, some policies exclude real estate unless such investments are directed or managed by a qualified professional asset manager (QPAM) as defined under DOL Class Exemption 84-14.[4] Trustees of plans with real estate investments of any kind—including construction loans, mortgage loans and joint real estate investment with other multiemployer plans—should give this endorsement special attention.

This endorsement excludes coverage for any claim related to the investment of plan assets in real estate or mortgages unless the investment is "directed or managed by" a QPAM with substantial experience in real estate and/or mortgages, as defined under DOL Class Exemption 84-14. If trustees are sued for a real estate decision they made as the result of a recommendation by the QPAM, the insurer will cover defense costs and settlement costs up to the limit of liability. On the other hand, if trustees make a decision without the assistance of a QPAM, defense costs for litigation arising out of such decisions would not be covered.

One of the reasons certain carriers are including this endorsement is that in recent years, DOL has stepped up its litigation against Taft-Hartley pension funds for (1) making construction loans or mortgage loans at below prevailing market rates, and (2) investing in "union-only" construction projects at rates of return less than the prevailing market rate. Funds usually end up with substantial defense costs for this type of litigation. Therefore, it is not surprising that some carriers want to limit their liability exposure in this area, and one way to do that is for the carrier to insist, under the endorsement, that trustees utilize the services of a QPAM and not rely solely on their own judgment.

If this endorsement is attached to a policy, trustees should discuss with legal counsel whether the endorsement is unduly restrictive. Trustees should also check to make sure they are currently employing a QPAM to direct or manage real estate investments. Otherwise, trustees have no coverage for litigation related to those investments.

* * *

Other exclusions that may be added by endorsement to a basic policy are:

- **Alleged discrimination under any municipal, state or federal law**—an exclusion that may be applied to apprenticeship training funds
- **Bankruptcy, insolvency or inability to pay benefits due to insufficient contributions**—added if a fund has major delinquency collection problems and/or inadequate delinquency control procedures
- **Alleged actuarial errors, omissions, assumptions or projections**—applied if there have been challenges to the actuarial interest rate assumption used to calculate withdrawal liability
- **Any legal action between or among the insured**—for example, a suit filed by one group of trustees against another group of trustees
- **Any alleged violation of the Racketeer Influenced and Corrupt Organizations Act (RICO)**
- **Items of noncompliance identified in a Fiduciary Audit® Operational Review**—the review conducted at the insured's request for obtaining enhanced IRS liability insurance coverage.

How Much Is the Policy Deductible and How Should It Be Applied?

The amount of a policy deductible and the conditions under which the deductible is applied vary by policy. Trustees should know the deductible amount and when it is applied.

Most carriers require payment of the deductible each time a new claim is filed against the insured during the policy period. There is one deductible that applies to both defense costs and other covered losses. Nevertheless, there are some exceptions:

- Many plans require just one deductible if a claim is related to an earlier claim involving the same wrongful act. In other words, the insured pays just one deductible regardless of the number of claims that result from the act.
- A few carriers require payment of a deductible only if damages are actually awarded to the claimant. Defense costs are covered on a first-dollar basis. This arrangement may be preferred, but trustees should carefully evaluate the total premium paid. Waiver of the deductible unless damages are awarded may end up costing the plan a significantly higher premium.

A typical deductible charged by carriers is $1,000 per claim (or $1,000 for a claim involving a class action suit or a series of related claims). This amount is not affected by the number of trustees, the type of benefits being provided by the benefit plan or the type of funding method used (insured vs. self-funded). In some cases, a carrier may offer a higher deductible—such as $5,000; $10,000; or $25,000—in exchange for a lower premium.

A carrier may also require a higher deductible as a condition of insurability if the carrier believes a particular benefit plan represents an above-average risk. In this case, this carrier may allow the plan to reduce the higher deductible to $1,000 by paying the difference between the higher

Tip for Trustees

Ask your plan's legal counsel to review the exclusions in your fiduciary liability insurance policy as well as any added as an endorsement or rider. It is important to know in advance what these exclusions are because you may be able to take certain actions designed to minimize the risk of litigation in areas where you have little or no coverage.

If your legal counsel is not sure whether a particular type of claim is excluded, ask your insurance broker or someone at the carrier's home office who can speak with authority.

You may find that carriers are sometimes reluctant to be "pinned down," and they generally do not like to deal with hypothetical situations. However, your plan is probably paying a healthy premium and you have a right to know what that premium is buying in terms of coverage. As trustees, you are not just concerned about protecting plan assets; you are also concerned about protecting your personal assets that are at risk if coverage is not there when you need it.

If you cannot get clarification on what your policy covers or if your plan experiences significant premium increases, do not hesitate to shop around. It is well worth the effort to fill out an application and obtain competitive premium quotes. You may be pleasantly surprised to discover you can purchase the same or better coverage with another carrier at a lower rate.

deductible and the $1,000 deductible as part of the basic premium charge. For example, if a $5,000 deductible is required, the fund may be permitted to reduce the deductible to $1,000 if it adds another $4,000 to the established premium charge.

Considerable variation exists among carriers with respect to deductibles and the way deductibles are applied (e.g., whether applied to every claim or only applied if damages are awarded to the claimant). For this reason, trustees should check their plan deductible and whether it applies to defense costs.

Periodically ask the current carrier what premium savings, if any, would result if trustees opted for a higher deductible. If a plan has had no litigation over a number of years and fund counsel believes the potential for litigation is minimal, it may be appropriate to choose a higher deductible that will reduce premium costs.

What Factors Should Be Considered When Selecting a Liability Limit?

Selecting an appropriate liability coverage limit represents a difficult decision for trustees because the need for protection must be balanced with what a plan can afford to pay.

The first step in this process is asking legal counsel what the risks of litigation and IRS monetary sanctions may be for trustees and their particular plan—these are the primary reasons to purchase a fiduciary liability insurance policy. If trustees are diligent performing their fiduciary duties, employ competent professional advisors and follow the advice of these professionals, liability risk will be relatively minimal under normal circumstances.

Liability risk also depends on the type of benefits involved. Though some have occurred, it is reasonable to expect few suits against apprenticeship training or vacation programs. On the other hand, welfare funds frequently experience benefit disputes not covered by fiduciary liability insurance unless the beneficiary claims compensatory damages. As a result, welfare plans end up absorbing the defense costs for most benefit claims—a fact that should be recognized when selecting an appropriate liability limit. Another factor exists concerning welfare plans. They primarily invest in short-term, fixed income assets requiring minimal investment decisions and therefore less liability risk.

This is not to say that welfare funds have no liability exposure just because most benefit claims are not covered and investment claims are unlikely. Many other types of claims are filed against welfare plans such as claims alleging failure to:

- Adequately fund health care benefits
- Collect delinquencies
- Maintain adequate records to determine eligibility
- Provide participants with information required by ERISA, and so on.

In contrast, a pension fund generally has a higher risk of litigation than a welfare plan. IRS monetary sanctions only apply to a qualified pension plan. There exists the long-term nature of pension plan investments and the wider range of investment options available to a pension plan. The risk of litigation for a pension fund might also be greater if a significant percentage of plan assets are invested in real estate and mortgages.

It is important to note that DOL gives top priority in its enforcement efforts to the examination of real estate investments made by Taft-Hartley trustees, especially if it appears such investments were made below prevailing market rates. Even if these decisions are delegated to a professional asset manager, this does not mean DOL will back off from filing a lawsuit if it thinks violation of ERISA's prudent man rule has occurred. Such litigation can lead to significant defense costs even though trustees are not held personally liable for their actions—this is a factor for pension fund trustees to consider when selecting a liability limit.

Many other factors may affect the risk of litigation. Trustees should ask legal counsel to assess the potential risks of litigation for their particular fund and use the assessment as a basis for determining what an appropriate liability limit might be.

What Liability Limits Are Available?

There is considerable choice in the liability limits available from carriers. Most carriers offer a minimum limit of $250,000. Maximum liability limits range from $5 million to $10 million. Higher limits are available from some carriers through a reinsurance arrangement.

These limits are usually applied on a policy-year basis, regardless of the number of claims filed during the policy period; once the limit is exhausted by one or more claims during the policy period, coverage ceases. As a rule, carriers are not willing to restore the liability limit for the remainder of the policy period.

In selecting an appropriate liability limit, a major consideration is whether the limit offered includes or excludes defense costs. Because defense costs are usually included in the limit, it is possible the limit will be exceeded by defense costs with no money left to pay damages awarded in court. Trustees should recognize they could be held personally liable for these damages if the liability limit is exhausted by defense costs.

Trustees may wish to ask plan counsel what they might anticipate in the way of defense costs if a major claim were filed against them. This figure can be a starting point for determining a minimum liability limit. A judgment still has to be made, however, as to how much cushion (if any) should be added to cover potential damages. Again, the advice of legal counsel will be helpful.

How Is the Premium Determined?

When determining the premium for a policy, the carrier considers sheer size. In the case of a pension plan, the number of plan participants, number of retirees and total assets determine size. In the case of a welfare plan, size is determined based on the number of plan participants and total annual contributions. Carriers are quick to acknowledge there are many other factors in the premium decision. These factors include, but are not limited to:

- The liability limit
- The deductible
- The annual amount of benefit claims paid
- Whether benefits are insured or self-funded (Higher premiums are usually charged if self-funded.)
- The litigation experience of the plan and its trustees before and after the policy was first put into effect
- The extent to which trustees delegate investment responsibility to a professional asset manager within written guidelines provided by the trustees
- The professional reputation of plan service providers (e.g., legal counsel, administrative manager and benefit consultant)
- The trade, craft or industry involved
- The geographic area covered by the plan's jurisdiction
- The specific union(s) represented on the board of trustees.

In addition to being the basis for setting the premium amount, many of these same factors also determine the insurability of a particular fund.

It is unknown how much weight a particular carrier gives to each factor, but any one factor could have a significant effect on how the carrier perceives a plan's liability risk, and the premium charged. If a plan has been experiencing significant premium increases in recent years—especially if no claims have been filed with the carrier—it is advisable to ask the carrier what factors are being used to set the policy premium. Once the factors are known, trustees can decide whether there are any actions they can take to reduce the risk.

What is a Reasonable Premium?

Every board of trustees is concerned about whether it is paying too much for its fiduciary liability insurance coverage. This concern has intensified in recent years because many Taft-Hartley funds have experienced significant increases in their fiduciary liability insurance policies premiums (even though they may have filed no claims with the carrier).

Trustees have a fiduciary obligation to act prudently in the expenditure of plan assets for fiduciary liability insurance. This means trustees are obligated to determine whether their current fiduciary liability insurance premium is reasonable. This is not an easy assignment because there are no comparable data readily available at a single source that trustees can use to determine how their plan's premium stacks up against what is charged other plans of similar size. Moreover, so many factors must be taken into consideration with respect to what liabilities are being covered and the unique features of a plan that direct comparisons even among plans of similar size have limited value.

The best way to find out whether a premium is in the ballpark is for the trustees to periodically ask for premium quotes from a number of different carriers, along with a *specimen* (sample) copy of the policy that legal counsel may use to compare cost and coverage.

There are at least four major carriers underwriting fiduciary liability insurance for Taft-Hartley plans; that fact alone suggests some degree of competition.[5] Although carriers may not be pounding down fund office doors trying to sell fiduciary liability insurance, some carriers are interested in new business.

What if a Policy Is Canceled?

Although trustees undoubtedly hope their policy will never be canceled, it is important to know what can be done to continue coverage in the event of cancellation.

Good sense dictates trustees and plan legal counsel sit down as soon as possible after a cancellation notice is received. This meeting should occur prior to the cancellation date (usually a period of 30 days or less from the date of notice) to identify any wrongful acts that may have been committed prior to the cancellation date that require reporting to the carrier.

Ask the carrier how much detail will ensure these potential claims are covered if eventually made. Although this may require some effort, the opportunity should not be missed. After all, the future coverage provided under a claims-made extension clause costs the plan absolutely nothing.

Extended Coverage

Most fiduciary liability insurance policies permit plans to purchase *extended coverage* for another six or 12 months for a premium 25% to 75% higher than the premium charged for the most recent policy period. Such coverage "extends" to wrongful acts occurring prior to—but not discovered until after—the policy was canceled. Extended coverage provides trustees with some additional protection in the event a claim arises that no one anticipated. No coverage is provided, however, for a claim based on a wrongful act committed after the cancellation date.

Policies vary widely in terms of the time allowed to purchase extended coverage. In some cases, this option must be exercised prior to the effective date of cancellation. In other cases, the extended coverage must be purchased no later than ten or 30 days after cancellation. Consequently, if a policy is canceled, trustees should ask plan counsel to check immediately on this time limit.

Whether or not extended coverage is worth the increased premium is a decision trustees, in consultation with their plan attorney, will have to make based on individual circumstances. If coverage is picked up immediately from a new carrier, then there may be limited value to purchasing the extension unless the new policy has limits coverage for prior wrongful acts. Since it will take some time before an application for coverage with a new carrier is processed, purchase of extended coverage may be essential—especially if trustees anticipate a major claim will be filed based on a wrongful act allegedly committed prior to the cancellation date.

Conclusion

Trustees should not expect to find fiduciary liability insurance that will provide all the protection they think they need at an affordable price. The fact is that all policies have coverage gaps. The typical fiduciary liability insurance policy provides no more than a minimum security blanket of protection for trustees.

Moreover, like most insurance policies, a fiduciary liability insurance policy always contains some fuzzy wording and legal terminology that creates uncertainties regarding protection under a specific set of circumstances. If a policy is not clear whether a particular type of claim is covered, legal counsel should seek further clarification the insurance broker or someone at the carrier's home office who can speak with authority regarding coverage. If the carrier

Questions to Ask

Plan Liability Risk and Protection

1. Does fund counsel periodically review with the entire board of trustees the coverages, exclusions, deductible, liability limit and other features of the current fiduciary liability insurance policy?
2. Do trustees know if the policy covers defense costs for these claims?
   - A wrongful act allegedly committed before the policy period?
   - A dispute over a benefit claim?
   - An allegation that a trustee engaged in a willful or reckless violation of a statute?
   - An allegation that a trustee obtained personal profit or advantage to which they were not entitled as plan fiduciaries?
3. Does the plan policy cover IRS monetary sanctions imposed against trustees for failure to operate a pension fund in accordance with IRC qualification requirements?
4. Is an endorsement regarding real estate and mortgage investments attached to the policy? If yes, does the plan meet the conditions set forth in the endorsement for coverage of claims arising out of these investments?
5. At the time of policy renewal, does legal counsel review with trustees any potential claim situations that should be reported on the renewal form? At the same time, does fund counsel make suggestions as to what the trustees should do to reduce the risks of litigation against the plan and its trustees?
6. Has the plan experienced any significant increases in its fiduciary liability insurance premium during the last several years? If yes:
   - Has legal counsel asked the carrier what factors explain the premium increases?
   - Have trustees asked legal counsel to obtain premium quotes from other carriers to determine whether the plan is being overcharged?
7. Has every trustee purchased a waiver-of-recourse provision eliminating the carrier's right to seek reimbursement in the event trustees are guilty of a fiduciary breach?

fails to provide a clear-cut answer, then it may be time for the trustees and plan counsel to check out the competition.

Another essential point to keep in mind is that fiduciary liability insurance policies change. Carriers are quick to recognize new laws and regulations that significantly increase their liability risk; their response is new coverage exclusions. It is important that trustees insist legal counsel stay abreast of new developments and keep trustees up-to-date on any new restrictions.

Endnotes

1. ERISA §502(d)(1).
2. ERISA §410(b)(1).
3. Dennis Kass, former Assistant Secretary of Labor, remarks made at the 32nd Annual Employee Benefits Conference of the International Foundation of Employee Benefit Plans, published in the *Digest*, February 1987: 3-6.
4. U.S. Department of Labor, Class Prohibited Transaction Exemption 84-14, published in the *Federal Register* on March 13, 1984, pp. 9494-9507.
5. These carriers include Aetna, Lloyd's, the Chubb Group, Union Labor Life Casualty Company, First State and National Union Insurance Companies.

Chapter 12

Fiduciary Liability Insurance: An Insurance Company Perspective

Daniel Aronowitz

Unlike most employers and organizations, a benefit plan cannot reimburse a fiduciary for the costs of a liability claim. If there is a fiduciary breach, a trustee's personal assets are at risk. This chapter focuses on how trustees and other benefit plan fiduciaries can protect themselves by purchasing fiduciary liability insurance coverage from a responsible carrier.

A *fiduciary liability insurance policy* protects trustees against claims alleging they breached their fiduciary duties to their plan or committed an error in the administration of the plan.[1] The insurance contract provides two important basic benefits—the *insurer* (the insurance company) generally (1) pays for the cost of defending trustees accused of violating their duties to their plan and (2) *indemnifies* (compensates) trustees for their financial liability if the alleged violations result in a financial settlement or judgment against them.

The following is a summary of key fiduciary liability policy provisions for multiemployer benefit plans and how these policies work when there is a claim.

Who Can Pay for Fiduciary Insurance?

The Employee Retirement Income Security Act of 1974 (ERISA) does not require benefit plans or trustees to purchase fiduciary insurance. But trustees and other fiduciaries face significant personal financial risk without this protection. Under ERISA, a benefit plan generally cannot:

- Excuse a fiduciary from liability for a breach of duty—or use plan assets to pay a liability—even if the breach was unintentional or in good faith.[2]
- Pay for the defense of trustees who breach their duties to their plan.

Waiver of Recourse Provisions

ERISA does allow plans to purchase fiduciary insurance coverage for its fiduciaries. To do so, however, the plan must give the insurance company the right to *recourse* against the breaching fiduciary. This ERISA-mandated *recourse provision* means that despite the insurance policy, the breaching fiduciary's personal assets are still at risk for all losses caused by the fiduciary. If an insurance company covers plan losses caused by a trustee's breach of duty, the insurer has the right to recover this money from the trustee.

To avoid this result, insurers typically offer a *waiver of recourse provision.* This provision generally means an insurance company will not make an effort to recover from a trustee any payments made for a trustee's liability. The insurance company must charge an additional premium to waive the right of recourse. Under ERISA, plan assets cannot be used to pay this extra fee; but the individual trustees, employers of the trustees, an employer association or union can pay it. The charge is typically a token \$25 to \$35. Though a small dollar amount, this is the most important portion of the policy premium for trustees.

What Is the Application Process for Fiduciary Liability Coverage?

Most insurance companies require a plan purchasing a fiduciary liability policy to complete an application. Certain documents such as benefit plan financials are also required as part of the application process. The application, sometimes called a *proposal form,* formally introduces the benefit plan and plan trustees to the insurance company; it helps the insurer evaluate the plan's liability risk. A typical application requests at least the following information and materials:

- The benefit plan name and address
- A statement of total assets, number of participants and annual contributions for the three prior plan years
- Details on plan amendments or any anticipated benefit reductions
- The total number of trustees and plan employees
- Names, addresses and employer affiliation of all present trustees, as well as former trustees from the prior six years
- Names and years of service for the plan's professional administrator, actuary or benefit consultant, legal counsel, certified public accountant, custodian of assets, and investment manager for investment decisions
- Details on current insurance—including the limits of liability and deductibles
- The claims history of the plan
- Details on any claim or circumstance that may give rise to a policy claim—including any investigation or audit by the Department of Labor (DOL), the Internal Revenue Service (IRS) or other governmental agency
- The most recent audited financial statement, investment schedule and portfolio, IRS Form 5500 (or 990), and all completed schedules.

The insurer uses the information provided during the application process to underwrite and price the policy. The most critical question on an initial application for insurance coverage is whether the plan's trustees and administrator know of any claim or circumstances that may lead to a claim under the policy.

What Happens if Application Information Is Misrepresented?

When information concerning a plan is misrepresented or omitted in a policy application, what the insurer does depends on policy language and state law. Potential actions include:

- **Denial of coverage for a particular claim.** The insurer may deny the specific claim, but allow coverage to continue for future claims not related to the claim denied.
- **Reformation of the policy.** This remedy allows the insurance company to change the policy to reflect more accurately the plan. Plan coverage continues but the policy and premium are modified to reflect the new information.
- **Rescission of the policy.** Rescission is a drastic remedy. The policy becomes void as if it never existed. The insurer is usually required to return to the plan the premium paid for the policy plus interest. In most states, an insurer that has valid rescission rights must act promptly or risk waiving the right to revoke coverage.

It is important to note insurance carriers rarely use rescission. In the event of a significant misrepresentation, insurers typically deny coverage rather than fight in public with a policyholder.

Severability Clauses

When a policy is *rescinded,* coverage is cancelled even for those who did not participate in the misrepresentation. As a result, trustees and administrators are advised to negotiate for "severability" in plan insurance policies. A *severability clause* typically provides that a misrepresentation by one of those who is insured will not affect coverage of others covered by the policy. To rescind an entire policy, the insurance company may have to prove that each and every one insured knew of the situation that was misrepresented in the application. The severability provision preserves insurance protection for those who were not aware of the misrepresentation.[3]

Warranty Provisions

The provision that most frequently leads to coverage issues is the application *warranty statement* saying no person covered by the policy is aware of any matter that may give rise to a future claim. A warranty statement is used when a policy is first issued, but generally not when it is renewed. Upon renewal, the insurer accepts the risk for prior potential claims.

On the other hand, when a plan's coverage limits are increased at the time of renewal, a warranty statement may be required for the change. If this is the case, plan fiduciaries should seek to have the warranty limited to the amount of the increase in policy limits.

Warranty provisions during the application process vary in two primary ways:

1. Some provisions refer to known "facts, circumstances or situations." This language is broader and does not require knowledge of specific conduct but rather knowledge of general circumstances that could give rise to a claim.
2. Others provisions refer to known "acts or omissions." These provisions describe the likelihood of future claims. Some insurers require disclosure of

known information that "might" or "may give rise to a future claim." Others require disclosure of known information only if the information is "likely" or "reasonably likely" to give rise to a claim.

What Are the Elements of a Fiduciary Liability Policy Agreement?

The key provision of every insurance policy is the *insuring clause* that describes policy coverage. Although the language will vary, an insuring clause will typically read as follows:

> *"The company shall pay on behalf of each of the insureds all loss for which the insured becomes legally obligated to pay on account of any claim first made against the insured during the policy period . . . for a wrongful act committed, attempted, or allegedly committed or attempted, before or during the policy period by an insured or by any person whose wrongful acts the insured is legally responsible."*

This clause includes four key concepts that are defined in the policy: (1) insured, (2) claim, (3) wrongful act and (4) loss. Each term is addressed below.

Insured: Who Is Covered?

The *insureds* that are protected by a fiduciary liability policy are the benefit plan and specific persons affiliated with the plan. If multiple benefit plans are covered by the same policy, policyholders should verify all are listed on the policy declarations page.

The persons covered by a fiduciary liability policy are plan trustees and employees. Be sure that past, present and future trustees are protected. Former trustees can be sued for an investment they made years earlier; they need coverage when the actual lawsuit is filed. If a change in trustees or employees occurs during a policy year, it is also essential to provide coverage automatically for these new individuals.

While the plan, trustees and plan employees are the key parties insured under a fiduciary policy, other persons or organization may be designated as additional insureds using a policy *endorsement* (an extra contract provision). Any additions should be evaluated carefully, since all persons and organizations protected by a policy share the same coverage limits. For this reason, a plan's third-party administrator and other service providers are not normally covered by a plan's fiduciary liability policy—even if these vendors are fiduciaries under ERISA. Claims filed against service providers are typically covered by their own errors and omissions insurance policy. Nevertheless, third-party advisors occasionally ask to be added to a plan's policy as an additional insured. Agree to this provision only after careful consideration of the risk.

Claim: What Triggers Coverage?

Most fiduciary liability policies are written on a *claims-made* format. This means the insurance company pays only for claims first made against the insured during the policy period—even if the alleged wrongdoing occurred prior to the policy period. The timing of fiduciary liability claims is different from liability claims for a home or car. The latter are triggered by the date a loss or injury occurs; for example, the day of an accident or bad weather. With fiduciary liability coverage, the policy that provides coverage is the one in force when a claim is made—not the policy in force when it is claimed a wrongdoing occurred. For this reason, it is essential that a fiduciary liability insurance policy be renewed every year.

Claim and when claims are made. To trigger coverage under a fiduciary liability policy, a person or organization must accuse the insured of having done something wrong with regard to the plan and demand relief—usually monetary relief. Although policies vary, a *claim* may be:

- A demand for monetary or nonmonetary relief
- The filing of a civil complaint or similar pleading in court
- A criminal proceeding begun by the return of an indictment or similar charging document
- A formal administrative or regulatory proceeding begun by the filing of a notice of charges, a formal investigative order or similar document
- A written notice by DOL or the Pension Benefit Guaranty Corporation (PBGC) that an investigation is underway. (Routine DOL audits are typically not considered investigations for this purpose.)

An evolving claims issue is whether fiduciary liability insurance covers mistakes. The most common example is when a plan administrator mistakenly overpays pension benefits by using an incorrect formula. An overpayment to multiple beneficiaries can be significant, and the administrator has a fiduciary responsibility to recover the overpayments. Obviously, the beneficiaries receiving the overpayment have no incentive to sue so there is no legal action against the plan that would trigger a claim. While fiduciary insurance is not designed to cover mistakes that do not rise to the level of a fiduciary breach, how insurance carriers will respond to such an issue varies.

Claim reporting requirements. A second trigger that fiduciary policies generally require is that the insured notify the insurer "as soon as practicable" that there is a claim. What this means varies.

- Some policies require the insurance company be notified no later than a defined number of days (e.g., 60 days) after the end of the policy period.
- Other policies are *claims-made-and-reported* requiring notice (1) as soon as practicable and (2) within the policy period. These policies give plans relatively narrow coverage. Claims made close to the end of the policy period may not be covered because the plan does not have sufficient time to notify the insurance company before the policy period ends.

Most policies have a *notice of circumstances* or *potential claim* provision that allows a plan to report, during the policy period, circumstances that *might* give rise to future claims. If the claim is made later, the insurer treats it as being made at the time the notice of the potential claim was given. Importantly, the policy will require that the potential claim notice be specific and detailed in order to "lock in" future coverage.

Trustees considering a switch in insurance companies should evaluate whether they know of any facts or circumstances that could give rise to a future claim, and give notice of the potential claim to their current carrier before switching coverage. Otherwise, any claim that later arises could be excluded by the new carrier.

Claim time limitations. The broadest fiduciary liability insurance policies provide coverage for any wrongful acts in the past. Frequently, however, policies have a *retroactive date limitation* or similar language that restricts coverage to claims arising from wrongful acts occurring after a "retroactive" date. Generally, insurers impose this type of time limit in one of two ways; the retroactive date is:

1. The same day that policy coverage began or
2. The expiration date of the expiring policy providing "prior acts" coverage.

If a policy has a provision stating all prior wrongful acts are covered, the policy provides *full prior acts coverage.* Many policies contain no reference to the timing of prior wrongful acts; most of these policies also provide full prior acts coverage.

To prevent multiple policies from providing coverage for the same or related claims, most fiduciary policies contain *interrelated claim provisions.* These provisions provide that the same insurance policy will respond to any later claim related to or arising out of an initial claim—even if it happens years later.

Wrongful Acts: What Violations Are Covered?

Once it is determined who is insured and when a claim is triggered, the next question is what alleged violations are covered by the insurance policy. What is considered a *wrongful act* varies from carrier to carrier and policy to policy, but most policies cover two primary categories of wrongful acts:

1. Breaches of fiduciary duty
2. Errors in the administration of a plan.

"Breaches of fiduciary duty" is very broad—including any actual or alleged breach of responsibility under ERISA as well any other law, rule or regulation. Examples of these other laws include the Health Insurance Portability and Accountability Act of 1996 (HIPAA) and the Consolidated Omnibus Budget Reconciliation Act of 1985 (COBRA). It is important for an insurance policy's definition of *wrongful acts* to be open ended and not limited to any particular statute; new legislation and changes in existing laws often create new fiduciary responsibilities.

Depending on the nature of the breach and the number of beneficiaries involved, a breach of fiduciary duty claim can result in significant plan liability. Historically, the most significant fiduciary liability losses have been the result of charges that trustees were imprudent when investing plan assets. The losses for these types of claims are typically lost investment principal and the money the plan would have received if the investment had been prudent. Other breach of fiduciary duty claims may also present significant liability potential, these include:

- Allegations a plan document was misinterpreted
- Administration of a plan in a way that does not comply with plan documents
- Providing imprudent investment options to participants in a defined contribution plan
- Misrepresentations of plan investments
- Failing to accurately communicate relevant information to plan participants.

Most fiduciary policies cover negligent administrative errors in the administration of a plan even if the error is not a fiduciary breach. In this context, *plan administration* is commonly defined to include handling plan paperwork and records, and providing interpretations or advice to participants regarding a plan. For example, plan participants have 30 days to add a newborn child to a health insurance plan. A plan employee mistakenly tells a participant there are 60 days to make the addition. As a result, the participant is late enrolling the child and denied a medical benefits claim. The participant might sue the plan—alleging the inaccurate enrollment information resulted in the claim denial. This claim could qualify as an administrative error covered by a fiduciary liability policy.

While breaches of fiduciary duty and administrative errors are the two most common wrongful acts covered under a fiduciary policy, some newer policies also attempt to address the growing number of claims connected to nonfiduciary functions of trustees. In addition to their fiduciary duties, multiemployer plan trustees often have *settlor functions* concerning the design of a plan: the level of plan contributions and decisions to terminate, freeze or merge a plan. Some insurance companies have responded by expanding the definition of *wrongful acts* to include any negligent act, error or omission by a plan trustee. This provides protection to a trustee even when the claim involves a settlor or some other nonfiduciary function.

Loss: What Will the Insurer Pay for?

A *loss* covered by fiduciary liability insurance generally includes damages, settlements, judgments and defense costs resulting from a covered claim. State laws sometimes place limits as to what losses a policy may insure.

With limited exceptions, virtually all fiduciary policies exclude penalties imposed by law as losses. Historically, the most common ERISA penalties incurred by benefit plans and trustees are Section 502(i), (l) and (c) penalties imposed by DOL. HIPAA penalties are also relatively frequent. Plan fiduciaries must make sure that penalties imposed under these three sections of ERISA are not part of a blanket exclusion of fines and penalties in a plan's fiduciary policy.

Penalty coverage for voluntary compliance programs. In addition to coverage for the ERISA violations just noted, many insurance carriers offer expanded coverage for costs associated with a plan's voluntary effort to bring a plan into compliance with certain ERISA rules and the Internal Revenue Code (IRC). The federal government allows plans to self-correct violations through the Employee Plans Compliance Resolution System (EPCRS). Administered by IRS, EPCRS is a system of three programs encouraging benefit plans to report and address violations free of the threat that a violation will cause a plan to be disqualified.

Voluntary compliance coverage makes it possible for an insured plan to file a claim without a third party charging wrongful acts have occurred. The amount of coverage is typically subject to a *sublimit*—meaning the liability protection for self-corrected violations is lower than the policy's overall liability limit. The sublimit is usually part of—and not in addition to—the policy's overall liability limit. Be aware that this coverage will not pay any funding obligations that are part of the self-correction process.

Voluntary compliance program claims for reimbursement of penalties paid to IRS and DOL are now among the most common fiduciary liability claims. Benefit plan trustees must make sure that they have an adequate coverage sublimit, and coverage for any potential penalties. Penalty coverage for compliance programs that is as broad as possible is recommended. For example, under the Patient Protection and Affordability Act of 2010 as amended (ACA), IRS may assess excise taxes upon group health plans for failing to comply with insurance market reforms. These penalties can be reimbursed under a fiduciary policy, but only if the penalty coverage is expressly provided in the policy.

Defense coverage. The most valuable feature of an insurance policy is payment of the expenses to defend a claim. Defense costs often exceed other losses covered by a policy. Defense coverage comes in two basic formats:

- ***Duty-to-defend coverage*** is most common. If a claim alleges a wrongful act by an insured, the insurance company has the right and obligation to defend the claim—even if the claim is groundless, false or fraudulent. The benefit of this form of coverage is that the insurance company must cover all allegations connected with the claim even if only one part is covered by the policy.
- ***Duty-to-reimburse coverage*** states that it is the responsibility of the insured—not the insurance company—to defend a claim. The insured controls the defense, but submits expenses to the insurance company for reimbursement. The advantage of this coverage is that the insured may select defense counsel and has more control over litigation decisions such as legal strategy, and when and whether to settle. These policies stipulate it is the "duty of the insured and not the insurer" to select a defense counsel. Contractually, the insurance company retains the right to approve the defense counsel selected, but consent cannot be "unreasonably withheld."

The insurance company reimburses defense costs at designated points during the claim process once any deductible is satisfied. Details regarding documentation, billing and communication with defense counsel should be addressed at an early stage in a claim to avoid problems later.

In some instances, even under duty-to-defend coverage, an insurance company will allow an insured to use its own defense counsel if approved in advance of a claim. Approval is usually given during the coverage negotiation process. As an alternative, a number of insurance carriers with duty-to-defend forms now provide defense coverage under *panel counsel*—a group of preapproved attorneys who handle claims on behalf of the carrier. Panel counsel attorneys are usually highly experienced lawyers with expertise in ERISA and fiduciary liability that can benefit those facing litigation. The insurance company also benefits from prearranged billing rates and reporting arrangements, which help the company better manage the litigation.

Fiduciary policies typically cover "reasonable and necessary" defense costs. Such expenses include attorney fees, expert fees and other costs incurred while defending or investigating a claim. On the other hand, defense costs frequently exclude any compensation or benefits to trustees, officers or employees of a benefit plan, and overhead costs. A primary dispute between a plan and an insurance company can be what constitutes "reasonable and necessary."

Most policies that do not have a duty-to-defend form require insurance company consent for settlement of claims and that such "consent shall not be unreasonably withheld." Many fiduciary policies also contain language giving the insurance company the right to recommend settlement. If the insured refuses to settle, there is a restriction on the amount the policy will pay. These provisions are commonly referred to as *hammer clauses.* If the insured rejects the insurer's recommendation to settle and instead chooses to litigate, the insurance company limits its liability to the proposed settlement amount plus defense costs incurred prior to the date the settlement was refused.

Many insureds feel that a settlement, rather than a decision by a judge in court, does not fully clear them of the alleged wrongdoings. They may also believe a successful defense in court may prevent or reduce the likelihood of similar future actions. Prior consent or hammer clauses can make it difficult to continue litigation because the insured will have to bear any defense costs and/or loss in excess of the recommended settlement. Insurers counter that without such clauses, they might be subjected to a loss far in excess of the value of the claim.

Fiduciary policies also require that the insured cooperate with the insurance company in the handling of a claim. Courts have held that an unwillingness to cooperate with the insurer on material matters is a violation of the policy that prevents recovery under the policy.[4] While a *cooperation clause* is often invoked by insurance carriers during the course of contentious claims, an insurer typically has a high burden to deny coverage for an alleged breach of cooperation. Indeed, the trend of cases appears to be that a *breach of the cooperation clause* will not relieve the insurer of its obligations unless the insurer can demonstrate substantial harm because of the breach.[5]

What Is Not Covered by a Fiduciary Liability Policy?

Policy Limits

Most fiduciary liability insurance policies are subject to a single *annual aggregate limit*—the most that the insurer will pay for claims during the policy year. Most policies also clearly state that the costs and expenses associated with the defense of the insured are included in, and not in addition to, the policy's limit on liability. Benefit plans need to purchase a policy with a limit sufficient to cover both defense and other potential losses.

The aggregate limit applies if a plan elects an *extended reporting period*—additional time for a plan to report a claim beyond the policy's expiration date. A plan's liability limits are not usually reinstated or increased by purchase of an extended reporting period. But reinstatement of full limits may be available in limited circumstances for an additional premium.

Policy Exclusions

A fiduciary liability insurance policy contains significant coverage limitations in the "exclusion section" of the contract. Exclusions are also throughout a policy—particularly in policy definitions of *wrongful acts* and *loss.* Two overarching issues should be considered with respect to policy exclusions:

1. Language in an exclusion often determines the scope and effect of the exclusion. For example, the language *for bodily injury* excludes only claims by a person who alleges bodily injury. In contrast, the words *based upon or arising out of bodily injury* are much broader and could exclude related claims.
2. The impact of policy exclusions is also affected by the "severability" clause that comes at the end of an exclusion section. The severability clause provides that the exclusion will apply only to insureds with knowledge of the wrongful act. This preserves coverage for innocent insureds.

Policy coverage exclusions generally fall into one of four categories: (1) conduct or uninsurable exclusions, (2) claimant exclusions, (3) laser exclusions and (4) other insurance limitations. An explanation of each follows.

Conduct or ***uninsurable exclusions*** try to eliminate coverage for actions considered sufficiently self-serving or egregious that insurance protection is inappropriate. Fiduciary policies typically exclude coverage for losses resulting from fraudulent acts of the insured and willful violations of the law. Most fiduciary policies also have a *personal profit exclusion* that excludes claims where a fiduciary has gained "personal profit, advantage, or remuneration to which they were not legally entitled."

Claimant exclusions bar coverage for claims by those who, for various reasons, present litigation risks that an insurer generally does not want to cover. A noteworthy claim exclusion is the filing of a claim by one insured party against another. Insurance companies want to prevent a plan and its trustees from trying to convert a policy to cash by suing others who are insured by the policy. These *insured versus insured exclusions* are problematic; trustees sometimes have an obligation under ERISA's co-fiduciary responsibility to bring a claim against another fiduciary to remedy a breach. The recent trend is to eliminate insured versus insured exclusions to address this issue.

Laser exclusions address specific risks unique to a particular insured that the insurance company has identified as inconsistent with its underwriting principles or other policies. As mentioned previously, fiduciary policies often bar coverage for claims that occur prior to a specific date such as the day policy coverage began. A policy may exclude claims for breach of contract, bodily injury, pollution or failure to comply with certain laws and regulations. The breach of contract exclusion arises frequently with courts making a distinction between what is fiduciary duty and voluntary contractual obligations. Some common laser claims exclusions relate to contributions, insufficient funding and withdrawal liability.

Benefits due exclusions state an insurance company will not cover benefits owed to a plan beneficiary; for example, a participant claim that a monthly pension payment was incorrectly calculated, or a medical claim was improperly denied. These claims reflect a voluntary contractual obligation as just discussed under laser exclusions. Benefit claims are the most common claims against plan trustees.

Though a fiduciary liability policy will not cover benefits a plan owes, the plan and other insured may still have coverage for legal defense costs connected to a benefit claim. Consider a suit by a retiree who charges a pension plan miscalculated and underpaid a lump-sum distribution. Fiduciary liability insurance would pay to defend the plan against the retiree's claim. The plan, however, would have to pay any settlement or judgment awarding the retiree the underpaid portion of the distribution.

Other insurance exclusions are the final category of exclusions; they may be found in a policy as an "other insurance" clause or with other exclusions. These exclusions state that if a loss is covered under any other valid insurance policy, no coverage exists under the fiduciary policy. The intent is to avoid covering risks typically covered by other forms of insurance. Some fiduciary policies, however, will cover losses in excess of the amount covered by the other insurance policy.

How Does an Insurer Respond to a Claim?

Reservation of Rights

When an insurance company first receives notice of a claim against an insured, the company must promptly do one of the following:

- Acknowledge receipt of the notice and advise the insured that it will provide coverage
- Advise the insured that it will defend the insured though it reserves the right to deny coverage on one or more specified grounds
- Deny coverage because the claim is either not covered under the policy, or the insured has breached a policy condition
- Rescind the policy if it appears the policy was gotten through fraud, mutual mistake of fact, or the misrepresentation of material facts in the application.

When a claim appears to be within the scope of coverage, the insurer acknowledges the claim and indicates to the insured that coverage will be provided. If the insurance company has reservations about whether the claim is covered, the company informs the insured of policy provisions that make it possible for the company to fulfill its duty to defend (or reimburse) the insured yet reserve the right to later get a judgment on its obligations to the insured. A *reservation of rights letter* should either quote or make specific reference to the policy provisions that are the basis for the company's assertion that there is no coverage for the claim.

Bad Faith

An insurer that wrongfully denies its duty to defend and *indemnify* (reimburse) an insured, or fails to settle a covered claim within policy limits, may be held liable to the insured for bad faith. Whether an insurance company has acted in bad faith generally requires a determination that coverage exists for the disputed claim.[6] Although the standard varies by state, an insurer typically must have a "rational, principled basis for denying liability" to avoid a finding of bad faith.[7] The test for determining whether an insurer has rejected a settlement in bad faith is "whether a prudent [insurer] without policy limits would have accepted the demand."[8] An insurer found to have acted in bad faith can be held liable for damages in excess of the insurer's policy limits.

How Much Coverage Should a Plan Purchase?

This is one of the most commonly asked questions about fiduciary insurance policies. The best answer will come from a qualified insurance broker or professional with experience in fiduciary liability insurance. The amount of insurance purchased depends primarily on the value of plan assets. Plans with less than $5 million in assets generally purchase at least $1 million in coverage; those with between $5 million and $10 million in assets usually purchase $1 million to $5 million; plans of $10 million to $50 million often purchase $5 million; and funds over $50 million purchase between $5 million and $10 million. When funds reach $100 million in size, insurance professionals begin to recommend $10 million or even higher limits. Funds with $250 million and above in assets often purchase $25 million or more in insurance, with multiple insurance companies participating in the program. Again, funds should seek professional advice from an experienced insurance professional.

Some fiduciary insurance policies contain a *retention provision* or other language requiring the insured to bear a portion of loss before the insurer pays any portion of the loss. This provision is essentially the same as a deductible found in other insurance policies. Because multiemployer plans cannot pay the retention and fiduciaries would have to pay this amount out of their personal assets, the trend is to eliminate any policy deductible for multiemployer plans. Fiduciaries should attempt to purchase a policy that has no retention provision.

How Much Should Coverage Cost?

This is another common question best submitted to a qualified broker or professional with experience in fiduciary liability insurance. Nevertheless, some rules of thumb are useful based on how insurance companies price benefit plan risks. The starting point for rating a policy is the value of plan assets and the number of plan participants. The larger the fund and the more participants, the more insurance is needed and the more expensive the policy will be. From this initial price estimate, an insurer will raise or lower the premium charged based on risk factors such as plan funding level and cash flow. Not surprisingly, better-funded plans often receive premium credits based on a lower level of risk for fiduciary exposure.

Endnotes

1. Fiduciary liability insurance and fidelity bonding are easily confused. A *fidelity bond* is a contract under which the issuer of the bond (typically a surety or insurance company) agrees to reimburse a benefit plan for certain losses caused by theft, fraud or other dishonest acts. A fidelity bond covers losses due to intentional acts that deprive a plan of its assets. As for a fiduciary insurance policy, it covers losses caused by acts or omissions not intended to cause a plan to lose assets. While fiduciary insurance is discretionary, ERISA mandates fidelity bonding.
2. See ERISA §410, 29 U.S.C. Section 1110 (Exculpatory Provisions; Insurance), which provides as follows:

   "(a) Except as provided in sections 405(b)(1) and 405(d), any provision in an agreement or instrument which purports to relieve a fiduciary from responsibility or liability for any responsibility, obligation, or duty under this part shall be void as against public policy.

   (b) Nothing in this section shall preclude: (1) a plan from purchasing insurance for its fiduciaries or for itself to cover liability or losses occurring by reason of the act or omission of a fiduciary, if such insurance permits recourse by the insurer against the fiduciary in the case of a breach of a fiduciary obligation by such fiduciary; (2) a fiduciary from purchasing insurance to cover liability under this part from and for his own account; or (3) an employer or an employee organization from purchasing insurance to cover potential liability of one or more persons who serve in a fiduciary capacity with regard to an employee benefit plan."
3. *Shapiro v. American Home Assurance Co. (Shapiro II)*, 616 F. Supp. 900 (D.Mass. 1984).
4. See *Utica Mut. Ins. Co. v. Gruzlewski*, 217 A.D.2d 903, 630 N.Y.S.2d 826 (N.Y. App. Div. 1995) (insured barred from recovering because of willful obstruction of an insurer's defense of underlying litigation).
5. *Talley v. State Farm Fire & Cas. Co.*, 223 F.3d 323, 326-28 (6th Cir. 2000).
6. *Republic Ins. Co. v. Stoker*, 903 S.W.2d 338 (Tex. 1995).
7. *Freidline v. Shelby Ins. Co.*, 774 N.E.2d 37 (Ind. 2002).
8. *Continental Cas. Co. v. United States Fid. & Guar. Co.*, 516 F. Supp. 384, 387 (N.D.Cal. 1981).

Chapter 13

Health Care Benefits and Service Providers: An Introduction

Jackson Loos

Creating and managing a health care plan involves several broad questions:

- What benefits will be provided?
- Who will be eligible for benefits and when?
- What delivery systems will be used to provide these benefits?
- How will the plan be financed and administered?

This chapter and those that follow explore many of the potential options available to multiemployer health benefit plan trustees when addressing these questions.

With respect to the first three questions, plan trustees have substantial choice as to what benefits are provided, who will be eligible for coverage and what delivery system(s) will be used to provide these benefits. How much a plan is able to customize its benefits is influenced by how it is financed and the size of the plan. Self-financed plans obviously will have more flexibility than plans purchased through an insurance company that may only offer "off-the-shelf" plan options. With a large number of participants, however, insurance companies and health care service providers are more likely to build a benefits package tailored to the desires of plan trustees. Federal and state mandates place some limits on coverage choices—various laws and regulations require health plans and insurers to provide coverage for certain benefits, care providers and persons. Chapter 21 provides an overview of federal mandates and some examples of requirements among the states.

Some plans purchase all services and programs from one provider in an effort to create a fully integrated health care system for participants. Other plans elect to contract with more than one provider, choosing those providers that are most efficient in providing a program or service. Some plans *carve out* specific benefits and provide them on a separate basis. Carving out prescription drug benefits is common now that pharmacy benefit managers (PBMs) have emerged that can provide cost savings through pharmacy networks and specialized drug management programs. Mental health and substance abuse benefits have also been carved out and are separately managed by many health plans.

The final question when considering the creation and management of a health benefit plan involves the relationship among the plan, service providers and participants. Some plans provide their benefits through an insurance

Tip for Trustees

With today's rising health care costs, it is easy to become immersed in how to keep plan costs in check. Cost considerations, however, must be balanced with equally important concerns:

- **Quality**—the providing of health care goods and services that improves patient health, quality of life and productivity
- **Access**—minimizing financial, geographic and other barriers to care
- **Participant satisfaction**—related to quality and access
  - Do participants feel their benefits are of high quality?
  - Are they affordable?
  - Are the goods and services easy to access in terms of location?
  - Do network providers provide courteous service?

company that reimburses participants and/or service providers. Trustees of larger plans may elect to self-finance benefits, eliminating the cost of using an insurance company. Chapters 14 and 15 discuss funding a plan through insurance and self-financing.

Trustees also determine how a plan will be administered. In other words, who will collect contributions, handle participant claims and reimburse providers. One option is hiring a *third-party administrator (TPA),* an independent company that handles some or all of these administrative functions. The scope of a TPA's services varies from plan to plan. Other health and welfare plans turn to insurance companies, preferred provider organizations (PPOs) or health maintenance organizations (HMOs) for assistance with plan administration. Another alternative is *self-administration,* with a plan having its own employees handling a full range of administrative functions. Often, a family of plans—health and welfare, pension, vacation and 401(k)—established by a set of collective bargaining agreements will jointly employ staff to administer all of the plans.

The remainder of this chapter examines the evolution of employee benefit plans and the organizations that help health care plans deliver benefits. Some of the many methods used to reimburse health care providers are introduced with a look at which ones have the most potential to help plans control benefit costs. The chapter concludes with practical advice on how to select and monitor health care service providers.

What Is Known About the First Employee Health Plans?

The first employer-sponsored health plan for employees is believed to have been a 1929 agreement negotiated with Baylor Hospital in Texas to provide health care to Dallas County public school teachers. The school system gave the hospital a set dollar amount in advance for providing care to plan participants. It can be argued this was the beginning of managed health care, as the hospital had some financial risk if the cost of caring for the teachers was greater than the fixed amount the hospital was paid to provide care. There was an incentive for the hospital to not provide services that would have little impact on a patient's condition and increase the cost of care.

The alternative means of providing health care coverage to employees in the early years—and the one that eventually became the preferred method for employers to provide coverage—was an *indemnity plan.* A health care indemnity plan reimburses providers for the specific health care services received by plan participants. Indemnity plans offer no incentive for health care providers to control the amount of care *(utilization)* that patients receive or the cost of this care. In fact, more patient visits to a doctor or longer stays in a hospital increase the income of the health care provider.

For nearly 40 years, the lack of an incentive to keep health care costs under control was of little concern to employers or anyone else because health care costs increased at about the same rate as the price of other goods and services. But by the 1970s, things were changing. Health care cost increases began to outpace other prices; managed care organizations looked promising as a solution to this problem.

What Is a Managed Care Organization?

Managed care organizations (MCOs) are health care organizations that use a variety of techniques to reduce the cost and improve the quality of health care. The earliest forms of MCOs were health maintenance organizations (HMOs). President Richard Nixon and Congress passed the Health Maintenance Organization Act of 1973 to encourage the formation of HMOs and managed health care. HMOs quickly gained popularity among plan sponsors and are widely credited with helping keep medical costs under control in the late 1980s.

Health Maintenance Organizations (HMOs)

Similar to the early Baylor Hospital plan, early HMOs assumed all the risk for the cost of participant care that exceeded a fixed prepayment provided by a plan sponsor. Other characteristics of HMOs vary and continue to evolve today, but generally, HMOs:

- Deliver comprehensive health care services with an emphasis on preventive care services such as immunizations, health screenings and wellness programs
- Operate and provide services in a limited geographic area
- Provide services for a fixed or prepaid fee rather than payments for specific services provided plan participants
- Place restrictions on which providers can be used by plan participants.

HMOs have different models that reflect how they contract with the physicians who serve plan participants (referred to as *HMO members*):

- **Group practice model.** The very first HMOs were typically comprised of an independent group of doctors practicing as a group and contracting with the

Checklist

Health Benefits Plan Review

Use this checklist as a starting point for periodic reviews of your health benefits plan.

Need

- What are the current health needs of participants? Their families?
- Are there any factors that will influence future needs? (e.g., average age of participants, income, industry, geographic location, hourly wages)
- Does the plan address these issues?

Eligibility

- Who is allowed to participate in the plan? Full-time employees? Part-time employees? Retirees? Spouses? Domestic partners? Children? Others?
- How long must a person wait before being eligible for participation?
- What are the requirements for continuing eligibility?
- Is there extended eligibility through an hours or dollar bank?
- Under what circumstances does eligibility end?
- How do the eligibility requirements compare with those of other plans?

Coverage

- What benefits are provided?
  - Is an emphasis placed on preventive care? Catastrophic care?
  - Are programs and services in place that will assist patients with (or at risk of) chronic conditions to maintain healthy lifestyles?
  - What alternative care options (e.g., chiropractic care, home health care) are available?
- What limits are placed on benefits?
- Are there other restrictions or exclusions?
- How do these benefits compare with those provided by other plans?

Access

- Are care providers in geographic locations that are convenient for participants?
- What happens when a participant needs care out of the provider area? While out of the country?
- Are participants able to access care (e.g., primary physicians, specialists, outpatient facilities, hospitals) in a reasonable amount of time?
- Are there any cost-sharing strategies, limits or restrictions that discourage patients from seeking care?

Choice

- Have participants been asked about their satisfaction with the service provider?
- Are participants satisfied with their service provider options?
- What incentives encourage participants to make cost-effective choices?
- What information or other support is available to help participants make choices regarding care providers and treatments that will provide the best outcomes? (e.g., newsletters, advice lines)

Claims

- Is the claim submission process easy for participants to use?
- Are participants able to appeal claim issues in person?
- Are claims resolved in a reasonable amount of time?
- Is the process for handling claim disputes reasonable and fair?

Legal requirements

- Are there any elements of the plan that are required as part of a contractual agreement with a union or other entity?
- Are there any plan features that are required by state or federal law?

Financing

- What do plan participants contribute to the cost of the plan?
- What other cost-sharing strategies are used? Deductibles? Copays? Coinsurance?

If you are looking for ways to improve cost and quality management, various strategies are discussed in Chapters 16 through 19.

HMO. The group may include only primary care physicians, physicians from multiple medical specialties (called a *multispecialty group*) or a mix of primary and specialty physicians. Individuals or health care plans pay the HMO a fixed fee for providing services through its affiliated doctors and hospitals.

- **Network model.** A variation on the group practice model, HMOs with a network model contract with more than one independent group practice and may also contract with independent physicians.
- **Staff model.** In a staff model, an HMO hires and pays its own doctors. Health care services are usually provided at HMO facilities. Services are generally provided exclusively to HMO members, though some staff model HMOs do have a small amount of fee-for-service business. The size and number of specialties in a staff model HMO tend to vary. Very large HMOs may have many specialists on staff while others may only have primary care physicians such as family practitioners, general practitioners, pediatricians and internists. HMOs with a small staff generally contract with independent doctors for specialty care.
- **Individual practice model.** This model of HMO contracts with a number of independent doctors and/or single specialty groups. There are no central or integrated HMO facilities.

HMOs grew quickly in the 1980s and 1990s, but a consumer backlash soon occurred. People did not like restrictions such as which health provider they could use, the number of days they could stay in the hospital and which drugs would be reimbursed. Another criticism was that patients had to visit a primary doctor and get approval to see a specialist. HMO cost-control efforts created a perception the plans were more interested in saving money than providing quality health care. MCOs, health benefit plans and insurers responded with new options including PPOs and POS plans.

Preferred Provider Organizations (PPOs)

Preferred provider organizations (PPOs), like HMOs, do not always fall into a neat category, but they do share some common features. PPOs:

- Are arrangements between health care providers and purchasers of health care in which the providers provide their services at a reduced cost in return for adjustments in plan design
- Generally have guidelines in place or other systems for controlling costs
- Allow plan participants to use preferred providers within the PPO network or nonpreferred providers, but participants are given a financial incentive to use those that are within the network.

Providers are reimbursed on a fee-for-service basis that is usually lower than what would be paid to other providers because of the negotiated discounts. PPO providers are willing to do this because of the volume of business they get from an agreement with a plan. When the provider networks of HMOs and PPOs are compared, HMO networks tend to be smaller and more geographically limited.

Point-of-Service (POS) Plans

A *POS plan* is a cross between a traditional HMO plan and a standard PPO plan that expands participant choice beyond network care providers. A plan sponsor either contracts with health care providers or a managed care company to provide medical care through a POS. A typical POS plan design offers a basic set of benefits if the participants use network providers. If a participant chooses providers outside the network, plan benefits are reduced and the participant has higher out-of-pocket costs such as greater deductibles or copays.

* * *

Today, the distinctions between MCOs have blurred, with larger delivery structures being created and new management strategies introduced. To be competitive with MCOs, other service providers have formed their own provider networks and other organizational structures to generate cost savings. Group practices, networks and so forth give formerly independent service providers the ability to establish contractual arrangements with plans and insurance companies.

The health care delivery system that now exists in the United States has service provider structures that vary dramatically in terms of organization, size and geographic service area. Some provider organizations are limited to a particular type of care or a specific region within a state, while other networks encompass hundreds of thousands of providers across the nation capable of providing almost any type of care. New provider organizations continue to emerge as virtually everyone seeks additional ways to control the increases in health costs. Developments of particular interest at present are:

- **Integrated delivery system (IDS).** In an IDS, multiple types of providers are part of one management structure providing health care services across the continuum of care. An IDS typically includes primary care doctors, specialty care doctors and one or more hospitals. Other types of providers may be included such as home health care providers and even service providers for vision and dental care. The amount of integration in terms of patient care varies by organization, as does the amount of financial integration.

- **Accountable care organization (ACO).** The term *accountable care organization* is relatively new. The inclusion of ACO in the health reform legislation of 2010 has solidified ACO in health management history. The Affordable Care Act (ACA) defines an *ACO* as multiple health care providers and/or provider groups with a shared governance structure. The law specifically allows group practices and integrated delivery systems to be ACOs. The law has certain requirements if an ACO wants to participate in certain programs created by ACA. For example, the organizations must be willing to become accountable for quality, cost and overall patient care. What an ACO will look like will be more clear as regulations implementing provisions of ACA are issued.

What Factors Must Be Considered When Choosing Health Care Providers?

Selecting health plan providers is an important fiduciary responsibility for trustees of a health and welfare plan—a careful evaluation process is required. Largely, the factors that must be considered when choosing providers depend on the type of provider or provider organization being selected. If selecting an MCO, trustees will have to be concerned with all of the criteria listed below.

Benefit Package

Much variation exists in the benefit packages offered by insurance companies and managed care companies. Among the questions to ask are:

- Can you provide all of the benefits provided by our current plan?
- What other benefits can you provide plan participants?
- Do you offer alternatives such as home health care and hospice care?
- Does your organization offer benefit design consulting services? What does this involve and what is the cost?
- What types of cost sharing (i.e., deductibles, copays and coinsurance) are used in the plan?
- What incentives are there for patients to make cost-effective health care decisions?
- Do you have any incentives to promote preventive care?
- Do you have any incentives to promote lower cost care such as the use of outpatient vs. inpatient services? Generic vs. brand-name drugs?
- Are these incentives sufficient to generate cost consciousness among participants?
- What kinds of limits or restrictions are there on coverage? (e.g., lifetime claim limits, drugs that will reimbursed, mental health services)
- Are there any cost-sharing strategies, limits or restrictions that discourage patients to seek care and result in outcomes that create demand for higher cost care in the long term?
- What patient education programs do you have? What are the objectives of these programs?
- Do you communicate with participants? If yes, when, how and for what reason(s)?
- How do you structure fees for benefits? (e.g., a flat annual fee, per participant per year, per member per month)

Provider Choice and Access

Trustees should carefully consider a provider network with respect to participant choice of and access to care providers.

- How many board-certified physicians are part of your network? What are their specialties?
- Must participants get approval from a primary care provider or other gatekeeper before seeing a specialist?
- Are OB-GYNs considered primary care providers or must female participants be referred by a primary care provider?
- What is the typical wait time for an appointment with a primary care provider? An appointment with a specialist? Admission to a hospital?
- What pharmacy delivery options are available to participants? Local retail pharmacies? Mail-order? The Internet?
- Do you have the ability to communicate in languages other than English? Which ones?
- In terms of geography, what is your primary service area?
- What care options are available to participants in the primary service area? Outside this area?
- Can participants use providers outside the network? What are the procedures for doing so? If there are additional costs for doing so, what are they and when do they apply?

Network adequacy in terms of both care providers and geographic dispersion is essential. Trustees should request a geographic analysis that compares health care provider locations to where participants work and live to ensure adequate access to all types of health care providers. The company must be of sufficient size and scope—in terms of services provided and geographic area—to fulfill the needs of the plan and plan participants. For small provider networks, the qualifications and experience of lead specialty physicians and other key providers are particularly important criteria.

Claims Management

In addition to provider quality and access, claims management is one of the keys to participant satisfaction with a plan. In some cases, claims management also affects service provider willingness to provide services to participants. Any organization handling claims for a plan should be asked questions such as these:

- What is your process for handling claims? Do you allow paper claims, online claims or both?
- What is the typical turnaround time for a claim?
- Do you offer financial guarantees for specific services?
- How can plan participants contact you when they have a question or need assistance? (e.g., phone, Internet)
- When are customer service representatives available to assist participants?
- Do you have representatives who are able to communicate in languages other than English?
- What is your average length of time for resolving an issue from start to finish?
- Do you survey claimants to measure their satisfaction with the handling of claims? How often? What are the results of your most recent survey?
- Do you conduct audits to ensure providers are complying with contract terms? To look for potential fraud or abuse? Do outside auditors conduct these?

Care Quality and Cost Management

All organizations providing health care to plan participants, not just MCOs, should be asked what they are doing to improve the quality and cost-effectiveness of the care they provide:

- What criteria do you use for choosing service providers? (See Exhibits 1 and 2 for examples of the types of criteria to use for assessing the quality of physicians and hospitals.)
- Do you conduct on-site reviews of care providers? How often, and what do you examine during these reviews?
- Do you survey patients and/or participants to determine their satisfaction with service providers? How often, and what are the results of your most recent survey?
- What quality improvement initiatives do you have in place? What evidence do you have of their success?
- What cost-management initiatives do you have in place with respect to patients and service providers? What evidence do you have of their success? Is there an additional fee for these programs and services?
  - Do you have any programs to encourage healthy behaviors or patient compliance with physician recommendations? Please describe how you influence provider or participant behavior.
  - Do you have a *precertification* (prior authorization) program in place for any services? Describe it.
  - Do you track the diagnostic and treatment patterns of physicians? If yes, do you intervene when their practice is not consistent with recommended practices or the actions of their peers? How do you intervene?
  - Do you have any programs to monitor the care provided for chronic diseases (e.g., diabetes, asthma, depression) or catastrophic illnesses (e.g., premature babies, burn victims, spinal cord injuries)?
  - Are there any incentives for service providers to provide cost-effective, quality care? On the other hand, are there any incentives that might encourage a provider to withhold necessary care?
- Do you have a formal process for identifying the most up-to-date treatment recommendations for what is most cost-effective and in the best interests of the patient concerning safety and effectiveness?
  - How are these recommendations communicated to service providers?
  - What methods do you use to encourage adoption of these practices?
- What types of utilization and cost reports will you provide our plan and how frequently will you provide them? What is included in your standard reports?
- Do you provide customized reports? If yes, what do you charge for them (if anything)?
- Will you provide any performance guarantees for the cost or quality of care you provide participants? What percentage of your fees are you willing to put at risk meeting these guarantees?

Management features must be compared in detail. For example, it is not enough to know that an organization has a program to help manage costs. Rather, trustees should understand the elements of the program, how it is administered and what the impact of the program is on plan costs. A report on the impact for a group of participants com-

Exhibit 1

Physician Selection

How do trustees assess the quality of physicians in a provider network? These are the types of questions that should be asked when an organization is determining whether to admit a physician into a network. Many of these questions are also useful when considering whether a physician should continue to practice within a network:

- Is the provider licensed to practice in states served?
- Is the physician licensed to dispense medication in his or her state and by the federal Drug Enforcement Administration?
- Is the physician certified by a specialty board recognized by the American Board of Medical Specialties?
- Has the physician had any additional certification or training in performing a procedure?
- Does the physician have active, unrestricted hospital privileges?
- How many procedures does the physician perform annually?
- What are the physician's complication and mortality rates for procedures performed?
- What is the physician's success rate for a procedure?
- What is the average length of hospital stay for a procedure?
- What is the physician's malpractice history? (Malpractice is not always a reflection of quality, but it can provide an indication of the likelihood of future malpractice claims with a provider.)
- Has the physician ever lost practice privileges, been reprimanded or censured?
- What are the results of any patient satisfaction surveys?

Most state boards that license physicians now post the licensing status of physicians online. The National Committee for Quality Assurance has developed programs to identify doctors who provide high-quality care for diabetes, cardiac conditions, strokes and other specific chronic illnesses. A database of these physicians and information on the program is available at www.ncqa.org. If a physician participates in any managed care organizations (MCOs), trustees may also be able to request the results of periodic performance reviews done by the MCO.

---

parable to those of the plan should be requested from the organization being considered.

If the service provider is an MCO, there are two independent organizations that can help trustees assess the quality of the MCO. The National Committee for Quality Assurance (NCQA) and the Joint Commission on Accreditation of Healthcare Organizations review and accredit most of the MCOs in the United States. Accreditation involves an examination of the MCO's quality improvement efforts, processes for reviewing and authorizing care, the quality of the provider network, and participant rights and responsibilities. NCQA also has a Health Plan Employer Data and Information Set (HEDIS®) for standardizing the measurement and reporting of performance measures produced by many health plans. For more information concerning NCQA programs, visit www.ncqa.org. Information concerning the Joint Commission is available at www.jointcommission.org. When assessing an MCO, these are questions worth asking:

- Are you accredited by either NCQA or the Joint Commission?
- If yes, when was your last review and what accreditation status were you given?
- Will you provide a copy of the findings from the accreditation process?

Creating a system to monitor and measure whether providers are meeting plan objectives and contract terms is as important as the selection of a provider. Many of the issues considered during the selection process should also be scrutinized on a regular basis after a contract is in place. Providers should be required to submit reports that plan trustees and other personnel can review to confirm provider performance meets expectations with respect to care quality, cost management, access to care and participant satisfaction.

Provider Compensation

How a service provider is compensated can influence the mix of benefits a health care plan can offer its participants, as well as the cost and quality of participant health care. Compensation arrangements with providers can be broadly classified as risk sharing and non-risk sharing.

Non-Risk Sharing. The early indemnity plans are an example of plans that were *non-risk sharing*. Care providers are reimbursed by plan sponsors and participants for any services provided plan participants. As stated previously, there is little or no incentive for providers to control patient utilization or the cost of this care. The following are common examples of reimbursement methods that are non-risk sharing—though some managed care programs have now addressed the lack of incentives by monitoring provider practices and intervening when practices appear out of line with current recommended care.

- **Fee for service.** Traditional indemnity plans pay providers a *fee for service;* the doctor or other provider bills the plan for the service to the participant, then the plan reimburses the provider. The plan bases the amount to pay the provider on what is reasonable and customary (R&C) in the geographic area; this *R&C payment* is the most frequent amount providers in an area charge for a service. Let's assume that what is typical in the community is $100 and the doctor bills $80. The doctor will be paid $80. If the doctor charged $120, the doctor would be paid the R&C amount of $100. The doctor may *balance bill*—send a bill to the patient for the remaining $20.
- **Fee schedule.** A variation on the fee-for-service arrangement is the use of a fee schedule with amounts negotiated in advance for each different service a provider performs. The provider is again paid whichever is less: the amount billed or the amount on the schedule. PPO physicians often agree to accept the amount on the fee schedule as full payment and promise not to balance bill the patient. The problem with this approach is that schedules must be reviewed and updated to remain relevant.
- **Discount.** A fee-for-service arrangement with a discount is one of the common reimbursement strategies used by a hospital; the health plan and hospital agree in advance to a discount. If a hospital bills $1,000 and the agreement is a 15% discount, the hospital will only receive $850 ($1,000 minus 15% or $150).
- **Per diem.** A fixed daily rate with a hospital is a *per diem.* Hospitals and plans sometimes negotiate in advance the payment for one day of care in broad categories such as medical/surgical, intensive care, delivery of a baby, etc. The hospital is paid this rate for each day the patient is in the hospital.

Risk Sharing. *Risk-sharing* arrangements transfer some of the responsibility for the cost of care from the plan to the health care providers, giving providers an incentive to control costs.

- **Case rates.** Some plans negotiate with hospitals a flat amount the plan will pay for a specific type of service such as the birth of a baby or outpatient surgery. The hospital must absorb any costs in excess of this fixed amount.
- **Diagnostic related group (DRG).** When Medicare adopted DRG reimbursement as the way it would pay hospitals in 1984, this method to compensate hospitals became more common among private plans. With a *DRG arrangement,* plans and hospitals prenegotiate payment for care of over 500 diagnoses. The hospital

Exhibit 2

Hospital Selection

A good starting place for evaluating the quality of a hospital is to check its license to operate and accreditation. When assessing the quality of hospitals, questions to ask include:

- Is the hospital licensed by the state within which it operates?
- Does it have accreditation from the Centers for Medicare and Medicaid Services for participation in Medicare and Medicaid?
- What is its accreditation status with the Joint Commission on Accreditation of Healthcare Organizations? Visit www.jointcommission.org.
- What volume of admissions does the hospital have for select conditions/procedures?
- What are the complication, morbidity and mortality rates for select conditions/procedures?
- What is the hospital's success rate for select conditions/procedures?
- What is the average length of hospital stay for select conditions/procedures?
- Has the hospital been designated as a center of excellence for any high-risk, high-cost condition or procedure such as heart surgery, organ transplants or burns?
- What are the results of any patient satisfaction surveys?

HealthGrades.com Inc. provides quality ratings for hospitals at www.healthgrades.com.

has an incentive to control the length of stay and the cost of services provided a participant during a stay.

- **Bundled payment.** Also referred to as *global payment,* compensation through a *bundled payment* arrangement pays providers a negotiated amount for a patient's episode of care. An *episode of care* is defined as all of the health care services that a patient needs for a specific medical condition or disease, for example, an occurrence of cancer or coronary artery disease. A bundled payment may include all the services provided by doctors, the hospital (both inpatient and outpatient), labs, radiology, home health care, etc. Providers receiving bundled payments have an incentive to control both the unit cost of services and the utilization of services.
- **Capitation.** Under *capitation,* providers are paid a fixed amount per participant per month to provide as many services as the person needs. A capitation arrangement may be limited to just one service or a full range of services. Behavioral health services (i.e., mental health, drug and substance abuse services) and home health care are commonly capitated with limited services. Capitation arrangements covering a broad range of services are typically between a health plan and an integrated delivery system that directly provides all (or the majority) of the arrangement's services. As with bundling, providers have an incentive to control patient utilization as well as the cost of care. But with capitation, providers assume even more risk; providers take on some of the financial consequences of less healthy plan participants.
- **Bonuses.** With this arrangement, providers are typically paid a fee for service but receive extra dollars if they meet preestablished performance measures. The performance measures are usually plan goals (or desired outcomes); the measures may be based on quality, utilization and/or costs per member per month. For example, if a plan wants to promote preventive care, it may give a group of physicians performance measures for the percentage of children given immunizations or the percentage of women over the age of 40 receiving a mammogram. To promote plan cost savings, a multispecialty group may be given measures for total physician/hospital claim costs per member per month. While these physicians do not directly control hospital costs, they have a big influence on them when they authorize inpatient admissions and outpatient services.
- **Withholds.** Another way to motivate providers to manage costs is a *withhold arrangement.* A percentage of the provider's payment is held until the end of a predetermined financial period; participant claims that exceed the budgeted costs for care are charged against the funds that were set aside. After any excess claims are paid, the providers receive any money that is left. Providers that hold costs below the amount budgeted are rewarded. If the costs exceed the amount withheld, an MCO usually must take responsibility for the rest.
- **Salaried physicians.** Under *salaried compensation arrangements,* physicians are employees of a service provider and paid a salary. The doctors may be provided bonus payments based on quality, patient satisfaction or other measures. Salaried compensation arrangements are most commonly associated with staff model HMOs.

In addition to the direct compensation a health care provider receives from a health and welfare plan, an organization may also receive compensation through provider discounts, prescription drug rebates and other sources. It is a trustee's fiduciary responsibility to ensure that any such compensation related to providing services to plan participants is appropriate and reasonable. Trustees should seek as much transparency as possible concerning both direct and indirect compensation received by a health plan service company.

Provider Organization and Finances

Health care service providers must also be judged as to how well they fit with plan values, needs and objectives. While some providers are not-for-profit, others are for profit. Some are independent while others are closely affiliated with another organization. The financial and operational status of a provider as well as their litigation history can influence both a provider's strategic and operational decisions. Health plan service companies will often provide this information in proposals if they are requested to do so.

Provider Management

Plan trustees and administrators value dealing with representatives who are easy to work with and can quickly resolve issues. Consideration should also be given to executive officers because they are responsible for changes in the financial status and future services of a provider. Trustees should review the qualifications and experience of the key management personnel to ensure good business partners are selected. The provider should notify trustees if there are key personnel changes, a merger or a sale.

Transition

When considering a change from one provider to another,

trustees should consider the ease of transition for plan participants, the administrator, and other parties as well as costs of the transition. It is helpful to request a disruption analysis that compares the location of participants' most-used current providers to the location of providers offered by the potential provider. The result will show whether providers are available in the communities where utilization is highest. In addition, it will reveal how many participants will have to switch providers if a new provider is chosen. Participants are more likely to accept the new provider network if there are minimal changes.

Conclusion

Trustees face many choices in the creation and management of a health benefit plan. A multitude of options exist with respect to what benefits are offered, who will receive benefits, how the benefits will be funded, which service providers will administer and deliver benefits, and the payment of these providers. An awareness of these options increases the likelihood that trustees will be able to make choices that are in the best interests of the plan and plan participants.

Chapter 14

Insured Financing for Health Plans

Arthur L. Wilmes and Jill S. Herbold

Insurance and self-funding are the primary ways multiemployer health plans are financed. Larger plans may rely on either of these options or a combination of both. Smaller and medium-sized funds typically rely almost entirely on insurance. This chapter explains how insurance works and various approaches to insured financing. Issues to consider when choosing an insured financing arrangement are provided at the conclusion to this chapter.

What Is Insured Financing?

Health benefit plans that pay premiums to an insurance company, health maintenance organization (HMO) or a Blue Cross and Blue Shield (BCBS) organization have *insured financing*. These plans pay *premiums* to an insurer in exchange for the insurer reimbursing health care providers for the care given to plan participants. In some cases, a participant may have to pay a provider for care from his or her own pocket then submit a claim to the insurer for reimbursement. Regardless of the arrangement details, insured financing allows a benefit plan to transfer its financial risk to an insurer. When the cost of providing care to participants exceeds the premium a plan pays an insurer, the insurer absorbs the difference.

The historic differences among commercial insurance companies, BCBS organizations and HMOs have blurred.

- The early BCBS organizations were not-for-profit and free of the pressure to earn a profit for shareholders, as for-profit insurance companies must do. Since the mid-1990s, however, many BCBS plans have converted to for-profit companies.
- Insurance and BCBS organizations historically provided health coverage through *indemnity plans* that reimbursed the fees charged by health care providers in exchange for payment of an insurance premium. Now, these insurance organizations typically offer a choice among traditional indemnity plans and various managed care options such as HMOs and preferred provider organizations (PPOs). Many insurance, BCBS and managed care organizations also offer a full range of health plan services, including claims administration, a provider network, utilization and quality management.

Since the historic differences have blurred and to simplify discussion in the remainder of this chapter, commercial insurance companies, BCBS plans and HMOs will collectively be referred to as insurers.

* * *

To sell health insurance in a particular state, an insurer must be licensed in that state. Insurers must meet state requirements regarding coverage, financial solvency, market pricing and so forth. The financial requirements help to ensure the insurer is able to fulfill its promise to provide the coverage promised. Some states control the price of health insurance or the amount that prices can increase. Some states have additional regulations that apply specifically to HMOs. The details and extent of HMO laws vary considerably from one state to another.

How Do Insurers Determine the Premiums They Charge Benefit Plans?

Insurers consider a number of factors when determining the premium paid by a health plan. In very broad terms, they consider:

- **Claims**—how much they anticipate they will pay for participant health care claims based on the prior experience of an insured group (i.e., plan participants) or a group of persons with similar characteristics
- **Risk charge or profit**—a contribution to an insurer's profit or surplus to compensate the insurer for the risk assumed
- **Commissions**—any money paid to an insurance agent or broker for helping trustees obtain insurance coverage
- **Taxes**—any taxes a state requires the insurer to pay on insurance premiums
- **Administration**—the expenses of handling a group's claims and providing other services
- **Conversion charge**—an optional fee that gives participants who exit the insured group the opportunity to continue coverage as individuals
- **Pooling charge**—an amount charged to all insureds to cover excess claims. The insurer puts a limit on the amount for individual claims that will be considered in analyzing the claims experience of the group. The excess claims are placed into an insurance company's *pool* of excess claims. Each insured group is charged a fee based on the claims experience of this pool that reflects the predicted claims the group will have beyond the limits set. Pooling charges for health care plans are normally a percentage of a group's annual claims or a fixed fee per employee.

What Options Are Available for the Insured Financing of a Health or Welfare Plan?

The size of a health and welfare plan group and the credibility of its prior claim experience will limit or enhance its ability to obtain insured financing. For large multiemployer plans with substantial prior claims history, insurers are able to predict with reasonable accuracy the cost of claims the group will have in a year. When a few participants in a large plan have very high medical expenses, these expenses have little impact as they are averaged out with the claims of the large number of participants. Large plans with a history of predictable health care claims have many insured financing arrangements to choose from as well as the possibility of self-financing their benefits.

Smaller groups or groups with little prior claim experience may have no option other than a guaranteed premium method. A few participants with high expenses in a small group can create dramatic fluctuations in both the average and total claims experienced from one year to the next. The inability to predict claims greatly reduces the options available to small benefit plans.

Adjusted Community Rating

For very small plans, insurers take into consideration the claim and expense experience for similar groups. The insurer may consider and make adjustments for the industry, age, gender, family status and geographic composition of plan participants. Insurers also use this *adjusted community rating* method when determining premiums for larger groups that do not have sufficient prior claims experience to predict accurately what future claims will be.

Using the adjusted community rating to determine the potential cost of claims, the insurer is able to establish the amount of money it will need to provide insurance coverage to the group. The charge is usually a fixed dollar amount per participant per month. An insurer that underestimates the costs of providing coverage must absorb the difference. The insurer cannot come back and ask a group to pay more money; hence, this approach to financing benefits is referred to as a *fixed premium arrangement.*

Experience Rating

For large plans with sufficient claims history, insurers use *experience rating* to determine premiums; the premium charged for insurance coverage is based on the actual claims experience of the group.

Prospective experience rating. With *prospective experience rating,* the amount the insurer charges a plan is based on the plan's past claim experience. If a group is very large and the insurer has sufficient past claims information to feel confident with its predictions on the group's claims for a future period, the premium amount will use *full prospective experience rating,* which is based completely on the group's past experience. Some relatively large plans do not have a sufficient number of participants or past claims experience for an insurer to feel entirely certain of a claims prediction—in these situations, the insurer may base the premium on a combination of the group's past experience and the insurer's experience with similar groups. *Partial prospective experience rating* combines prospective experience rating and adjusted community rating. Like fixed premium insurance, premiums set through prospective experience rating are guaranteed to the insured group for the period they are paid.

Retrospective experience rating. Insurers may also use *retrospective experience rating* for groups with sufficient claims experience. With this approach, a surplus is created if a group's claim experience during the insured period is lower than assumed when the premium was set for the period. Of course, there could also be a deficit if claims are more than what was anticipated. Precisely how surpluses and deficits are calculated and handled is determined by the initial contract negotiated between the insurer and the health benefit plan.

The insurer can return some or the entire surplus to the plan. Another option is to have the insurer place some or all of the extra dollars into a *stabilization reserve*—an account set up by the insurer that can be used to cover future deficits. A deficit may be carried forward then offset by future surpluses. Often, the plan has to pay interest on this amount until it is repaid, much as a plan would have to pay interest on any loan.

A typical retrospective experience rating formula is illustrated in Exhibit 1. The first column of numbers shows a plan with a surplus of $108,100 while the second column reflects a $67,900 deficit in the plan's retrospective account balance.

Are There Any Alternative Insurance Arrangements That Might Benefit a Plan?

Insurers offer plans some options that can reduce the premium amount. Options are also available for delaying premium payments that can improve a plan's cash flow.

Minimum Premium. A *minimum premium arrangement* is a modification made to a guaranteed insurance (i.e., fixed premium or prospective rated) contract. A rider is attached to the insurance contract that requires a portion (90% is common) of the premium be placed in a special trust fund used to pay claims. If claims exceed the amount in the trust fund, the remaining claims are paid directly by the insurer. The amounts deposited in the trust fund are not subject to premium taxes in many states. This may be a significant cost advantage for large groups.

Retrospective Premium. With some policies using a retrospective experience rating method, the insurer charges less than the normal insurance premium. For example, an insurer might accept 90% of the premium typically charged. At the end of the coverage period, the benefit plan must pay an additional premium *(retrospective premium)* if claims plus other expenses exceed the initial 90% paid. This type of arrangement generally limits a group's total premium liability to a percentage (e.g., 125%) of the initial premium paid. Amounts due in excess of the limit are paid by the insurer. Reducing the initial payment improves a plan's cash flow and creates opportunities to generate investment earnings on the difference. The downside is that a plan is liable for claims up to the limit, which is more than the premium paid under a fixed premium or experience-rated contracts.

Exhibit 1

Retrospective Experience Rating Formula Example

	Claim Experience Scenario	
	SURPLUS (90% of Projected)	DEFICIT (110% of Projected)
Income		
Earned premiums[1]	$1,000,000	$1,000,000
Investment income[2]	22,500	22,500
Total income	$1,022,500	$1,022,500
Expenses		
Incurred claims[3]	$792,000	$968,000
Conversion charges	2,400	2,400
Commissions	15,000	15,000
Administrative expenses[4]	60,000	60,000
Risk/profit charge[5]	25,000	25,000
Premium tax	20,000	20,000
Total expenses	$914,400	$1,090,400
Retrospective credit/(charge)	$108,100	$(67,900)

1. **Earned premiums**—premiums paid by the policyholder, less any increase in the *unearned premium reserve* (premiums paid in advance for which insurance has not yet been provided).
2. **Investment income**—the income earned on any reserves that are held on deposit with the insurer. Examples of reserves for which investment income would be credited include unearned premium reserves, claim reserves (funds set aside for claims that an insurance company is aware of but that have not yet been settled) and *claim stabilization reserves* (funds set aside for years with unusually high claims).
3. **Incurred claims**—the claims paid by the insurer during the contract period, the change in claim reserves held for the group and any pooling charges related to the group. The *change in claim reserve* is the amount held in the plan's claim reserve account at the end of the period minus the amount in reserve at the beginning of the insurance period. This amount is added to paid claims. The *pooling charges* are a group's claims subject to pooling provisions less the group's share of the claim pool. This item is deducted from paid claims.
4. **Administrative expenses**—this may be a fixed percentage of earned premium, or a fixed per employee or per member amount per month.
5. **Risk/profit charge**—insurers generally do not show company profit in their experience rating formula. Rather, they combine profit with the risk charge. The *risk charge* assessed by insurers is used to offset losses incurred on insured groups that cancel their coverage while their retrospective fund has a deficit.

Premium Drag. Group insurance contracts generally have a 30-day grace period for paying premiums. The insured group can delay payment for 30 days with no penalty. A *premium drag arrangement* extends this grace period an additional 30 to 60 days. By extending the grace period, the insurer allows the insured group to delay payment of premiums by as much as 90 days. Cash flow for a benefit plan can be improved through this arrangement since a portion of the premium normally due is withheld. Insurers may charge a higher risk fee to the group and/or interest on the premium withheld.

No-Reserve. Under a *no-reserve arrangement,* the plan is responsible for funds normally held by the insurer. Cash flow for a plan can be improved because the funds normally paid to the insurer are reduced. With this arrangement, trustees must be sure their plan has sufficient assets to pay the insurer later. In addition, insurers may charge the group a higher risk fee.

What Should Be Considered When Choosing Insured Financing?

Trustees must go through a careful evaluation process to determine whether and which insured financing approach is most appropriate for their plan. What financing arrangements are appropriate—or even available—can vary greatly from plan to plan. Issues to consider are:

Cash Flow

As just explained, a plan's cash-flow position can be improved by retaining some of the assets normally held by an insurer through a retrospective premium arrangement, a premium drag arrangement or a no-reserve arrangement. While cash flow is enhanced by these arrangements, trustees must also consider any additional costs and risks of doing so. This analysis must include whether the interest a plan can earn on retained funds will exceed the interest paid by the insurer.

Asset Position

Funds with a healthy asset position will be better positioned to absorb unexpected fluctuations in claims experience than may occur with some insured financing arrangements. If a fund's asset position is weak, it may not be advisable to finance the benefits through anything other than a guaranteed premium plan.

Benefit Type

The type of benefit to be financed also affects the financing decision. Benefits subject to low claim frequency but high claim amount (e.g., accidental death and dismemberment insurance) may be more suitably financed through a guaranteed premium plan. Other financing methods are more practical for benefits with more stable (predictable) claims.

Risk Aversion

Trustees who are not comfortable with a big change in financial results from one year to the next may prefer guaranteed premium arrangements that provide more stable results than other insured financing methods.

Chapter 15

Self-Financing of Health and Welfare Plans*

Arthur L. Wilmes and Jill S. Herbold

Self-financing offers multiemployer benefit plans an alternative to conventional insurance for the financing of health and welfare benefits. Medical, dental and short-term disability benefits are most frequently self-financed. Claims for these benefits tend to have higher frequency and relatively low claim amounts compared to benefits for death, long-term disability, and accidental death and dismemberment.

This chapter explores how plans self-finance, the advantages and disadvantages of self-financing, and what trustees should think about if they are considering self-financing of health and welfare benefits.

What Is Self-Financing?

A plan that self-finances assumes all the responsibilities and financial risk of providing benefits to plan participants:

- **Total liability.** With a fully self-financed plan, the plan assumes the financial risk *(liability)* for all benefit claims incurred by plan participants. Many plans are partially self-financed; they purchase stop-loss insurance to provide protection for situations where claims exceed a predetermined amount. Partial self-financing and stop-loss insurance are discussed later in this chapter.
- **Administration.** All multiemployer plans must have systems for maintaining records concerning participant eligibility and plan contributions. Self-financed plans need claims administration capabilities such as the receipt and payment of claims, a process for handling claim disputes, and guidelines and procedures for coordinating benefits if other insurance coverage is available to plan participants. Self-financed health and welfare plans often contract with a health care service company to provide some or all of these administrative functions.
- **Other responsibilities.** What can easily be overlooked is that self-funded plans must also take on the behind-the-scenes tasks of a conventional insurer. Loss prevention, actuarial, legal, investment and accounting functions are performed in-house by plan employees or contracted to outside consultants.

Self-financed plans have two funding method options:

1. **Unfunded.** There is no specific trust instrument used for funding benefit claims when plans are *unfunded.* Rather, cash benefits are paid when due from either plan assets or cash flow.
2. **Funded.** The alternative *funded* method uses a trust instrument to fund the cost of claims, as well as accrued-but-unpaid claims. The trust instrument most often used by a funded plan is a voluntary employees' beneficiary association (VEBA) trust, also called a *501(c)(9) trust* since this is the section of the Internal Revenue Code that exempts VEBAs from income tax.

What Services Do Third-Party Administrators Offer Self-Financed Plans?

A self-financed plan can hire a *third-party administrator* (TPA) to handle plan operations and management. In addition, a TPA can be assigned certain fiduciary powers for

*Many different terms are used to describe a health and welfare plan that provides benefits directly rather than through an insurer. Other terms frequently used include *self-insurance* and *self-funding.*

plan administration. Typical services provided by a TPA (as well as some insurance companies) include:

- Claims processing
- Banking arrangements
- Administrative and financial reports
- Government reports and compliance
- Plan descriptions for plan participants
- COBRA notifications and administration
- Individual conversion policies.

Third parties, however, cannot take on the financial responsibility for the plan. Claims payments are drawn from the assets of the plan's trust fund.

The primary reason that plans purchase third-party services is for cost efficiency. Many expenses associated with administering a plan (e.g., the establishment and maintenance of computer hardware, software and systems) is spread among the many clients of the third party. Keeping staff up to date on changes in government regulations and health care can also be costly and time-consuming for plans, and more efficiently provided through outsourcing. TPAs are discussed more thoroughly in Chapter 49.

What Is Stop-Loss Insurance?

To mitigate the risk of large claims, many self-financed health and welfare plans purchase stop-loss insurance from an insurance company. There are two types of stop-loss insurance: specific and aggregate.

Specific stop-loss insurance. With *specific stop-loss insurance,* also referred to as *individual excess loss insurance,* an insurance company agrees to pay claims of any plan participant that exceed a dollar limit set for the plan year. The limit, established in the insurance contract, is referred to as the *specific deductible.* Lower specific deductibles transfer more risk from the self-financed plan to the insurer than higher specific deductibles. As a result, plans pay higher premiums for lower specific deductibles.

Aggregate stop-loss insurance. The term *aggregate excess insurance* is used interchangeably with *aggregate stop-loss insurance.* With this coverage, the plan and the insurer establish a dollar limit for annual claims incurred or paid for the entire group. The insurer pays all claim costs of the group that exceed the aggregate limit. This limit is known as the *aggregate attachment point* and is usually set at 120% to 140% of expected claims for the group. A plan still has the risk for some of its adverse claims experience, but the rest transfers to the insurance company.

Aggregate stop-loss insurance is not as common as specific stop-loss insurance. Insurance companies typically require a plan to purchase specific stop-loss insurance before it can purchase aggregate stop-loss insurance.

How Do Self-Financed Plans Calculate Their Liabilities?

Trustees have a responsibility to periodically calculate financial obligations to plan participants and determine whether plan assets are sufficient to cover fully this liability if the plan were to terminate.

IBNR

The largest liability for a self-financed health and welfare plan is typically an *unpaid claim reserve* representing claims *incurred but not reported* (IBNR) to the plan at the end of an accounting period. These claims are the outstanding bills for participant care the plan expects to receive but that have not been filed. For medical benefits, the IBNR is often 20% to 30% of annual incurred claims.

Other

Self-financed health and welfare plans can have other liabilities beyond IBNR. For example, a plan that waives the premium for disabled plan participants must estimate the likelihood that participants might be disabled and establish a *waiver of premium reserve* to provide these persons with the promised continuation of benefits. A reserve is also needed if plan participants are eligible for coverage in a future period based on their service in a prior period.

* * *

Trustees should ask their actuarial consultant to estimate how much money to place in reserve to meet these obligations. Trustees typically establish liabilities with a conservative margin to cover adverse fluctuations from best estimates of the liability. How conservative the margin is depends on trustee aversion to risk, the cash-flow needs of the plan and plan asset strength.

Tip for Trustees

Trustees considering self-financing as an alternative to conventional insurance should have an actuarial analysis prepared to study the impact of self-financing on the health and welfare plan. The case study on page 110 provides an example of such an analysis.

What Are the Advantages of Self-Financing?

Self-financing a health and welfare plan can provide financial advantages.

Cost Reduction

Self-financing can eliminate some of the costs associated with a conventional group insurance contract.

- **Premium tax.** One such cost is the *state premium tax* that insurance companies pay states on premiums received. The premium tax may make up to 20% or 30% of insurer charges excluding claims. Of course, this advantage applies only in states where self-financed plans are not subject to a premium tax.
- **Profit and risk charges.** A second area of cost savings involves the insurer's profit and risk charge. The *profit charge* compensates the insurer for its services and assumption of plan risk. It also provides the insurer with a return on its business investment. The *risk charge* for an insurer represents an additional margin to cover fluctuations in claim experience.
- **Commissions.** A third cost savings is the elimination of commissions paid to an insurance agent or broker. Self-financing does not involve the sale of a product by an agent paid a commission by an insurer.

Improved Investment Return

Like a self-financed plan, insurers also maintain an IBNR reserve equal to two to three months' premiums or 20-30% of annual incurred claims. A self-financed plan may receive a better investment return, net of investment expenses and taxes, if it holds its own reserves. The extent of this advantage depends on whether the insurer pays an insured plan a competitive rate of investment return on the reserves it establishes under the group insurance contract.

Improved Cash Flow

Any realized cost savings that result from self-financing can be invested by the plan. Improved cash flow also results from improved investment return. In addition, cash flow may be improved if the self-financed plan is responsible for setting its own plan reserves.

Insulation From Market Conditions

Insurance pricing practices tend to be cyclical with market conditions dictating the level of rate increases. When insurers are in heavy competition for a larger proportion of market share, the market gets soft and small rate increases result. When insurer results worsen and the industry's balance sheets begin to reflect the extended period of underpricing, the market hardens and large rate increases are not uncommon. Self-financing may provide some insulation from these types of cyclical pricing patterns.

What Are the Disadvantages of Self-Financing?

Self-financing may result in some cost savings due to the elimination of premium taxes, sales commissions, profit and risk charges and retention of the reserve. The magnitude of the cost savings, however, can sometimes be overstated if not properly balanced against the costs of self-financing. Self-financed plans have some costs they would not have if they used conventional insurance. An analysis of self-financing should reflect the expenses removed as well as the expenses added.

Trustees should not assume claim costs will remain the same if their plan is switched from an insured to self-financed plan. A self-financed plan that liberally interprets its benefits may find it has higher total claim costs than a conventional insured plan with strict interpretations. Self-financed plans may also lack the sophistication to interpret benefits as detailed in the policy; borderline claims may not be settled to a plan's advantage, or coverage from other insurances may unknowingly be duplicated. In addition to increased benefit costs, there are other potential disadvantages with self-financing:

- **Risk shifting.** A self-financed plan may find it is shifting insurance risk to plan participants or employers. Without stop-loss insurance, a self-financed plan runs the risk of not having sufficient funds to pay for large claims. The cost of these claims would have to be shifted to participants or contributing employers.
- **Conversion privilege.** A self-financed health and welfare plan may not be able to provide a terminating employee with a conversion privilege to an individual plan.
- **Set-up costs.** There will be development and maintenance costs for a self-financed plan. The plan must perform loss prevention, actuarial, legal, accounting, and administrative duties or contract these responsibilities to outside service companies.
- **Time.** Considerable trustee time must be spent to ensure plan benefits remain competitive with the current employee benefits market. Substantial staff time may be required to remain up to date on changes associated with technology, health care practices and government regulations.
- **Participant satisfaction.** A self-financed plan is

Self-Financing Versus Insurance: An Analysis

This table compares the actual financial results under an insured plan with the results projected if a plan were partially self-financed. The analysis assumes that contributions, claims, changes in reserves and administration expenses do not change if the plan is self-financed. These assumptions are not valid for all plans; the purpose of this example is to illustrate how the financials might look when exploring such a change.

In this analysis, investment income increases if trustees elect to self-finance their plan. The increase results from a higher investment return on reserves and the investment income earned on the additional cash flow. Self-financing reduces expenses because premium taxes and insurer risk charges are eliminated. (There is no line item for profit as most insurers include the profit charge for what they label their risk charge.) The self-financed option has additional expenses for the purchase of stop-loss insurance and actuarial services. The plan would reduce its total insurance costs by $62,147 or 4.6% of end-of-year assets.

Be aware that this is a retrospective analysis based on prior claims and an assumption there will be no difference in the cost of claims under insured versus self-financed funding. A complete analysis would also include a prospective review of projected claim costs for the next one to three years. The prospective analysis would involve a scenario of reasonable claim results in order to test the sensitivity of self-financing results to deviations in the expected claims.

Health and Welfare Fund

Restated Financial Statement

		Insured	Self-Financed
Contribution income			
Major medical	$239,018		
Other	898,550	$1,137,568	$1,137,568
Investment income		7,000	31,939
Total income		$1,144,568	$1,169,507
Claims		$946,505	$946,505
Change in reserve			
Beginning	$446,771		
Ending	441,164	(5,607)	(5,607)
Premium tax		22,751	0
Insurer expense		33,558	0
Insurer risk charge		22,751	0
Claims and general administration		34,127	34,127
Stop-loss		0	31,852
Actuarial fees		0	10,000
Total expenses		$104,085	$1,016,877
Surplus (deficit)		$90,483	$152,630
Estimated gain (deficit) from self-funding			$62,147
As a percent of end-of-year assets			4.6%

responsible for settlement of its claims. This places the burden of difficult decisions and the resulting employee complaints on trustees rather than on an impartial third party. This disadvantage occurs to a lesser degree when there is a trustee appeal process.

Why Do Many Self-Financed Plans Use a Partial Versus Fully Self-Financed Approach?

Despite the economic advantages of self-financing, many funds use partial self-financing for the following reasons:

- **Risk exposure.** Self-financing a plan requires a sufficient number of participants to project annual benefit costs. With a small number of participants, it may be difficult to predict confidently these costs. Modified arrangements using stop-loss insurance allows smaller groups to partially pool benefit risk.
- **Predictability.** Even with larger groups, claim amounts fluctuate from year to year. An insured program such as stop-loss coverage helps plans stabilize annual benefit costs and plan finances.

What Should Be Considered When Choosing Self-Financing?

Trustees considering self-financing should carefully evaluate this alternative before making a final decision. The following general guidelines have been prepared to assist trustees in their evaluation.

Asset Strength

A strong asset base may increase the feasibility of self-financing since it increases a plan's ability to deal with random fluctuations in claim experience. The need for asset strength may be reduced if the plan purchases stop-loss insurance.

Risk Aversion

Not all trustees are willing to accept the ups and downs in financial results that can occur with self-financing from year to year. Conventional insurance arrangements can provide more predictable and stable results.

Claim Experience

Self-financing may be more feasible for groups that have a history of consistent claim experience from one year to the next. Larger groups are more likely to have this consistency. In addition, medical and short-term disability benefits are better candidates for self-financing because their experience tends to be more stable. Death, long-term disability, and accidental death and dismemberment benefits are lesser candidates since claims for these benefits are lower in frequency and have a higher cost per claim potential—factors that reduce the predictability of claims and financial stability.

Actuarial Analysis

A self-financing decision should include an *actuarial analysis* (cost impact study) estimating the potential gain or loss expected under a self-financed plan. The analysis should estimate the risk faced by a self-financed plan due to claim fluctuations.

Taxes

Benefits received from a self-financed benefits plan are, in general, subject to the same income tax treatment as conventionally insured benefits. An exception is a self-financed life insurance benefit. While life insurance benefits paid by an insurance company are not taxed, self-financed life insurance benefits in excess of $5,000 are taxable as income.

Administration Capability

Self-financed plans take on the responsibility for plan administration. Trustees must decide whether plan administration will be done internally or outsourced.

Conclusion

While self-financing can appear less costly, trustees should consider the issues raised in this chapter. Remember, the handling of claims disputes falls on the trustees in self-financing.

Chapter 16

Current Trends in Health Benefit Plan Design

Edward A. Kaplan

For many years, plan sponsors and trustees have worked to maintain health plan designs that provide participants with 80-90% reimbursement for eligible charges, low deductibles and copayments, and reasonable out-of-pocket (OOP) maximums. Despite decades of medical inflation, plan innovations have helped keep the cost of this generous coverage from reaching a breaking point for plan sponsors and participants.

The health care delivery system has been plagued by factors that put pressure on costs: an aging workforce, growing obesity that fuels higher rates of chronic diseases, expensive new medical technologies, overutilization of services and direct-to-consumer prescription drug advertising. Then, tough economic times arrived and the Patient Protection and Affordable Care Act as amended (ACA) added new health care coverage requirements—both adding more pressure to an already stressed system.

Annual health claim costs continue to outpace inflation. Exhibit 1 shows that the annual per member plan costs for 2011 are expected to increase at a rate that is four to five times the rate of inflation as measured by the Consumer Price Index.

Exhibit 1

Estimated Expected Cost Increases for 2011

	Expected Increase
Preferred Provider Organization (PPO)	11%
Health Maintenance Organization (HMO)	10%
Prescription Drugs	9%
Consumer Price Index	2-3%

Source: The 2011 *Segal Health Plan Cost Trend Survey.*

Today's health benefit plan trustees are grappling with:

- How to finance current and emerging health care costs
- The level and intensity of cost management to be adopted
- Participant ability to bear increased OOP expenses
- Increased focus on investing in healthy behaviors
- Increasingly complex legal and compliance issues.

For health benefit plans, no single solution is likely to fix the problem of rising health care costs. Success will require a combination of strategies and actions addressing the unique needs of each plan and each plan's participants. Because conditions continue to change, efforts will have to be revisited regularly to determine what still works and what needs to be eliminated or modified.

Plan trustees facing these challenges can organize their thinking from three perspectives:

1. **Vendor management (the supply side).** Many plans aggressively manage service provider contracts. These plans use competitive bids for market leverage, diligently negotiate deeper discount guarantees, cap administrative fees, and monitor and audit performance results.
2. **Population health management and wellness**

programs (the demand side). A growing number of plans are establishing wellness programs that use plan design incentives. A few have aggressively redesigned their medical benefit offerings with encouraging results.

3. **Plan design (allocation of coverage dollars).** More plans are paying close attention to creative plan design. Plans are introducing changes that significantly reduce the cost of providing health coverage without compromising the overall quality of the coverage.

An aggressive and innovative three-pronged approach can keep plan cost increases well below the projected 10% per year rates that have been stressing most health plans. The remainder of this chapter will focus on the third component of this trio—plan design that can, in many cases, be the critical element in cost containment.

What Are Some Plan Design Options?

There are many major plan design choices available. Following is a list of key areas to consider:

- **Eligibility and coordination of benefits.** Trustees may want to revisit the rules for active employees, retirees and dependents. One multiemployer plan that had significant costs due to offering extended eligibility decided to make changes to help reverse deficit spending. Originally, coverage was extended for six months to any worker who lost full-time hours and met the plan's eligibility rules. The trustees later adopted a vested eligibility rule. Workers with five or more years of service continued to receive the six-month extension of coverage. Workers with fewer than five years of service received a reduced extension of 30 days. This resulted in a noticeable reduction in the fund's claim liability.
- **Employee contribution strategies.** Many contribution strategies are used to control costs. A plan might pay the full cost of basic coverage and require participants to purchase any additional coverage. A small but growing number of plans require premium sharing for spousal and dependent coverage. Plans that require little or no premium contributions for working spouses generally end up subsidizing other employers that provide less generous benefits and/or require their employees to contribute toward the cost of their benefits. Requiring employee contributions for working spouses and dependents can produce valuable savings.
- **OOP costs.** Copays, deductibles, coinsurance, health care reimbursement arrangements and health savings accounts should be reviewed with an eye to participant costs and plan affordability. Comparing a plan's benefits and costs with others in the industry can help a plan remain in step with trends and identify changes that others are making that successfully address similar cost challenges.
- **Benefits exclusions and limitations.** It is important periodically to update policy definitions, limits and exclusions so plans keep pace with treatment advances and changes in medical practice. For example, plans that do not set limits on high-cost procedures like bariatric surgery can end up entirely paying for the procedure, adding costs to the plan.
- **Network incentives.** Many plans have high participant utilization rates for network service providers. Effective financial incentives and a larger number of network providers to choose from are among the reasons participants are willing to accept care within a network. In the future, plans may have to consider provider networks with fewer but more efficient service providers offering even deeper savings. For example, a plan might select a small number of hospitals that offer the best outcomes and cost savings for heart disease and oncology patients. More incentives will be needed to encourage patients to use network providers.
- **Value-based design.** Incentives can also be used to reward behaviors and cost-effective choices that result in better health outcomes. Trustees might consider coverage and payment differentials to encourage the use of proven low-cost treatments. Higher cost-sharing might be expected of participants who elect expensive treatments with little proven value or the greatest potential for abuse. Incentives are also used to encourage participation in wellness programs. For more information concerning value-based health management (VBHM), see Exhibit 2.
- **Prescription drug benefit design.** Encouraging the use of generics through lower copays and limiting coverage for expensive brand-name medications is an effective way to cut prescription drug costs. Step therapy, copays, coinsurance, deductibles, formularies, mail service, limited supplies for targeted substances and precertification are all strategies that should be considered. Chapter 19 provides a more in-depth review of pharmacy design elements.
- **Care management.** Professional advisors can help trustees explore strategies that promote best practices among both care providers and patients. Specific strategies being used to influence treatment choices include using primary physicians as gatekeepers to other

Exhibit 2

Value-Based Health Management (VBHM)

In plan design, health care benefits and cost-sharing have historically been equal among plan participants. Everyone pays the same premium for the same coverage. VBHM is an approach to health care design that tailors cost-sharing to the evidence-based value of specific services for targeted groups of patients. Currently, cost-sharing is nearly always based on the expense of the service or medicine and rarely is related to its potential benefit to a patient. VBHM helps control company health care costs by:

- **Removing Barriers.** High OOP (i.e., copays, coinsurance) and coverage limits/exclusions can keep people from getting the care they need—possibly leading to more costly care in the future. VBHM emphasizes removing these barriers and providing greater access to care in order to keep people healthy longer. For those who have a chronic condition, the goal is to prevent the condition from getting worse and more costly. Plans using a VBHM approach offering incentives by waiving or reducing OOP costs can help people get the treatment they need and stay with it.
- **Using Integrated Care Management.** Another feature of VBHM is creating care provider teams—physicians, pharmacists, nurses and health coaches—to support patients through wellness programs, medical decision making and care management. This approach helps patients better manage their health conditions, reduce excess health risks, achieve desired clinical outcomes and improve their quality of life.
- **Focusing on Prevention.** Preventive care provides such benefits as smoking-cessation programs, weight management and nutrition classes, vaccination programs, and screenings to help prevent chronic health problems before they start.

health care providers, treatment precertification, large case management and utilization review. Chapter 17 provides a basic introduction to these strategies.

How Do Changes in OOP Costs Impact Total Plan Costs?

The typical health plan covers 80-85% of allowable claim costs submitted by patients. Changes in OOP costs, however, can yield radically different claim costs. Before making any changes to a plan's design, trustees need to have the facts regarding their plan's cost-sharing levels and grasp how OOP costs influence patient ability and willingness to pay for care. This is a basic premise of value-based design—creating incentives and programs to encourage treatments proven to provide clinical benefit, yet lowering financial and behavioral barriers to such treatment.

Utilization

A key to effective value-based design is to make sure that cost-sharing does not discourage appropriate utilization or promote excessive utilization. According to a Rand Corporation study, very high deductibles and OOP costs result in drops in health care utilization, including the use of desired preventive care treatments and diagnostics.[1] Such choices can actually increase plan costs versus providing cost savings.

One multiemployer health plan discovered that diabetes accounted for 12% of its total health costs. Cardiovascular diagnoses (hypertension, coronary artery disease, congestive heart failure and stroke) accounted for the next largest percentage. Previous increases in prescription deductibles and copays had resulted in a significant drop in prescription drug utilization—people were not getting the medications they needed.

The plan instituted a value-based design with lower copays for a select group of drugs used for patients with these chronic conditions: diabetes, high blood pressure/heart disease, high blood cholesterol and asthma. The plan also expanded its wellness program to promote healthier lifestyles and other prevention activities. After 22 months, the medicine possession rate increased from 79% to 88%—an indication that patients were increasingly getting their medications as recommended by their physicians. More importantly—although diabetes remained the most costly condition for the plan—the cost of treating the condition dropped from 12% to 7.5% of plan costs.

Cost-Effective Choices

Many plans do not have adequate incentives for participants to seek out the most cost-effective care. Raising copays for specialist visits while lowering or maintaining them for primary care visits may redirect patients to lower cost treatment with the same health care outcome. A low copay for specialists or emergency room visits may encourage overuse of costly providers and services.

One plan developed a tiered design to encourage appropriate use of emergency care. The copay for treatment at a nonurgent care facility was $25, while the copay for a trauma emergency room visit certified by the patient's physician as "necessary and appropriate" was $75. The copay was $200 for an emergency room visit that was not certified. This change helped lower the number of costly emergency room visits and steered patients to widely available lower cost urgent care centers, when appropriate.

Why Is There so Much Interest in Behavioral Intervention?

Evidence suggests that many health care services are avoidable, overused and ineffective. Individuals also do not follow lifestyle advice and health care provider instructions that would result in a better health outcome. Consider the following:

- The Centers for Disease Control and Prevention (CDC) has determined that more than 50% of children prescribed antibiotics did not test positive for a bacterial infection.
- CDC reports that as the number of obese persons continues to rise, there are corresponding increases in the risks of diabetes, heart disease, musculoskeletal conditions and even cancer.
- Segal Company data shows that less than 20% of the health plan population over the age of 50 gets a colonoscopy to detect early cancers. Colonoscopies improve patient outcomes and lower plan costs.
- Ongoing research sponsored by the American Diabetes Association reveals Type II diabetes patients were able to control their blood sugar levels through diet and exercise at levels equal to or better than those taking oral medications.
- Quitting smoking can significantly reduce both the rates of cancer and heart disease—producing long-term reductions in catastrophic claim amounts for health plans. Today, nearly 50% of multiemployer health plans offer smoking-cessation programs, up from about 25% just a few years earlier.[2]

The point of these studies, and others, is that much can be done to change patient behavior and treatment options to avoid costly claims. There are savings opportunities if plans address obesity, smoking, early cancer detection and other manageable conditions.

To encourage behavioral changes, trustees must determine which rewards (or penalties) will be most effective given the plan participants being targeted. Compliance is another major consideration and should be discussed with fund counsel. Provisions of ACA specifically address when incentives for wellness programs are allowed and their amounts.

What Plan Design Changes Are Best?

There is no one-size-fits-all strategy for health care plan designs. While some plans may be able to achieve their goals by modestly adjusting current benefit offerings, others may require more dramatic changes. Digging into plan data is a good place to start when considering modifications in plan design. Statistics give trustees the information necessary to make decisions that address the specific needs of their plan and plan participants.

Gathering information that answers these questions helps trustees identify design elements that will lower plan costs while maintaining or even enhancing the quality of care provided participants:

- What medical, drug and laboratory claims are most common by provider type, setting (i.e., inpatient or outpatient), treatment/procedure and primary diagnosis?
- Are there specific claims that are increasing or decreasing in prevalence?
- Which conditions and illnesses consume the largest portion of claim costs?
- Is participant use of preventive care strategies (e.g., participation in health risk assessments, prescreening programs and wellness activities) increasing or decreasing?
- Are the cost-management strategies (e.g., cost-sharing, precertification, utilization management) that are already in place encouraging patients to:
  - Make lifestyle changes that will improve their health status?
  - Participate in early screening and preventive care programs?
  - Adhere to drug therapies and other treatments recommended by their health care providers?
  - Use cost-effective treatments, providers and care settings?
- Are there additional strategies that might encourage the behaviors just identified?
- Are there any excessive OOP expenses that are encouraging participants to underuse plan benefits and risk developing costly future problems?

Conclusion

When designing a health benefit plan, the goal of most trustees invariably comes down to maximizing participant value and coverage within the fiscal constraints faced by the plan and plan participants.[3] Plan design changes can help trustees better manage costs and position a plan for long-term stability. A growing number of health plans are already taking these steps and are seeing results.

Endnotes

1. Melinda Beeuwkes Buntin, Amelia M. Haviland, Roland McDevitt and Neeraj Sood. "Healthcare Spending and Preventive Care in High-Deductible and Consumer-Directed Health Plans," *The American Journal of Managed Care,* v.17, no. 3, (Mar. 2011).
2. Segal Multiemployer Health Plan Database.
3. When this chapter was written in early 2011, ACA had already begun to reshape how plan sponsors address health benefit design. At the same time, legislative and judicial challenges to the law were underway. As we went to press, it remained unclear how these rules and regulations would play out.

Chapter 17

Health Care Cost Management

Arthur L. Wilmes and Jill S. Herbold

For many years, the cost of health care in the United States increased at about the same annual rate as the price of other goods and services. In the 1970s, however, the rate of the increase in health care costs began to pass price increases for other items as measured by the Consumer Price Index (CPI). The gap between the price of health care and the CPI has been increasing ever since.

The increase in the cost of health care has meant employer expenditures for health benefits have become an increasingly larger portion of total employee benefit dollars. Employers and health insurance carriers have responded with a variety of management strategies in an attempt to reduce the rate of growth in health care costs.

This chapter begins by providing a brief explanation of why health care costs have been on the rise. With a better understanding of what has led to the increases, the rest of the chapter considers some solutions in the form of health care management techniques—including their effectiveness and some of the legal aspects of adopting these strategies. Some guidelines are also offered for trustee consideration when incorporating these strategies into health and welfare plans.

Why Have Health Care Costs Increased More Than Other Costs?

A combination of factors has led to the increase in health care costs. Some of the primary causes are:

- **Inflation.** Health care costs are subject to price increases *(inflation)* much like any other good or service. Consider the cost of hospital care. The salaries of hospital personnel, utilities, hospital maintenance and so forth are sensitive to inflation. As the prices of the goods and services needed to operate a hospital increase, the costs to compensate providers for a hospital room, surgery, nursing care, etc., increase. Likewise, physician fees increase with the increased cost of operating their offices.
- **Utilization.** Health care costs are also influenced by how much medical goods and services are used. If people use more services, the total cost of providing these services will increase regardless of whether the cost per service increases. An aging population and increased obesity are just two of the reasons the utilization of health care has increased in the United States.
- **Medical technology.** Changes in medical technology also have had an impact on health care costs. For example, the introduction of CAT scans resulted in a new procedure with an expensive price tag. To remain competitive and provide the latest care, hospitals purchase the latest equipment. The cost of the new technology is passed to others paying for patient care. Of course, technology is not just hardware. New drugs called *specialty drugs* that have become increasingly available in recent years can cost thousands of dollars a month for the treatment of one patient.
- **Defensive medicine.** Lawsuits against health care providers for malpractice led to the defensive, or conservative, medicine practiced by today's physicians. Defensive medicine increases utilization as doctors order additional procedures to reduce malpractice risk.
- **Plan design.** Plan designs, historically, have been rich in benefits. In other words, the plans were designed with very little out-of-pocket (OOP) payment by the insured. Over time, these low OOP payments have

not kept pace with medical cost inflation. Payments that may have been meaningful years ago when first incorporated into a plan have had their effectiveness eroded by inflation.

- **Third-party payers.** The growth in commercial and Blue Cross and Blue Shield insurers following World War II—and the growth in employer-provided insurance benefits—have resulted in an environment in which the recipient of medical care often is removed from the cost of the care. Third-party payers (e.g., insurance companies, employers and government) pay for most health care costs rather than the recipients of the care. With costs often passed on to third parties, there is little incentive for the recipients (i.e., plan participants and their family members) to reduce their use of medical benefits or to seek less costly treatment.
- **Medical care economics.** The economic laws of supply and demand do not generally apply to health care. A person who is seriously ill or injured needs health care *now*—he or she does not have time to shop around for the best deal or wait until a better deal comes along. In addition, as the supply of health care goods and services increases, demand for these same goods and services increases. When the number of physicians and hospitals increases in a community, the use of physicians and hospitals also tends to increase.
- **Cost shifting.** The health care payments provided to hospitals and physicians from government insurance programs—notably Medicare and Medicaid—have decreased. Hospitals and physicians sometimes replace these reductions by increasing the amount charged to individuals who are privately insured.

What Strategies Are Being Used to Control Health Care Costs?

Diverse health care management strategies are being used in efforts to control health care spending. A list illustrating the variation in efforts is shown in the Exhibit below.

Cost Sharing

Cost sharing passes a portion of health care costs to plan beneficiaries. These are among the major cost transfer methods:

- **Deductibles** represent the OOP costs that a plan participant must pay before plan coverage begins. Increasing OOP payments yields a direct reduction in plan costs. In addition, higher deductibles provide a financial incentive for more prudent use of medical services by plan participants.
- **Coinsurance** represents the percentage of health costs (in excess of the initial deductible level) that is paid by the plan participant OOP versus the plan. A very com-

Exhibit

Health Care Cost-Management Strategies

Cost Sharing
- Deductibles
- Coinsurance
- Limits (maximums)
- Employee contributions
- Medical expense budgeting

Utilization Management
- Preadmission testing
- Second opinions
- Outpatient surgery
- Precertification
- Concurrent review
- Retrospective review
- Physician profiling

Alternative Care Management
- Large-case management
- Disease management
- Hospice care
- Extended care facilities
- Home health care

Preventive Care Management
- Wellness programs
- Periodic health examinations
- Participant communications
- Health risk appraisals
- Demand management

Financial Management
- Negotiated reimbursement arrangements
- Hospital audits
- Participant audits
- Participant bonus programs

mon cost-sharing arrangement requires a participant to pay 20% of a medical procedure while the plan pays the remaining 80%. Similar to deductibles, a higher coinsurance percentage for the plan participant not only reduces plan costs, but also provides an economic incentive for more prudent medical benefit use.

- **Limits** are the caps (or maximums) placed upon the cost or number of services that a plan will provide for benefits. Some plans place internal limits on specific plan benefits such as physical therapy. Internal limits are generally used when plan participants have some control over how much of the service they will use. Some health plans also have annual maximum benefits that will be paid for each person covered, although these are becoming less common due to provisions in the Patient Protection and Affordable Care Act of 2010.
- **Employee contributions** not only reduce an employer's health benefit costs, they also increase employee awareness as to the total cost of a health insurance program—especially if the contribution increases automatically each time the cost of coverage increases. Employees may be required to pay a portion of the health care premium or benefit cost. Plans frequently adjust the employee contribution amount depending on who is covered: just the employee, the employee and the employee's spouse or the entire family.
- **Medical expense budgeting** is the allocation of a set dollar amount that each employee can use to purchase health insurance benefits. Employees are typically allowed to choose from a variety of insurance options. If an employee selects a benefit-rich plan with a cost that exceeds the amount set aside, the employee makes up the difference. The plan controls medical benefit cost increases by controlling the amount budgeted for each employee.

Utilization Management

The primary goal of utilization management is reducing unnecessary or inefficient use of health care services.

- **Preadmission testing** is the completion of certain examinations (e.g., blood tests, x-rays) on an outpatient basis prior to hospital entry. Requiring testing before admission often reduces the number of hospital days required. In addition, tests taken on an outpatient basis often cost less than those done as an inpatient.
- **Second opinions,** given after a second physician consults with the patient, often reduce unnecessary surgeries and other treatments. While some second opinion programs are voluntary, others are mandatory. In either situation, the second-opinion physician is usually reimbursed in full. The reasoning is that savings from unnecessary treatment will make up for the cost of the extra doctor visit.
- **Outpatient surgery** is another effort to reduce health care costs by having low-risk procedures performed in a facility that is less costly than a hospital, such as a clinic or a doctor's office.
- **Precertification** requires patients to get plan approval prior to treatment. As with second opinions, the purpose is to avoid unnecessary treatment and provide an opportunity to consider alternative care that may be as effective but less costly. Generally handled by the patient's physician, precertification is only required for nonemergency situations. For hospital precertification, the patient's doctor will typically discuss the diagnosis and recommended course of treatment with a preadmission certification specialist. The specialist is usually a registered nurse or a physician who authorizes the length of the hospital stay. If the length of stay exceeds the preapproved limit, an additional request must be made of the specialist. When a certification specialist does not approve treatment, there is generally an appeals process.
- **Concurrent review** is the monitoring of a patient during hospitalization or other treatment by a registered nurse or the attending physician. Concurrent review evaluates whether the patient care program is consistent with what was preauthorized. Staying abreast of patient treatment helps ensure that the patient receives medically appropriate yet cost-effective treatment.
- **Retrospective review** is the tracking of a patient's care after a hospital discharge or other treatment. Some retrospective reviews are similar to an audit in

Tip for Trustees

Some plans have banded together into *purchasing cooperatives* that use larger volume purchasing to increase buying power in the marketplace. This approach to buying goods and services can be particularly attractive to smaller plans that would not be able to get the same kinds of discounts as larger plans. The role of the cooperative is similar to the role insurance companies and managed care organizations are taking in negotiating prices with health care providers.

that errors or inappropriate services can be corrected, and bill adjustments made. Other reviews involve the monitoring of physician practice patterns and hospital length-of-stay averages. This monitoring allows a health care plan to identify providers that consistently deliver cost-effective and quality health care. In addition, it provides an opportunity to suggest alternatives to physicians whose practice patterns appear to be outside of the norm.

- **Physician profiling** also looks at individual doctors to determine if individual physicians follow certain patterns of use. Data on the practices of individual doctors is compared to that of their peers to identify significant differences. Practices that may be analyzed include the frequency of basic diagnostic tests, forms of preventive care, specific medications prescribed or referrals made. Profile results are sent to each physician to create an awareness of how his or her practice differs from that of others. Profiling programs may use the information as the basis for corrective action and possible removal of a doctor or facility as a care provider.

Alternative Care

Alternative care programs seek to provide patients with the highest quality care in a cost-effective manner.

- **Large-case management** is generally used with catastrophic cases such as AIDS, burn victims, premature babies or injuries of the central nervous system. With these programs, a case manager or treatment specialist consults with the primary physician at the onset of the catastrophic claim to ensure that the patient receives the highest quality and most cost-effective treatment.
- **Disease management** focuses on controlling the course of a specific disease, for example, diabetes, asthma, chronic obstructive pulmonary disease or depression. The rationale is that these proactive programs will result in improved patient outcomes and will avoid more costly care in the patient's future. Disease management involves many clinical professionals such as physicians, pharmacists, social workers and therapists.
- **Hospice care** is starting to be recognized as a cost-effective method of caring for terminally ill patients in their last months of life. While not historically covered by health care plans, some plans are now adding this benefit as a less costly alternative to inpatient hospital benefits. Hospice care is often available in a patient's home as well as at residential nursing facilities.
- **Extended care facilities** (e.g., residential nursing homes) generally have daily charges less than those charged by hospitals. Physicians are encouraged to transfer patients from the hospital to an extended care facility as soon as it becomes medically appropriate.
- **Home health care,** like care in an extended care facility, costs much less than care in a hospital. Physicians are encouraged to discharge patients to a home setting with an at-home caregiver and visiting health care professionals as soon as medically appropriate.

Preventive Care

Preventive care strategies seek to reduce health care costs through prevention. The following list summarizes some of the primary preventive care management methods.

- **Wellness programs** seek to improve the quality of a plan participant's health by encouraging healthy behavior and lifestyle. Smoking cessation programs, weight loss programs, on-site exercise facilities, and blood pressure and cholesterol screenings are all examples of wellness programs introduced by employers and health care plans to promote change and reduce long-term health care costs. Other benefits associated with a wellness program may be an improvement in employee productivity and a reduction in employee absenteeism in the workplace. Employees often find they feel better about themselves and the quality of their lives both at work and at home. Various provisions of the Patient Protection and Affordable Care Act of 2010 provide incentives for wellness programs.
- **Periodic health examinations** are often part of a wellness program. The goals of a periodic health examinations are twofold: (1) early detection of illnesses and (2) employee education on preventive care strategies. Periodic health examinations build awareness among participants of personal health changes, trends and potential health issues. The examination often motivates participants to make changes that reduce the risk of illness or death. Information gathered from a health examination can identify health education and information issues that need attention.
- **Participant communications** provide information and education to plan participants concerning health issues, wellness programs, plan services, etc. Communications in the past were primarily mass communications to all participants, but new technology

offers opportunities to target communication for specific age groups, health risks, etc.

- **Health risk appraisals** have been used by doctors for a long time to identify medical conditions and risk factors associated with new patients. Information is collected on the health history of the patient and patient's family—diet, weight, physical activity, blood pressure, cholesterol levels, current medications, etc.—to determine the likelihood that a patient might have or develop a chronic illness such as diabetes. This information is now used more proactively to develop patient-specific treatment plans that will reduce the chance of disease and long-term treatment costs.
- **Demand management** provides patients with the information they need to make wise decisions concerning their personal health care. Strategies range from the distribution of home health care manuals and the use of 24-hour nurse advice lines to expanded clinic/office hours. All of these programs have the potential to reduce costly emergency room visits.

Financial Management

Financial management strategies seek to reduce the cost of health care by focusing on what the plans are being charged for health care goods and services—and finding ways to reduce these charges.

- **Negotiated reimbursement arrangements** reduce the cost of health care via contractual arrangements between a plan and a health care provider. Examples are preestablished daily rates for hospital stays and discount prices for medications.
- **Hospital audits** are generally used when there is a large claim to ensure that there were no billing errors. Audits check whether the patient received the billed goods and services and that the dollar amounts were consistent with any contract agreements.
- **Participant audits** are voluntary programs in which plan participants are encouraged to review their hospital and physician bills prior to payment by the health plan. As with hospital audits, the goal is to find billing errors. To encourage participants to conduct a review, financial incentives are used such as giving the participant a fixed dollar reward or a percentage of any error the participant finds.
- **Participant bonus programs** encourage the wise use of medical services. The bonus is a portion of the difference between a plan's total health costs for a period and the amount the plan anticipated would be spent. Not all of the difference is typically shared with the participant—some funds are retained by the plan as a contingency reserve.

How Effective Are Cost-Management Strategies?

The savings resulting from health care management are difficult to estimate. Often, there are not accurate records of claims experience prior to implementation of a program. This makes before and after comparisons difficult. In addition, when multiple programs are implemented, the savings in one area may be offset by cost increases in another area.

The savings that result depend upon a number of factors:

- **Current utilization levels.** Utilization management programs achieve savings by encouraging prudent utilization of health care. If current utilization levels are high with respect to national norms, relatively large savings can be expected. Lower savings can be expected if current utilization levels are relatively low.
- **Voluntary versus mandatory programs.** The expected cost savings also depend upon whether a program is mandatory or voluntary. When a voluntary program uses a reduced copay, a bonus or other financial incentives to encourage participants to make different health care choices, some of the savings goes back to the plan participants. On the other hand, a financial incentive may increase the number of participants willing to make more cost-effective choices. With some mandatory programs, there are no choices—compliance is required. A few plans now impose a financial penalty such as requiring participants to pay a higher portion of their health care program if they refuse to participate in a disease management program.
- **Multiple programs.** As stated previously, the introduction or use of more than one program at the same time makes it difficult to isolate the savings associated with any specific program. Savings can overlap or in some cases, the success of one strategy can make it appear that another strategy has failed. For example, a precertification program may reduce or eliminate any potential savings resulting from an outpatient surgery program since some inpatient surgeries may be denied by the precertification process and referred to an outpatient facility yielding an increase in outpatient costs.
- **Negotiated reimbursement arrangement.** Savings from these arrangements vary greatly according to the deal negotiated. Obviously, the savings resulting from a discount program depend on the size of the discount.

- **Cost of administration.** Cost-management efforts typically increase a plan's administrative costs. These costs must be recognized in evaluating the net effect a strategy will have on overall health care costs.

It is reasonable to expect savings from health care management strategies in the range of 0-10%. These percentages reflect an estimate of the cost reduction for the year in which the strategy is first implemented. It is important to realize that these programs will affect not just current health care costs, but also costs far into the future.

What Are the Steps in Implementing a Strategy?

Trustees considering the implementation of a new health care management strategy should go through a careful evaluation process prior to making a final decision. Some general guidelines to follow are:

- **Analyze current data.** Review current utilization of plan participants and the practice patterns of plan providers. Compare this information with national data on an age- and sex-adjusted basis. In addition, compare the information from one plan with other comparable plans. This analysis will indicate areas where improvements and cost savings can be reasonably expected.
- **Identify appropriate strategies.** Explore what strategies best address areas of concern and are most appropriate given any unique features of the plan and plan participants. Does the plan have access to the data and other resources required to implement the strategy? How will participants respond to the new program? Will they welcome the change or might there be substantial resistance? It can be very valuable to take a look at what has and has not worked for similar plans.
- **Cost analysis.** Estimate reasonable cost reductions that can be expected from the implementation of the strategy. Consider not only the estimated savings for the next plan year, but also the potential savings for the program over the next three to five years. This analysis should reflect any extra plan administration costs.
- **Management information systems.** Management information systems (MIS) should be developed to monitor the effects of the health care management program. The MIS should be capable of producing utilization reports on an age- and sex-adjusted basis, as well as reports summarizing hospital and physician treatment patterns.
- **Legal exposure.** Ask legal counsel to prepare a report on the potential liability risk associated with implementation of the new strategy. Also, request that the report provide recommendations on how to minimize liability exposure.

Chapter 18

Consumer-Directed Health Plans and Savings Accounts

Arthur L. Wilmes and Jill S. Herbold

Consumer-directed health plans (CDHPs) are a type of health plan design that encourages participants to engage actively in their health care. Participants are typically given more choices with respect to their health care decisions as well as incentives for seeking out the most cost-effective care. CDHPs typically combine high-deductible health plan (HDHP) coverage—providing protection from catastrophic medical expenses—with a prefunded, consumer-controlled savings account used to directly pay for routine health care expenses not covered by the HDHP. Dollars placed into these savings accounts and used to pay for qualified medical expenses are not taxed by the federal government.

This chapter provides a description of HDHPs and a comparison of the various types of tax-advantaged savings accounts. The chapter also identifies trends concerning the use of CDHPs and issues to consider when exploring the adoption of such a plan.

What Is an HDHP?

The Internal Revenue Service defines an HDHP as having:

- A higher annual deductible than typical health plans
- A maximum limit on the sum of the annual deductible and out-of-pocket (OOP) medical expenses that the insured pays for covered expenses. OOP expenses include copayments, coinsurance and other costs, but not plan premiums.

An HDHP may cover a participant's preventive care expenses without a deductible or with a deductible below the plan's overall annual deductible.[1]

As with traditional health plan design, the insured with an HDHP is responsible for the cost of health care services up to the deductible amount as well as coinsurance and copayments after surpassing the deductible. The difference with HDHPs is that the deductible is much higher than with traditional health plans. Savings accounts can provide a tax-advantaged vehicle for the consumer to fund the deductible and other cost-sharing amounts.

HDHPs provide an incentive for consumers to engage actively in their health care decisions because of the direct financial responsibility they have via the higher deductible and other OOP costs. Various support services are often available to help insureds make health care decisions.

What Tax-Advantaged Savings Accounts Are Available?

Health savings accounts (HSAs), health flexible spending arrangements (FSAs) and health reimbursement arrangements (HRAs) give consumers tax advantages when paying for their health care services. The accounts vary with respect to funding, portability and other key characteristics, as summarized in Exhibit 1. It is important to note that FSAs and HRAs can be used with both traditional health plan designs and HDHPs, while HSAs can only be used in conjunction with HDHPs.

Archer and Medicare Advantage medical savings accounts (MSAs) are other types of savings accounts that can be used to pay for health care expenses. Archer MSAs are similar to HSAs but eligibility is limited to self-employed persons and employees of small employers. Eligibility for Medicare Advantage MSAs is limited to individuals enrolled in Medicare; contributions can only be made by Medicare.

Exhibit 1

Comparison of Savings Accounts

	Health Savings Account (HSA)	Flexible Spending Arrangement (FSA)	Health Reimbursement Arrangement (HRA)
Eligibility	Participant must be covered under an HDHP and have no other health coverage or savings account (some exceptions).	Employer-specified. Other health coverage is not required.	Employer-specified. Other health coverage is not required.
HDHP Requirements*	Minimum annual deductible $1,200 single/$2,400 family. Maximum annual deductible and out-of-pocket in-network $5,950 single/$11,900 family. All benefits subject to deductible except preventive care.	None	None
Account Funding	Employer, employee and/or any other person	Employee and/or employer	Employer only
Contribution Limits*	Total contributions limited to $3,050 single/$6,150 family	Employer-specified	None
Contribution Tax Treatment	Employer contributions not included in income. Other contributions are tax-deductible.	Employer contributions not included in income. Employee contributions are tax-deductible.	Employer contributions not included in income
Distribution Tax Treatment	Payments for qualified medical expenses are not taxed. Other withdrawals subject to tax and penalty.	Payments for qualified medical expenses are not taxed. Other withdrawals are not permitted.	Payments for qualified medical expenses are not taxed. Other withdrawals are not permitted.
Account Structure	Tax-exempt trust or custodial account. Trustee-administered. Individual owns account.	Typically, a bookkeeping account administered by the employer.	Typically, a bookkeeping account administered by the employer.
Portability	Yes, employee can take with him or her if employment terminated.	Not portable	Employer-specified
Carryover	Contributions remain in account until used.	Contributions not spent by the end of the plan year are forfeited.	Employer-specified. Contributions typically remain in account until used.

*2010 level. Future years are indexed to inflation

What Design Features Are Common to CDHPs?

The design of a CDHP centers on an HDHP used in combination with a tax-advantaged savings account and the provision of information that supports the participant's ability to make wise health care choices.

HDHP Cost Sharing

Participant share of cost via deductibles, copays, coinsurance and other plan design elements must be high enough to provide members an incentive to engage actively in their health care decisions—yet remain affordable. The amount of the employer contribution to a savings account needs to be coordinated with the HDHP cost sharing to ensure that the total health benefit package has the desired financial incentives.

Savings Account

The type of savings account utilized is determined by the account features and federal guidelines as summarized in Exhibit 1. If an HSA is offered, plan trustees may set up the accounts for the participants, or allow participants to open HSAs on their own.

Price and Quality Transparency

To be actively engaged in health care decisions and make wise choices, plan participants need information about their health care options. Many insurers now make information regarding hospitals and physicians available via a website that allows comparisons of health care provider quality and costs. Substantial improvements have been made with respect to the amount and reliability of information available to plan participants via the Internet, and many more improvements are expected in the years ahead.

Health Education

Educating members on what preventive care they should be receiving, habits to promote long-term health and ongoing support for chronic conditions are common health educational programs used in conjunction with CDHPs.

Communication

A communication program is required to educate participants on the design of their HDHP, savings account funding and administration, incentives for healthy behaviors (e.g., weight loss, quitting smoking), decision-making tools available and health education. The communication program needs to encourage consumer engagement and support the objectives of the health and welfare plan. A strong communication program is a key component for the success of a CDHP.

Tip for Trustees

When considering whether a CDHP is the right choice for your health and welfare plan, you will need to think about whether the CDHP will be understood and accepted by your plan participants, engage participants and other beneficiaries, and be effective in meeting plan objectives.

- **Objectives.** CDHPs are offered for a variety of reasons including cost control, tax advantages, competitive benefits, and to promote both the health and productivity of employees. A health and welfare plan should prioritize its objectives for offering a CDHP and make the objectives an integral part of the health plan design.
- **Financial feasibility.** An actuarial analysis should be developed to show the potential cost or savings anticipated with a CDHP. The analysis should consider the population and an assumption as to which plan participants will choose if both a CDHP and a traditional plan are offered. When people are given a choice between a traditional heath plan and a CDHP, studies have shown that healthy people are more likely to enroll in a CDHP than nonhealthy people. When researchers adjust for this fact, there are still some cost savings associated with CDHPs. These savings, however, are not automatic—the amount of savings depends on plan design. An actuary can help analyze design options to produce optimal results for your participants.
- **Organizational readiness.** CDHPs are a major change for an organization that has only known traditional health plan designs—they need to be embraced by participants and their families to be successful. Many sponsors have opted for a phased approach, providing health education and communication for a year or more prior to the introduction of an HDHP and savings account.

What Are the Trends in the Marketplace?

Employers first offered CDHPs with HRAs in 2001. The Medicare Prescription Drug, Improvement, and Modernization Act of 2003 introduced HSAs. Since then, the percentage of employers offering CDHPs—and enrollment in CDHPs—has risen. Several surveys provide statistics similar to the following for 2010:

- **Employers offering CDHPs.** Approximately 16% of employers with fewer than 500 employees, 23%

of employers with 500 or more employees and 51% with 20,000 or more employees offered CDHPs.[2]

- **CDHP enrollment.** Approximately 11% of all covered employees were enrolled in a CDHP.[3] Enrollment in CDHPs with HSAs is roughly twice the enrollment in CDHPs with HRAs.
- **FSA enrollment.** Approximately 24% of all covered employees had an FSA.

The prevalence of employers offering CDHPs—and enrollment in CDHPs—is expected to continue to grow as (1) employers and employees become more comfortable with HDHPs and savings accounts, and (2) health care inflation continues to outpace other inflation components. Additionally, plan sponsors with CDHPs continue to modify cost sharing, enhance the information available to members, and adjust other CDHP elements to achieve optimal efficiency for their populations.

References

U.S. Department of the Treasury, Publication 969. "Health Savings Accounts and Other Tax-Favored Health Plans," (November 2009).

Mercer's National Survey of Employer Sponsored Health Plans, (November 2010).

R.A. Cohen and M.E. Martinez. "Health Insurance Coverage: Early Release of Estimates from the National Health Interview Survey, January-March 2010," *National Center for Health Statistics.* (September 2010).

Chelsey Ledue. "CDHP growth slows, enrollment decline," *Healthcare Finance News.* (August 2010).

Thomas Kess. "Determining if a CDHP Makes Sense for Your Business," *Milliman Health Perspectives.* (Winter 2007).

Rob Pipich. "Designing Effective Consumer-Driven Healthcare," *Milliman Health Perspectives.* (Summer 2008).

Paul Fronstin. "What Do We Really Know About Consumer-Driven Health Benefits?" *EBRI Issue Brief,* no. 345. (August 2010).

Endnotes

1. IRS Publication 969 (2009).
2. Mercer's National Survey of Employer Sponsored Health Plans, November 2010.
3. Ibid.

Chapter 19

Prescription Benefits: Trends and Strategies for Cost-Effectiveness

Sean M. Brandle

Two trends influence everything said in this chapter:

1. **The rising cost of prescription drugs.** Costs of medications continue to rise both in real terms and relative to all health care benefits.
2. **The increasing influence of pharmacy benefit managers (PBMs).** Almost all plan sponsors purchase their prescription drugs for plan participants through a PBM.

After a long period of double-digit annual cost increases, prescription drug costs finally dipped to the single digits in 2004 (see Exhibit 1). This decline, however, is likely to be short term and the cost increases are still significant. Most plan sponsors have seen a steady increase in the percentage of total health care dollars represented by prescription drugs. Attention must continue to be given to controlling these expenditures.

Today, PBMs control many of the processes associated with drug plan administration and have become critical links in drug delivery to plan participants—including mail-order and specialty drug delivery. Virtually all prescriptions flow through PBMs that negotiate drug prices with retailers and drug manufacturers. PBMs also help plans in many other ways; just a few of these services are recommending how to optimize a drug plan's design, recommending the most effective and economical drug therapies, monitoring customer utilization, and educating both plan participants and prescribers.

This chapter examines what is driving the continuing increases in prescription drug spending and strategies that can help trustees provide a cost-effective, quality benefit program for participants.

Exhibit 1

Average Annual Percentage Increase in Selected U.S. Health Expenditures

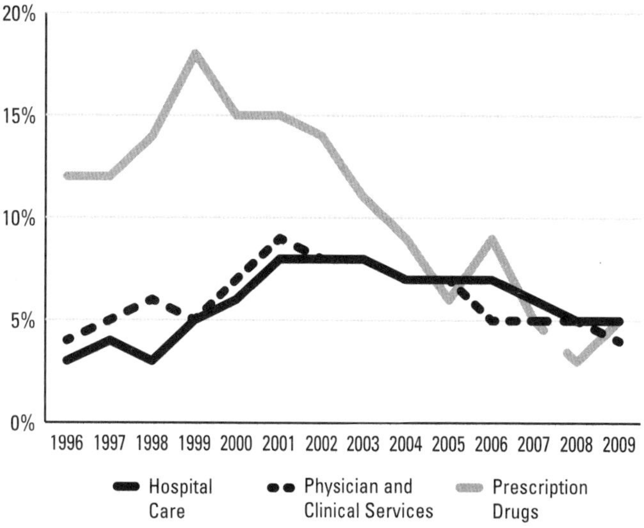

Source: Centers for Medicare and Medicaid Services.

What Is Driving Higher Prescription Drug Costs?

A mix of factors have transformed the environment in which prescription benefit plans operate and contributed to increases in both prescription drug prices and utilization—hence higher prescription costs for health plans.

New Drugs

The creation and introduction of new products to the prescription drug market usually means higher drug plan costs for sponsors. Even though these new drugs may increase total drug spending, plans are often willing to pick up the cost because the drugs improve participant health and offset potential future costs by controlling and monitoring existing conditions. Medications that manage chronic conditions such as high cholesterol and diabetes fit into this category. In some situations, drug therapy is also a less costly therapy. Consider modern cholesterol drugs such as statins. While these new cholesterol medications have increased a plan's total spending for prescription drugs, the drugs also have been shown to reduce the incidence of heart attack, and thus total health care costs.

Not all new drugs, however, are a medical necessity. Some provide benefits geared more toward improving a user's lifestyle than saving or extending lives. In recent years, many new "life-enhancing" medications have been introduced. The availability of and demand for these treatments targeting such conditions as acne, baldness, impotence and wrinkles have also increased prescription drug costs for plans.

Cost Inflation

Patent protections give developers of new medications a period to recoup their research, government approval and marketing costs before competitors can enter the marketplace with their own versions of the new drug. It should not be surprising that these new brand-name drugs have higher prices than drugs that have been available for a while. The inflation rate for brand-name drugs consistently outpaces the Consumer Price Index (CPI). As shown in Exhibit 2, brand-name drug inflation is significantly higher than generic drug inflation and the Consumer Price Index for All Urban Consumers (CPI-U).

Specialty/Biotech Products

An increasing proportion of medications being introduced as brand-name products in the marketplace are specialty medications and biotech products. With the mapping of the human genome, drug manufacturers are increasingly focused on developing therapies that address

Exhibit 2

Prescription Drug Inflation

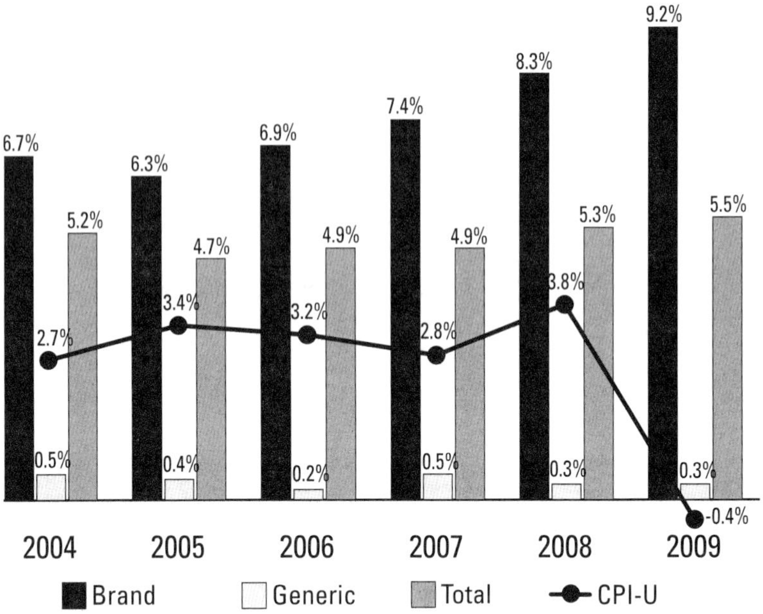

Source: Medco *2010 Trend Report.*

Exhibit 3

Top Five Specialty Drug Therapy Classes, Ranked by 2009 Per Member Per Year Cost

Therapy Class	Per Member Per Year Cost to Plan	Percent of Total Specialty Drug Cost	2009 Cost Increase
Inflammatory Conditions	$30.94	27.8%	17.7%
Multiple Sclerosis	$25.76	23.2%	34.4%
Cancer	$17.40	15.7%	23.1%
Anticoagulant	$6.00	5.4%	10.6%
Growth Deficiency	$5.06	4.6%	5.6%

Source: Condensed from Express Scripts *2010 Trend Report.*

specific health conditions (e.g., hemophilia, rheumatoid arthritis, Gaucher's disease, HIV and cancer).

To ensure appropriate health outcomes and cost-effective utilization, these drugs often require special handling and close patient monitoring. While used by only a very small proportion of plan participants, these medications represent a significant portion of a health plan's total drug spending. As Exhibit 3 illustrates, these therapies are expensive and costs are increasing at rates well above the cost of prescription medications overall. For comparative purposes, consider that the rate of increase for all brand-name prescription drugs in 2009 was 9.2%.

A complicating factor associated with specialty medications and biotech products is their limited distribution and availability. Due to their special handling and distribution requirements, they are not readily available at most pharmacies. Specialty pharmacies have sprung up that focus solely on the purchase, distribution and patient management aspects of these products. Larger PBMs also have become prominent in this area through the purchase of boutique, specialty pharmacies. This can result in increased prices because distribution is more costly and there is a lack of market competition.

New Indications for Existing Drugs

Drugs approved by the Food and Drug Administration (FDA) for one purpose are often shown to be effective for other purposes. These so-called new *indications* also add to drug plan costs. For instance, a drug used in the treatment of autism was later found also to be useful in treating schizophrenia, bipolar disorder and major depression.

Direct-to-Consumer (DTC) Advertising

The relaxation of DTC advertising regulations in 1997 created a new avenue for drug companies to promote their products. No longer confined to communicating with physicians, drug manufacturers began advertising their products to the general public. Being allowed to communicate directly with consumers gave drug companies a powerful new mechanism to stimulate demand—particularly for more expensive brand-name medications. DTC ads enforce consumer expectations that there is a drug for every ailment and increase the likelihood a person will seek out a remedy.

Utilization and Demographics

Changing utilization patterns caused by the aging of a population are a prime driver of increased plan costs. Exhibit 4 illustrates the vast differences in benefit costs as a population ages. Utilization increases are occurring most prominently at younger age groups, as illustrated in Exhibit 5.

Exhibit 4

Net Plan Cost for Prescription Drugs Per Person by Age Group, 2009

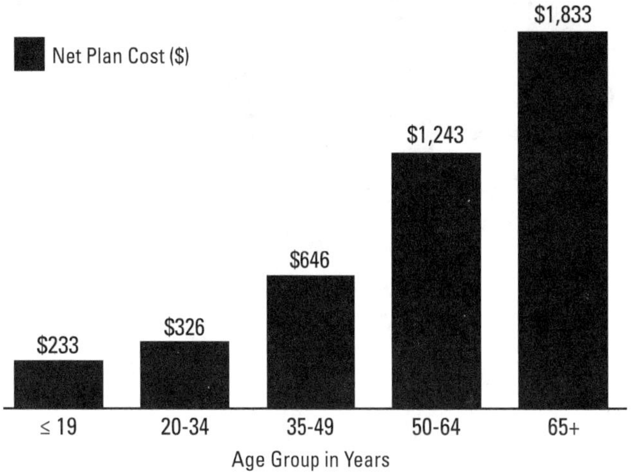

Source: *2010 Drug Trend Report,* Medco.

Exhibit 5

Changes in Drug Utilization and Spending by Age Group, 2009

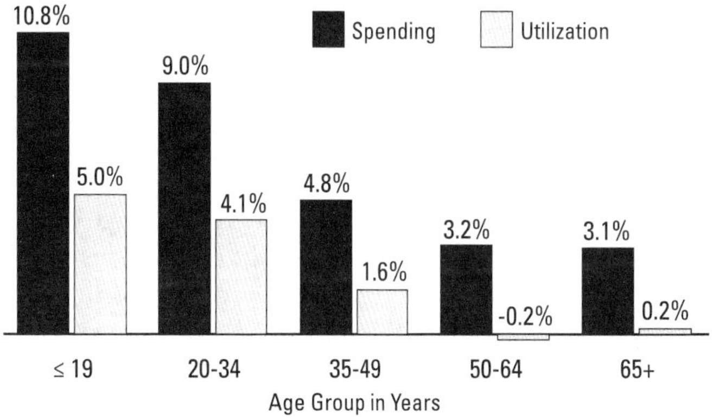

Source: *2010 Drug Trend Report,* Medco.

What Strategies Can Help Control Pharmacy Costs and Quality?

By working with a PBM and implementing a well-designed clinical program, it is possible to manage pharmacy benefit costs and maintain a quality pharmacy benefit plan. Exhibit 6 illustrates a proven three-pronged approach.

Exhibit 6

A Three-Pronged Approach to Controlling Prescription Drug Costs and Quality

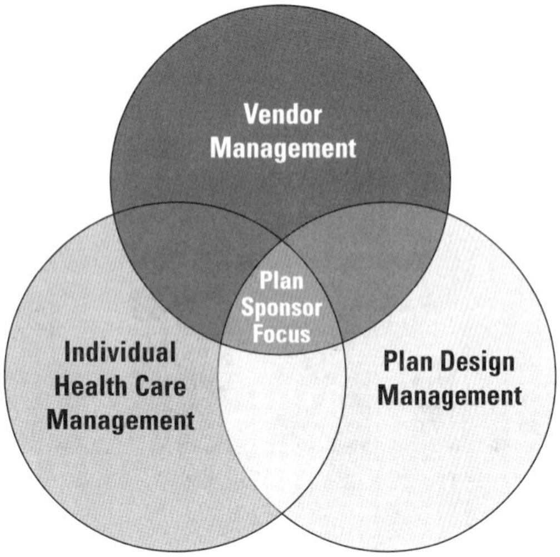

Source: The Segal Company.

A sensible place to begin is vendor management. Increased discounts and/or lower administrative fees may provide savings with no changes for participants. Potential actions in the other arenas—plan design and individual health care management—will vary with factors such as the benefit philosophy of trustees, the capabilities of a plan's PBM, acceptable member cost and the disruption to plan stakeholders caused by a change.

In this data-driven benefit environment, PBMs can quickly provide trustees with valuable information such as how many participants would be affected by a change in plan design or management. Trustees should work with their plan's PBM to estimate both the financial impact and potential disruption of any revisions to a prescription benefit program.

Vendor Management

Given the rapidly changing prescription drug and PBM market, trustees of health benefit plans must actively monitor and manage PBM performance. The data that supports plan design decisions can also be used by trustees to measure PBM performance and fine-tune a plan's relationship with a PBM. An independent audit of a PBM's financial performance is another valuable cost-control mechanism.

While most multiemployer health plans have done a commendable job seeking out PBM arrangements with advantageous financial terms and robust support services, it may be possible to cut costs even further. For example:

- **Closely inspect the PBM contracts.** Corporate data—available from consulting firms and independent studies that take into consideration factors such as number of plan participants, demographics and the mix of drugs being dispensed—should be used to assess contract terms.
- **Periodically subject PBMs to competitive bids.** In some studies, the financial terms with a PBM vary dramatically. The competitive bidding process often reveals wide discrepancies in fees for a similar scope of services. Opening contracts to other service providers has the potential to not only reduce program costs, but to also improve participant benefits and services.
- **Reduce drug cost expenses.** Corporate data provides insight into whether the contractual discounts and fees on medications are appropriate given program cost and utilization characteristics.
- **Cut administrative expenses.** Corporate data can be used as a guideline to determine whether administrative expenses represent an appropriate percentage of total program costs.
- **Require vendors to agree to performance guarantees.** The timeliness of payments, efforts to detect fraud and high-accuracy results, (e.g., claim dispensing and processing accuracy) are examples of performance guarantees. Trustees should insist on dollar-for-dollar reimbursement if a PBM does not attain what has been guaranteed. There should be no fixed dollar amount or "cap" on a PBM's liability. Of course, guarantees are of value only if there is monitoring to be sure that the contractual promises made are actually met.
- **Evaluate the results of PBM efforts to control costs and improve patient outcomes.** PBMs frequently offer clinical intervention programs (paid for by the plan and plan sponsors) to reduce costs and/or improve patient outcomes. For some programs, there is little evidence that program goals have been achieved. In fact, the result may actually be the promotion of alternative drug therapies that produce greater revenue for the PBM and increased plan costs.
- **Audit claims-processing results.** An audit of claims may uncover situations in which benefits were improperly paid due to a misinterpretation of plan rules. Audits provide an opportunity to rectify problems and administer the plan as trustees intended.
- **Review claims for potential fraud and abuse.** Periodic reviews of claims for appropriate utilization can also reduce plan costs and protect participants.

Plan Design Management

Plan design is probably the most effective way to control prescription benefit costs. Health and prescription drug plan sponsors have introduced a variety of design features to preserve valuable levels of coverage within plan cost constraints:

- **Generic alternatives.** For most of the 20th century, generic drugs were a very small share of the U.S. pharmaceuticals market. In recent years, less costly generic substitutes for brand-name medications have become increasingly available and a major reason that prescription drug spending did not increase even more. Expanded consumer acceptance of generics and the fact that a handful of blockbuster brand-name drugs are scheduled to lose patent protection relatively soon presents plans with opportunities for prescription drug savings.
- **Limits and exclusions.** As stated previously, not all medications are medical necessities. Some plans have chosen to exclude coverage for medications such as appetite suppressants, smoking-cessation drugs, fertility drugs, oral contraceptives, prescriptions used for cosmetic purposes and vitamins. An example of a limit increasingly being used by plans is establishing a maximum quantity of drugs that may be dispensed at one time. Restricting dispensing to a 30-day supply (versus a 90-day supply) for a new therapy reduces the likelihood the medication will be wasted if it is ineffective or the patient experiences a serious side effect.
- **Formularies.** Also known as a *preferred drug list,* a *formulary* is a list of drugs for which a plan will provide reimbursement. Formularies encourage clinically appropriate and cost-effective prescribing by physicians. A formulary provides a way for a plan to promote new medications that are truly an advance in treatment while discouraging expensive copycat versions of drugs that are equally safe and effective.
- **Cost sharing.** High deductibles, copays and coinsurance can deter plan participants from getting essential medications and adhering to their drug therapies—behaviors that can increase overall health care expenditures. The goal of cost sharing should be to encourage behavior that lowers overall health expenditures versus a simple shifting of costs to plan participants.
- **Cost-sharing differentials.** Different levels of cost sharing are often used to encourage participants to seek the most cost-effective course of treatment—for example, a lower copay for generic versus brand-name drugs provides a financial incentive for participants to choose the generic. Cost-sharing differences can also provide an incentive to use a less expensive mail-order or retail pharmacy. Lower out-of-pocket costs for select drug therapies (including treatments for asthma, diabetes and heart disease) have been found to increase patient adherence to drug therapy—a financial benefit for both plan participants and plan sponsors.
- **Program incentives.** Financial incentives are a useful tool for motivating participants to use programs created to complement drug treatment. For instance, participation in wellness programs such as weight loss or asthma, with appropriate incentives, may provide valuable member lifestyle changes.
- **Precertification.** A *precertification* or *prior authorization program* requires case-by-case approval of a drug therapy by a plan administrator or benefits manager before reimbursement for the prescription is allowed. Broad-based, nonspecific precertification rules that ultimately result in approval of all requests are a waste of time and money. To be effective, precertification rules should target treatments that (1) are expensive, (2) require monitoring to reduce potential side effects, (3) have the potential for abuse or (4) have limited effectiveness in certain situations. For instance, some participants improperly use narcotic painkillers—an indication of possible addiction. Requiring precertification for these specific medications can identify potential cases of abuse.
- **Step therapy.** As more medications move from a single source brand to generic—and even over the counter—plans are looking at step therapy as another means for cost savings. *Step therapy* allows a doctor to prescribe a more expensive drug only after another appropriate but less costly treatment has been tried with a patient.

Individual Health Care Management

As PBMs continue to evolve, distinct drug management strategies are emerging. These efforts increasingly focus on patient drug utilization and acquisition.

- **E-prescribing.** One of the newest tools for achieving cost-effectiveness is *electronic prescribing*—using technology to provide prescribers with clinical and cost information on treatment options. Access to this information makes it possible to better counsel patients and make optimal choices in terms of effectiveness, safety and cost.

- **Patient counseling.** The most frequented providers in the health care delivery chain are pharmacists. The face-to-face interaction pharmacists have is extremely useful for educating patients about their medical condition and associated drug therapy. An attentive pharmacist can also improve a patient's medication compliance—identifying and correcting counterproductive behaviors. All of these activities have the potential to improve the outcome of a drug therapy and reduce plan costs.
- **Medication therapy management.** Many patients are prescribed multiple medications by multiple physicians, with little or no oversight or coordination. Pharmacists are in a position to bring together physicians and help control plan costs. *Medication therapy management (MTM)* is a service in which a pharmacist evaluates all of a patient's medications (i.e., prescription, nonprescription, alternatives, nutritional supplements, etc.) to determine whether the drugs are appropriate given the patient's medical condition(s). Many of these programs focus on common diseases, such as diabetes, that typically involve patients taking three or more medications a month.
- **Utilization review.** *Drug utilization review (DUR)* monitors the use and improves the delivery of prescription medications. The most basic type of DUR is an audit that examines such concerns as the amount of a medication prescribed, whether the prescription is appropriate, the cost of the drug and adverse reactions. The review may examine this data for a particular drug or group of drugs, prescribing physicians or even individual patients. Potential problems are identified and recommendations made to the appropriate persons that can improve patient outcomes and lower costs. For example, prescribers identified as having high-cost prescription patterns might be contacted with information recommending lower cost but equally effective alternative drug therapies.
- **Mail order.** Handling prescriptions via mail can offer both consumer convenience and plan cost savings. Due to the largely automated nature of the dispensing process, pharmacists who work in a mail-order setting are more readily available to provide patient counseling via phone or e-mail.

Many of the emerging health care strategies give pharmacists a larger role as drug therapy counselors and managers. A targeted, well-designed, pharmacist intervention strategy can produce benefits for both participants and plan sponsors. Plan sponsors may see savings from:

- An appropriate decrease in the number of medications a patient takes
- The substitution of expensive brand-name medications with less expensive alternatives
- Changes in medications or doses for safety reasons
- The elimination of duplicate therapies
- The promotion of proper dispensing in accordance with national guidelines
- Increased patient adherence with prescribed therapies.

Trustees who want to increase pharmacist involvement in their health care plan's drug management should begin by obtaining prescription cost and utilization data for their plan. For most plans, the plan PBM will be able to provide this information. Once the data is obtained, costs and utilization can be summarized by dispensing pharmacy and medication categories. Reviewing this data, it is not uncommon to find most drug utilization and costs for a plan involve a handful of pharmacies or pharmacy chains. These pharmacies are a potential focus for management strategies. When considering which drugs to focus on, the best candidates are those prescribed for chronic conditions and used over long periods.

Conclusion

The difficult prescription benefit plan choices faced today are expected to continue for years to come. The good news is that while there are no silver bullets, many options are available that can yield more cost-effective approaches for quality participant health care. Trustees who want to rein in spending while preserving effective prescription coverage will want to consider taking steps in all three categories of cost management: vendor, plan design and individual health care. Before pursuing one or more of the strategies, trustees should gather data, understand the different programs and changes that are possible, and consider how the options match up with plan goals and objectives.

Chapter 20

Retiree Health (Postretirement) Benefits

Michael I. Helmer

This chapter examines the evolution of multiemployer retiree health benefits from their beginnings as relatively inexpensive components of benefit programs to their current status as significant financial concerns for most health and welfare plan sponsors. Possible plan design and funding strategies for postretirement health benefits are also explored, with an eye to managing related costs.

What Is the History of Retiree Health Benefits?

During the middle of the 20th century, employer-sponsored health care coverage gained popularity as a tool for attracting and retaining employees without significantly increasing payroll expense. The U.S. Congress enhanced the appeal of providing health care benefits by allowing employers to deduct health insurance expenses from their federal taxes.[1]

Medicare, the federally subsidized insurance program offered to older and disabled Americans, followed in 1965. During its infancy, Medicare covered most medical costs (with the exception of prescription drugs) of retirees from age 65 until their deaths. To promote themselves as providing retiree health coverage, employers needed only to bridge the period from retirement to Medicare eligibility at the age of 65. Many health plan sponsors added retiree benefits "because they needed them to make their retirement packages work, because they were attractive to labor in competitive labor markets and because the costs were rarely significant."[2]

The employer cost to provide coverage to a pre-Medicare retiree can be significantly higher than the employer cost for a Medicare-eligible retiree. The high cost exists because once a retiree reaches age 65, Medicare covers about 65% to 75% of the costs that the fund would incur without Medicare.

Funding

Historically, retiree health benefits were financed on a pay-as-you-go basis with these sources of funding:

- Employer contributions resulting from hours worked by active employees
- Contributions from retired participants
- Investment returns on fund assets.

For all practical purposes, a zero reserve exists for retiree health benefits funded in this manner. Alternatively, trustees may elect to earmark portions of a welfare fund's reserves to fulfill part or all of a plan's obligations for retiree health care. Where reserves exist, the amount can vary significantly. In some industries, a separate jointly managed fund exists only to provide postretirement medical benefits.

Legal Requirements

Qualified defined benefit (DB) pension plans must be funded during a plan participant's working years to ensure financial solvency. However, retiree health benefits are not subject to regulatory funding requirements. There is also no established legal requirement that welfare plans must be continued at their current level of benefits—or that they must be continued at all.[3]

Accounting Standards

In December 1990, the Financial Accounting Standards Board (FASB) issued Statement of Financial Accounting Standards No. 106 (FAS 106) concerning postretirement.[4] Simply put, FASB decided that employer accounts should recognize the cost of postretirement health benefits as the costs are accrued during employees' working careers, even if they are not funded that way.

Subsequently, the American Institute of Certified Pub-

Exhibit 1

Increases in Health Insurance Premiums Compared to Workers' Earnings

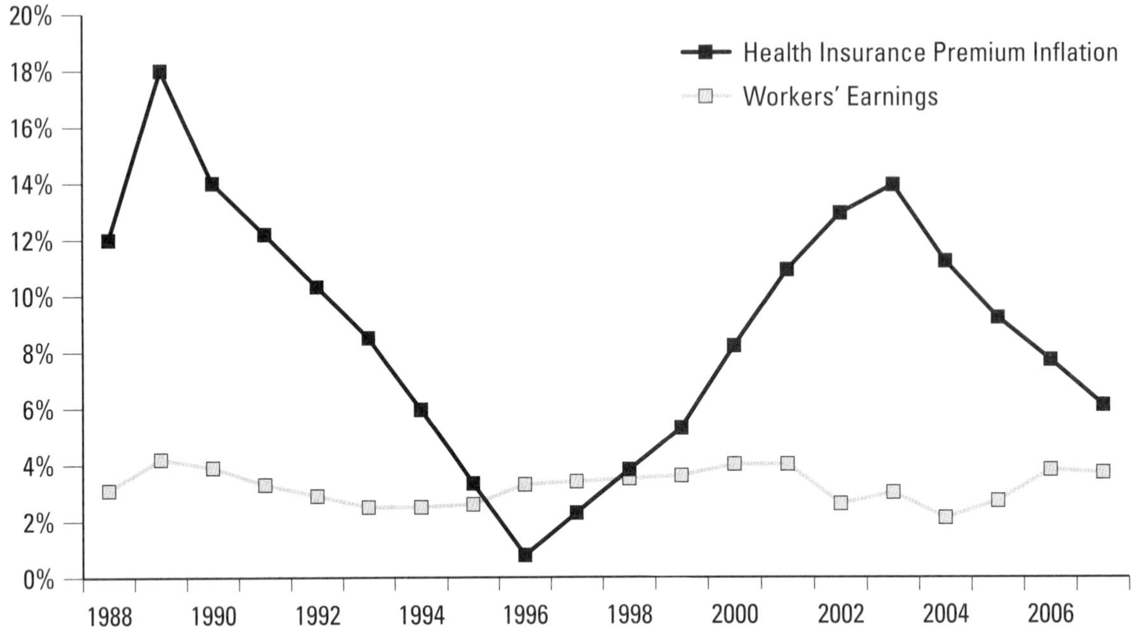

Sources: Kaiser Family Foundation. *Trends in Health Care Costs and Spending.* (September 2007). Kaiser/HRET. *Survey of Employer-Sponsored Health Benefits.* (1999-2007). KPMG *Survey of Employer-Sponsored Health Benefits.* (1993,1996). The Health Insurance Association of America (HIAA) (1988, 1989, 1990). Bureau of Labor Statistics. *Consumer Price Index, U.S. City Average of Annual Inflation (April to April).* (1988-2007). Bureau of Labor Statistics, *Seasonally Adjusted Data from the Current Employment Statistics Survey (April to April).* (1988-2007).

lic Accountants (AICPA) required welfare benefit plans (including multiemployer health and welfare funds) to disclose—but not to fund—the postretirement benefit obligation calculated in accordance with FAS 106.[5] The obligation is determined by an actuary who projects the sizes of specific active and retiree populations into the future and then assesses the value of the future cost of providing postretirement benefits in current dollars. The actuary achieves this by making assumptions regarding such future events as health care inflation, retirement, mortality and the utilization of health care at older ages.

Development of the Perfect Storm

During the mid-1990s, medical inflation rates fell to single digits as plan sponsors began addressing two key components of health care inflation: utilization and price. Utilization was reduced by implementing elements of managed care, such as preauthorization review, case management and gatekeeping practices (e.g., requiring a patient to get a referral from a primary physician before seeing a specialist). A discussion of these and other cost-management strategies is provided in Chapters 16 and 17. Price was reduced by leveraging participant volume to obtain pricing discounts. In addition, price was affected by prescription drug advances that helped prevent acute conditions requiring hospitalization and other expensive medical treatment. As illustrated in Exhibit 1, these strategies were effective for a short time only. In the early 2000s, health care inflation returned to double-digit rates.

A major contributor to high health care inflation is the increasing average age of the population. Typically, the older the population gets, the more health care services are required. By 2020, the number of individuals aged 55 to 65 is projected to increase by 75% and, by 2030, the number of those over age 65 is expected to double.[6]

With the retirement of the baby boom generation, there will be fewer active employees in the workforce to subsidize the health care costs of retirees. As the ratio of retirees to active workers increases, the cost burden per active worker increases. Consider a health benefits fund that currently has one retiree for every two active employees, with a retiree subsidy of 50¢ per hour. In five years, if the ratio increases to one retiree for every 1.5 actives, the hourly subsidy will have to increase from 50¢ to 67¢ per hour, even before health care inflation is taken into account. If health care inflation grows even modestly, at 8% per year over the same five-year period, the subsidy will need to nearly double from 50¢ to 98¢ per hour. These challenges are compounded during periods of difficult investment environments and reductions in employment levels.

What Options Are Available for Establishing a Reserve Fund?

Trustees who are committed to providing postretirement subsidies but are concerned about the impact of rising subsidies may establish a retiree-only reserve. This reserve could be within an existing fund or operate as a separate trust fund. The benefit of having the retiree-only reserve within an existing fund is that the reserve becomes a bookkeeping entry. Plan sponsors can use or borrow money from the reserve as they deem necessary to satisfy other health-related fund obligations. There is no real requirement that the spent money be replenished. A separate fund or postretirement benefit established as a voluntary employees' beneficiary association (VEBA) does not provide the same flexibility. With a VEBA, reserves are specifically earmarked within the health and welfare fund. On the other hand, a separate retiree health VEBA increases the likelihood that contributions are used specifically to provide postretirement health benefits.

When starting a retiree reserve, there is a "build-up period" during which annual contributions are made to the retiree reserve (in addition to general fund contributions). Upon an employee's retirement, there is a "pay-down period" when benefit payments are made from a combination of the retiree reserve and contributions by participants after their retirement.

When deciding how to design a reserve fund, there are many types of participant cost-sharing arrangements. Here are three general approaches to consider:

- **Standard retiree subsidy approach.** On an annual basis, the plan examines the cost of providing postretirement benefits and establishes the retiree contribution to achieve the desired subsidy level. This is by far the most common practice and is probably already understood by trustees.
- **Defined benefit (DB) approach.** This approach is similar to a DB pension plan. Retirees are given credits based on years of service and/or age. Credits are applied after retirement. For example, retirees could receive $10 per year of service or 2% of the expected cost per year of service.
- **Defined contribution (DC) approach.** Employer contributions are put in the individual accounts of active participants and grow with or without interest, depending on plan sponsor preference. At retirement, the value of the individual account can be used to defray the cost of postretirement health care coverage. Multiemployer plans typically apply the DC approach using health reimbursement accounts (HRAs). These are accounts established by an employer to pay for qualified health care expenses approved by trustees and defined in the plan's language. Trustees may set up "lock box" HRAs so that HRAs are restricted for use only at retirement. Trustees can also define how HRAs are forfeited or passed on to survivors.

For a look at the advantages and disadvantages of the DB and DC approaches, see Exhibit 2.

What Strategies Can Help Contain Retiree Health Plan Costs?

Until recently, participants who retired at age 55 with ten years of service received fully subsidized health benefits. Unlike pension plans, there was no adjustment for early retirement or number of years of service. This is now changing—workers who retire early or have less service, receive less than a full subsidy for their health benefits.

Recently, trustees have focused on the following key areas to provide a level of retiree health benefits consistent with available resources:

- **Eligibility.** Restricting eligibility holds down postretirement benefit costs and promotes longer active service along with the related contributions. One approach has been to increase the participant minimum age and/or service requirement for receiving postretirement benefits. An alternative solution has been to reduce the subsidy for early retirees who have fewer service credits. The subsidy reduction is usually implemented by increasing the self-pay requirement for these early retirees.
- **Coinsurance versus copays.** Under a copay structure, the entire impact of health care inflation is borne by the health benefit plan. As a result, many plans are shifting from copays to coinsurance which provides automatic participant cost-sharing adjustments. Assume that a $100 prescription has a $20 copay. The cost to the fund is $80 in a year. The next year, the cost of the same prescription increases by

Exhibit 2

Defined Benefit Versus Defined Contribution Retiree Health Plans

	Defined Benefit Approach	Defined Contribution Approach
Advantages	Ensures a specified level of benefits to retirees	Financing level established and maintained
	Allows for significant benefits to those nearing retirement	No actuarial valuation required
Disadvantages	Requires regular actuarial valuations	Participants approaching retirement may not be able to accrue a sufficient benefit.
	Welfare fund at risk for assets and demographics not meeting expectations	Level of postretirement subsidy is unknown before retirement.

15% to $115. If the copay remains the same, the cost to the fund will now be $95 ($115 cost with a $20 copay). This represents an 18.75% increase to the fund versus the 15% market price increase. If the plan uses coinsurance versus a copay, the increased cost to the fund is the same as the increase in the market price: 15%. The difference is made up with the automatic adjustment provided by having coinsurance.

- **Retiree contributions.** Plans are reviewing the methods currently used to establish the amount contributed by participants after retirement. Trustees can set contribution levels to help control active subsidy levels and reward participants with longer service. Retiree contributions can also be set to adjust for who is covered (e.g., retiree only, couple, family) and level of benefits (pre-age 65 versus post-age 65).
- **Coordination of benefits (COB) with Medicare.** Plans that offer medical benefits to retirees are reviewing how they coordinate with Medicare. Plans that self-fund their post-age-65 benefits are typically coordinated using one of these methods:
  - **Full coordination of benefits.** The plan pays the lesser of these two amounts: (1) what the plan would have paid in the absence of Medicare or (2) the remaining expenses after Medicare has paid its portion. This approach is the most generous to participants and the most expensive to a fund.
  - **Exclusion.** The balance of expenses after Medicare's payment are reviewed by the administrator and split between the participant and the plan according to the plan's deductible and coinsurance provisions. This approach shares the Medicare savings between the participant and the plan.
  - **Carve-out.** The plan reduces the amount it would have paid in the absence of the Medicare payment. This approach to coordinating benefits with Medicare is the least expensive for a plan.

Instead of self-funding the post-age-65 medical benefits, trustees may find financial opportunities to contract with Medicare Advantage or other fully insured Medicare supplemental products. Many of these programs include wellness programs (such as gym memberships, dieting and stop-smoking programs) as part of their premium package.

The Medicare Modernization Act (MMA) signed by President George W. Bush in 2003 created opportunities and incentives for plan sponsors that provide postretirement health benefits. The act offers direct cash reimbursement for a portion of the prescription drug costs incurred by plan sponsors for its Medicare-eligible retirees. This is provided the plan sponsor can show that the drug benefit design is at least as generous as Medicare's standard Part D coverage. This reimbursement is known as the retiree drug subsidy (RDS) program.

MMA also provides significant reimbursements to sponsors that provide prescription drug coverage beyond Medicare eligibility age. For these plan sponsors, it may be financially attractive to contract with or become a prescription drug plan (PDP) instead of self-funding prescription drugs for Medicare retirees. Reasons for considering a move away from self-funding to use of an insurance carrier are:

- Value is driven by competition among carriers to gain Medicare dominance.
- Carriers are able to spread risk and administrative

costs among a larger group of individuals.
- Plan sponsors can more easily and accurately budget for PDP insurance rates than they can for expected prescription drug claims minus the RDS reimbursement.
- Recent changes to the law will have the effect of giving preference to PDPs over the now more prevalent RDS programs.

Conclusion

With the aging workforce and baby boomer retirements, welfare fund trustees should take a hard look at their fund's postretirement benefit obligations. Trustees are encouraged to pay particular attention to whether providing postretirement health benefits will affect their fund's ability to provide a level of benefits that match participants' needs. Reviewing financial issues and demographics allow trustees to determine the funding and plan design strategies that will enable both short- and long-term success.

Endnotes

1. The federal government enhanced the attractiveness of providing health care benefits by passing legislation in 1954—Section 61(a) of the Internal Revenue Code—that made the costs associated with providing health insurance exempt from federal taxes.
2. G. Lawrence Atkins. "The Employer Role in Financing Health Care for Retirees," in Judith Mazo, Anna Rappaport and Sylvester Schieber, eds., *Providing Health Care Benefits in Retirement,* p. 108.
3. Although *UAW v. Yard-Man* extended the concept of "vested" benefits to certain retiree health benefits established through collective bargaining, thereby preventing their reduction by subsequent plan changes after the employee had retired, other circuit courts around the United States have been generally unreceptive to this position. Thomas H. Bergh, Varnum LLP, Attorneys at Law, "Appeals Court Limits Reach of 'Vesting' of Retiree Health and Welfare Benefits."
4. "Statement of Financial Accounting Standards No. 106," paragraph 4.
5. Statement of Position 92-6 (SOP 92-6) and FASB Accounting Standards Codification 965 (FASB ASC 965).
6. General Accounting Office (GAO)—01-374.

Chapter 21

Compliance With Federal Health Regulations

Kathryn Bakich

Federal statutes that affect multiemployer health plans are the focus of this chapter. All of the laws discussed apply to group health plans and health insurers. In general, there are no distinctions in compliance obligations for a self-financed versus a fully insured plan. Trustees should note that their plan as well as plan sponsors might be liable when a plan vendor (e.g., third-party administrator) fails to perform functions required by law.

After years of tackling compliance with the privacy and security requirements of the Health Insurance Portability and Accountability Act (HIPAA), plan sponsors must now broaden their attention to other health laws. The Employee Benefits Security Administration (EBSA) of the Department of Labor (DOL) has rekindled its enforcement efforts, auditing many group health plans for compliance with the following laws:

- HIPAA's portability and nondiscrimination requirements
- The Children's Health Insurance Program Reauthorization Act (CHIPRA)
- The Newborns' and Mothers' Health Protection Act (NMHPA)
- The Mental Health Parity and Addiction Equity Act (MHPAEA)
- The Women's Health and Cancer Rights Act (WHCRA)
- The Genetic Information Nondiscrimination Act (GINA)
- The notice provisions of the COBRA continuation coverage law.

A list of common violations and the consequences of noncompliance are near the end of this chapter.

What About State Regulations?

Each state has its own set of laws and regulations governing the provision of insured health benefits. Laws and regulations can vary substantially from one state to another. There are some insurance laws that mandate coverage of specific health benefits, generally known as *insurance mandates.* Insurance mandates are found in nearly every state. For example, regulations regarding mammograms and the length of maternity stays exist in almost all 50 states. Forty-eight states have mental health parity mandates in addition to the federal mandate. Forty-five states require the provision of diabetic supplies.

Some mandates require coverage of specific types of health care providers or persons related to a participant. Forty-five states require coverage for health care provided by chiropractors, while 12 states require coverage of services provided by an acupuncturist. States also often require coverage of certain dependents. Instances where states require specific persons to be covered by a plan include disabled dependent adults (42 states), domestic partners or civil unions (18 states) and grandchildren (9 states).[1] The Council for Affordable Health Insurance (www.cahi.org) annually publishes a report summarizing these mandates.

Although state insurance laws are preempted by ERISA for self-financed group health plans, plan sponsors of such plans often look to the laws for information about what coverage is available under insured plans in particular states.

Although the Department of Labor (DOL) is generally responsible for auditing multiemployer plans, regulations are issued jointly by three departments: (DOL) through the Employee Benefits Security Administration (EBSA)); the Treasury Department (and the Internal Revenue Service (IRS)); and the Department of Health and Human Services (HHS) (as well as its agency, the Centers for Medicare and Medicaid Services (CMS)).

* * *

Most of the laws discussed in this chapter contain a delayed effective date for collectively bargained plans: The law does not apply until the first plan year after the expiration of the collective bargaining agreement in existence when the law was passed. While most plans complied with HIPAA as this book was written, many plans were not yet in compliance with MHPAEA because they were still in the collective bargaining delay period.

The Consolidated Omnibus Budget Reconciliation Act of 1985 (COBRA) Continuation-of-Coverage Rules

COBRA contains the law requiring employers to provide continued health care coverage to individuals who lose their health care coverage because of certain circumstances. Due to space constraints, this chapter highlights COBRA requirements, including the notification obligations that DOL typically examines during an audit. Typically, plans that have good notice procedures have fewer participant lawsuits claiming violations of COBRA.

Exhibit 1 summarizes who is entitled under COBRA to continuation of health plan coverage (the *qualified beneficiary*), when (the *qualifying event*) and for how long. A qualifying event occurs only if health care coverage is lost. To *lose coverage* means a covered employee, spouse or dependent is no longer covered under the terms and conditions in effect immediately prior to the qualifying event. The law defines loss of coverage also to include an increase in the premium or contribution that a beneficiary must pay for plan coverage.

COBRA limits the period of continuation coverage to a maximum period of 18, 29 or 36 months, depending on which qualifying event triggered application of the law. This period generally begins at the time the qualifying event occurs. The 18-month period of COBRA continuation coverage may be extended for up to 11 months under certain circumstances for disabled individuals. All maximum periods may be cut short for specific reasons.

Notice Requirements

When an employee is initially covered by a group health plan, COBRA requires the employee and his or her spouse be given a written notice advising them of their rights under COBRA. For example, this notice must describe the circumstances under which an employee who declines cov-

Exhibit 1

COBRA Continuation Coverage

	Qualified Beneficiary		
	Employee	Spouse	Dependent Child
Qualifying Event	Length of Continued Coverage		
Employee terminated (for other than gross misconduct).	18 months	18 months	18 months
Employee workhours reduced (making employee ineligible for the same coverage under the terms of the plan).	18 months	18 months	18 months
Employee dies.	N/A	36 months	36 months
Employee becomes divorced or legally separated.	N/A	36 months	36 months
Employee becomes entitled to Medicare.	N/A	36 months	36 months
Dependent child ceases to have dependent status.	N/A	N/A	36 months

Source: The Segal Company.

erage may later enroll himself or herself or family members. It must also inform them of their rights to continue coverage for a limited time under COBRA when a qualifying event occurs. The notice may be provided in the summary plan description (SPD). Other notice requirements apply when an individual becomes entitled to elect COBRA coverage or COBRA coverage is denied.

Substantial penalties (as much as $100 a day for each day a notice is not given to an individual with family coverage) can be imposed for a delay in giving the initial COBRA notice to new employees and their spouses.

Temporary COBRA Subsidy

When persons lose their jobs, they are often unable to afford to take advantage of their right to continue health coverage under COBRA because of the expense. President Obama signed the American Recovery and Reinvestment Act of 2009 (ARRA) on February 17, 2009 to provide a temporary subsidy to help the unemployed with COBRA premiums. The subsidy covered 65% of the COBRA premium charged to the former employee. Although the subsidy program was extended several times, the program is largely over as of this writing.

Health Insurance Portability and Accountability Act of 1996 (HIPAA)

HIPAA Portability Rules

When Congress passed HIPAA in 1996, a major objective was to improve access to health insurance when employees changed jobs. The HIPAA portability rules:

- **Limit preexisting condition exclusions.** If an individual receives medical advice, diagnosis, care or treatment for a condition in the six months prior to enrollment in a new group plan, the plan may not exclude this *preexisting condition* from coverage for more than 12 months after the individual's enrollment date. This 12-month exclusion period must be reduced by any *creditable coverage* the individual had under a previous health plan unless the person had a break in coverage of 63 days or more. Enrollment under most health benefit programs is considered creditable coverage; this includes single employer and multiemployer group health plans, individual health insurance policies, Medicare, Medicaid, state and local governmental programs, etc. See the online chapter at www.ifebp.org/Handbook7 concerning the Patient Protection and Affordable Care Act

Tip for Trustees

No matter what question arises regarding COBRA, it is always best to keep the following basic principles in mind:

- COBRA participants must be given the same coverage and rights that are available to similarly situated non-COBRA beneficiaries. In almost every situation, this means that what is done for a similar but active employee (or family dependent) must be done for the COBRA participant.
- COBRA requires continuation of coverage. Generally, plan coverage and all rights under a plan must be continued without interruption from the date of the qualifying event that caused coverage to end until the end of the COBRA continuation period. Only one thing changes; the qualified beneficiary may be required to pay the *applicable premium*, which is the full cost of the coverage plus a limited surcharge.

There is more to a health care plan than the schedule of health care benefits. Plans often provide rights that go beyond specific benefits for health care expenses. Whenever these or any other additional rights exist, they too are subject to COBRA's requirements. Some common examples of these rights are:

- **Covering newly acquired dependents.** Most plans allow employees to add newly acquired spouses and children to their coverage. Indeed, under HIPAA, such plans are required to allow employees of such plans to add dependents acquired through marriage, birth or adoption.
- **Allowing special enrollment under HIPAA.** In addition to adding newly acquired dependents, a COBRA participant must be allowed to enroll dependents who lose their other health care coverage if they would be entitled to special enrollment under HIPAA.
- **Disability extension of benefits.** Many plans provide an extension of benefits if coverage ends while a covered person is totally disabled or hospitalized or in the course of active treatment for a particular medical or dental problem.
- **Conversion.** Practically all insured medical benefit plans provide a right to convert the plan to a personal medical expense policy when coverage ends.

of 2010 as amended (ACA) for a discussion of how preexisting conditions are eliminated by the act, first for children and in 2014 for adults.

- **Provide special enrollment rights.** Under certain circumstances, persons are allowed to enroll for health coverage without having to wait for late or open enrollment:
  - An employee may enroll if he or she loses eligibility for other health coverage, gets married or adds a new dependent through birth or adoption.
  - Employees may also enroll if employer contributions toward other coverage terminate.
  - A spouse or dependent of the employee may enroll if the dependent reaches a lifetime limit on all benefits under the dependent's plan. ACA eliminated lifetime limits on benefits for plan years beginning on or after September 23, 2010.
- **Require a notice of special rights.** Group health plans must provide all employees—both those who enroll in a plan and those who do not—with a notice describing their special enrollment rights before or at the time an employee can first enroll in the plan. The final rules for this legislation contain model language for the notice that should be included in an employee's enrollment materials.
- **Require a notice of creditable coverage.** When an individual loses coverage under a plan, becomes entitled to elect COBRA continuation coverage or exhausts COBRA continuation coverage, his or her plan must automatically provide a notice that states how long the person and any dependents were covered by the plan. This notice offsets a new plan's preexisting condition exclusion limitation as described previously. A certificate of creditable coverage must meet specific content requirements; using the model certificate provided in the final regulation ensures these rules are met. An individual may also request a certificate within 24 months after losing plan or COBRA coverage.
- **Require written request procedures.** HIPAA rules also require plans to have a written procedure for individuals to request and receive certificates of creditable coverage. The certificate must be provided free of charge upon request when a person has health coverage or any time within 24 months after coverage ends.

Tip for Trustees

To help plans comply with federal health benefit laws that it enforces, DOL has issued a *Compliance Assistance Guide* (www.dol.gov/ebsa/pdf/CAG.pdf), extensive fact sheets and *Frequently Asked Questions*. These materials and others are available online at www.dol.gov/ebsa/compliance_assistance.html. Use these materials to check whether your plan is in compliance. Most violations are addressed by simply amending or eliminating certain plan provisions and making sure certain notices are provided. Many of the model notices discussed in this chapter are also provided.

Instead of meeting all of the HIPAA rules concerning preexisting condition exclusions, many group health plans eliminated these exclusions years ago. However, certain provisions will be considered exclusions if the availability of benefits is determined by when a medical condition arose compared to the effective date of coverage under the plan. Plans are not prohibited from having these so-called hidden preexisting condition exclusions, but these exclusions must meet all HIPAA regulations. For example, HIPAA allows exclusions to apply only on conditions treated within the first six months of the enrollment date.

Hidden preexisting condition exclusions which must be either removed or changed to be treated as if they are preexisting condition exclusions that comply with HIPAA include the following:

- A lifetime limit on coverage for the treatment of diabetes for those diagnosed with diabetes before the effective date of coverage under a plan
- Coverage for an accidental injury only if the injury occurred while covered under the plan
- Excluding benefits for a congenital condition (such as a congenital heart problem) when the plan otherwise provides benefits for the condition when it is not congenital.

Exceptions. Certain types of plans are "excepted" from HIPAA's portability requirements. These exceptions are particularly important, because these same plans are also not required to comply with the health plan mandates of ACA. Excepted plans are:

- **Plans with fewer than two current employees as participants.** Thus, retiree-only plans probably do not have to comply with HIPAA portability.
- **Limited scope dental and vision benefits.** HIPAA portability does not apply to dental and vision benefits if (1) the benefits are provided under a separate policy, certificate or contract of insurance; or (2) participants have both the right not to elect coverage for the benefit and must pay an additional premium or contribution for the coverage.

- **Health flexible spending arrangements (FSAs).** Generally, health FSAs are not subject to HIPAA portability rules. A special regulation provides that portability does not apply if a plan (1) makes other benefits not excepted by HIPAA available to participants and (2) the maximum benefits payable to the participant under the FSA do not exceed two times the participant's salary reduction election (or, if greater, does not exceed $500 plus the amount of the participant's salary reduction). Multiemployer plans do not generally have an FSA, because it generally involves a Section 125 cafeteria plan and salary reduction contributions.
- **Insurance provided under a separate policy, certificate or contract of insurance that supplements group health coverage.** Supplemental insurance includes insured Medigap policies. However, self-insured plans that are secondary or supplemental to Medicare under coordination-of-benefits provisions are not excepted benefits. This generally means that group health plans covering both actives and retirees that limit coverage for retirees to coverage that supplements Medicare benefits do not meet the requirements of this exception and must comply with the HIPAA portability requirements.

HIPAA Nondiscrimination Rules

HIPAA prohibits discrimination in enrollment and in premium contributions based on a health status factor. Basically, this means that a group health plan cannot treat people differently based on their health status, receipt of health care or submission of claims. Plans cannot exclude individuals from coverage due to their health problems (ever) or charge these persons more than other enrollees (with one exception). The one exception is that HIPAA allows plans to provide premium discounts, rebates and cost-sharing modifications as part of a wellness program that meets the HIPAA wellness rules. The narrow exception allows plans to reward healthy people while less healthy people are treated less favorably. Two types of wellness programs are allowed:

- **Group 1** programs (1) do not require individuals to meet health-related standards to obtain a reward or (2) have no reward.
- **Group II** programs require individuals to meet health-related standards to obtain a reward.

Because Group II programs link rewards to health-related standards, these programs have to meet five additional rules. Exhibit 2 offers examples for the two types of programs as provided by the wellness rules and from

Exhibit 2

Programs Allowed Under HIPAA Wellness Rules

Group I—Automatically Allowed

- Reimburse cost of fitness center or gym
- Reward for participation in screening/testing programs—not for test outcome
- Waive cost sharing for prenatal care or well-baby visits
- Waive cost sharing for diabetics who enroll in a disease-management program that consists of attending educational classes and following doctor's recommendations on exercise and medication
- Reimburse cost of smoking-cessation aids without regard to whether the person quits smoking
- Reward for attending health education seminars
- Reward for completing a Health Risk Assessment (HRA) questionnaire—with the actual answers not used to provide rewards

Group II—Must Comply With Extra Rules

- Reward for achieving or having a certain health outcome such as certain cholesterol level, weight or body mass index (BMI)
- Premium discount for stopping smoking or being a nonsmoker
- Rebate for exercising a certain amount
- Reward for diabetics who meet certain standards (e.g., maintain certain BMI) while participating in a disease management program
- Reward based on the information provided in answers to questions on an HRA

These programs must:

- Limit reward to 20% of total cost of health plan coverage (subject to increases under ACA)
- Be reasonably designed to promote health
- Allow enrollment at least once per year
- Provide a reasonable alternative for people who cannot meet (or attempt to meet) the objective due to a medical condition
- Disclose alternatives in program materials

DOL's Wellness Program Checklist (www.dol.gov/ebsa/regs/fab2008-2.html). The exhibit also lists the five rules that apply to Group II programs.

ACA puts the HIPAA wellness regulations into federal statute and makes one significant change. Effective in 2014, plans are permitted to increase the reward from 20% to 30% of the total cost of health plan coverage. ACA also authorizes the federal departments implementing HIPAA (referred to as the *HIPAA agencies*) to increase the reward to up to 50% if they deem it appropriate. As under the HIPAA regulations, the total cost of coverage is based on employer and employee contributions for employee-only coverage. If dependents participate in the wellness program, the total cost of coverage is based on the total cost of coverage of these same dependents.

HIPAA agencies have stated that before 2014, they intend to use their existing pre-ACA regulatory authority to propose an increase in the total reward to 30%.[2] The FAQs note that these regulations will include consumer protections to prevent wellness programs from being used as a subterfuge for health status discrimination. The FAQs also state that more guidance is expected. At the time this chapter was written, this additional guidance had not yet been released.

HIPAA Privacy and Security Rules

In addition to the portability and discrimination rules, HIPAA also requires that group health plans transmit electronic data related to claims payment and eligibility using a standard format set by industry and adopted by regulations issued from the Department of Health and Human Services (HHS). To facilitate these electronic transactions, plans are required to keep individually identifiable health information (including demographic information) private and secure. HHS has issued extensive procedures for organizations to safeguard and internally police the use and disclosure of private health information. The privacy rules apply to all ERISA-governed health plans. HIPAA:

- Allows plans to use *private health information (PHI)* without written authorization from an individual for plan administration purposes—this includes claims payment, treatment, utilization review, case management, audit and other health care operations. However, plans must make all reasonable efforts to use the minimum amount of information necessary to accomplish these functions.
- Permits plans to use and disclose PHI without written authorization in other limited circumstances that include but are not limited to public health activities, health oversight activities, certain judicial and law enforcement purposes, research, emergencies, disclosure to next of kin, other specialized uses (such as for military purposes) as well as other uses or disclosures required by law. The plan must obtain a written authorization from the individual for other uses or disclosures of PHI not addressed in the privacy rules.
- Prohibits plans from giving PHI to a business associate (e.g., an administrator, lawyer or consultant) unless there is a contract between the health plan and the associate establishing how the associate can use and disclose PHI.
- Requires plans to provide individuals a notice that tells how the plan will use the their medical information.
- Requires plans to have written privacy policies and procedures and to train plan employees on these policies and procedures. Plans must designate a privacy official to be responsible for developing and implementing the policies.
- Gives individuals the right to inspect, get copies of and propose corrections to medical records.

The HIPAA security rules are intended to ensure the confidentiality, integrity and availability of *electronic protected health information (ePHI)*—individually identifiable health information that is created, transmitted or maintained electronically. Such information must be protected from reasonably anticipated threats, improper use and disclosure. Exhibit 3 briefly summarizes the HIPAA security standards and implementation specification(s). The matrix also denotes whether the implementation is *required* (as indicated by the letter R in the second column) or *addressable* (indicated in the same column by the letter A).

Security Breach Notification

One of the most significant revisions to HIPAA privacy and security rules has been a breach notification requirement that applies to HIPAA-covered entities and their business associates. Fulfilling a mandate of the Health Information Technology for Economic and Clinical Health Act (HITECH), HHS released interim final regulations for breach notification that took effect on September 23, 2009.

As HIPAA-covered entities, multiemployer health plans must notify individuals when there is a breach of *unsecured* PHI (as defined by HHS) that affects the individual. This breach of notice rule applies to all types of PHI—information that is written and spoken, as well as ePHI that is in an electronic format. Plans must provide notice to each affected individual without *unreasonable delay.* In no case can notice be more than 60 days after a breach is discovered.

Exhibit 3

HIPAA Security Standards and Implementation Specification(s)

	Standards (in Bold) and Implementation Specification(s)	*	Brief Explanation
Administrative Safeguards	**Security Management Process** • Risk analysis • Risk management • Sanction policy • Information system activity review	 R R R R	One of the most important elements of the security rules is the required risk analysis. Security risk management involves, among other things, the implementation of measures to eliminate or reduce the risks and vulnerabilities identified by the risk analysis. The sanction policy should apply to all personnel who have access to ePHI. An information system activity review entails regular review of all nonsoftware systems logs (e.g., audit logs, access card reader reports and security incident tracking reports).
	Assigned Security Responsibility	R	A person must be delegated to be the security officer. This can be the same person assigned as the HIPAA privacy officer.
	Workforce Security • Authorization and/or supervision • Workforce clearance procedure • Termination procedures	 A A A	Policies and procedures must be put in place to ensure that only authorized members of the workforce have access to ePHI.
	Information Access Management • Access authorization • Access establishment and modification	 A A	Policies and procedures should be in place for granting access to ePHI (e.g., through a particular workstation or software program) and for documenting, reviewing and modifying a user's right of access.
	Security Awareness and Training • Security reminders • Protection from malicious software • Log-in monitoring • Password management	 A A A A	Security and awareness training is required, however, plans do not need to conduct this training themselves.
	Security Incident Procedures • Response and reporting	 R	Formal, documented report and response procedures must be implemented so that security incidents are reported and handled promptly.
	Contingency Plan • Data backup plan • Disaster recovery plan • Emergency mode operation plan • Testing and revision procedures • Applications and data criticality analysis	 R R R A A	Formal procedures must be established and documented for backing up and retrieving data. A disaster recovery plan with procedures for restoring any loss of data is also required. The emergency operation plan must describe how the plan will keep critical business processes operational in the event of a disaster or emergency. To develop a contingency plan, a method for identifying critical data and systems applications is needed.
	Evaluation of Security Policies • Periodic technical and nontechnical evaluation	 R	Evaluations must be undertaken in response to environmental and operational changes that could compromise ePHI security (e.g., allowing personnel to access the plan network from home with a remote connection for the first time or the addition of a health benefits software system).
	Business Associate Contracts and Other Arrangements • Written contract or other arrangement	 R	Business associates may receive, use or transmit ePHI only after providing satisfactory assurances they will appropriately safeguard the data.

* This column indicates whether each standard or implementation specification is required (R) or addressable (A).

HIPAA Security Standards and Implementation Specification(s) *(continued)*

	Standards (in Bold) and Implementation Specification(s)	*	Brief Explanation
Technical Safeguards	**Access Controls** • Unique user identification • Emergency access procedure • Automatic log-off • Encryption and decryption	 R R A A	A unique user identification must be created for each person who has access to plan software systems that store or transmit ePHI. An emergency access process is required that documents all possible means by which personnel can access software systems containing ePHI if business as usual is interrupted. An automatic log-off terminates an electronic session after a predetermined amount of inactivity. Encryption and decryption are mechanisms to prevent unauthorized access to ePHI.
Technical Safeguards	**Audit Controls**	R	Procedures are required for recording and examining information systems that contain or use ePHI. For example, a procedure might call for review, every two months, of the log showing who has logged onto the network or has attempted to log into the primary software used for managing the participant data.
Technical Safeguards	**Integrity** • Mechanism to authenticate ePHI	 A	Mechanisms must be in place that ensure ePHI has not been improperly altered or destroyed. This standard may be met with error-correcting memory and magnetic disk storage, mechanisms found in most benefit office hardware and operating systems.
Technical Safeguards	**Person or Entity Authentication**	R	Procedures must be implemented to verify the identity of anyone seeking access to ePHI.
Technical Safeguards	**Transmission Security** • Integrity controls • Encryption	 A A	Steps are needed to ensure data confidentiality and *integrity* (i.e., data is not altered or destroyed) while ePHI is being transmitted over an electronic network. Some form of encryption is encouraged, especially for transmission over the Internet.
Physical Safeguards	**Facility Access Controls** • Contingency operations • Facility security plan • Access control and validation procedures • Maintenance records	 A A A A	The security of office premises includes ensuring that only properly authorized access is permitted. Security must be maintained during an emergency, when staff may need to restore lost data or continue critical operations. Repairs or modifications to physical structures (e.g., changing locks) can have security implications.
Physical Safeguards	**Workstation Use**	R	All workstations used to store, work with and/or transmit ePHI must be protected by a proper use policy that covers the proper functions to be performed on the workstation (e.g., it may only be used to view and update member eligibility), the manner in which those functions are to be performed (e.g., accessing data with a unique password) and the attributes of the physical surroundings of a specific workstation (e.g., monitors may only be viewed by benefits office personnel).
Physical Safeguards	**Workstation Security**	R	Access to all workstations used to store, work with and/or transmit ePHI must be restricted to authorized users only. If a secure separate and lockable room is unavailable, workstations may be grouped behind partitions at one end of a room in the benefits office.
Physical Safeguards	**Device and Media Controls** • Disposal • Media reuse • Accountability • Data backup and storage	 R R A A	Policies and procedures must be implemented that manage the receipt and removal of hardware and electronic media containing ePHI into and out of a facility, as well as the movement of these items within the facility. The disposal and reuse of disks, old workstations, magnetic tapes and any other media containing ePHI must be documented.

* This column indicates whether each standard or implementation specification is required (R) or addressable (A).

If a breach involves 500 or more individuals, HHS must be given notice at the same time individuals are notified. When a breach involves fewer than 500 persons, HHS can be notified annually. In some cases, prominent media outlets must also be notified. The rule sets forth standards for the notice; these include the notice being written in plain language. If a business associate is responsible for the breach, the business associate must notify the plan and provide the information the plan needs to provide the required notice.

The HITECH security breach rule only applies to *unsecured PHI*—protected health information that has not been secured through the use of a technology or methodology specified by HHS. In April 2009, HHS released a safe harbor rule stating that encryption and destruction are the only two ways to secure PHI and thus avoid breach notification under the act.

The HITECH regulations provide the following guidance concerning a breach and notification of a breach:

- **Use or disclosure must violate privacy rule.** There is no breach unless the unauthorized use or disclosure of PHI violates the HIPAA privacy rules. A use or disclosure that involves more than the minimum necessary PHI may qualify as a breach requiring notification.
- **Risk-of-harm threshold.** Notification is not required unless the unauthorized use or disclosure of PHI poses a "significant risk of financial, reputational or other harm to the individual." The plan or business associate must assess and document the level of harm to consider whether notification is required. Factors to consider in the assessment are:
  - The type and amount of PHI involved—for example, names alone would not be as sensitive as names and Social Security numbers.
  - The level of risk—in an example, HHS indicates that a list of names of people who received services from a general hospital poses less of a risk than a list of people treated at a substance abuse facility.
  - The identity of the unauthorized person who used the PHI or to whom the PHI was disclosed
  - Whether the disclosure was to another covered entity (e.g., plan, service provider) with its own legal obligation to protect the PHI—this would pose less risk than disclosure to an entity without such a duty.
  - Whether immediate steps have been taken to limit harm
  - Whether the PHI is returned prior to being accessed for an improper purpose.

Tip for Trustees

As of this writing, HHS has stated it is reconsidering some of the issues in the HITECH regulations. Check with your plan's legal counsel to see if there have been changes since publication of this handbook.

- **Concrete examples of breach exceptions.** HITECH includes exceptions for certain unintentional actions and situations where the unauthorized recipient could not reasonably have been able to access the PHI. Consider an employee acting in good faith who opens an e-mail sent by mistake by another employee. There is no breach if the recipient alerts the sender of the misdirected message, deletes the e-mail and makes no further use of the information. In another scenario, a health plan mails an Explanation of Benefits (EOB) form to the wrong person and the letter is returned unopened by the post office. This is not treated as a breach. On the other hand, if a plan knows an EOB was sent to the wrong person and it was not returned as undeliverable, this situation should be treated as a potential breach.
- **Flexibility in dealing with business associates.** While business associates are required to notify a covered entity of any breach, covered entities and their business associates may still allot duties in their business associate contract. As an example, a plan might require a vendor to provide notices and clarify the circumstances in which the vendor must take responsibility for a breach.
- **Policies and procedures.** Plans must develop written policies and procedures on breach notification and train their workforce members on those rules.

The Mental Health Parity and Addiction Equity Act of 2008

The original Mental Health Parity Act (MHPA), effective in 1998, required people with mental health conditions (e.g., depression and bipolar disorder) to be provided mental health benefits similar to those with physical medical conditions. The law prohibited annual or lifetime dollar limits on mental health benefits that are different from those for medical/surgical benefits. Plan sponsors could and did introduce plan designs that limited the scope and duration of covered treatment for mental health benefits. MHPAEA, the 2008 amendments to MHPA, provides broader protection by prohibiting unequal treatment limits and financial requirements, such as cost sharing. The amendments also expand the scope of protection to include benefits for addiction treatment.

It is important to note that like the original legislation, the new federal legislation does *not* require group health plans to provide mental health or addiction benefits or to cover any specific conditions or treatments. However, if a plan does cover mental health or substance use disorder benefits, plans must provide for parity in the following areas according to the MHPAEA regulations:

- **Parity in Financial Requirements and Quantitative Treatment Limit.** Plans may not impose financial requirements such as cost sharing or place limits on the number of treatments for mental health or substance abuse disorders that are more restrictive than those for all or substantially all medical/surgical benefits. In addition, plans cannot have cumulative financial requirements or treatment limits. This means plans cannot have deductibles, out-of-pocket maximums or day/visit limits that accumulate separately for medical and mental health/substance use disorders.
- **Parity in Nonquantitative Treatment Limits.** The regulations also prohibit disparities in the limits on the scope or duration of treatment under the plan. This prohibition applies to medical management tools such as prior authorization, the use of an employee assistance plan as a gatekeeper to care, step therapy, standards for provider admission to participate in a network (including reimbursement rates) and plan methods for determining allowable charges. The standards must be comparable and not more stringent than those used for medical benefits. Differences are allowed only where recognized clinically appropriate standards of care permit a difference.

Tip for Trustees

In addition to the federal laws concerning mental health, many states have passed laws that require fully insured plans to provide a minimal level of coverage for mental health and substance abuse treatment. When preparing plan documents for fully insured plans, it may be helpful to review applicable state insurance law for mental health benefits. In addition, insured plans need to identify any state rules concerning newborns' and mothers' rights to stay in the hospital for specific time periods.

The MHPAEA regulations require parity in aggregate dollar limits and require plans to provide specific plan disclosures upon request. The regulations also require that any definitions of what is medical versus mental health/substance use disorder benefits be consistent with generally accepted recognized independent standards of current medical practice.

The Newborns' and Mothers' Health Protection Act of 1996

NMHPA prohibits group health plans from restricting hospital stays in connection with childbirth to less than 48 hours following a vaginal delivery or 96 hours following a cesarean delivery. After consulting with the mother, the attending provider may discharge the mother and/or her newborn child earlier. Plans may not offer incentives to mothers to accept a shorter hospital stay. Plans that provide maternity or newborn infant coverage must advise individuals of their rights under the law in the summary plan description.

Many states have enacted laws preventing discharge before a certain stay after birth. In states with these laws, plans with insured coverage must notify individuals of both their state and federal rights.

The Women's Health and Cancer Rights Act of 1998

President Clinton signed WHCRA on October 21, 1998 as part of the massive Omnibus Appropriations Bill (H.R. 4328). The law requires plans that provide medical and surgical benefits for mastectomies to cover reconstructive surgery, as requested by the patient in consultation with her physician. Plans cannot circumvent the law by denying eligibility, penalizing providers or providing incentives to induce providers to give care in a manner inconsistent with the law.

When a person enrolls in a health plan, this legislation requires a plan to issue a detailed notice describing the benefits required under the law. Another notice must be furnished annually. DOL guidance clarifies several issues about the annual notice and provides model language. For example, the guidance states the annual notice:

- May be issued at any time during the plan year
- May be sent by itself or included in any of the following documents: the SPD; a summary of material modifications; a summary annual report; a union newsletter (or a benefits newsletter); open enrollment materials; or any other written communication by the plan.

- Does not have to contain the same information or detail as the notice provided to participants at enrollment (and that should be included in the SPD). The annual notice must simply describe the availability of benefits for the treatment of mastectomy-related services including reconstructive surgery and surgery to achieve symmetry between the breasts, prostheses and treatment of complications from a mastectomy (including lymphedema), and provide information on how to obtain a detailed description of these benefits.

The Children's Health Insurance Program Reauthorization Act of 2009

CHIPRA was enacted in February 2009. Many states offer premium-assistance programs as part of their Medicaid and/or Children's Health Insurance Program (CHIP). Under these programs, states can pay the employee share of the premium for certain group health plan coverage for low-income children (and, in some cases, coverage for the parent and other family members as well). Some programs also assist with cost-sharing and other out-of-pocket expenses, and provide benefits supplementing the coverage provided by the group plan. Forty states offer some type of premium-assistance program at this time; generally, only children in low-income families are eligible for premium assistance.

CHIPRA has several requirements applicable to group health plans:

- Plans must allow the enrollment of individuals who become eligible for a premium-assistance program or who lose eligibility for CHIP or Medicaid.
- When requested, plans must share specific information with state agencies to promote coordination of benefits with state premium-assistance programs.
- Employers that provide health benefits must notify individuals about the premium-assistance programs available in their state. DOL has issued a three-page model notice for this requirement that provides contact information for each of the 40 states offering premium assistance, as well as contact information for DOL and HHS.

CHIPRA expressly requires "employers" to provide the notice. It is unclear who has the obligation to provide the notice in a situation involving a multiemployer plan and its contributing employers. Multiemployer plans may elect to send the notice because they are the most efficient way to inform participants about the availability of public health benefits. Plans may also be the most appropriate resource to answer participant questions or to provide referrals to an appropriate public resource.

Every employee who resides in a state offering assistance must receive a notice, regardless of whether the employee is enrolled in the employer's group health plan. Employers may choose to send the model notice to every employee or may distinguish between employees based on their state of residence. The same is true for multiemployer plans that choose to send these notices.

The Genetic Information Nondiscrimination Act of 2008

On May 21, 2008, President Bush signed GINA into law. Modeled on HIPAA, Title I of GINA regulates group health plans and health insurance issuers (i.e., state-licensed entities in the business of health insurance). The act took effect with the plan year that began one year after enactment (for calendar year plans, January 1, 2010). Title II of GINA regulates employers, employment agencies, labor organizations and training/apprenticeship programs controlled by joint labor-management committees. It took effect 18 months after enactment.

On October 7, 2009, guidance on wellness and disease management program incentives was published. The regulations apply to plan years beginning on or after December 7, 2009 (for calendar years plans, as of January 1, 2010). The federal agencies may impose a civil monetary penalty of $100 per violation on a plan sponsor for a GINA violation.

GINA prohibits group health plans and health insurance issuers from:

- Adjusting premium or contribution rates for a group on the basis of the genetic information of individuals in the group
- Requiring or requesting that an individual or family member undergo a genetic test
- Requesting, requiring or purchasing genetic information for underwriting purposes or prior to enrollment in a plan
- Using or disclosing protected health information (PHI) that is genetic information for underwriting purposes. (This prohibition applies to HIPAA-covered entities and will be accomplished through amendments to the HIPAA Privacy Rule.)

To be clear, GINA does not prevent an insurance issuer from increasing a group health plan's premium as a whole due to an individual's disease or disorder—even if the disease or disorder has a genetic basis. Nor does GINA prevent a group plan or issuer from obtaining and using the results of a genetic test in deciding whether to pay a claim. For example, a plan could condition payment for a preventive mastectomy upon receiving results that a patient's genetic test detecting genetic mutations associated with breast cancer.

Any time a health risk assessment (HRA) or similar tool asks a question about an individual's family medical history (or any other form of genetic information), GINA must be considered. Group health plans may *not:*

- Ask questions concerning a person's family history before a person has enrolled in a plan
- Provide a reward to an individual who completes an HRA with a question about family medical history even if the request to complete the HRA comes after enrollment in the plan and completing it has no impact on enrollment in the plan. Rewards include premium reductions, discounts, rebates, payments in kind and any other premium differentials regardless of the amount. A change in a deductible or other cost-sharing mechanism is also a reward when offered in return for providing family medical history (or any other form of genetic information).
- Collect genetic information to determine eligibility for additional plan benefits such as a disease management program.

On the other hand, group health plans may:

- Collect genetic information through an HRA after an individual enrolls in a plan as long as no reward (as defined above) is provided
- Administer two distinct HRAs—one that does not request genetic information (for which an award may be provided upon completion) and one that does request genetic information (for which no award is offered). The second HRA must make it clear that its completion is voluntary and will not affect the reward given for completing the other HRA.
- Ask HRA questions that do not directly seek genetic information (e.g., "Is there anything else concerning your health that you would like us to know or discuss with you?") as long as the HRA includes a clear instruction not to provide genetic information. The regulations provide a sample instruction: "In answering this question, you should not include any genetic information. That is, please do not include any family medical history or any information related to genetic testing, genetic services, genetic counseling or genetic diseases for which you believe you may be at risk."
- Request genetic information (such as family history) to determine whether a benefit is medically appropriate for an individual after the enrollee seeks the plan benefit. For example, a plan may offer a program for people at risk of diabetes. After an individual asks to participate in the program, the plan may ask about the person's family history of diabetes. Nevertheless, the plan must request only the minimum amount of genetic information necessary to determine medical appropriateness. The plan is also prohibited from using the information for an improper purpose.

Title II of GINA also prohibits employers, labor organizations and other entities from:

- Engaging in certain employment practices based on genetic information. For example, it is illegal to refuse to promote individuals because they have a family history of cancer.
- Requesting, requiring or purchasing genetic information except in certain listed circumstances such as the acquisition of information in connection with health or genetic services offered by these entities. This includes services offered as part of a wellness program, provided
  - The employee provides prior, knowing, voluntary and written authorization.
  - Only the employee (or family member) and the licensed health care professional or board-certified genetic counselor involved in providing the services receive the individually identifiable information concerning the results of such services.
  - Any individually identifiable genetic information provided is only available for the purposes of the services offered and not disclosed to the sponsoring entity except in general terms that do not disclose the identity of specific employees.

Final regulations implementing this part of GINA, issued by the Equal Employment Opportunity Commission, took effect January 1, 2011. These regulations also prohibit the offering of a financial inducement for individuals to provide genetic information.

Under Title II, genetic information must be kept confidential and separate from employment records in a manner similar to that required by the Americans with Disabilities Act (ADA).

Michelle's Law

On October 9, 2008, President Bush signed Michelle's Law, named for a New Hampshire college student who died from cancer in 2005. This law requires group health plans and health insurers to provide:

- Up to one year of extended coverage to college students who would otherwise lose health coverage when they take a medically necessary leave of absence

- Notice about a student's rights under the law.

This law is effective for plan years that began on or after October 9, 2009 and applies to medically necessary leaves of absence beginning during that plan year.

Michelle's Law applies only if a group health plan provides coverage to dependent children based on their student status at a postsecondary educational institution (whether attending full-time or not). The law's protections are triggered when a medically necessary leave of absence (or other change in enrollment) causes a child to lose student status under the terms of a plan. Plans that do not require student status for older children to be covered do not have to comply with Michelle's Law. Some plans (such as insured plans in states with dependent extension laws) no longer require student status for older children and instead impose age and other requirements (e.g., financial dependency).

ACA requires group health plans to provide coverage for adult dependents up to the age of 26. This provision was effective for the first plan year beginning on or after September 23, 2010. As a result, Michelle's Law is not of concern for adult children under the age of 26. However, if a plan covers students aged 26 or older based on student status, the plan would still have to comply with Michelle's Law.

Medicare Part D Notices of Creditable Coverage

Under the Medicare Modernization Act of 2003 (MMA), group health plans and others that provide prescription drug coverage to Medicare Part D-eligible individuals are required to inform these individuals whether plan drug coverage is "creditable." *Creditable coverage* must provide a benefit that is "on average at least as good" as the standard Part D benefit. In other words, the amount a plan expects to pay for prescription drug claims must be at least as much as the expected amount of claims paid under the standard Part D benefit. Plans must provide these individuals with a Notice of Creditable (or Noncreditable) Coverage. The purpose of the notice is to help persons avoid a late enrollment penalty under Part D.

A group health plan that covers Part D-eligible individuals must provide this notice unless the plan (1) has applied to CMS to become a Prescription Drug Plan under Part D or (2) contracts with a Part D plan to provide a prescription drug benefit.

Notices must be sent to all Part D-eligible individuals—including employees and former employees who are actives, retirees, disabled or receiving COBRA benefits. The notices must also be sent to Part D-eligible spouses/dependents under active or retiree coverage, as well as those who are disabled or receiving COBRA benefits. According to the Centers for Medicare and Medical Services (CMS), plans may send a single notice to the employee/participant and his or her Part D-eligible spouse/dependents. However, the plan must send a separate notice if the plan knows that a Part D-eligible spouse/dependent resides at a different address.

In general, plans must send the notices at the following times:

1. Prior to the Medicare Part D annual election period, which starts on October 15 (and runs through December 7)
2. Prior to an individual's initial opportunity to enroll in Part D; an individual's initial enrollment period spans seven months, beginning three months before the month he or she is eligible for Medicare and ending three months after that month
3. Prior to the effective date of coverage for any Medicare-eligible individual who joins the plan
4. When the plan's prescription drug coverage is no longer creditable or becomes creditable
5. Upon request by a participant or beneficiary.

CMS will consider (1) and (2) to be met if the plan provides the notice to all plan participants annually.

What Are Some of the Common Errors Found With a DOL Audit?

These are some of the common errors discovered through a compliance audit of a health plan:

- **HIPAA certificate of creditable coverage.** This is the notice to former participants and covered dependents detailing the period they were covered by a health plan. A group health plan must automatically issue the certificate when a person loses coverage as defined by COBRA. DOL has found information—particularly that regarding dependents and the date a waiting period began—is often missing from the certificate.
- **Prohibition against nonconfinement clauses.** *Nonconfinement clauses* delay the effective date of health coverage until an individual (usually a dependent) is released from the hospital. Nonconfinement clauses violate HIPAA nondiscrimination and preexisting condition rules and should be eliminated.
- **HIPAA special enrollment notice.** A special enrollment notice must be provided prior to or when an employee is first offered an opportunity to enroll in the plan. Some plans are not providing these notices in a timely fashion. For instance, if this notice is provided along with the SPD 90 days *after* an individual's enrollment in the plan, there is a violation of the timing requirement.

- **Effective date of HIPAA special enrollment.** Plan enrollment of a dependent must be effective as of the date of the dependent's birth, adoption or placement for adoption. Enrollment due to a person's loss of other health coverage must be effective no later than the first day of the first calendar month following the date a request for special enrollment is received. Many plans have not applied the proper effective date.
- **SPD disclosure requirement under NMHPA.** An SPD must describe the federal NMHPA law and any state law that applies to insured benefits relating to hospital length of stay. Many plans do not describe applicable state length-of-stay laws.
- **Notice requirement under WHCRA.** WHCRA contains three separate notice requirements: (1) a one-time notice was required in January 1999, (2) upon plan enrollment and (3) annually.

What Are the Consequences of Noncompliance?

Noncompliance can be costly. A group health plan that does not comply with federal health plan mandates under ERISA could be subject to individual lawsuits as well as civil penalties of $110 per day for failure to produce documents. In addition, IRS may impose an excise tax on any group health plan that fails to meet the requirements in the amount of $100 per day for each day of noncompliance for each individual to whom the failure relates. Moreover, DOL can impose a civil penalty of up to $1,100 per day for failure to file a Form M-1 if the entity is a Multiple Employer Welfare Arrangement (MEWA) or meets the standards for filing a Form M-1 (e.g., a new multiemployer plan).

Although DOL does not directly address enforcement in its guidance, group health plans cited with a violation have generally been asked by DOL auditors to "right the wrong" that has been cited. For example, if a required notice was not in a summary plan description (SPD) or had not been provided to individuals, DOL may ask the plan to issue the notice. In addition, if a substantive violation resulted in a person's benefits being denied, plan sponsors have been asked to make the individual whole for the benefits that they were improperly denied. However, even if DOL auditors approve a plan's compliance program, there is no guarantee that an individual will not file a lawsuit seeking employee benefits under one of these laws.

COBRA

For each day a plan does not comply with COBRA, the current penalties are a nondeductible excise tax of $110 per qualified beneficiary. The maximum penalty for a plan is $500,000 or 10% of the total amount paid or incurred by the plan for medical coverage during the preceding taxable year, whichever is less. The maximum penalty for an insurer or third-party administrator that is responsible for a plan's failure to comply with COBRA is $2 million. If a plan or fund administrator identifies areas of noncompliance and takes action to rectify them before the government finds them (or serves notice of an audit designed to identify them), the penalties will not apply.

HIPAA

HIPAA penalties increased in 2009 under HITECH. There are now minimum penalties (ranging from $100 per violation to $50,000 per violation, depending on the degree of fault) and maximum penalties (per violation and per year). The maximum annual penalty for multiple violations of one specific requirement is now $1.5 million. HIPAA also established a criminal penalty for any person who wrongfully discloses individually identifiable health information. This penalty for this crime is a fine of not more than $50,000 and/or imprisonment of not more than one year. Penalties are higher for offenses committed with the intent to use the information for commercial advantage, personal gain or malicious harm. HITECH also clarified that individuals (such as a plan employee) as well as the plan may be subject to criminal prosecution. There is no individual right to sue a plan for a violation of the privacy or security regulations.

Conclusion

Just over ten years passed between the enactment of COBRA in 1985 and HIPAA in 1996. Since that time, however, Congress has passed many laws regulating group health plans, adding much complexity to the compliance landscape. Many of these laws and their implementing regulations (such as HIPAA's wellness program rules and MHPAEA) will have important implications for plan design decisions made by trustees. While many other requirements (such as HIPAA privacy/security and COBRA) present largely administrative challenges, compliance with them will nonetheless require significant resources and expertise. Trustees and plan administrators need to rely on legal counsel for authoritative advice on how these various laws affect plan design and operations.

Endnotes

1. Council for Affordable Health Insurance, www.cahi.org/cahi_contents/resources/pdf/MandatesintheStates2010.pdf
2. Department of Labor Compliance Assistance Guide. FAQs released December 22, 2010. www.dol.gov/ebsa/faqs/main.html

Chapter 22

Ancillary Insurance Coverages

Daniel Wolak

A wide range of *ancillary coverages*—like life, disability, dental and vision insurance—can protect plan participants and their families from unexpected expenses and financial hardship. An advantage of providing these coverages through a group such as multiemployer plan participants is the low cost that participants would be able to get if they purchased an individual insurance policy. This chapter provides an overview of ancillary coverages offered today.

Multiemployer plans can provide ancillary protection through insurance arrangements or through self-funding. Which option is chosen depends on the characteristics of the liabilities and tax consequences. For a more thorough chapter on funding benefits through an insurance company and self-funding, read Chapters 14 and 15, respectively.

LIFE INSURANCE

Life insurance is a low-cost benefit provided to many workers. In fact, more individuals today are covered by a group life insurance policy than by individual policies.[1] Initially, group life policies were a way to provide for final expenses if a worker died. The amounts of and types of coverage have expanded such that according to a recent survey, the average amount of life insurance protection is now $78,000.[2] Basic life insurance is the most common way employees are provided a death benefit.

What Is Basic Life Insurance?

Basic life insurance typically offered as a flat dollar amount provided upon the death of a participant may vary by whether a participant is active or retired. Coverage can also be offered as a percentage of salary and may vary by years of service or job class. Plans commonly reduce coverage by 35% once a participant reaches the age of 65. Basic life insurance can be *noncontributory,* wherein all active participants are covered at no cost to the participants.

Most workers are provided basic life insurance at no cost or limited cost. If a plan requires a payment on the part of participants, the insurance carrier generally requires 75% of the group be covered to reduce the chance that *antiselection* will occur—only those participants most likely to benefit from the insurance elect to purchase the coverage. The affordable cost of group insurance requires a large number of insured persons among whom the insurance carrier can spread the cost of death benefits paid out.

Group life coverage is primarily an arrangement with an insurance company. The reason insurance is preferred over self-funding is the tax benefit. Death benefits paid by an insurance carrier are nontaxable income when paid by the insurance carrier, while benefits paid by other sources are taxable. More on the taxation of life insurance contributions and benefits will come later.

To keep the cost attractive, the insurance carrier may require individuals with coverage exceeding a specific dollar amount—the *guarantee issue limit*—to complete a *statement of good health* (also referred to as *evidence of insurability*). This statement usually has three to five questions concerning the insured participant's health.

How Is the Premium for Basic Life Insurance Determined?

A plan's monthly premium for group life insurance is the number of participants insured multiplied by a flat monthly rate per $1,000 of insurance. The rate is an average of the group's insurance weighted for the covered participants' ages and gender. The important drivers for determining the premium for a group are:

- **Average age**—For every five-year increase in average participant age over 40, the premium cost increases 50%. Therefore, the premium for a group with an average age of 45 will pay 50% more than a group with an average age of 40.
- **Percent female**—Females have premium rates that are normally 50% to 60% of males' cost, so a group with a large percentage of females will have a significantly lower premium than a group that is mostly males.
- **Occupation**—Studies show that higher income professions/trades have lower mortality rates than lower income trades. The difference can be 50% to 75% higher mortality between the lowest (e.g., teachers) and the highest cost groups.

What Are the Standard Provisions of Basic Life Coverage?

Group basic life policies—as well as supplemental and voluntary life insurance policies discussed in this chapter—have several standard provisions.

Eligibility Requirement

All policies have an *eligibility requirement*—for coverage, the participant must be actively at work (or actively available for work) on the day coverage begins.

Conversion Provision

A *conversion provision* gives participants who experience a reduction or loss in coverage under their group policy the right to convert to a whole life policy. Participants who lose coverage eligibility (e.g., they change jobs or are unable to work) may purchase the same or a reduced amount of individual coverage. This can be a valuable benefit for those who lose coverage due to a health condition and otherwise would not be approved for insurance coverage or would have a premium they cannot afford. If coverage is lost because a group policy is terminated, a limited amount of individual coverage can be purchased, normally up to $5,000. Participants who lose coverage have 31 days from the date they lose coverage to elect a conversion policy.

Disability Waiver of Premium

Many policies have a *disability waiver of premium* provision that continues the life insurance protection at no cost if a worker becomes disabled. A standard provision covers an approved disability lasting at least nine months and that occurs before the participant reaches the age of 60. The coverage normally continues until reaching a specific age, most commonly the age of 65. There are variations of this coverage that cover disabilities before the age of 65 or that continue to waive premiums to the age of 70 or for life. These provisions will increase the cost of the group life coverage. To be eligible for waived premiums, the participant must provide proof of disability to the insurance company at least every two years.

Payment of Death Benefit

A standard policy provides several ways for a death benefit to be paid. These options include paying the benefit as a lump sum, in monthly installments or as a transfer to an interest-bearing account *(retained assets account)* with check-writing privileges for the beneficiary.

Are There Insurance Options Available Besides Basic Life?

As the name suggests, the basic life insurance policy provides a "basic" amount of coverage for all participants. Because basic insurance protection is often inadequate for workers with families and other obligations, many plans provide participants an opportunity to purchase additional coverage.

Supplemental Life

Supplemental life insurance is a rider to a basic life policy. Participants can elect protection over and above their basic coverage. A supplemental insurance policy requires significant participation of a group.

Each participant selects an amount of coverage that better meets his or her needs. To keep the cost of this coverage low and limit adverse selection, the insurance carrier requires a minimum portion of the group to participate (e.g., 25% participation) and/or medical evidence must be provided. A limited amount of extra coverage can be offered *guarantee issue* without participants completing a statement of good health. The amount in excess of the stated guarantee limit requires a statement of good health. In some cases, depending on the participant's age and amount of coverage requested, the participant may need to complete a medical exam.

Voluntary Life

Voluntary life insurance is similar to supplemental, except a separate policy is used and the participant typically pays the entire cost. Voluntary coverage provides participants flexibility in the amounts of insurance they purchase, but it may have lower guarantee issue amounts because the insurance company faces a greater risk of adverse selection. Generally, the carrier providing voluntary coverage is not the same carrier providing basic insurance.

How Are Premiums Determined for Additional Coverage?

The premium rates for supplemental and voluntary coverage normally vary by five-year age bands and must be unisex. The employer or plan collects premiums through payroll deduction or another method, and then sends the money to the insurance company. This approach provides lower rates than if the insurer billed each worker separately, since participants are paying most or all of the cost for the plan.

What Provisions Are in These Additional Coverages?

Portability

A common provision in supplemental and voluntary coverage is the *portability option,* which allows participants to continue coverage if they are no longer eligible for coverage through employment. The participant can continue the insurance at a low group rate, rather than convert to an individual policy. The insurance carrier will bill the insured directly. Some carriers charge an additional billing fee for doing so.

Dependent Coverage

Many supplemental plans offer *dependent coverage* for a worker's spouse and dependent children. The amount of coverage is usually small, with a flat monthly premium covering the entire cost paid by the worker who chooses coverage. The premium rate is the same whether the member has one dependent or ten dependents. Coverage for the spouse is typically $5,000 or $10,000. Children aged 15 days to a maximum age (e.g., 19 or 23 years) are covered in amounts such as $1,000 or $2,000. Recent social trends have resulted in employers expanding the definition of spouse and children.

Dependent coverage in greater amounts may be available. Maximum spouse coverage might be limited to $100,000, while coverage for a child is limited to $10,000. To limit antiselection, a carrier may restrict coverage for the spouse to no more than 50% of the employee's coverage. When larger amounts of coverage are provided for a spouse, a health statement may also be required.

How Is Group Life Coverage Taxed?

Group life insurance has tax benefits for employers, employees and the beneficiaries of employee policies.

Premiums paid by an employer, union or multiemployer plan are deductible business expenses.

Payments drawn from a policy before a participant's death as an *accelerated death benefit* are tax-free if a physician certifies the insured has an illness that can reasonably be expected to result in death within 24 months.

Life insurance benefits are not part of a beneficiary's gross income—these benefits are tax-free. In the past, a plan could make a tax-free death benefit payment of up to $5,000 to a deceased participant's family. A change in tax law now requires these death benefit payments be taxed and reported on IRS Form 1099. Life insurance is now a tax-saving alternative to even the small death benefits made by plans.

Even some of the money used to purchase group life insurance is tax-free income to the employee. The cost of the first $50,000 of group insurance that an employer or benefit plan provides an employee is tax-free income for the employee. For coverage over $50,000 purchased by an employer or plan, employees must report the cost of the insurance as income on their W-2 form. If the employee pays part of the cost of the insurance and has more than $50,000 coverage, an IRS calculation determines how much paid for the employee is taxable income.

ACCIDENTAL DEATH AND DISMEMBERMENT (AD&D) INSURANCE

AD&D coverage is typically a low-cost rider to a group life plan. The amount of coverage is typically the same amount as for group life.

What Is Covered by AD&D?

A&D coverage provides a cash benefit for two types of events:

1. Deaths due to accidental causes, whether on or off the job
2. Dismemberment due to an accident.

Accidental Death

When there is an *accidental death,* the full coverage amount (the *face amount*) is paid to the beneficiary. Accidents normally excluded are those connected with committing a felony; driving while legally intoxicated; being under the influence of drugs; suicide; and participating in certain dangerous activities such as parachuting, skydiving, and competing or practicing for a vehicular race. In addition, medical-related causes such as an infection "accidentally" contracted are excluded.

Dismemberment

All or a portion of the face amount is paid for covered injuries resulting from an accident—depending on the severity of the injuries. *Dismemberment* includes loss of eyesight, hearing, speech or a limb. For the loss of two limbs, quadriplegia, loss of speech and hearing, or sight of both eyes, the full policy amount is usually paid. Accidental loss of one limb, paraplegia, hemiplegia, loss of speech or hearing, or loss of one eye results in one-half of the face value being paid. Some policies also provide that accidental loss of a thumb and index finger on the same hand or hearing in one ear pays one-quarter of the face value. If the injury is work-related, the dismemberment benefit is paid in addition to any workers' compensation payments.

Over the past 30 years, as work and safety conditions have generally improved, the number of dismemberment claims have become a small percent of claims compared to accidental death. Less than 10% of the claims are now due to dismemberment.

Common Carrier Benefit

Another standard benefit under an AD&D policy is a *common carrier benefit* paid if the insured person dies while riding or traveling as a fare-paying passenger in a common carrier (e.g., bus, train or commercial plane). An additional amount above the accidental death benefit is paid; it may be the same amount as the accidental death benefit or a flat amount such as $25,000 or $50,000.

How Much Does AD&D Coverage Cost?

The cost for AD&D coverage is a monthly rate per $1,000 of coverage and usually relatively low. Rates normally are not adjusted for age or gender, but some occupations are taken into consideration. Typical premiums range from $0.02 to $0.05 per $1,000 per month, though they can be $0.10 or more for occupations with hazardous work conditions. As shown in Exhibit 1, accidental death rates in the United States have declined over the last 40 years though they have crept upward in the past decade.

As claim rates have improved, insurance companies have gradually enhanced AD&D benefits with features such as a rehabilitation benefit and child-care coverage when there is dismemberment. Some carriers also have begun to waive the premium for those who are disabled.

Exhibit 1

Annual Accidental Death Rates in the United States

Year	Deaths per 100,000 Population
1970	62.2
1980	46.4
1990	36.3
2000	34.9
2007	40.0

Source: U.S Census Bureau, Statistical Abstract of the United States, 2011.

Another common benefit is a repatriation benefit that pays the cost of preparing the body of an insured who dies in a foreign country and returning the body to the home country. Finally, some carriers have begun to offer coverage for third-degree burns.

AD&D is an attractive additional supplemental benefit because it can be purchased at a low cost when compared to life insurance. The coverage can be purchased in relatively high amounts with no medical exam required. For workers under the age of 45, the major cause of death is accidents; AD&D coverage can meet a significant portion of financial security for younger participants who otherwise might have minimal or no life insurance coverage at all.[3]

DISABILITY INSURANCE

Disability insurance is available for either short-term disability (STD) or long-term disability (LTD) protection. Carriers are increasingly selling policies that combine STD and LTD coverage in one policy.

What Should Trustees Know About Short-Term Disability Coverage?

Short-term disability coverage typically provides payments to insured persons who have disabilities that are not work related. (Occupation-related disabilities are paid through workers' compensation benefits.) As the name implies, STD coverage is for a relatively short period of time—typically 90 days to one year. Benefit payments begin after a short *elimination period*—the insured must be out of work due to sickness or an accident for seven days, with payments starting on the eighth day. If a person has paid sick days, these days must also be used before STD payments start.

STD coverage can be offered through an insurance carrier or be self-insured by the plan. Because claims are relatively consistent from year to year for large groups and the maximum benefit paid per participant is relatively small compared to medical and other coverage, plans often self-fund this benefit. Many multiemployer plans self-insure but use a third-party administrator for claim approvals and processing.

STD coverage is straightforward with benefit amounts paid as a percent of salary or as a flat dollar amount (e.g., $200 per week) as established in the insurance policy. STD benefits are typically not reduced if a participant receives other payments.

For STD benefits, insurers typically consider workers who are unable to perform all duties of their occupation as disabled. An updated proof of disability is generally required every two to four weeks to remain eligible for a benefit payment.

California, New Jersey, New York, Rhode Island, Hawaii and Puerto Rico have mandated STD programs for workers in their states.

What Should Trustees Know About Long-Term Disability Coverage?

Long-term disability coverage provides benefit payments when a worker has a disability that lasts longer than the STD period and provides benefits until a worker reaches normal retirement age. LTD benefits are commonly a percent of salary. Unlike STD coverage, LTD coverage typically covers both occupational as well as nonoccupational disabilities. Another difference between STD and LTD coverage is that LTD benefits are typically reduced by income from certain other sources including Social Security Disability Insurance (SSDI), workers' compensation benefits, earnings from part-time employment and any retirement benefits. The most common reduction in disability benefits is for SSDI. For more on how benefits are offset (reduced), see Exhibit 2.

Most LTD plans have an elimination period of three to six months of continuous disability before benefits begin. For plans that also have STD coverage, LTD coverage starts at the end of the short-term coverage. To encourage the disabled to try to return to work, most policies do not require a new full elimination period be met if workers subsequently return to disability leave.

Exhibit 2

Integrating Private Long-Term Disability and Social Security Disability Benefits

The benefit from a long-term disability (LTD) insurance policy is not offset by Social Security Disability Insurance (SSDI) benefits until the Social Security Administration (SSA) officially approves a disability. To be eligible for SSDI, a worker must have sufficient credit for working in jobs covered by Social Security and have a disability that does not allow the person to (1) perform the work done before or (2) make an adjustment to do other work. SSA uses a broad "any occupation" definition of *disability*—the person is unable to do their job or adjust to another job due to a medical condition. SSA also requires that the disability be expected to last at least one year.

Individuals cannot apply for SSDI until at least five months have passed. Many times the approval for SSDI can take several years. Once approved, any back SSDI payments are shared with the LTD insurance carrier to reduce the benefit payments the company had already made. Going forward, LTD benefits are *integrated* (reduced) by the SSDI benefit amounts. For low- and medium-paid workers, SSDI benefit amounts could be equal to 50% to 100% of LTD benefits.

LTD and SSDI benefits can be integrated in several ways:

- Reduce only the LTD benefit amount for the insured worker
- Reduce the LTD benefit amount for the insured worker plus any amounts for other family benefits
- A combination of the SSDI benefit and other disability benefits is reduced by the amount that exceeds some percent (such as 70%). This is commonly referred to as *all sources.*

The method for integrating the payments is stated in the policy.

Integrating the benefit payments prevents situations in which an insured worker receiving full LTD and SSDI benefits might earn close to or more than the predisability income. Integration also reduces the cost of the LTD premium because LTD benefits are less. For an insured who is not granted SSDI coverage, LTD still provides a significantly portion of salary as a disability benefit.

Future cost-of-living adjustments to the SSDI benefit payment do not cause an additional offset by the insurance carrier. The adjustment is extra income for the disabled worker.

The maximum length that LTD benefits are paid—the *benefit period*—varies with the plan. Most plans provide coverage for two years, five years or until the worker reaches Social Security "normal retirement age." The premium for an LTD plan is highly dependent on the maximum length of disability. A shorter benefit period may allow a plan to provide benefits at an affordable cost for a group that would otherwise not have coverage.

The definition of *disability* can vary from one LTD policy to another. A *disability* may be defined as either:

- **Any Occupation.** The worker is unable to perform any suitable occupation based on the disabled's training, education and experience. This is the broadest definition.
- **Own Occupation.** The worker is unable to perform his or her occupation. With this narrow definition, a worker may not be considered disabled if he or she can do other types of work.

For a warehouse worker who lifts boxes, a bad back means the worker is disabled for his or her own occupation, but not any occupation. A policy that defines disability as *any occupation* would not pay the warehouse worker a benefit because the worker might still be able to do work that does not require lifting. On the other hand, a policy that defines disability as a worker's inability to do his or her *own occupation* would pay benefits to the warehouse worker. Naturally, a policy with the "own occupation" definition will pay more claims than an "any occupation" policy; it will also have a higher premium. Many of today's plans require an insured be defined as disabled from his or her "own occupation" for the first two years and "any occupation" thereafter.

Like life insurance, LTD insurance is mostly offered as an insured contract. An insurance carrier is better suited to manage and monitor claims and establish a necessary financial reserve given the long-term nature of claims.

How Are Premiums Determined for Long-Term Disability Coverage?

The premium rates for LTD coverage are normally a percent of a worker's salary or a rate per $100 of monthly benefit. An insurance carrier considers these factors when setting the premium rate:

- Occupation and industry of the insured
- Age and gender of the insured
- Benefit level as a percentage of salary
- Plan design including the elimination period, maximum benefit period and any limits
- Definition of disability
- SSDI integration approach
- Geographic area.

Occupation is a key factor in cost. More physical jobs such as construction, public safety (i.e., firefighters and police) and trucking have a much higher rate of disability than typical work. As a result, they also have higher LTD premium rates. To offset the higher risk, a plan may be given a shorter benefit period, a benefit that is a lower percent of salary, an "any occupation" definition of disability or a combination of these three features. Industry is a rating factor because those that are growing or recessionproof are less likely to have active workers with health issues deciding to take disability with a reduced income compared with risking the loss of their job and all of their income.

A common restriction on LTD benefits is to limit payments to two years if the disability is for (1) mental and nervous conditions, or (2) drug and alcohol dependence. Both conditions are more subjective in nature and diagnosis. There may be an exception made, however, if other medical conditions are contributing to these disabilities.

How Are Disability Benefits Taxed?

When a worker pays the full cost of STD or LTD benefits, the federal government treats benefits paid as tax-free income. On the other hand, if the plan covers the full cost, the entire benefit is taxable income. Sometimes, the cost is paid through a combination of worker and employer contributions; the percentage of the cost paid by the employee determines the proportion of the benefit that is tax-free. The remainder reflecting the employer's contribution is taxable.

LONG-TERM CARE INSURANCE

What Should Trustees Know About Long-Term Care Coverage?

Long-term care (LTC) insurance is a relatively new type of insurance developed specifically to cover the costs of medical care and assistance with daily living at home as well as in a variety of community and institutional settings (e.g., nursing homes). Traditional health insurance and Medicare do not cover most of this care. LTC benefits are triggered when an insured is unable to perform at least two of the six *Activities of Daily Living;* these are:

- Bathing
- Continence
- Dressing
- Eating

- Toileting
- Transferring.

In addition, severe cognitive impairment can be a qualifying event. It is typical to include a waiting period of 30, 60, 90 or 100 days before benefits begin. LTC excludes coverage for mental and nervous disorders and claims due to alcoholism and drug addictions.

The cost of the insurance reflects the type and amount of services chosen. There is a great deal of choice and flexibility in LTC insurance policies with respect to care options and benefits. When choosing an LTC policy, decisions must be made regarding the following options:

- The daily benefit amount (e.g., $100/day)
- The amount paid for other care settings (e.g., 50% or 75% for home health care)
- A maximum period of coverage or dollar limit for benefits paid. Common benefit periods are two, three, four and five years as well as lifetime or unlimited coverage. Options between five years and lifetime/unlimited coverage are also available. Most policies translate time periods into dollar amounts and do not actually limit the number of days. There are fewer companies today offering a lifetime/unlimited policy, although some have a *high-coverage option* such as a $1 million lifetime limit.
- Comprehensive or facility care-only coverage. *Comprehensive* policies cover a broader range of care settings and services including care at home and in various types of facilities. *Facility care-only* policies pay for care in a nursing home or assisted living facility, but not for care at home or in the community.
- Additional optional benefits or riders to customize coverage. One important option is *inflation protection,* which helps protect the insured from the rising cost of care over time.

LTC coverage is always offered as an insured contract because of the voluntary nature of purchases and the long period over which payments for claims are made. The tax treatment of qualified LTC plans is like that of qualified pension plans. An employer can deduct employer–paid premiums for workers as a business expense. The employer contribution is tax-free to employees, and benefits received are not taxed.

DENTAL INSURANCE

What Should Trustees Know About Dental Coverage?

Dental coverage is frequently offered along with medical coverage. In contrast to medical insurance, dental insurance has no catastrophic claims and is much less expensive. The insured and a dental provider are more likely to be aware of the cost of different dental procedures and make care decisions based on their coverage. While a medical procedure may be the difference between life and death, many dental procedures can be postponed or not done at all.

Dental plan design is important. Most plans require participants to pay part of the cost of the care; the level of cost sharing varies with the type of treatment:

- **Preventive and diagnostic**—100% coverage is common for oral exams, x-rays, fluoride and sealant treatments.
- **Basic restorative, endodontic, periodontics**—80% coverage is common after a deductible for services such as filling cavities, gum treatments and root canals.
- **Major procedures (restorative and prosthodontics)**—50% coverage is typical after a deductible for services such as bridges, inlays, crowns, posts, full and partial dentures
- **Orthodontic**—an option that can be added to a plan that typically covers a fixed dollar amount up to some percentage of actual charges (e.g., 25-50%).

Policies generally include a limitation that one exam is covered every six months. In addition, the frequency that x-rays are covered is defined in the policy.

Dental claims are small relative to coverages such as health, life and disability benefits. In addition, for large groups, the claims are predictable from one year to the next. As a result, plans often choose to self-fund dental coverage.

When an insurance company is setting the premium for dental coverage, the carrier considers whether or not the group currently has dental insurance coverage. If not, premiums are higher because claims in the first year are expected to be higher as the insured population takes care of existing unmet dental needs. If coverage is optional and participants pay part of the cost of coverage, insurers typically require participation by 75% of workers eligible to participate. Insurers often discount the premium if 100% of the group is covered.

VISION BENEFITS

What Should Trustees Know About Vision Coverage?

Vision insurance is a popular plan that provides coverage for an annual eye exam as well as reimbursement for lenses, frames and contact lenses. Reimbursements are in dollar amounts, and one purchase is allowed every one or two years. Some insurance carriers offer lower premiums if only services through a covered network provider are used.

Vision plans are relatively low premium coverage when compared to medical, disability and dental coverage. However, the age of a group significantly affects the cost, as the need for eye care increases as people age. Offering vision coverage as an optional coverage to participants is challenging, as people tend to choose coverage when they anticipate they will need vision services. Premium rates are more attractive when this benefit is provided to all participants.

HEARING AID BENEFITS

What Should Trustees Know About Hearing Aid Coverage?

For some occupations, noise levels create a hazard to hearing that makes hearing aid coverage particularly valuable. The monthly cost of the benefit is relatively low. Plans normally pay for the purchase of a hearing aid once every four or five years. The insurer may offer a discount on the amount paid by the insured for the hearing aid if a vendor that is part of a network is used. A plan may offer coverage for the worker only or for the worker and the worker's family.

CRITICAL ILLNESS INSURANCE

What Should Trustees Know About Critical Illness Coverage?

Critical illness (CI) coverage provides a benefit when a person is diagnosed with one of the illnesses listed in the policy. A typical CI plan pays a lump-sum amount (i.e., $50,000 or $100,000) when there is a diagnosis such as cancer or the insured has a heart attack or stroke. The coverage can be included as a rider on life insurance coverage or sold separately as health insurance coverage.

CI is a popular coverage in Canada, Europe and South Africa. The market in the United States is beginning to grow as the product is better understood and marketed. Some plans include a CI benefit as part of group life insurance. The coverage is also being marketed as an individual policy product in the workplace. A 2010 study found a little more than 50% of individual CI coverage was purchased by buyers under the age of 45.[4]

For the individual insurance market, it is common to have a benefit that steps up after two years; the benefit is reduced for conditions diagnosed in the first two years of coverage. The premium is based on the age of the insured when the policy is issued and remains at that level thereafter. The benefit can be a way to offset loss of earnings or higher medical costs due to serious illness.

LEGAL BENEFITS

What Should Trustees Know About Legal Aid Coverage?

Some plans offer a benefit that provides limited or comprehensive legal services. For example, limited services might include a set number of phone hours and preparation of a will. A medium-service plan might add legal services such as real estate transactions and adoptions. Divorce services might be part of a full-service plan. Legal benefits are usually offered through a network of lawyers who have agreed to work at a stated hourly fee.

HOSPITAL INCOME PROTECTION INSURANCE

What Should Trustees Know About Hospital Income Protection Coverage?

Hospital income protection (HIP) is generally a supplemental or voluntary coverage versus basic coverage on all plan participants. The premium is paid by participants. HIP can supplement lost income or medical expenses that result from hospitalization of the insured. The coverage pays a flat dollar amount per day in the hospital. Additional amounts may be paid for days in an intensive care unit. The coverage may include a payment for other types of medical visits such as annual physicals or other wellness-related services.

Conclusion

Ancillary benefits can provide a valuable level of protection for risks such as death, disability and health expenses not covered by the typical health insurance as well as unexpected expenses such as legal costs. Participants and their families greatly appreciate the extra security.

Endnotes

1. American Council of Life Insurers, *Life Insurers Fact Book*, 2008.
2. JHA Gen Re 2010 U.S. Group Life Mid-Year Market Survey.
3. U.S. Census Bureau, Statistical Abstract of the United States, 2011.
4. AACIII study, published 2/21/2011 in National Underwriter Life & Health.

Chapter 23

Apprenticeship and Training Funds

Richard T. Kennedy and Joseph A. Vater Jr.

Apprenticeship and training funds (referred to as *apprenticeship funds* or *funds* throughout this chapter) have a long history of providing skilled workers for a number of industries. These funds are employee welfare benefit plans under the Employee Retirement Income Security Act of 1974 (ERISA) and are typically exempt from federal income taxation under the Internal Revenue Code (IRC). As a result, the funds are subject to many of the same laws and requirements that apply to other multiemployer welfare plans. Because of their training and education function, it is important to know that these funds are subject to additional laws and requirements.

Apprenticeship funds seem to be largely ignored in the benefit literature. This chapter helps remedy this—discussing how these funds are similar to other benefit plans and highlighting some unique characteristics, laws and regulations.

What Laws and Regulations Apply to Apprenticeship and Training Funds?

The Taft-Hartley Act

The Taft-Hartley Act of 1947 applies to all multiemployer benefit trust funds including apprenticeship and training funds. The act prohibits payments from an employer to a union or employee representative. Violations can result in criminal penalties. There is an exception, however, for contributions to employee benefit trust funds that include apprenticeship and other training funds. To be covered by the exception, there must be:

- A written agreement with the employer that sets forth the detailed basis on which such payments are made to the trust fund
- Equal representation by employers and employees in the administration of the fund
- Procedures to resolve a deadlock in fund administration between the employer and employee groups
- Provisions for an annual audit of the fund.

ERISA

ERISA is a key statute that protects the interests of employee benefit plan participants and establishes requirements for employee benefit plan administration. Apprenticeship and training plans, like other plans covered by ERISA, must be established and maintained pursuant to a written plan document. All plan assets must be held in trust, which requires a trust agreement. Plan trustees are named in the plan document, trust agreement or appointed by a named fiduciary. An explanation of the operation of plans under ERISA is in Chapter 5.

Federal and State Tax Laws

The IRC governs the federal income tax treatment of plan contributions, trust income, instructor compensation and other apprenticeship fund payments.

Like other multiemployer benefit plans, apprenticeship funds can qualify for tax-exempt status under the IRC. The trust income of tax-exempt funds is not subject to federal income tax. Funds that are exempt from federal income tax may also qualify for exemption from a number of state and local taxes, such as income, sales and property taxes. For apprenticeship funds, the tax savings can offset the costs of training and education programs. Tax laws must be reviewed on a case-by-case basis—a fund accountant can help determine what state and local taxes apply.

Apprenticeship funds can qualify for federal income tax

exemption as a 501(c)(3) charitable and educational organization, a 501(c)(5) labor organization or a 501(c)(9) voluntary employees' beneficiary association. These refer to sections in the IRC. Most, if not all, apprenticeship funds are tax-exempt organizations. To establish tax-exempt status, an application is filed with the Internal Revenue Service (IRS).

As an interesting side note, IRS lists 501(c)(3) organizations in its Publication 78, *Cumulative List of Organizations described in Section 170(c) of the Internal Revenue Code of 1986.* Even though an apprenticeship fund's tax exemption is actually evidenced by an exemption letter issued by IRS, Publication 78 can be used to determine or confirm the 501(c)(3) tax-exempt status of an apprenticeship fund. An online searchable version is available on the IRS website at www.irs.gov/app/pub-78.

National Apprenticeship Act

The National Apprenticeship Act authorizes the U.S. Department of Labor (DOL) to (1) issue regulations and standards that safeguard the welfare of apprentices, (2) encourage the establishment of apprenticeship programs and (3) cooperate with states in the formulation and promotion of apprenticeship standards.

DOL has issued regulations found at 29 C.F.R. Part 29 and Part 30. Part 29 covers the registration of apprenticeship programs, including the required "standards of apprenticeship" and "apprenticeship agreements." Part 30 covers antidiscrimination and equal opportunity requirements that apply to apprenticeship programs.

Apprenticeship programs register with the DOL (Office of Apprenticeship, Employment and Training Administration) or with a state apprenticeship agency authorized by DOL. Registration requires compliance with the standards established by DOL. Most apprenticeships are registered. Programs must also be reviewed and approved by DOL or the state agency with which the program is registering. The standards for registration are detailed in 29 C.F.R. Part 29. They include the preparation of the standards of apprenticeship and apprenticeship agreements discussed later. The registration agency can provide guidance and assistance on the requirements for registration and the registration process.

DOL regulations require registration agencies to evaluate the performance of a registered apprenticeship program. Program elements considered include quality assurance assessments, equal employment opportunity compliance reviews and completion rates. The DOL regulations also identify factors for both voluntary and involuntary deregistration of an apprenticeship program, and provide for hearings and appeals of an involuntary termination.

Laws Prohibiting Discrimination in Employment or Training

Although not addressed here, many state and local laws prohibit discrimination in employment or training. The state and local laws often coincide with federal antidiscrimination laws—some state and local laws provide more protections to workers and trainees than federal law. For example, there are state and local laws that prohibit discrimination based on sexual preference. There is no such federal protection. Trustees need to be aware of all of the antidiscrimination laws applicable to apprenticeship and training programs and keep abreast of changes.

The Equal Pay Act of 1963 (EPA)—an amendment to the Fair Labor Standards Act—requires employers to pay the same wage to men and women who perform jobs that require substantially the same skill, effort and responsibility, and that are performed under similar working conditions within the same establishment. Pay differences are permitted when based on seniority, merit, quantity or quality of work, or factor other than gender.

The Age Discrimination in Employment Act of 1967 (ADEA) prohibits discrimination based on age if an individual is 40 years of age or older. ADEA also prohibits harassment because of an individual's age. This federal law treats the apprenticeship fund as an employer if the fund employs 20 or more persons. If a fund has fewer than 20 employees, a fund may still be subject to state or local laws prohibiting age discrimination in employment. Most state and local age discrimination laws apply to employers with far fewer employees. For example, the threshold in Pennsylvania for age discrimination protection is four employees. For most apprenticeship programs, ADEA also applies to the selection, discipline and training of apprentices.

Title VII of the Civil Rights Act of 1964 (Title VII), as amended, makes it unlawful for an employer to discriminate against any individual on the basis of race, color, religion, sex or national origin. Title VII also prohibits racial, religious, ethnic or sexual harassment in the workplace. If a fund has 15 or more employees, Title VII applies to fund hiring, discipline and termination of employees. If the fund has fewer employees, most states and many local governments have similar prohibitions against employee discrimination and harassment that may apply. For most apprenticeship programs, Title VII also prohibits discrimination in the selection, discipline and training of apprentices.

Title I of the Americans with Disabilities Act of 1990 (ADA) prohibits discrimination against qualified disabled individuals with respect to application procedures, job training and other conditions of employment. Persons are considered disabled if they have a physical or mental impairment (or a record of impairment) that substantially limits one or more of their major life activities. Major life activities include hearing, sight, learning, speaking, walking and breathing. A *qualified* individual is an individual who, with or without reasonable accommodations for the disability, can perform the essential functions of a job.

ADA applies to an apprenticeship fund as an employer if the fund employs 15 or more employees. In most cases, ADA also applies to the selection and treatment of apprentices. Many state and local laws also prohibit discrimination based upon disability.

The ADA's impact can extend beyond employment and training. ADA might also be applicable to a building owned or operated by a fund. **Title III of ADA** requires accessibility to buildings where people are employed or trained.

DOL Regulations

In addition to the above statutes, DOL has issued equal employment opportunity regulations that apply to the recruitment and selection of apprentices and to all conditions of training during the apprenticeship.

Other Statutes

There are other employment-related laws that can apply to a fund. For example, the **Family and Medical Leave Act (FMLA)** (applicable if an apprenticeship fund has 50 or more employees) provides employees with the right to take an unpaid leave of absence for specified family-related reasons. Another is the **Uniformed Services Employment and Reemployment Rights Act (USERRA)** that provides eligible apprentices and employees returning from qualified military service with federal reemployment rights and prohibits discrimination based on military service or obligations.

Apprenticeship funds must be aware of and comply with these obligations. Legal counsel or another professional advisor can offer advice and additional information.

What Are the Standards of Apprenticeship?

To qualify for approval and registration by a registration agency, an apprenticeship program must have written standards covering the training and employment of apprentices. The provisions required for these *standards of apprenticeship* are covered in detail in DOL regulations at 29 C.F.R. Part 29. Among the provisions that must be addressed in the standards are:

- The training and employment of the apprentice in a skilled occupation
- The terms of the apprenticeship, which can be measured by on-the-job learning, the attainment of skill competency, or both
- The supervised work experience and on-the-job training that the apprentice will receive
- The instruction in technical subjects related to the occupation that will be provided, with an annual minimum of 144 hours recommended
- A progressively increasing schedule of wages consistent with the skills acquired
- A periodic review of apprentice performance on the job and in the classroom
- The minimum qualifications for apprenticeship
- Compliance with the nondiscrimination and equal opportunity requirements of 29 C.F.R. Part 30, including an equal opportunity pledge and adoption of an affirmative action plan
- The requirement for a written apprenticeship agreement and the registration of the apprenticeship agreement
- The registration of the apprenticeship program.

The standards of apprenticeship are the core documents for apprenticeship programs and cover in detail the terms and conditions for the recruitment, selection, employment and training of apprentices. In addition to DOL and state agencies, advice and assistance on the preparation and administration of standards of apprenticeship may be available from the international union or a national apprenticeship and training program.

What Is an Apprenticeship Agreement?

DOL regulations also require an *apprenticeship agreement.* Generally, this is a written agreement between the program sponsor and the apprentice. The agreement sets forth the terms and conditions for the employment and training of the apprentice. The apprenticeship agreement is registered with the registration agency as evidence of the apprentice's participation in the apprenticeship program.

DOL regulations specify the contents of the agreement. In addition to incorporating the standards of apprenticeship, the agreement must (among other things):

- Identify the apprentice and the apprenticeship program
- List the occupation in which the apprentice is to be trained
- Specify the term of the apprenticeship program

- State the graduated scale of wages to be paid
- Include statements on the required cancellation provisions
- Provide contact information for the party designated to receive and resolve complaints.

Apprenticeship agreements are prepared in conjunction with the standards of apprenticeship. Again, DOL, state agencies, the international union or a national apprenticeship and training program can provide advice and assistance on preparation.

Who Manages Apprenticeship and Training Programs?

Joint Apprenticeship and Training Committee

A Joint Apprenticeship and Training Committee (JATC) is typically the sponsor of an apprenticeship and training program. The JATC is responsible for the administration and operation of the program under the National Apprenticeship Act. In accordance with this federal legislation, programs are usually registered with DOL or a state apprenticeship agency using the name of the JATC.

A JATC is not necessarily the ERISA plan administrator and/or board of trustees, but it can be. Often, this is determined by the size of the fund. For a fund covering a single registered program, a board of trustees appointed in accordance with the Taft-Hartley Act can serve as the JATC, the ERISA plan administrator and the ERISA trustees. For a larger fund covering a number of registered apprenticeship programs, each program may have its own JATC while the overall operation of the fund and the investment of the assets is administered and managed by a different (or smaller) board or committee.

Apprenticeship Training Coordinator

Many apprenticeship funds have a *training coordinator* (or *manager*). The coordinator most often is a fund employee responsible for carrying out the daily administration and operation of the program within the guidelines of the fund's standards of apprenticeship and the JATC.

The coordinator may also serve in any or all of these roles:

- Member of the JATC
- ERISA plan administrator
- ERISA trustee.

Fulfilling these additional functions does not seem to be a typical practice. If done, it should be carefully structured and reviewed for compliance with the ERISA prohibited transaction provisions.

Whether a coordinator has fiduciary responsibilities under ERISA depends upon the discretion and authority given to the coordinator. Most funds treat an apprenticeship coordinator as a fiduciary.

Are There Any Regulations Concerning Program Instructors?

Instructors typically are employees of an apprenticeship fund, but not always. Instructors are sometimes hired as "independent contractors." Without going into detail, an employee relationship exists for federal employment and tax law purposes when an employer has the right to direct and control a worker with respect to not only what a worker does, but also how the worker does the work. It is very important that instructors be properly classified. An apprenticeship fund has very different duties, responsibilities and obligations to employees and independent contractors, and it could incur significant liability if instructors are misclassified.

Perhaps stating the obvious, an apprenticeship fund should hire instructors with the necessary expertise, background and skills to be an effective teacher. In this regard, the DOL regulations establish two specific requirements for an apprenticeship instructor:

1. The instructor must either meet state department of education requirements for a vocational-technical instructor or be a subject matter expert. A *subject matter expert* is an individual who is recognized within an industry as having expertise in a specific occupation. This would include journeymen with the necessary expertise.
2. The instructor must have training in teaching techniques and adult learning styles. This training can occur before or after the instructor has started teaching; it can be provided by the fund or by an accredited institution of higher learning.

What Policies Are Needed to Comply With Laws That Prohibit Discrimination?

The laws prohibiting discrimination in employment and training have a major impact on the operation of apprenticeship and training programs. Besides the operational impact, the remedies and penalties for a violation can be significant. The remedies for violating Title VII of the Civil Rights Act or Title I of ADA include back pay; front pay in lieu of reinstatement; damages for loss of benefits; compensatory damages including damages for emotional distress, pain and suffering; as well as punitive damages. The remedies for a violation of ADEA include back pay, front pay in lieu of reinstatement and damages for loss of benefits. Damages double when there is a willful violation of ADEA.

Trustees need to be aware of the basic application of these laws to employees and apprentices. Two key issues to consider are an antiharassment policy and the equal employment opportunity standards for apprenticeship and training.

Antiharassment Policy

Title VII prohibits racial, religious, ethnic or sexual harassment. *Harassment* for this purpose is verbal or physical conduct where the conduct has the purpose or effect of unreasonably interfering with an individual's work performance or creates an intimidating, hostile or offensive work environment. The Equal Employment Opportunity Commission (EEOC) administers Title VII. EEOC regulations define the term *harassment* broadly to include epithets, slurs, negative stereotyping, threatening or hostile acts, and written or graphic material that denigrates or shows hostility to a person in a protected class or the protected class itself. The standard for determining harassment is whether a reasonable person in the same or similar circumstances would find the conduct intimidating, hostile or abusive.

Harassment also includes unwelcome sexual advances or requests for sexual favors and other verbal or physical conduct—where acceptance or rejection of the conduct is the basis for a favorable or unfavorable action toward an employee or apprentice. A fund may be liable for the conduct of its employees or apprentices if the fund (1) knew or should have known about conduct that occurs at an apprentice function and (2) fails to take action to stop the conduct.

To minimize liability, every fund should have a written policy against harassment that is clearly and regularly communicated to employees and apprentices. An antiharassment policy should provide procedures by which harassment victims can (1) make their complaints known and (2) have their complaints promptly and confidentially investigated. The policy should provide an opportunity for a person to make a complaint to the apprenticeship coordinator or to a union- or employer-appointed trustee. A policy that allows a complaint to be filed with a number of persons may avoid circumstances where a person is reluctant to bring a complaint involving the person with whom the complaint is to be filed. The policy should also provide for an investigation and action that stops the harassment. Trustees often rely on professionals to draft and implement an antiharassment policy and to assist with claims.

Equal Employment Opportunity Standards for Apprenticeship and Training

DOL regulations set forth the general equal employment opportunity requirements for apprenticeship and training programs.[1] These regulations prohibit discrimination based on race, color, religion, national origin or sex in the recruitment, selection, employment and training of apprentices. The regulations also require uniform application of rules and regulations to all conditions of training during the apprenticeship and that the apprenticeship fund take affirmative action to provide equal opportunity in apprenticeships.

Notably, the regulations require an apprenticeship program (with five or more apprentices) to adopt a written affirmative action plan. Affirmative action plans must include the process by which the apprenticeship program reaches out to qualified women and minority applicants. Percentage goals and timetables may be necessary. Regular review of an affirmative action plan to assess its effectiveness and to ensure that current recruitment efforts are consistent with the plan is recommended.

An apprenticeship program is required to maintain records that include the affirmative action plan, summary of each applicant's qualifications, and the basis for selecting or rejecting each applicant. DOL has the authority to conduct affirmative active compliance reviews (as well as general compliance reviews) and to investigate complaints filed by an apprentice or applicant for apprenticeship. DOL has the power to impose sanctions for not operating in accordance with the equal employment opportunity requirements that include instituting proceedings to deregister the apprenticeship program.

DOL regulations require that a fund's affirmative action program use one of four methods when selecting apprentices:

1. **Selection based on rank from a pool of eligible applicants.** Generally, this is the rank order of scores on one or more permitted qualification standards.
2. **Random selection from a pool of eligible applicants.** This method is subject to DOL approval and must be supervised by an impartial person or persons.
3. **Selection from a pool of current employees.** Apprentices are usually selected from a pool of workers already employed by the program sponsor in a manner prescribed by a collective bargaining agreement when one exists, or by the sponsor's established apprenticeship promotion policy.
4. **An alternative selection method approved by DOL.**[2]

There is very detailed guidance in the regulations on the application of each of these selection methods, including the creation of applicant pools and qualification standards.

Selection Procedures

A fund's standards of apprenticeship generally establish the time frame for notifying the public it is accepting applicants. These time frames should be followed.

If applicants are required to take a written test, the test and test scores must be directly related to performance on the job and in the apprenticeship program. This requirement is also true for tests administered by state employment agencies. If an aptitude test is used, consider hiring a consultant to assist in the preparation of the test. A consultant can validate the test, certify the test is not discriminatory, and substantiate there is a relationship between test scores and the ability of applicants to succeed with training in class and on the job.

Oral interviews cannot be used to determine admission into an eligibility pool. However, once a group has been determined to be eligible based upon the application and/or an aptitude test, oral interviews are permissible. During the interview, take care not to ask for any information that cannot be requested on an application. The interviews should not request information concerning the applicant's race, sex, religion, age, national origin or disability. Interviewers should be consistent in the information they seek from each applicant. One way to accomplish this is to develop a written set of questions before the interview and to use the same questions for each applicant. This helps maintain the objectivity of the interviews and helps provide evidence that all individuals interviewed were treated equally.

One danger of an oral interview is that an applicant may voluntarily disclose information that interviewers are not allowed to request. For example, an applicant may begin to discuss a workers' compensation case in which he or she is involved. If this happens, interviewers should advise the applicant the information is not relevant and will not be considered in the selection process. This type of information should not be considered during the decision-making process, nor should followup questions ever be asked.

Establish weights for factors such as work experience, test scores and interview responses. An applicant who has not been selected may challenge the decision with DOL, EEOC, a state agency or in another forum. If emphasis is on objective factors such as work experience and test scores, it is easier to respond to a legal challenge. If more weight is given to the interview process, which tends to be more subjective, it is more difficult to have a challenge dismissed. This is especially true if the applicant's objective scores are higher than the objective scores of individuals who were selected.

The effect of ADA (Title I) on the selection process is especially significant. Disability-related inquiries should not be included on an application or in an interview. Such inquiries include questions whether an applicant:

- Has a disease
- Was sick in the previous year
- Has been injured or treated for alcohol or mental health problems
- Is currently taking prescription drugs.

ADA does not allow an apprenticeship program to require a physical examination or completion of a medical questionnaire prior to applicant selection. A physical exam after a person has been conditionally selected for the apprenticeship program, however, is permitted. A conditional offer may be revoked if the condition discovered is job related and is consistent with business necessity.

Drug testing is not a medical examination under ADA. A current user of illegal drugs is not a qualified disabled individual.

ADA requires examination results be kept confidential and in a separate file from the applicant's regular file. Information obtained from post-offer physicals or other medical information that comes to the attention of the program is also confidential and should be accessible only to persons who have an absolute need to know the information.

Regular review of apprenticeship program application and selection procedures helps ensure the process continues to be relevant and legal.

What Are the 501(c)(3) Tax Exemption Provisions ?

An apprenticeship fund may qualify for federal income tax exemption as a 501(c)(3) educational organization. This requires the apprenticeship fund to satisfy an organizational test and an operational test.

Well-run apprenticeship funds should have little difficulty in satisfying the basic 501(c)(3) exemption requirements:

- The organizational test requires that the exempt purpose be properly described in the operating documents.
- The operational test generally requires that an apprenticeship fund engage primarily in activities that further its exempt educational purposes.
- No part of the net earnings of the trust fund may inure to the benefit of any private shareholder or individual; the tax exemption can be jeopardized if the fund serves a private interest, rather than a public interest.

- An apprenticeship fund may not engage in any political campaign activity whatsoever and may engage only in "insubstantial" legislative activities unless it makes a special election to be subject to specified limitations on lobbying expenditures.

As a "private school," an apprenticeship fund must satisfy all of the following additional exemption requirements:

- The operating documents (or a resolution) must include a statement of its racially nondiscriminatory policy.
- A notice of the nondiscriminatory policy must be included in brochures and written advertising and may need to be publicized in local newspapers.
- The apprenticeship fund must be operated in a racially nondiscriminatory manner, including with respect to any scholarships or loans.
- Compliance must be certified annually (Schedule E, Form 990 or 990-EZ).
- Proper and specific records must be maintained.

Are ERISA Reporting and Disclosure Requirements the Same as for Other Benefit Plans?

DOL regulations waive ERISA (Title I, Part 1) reporting and disclosure requirements for an apprenticeship fund providing only apprenticeship and training benefits, if the fund does all of the following:

- Files a one-time notice with DOL
- Takes reasonable steps to disclose information in the notice to employees of contributing employers who may be eligible for any of the fund's training or education programs
- Makes the notice available to employees upon request.

If this exemption does not apply, an apprenticeship fund is subject to ERISA's reporting and disclosure requirements—most notably the requirement to file the Annual Return/Report of Employee Benefit Plan (Form 5500). DOL can assess a penalty of up to $1,100 per day against a plan administrator for a failure to file the form in a timely fashion when it is required.

IRS requires most 501(c)(3) organizations (and other tax-exempt organizations) to file a Form 990, Return of Organization Exempt from Income Tax (or if eligible, a Form 990-EZ, Short Form, Return of Organization Exempt from Income Tax). Financial penalties can also be assessed for failing to file the Form 990. Failure to file a Form 990 for three consecutive years will result in the loss of tax-exempt status.

How Are the Unique Facility and Equipment Needs of Apprenticeship and Training Programs Addressed in ERISA?

Unlike other ERISA welfare plans, apprenticeship funds own or lease training facilities, equipment and/or materials used to train apprentices and journeymen. This distinguishes apprenticeship funds from other ERISA welfare plans. More importantly, this often means apprenticeship funds enter into more transactions with unions or contributing employers that require a heightened review of potential prohibited transaction issues. For example, it is not unusual for an apprenticeship fund to lease a union-owned training facility or to purchase supplies from a contributing employer working in the same industry. Both of these would be a party in interest prohibited transaction if ERISA or DOL did not provide an exemption.

A key ERISA statutory exemption permits plans to pay a party in interest, including a fiduciary, for office space or for services and incidental goods if these three criteria are met:

1. The office space or service is necessary for the establishment or operation of the plan.
2. The office space or service is furnished under a reasonable contract or arrangement.
3. No more than reasonable compensation is paid.

This exemption applies to the party in interest prohibited transaction provisions, but not to the self-dealing/conflict of interest prohibited transaction provisions. For a fuller explanation of prohibited transactions, see Chapter 5.

DOL has issued three important prohibited transaction class exemptions of particular interest to multiemployer plans and apprenticeship and training programs.

1. PTE 76-1 permits multiemployer plans to do the following with an employer, employer association, union or another multiemployer plan that is a party in interest:
   a. Lease office space to each
   b. Provide administrative services to each
   c. Sell or lease goods to each.

This exemption applies to the party in interest prohibited transaction provisions, but not to the self-dealing/conflict of interest prohibited transaction provisions.

2. PTE 77-10 complements PTE 76-1 by enabling a multiemployer plan to do the following with an employer, employer association, union or another multiemployer plan that is a party in interest:
   a. Share office space, administrative services and goods with each
   b. Lease office space to each
   c. Provide administrative services to each

d. Sell or lease goods to each.

This exemption applies to the conflict of interest (but not self-dealing) prohibited transaction provisions.

3. PTE 78-6 permits an apprenticeship plan to
   a. Purchase personal property from a contributing employer
   b. Lease personal property or real property (other than office space) from a contributing employer
   c. Lease real property (other than office space) and incidental personal property from a union.

This exemption applies to the party in interest prohibited transaction provisions, but not to the self-dealing/conflict of interest prohibited transaction provisions.

It is essential to consider carefully the circumstances when relying on an exemption from the prohibited transaction provisions.

These statutory and class exemptions typically provide the relief necessary for the operation of apprenticeship and training programs, but not always. For example, an apprenticeship fund purchase (or sale) of a training center from (or to) the (bargaining party) union is a party in interest prohibited transaction not covered by the foregoing exemptions—or any other statutory or class exemption. This is true even though the fund's leasing of a training center from the same union would be exempt under PTE 78-6. As another example, a loan to an apprenticeship fund by another fund with common trustees would be a conflict of interest prohibited transaction for which there is no exemption. It cannot be emphasized enough that all transactions with a party in interest or where a fiduciary may be operating under a conflict of interest should be carefully reviewed.

What Insurance Does an Apprenticeship and Training Fund Need?

Like other ERISA plans, an apprenticeship fund must purchase ERISA fidelity bond coverage and should purchase fiduciary liability coverage to protect its plan assets. With respect to fiduciary insurance, it is important not to overlook the "waiver-of-recourse" endorsement. ERISA requires that an insurer have a right of *recourse* (recovery) against a breaching fiduciary when plan assets are used to purchase fiduciary insurance. Insurers will waive this right of recourse or recovery under a waiver-of-recourse endorsement. Obtain this endorsement to protect the personal assets of fiduciaries. A minimum insurance premium is charged for the endorsement. The premium cannot be paid with plan assets. The fiduciary or the respective appointing bargaining party typically pays for it. Details concerning fidelity bond coverage and fiduciary coverage are provided in Chapters 11 and 12.

Because apprenticeship funds own or lease training facilities, equipment and materials, the insurance needs of an apprenticeship fund are far more complicated than those of most other benefit plans. In addition to the more obvious types of insurance such as fire, theft, casualty, marine, general liability and workers' compensation, trustees may also want to consider employee practice liability insurance depending upon the number of employees, business disruption insurance and educational liability insurance.

Trustees should engage a knowledgeable insurance broker to assist them in determining fund insurance needs and to assist in obtaining the lowest possible premium. Failure to consider the insurance needs of an apprenticeship program and to protect the assets of the apprenticeship fund could be a breach of fiduciary duty.

Conclusion

Service as a trustee of an apprenticeship fund may initially seem to be a daunting task with many things to know and many responsibilities. It has been the authors' experience that the vast majority of trustees approach their responsibilities seriously and with the goal of providing the best training and education possible for apprentices and journeymen. This approach, along with a reliance on experienced trustees and knowledgeable advisors as needed, will enable all trustees to perform properly their important role in the operation of apprenticeship funds.

Endnotes

1. 29 C.F.R. Part 30.
2. 29 C.F.R. Part 30.

Chapter 24

Preservation of Plan Assets Through Subrogation and Reimbursement Rights

Philip R. O'Brien

Trustees of self-financed health plans are likely to find the subject of subrogation either foreign or uninteresting. However, since unpredictable markets are making the return on plan assets less than a sure thing, recovery of dollars through subrogation and reimbursement rights has become, along with securities investments and employer contributions, the "third rail" of asset generation for plans. It is essential that trustees have a working knowledge of subrogation to fulfill their fiduciary responsibility to pursue reasonably and diligently money owed to their plan—in this case, reimbursement for benefits advanced to participants for medical and loss-of-time claims.

What Is Subrogation and Why Is It Important to Trustees?

Subrogation is a legal technique used by self-financed benefit plans trying to recover expenses paid for a participant claim that should have been the responsibility of another party. The Employee Retirement Income Security Act of 1974 (ERISA) forbids multiemployer benefit plans from providing coverage for medical treatment for an injury caused by a third party. The most common examples of these types of health care claims are injuries that result from (1) an auto accident, (2) dangerous property conditions, (3) a faulty product or (4) danger on the job. Because these incidents require formal claims to an insurance company and/or legal action, participants must wait a number of months, and sometimes years, for resolution and often a monetary award.

Despite the ERISA prohibition on coverage, multiemployer plans have traditionally covered these types of participant medical and loss-of-time claims while legal action is pending. This is done with the condition that participants reimburse the plan when the third-party insurer pays them or the case is settled.

While ERISA does not explicitly state trustees must assert subrogation and reimbursement rights, it does require trustees to discharge their fiduciary duties prudently and solely in the interests of all plan participants and beneficiaries. If trustees do not seek reimbursement for plan expenses when a participant has received a third-party payment for the same expenses, trustees are not acting in the best interests of the plan and plan participants as a whole.

What Must Trustees Do To Protect Plan Subrogation Rights?

The most important step plan trustees and administrators can take to protect plan subrogation rights is to review and update the language contained in plan documents and summary plan descriptions. The other critical action is for trustees and administrators to be vigilant in following plan policies and procedures for obtaining reimbursement.

Subrogation Provisions

Subrogation language should be consistent across plan documents to avoid challenges regarding which document controls plan actions. Subrogation provisions should address a number of principles; each principle should be reviewed individually and tailored to the law of the state in which the self-financed plan is located. The principles should also be consistent with current plan terms, administrative policies and procedures.

Decisions from the Courts

The U.S. Supreme Court Solidifies ERISA Plans' Subrogation Rights

Joel and Marlene Sereboff were beneficiaries of a self-funded health plan for which Mid Atlantic Medical Services served as the claims fiduciary. Plan documents gave the plan the "right to recover any payments" made to beneficiaries by third parties for injuries caused by the acts of "another person or organization." When the Sereboffs were involved in an automobile accident in California, the plan advanced the couple $74,869 for medical expenses. On a number of occasions—both before and after the Sereboffs filed their personal injury lawsuit in California state court—the plan informed the couple of its rights to recover this money and asked the couple to sign a reimbursement agreement. The Sereboffs refused to sign. The plan paid additional benefits but continued sending regular correspondence to the Sereboffs updating the dollar amount of the plan's claim and reasserting the reimbursement rights of the plan.

Without notifying Mid Atlantic or seeking its consent, the Sereboffs settled their case against the responsible third parties for $750,000. After the amount owed the attorneys was deducted, the Sereboffs placed the remaining money into a personal investment account. When Mid Atlantic discovered the case had been settled, it sued the Sereboffs on behalf of the plan in the federal District Court of Maryland (the Sereboffs' home state). Mid Atlantic claimed the Sereboffs were obligated to pay the plan out of the settlement money the couple had received. The Sereboffs argued the plan was seeking monetary damages, which were not permissible under ERISA.

The district court and, on appeal, the Fourth Circuit, agreed with Mid Atlantic that the funds were in the possession and control of the Sereboffs and that the money could properly be used to reimburse the plan. The Sereboffs appealed to the U.S. Supreme Court in 2006. In the case called *Sereboff v. Mid Atlantic Medical Services, Inc.*, 547 U.S. 356 (2006), the Court unanimously preserved the plan's right under ERISA to be reimbursed from a participant who had recovered damages from a third party in a personal injury tort action.

Individuals covered by provision. Plan documents should state that plan subrogation rights extend to all plan participants and beneficiaries, including any individuals or entities that may receive payments on behalf of a participant or beneficiary such as dependents, heirs, estates and trusts. It is helpful to define this entire group of people as the *claimant* or *covered person.*

Right to subrogate. The provision should state the plan is subrogated to "any and all rights of recovery and causes of action" that the claimant may have against any third party. These third parties may include spouses or other family members and various forms of insurance coverage (uninsured, underinsured, no-fault, medical payments, personal injury protection, etc.) for either the claimant or the individual responsible for the claimant's injuries.

Right to reimbursement. The provision should give the plan a specific and first right of reimbursement from any money a claimant receives from a third party to the extent of benefits paid—or to be paid—by the plan on the claimant's behalf. In other words, once a claimant receives payment from a third party, the benefit plan is reimbursed before the money is used for any other purpose. The sources of recovery from which the plan expects reimbursement should also be specified. These include: a responsible party and/or responsible party's insurer (or self-financed protection); no-fault protection; personal injury protection; medical payments coverage; financial responsibility; uninsured or underinsured insurance coverage; an employer under the worker's compensation law; and an individual policy of insurance maintained by the claimant.

First priority/rejection of make-whole doctrine. In an attempt to deny or limit a plan's subrogation and reimbursement rights, participants often cite the *make-whole doctrine,* claiming they must be fully compensated for the harm done to them before they have any obligation to repay the benefit plan. A plan's subrogation provision should state that the plan is reimbursed first, even if (1) participants do not recover all their claims for damages or (2) the payment received is for nonmedical expenses. If possible, the document should specifically reject the make-whole doctrine by name.

Right to lien and participant consent. It should be stated specifically that the plan is granted, in the magic words of the *Sereboff* decision, an "equitable lien by agreement and constructive trust to which the claimant consents." This means that the participant (claimant) agrees that money advanced by the plan is to be set aside and protected if the participant's legal claim against the responsible party is successful.

Cooperation. Plan participants must cooperate with the plan to enforce plan subrogation and reimbursement rights; this includes a requirement to execute a separate subrogation and reimbursement agreement that reflects the plan and/or summary plan description provisions. The claimant should be prohibited from evading, innocently or otherwise, plan subrogation and reimbursement rights.

Nonrecognition of other common law doctrines. Many circuit courts have upheld a plan's rejection of common law doctrines such as the make-whole doctrine or the *common fund doctrine* (which can require the plan to pay a portion of the participants' attorney fees). This means that in all likelihood, a plan can immunize itself from these defenses if it includes such language of disavowal.

Subrogation and reimbursement agreements. Though the *Sereboff* Supreme Court decision featured earlier in this chapter suggests it is not necessary to have a plan participant sign a subrogation and reimbursement agreement when a third party is involved, it is still worth inserting language that requires participants—and possibly his or her attorney—to sign an agreement as a condition for receiving medical benefits from the plan. The subrogation and reimbursement agreement is another opportunity for the plan to notify the participant of plan rights and requires the participant to acknowledge these by signing the document. Such agreements also help create a time line of plan efforts to recover benefits advanced and place participant attorneys on notice regarding the plan's right to recovery.

Right to offset against future payments. Finally, the subrogation provision should state that the plan has the right to offset or reduce future benefit payments due to participants and beneficiaries to recover money owed to the plan. Offsets are a common practice and provide a useful tool when negotiating reimbursement payments with uncooperative participants.

Administrative Vigilance

ERISA imposes a fiduciary duty on trustees to "reasonably, diligently and systematically" seek recovery of money a plan is owed. Staff members at the Department of Labor recently confirmed this means designated plan administrators must investigate each potential subrogation or reimbursement claim and determine whether the time, effort and expense of pursuing the claim is in the best interest of the plan and plan participants.

Trustees should ensure that plan administrators periodically review plan policies and procedures, and, if necessary, implement new measures to identify and evaluate these potential claims. Plan administrators should also follow previously adopted procedures that allow their plan to protect subrogation and reimbursement rights quickly and effectively when pursuing a claim.

If plan documents permit, the plan administrator should consistently require participants to sign a subrogation and reimbursement agreement as a condition for receiving benefits. Regardless of whether plan documents permit suspension of benefits until the reimbursement agreement is executed and returned, plan administrators should regularly notify all interested parties (the plan participant, the participant's attorney, third-party insurers, etc.) of the plan's right to recover anything the participant receives from a third party.

Typical notices consist of written correspondence to interested parties and include obtaining a signed reimbursement agreement from the plan participant. While a plan may not need a signed agreement to assert its reimbursement rights, a plan cannot recover unless the money that is awarded to a plan participant is held in an identifiable fund. The reimbursement agreement provides additional notification to the participant of the plan's subrogation and reimbursement rights and interests. A sample Subrogation and Reimbursement Agreement is set forth in the accompanying Appendix A.

Plans must have administrative protocols in place to refer appropriate claims to plan counsel before the participant receives money from the third party. Referral to plan counsel is vital to ensure prompt action: The option of enforcement in federal district court under ERISA section 502(a)(3) is taken to protect the plan's subrogation and reimbursement rights.

What Happens If Trustees Need to Use the Courts to Assert a Plan's Subrogation and Reimbursement Rights?

The Supreme Court made it clear in *Sereboff v. Mid Atlantic Medical Services, Inc.* that subrogation and reimbursement are appropriate tools for use by employee benefit plans under ERISA. In the cases that have been decided since *Sereboff*, most lower courts have concluded the same when they believe the circumstances match those of the *Sereboff* case. While it is impossible to predict how a court will rule in particular case, a close reading of court decisions to date suggests the following lessons.

Sue the Right Parties

Plan administrators and trustees must make sure plan documents allow their plan to seek reimbursement from any party that could hold a third-party recovery on behalf of a participant. In addition to the plan participant, the plan should have the right also to recover funds from a legal guardian, representative or trustee.

The ability to sue the correct individual could be the difference between success and failure in court. For example, in *Great-West Life & Annuity Co. v. Knudson,* 534 U.S. 204 (2002), the plan sued the plan participant (Knudson) but did not sue the trustee of the special-needs trust set up for Knudson where settlement money had been placed. The Supreme Court denied the plan's claim to money in the trust fund because the trustee of the trust, not Knudson, had actual possession of the settlement dollars.

Compare the result in *Knudson* with the result in a different case decided after *Sereboff:* An ERISA plan successfully pursued a claim against the trustee of a special-needs trust for a participant. In *Administrative Committee of Wal-Mart Stores, Inc. Associates' Health and Welfare Plan v. Shank,* 2006 WL 2546797 (E.D. Mo. Aug. 31, 2006), the plan paid more than $450,000 in medical bills for a participant injured in an auto accident. The participant settled a case against a responsible third party for $700,000. After deducting attorney fees and costs, the balance ($414,477) was placed in a special-needs trust for the participant. The plan sued the trust and the trustee, not the participant, for reimbursement. The court confirmed the plan's right to reimbursement.

Document Consistency

In a case from the Court of Appeals for the Eighth Circuit, *Administrative Committee of the Wal-Mart Stores, Inc. Associates' Health and Welfare Plan v. Gamboa,* 479 F.3d 538 (8th Cir. 2007), a plan participant was permanently disabled in an auto accident. The personal injury lawsuit settled all claims for $1 million. The plan had advanced $177,136 in medical benefits for Gamboa and demanded reimbursement based on the subrogation provision in the plan associates' benefits handbook. Gamboa claimed the subrogation provision was not officially part of the plan because it was only found in the benefits handbook, but not in the formal plan wrap document. The court concluded the plan's decision to consider the subrogation provision of the associates' benefits book as part of the formal plan document was reasonable. However, this case magnifies the importance of making sure subrogation language not only exists in both the summary plan description and the formal plan document, but also that the provisions accurately mirror each other.

Avoid Common Law Defenses

Plan participants frequently use the make-whole doctrine or the common fund doctrine as reasons to deny a benefit plan's right to reimbursement. Recall that with the make-whole doctrine, participants typically argue that the recovery did not cover all of their losses—failing to make them "whole"—and thus, they should not have to repay the plan. Courts differ whether and how this doctrine applies: Several have supported this argument unless the plan expressly disavows it.

In *Providence Health System–Washington v. Bush,* 461 F. Supp. 2d 1226 (W.D. Wash. 2006), a Washington State district court found that the plan failed to "expressly" disclaim the doctrine. While the plan document stated the plan had a right to be reimbursed up to 100% and that the plan would not provide benefits that duplicate other coverage, the court held the plan failed to disavow the doctrine because (1) plan documents did not mention the doctrine specifically and (2) the doctrine could be applied without being inconsistent with plan provisions. Sample language in Appendix B provides a good example of the language courts will accept as a clear disavowal of the make-whole doctrine.

Another common law defense that participants routinely assert is the common fund doctrine that claims plan recovery should be reduced by a fair share of the attorney fees and costs incurred by a participant in pursuit of a third-party recovery. This doctrine is based on the theory that the participant's legal actions benefit the plan; therefore, the plan should pay a portion of the costs incurred on behalf of the plan. Plans can avoid the application of the common fund doctrine by stating in plan documents that this defense specifically does not apply to the plan's subrogation and reimbursement rights.

Quickly Assert the Plan Rights

A major problem inherent in the *Knudson* case is the requirement that settlement funds be identifiable and not paid out; this requirement provides an incentive for plan participants to try to hide or spend settlement monies. Wherever possible, plans must quickly notify participants of plan reimbursement interests. Notice must be followed by continuous monitoring of participant actions to ensure funds are not spent before plan reimbursement.

Offset Other Payments

When participants or beneficiaries who owe reimbursement remain eligible participants, plans might consider asserting the plan document provision that allows for the offsetting of future payments against the amounts owed. With this tactic, plans typically do not need to institute action in court or hunt for the settlement funds paid. Of course, participants might still sue the plan for payment of benefits.

Recover Funds Spent To Recover Funds

Plans must spend more money to enforce reimbursement and subrogation rights. It may be possible to recover the costs of litigation by asking a court to order the participants who refuse to reimburse the plan, and sometimes even their attorneys, to pay plan attorney fees and costs. ERISA §502(g) expressly provides that courts may, in their discretion, order attorney fees to be paid to the party that wins in litigation.

Attorneys representing participants who withhold funds may face both ethical and legal complaints. State ethics rules contain provisions relating to how an attorney must treat client trust accounts and settlement funds. In at least one case, *Trustees of Teamsters v. Papero,* 485 F. Supp. 2d 67 (D. Conn. 2007), a court permitted an ERISA action to proceed against attorneys on the grounds that they were ERISA fiduciaries to the extent the attorneys held or controlled "plan assets."

Conclusion

Trustees should make sure the subrogation provisions in plan documents and summary plan descriptions are in line with the suggestions contained within this chapter. Practical administrative procedures must also be in place and followed in vigilant fashion in order to ensure maximum recovery from responsible third parties of dollars advanced on behalf of participants. Following these basic guidelines will result in the recovery of significant plan assets.

Sample Subrogation And Reimbursement Agreement

The following is a description of the principal provisions of the ________**Health and Welfare Fund's** (the "Fund") reimbursement and subrogation rights. This list is not exhaustive and the language of the Fund document will control to the extent that there are any differences between the following descriptions and the Fund document.

The Employee and/or his or her Dependent understands and agrees that:

(a) The Fund has the right to reimbursement from monies recovered by the Employee and/or Dependent from any source relating to a claim, resulting from an injury, sickness, accident or condition, including an individual policy of insurance which is maintained by the Employee and/or Dependent.

(b) The Fund's subrogation and reimbursement rights attach to all monies recovered by the Employee and/or Dependent regardless of how the amounts are characterized. The Fund's subrogation and reimbursement rights extend to monies recovered for medical and loss-of-time benefits paid and to monies recovered for other than medical and loss-of-time benefits paid including, but not limited to, monies recovered for pain and suffering. This means that the Fund specifically will not recognize any claim by the Employee and/or Dependent that monies recovered were insufficient to allow the Employee and/or Dependent to be "made whole."

(c) The Fund has the right to reimbursement for all benefits the Fund has paid to or on behalf of the Employee and/or Dependent as of the date the Employee and/or Dependent recovers monies and for all other benefits the Fund pays after the date of recovery to or on behalf of the Employee and/or Dependent.

(d) The Fund has the right to suspend and withhold all future benefit payments due to an Employee, Dependent and/or any other Dependent of the Employee if the Employee and/or Dependent fails to complete and return this Subrogation and Reimbursement Agreement, the subrogation and reimbursement questionnaire and/or any other documentation to be used to enforce the Fund's subrogation rights until the Fund has recovered the full amount of monies advanced on behalf of the Employee and/or Dependent. If the Employee and/or Dependent recovers monies from any source but does not reimburse the Fund, the Fund also has the right to withhold future benefits on any claims submitted by the Employee, Dependent and/or any other Dependent of the Employee until the Fund has recovered the full amount allowed under the subrogation and reimbursement terms of the Fund.

(e) The Employee and/or Dependent shall be solely responsible for paying all legal fees and expenses in connection with any recovery for the underlying claim, resulting from an injury, sickness, accident or condition, and the Fund's recovery shall not be reduced by such legal fees or expenses.

(f) The Employee and/or Dependent has the duty to cooperate with the Fund regarding its subrogation and reimbursement rights. The Employee and/or Dependent cannot alter the Fund's subrogation and reimbursement rights by an agreement with the third party.

(g) The Employee and/or Dependent, and/or any agent of the Employee and/or Dependent, including any attorney, agrees to hold any money recovered in constructive trust for the benefit of the Fund to be paid to the Fund immediately upon recovery thereof.

The undersigned expressly understands and agrees that all benefits paid or to be paid by the Fund, including those amounts to be paid pursuant to this specific Subrogation and Reimbursement Agreement, are conditioned upon the Fund's rights of subrogation and reimbursement and create an equitable lien by agreement. The undersigned agrees to notify the Fund of any recovery by the undersigned relating to his or her claim and to repay the Fund from any and all recoveries once the undersigned has recovered monies. The undersigned understands and agrees that this Subrogation and Reimbursement Agreement creates contractual and equitable rights, in addition to those created under the Fund's Rules and Regulations, for the Fund to assert its subrogation and reimbursement rights against the undersigned in a court of competent jurisdiction.

____
Employee's Signature

____
Dependent's Signature (If of Legal Age)

____
Date

Sample Plan Document Language

Individuals Covered by Provision

The plan shall be entitled to subrogation and/or reimbursement of all rights of recovery of a participant, his or her parent(s) and dependent(s) or a representative, guardian or trustee of the participant, parent(s) or dependent(s) (hereinafter, collectively "claimant").

Right to Subrogate

The plan is subrogated to any and all rights of recovery and causes of action that the claimant may have against any third party, whether by suit, settlement or otherwise, that may be liable for a claimant's injury or illness for which the plan has paid or is obligated to pay benefits on the claimant's behalf.

Rights to Reimbursement with Source of Funds Specifically Identified

The plan shall also be entitled, to the extent of payments made or to be made on account of the claim, to the proceeds of any settlement, judgment or payment from any source liable for making a payment relating to the claimant's injury, illness or condition. A source includes, but is not limited to, a responsible party and/or responsible party's insurer (or self-financed protection), no-fault protection, personal injury protection, medical payments coverage, financial responsibility, uninsured or underinsured insurance coverage, an employer under the provisions of a workers' compensation law and an individual policy of insurance maintained by a claimant.

Rejection of Make-Whole Doctrine

Such subrogation and reimbursement rights shall apply on a priority, first-dollar basis to any recovery, whether by suit, settlement or otherwise, whether there is a partial or full recovery and regardless of whether the amounts are characterized or described as medical expenses or as amounts other than for medical expenses.

Equitable Lien by Agreement

Once the plan makes or is obligated to make payments on behalf of a claimant, the plan is granted, and the claimant consents to, an equitable lien by agreement or a constructive trust on the proceeds of any payment, settlement or judgment received by the eligible employee or dependent from any source to the extent of payments made or to be made by the plan on the claimant's behalf.

Claimant Must Set Aside Funds

The claimant shall hold in trust for the plan's benefit that portion of the total recovery from any source that is due for payments made or to be made. The claimant shall reimburse the plan immediately upon recovery. The claimant shall immediately notify the plan if he or she is involved in or suffers an accident or injury for which a third party may be liable. The claimant shall again notify the plan if he or she pursues a claim to recover damages or other relief relating to an injury or illness for which the plan may make payments on the claimant's behalf. The claimant shall do nothing to impair, release, discharge or prejudice the plan's rights to subrogation and/or reimbursement. The claimant shall assist and cooperate with representatives the plan designates. The claimant shall do everything necessary to enable the plan to enforce its subrogation and reimbursement rights. The claimant shall immediately notify the plan upon receiving a judgment, settlement offer or compromise offer and shall not settle or compromise any claims without the plan's consent.

First-Dollar Recovery

The plan's subrogation and reimbursement rights shall apply on a priority first-dollar basis to any recovery whether by suit, settlement or otherwise, regardless of whether a claimant is made whole.

Disavowal of Common Fund Doctrine

The plan's subrogation and reimbursement rights apply to any recovery by the claimant without regard to legal fees and expenses of the claimant. The claimant shall be solely responsible for paying all legal fees and expenses in connection with any recovery for the underlying injury, sickness, accident or condition, and the plan's recovery shall not be reduced by such legal fees or expenses, unless the plan administrator, in his or her sole discretion, agrees in writing to discount the plan's claim by an agreed-upon amount of such fees or expenses.

The plan specifically disavows any claims that an eligible employee or dependent may make under any federal or state common law defense including, but not limited to, the make-whole doctrine and/or the common fund doctrine.

Cooperation

The plan administrator may require the claimant to complete and/or execute certain documentation to assist the plan in the enforcement of its subrogation rights including, but not limited to, a subrogation and reimbursement questionnaire and a repayment agreement. The completion and/or execution of any documents requested by the plan administrator shall be a condition to receiving payment for a claim. Further, the plan shall have the right to suspend all benefit payments due to a claimant, the employee of whom a claimant is a dependent and/or any other dependent of such an employee if the claimant fails to complete and/or execute such documentation.

Chapter 25

Merging Multiemployer Health and Welfare Funds

Mitchell D. Whitehead and Carrie J. Grove

When there is a merger between multiemployer pension plans, there is no shortage of rules and regulations that apply—from the funding, notice and procedural rules contained in the Employee Retirement Income Security Act of 1974 (ERISA) to the requirement that mergers be submitted to the Pension Benefit Guaranty Corporation (PBGC) for advance approval. In addition, numerous books, articles and other publications provide guidance on this subject.

In contrast, mergers between multiemployer health and welfare plans are subject to almost no federal regulation and require no advance approval by federal agencies. There is very little published guidance on the topic. The purpose of this chapter is to give plan trustees and administrators a practical guide to the merger of two or more multiemployer health and welfare funds. A general form of merger agreement in the appendix of this chapter illustrates many of the issues addressed during a merger.

What Legal Requirements Apply to Health and Welfare Plan Mergers?

As noted above, and somewhat incredibly, ERISA does not include any substantive requirements for mergers involving multiemployer health and welfare funds. Moreover, there are few court cases that involve health fund mergers; none deal meaningfully with requirements during a merger. A rare exception is some judicial guidance on the related issue of whether participants who withdraw from a welfare plan and move to another are entitled to a transfer of a portion of reserves from the original plan.

Settlor Function vs. Fiduciary Decisions

The merger of two or more multiemployer health funds has two separate and distinct stages: (1) the initial decision to merge the funds and (2) the process of implementing the decision. The decision to merge multiemployer health funds is most frequently made by the bargaining parties with a collective bargaining agreement instructing trustees of the merging funds to take all necessary steps to implement the merger.

Even if plan fiduciaries make the decision to merge, the first stage of the process is usually considered a "settlor" function. The courts and the Department of Labor (DOL) generally have recognized the establishment, design, amendment and termination of a benefit plan as *settlor functions.* Actions related to administration of a plan and those implementing a decision are considered *fiduciary.* Decisions characterized as settlor functions do not trigger ERISA's fiduciary rules.[1] Nevertheless, once a decision to merge is made, trustees must implement the decision in compliance with ERISA's fiduciary duties to act prudently, for the exclusive benefit of participants and in accordance with plan documents.

Despite possible application of the settlor function rule to the merger decision, trustees are well advised to be prepared to defend (1) the rationale for the merger as benefiting plan participants over time and (2) their due diligence as trustees. The due diligence process, at a minimum, should address (1) whether the transaction will cause a material funding problem for either of the plans and (2) whether the merger will cause any material disadvantage to plan participants over time.

Due diligence does not present a serious problem for most multiemployer plans given the bargaining parties and the trustees are often the same people. In addition, the plan sponsors (the employers and unions) generally work with consultants and advisors to assess the workability, financial impact and other implications of a merger well before merger negotiations begin.

If trustees are not satisfied with the due diligence process, they determine that the merger isn't workable, or perhaps they feel the merger is not justified from a fiduciary standpoint, they have to confront the question of whether they have the authority to disregard a directive in the collective bargaining agreement and refuse to merge the funds. The answer to this very difficult question ultimately depends on the rights and responsibilities of the trustees versus those of the bargaining parties in the trust agreement and collective bargaining agreements for the funds.[2]

Fiduciary Duties—Do the Deal Right

Quite apart from the decision of whether to merge, trustees must make sure their actions and decisions during implementation are fully consistent with their fiduciary responsibilities under ERISA. A key element in trustee compliance is performance of *transactional due diligence* (i.e., making sure the deal is done right).

Trustees should not hesitate to insist that plan professionals spell out exactly what due diligence steps are required and/or recommended while implementing the deal. The process should involve all key plan professionals, including administrative staff, attorneys, consultants and accountants. There should be a thorough review of all relevant plan documents including:

- The trust agreement
- Plan rules, regulations and procedures
- Applicable collective bargaining agreements
- Summary plan description, financial statements
- Form 5500 filings
- Fiduciary liability insurance (including any pending claims against the policy)
- Fidelity bond
- Service provider agreements and reports (e.g., HMOs, PPOs and other insured arrangements).

Trustees and plan professionals should also review all existing investments and analyze the impact of the merger on these investments, as well as determine how the merger will affect administrative and other costs.

A useful tool to manage this process is a *due diligence checklist* prepared by plan professionals showing all steps required to complete the merger, along with a timeline showing when each step will be completed. There is no more effective way for trustees to get the "big picture" on a merger and fully appreciate the timeframes involved. Experience indicates mergers generally take more time and effort to finalize than originally expected.

Fiduciaries are obligated to act in accordance with the documents that govern the plan as long as these documents are consistent with ERISA. Therefore, while reviewing documents, trustees should determine whether any contract conditions, notices, filings or other steps must be satisfied prior to completion of the merger. This review also helps ensure the obligation of each employer to contribute will pass to, and be enforceable by, the surviving fund. Employers may need to sign a new agreement confirming their obligation to contribute to the surviving fund.

Another important reason for the document review is to ensure that trust agreements specifically address trustee ability to authorize a fund merger and/or implement a merger authorized by the bargaining parties. Trustees may have the power to authorize and implement a merger under the general powers provided to them in their trust agreements. If the power to authorize or implement a merger is not specifically mentioned, trustees should consider adopting amendments to the trust agreements that specifically grant the trustees these powers.

Prohibited Transactions

ERISA's prohibited transaction rules must also be considered during a merger—these are the rules that forbid certain transactions between plans and "parties in interest." The rules come into play if any of the plans involved are "parties in interest" to each other, or if the plans have common trustees (since ERISA's fiduciary self-dealing rules prohibit trustees from acting on both sides of a transaction).

It is not always easy to determine whether funds involved in the merger are parties in interest. Funds often have common trustees or the same administrator. They may also be in the same industry or have the same sponsoring employers or unions. These relationships alone do not automatically cause the funds to be parties in interest to each other. Funds would likely be parties in interest only if one of the funds provided services to the other (e.g., administrative services, leasing office space, etc.) or they provide coverage to each other's administrative employees.

Because it may be difficult to determine whether a fund is a party in interest, trustees should request that legal counsel review the current relationships between the funds and any anticipated transactions with other parties in connection with the merger. Counsel should determine whether any of the transactions involving parties in interest violate the prohibited transaction rules.

Similarly, ERISA's self-dealing rules can pose a problem for a merger—particularly if there are trustees serving the merging plans.[3] Although Congress created an exception to the prohibited transaction rules for pension fund mergers involving common trustees, the exception does not explicitly extend to mergers of health and welfare funds.[4] There are a number of strategies for dealing with this problem, including having the common trustees abstain from all relevant discussions and votes. This is another occasion when the advice of legal counsel is essential.

What Notices Are Required During a Merger?

Although there is no legal requirement to provide advance notice of a multiemployer health funds merger, certain notices should be provided both before and after the merger becomes effective.

Advance Notice to Affected Parties

Although not legally required, mergers often have elaborate communication campaigns to:

- Inform participants
- Minimize anxieties about the deal
- Avoid enrollment, eligibility, benefit change and other transition problems.

These campaigns often involve one or more meetings with participants to answer questions and to assist with enrollments, applications, etc.

At a minimum, the trustees of plans involved in a merger should provide participants, beneficiaries, contributing employers, affected unions and any other interested parties with advance written notice of the merger. Ideally, the notice should:

- Describe the impending transaction
- Set forth the date of the merger
- Describe the benefit changes that become effective after it closes
- Explain any required enrollment, elections and eligibility steps including any deadlines for these actions
- Provide contact information for addressing any issues that arise during the transition period.

The notice to contributing employers must also specify where contribution checks are sent after the merger.

Of the information in the notice, it is particularly important to provide participants and beneficiaries detailed information regarding timing, enrollment deadlines and elections, and how the benefits will change after the merger. Since it is unlikely that any two funds will have the same benefit structure, the trustees or bargaining parties of the funds to be merged will need to decide what benefits will be offered under the merged plan. The trustees should inform the participants and beneficiaries of these changes as soon as possible after the benefit structure is finalized, and well in advance of the implementation of the new benefit changes. Funds are advised to provide notice of the merger (including all benefit changes) to the affected parties at least 30 to 60 days prior to the merger effective date.

Summary of Material Modifications

Trustees of each fund to be merged are legally required to provide a *summary of material modifications* (SMM) to all fund participants and beneficiaries explaining the merger and the new terms of the merged fund. Where practical, the advance notice to the participants and beneficiaries described above should meet the SMM content requirements; otherwise a separate SMM will need to be provided. DOL requires the SMM be given to participants and beneficiaries receiving health benefits within 60 days after an adoption or modification of benefits occurs if any of the changes are a material reduction in benefits. When applied to mergers, this requirement must be met for all plans being merged. If changes to the plans are not material reductions, the SMM is due within 210 days after the end of the plan year in which the changes are effective.

Notice to Affected Vendors

All vendors should be notified of a merger at the earliest possible date. Vendors should be asked to confirm that they will continue to provide services to the surviving fund, if they are requested to do so. If a vendor agreement will be terminated or a vendor will be assigned to another fund as a result of the merger, the agreement should be reviewed to determine the form and timing of any required notice to the provider. Legal counsel should be involved as early in this process as possible to allow adequate time to evaluate each agreement and notify the provider accordingly.

What Operational Issues Are Addressed Prior to a Merger?

Apart from legal considerations, many practical and operational issues are addressed prior to the merger and, where appropriate, covered by provisions in the merger agreement. This phase of the merger process usually requires a substantial commitment of time and resources on behalf of plan professionals and administrative staff. Funds should allow from three to six months for this part of the process. Some of the most relevant practical issues faced when implementing a merger are discussed below.

Prepare Merger Agreement

The parties involved will need to prepare and sign a written *merger agreement.* Given the requirement that fiduciaries follow the terms of a plan's governing documents, the merger agreement can serve as an amendment to these documents for the plans involved in the transaction. The agreement should contain all of the material terms of the merger, such as:

- The merger effective date
- The merger closing date
- The amount of assets to be transferred
- Any representations and warranties made between the funds
- A summary of the new benefit structure.

In addition, the agreement should incorporate other relevant items including:

- The procedure for appointing trustees to the new merged fund
- An indemnification provision whereby the surviving fund indemnifies the trustees of the other fund
- A description of how fiduciary liability insurance coverage will be provided for the surviving fund and the fund (or funds) that do not survive
- The treatment of participants under the merged fund.

The agreement should also address the administrative and transition issues discussed below. Once drafted, the agreement should be reviewed by each fund's trustees, legal counsel and consultants to ensure all issues are accurately addressed and reflected in the agreement.

The sample merger agreement in the appendix of this chapter illustrates the types of issues that might be addressed in a typical merger transaction. An agreement will need to be tailored by legal counsel for each separate merger transaction.

Review Compliance Issues and Completion of Due Diligence

Prior to the closing date, trustees should verify all recommended due diligence items are complete. The status of any outstanding items should be checked. Again, trustees should confirm that the due diligence process is properly documented.

Verify Post-Merger Benefit Design

It is virtually assured that at least one (if not all) of the plans involved in a merger will be changing the benefits provided its participants. Trustees and plan professionals of the affected funds will have to work together to design a post-merger benefit structure—this structure may be dictated by the bargaining parties.

Resolve Administration and Transition Issues

A merger of multiemployer health and welfare funds is also a merger of administrative, claims processing, information technology, trustee and operational cultures. Thus, there are a number of issues that should be resolved before, during and after the merger. Following is a list of some of the more significant administrative and operational issues:

- Who will handle the administration and claims processing for all of the affected participants after the merger closing date? Where will the administrative operation be located?
- Will the administrative operation of the nonsurviving fund(s)—or specific individuals who work for that operation—be engaged to provide transitional or ongoing administrative services? Will offices be combined or relocated?
- If a third-party administrator (TPA) is used for one or more of the funds being merged, will this TPA be terminated? Does it make sense from a practical and/or financial standpoint to self-administer the merged fund going forward?
- How will the transfer of documents and records be accomplished in order to comply with HIPAA privacy and other rules? How will records physically be transferred and where will they be kept?
- What arrangements will be made for any non-collectively bargained administrative staff who participate in any of the affected funds?
- What will happen to leases or other arrangements for office space currently being used by plans' administration?
- If the existing administrative operation and/or staff are not retained, how will existing policies, procedures and practices be communicated to the successor operation?
- Is there any propriety or licensed administrative/claims-processing software or hardware that must be assigned or transferred to the resulting fund? Does existing software access allow for the merger and added lives, and does it allow for use at a different location or "site"?
- How will arrangements be handled for the payment of employer contributions? Will contributions be payable at the same location, at the same time, and using the same lockbox and remittance report—or will these procedures change?

- Will there be any impact on the methods currently used for allocating employer contributions among related funds?

A health and welfare fund merger requires intensive effort and numerous meetings between the plan professionals and the administrative staff of all funds involved in the merger to work through these issues. The administrative and practical issues generally take months to resolve and will undoubtedly affect the merger closing date.

Obtain Fiduciary Liability Insurance

The trustees of each affected fund (other than the surviving fund) should consider obtaining at least six years of "tail coverage" under their existing fiduciary liability insurance policy. Such coverage is standard and is normally purchased at a reasonable premium. This type of coverage should be addressed in the merger agreement. The trustees of the funds that are merging should also be added to the surviving fund's fiduciary liability insurance policy as additional insureds.

Request Indemnification

If the trust agreements of the merging funds contain an indemnification provision protecting the trustees in connection with their actions as trustees, the trustees of the merging funds should request that the surviving fund indemnify and hold them harmless on the same basis. If this occurs, the surviving fund would assume the post-merger obligation of the nonsurviving funds to provide trustee indemnification. This indemnity could cover any liability connected with or resulting from the merger. In addition, trustees of each merged fund may want to review their current indemnity provision to ensure that it (1) provides them with state-of-the-art protection and (2) advances their liability expenses to the maximum extent permitted by law.

Provide for Continuation of the Fidelity Bond

Apart from fiduciary liability insurance, trustees of merged funds may want to continue the ERISA-mandated fidelity bond coverage for these funds for an appropriate period.

Determine Board Composition

Prior to the merger closing date, the trustees of all affected funds should clarify and have in writing the number of initial trustees that are to serve on the board of the resulting fund. The procedure for selecting or appointing trustees should also be established. Both of these decisions should be included in the merger agreement.

Conclusion

While there are no ERISA rules or regulations that specifically address the undertaking, the merger of multiemployer health and welfare funds can still be a daunting, difficult and time-consuming task that demands careful attention from the trustees of the affected plans. Not only is it essential to exercise due diligence and prudence, it is also important to document carefully what was done. This documentation includes maintaining evidence that appropriate input and advice was obtained from the plan professionals. The negotiation and drafting of a comprehensive merger agreement is a key step in any merger transaction. The sample provided for this chapter is a good starting place.

Endnotes

1. In its decision in 2007 in *Beck v. Pace*, the U.S. Supreme Court recognized that an employer's decision refusing to merge its pension plan into a multiemployer pension plan was a settlor function immune from the fiduciary considerations of ERISA 551 U.S. 96 (2007). It should be noted, however, that the application of the *Beck* decision in the multiemployer context is not completely settled, and there is some question about how a merger decision made by the trustees of a multiemployer plan (unlike the single employer plan in *Beck*) would be treated.
2. A detailed discussion of this issue is beyond the scope of this chapter, but it is generally believed that trustees are compelled to implement the instructions of bargaining parties unless to do so would cause a violation of law or some other very serious harm to the plan.
3. ERISA §406(b)(2) prohibits a fiduciary from acting "in any transaction involving the plan on behalf of a party ... whose interests are adverse to the interests of the plan." In a merger context, the interests of each fund are technically adverse to all other funds merged, since they are on "opposite" sides of a merger transaction.
4. ERISA §§408(b)(11), 408(f) and 4231.

MERGER AGREEMENT AND PLAN AMENDMENT

BETWEEN

[FUND A)

AND

[FUND B]

This **MERGER AGREEMENT AND PLAN AMENDMENT** (the "Agreement"") is made and entered into on this day of ___________ 20__, by and between the __________________ ("**[Fund A]**") and __________________ ("**[Fund B]**"), which hereby agree to be bound by the terms and provisions herein.

WHEREAS, [Fund A] is maintained pursuant to various collective bargaining agreements between and (the "Bargaining Parties") for the exclusive purpose of providing health and welfare benefits to its participants and their beneficiaries;

WHEREAS, [Fund B] is maintained pursuant to a collective bargaining agreement between the Bargaining Parties for the exclusive purpose of providing health and welfare benefits to its participants and their beneficiaries;

WHEREAS, the Bargaining Parties have directed the Trustees of **[Fund A]** (the "**[Fund A]** Trustees") and the Trustees of **[Fund B]** (the "**[Fund B]** Trustees") to merge **[Fund A]** into **[Fund B]**;

WHEREAS, the **[Fund A]** Trustees and the **[Fund B]** Trustees have determined that a merger of **[Fund A]** into **[Fund B]** (the "Merger") would be in the best interests of their respective participants and beneficiaries for reasons including, but not limited to, economics of scale in administration of a merged plan, the creation of a larger and more stable participant base with improved prospects for future growth, improved portability of benefits for plan participants and improved investment opportunities;

WHEREAS, the **[Fund A]** Trustees and **[Fund B]** Trustees have independently determined that the Merger is not inconsistent with their duties and responsibilities under the Employee Retirement Income Security Act of 1974, as amended ("ERISA");

WHEREAS, the **[Fund A]** Trustees are authorized to merge **[Fund A]** under the terms of the trust agreement under which **[Fund A]** is established:

WHEREAS, the **[Fund B]** Trustees are authorized to merge **[Fund B]** under the terms of the trust agreement under which **[Fund B]** is established; and

WHEREAS, the parties desire to merge **[Fund A]** into **[Fund B]** effective as of 12:00 a.m. on ______________, 20__ (the "Merger Effective Date"), with the resulting fund to be called the "**[New Fund]**."

NOW THEREFORE, in recognition of the promises and mutual covenants set forth herein, and for good and valuable consideration, the **[Fund A]** Trustees and the **[Fund B]** Trustees hereby agree as follows:

1. Effective as of the Merger Effective Date:

   (a) **[Fund A]** shall be merged into **[Fund B]**;

(b) **[Fund A]** shall cease to exist as a separate legal entity;

(c) all of **[Fund A]**'s assets and liabilities shall be merged into (and become a part of) **[Fund B]**; and

(d) **[Fund B]** shall assume all of the purposes, powers, rights, immunities and obligations of **[Fund A]**, including the obligation of providing benefits to all individuals who are participants (and beneficiaries) in **[Fund A]** on the day before the Merger Effective Date.

2. Effective as of the Merger Effective Date, **[Fund B]** shall be the sole surviving fund, shall be renamed the "**[New Fund]**" and shall be operated and administered pursuant to the plan of benefits of **[Fund B]** and the Agreement and Declaration of Trust establishing **[Fund B]** (the "**[Fund B]** Trust Agreement").

3. Effective as of the Merger Effective Date, health and welfare benefit of former **[Fund A]** participants shall be provided under **[Fund B]** in accordance with the attached Schedule A.

4. Effective as of the Merger Effective Date, the **[Fund A]** Trustees shall transfer to the **[Fund B]** Trustees all real and personal property, securities, cash, bank accounts and any and all monies and other assets of whatever nature of **[Fund A]** (including, without limitation. all reserves and contractual rights to contributions due but not yet paid), all documents, books and records, and any and all other things of value in the possession, custody or control of **[Fund A]** or the [Fund A] Trustees relating to **[Fund A]** (collectively, the "**[Fund A]** Assets").

5. Effective as of the Merger Effective Date, except as provided by ERISA or other applicable law, neither the **[Fund A]** Trustees nor the employers that contribute to **[Fund A]** (nor their former or present employees) shall have any right, title or interest to any **[Fund A]** Assets or any of the monies, assets, or other things of value in the possession, custody or control of **[Fund B]**.

6. Effective as of the Merger Effective Date, employees of every employer that becomes a contributing employer to **[Fund B]** shall be eligible to participate in the **[New Fund]**, provided such individuals continue to meet the requirements for participation and eligibility established by the **[Fund B]** Trustees on or after the Merger Effective Date.

7. Notwithstanding anything in this Agreement to the contrary, the **[Fund B]** Trustees, in their sole and absolute discretion and subject to applicable law, following the Merger Effective Date, shall have the right to reduce, modify or discontinue benefits and to modify any other rules and regulations governing such participants, to the extent permitted by applicable law.

8. Notwithstanding anything in this Agreement to the contrary, the plan year of the **[New Fund]** shall continue to be the 12-month period beginning on January 1 of each calendar year, subject to amendment by the **[Fund B]** Trustees in their sole and absolute discretion.

9. As soon as practicable after the execution of this Agreement, the **[Fund B]** Trustees and the **[Fund A]** Trustees shall notify all participants in **[Fund A]** of the Merger contemplated by this Agreement.

10. To the extent permitted by law, effective as of the Merger Effective Date, the **[Fund B]** Trustees will use commercially reasonable efforts to obtain, at the expense or **[Fund B]**, an extension of the reporting period for the fiduciary liability insurance in the amount in force at the date of execution of this Agreement with respect to **[Fund A]** and each of the **[Fund A]** Trustees members presently covered under **[Fund A]**'s fiduciary liability insurance policy or similar coverage for a reasonable period, not to exceed six (6) years, if reasonably available.

11. (a) The **[Fund A]** Trustees and the **[Fund B]** Trustees each hereby certify and represent to the other that, to the best of their knowledge and except as disclosed in the attached Schedule B, effective as of the Merger Effective Date:

(i) there are no pending (or threatened) litigations, disputed claims (other than routine claims for benefits), obligations, issues or liabilities of any type against their fund or its assets, employees, fiduciaries or agents. nor do any facts exist which could give rise to any such actions. Furthermore, no audit or investigation by a government agency has occurred in the last five years or is currently pending or threatened with respect to their fund, nor has their fund received, at any time during the last five years, any notice or other communication (whether oral or written) from any governmental body or any other person regarding any actual, alleged, possible, or potential violation of, or failure to comply with, any legal requirement. Except for qualified domestic relations orders (copies of which will be made available, if requested), their fund is not subject to any order by a court or other governmental body;

(ii) no prohibited transaction (as such term is defined in Sections 406 and 407 of ERISA and Section 4975 of the Internal Revenue Code of 1986, as amended (the "Code")) has occurred with respect to their Fund;

(iii) their fund has been operated at all times in accordance with its terms and in material compliance with the Code, ERISA, and other applicable law;

(iv) all applicable reports, documents and notices regarding their Fund required by ERISA or the Code to be filed with the Secretary of Labor or the Secretary of the Treasury (or distributed to participants of their Fund) have been filed (or distributed) in a timely fashion;

(v) every fiduciary of their fund, and every other person who handles fund assets, has been bonded in accordance with the requirements of Section 412 of ERISA;

(vi) their fund has no outstanding material liability not reported on the most recent financial statement provided to the other fund other than the obligation to pay benefits as they become due;

(vii) they are not aware of any reason that the financial statements and notes provided hereunder do not fairly represent the financial condition and results of operations and cash flow of their fund at the respective dates of and for the periods referred to in such financial statements;

(viii) except as disclosed in Schedule B, there are no known or suspected material delinquencies with respect to any contributions due and owing to their fund. There is no contest, claim, or right of set-off relating to the amount or validity of such delinquency. Each fund has disclosed a complete and accurate list of unpaid delinquent contributions as of the date hereof, and such list sets forth the aging of such amounts;

(x) except as disclosed in a schedule to this Agreement, since the date of the last audited balance sheet, there has not been any:

(A) damage to or destruction or loss of any asset or property of their fund, whether or not covered by insurance, materially and adversely affecting the properties, assets or financial condition of their fund;

(B) sale, lease, or other disposition of any asset or property of their fund or mortgage, pledge, or imposition of any lien or other encumbrance on any material asset or property of their fund; or

(C) cancellation or waiver of any claims or rights of their fund in excess of $10,000;

(xi) no claims have been made under their fund's fiduciary liability insurance policy in the past three years;

(xii) all insurance policies under which their fund is covered are valid, outstanding, and enforceable and provide adequate insurance coverage for the assets and the operations of their fund for all risks normally insured against by a retirement plan. Furthermore, their fund has fulfilled all of its obligations under such policies and has given notice to the insurers of all claims that may be insured thereby; and

(xiii) their Board has, by appropriate action, duly authorized the execution and implementation of this Agreement, which has been executed on behalf of their trustees by a person (or persons) authorized to do so, and such authorizations and execution do not violate any obligation or legal requirements by which their trustees are bound, such that this Agreement is a legal, valid and binding obligation of their fund.

(b) Both funds agree that they will immediately notify the other in the event that, to the best of their knowledge, any of the certifications in subparagraph (a) become not true at any time on or prior to the Merger Effective Date. Both funds further agree that they will not increase benefits at any time on or prior to the Merger Effective Date, unless directed to do so by the Bargaining Parties.

12. (a) The **[Fund A]** Trustees hereby certify to the **[Fund B]** Trustees that, effective as of the Merger Effective Date:

(i) the current insurance carrier providing fiduciary liability insurance to **[Fund A]** and the **[Fund A]** Trustees has been notified in writing of the Merger contemplated herein and it will not cancel the fiduciary liability insurance policy presently in full force and effect prior to the Merger Effective Date (unless "tail'" insurance has been purchased); and

(ii) the **[Fund A]** Trustees has not taken any action that would prohibit the **[Fund B]** Trustees from amending or terminating its plan or any contract or agreement entered into by **[Fund A]**.

(b) The **[Fund A]** Trustees agree that they will immediately notify the **[Fund B]** Trustees in the event that, to the best of their knowledge, any of the certifications in subparagraph (a) become not true at any time on or prior to the Merger Effective Date. The **[Fund A]** Trustees further agree that they will not increase benefits under their plan at any time on or prior to the Merger Effective Date.

13. As soon as practicable following the execution of this Agreement, there shall be a closing accounting of **[Fund A]** (stipulating, *infer alia*, the amount of assets transferred from **[Fund A]** to the **[New Fund]**), which accounting shall be conducted by a certified public accountant retained by **[Fund B]**.

14. The parties hereto agree that they shall take all such further required action, as may be necessary or desirable in order that this Agreement and the Merger provided for herein shall comply with all applicable law (including, without limitation, ERISA and the Code).

15. The **[Fund A]** Trustees and the **[Fund B]** Trustees agree to make any necessary government filings, notifications and/or amendments to their respective plans, trust agreements, summary plan descriptions, or related documents, and to terminate at the request of the **[Fund B]** Trustees service provider agreements, as may be necessary or appropriate in order to effectuate the provisions of this Agreement and the Merger provided for herein.

16. All questions of the interpretation of this Agreement, and all questions arising out of the Merger, shall be resolved by the **[Fund A]** Trustees and the **[Fund B]** Trustees. Should the parties be unable to resolve any disputes under this Agreement amongst themselves in accordance with the preceding sentence, then the parties hereto agree that such matter shall be referred to binding arbitration before a mutually agreed upon arbitrator selected pursuant to the Labor Rules of the American Arbitration Association, and the arbitration shall be governed by such rules.

17. Should any provision of this Agreement require interpretation or construction, it is agreed by the parties hereto that the arbitrator or other entity interpreting or construing such document shall not apply a presumption that the provisions hereof shall be more strictly construed against one party by reason of the rule of construction that a document is to be construed more strictly against the party who itself or through its agents prepared the same, it being agreed that all parties (either directly or by their respective counsel) have fully participated in the negotiation and preparation of all provisions of this Agreement.

18. Except to the extent preempted by ERISA, this Agreement and the Merger contemplated herein shall be governed by, construed and enforced in accordance with the internal laws of the State of California applicable to contracts made and to be performed in the State of California (without giving effect to the principles thereof relating to the conflict of laws).

19. This Agreement sets forth the entire agreement of the parties hereto, is intended to be a complete and exclusive statement of the terms hereof, and may not be modified or amended except by a writing signed by the parties hereto.

20. Notwithstanding anything in this Agreement to the contrary, no provision of this Agreement shall be construed so as to violate ERISA, the Code, or other applicable law.

21. In the event that any provision of this Agreement shall be held by any court of competent jurisdiction to be illegal, void or unenforceable, such provision shall have no effect upon, and shall not impair the enforceability of, any other provision of this Agreement, unless the **[Fund B]** Trustees determines, in their sole and absolute discretion, that the enforcement of such other provision would defeat the purpose of this Agreement.

22. This Agreement shall inure to the benefit of the parties hereto, and their successors and assigns. This Agreement is not intended to confer any right or benefit upon any other person or entity. No other person or entity shall have any legally enforceable right hereunder.

[bottom of page intentionally left blank}

23. This Agreement may be executed in any number of counterpart copies, each of which shall be deemed to be, and have the force of, an original, but all of which shall be considered the same instrument.

IN WITNESS WHEREOF, the parties hereto, in consideration of the mutual promises and undertakings set forth herein and intending to be legally bound hereby, have caused this Agreement to be executed pursuant to the authority duly granted them by the party for which they act, as of the day and year first above written.

ON BEHALF OF THE BOARD OF TRUSTEES OF [FUND A]

____

____

ON BEHALF OF THE BOARD OF TRUSTEES OF [FUND B]

____

____

Chapter 26

Defined Benefit Plan Design

Steven A. Brannon and Joseph A. Brislin

Historically, multiemployer plans have favored a defined benefit (DB) approach to providing workers with retirement benefits. DB plans:

- Provide retirees with a fixed retirement payment determined in advance
- Are funded through employer contributions sufficient to provide the amount promised.

Plan participants know throughout their working years what their exact pension benefit will be, making it much easier to plan for retirement. Participants know this predetermined benefit amount will be paid for the rest of their life (and often for the rest of their spouse's life).

Contributions to a DB plan are pooled to provide benefits for all participants who meet requirements stated in plan documents. Once a participating employer contributes dollars for the hours an employee works, the money is no longer associated with that specific employee. Instead, employees are given credit for the time they have worked and their individual benefits are based on these credits. The collective bargaining agreement (CBA) and plan participation agreement specify the contributions an employer must make on behalf of each employee working in covered employment.

Trustees are responsible for making sure contributions from employers and investment earnings are sufficient to pay the retirement benefit promised each participant. Trustees must understand the basics of how pension plans work and what it costs to provide different pension benefits for normal retirement, early retirement, disability, spousal benefits, death benefits, etc.

The pension environment is highly regulated; 33 federal laws regulating pension plans have followed the passage of the Employee Retirement Income Security Act of 1974 (ERISA). Each of these laws also has agency regulations and court cases interpreting the law. Benefit changes are a reality of the government regulations, collective bargaining process and today's financial uncertainty. Trustees must rely heavily upon the knowledge and expertise of plan advisors to comply with these laws.

The purpose of this chapter is to provide an overview

Qualified Pension Plans

A *qualified plan* offers tax advantages to both plan participants and contributing employers. The Internal Revenue Service (IRS) treats employer contributions to a plan as a tax-deductible business expense. In addition, plan contributions and the investments earnings made on these funds are not taxed. Money contributed accumulates tax-free until the plan begins paying out benefits. It is only then that recipients must pay federal income tax on the benefit amount received.

A qualified plan must meet various rules of the Internal Revenue Code (IRC) that restrict the design of the plan and how it is funded. There are also strict reporting requirements. A plan's attorney typically submits plan documents to IRS for review. If the documents pass review, IRS issues a determination letter indicating the plan is qualified.

In contrast, a *nonqualified plan* has very little in the way of rules on plan design or funding. Because they lack the favorable tax treatment, however, nonqualified plans are not very common.

of the key questions considered in the design of DB plans and some of the approaches used in addressing these issues. The input of a plan actuary and legal counsel will be essential in making these decisions.

Who Will Be Eligible for Benefits?

A multiemployer retirement plan can cover full-time, part-time, hourly or seasonal employees. Plan documents typically define what jobs are *covered employment*—work for which an employer is required to make plan contributions on behalf of an employee.

Service Requirements

Service for a retirement plan can be measured in hours, days, weeks, months or quarters during a plan year. The measure used is set by plan documents and the CBAs. An employee's service as a covered employee determines when an employee becomes a plan participant. ERISA requires that employees over the age of 18 be allowed to participate in a retirement plan no later than the earlier of:

- The first day of the first plan year beginning after the employee has one year of service, or
- Six months after the employee completes one year of service.

A standard year-of-service credit is earned when an employee accumulates 1,000 hours of covered employment within a continuous 12-month period from the date of hire. If an employee fails to earn 1,000 hours within this period, then the 12 months may be measured:

- From the anniversary of the employee's hire date, or
- As plan years.

Trustees should seek the advice of their plan legal counsel as to what service requirements are mandated by federal law and expect counsel to inform them when legal changes occur. Plan administrators should advise trustees on enrollment of new participants and recordkeeping.

Calculating Hours of Service

Hours of service is defined by federal law as the hours an employee is paid directly or indirectly by a contributing employer. Hours of service must include any time for which an employee is compensated—this includes not just hours worked but also hours when an employee is on a leave of absence, jury duty, disability, layoff, vacation and holiday. If an employee is granted back pay, the value of this pay must be converted into hours of service.

The federal government also mandates some leave hours be credited as service; for example, the hours an employee is in military service. The Uniformed Services Employment and Reemployment Rights Act (USERRA) requires plans to give service credit for vesting and benefits to participants called to active military duty (including reserve duty). A legal counsel can advise trustees of the federal requirements for recognizing and calculating hours of service for both work and nonwork time.

Service Outside the Bargaining Unit

On occasion, new employers become sponsors of a multiemployer plan. Trustees may adopt a plan provision that grants service credit for prior service to current employees of these employers at the time employers join the plan. These credits are referred to as *past service credits.* Trustees can establish limits on the number of past service credits for vesting and benefits.

There also are situations when an individual employee who works for a contributing employer in a nonbargained position then moves to a bargaining unit job. For plan eligibility purposes, the service these employees had outside of a bargaining unit that is *contiguous* (immediately prior) to their bargaining unit service must be counted as vesting service credit but not benefit service credit. As a result, some of these employees may have sufficient service credits to be immediately 100% vested. This does not mean, however, that the nonbargained service must be included in the calculation of their benefits.

When Will Participants Become Vested?

Vesting is the process by which plan participants obtain rights to their benefits. If a vested participant is terminated or switches to a job that is not covered employment, benefits *accrued* (earned) cannot be taken away from this participant. A vesting requirement may be a specific length of worked time (e.g., hours, months, years) or a specific number of service credits earned by the participant (e.g., five service credits). Generally, counting years of service for vesting starts with the first day a person has covered employment.

Participants earn service toward vesting in the same way they earn service for plan eligibility. The same Department of Labor (DOL) rules for 1000, 870 and 750 hours apply as well as other alternatives; but, again, a multiemployer plan has the option to adopt rules that are more liberal. Federal guidelines require that plan benefits become vested according to one of these schedules:

- **Five-year cliff vesting.** Participants who have at least five years of service must be granted a *nonforfeitable* *right* to 100% of their accrued benefits. In other words, the participant's right to benefits cannot be taken away. Prior to the five-year point, participants are considered *nonvested* and have no rights to their accrued benefits.

- **Three- to seven-year graded vesting.** As of January 1, 1989, participants with three years of service must have a nonforfeitable right to 20% of their accrued benefits after three years of service. This required vesting percentage increases 20% each year until participants are fully vested (100%) at the end of seven years.

Since it is simpler to explain and administer, most multiemployer plans currently use the five-year cliff-vesting schedule. For plan participants whose entire service was before 1997, prior vesting standards apply that allowed ten-year cliff vesting. Of course, plans may allow these participants to vest earlier than ten years.

Active Versus Terminated Vesting

Vested employees fall into two categories: active and terminated. *Active vested participants* currently work for employers that are submitting contributions on their behalf. *Terminated vested participants* are previously active participants who have worked a sufficient period to meet plan vesting requirements but are not presently working for an employer that is making plan contributions. When terminated vested participants meet plan requirements for retirement, they may apply for and draw benefits just like active vested participants.

Forfeiture Rules

Cyclical industries such as home construction and fishing have years when there is a lot of work available and other years when many employees are temporarily out of work. Plans may establish a minimum number of years in which an employee's service applies to vesting or the service is *forfeited* (lost). For example, assume a plan for carpenters has a ten-year forfeiture rule. A carpenter works two years, then switches to work as a plumber for the next 11 years. When there is a booming demand for carpenters, the worker decides to go back to carpentry work. Because more than ten years have passed, the worker loses credit for the two years of prior service as a carpenter and must start anew. If the worker had returned to carpentry jobs before the end of the ten-year forfeiture period, the prior two years of service would have been counted and the carpenter would have been able to start earning a third year of service. The worker's break in service as a carpenter is erased.

ERISA dictates forfeiture rules. However, other laws, such as the Pregnancy Discrimination Act and the Family and Medical Leave Act (FMLA), provide that time away from work for pregnancy and other covered leave cannot be used to calculate forfeiture. Like so many other pension benefit laws and regulations, a plan attorney should be responsible for keeping trustees up-to-date on federal guidelines that affect forfeiture.

What Is Normal Retirement Age?

Federal law requires plans to specify a *normal retirement age*—no later than the age of 65—when a vested participant can apply for and receive retirement benefits. In general, the benefit paid at normal retirement age must be calculated using the same benefit formula for all vested participants regardless of whether they are *active* (i.e., working for a contributing employer) or *inactive* at the time they retire.

The normal retirement age of most pension plans is the age of 65. However, a plan may adopt a lower normal retirement age. Typically, a plan that wishes to provide full benefits at an earlier age will keep the normal retirement age at 65 and allow unreduced early retirement.

Will Early Retirement Be Allowed?

Almost all plans allow participants to retire before they reach normal retirement age. In most plans, *early retirement* is permitted in the ten years prior to normal retirement age. While ERISA mandates the age of 65 for normal retirement, there are no federal standards for early retirement. Trustees have the option to set higher eligibility standards for early retirement; many plans require participants to have at least ten years of service to do so.

Early retirement may be with a reduced benefit or with the full accrued benefit. Some plans allow participants to retire with full benefits at any age if the participant (1) has 25 to 30 years of covered service or (2) under a *Rule of 85* or *80* has a combined age and years of service equal to either 85 or 80, respectively.

Plans offering early retirement may reduce the benefit amount for each month the participant retires prior to normal retirement age. This *actuarial reduction* is to make up for the additional time the retiree will receive benefits. Plans that offer early retirement are required to extend the early retirement option to vested participants who are active as well as those who are inactive. However, it is common that participants retiring from active service receive better factors or more retirement options.

From a practical point of view, unless the benefit level is quite substantial, experience shows that many employees will not retire until they qualify for Social Security benefits. Since reduced Social Security benefits are first payable at the age of 62, a substantial number of early retirements under a retirement plan occur at the age of 62.

How Will Benefits Accrue?

An hour of service for determining benefits does not have to be the same as an hour of service for vesting. Vesting credit must include all covered hours of service for which a participant received either direct or indirect compensation. In contrast, benefits credits may be based only on a participant's covered service for which employer contributions were required. The phrase "contributions were required" is very important because it indicates there may be occasions when contributions are not actually made. The employer may have declared bankruptcy or the plan never receives the contributions due for other reasons.

With this in mind, it is important to establish a limit on the benefit accrual in a plan document, summary plan description (SPD) and employer participant agreement for situations when an employer is delinquent. For example, these documents might state the employer and the employer's employees are suspended from plan participation and benefits cease accruing if contributions are more than three or six months' delinquent. This safeguard is essential to maintaining a healthy financial position for a plan.

In a multiemployer pension plan, a unit of benefit credit is usually granted for each full year a participant has covered service; the specific benefit accrual rules must reflect both the terms of the bargaining agreement and federal law. Trustees of DB plans may increase the benefit amount earned on past or future benefit credits, but only future benefits can be decreased.

Prorating Benefit Credits

ERISA requires participants be given a prorated benefit credit if they accrue a vesting service year during a plan year. Assume a plan requires employees to work 1,000 covered hours to earn one year of vesting credit and 1,800 hours of service to earn a full benefit credit. If employees work the 1,000 hours and earn a vesting credit, they must accrue at least 55.6% (1,000 ÷ 1,800 = .556) of a benefit credit. Trustees may also grant more than one benefit credit per year of service. For example, if a plan's benefit credit is based upon 1,800 hours worked in a plan year, the plan can provide an employee who works 2,000 hours in the plan year 1.11 credits (2,000 ÷ 1,800 = 1.11). Formulas for benefit credits can vary. Some plans use hours of service, others use months or quarters.

How Will Benefits Be Calculated?

There are essentially three broad categories of formulas used to calculate plan benefits; with each, there is wide variation. Benefit formulas reflect the anticipated needs of participants, the level of contributions paid to plans and the demographic characteristics of participants.

Unit Benefit

Most benefit formulas provide dollar benefit units per year of employee service. Assume a participant has 20 benefit credits and the benefit level is $50 per unit of credit. In this example, the participant's retirement benefit at normal retirement age (or the age for full retirement) will be $1,000 per month (20 credits × $50 per credit = $1,000).

Trustees may have benefit levels for different categories of service based upon the CBA, for example:

Past service	$30 per unit of past service credit
Service from January 1, 1990 to December 31, 1998	$40 per unit of service credit
Service from January 1, 1999 to December 31, 2005	$45 per unit of service credit
Service from January 1, 2006 to present	$50 per unit of service credit

Final Contribution Rate Benefit

In collective bargaining, the contracting parties may increase prior benefit rates retroactively. However, in many cases, only the current active participants in the plan on a specific date will receive the retroactive increase. Terminated vested participants cannot receive the retroactive increase. In the example above, the $40, $45 and $50 benefit rates may be increased to $60 for all active participants in the plan as of January 1, 2011. However, a participant who terminated on June 1, 2010 would have the $30, $40, $45 and $50 benefit rates.

Percentage-of-Employer-Contributions Benefit

Another formula that has come into frequent use in recent years establishes the monthly pension benefit for an employee as a percentage of the employer contributions; for example, the formula might be 1.5%, 2% or 2.5% of employer contributions. Assume the formula is 2.5% and the participant has 20 years of contributions at $3 per hour for 2,000 hours per year. The participant's benefit will be $3,000 per month (20 years × 2,000 hours per year × $3 per hour × 2.5%). Sometimes, *step-rate percentages* are applied, granting a higher percentage after an individual has accumulated 15 or 20 years of service.

How Can Benefits Be Protected From Inflation?

Although benefits are most often expressed as a fixed amount, it is generally accepted that inflation reduces the actual purchasing power of pension payments over a retiree's lifetime. Trustees, therefore, must determine if the plan will provide a cost-of-living adjustment (COLA).

Automatic COLAs are very rare in multiemployer plans. This does not mean that multiemployer retirees and beneficiaries never receive a benefit increase; trustees may decide from time to time to issue a COLA. The adjustment may apply to current retirees, current beneficiaries or both. It may apply only to those who have been retired for a certain number of years or those with a benefit below a certain minimum. The plan attorney and actuary can inform trustees concerning the legal issues and costs of a COLA benefit.

What Payout Options Will Participants Have?

Although there are exceptions, which will be dealt with later in this section, pension benefits are usually paid out as a lifetime annuity.

Annuities

Annuity benefit payments are typically a fixed dollar amount paid monthly for the life of the retiree (and often the life of the retiree's spouse). Some pension annuities guarantee a certain number of payments or some other death benefit. In most cases, the retiree will be offered the chance to take a reduced monthly lifetime benefit in exchange for some (or additional) death benefits. The most common death benefit is a monthly lifetime pension to a named survivor. This benefit, known as a *contingent annuity* or a *joint and survivor benefit,* is discussed in more detail below.

The other common death benefit is a guarantee of a certain number of payments, paid to a beneficiary if the retiree dies before all the guaranteed payments are made. Not all plans offer this as an option, and others may include it as part of the nominal benefit, so the participant does not need to make a special election to take advantage of this feature. For example, a plan may promise to pay the retiree $1,000 per month for a minimum of 60 months. If the retiree dies before these 60 payments are made, the remaining payments are made to the retiree's beneficiary.

Mandatory Distributions

Normally, benefits begin on a date chosen by the retiree. However, federal law requires benefits to begin no later than April 1 following the calendar year the participant reaches the age of 70½ unless the participant is still working. If benefits have not begun by this mandatory date, the Internal Revenue Service can disqualify the plan and the participant can be taxed 50% on all payments that should have been paid.

Because of this mandatory distribution rule, plans must try to locate vested terminated nonworking participants who have not applied for benefits so their payments can start by the required distribution date.

Annuity Cashouts

In cases where a participant is eligible to begin benefit payments, but the present value of those payments is $5,000 or less, some plans opt to pay the benefit as a single lump sum. This is done as an administrative convenience to avoid mailing a lot of little checks. If the present value exceeds $5,000, plans may offer to pay the benefits in a single lump sum. An annuity cashout is not common with multiemployer plans; they almost always prefer to pay monthly benefits.

What Benefits Will Be Provided to Spouses?

Both ERISA and the Retirement Equity Act of 1984 (REA) require DB plans as well as defined contribution (DC) plans to provide married participants with pension benefits in a *joint and survivor (J&S) form* automatically unless both the participant and spouse submit a written notarized waiver. In a DB plan, the J&S benefit pays the married couple a monthly annuity for the lifetime of both the participant and the surviving spouse.

Some plans offer only the 50% and the 75% J&S required by law. A 50% J&S is a fixed monthly sum paid as long as the participant lives. If the participant dies, the spouse receives one-half (50%) of the benefit that was paid during the participant's life. A 70% J&S works the same way. Some plans offer a 100% J&S option. To make up for the amount the surviving spouse receives, the monthly benefit during the lifetime of the participant may be reduced. In some cases, the plan may subsidize the 50% J&S benefit so there is no (or a smaller) reduction to the benefit.

Notification

Federal law requires plans to send information concerning the automatic J&S annuity form to active participants nine months before the participants reach early retirement age. Plans with no early retirement provisions must communicate the information nine months before normal retirement age. The information provided must indicate the financial effect of the participant's retirement choices. The information may be delivered by mail, employee newsletter or in person. It can also be permanently posted with employers and the union if there is reasonable assurance all participants will see it. If newsletters or postings are used, the information must be distributed regularly and continually.

Will Preretirement Death Benefits Be Provided?

Married Vested Participants

ERISA requires plans to offer married vested participants the right to elect a death benefit in the form of an annuity to surviving spouses that starts when the plan participant would have qualified for early retirement. ERISA allows plans to charge the participant for the cost of the preretirement death benefit protection (usually by a reduction in benefits at retirement), but most multiemployer plans absorb the relatively small cost. Trustees typically decide the complexity of administering the elections and reductions outweighs the cost that would be recovered. The administrative burden is reduced to the processing of claims for deaths that actually occur.

Unmarried Vested Participants

A death benefit may be paid to a beneficiary (e.g., parent, child or friend) of an unmarried vested participant who dies before retirement. This benefit, when offered, is most often a lump sum or a temporary life annuity. Not all pension plans offer a nonspouse death benefit because it is more like life insurance than a pension benefit. Other plans choose not to do so because the employee's health and welfare benefits provide a death benefit through life insurance.

Qualified Domestic Relations Order (QDRO)

In most states, the spouse of a plan participant has a marital property interest in retirement benefits earned by a participant during marriage. The rules governing joint and survivor annuities discussed in this chapter protect the nonemployee spouse's interest in these benefits. However, what happens when there is a divorce? The general rule is that a participant's earned benefits may not be assigned or conveyed to others. However, a court's qualified domestic relations order (QDRO) may do so. A QDRO may require the payment of part or all a plan participant's retirement benefits to the participant's divorced spouse.

Benefit plans must provide an explanation kit and procedures to the divorced spouse (or the spouse's representative) to obtain the QDRO. When the divorced spouse follows the procedures and submits the proper forms and documentation, the plan administrator records the QDRO. The administrator must notify the divorced spouse (or representative) if the QDRO qualified and when benefit payments may begin. The divorced spouse may use any benefit option that is available to the plan participant. For example, the divorced spouse may apply for an early retirement benefit even if the plan participant is still working.

The type or form of benefit paid the divorced spouse must be currently available under the plan. In other words, the court order cannot require the plan to pay a type or form of benefit not provided under the plan.

The plan administrator receiving a proposed QDRO must notify the participant and spouse that the order has been received and provide the plan's procedures for determining whether the order is qualified. Each plan must establish reasonable procedures to determine the qualified status of these orders. If the plan administrator determines the order is qualified, the plan must abide by the order and pay the former spouse the specified portion of the participant's pension.

One effect of a QDRO is that the payment of benefits to a former spouse may begin before the participant actually retires. Consider a former spouse who is granted the right to a portion of a participant's benefits. Benefits to this spouse can begin at the point of time when the participant is eligible for early retirement. The plan member could be working in covered employment and earning additional pension credits while his or her former spouse (or spouses) is receiving a court-ordered share of his or her pension earned up to the date of the divorce.

Will Disability Benefits Be Provided?

Most multiemployer DB plans have adopted some form of disability income protection for plan participants. Trustees can establish minimum service requirements to be entitled to a disability benefit. For example, the plan can provide that a participant must have a minimum of ten years of service credit to be eligible for the disability benefit. Most plans use the Social Security Administration (SSA) definition of a *disability* and often require a physician's certification. SSA requires that an employee be totally disabled for at least one year or that the disability is expected to result in the worker's death. SSA defines *total disability* as being unable to do work of any kind, not just the person's current job. SSA does not provide benefits for short-term or partial disabilities.

Given SSA's strict definition of *disability,* there are plan participants who cannot perform their trade or craft that are ineligible for Social Security benefits. These are persons SSA believes could do other kinds of work. To assist these workers and their families, some DB plans grant a partial disability pension if the participant can provide "objective evidence" of a disability. The evidence may involve a medical and/or psychological exam by one or more doctors designated by the plan administrator. Sometimes a board of trustees retains a doctor as a consultant to provide certification of a disability. Physicians providing this service should be qualified by a medical board to perform the examination and to give an informed professional opinion.

A disability benefit is usually the most costly benefit (other than retirement) a DB pension plan provides participants. As a result, trustees normally establish administrative procedures to check periodically on the disabled participant's disability status. Plans normally require persons receiving disability benefits to requalify periodically through a doctor's certification and income tax statements.

Plans typically pay a monthly disability benefit that is (1) a fixed percent (usually between 50% and 100%) of the participant's earned pension benefit, or (2) if greater, the benefit the participant would receive if he or she retired early. A number of plans with relatively high contribution rates pay a full pension benefit with no reduction if a participant is disabled.

While ERISA mandates a standard for normal retirement, it has no standards for disability or early retirement. A plan might require 15 vesting credits for early retirement and five vesting credits for disability retirement.

What Happens if a Participant Continues Working Beyond Normal Retirement Age?

In many instances, employees are eligible to retire but they continue to work in jobs covered by their plan: the income they earn may be greater than their pension and their health is such that they can continue to perform their job well. While these participants continue to work, the pension benefits they would have earned if they had retired are increased to reflect (1) the additional investment income the plan earns on their benefits not paid out and (2) the participant's shorter expected lifetime once the participant does retire. If an employee *defers* (postpones) retirement, plans usually reduce or eliminate any death benefits provided prior to normal retirement age.

How Will Benefits Be Treated if a Retiree Returns To Covered Employment?

Sometimes employees decide to return to work after they retire. Benefits payable to a participant who has reached the plan's normal retirement age may be suspended upon reemployment when the individual earns 40 or more hours of service a month and the plan gives appropriate advance notice of benefit suspension.

If a retiree reaches a plan's normal retirement age and decides to return to work, a suspension of pension benefits is allowed only through *suspendible employment* during which the participant completes 40 or more hours of service in a month in the same trade in the geographical area of the plan. Under DOL regulations, suspendible employment generally is considered work as a regular employee or a self-employed person in:

- Any industry covered by the plan
- An industry that employed the retiree when the employee was covered by the plan
- A trade or craft in which the retiree was employed in the geographical area covered by the plan.

Plans may apply more restrictive rules to those who have retired and who return to covered employment before they reach their plan's normal retirement date. The benefits for retirees who have not reached normal retirement age do not have to meet the definition of suspendible employment. For example, the retiree's benefits could be suspended for service in a geographical area covered by a reciprocal agreement or for nonunion employment in the plan's geographical area. However, when suspension before the normal retirement date is not suspendible employment, the suspended benefits must be actuarially increased once the individual reaches the plan's normal retirement age.

How Are Benefit Claims Appealed?

Federal retirement law requires all plans to have a reasonable written procedure for processing benefits claims and appeals if a claim is denied. The SPD must include a plan's claims procedures. The procedures and time limits for both filing and responding to a claims appeal are very specific. In addition, the federal rules change periodically. The plan's attorney and administrator will keep the trustees up-to-date.

What Features Distinquish Multiemployer Defined Benefit Plans From Other Retirement Plan Options?

Certainty and Ease of Planning

Throughout a participant's working years, the participant knows what his or her pension benefit will be. This simplifies planning for retirement. For example, if the current pension benefit is $50 per benefit credit and the participant expects to have 20 benefit credits, the participant knows that at normal retirement age he or she will receive an annuity of $1,000 ($50 per credit × 20 credits) per month for life.

Lifetime Payments

Retirees (and the retiree's spouse if the spouse has retained the J&S benefit) do not outlive their benefits. This is in contrast to a plan where benefits are an account balance that may be drawn down to zero.

Additional Benefit Objectives

Retirement benefits in a DB plan can be designed to meet specific objectives. Trustees might have an objective to protect participants who become disabled before retirement age from loss of income. Trustees could also have an objective to provide a retirement benefit equal to 50% of the average industry wage to participants with 20 years of service. Or trustees may want to provide a meaningful survivor benefit, even during a worker's early years of participation.

Limited Risk

An individual participant does not have the risk of investment loss of accrued benefits because plan assets are pooled, nor does the individual participant benefit from investment gain. A participant is entitled to receive his or her promised retirement benefit regardless of the plan's return on investments. If the plan has insufficient assets and investment return on these assets, the loss must be made up by increased employer contributions and/or future investment gains.

Underfunding

Although the plan bears the risk of poor investment return, participants' future benefits can also be affected. If a plan is *underfunded* (the current market value of the assets is less than the actuarial accrued liability), the Pension Protection Act (PPA) permits a combination of benefit reductions and increased employer contributions to resolve the underfunding.

Younger Participants Subsidize Older Participants

Although the same amount may be contributed on behalf of two employees and generate the same number of credits, this does not mean the value of the benefit credit for these employees is identical. Credits of older employees are more costly to plans because these persons retire earlier than younger employees and there is less time to accumulate investment earnings on the contributions for older employees. Thus, from a fixed pool of contributions and investment income, a plan must allocate more assets to providing the older employees' benefits. The extra earnings on contributions for younger workers subsidize the limited investment earnings on the contributions made for the older workers.

Portability

If an employee changes occupations and enters another industry not covered by the plan, the employee is not able to take the multiemployer plan with him. On the other hand, if an employee moves from employer to employer covered by the same multiemployer plan, the employee experiences no interruption in his pension credits. Some plans cover employment in several industries. In addition, it is common for multiemployer plans to have reciprocal agreements with other plans in the same industry, but covering other geographic locations. Although it is beyond the scope of this chapter to go into reciprocal arrangements in detail, suffice to say that participants under reciprocal agreements typically would start earning and vesting in the second plan as if all their previous service counted for that plan.

Withdrawal Liability

There is potential withdrawal liability for an employer. Even if an employer will never withdraw from the plan, the employer may have to identify this potential liability on its corporate balance sheet. Such a liability may affect the employer's ability to obtain bonding, loans or credit. In some competitive industries, this can cause loss of jobs.

PBGC Premiums

DB trusts must pay premiums to PBGC, which is an added administrative expense that DC plans do not have.

Chapter 27

Funding the Pension Promise: An Actuarial Perspective

Scott Gregory

This chapter discusses how to fund a defined benefit (DB) pension plan. In theory, the cost of any benefit plan is simply:

- The sum of all the benefits paid, plus
- The expenses to administer the plan, minus
- Any investment income earned on plan assets.

Funding a pension plan has one big difference—the time frame. A health and welfare plan is funded a year at a time. Money is put in, benefits are paid and trustees look at where the fund stands at the end of the year. A pension plan is funded one life at a time. Money is put in, grows and is used to pay benefits, and trustees see where the fund stands when the last participant dies.

What Is the Pension Promise?

A DB pension plan makes a unique promise. It promises to pay

- An **unknown** amount of benefit—because no one knows how much benefit each plan participant will earn between now and retirement
- To an **unknown** number of people—because no one knows how many of today's participants will actually reach retirement and collect a benefit
- Beginning at an **unknown** time in the distant future—because no one knows when participants will actually retire
- For an **unknown** number of years—because no one knows how long people will live
- To an **unknown** other person following the participant's death—because no one knows if the participant will be married at retirement or how long this spouse will live.

For a participant who is aged 25, this promise might reach 50 or more years into the future. The long-term nature of the pension benefit makes it extremely hard to figure out how to pay for it. Trustees need answers to several basic questions:

- What is the value of all the promises the plan has made to date?
- How do plan assets compare with the value of these promises?
- How should the plan pay for these promises?
- Finally, looking to the future, is the plan on the right path to meet these promises?

Trustees hire an actuary to help answer these questions. Measuring the value of the promise and figuring out how to pay for it is called an *actuarial valuation.*

Trustees do not need to know all of the details of the actuarial calculations. Nevertheless, trustees should understand some basic concepts.

What Is the Pension Promise Worth?

In other words, how much money does a plan need right now to keep the benefit promises made to participants?

Let's look at a simple example. Pretend a plan promises a single payment of $1,000 to each participant who is still living at the age of 65. To estimate the amount of money required, think about the following:

- Some participants will die before the age of 65. The plan will not have to pay these participants. If 20% of a plan's current participants die before the age of 65, the plan will have to pay only the remaining 80%. This means the plan needs only $800 for each current participant, not $1,000.

- Some of the promised benefit will be paid using income earned by investing plan assets. The more income earned, the less money needed today. An actuary may calculate that $400 invested today can grow to $800 by the time a participant reaches the age of 65. The process of figuring out how much money is needed today so that it will grow to $800 when the participant reaches the age of 65 is called *discounting*.

In this example, the actuary determines $400 is needed for each participant TODAY in order to pay $1,000 to every participant who lives to the age of 65. Since this amount is measured in today's dollars, it is the *present value* of the benefit that will be paid in the future. It is also called the plan's *liability*.

The actuary does this calculation for every single payment it is expected the plan will have to pay to every single participant. This includes normal retirement benefits, early retirement benefits, benefits to survivors, benefits paid to disabled participants, benefits for death before and after retirement, etc. The actuary considers all of the factors that can influence the amount of the benefit, the likelihood it will be paid and the income that will be earned on plan assets. These calculations estimate what the pension promises are worth today.

How Do Plans Pay for This Promise?

Theoretically, a plan could wait until a benefit is due (at retirement) and pay it then—for example, using the money contributed for current employees to pay for retirees. This approach was used a long time ago, but it had serious problems and is no longer legal for qualified plans. Most (if not all) multiemployer plans are *qualified*—the plans are given favorable tax treatment by the federal government because they meet certain guidelines.

Today, plan benefits must be paid for as they are earned. By the time a participant retires, the participant's benefits should be fully funded. Think about what this means for a participant promised a benefit. By the time the worker retires, all the money needed to pay the worker's benefit for the rest of his or her life should be set aside in the pension fund. There are several advantages to this approach:

- The benefit is not dependent on the future health or willingness of employers to make payments after the worker retires.
- Today's participants do not pass the cost on to a future generation of workers (i.e., their children and grandchildren).
- The cost of the pension is included in the cost of the product manufactured or the service provided by the plan participant. Workers are not depending on future consumers to pay an inflated cost for something that does not benefit them.

The solution is to project what will happen in the future and pay for all of the benefits as they are earned. This sounds nice but it is not that easy.

- The experience of the plan (e.g., investment return, death rates, retirement ages) will never be exactly what the actuary assumed.
- Trustees periodically improve a plan by increasing benefits for past years of service. This creates an immediate liability for which there is no money.
- The cost of a benefit earned by young participants is low because the money contributed by employers on their behalf can be invested and earn interest for many years. The cost of a benefit for participants near retirement is very high because there is little time to earn interest. To address the sharp increase in benefit costs as participants get older, actuaries use different methods to spread pension benefit costs over time. One approach is to collect more for younger participants to prefund the higher costs later on.

For these reasons, plan liabilities rarely equal plan assets. A plan's cost in any one year must take into consideration:

- The value of the benefits earned by participants during the year (or assigned to the year under the actuarial cost method, which is called the *normal cost*)
- An amount to pay for any increases in past benefits awarded by trustees. Such benefit increases are usually funded over several years, sort of like a home mortgage.
- An amount to make up for any differences between what the actuary assumed and what actually happened. (These are called *actuarial gains* or *losses*.)

What Is the Actuarial Valuation Process?

Gather Information

The process of calculating all of these values and determining annual cost is called an *actuarial valuation*. To do this work, an actuary first must gather detailed information about the plan:

- All of the benefits promised. Some plans offer a broad range of benefits and have complex benefit formulas and eligibility requirements.
- Enough participant information to determine all of the benefits each participant might receive. This infor-

mation includes birthdate, hire date, date of entry into the plan, annual service history, contribution rates and pay. This information is required for participants who are active and earning benefits, inactive persons with a right to future benefits, those who are retired and receiving benefits, survivors of participants with a right to benefits, and divorced spouses of participants who will get some benefits under a divorce agreement.
- The value of current plan assets and how asset values have changed over time. An actuary will also ask about plan investment policies.

Make Assumptions About the Future

The present value of a plan's promises depends on many things that happen in the future. The actuary must make *assumptions* about what is likely to happen. Some of the assumptions are:

Benefit amount
- How much service credit will participants earn each year?
- How much credit are participants likely to earn in the future?
- If benefits are based on participant pay, how will pay grow?
- Do (or will) participants qualify for special or subsidized plan benefits?

Demographics
- What is the chance participants will leave before vesting?
- What is the chance that participants will be disabled before retirement?
- What proportion of participants is likely to die before they retire?
- When are participants likely to retire?
- How long are participants likely to receive benefit payments after retirement?
- What is the likelihood a participant will have a spouse receiving benefits, and how long will benefits be paid to the spouse?

Economics
- Is the long-term economic outlook different from the past?
- How much investment income is likely to be earned on plan assets?
- What rates of inflation are likely in the future?
- How are the industry and hours of work likely to change in the future?
- What is the plan's projected future cash flow?

Actuaries are not fortune-tellers—they make assumptions considered reasonable based on (1) what has happened in the past and (2) predictions of how the future might be different. Consider rates of *mortality*—the likelihood participants will die each year in the future. Rates of mortality have been declining, and life expectancy has been increasing for many years. These trends are expected to continue. Actuaries know when people have retired in the past but also realize a change in plan or government retirement benefits may influence the age at which people will retire in the future. Actuaries examine how plan investments have performed in the past but also consider future economic conditions and changes that plan trustees are making to get better future returns.

Under the Employee Retirement Income Security Act of 1974 (ERISA), the assumptions for a multiemployer plan had to be reasonable "in the aggregate." This means an "individual" assumption could be less than reasonable if it was offset by another assumption. The Pension Protection Act of 2006 (PPA) changed this to require that each assumption must be reasonable on its own. It is not acceptable for one questionable assumption to be offset by another.

Over time, federal law and accounting requirements have increasingly determined certain assumptions—primarily the investment return assumption and the mortality assumption. In these instances, the actuary no longer has the right to select these assumptions.

Calculate Liabilities and Costs

Using the information gathered and the assumptions selected, an actuary calculates the present value of plan benefits. Actuaries typically calculate the present value of

- All benefits earned by plan participants in the past—the *liability for accrued benefits*
- Benefits that plan participants are expected to earn in the next plan year—the *normal cost*
- All benefits plan participants are expected to earn up to retirement—the *liability for projected benefits.*

It can be confusing when so many different things are called *liabilities.* A *liability* may be benefits earned in the past, benefits expected to be earned in the future, vested benefits or total benefits. Liability is also used for different purposes—like funding, withdrawal liability, accounting disclosure or plan termination. A liability may be based on assumptions of the actuary, those required by the Internal Revenue Service (IRS) or those established by accounting rules. Trustees must understand what each liability is measuring and how it should be used.

A plan's actuary will also calculate the minimum contribution that employer sponsors must contribute annually to a plan under IRS rules. In general, the minimum contribution is the sum of:

- The value of benefits that participants will earn in the next year (the *normal cost*)
- Amortization payments to fund retroactive benefit increases a plan has given
- Amortization payments to make up any past actuarial gains or losses such as investment losses
- Any technical adjustments, for example, changes in actuarial methods, assumptions or amortization periods.

Amortization payments are regular dollar amounts put aside to cover a debt, much like a homeowner making regular payments on a mortgage for a set period.

In a multiemployer plan, labor and management typically negotiate a contribution rate (i.e., cents per hour) so the contribution is fixed for the term of the contract. Trustees then control the annual cost of the plan by setting the level of pension benefits.

The Valuation Report

Plan actuaries put all of this information into a report and present it to plan trustees. The report includes the calculation results and the key information on which the calculations are based.

Even though it looks imposing, trustees should take the time to go through it. It is the only document given to trustees that provides a complete picture of a plan. It has a summary of plan benefits, offers an overview of participant characteristics, summarizes plan assets and states the assumptions the actuary is making about the future. It also includes the details of the actuary's calculations. Trustees do not need to understand these details, but they should understand the basic concepts. With this information, trustees can answer important financial questions:

- Has the plan put aside enough money to fulfill the promises made so far?
- If not, what steps are needed to make up the shortfall?
- Are plan contributions sufficient to meet IRS funding requirements?
- What is the outlook for the future—is the plan heading in the right direction?
- Can the plan afford to improve benefits?

What Federal Laws Control Pension Plans?

After a series of pension disasters in the 1970s, the federal government stepped in and established benefit plan design and funding requirements. Over the years, these rules have become more and more complex. Here is a brief overview of the history of these funding rules.

Employee Retirement Income Security Act

ERISA introduced minimum standards to help ensure plan participants received the benefits they have been promised. In general, this federal law:

- Established minimum funding requirements for pension plans. These requirements define how an employer's required contribution on behalf of participants is calculated. These costs are based on the funding method, the method for valuing plan assets and assumptions about the future. (More information on two of these factors is provided in the next two bullets.)
- Approved the use of several different *funding methods*—the mathematical processes for spreading the cost of a pension over a participant's working life. Some methods try to pay for benefits as they are earned. Others try to prefund benefits in preparation for the benefit cost increases as participants get older.
- Allowed plans to use a different value for plan assets when calculating cost for the current year. The *market value* of an asset is what someone else is willing to pay for the asset. This value tends to bounce around from day to day and year to year. If the market value is used to determine cost, it should not be a surprise that the annual cost will bounce around from year to year. To lessen this volatility, plans were allowed to *smooth out* year-to-year fluctuations by averaging asset values over several years.
- Required that plan changes that increase or decrease liabilities must be paid (amortized) over a specified number of years
- Required that unexpected fluctuations in plan experience (such as investment gains or losses) be made up with contributions over a specified number of years
- Established some requirements for the assumptions actuaries make about the future
- Established a device to measure whether a plan sponsor is meeting these new funding requirements. This device, called a *Funding Standard Account,* adds up all contributions actually made to a plan since about 1976 and compares it to all the contributions required under ERISA. If contributions paid over the years are larger than the required contributions, the plan has a *credit balance* and all is well. On the oth-

er hand, if contributions are less than the required amount, the plan will have a *funding deficit* that triggers federal penalties and sanctions. For more detailed information on the Funding Standard Account, see Chapter 28.

Pension Protection Act of 2006

In the early part of this century, investment markets tumbled and most pension plans fell on hard times. Asset values declined, liabilities increased and unfunded liabilities rose sharply. In 2006, the federal government passed PPA to strengthen funding requirements (and pension security). In general, this law:

- Established new standards to measure the financial health of pension plans. These new standards require actuaries to project the financial condition of a plan into the future. This was a change from past practice where the rules required looking only at the current year.
- Classified plans as *critical* if there is a projection the plan will have a funding deficiency in the near future
- Classified plans as *endangered* if they are not in critical status, but the value of plan assets is less than 80% of accumulated plan benefits (liabilities)
- Considers plans that are not in critical or endangered status to be reasonably healthy
- Requires trustees of plans in critical or endangered status to develop a program to return to healthy status over a short period. A plan in critical status must create a *Rehabilitation Plan.* A plan in endangered status must create a *Funding Improvement Plan.*

Worker, Retiree, and Employer Recovery Act of 2008 (WRERA)

The new requirements of PPA took effect in 2008. At the beginning of that year, most plans had returned to reasonable health and the law did not have a significant impact on them. But during 2008, investment markets crashed and the vast majority of multiemployer plans fell into endangered or critical status. In late 2008, the U.S. Congress passed WRERA to provide some temporary relief from PPA requirements. See the exhibit on the next page for more information on the funding status and the programs to return plans to healthy funding levels.

Pension Relief Act of 2010

With many plans still struggling, the federal government passed the Pension Relief Act of 2010. This law introduced several changes that spread funding requirements a bit further into the future and reduced current contribution requirements.

Over time, these changes have made the calculation of minimum required cost increasingly complex. The plan actuary performs the calculations and reports the required cost to trustees. The actuary will also project costs into the future and compare them with the contributions expected in the future under the collective bargaining agreement.

How Is Plan Financial Health Measured?

Whether a plan is healthy or unhealthy is based primarily on the following measurements (and in some cases additional measurements):

- **Do employer contributions meet minimum funding requirements?** If contributions exceeded the minimum requirements in past years, the prior overpayments can help cover the current year's minimum cost. Prior overpayments are measured with the Funding Standard Account and are called a *credit balance.* Let us say a plan has a minimum funding requirement of $1 million and a credit balance of $100,000 from previous years' contributions. Contributions for this year need be only $900,000—the $1 million less the $100,000. After the end of each plan year, the actuary must report whether the plan has met the minimum contribution requirements by submitting Schedule MB to IRS.
- **Is there enough money to pay the benefits promised?** The *funded ratio* (or *funded percent*) is the value of a plan's assets divided by a plan's liability for accrued benefits. If this ratio is more than 100%, there are enough assets to pay all of the promised benefits and the plan is financially healthy. If the ratio is less than 100%, trustees must take steps to make up the shortfall. If the ratio is less than 80%, the plan is unhealthy under PPA and trustees may be required to take additional steps to fix this.
- **Will the plan be able to make future benefit payments as they come due?** Projecting plan assets will answer this question. If the plan is projected to run out of money, it will not be able to pay benefits and will soon become insolvent.

PPA introduced a number of tests based on the above measures. A plan actuary performs these tests and reports to trustees on the condition of a plan.

PPA requires that a plan's actuary report the financial health of the plan to IRS each year. This *actuarial certification* is submitted within 90 days following the end of each

Exhibit

Plan Financial Health

Critical Plans (Red Zone)

A plan is certified as *critical* (or in the *red zone*) if it fails any one of four tests, generally related to whether it is projected to have a funding deficiency or cash flow problems within the next four years (five years for certain less-well-funded or mature plans).

Bargaining parties of a plan in the red zone are required to develop a *Rehabilitation Plan* (RP)—a schedule or schedules showing revised contribution and/or benefit structures that address the plan's funding problems. The changes may include reductions or elimination of some accrued benefits. If the bargaining parties do not adopt a schedule for the next contract, a plan's board of trustees is required by law to reject the contract. Prior to adopting one of the RP schedules, employers may be required to contribute a surcharge to the plan.

The RP must be reasonably expected to bring the plan out of the red zone within ten years and keep the plan out of critical status for at least ten more years. The Worker, Retiree, and Employer Recovery Act (WRERA) allowed trustees of a plan in the red zone for the first time in 2008 or 2009 to extend this ten-year period to 13 years.

Endangered Plans (Yellow and Orange Zones)

A benefit plan is certified as *endangered* (in the *yellow zone*) if it is not critical (in the red zone) and either (1) its funded ratio is less than 80% or (2) it is projected to have a funding deficiency within seven years. A plan is *seriously endangered* (in the *orange zone*) if both of these conditions are true.

Trustees of plans in the yellow or orange zone must develop a *Funding Improvement Plan* (FIP)—a schedule or schedules showing revised contribution and/or benefit structures that address the plan's funding problems. The schedule(s) must be adopted by the plan's bargaining parties for the next contract. If they do not do so, the law requires the board of trustees to reject the contract.

For a plan in the yellow zone, the FIP must be designed to improve the funded ratio by one-third of the underfunding and eliminate any funding deficiencies projected to occur within ten years. If a plan was 73% funded when it was certified as yellow, the schedule must increase the funded ratio to at least 82% by the end of the improvement period. Where did the 82% come from? In this example, assume a plan was 73% funded. Subtract this 73% from 100% and then divide the answer by three (representing a one-third improvement). The one-third improvement is 9%. Add 9% to the plan's current funding of 73%, and the result is 82%. WRERA allows plans to extend this funding improvement from ten years to 13 years if the plan was yellow for the first time in 2008 or 2009.

For a plan in the orange zone, the FIP must be designed to improve the funded percentage by 20% of the underfunded amount in 15 years. For example, if a plan was 75% funded when it was certified as orange, the FIP must be designed to increase the funded percentage of the plan to no less than 80% at the end of 15 years (20% of 100% less 75% is 5%. 75% plus 5% is 80%). WRERA allowed trustees to adopt an optional extension to 18 years for a plan first certified as orange in 2008 or 2009.

---

plan year. A copy of this document must also be provided to all plan participants.

The actuarial certification uses the same assumptions used for the annual actuarial valuation with one important exception. The projection of future funding standard account balances requires an assumption on future contributions. This involves projecting both the amount of participant work and contribution rates per credit. This *projected industry activity* assumption is based on information provided to plan trustees.

Are There Any Limits on How Much Can Be Contributed to a Plan?

To encourage retirement saving, federal tax law allows employers to deduct their contributions to qualified employee benefit plans on their tax return. IRS, however, does not want this tax break used unfairly to avoid taxes. There is a maximum limit on how much employers can contribute to plans and deduct on their taxes. Any contributions in excess of this maximum cannot be deducted. In addition, the excess contributions are subject to a 10% excise tax.

Prior to 2002, this limit was low and a number of plans bumped into it. A common solution, at that time, was to increase plan benefits. Trustees often felt that they had little choice but to do this. In 2002, the rules were changed to allow employer contributions to be fully deductible as long as they did not exceed the unfunded *current liability* of the plan. Current liability is calculated using a current interest rate and a mortality table specified by IRS. In 2006, the limit was raised to 140% of current liability. In recent years, current liability has been much larger than the liability used for funding. Using a larger liability gives employers more room to claim a tax deduction. The rule changes, in combination with recent low-interest rates, have meant that almost all plan contributions made by employers' multiemployer plans have been fully deductible.

If a plan runs into this limit, trustees might consider several things:

- **Increase plan benefits.** Trustees often used this strategy in the past. Increasing benefits generally increases the limit on deductible contributions, but it also will increase plan costs—not just in the current year but for future years as well.
- **Reduce contributions.** Since contributions to multiemployer plans are usually determined by collective bargaining agreements, it is not easy to reduce them. Participants believe this money is owed to them and should be used for benefits.
- **Adopt one-time benefit improvements.** These improvements do not affect future years, such as a one-time lump-sum increase to retirees (a 13th check).
- **Change to a lower (and more conservative) interest assumption.** This approach can increase benefit security and allow continued deductibility of employer contributions.
- **Divert contributions to other participant benefits.**
- **Temporarily park excess contributions in an escrow fund.**

How Should We Talk to Our Actuary?

Actuarial stuff can get technical, but trustees must understand enough to make important plan decisions. Here are a few suggestions to help improve communication with a plan actuary:

- **Ask questions.** Actuaries usually arrive with a business suit, a briefcase, a computer and a bunch of initials after their name. This can make them a little imposing. "I don't want to look stupid so I don't ask questions." That is the wrong approach. Actuaries work for plan trustees, not the other way around. Trustees have hired the actuary. Trustees pay him or her. In addition, trustees need to be sure they get their money's worth. ASK QUESTIONS. It is a lot worse to make a bad decision for a plan than to ask a silly question.
- **Insist on plain English.** Actuaries use a lot of jargon, and not everyone understands all of the buzzwords. Trustees must stop and think—they probably use many words in their work that others do not understand. Ask actuaries to speak in plain English. If trustees do not understand a word or concept, they should ask for an understandable explanation. Trustees must keep asking questions until they understand what the actuary is trying to say.
- **Understand the assumptions.** Ask the plan actuary about the assumptions used in calculations. These are the actuary's best predictions about what is going to happen in the future. Trustees should consider whether they think the assumptions are reasonable. Are investment decisions made to meet the actuary's assumptions, or do the assumptions reflect how trustees have chosen to invest plan assets?
- **Share special knowledge.** Trustees know their industry and the things that are happening that may affect the future. Trustees know plan participants, how participants think and what motivates them. Trustees may know about a big new project, a new collective bargaining agreement, pending layoffs or a plant shutdown. The actuary needs this information to do a better job. So share it.
- **Let the actuary know plan objectives.** Some trustees include the actuary as a trusted advisor. The actuary attends full trustee meetings and gets to know trustee concerns and challenges. Other trustees view the actuary as a numbers geek—the actuary is invited to attend one meeting a year to present a report and then he or she is dismissed until the following year. An actuary that is seen once a year cannot know much about plan needs and challenges. The actuary that knows plan issues can do a better job helping trustees find solutions.
- **Be fair.** Sometimes labor and management trustees do not get along very well. They disagree on what is best for plan participants. Labor wants larger benefits. Management wants better funding. Sometimes one side will try to use the actuary to support its position and browbeat the other side. The actuary is not the actuary for labor or management. The actu-

ary is responsible to the plan. Trustees should use the actuary to get good information so they can make informed decisions but not try to get the actuary to take a side.

What Responsibility Does a Plan Have When an Employer Withdraws From a Plan?

ERISA requires single employers to keep the pension promises they make to their employees. This means that even if the employer decides to terminate a pension plan, the employer is still required to pay for any unfunded benefits. They cannot just walk away from their promise. If the employer goes bankrupt—then and only then—a government insurance program (the Pension Benefit Guaranty Corporation (PBGC)) steps in to pay unfunded benefits.

Multiemployer plans were a unique problem when ERISA was drafted because multiemployer plans have many participating employers. The departure of one employer does not cause the plan to terminate. It took Congress six years after the passage of ERISA to come up with a way to deal with multiemployer plans through the Multiemployer Pension Plan Amendments Act (MPPAA) of 1980. The philosophy is the same—a pension promise made by an employer must be kept—but the mechanics are different. An employer that chooses to withdraw from a multiemployer plan must pay its share of any unfunded vested benefits.

Trustees have several responsibilities when a withdrawal occurs:

- Identify employers when they withdraw
- Calculate the amount of their withdrawal liability
- Assess and collect the liability.

Identify Withdrawn Employers

MPPAA defines what it means to withdraw. A *complete withdrawal* occurs when an employer:

- Permanently ceases to have an obligation to contribute under the plan, or
- Permanently ceases all covered operations under the plan.

While this may seem relatively straightforward, there are many complications and a number of exceptions. There are special rules for building and construction plans, the entertainment industry and the trucking industry. There are special rules to deal with the sale of a company. There are even special rules dealing with a *partial withdrawal*—a situation where an employer has a sharp decline in contributions or only partially meets its contribution obligation.

Trustees must work with their plan administrator and attorney to determine when an employer withdraws. Partial withdrawals can be particularly hard to identify as it can take three years before the legal definition is met. It is important that a plan administrator have procedures to track and identify withdrawals.

Calculate the Amount of Withdrawal Liability

Determining an employer's withdrawal liability starts by calculating the value of vested benefits of the plan. Note that this is not the value of all benefits promised to these employees—it is only the value of vested benefits. This value is calculated as of the end of the plan year prior to withdrawal. The liability at December 31 may not be the same as the liability on the next day—January 1.

The choice of assumptions is an important issue. In the past, many plans used the same assumptions used to determine plan cost. These assumptions use a long-term outlook. One major actuarial firm introduced a different approach many years ago. It used an interest assumption that was partly based on a long-term assumption and partly based on a termination assumption using interest rates published by PBGC. This increases the size of the liability and the amount charged the withdrawing employer. More recently, a number of plans have started to base liability on termination-type assumptions. These assumptions produce even larger values for vested benefits. This is a reaction to the unfavorable investment markets of the last decade and the weak funding position of many plans.

The value of plan assets is subtracted from the value of vested benefits to get *unfunded vested benefits (UVB)*. MPPAA does not specify how to value the assets. Many plans use the market value, but as noted previously, this tends to bounce around from year to year. Other plans use the actuarial (or smoothed) value of assets. This value tends to be more stable from year to year. No matter which value is used in any one year, someone can argue the other value should be used.

UVB are allocated among all participating employers. The big question is, "How do you divide it up among all employers?" The law describes an automatic (or *presumptive*) procedure, but it also includes a number of optional procedures. The law also allows a plan to apply to PBGC for other procedures. The different allocation options are an attempt to find a balance between what is fair and what is doable. The "fairest" methods tend to be very complex, requiring extensive records and complex calculations. The "simpler" methods tend to sacrifice some of the "fairness." Plans in certain industries like the construction industry are required to use a specific allocation method. If the trustees do not formally select one of the options, the presumptive method automatically applies. An actuary can discuss this with trustees when the situation arises.

The amount calculated above may then be adjusted for a *de minimis rule.* The intent of this rule is to eliminate or reduce the amount of withdrawal liability charged to small employers. A withdrawal liability of less than $50,000 is forgiven. If it is between $50,000 and $100,000, it is reduced by $50,000. Above $100,000, the offset is reduced but by an amount less than $50,000. Above $150,000, there is no reduction.

Assess and Collect the Withdrawal Liability

A plan attorney has confirmed an employer withdrew. A plan actuary has calculated the amount of withdrawal liability. Now the plan must notify the withdrawn employer what the amount of withdrawal liability is and provide a schedule of payments.

In general, the law wants the withdrawing employer to continue contributing to the plan at the same rate as prior to withdrawal until the full liability is paid. The required payment is based on the employer's highest contribution rate in the last ten years multiplied by the number of contribution units (hours, shifts, weeks, etc.) for the highest consecutive three years in the last ten years. Contributions are limited to 20 years, and interest is included in the calculation.

Once an employer is sent notification, the business must start making payment. If payments are not made when due, a plan can demand payment in full of the outstanding balance.

An employer has the right to challenge the liability assessed, but the appeal process must begin within 90 days of the assessment. If there is no challenge within 90 days, the employer loses the right to challenge. Scheduled payments must be made during the challenge.

The challenge of a withdrawal liability starts a legal process. If an employer challenges a plan and requests additional information, the plan must respond and provide the information requested. The dispute then goes to arbitration. The law assumes the plan's assessment is correct unless the employer can show the assumptions and methods used were unreasonable or the actuary made a significant error in the calculations.

Recent Issues

PPA made several technical changes to previous law and regulations concerning withdrawal liability:

- **Allocation procedures.** Trustees are now allowed to revise the allocation procedure for plans that have no UVB for withdrawals occurring on or after January 1, 2007. Doing so can simplify the presumptive allocation method.
- **Withdrawal liability when plans are in the red zone.** As mentioned previously, plans that are in the red zone must adopt a Rehabilitation Plan that includes surcharges on participating employers and may include benefit reductions applicable to past service. Both these surcharges and benefit reductions are disregarded in determining a withdrawing employer's liability.

In 2010, the Financial Accounting Standards Board (FASB) issued a proposed rule that would require employers to disclose the withdrawal liability that might be assessed if they withdrew from a multiemployer pension plan. Much of this information would have to be provided by plan administrators. There is concern that this information may be misleading for employers that have no intent to withdraw. Further, this may create significant additional work for the plan administrator that would have to provide much of this information. At the time of publication, FASB was still considering this issue.

Other Observations

Employers met the withdrawal provisions of MPPAA with disapproval. From an employer's point of view, the employer agreed to a collective bargaining agreement that requires contributions to a plan. He paid the negotiated contributions and fulfilled his obligations. He did not agree to pay benefits. He had no role in determining the amount of the benefits. So, many employers believe this law is unfair.

This solution has also had a mixed effect on multiemployer plans. Employers cannot withdraw and leave unfunded liabilities for the remaining employers to pay. This has, perhaps, made plans a little stronger financially. On the other hand, this law has made it much harder to bring new employers and participants into these plans. A new employer may look at the potential for withdrawal liability and conclude that it does not want to participate.

Many employers challenge an assessment of withdrawal liability. The law clearly favors the plan, but there have been occasions when assessments have been successfully challenged. These include:

- The trustees did not take proper, formal actions and clearly document their decisions.
- The trustees did not properly notify participating employers of their actions.

- The actuary did not properly distinguish between vested and nonvested benefits.
- The trustees made decisions after an employer withdrew and then tried to apply their changes retroactively.
- The actuary made decisions for the trustees that were not communicated to, or approved by, the trustees.

It is important that trustees take the time to properly define and document their procedures, communicate them to all interested parties and properly perform the calculation.

Chapter 28

Pension Funding and the Role of the Actuary

Ralph Weinberg and Ken Friedman

The trustees of multiemployer defined benefit pension plans employ the services of a group of professionals to assist in plan operations. This chapter focuses on the role of one of these professionals—the actuary—whose primary function is to help trustees maintain the financial well-being of a plan. The primary tool for doing so is the annual actuarial valuation. The Pension Protection Act of 2006 (PPA) requires pension plan actuaries to annually submit to the federal government an actuarial certification that reports the general health of their plan. This chapter introduces the annual actuarial valuation, implications of recent legislation such as PPA on pension plan funding and four key pension-funding issues that require trustee awareness: minimum contributions, maximum contributions, underfunding and employer withdrawal liability.

What Is an Annual Actuarial Valuation?

An *annual actuarial valuation* determines the accrued and projected future benefit obligations of a defined benefit pension plan. More specifically, this valuation calculates:

- The minimum required employer contribution under the Employee Retirement Income Security Act of 1974 (ERISA)
- The maximum allowable deductible contribution employers may make under the Internal Revenue Code
- The present value of vested benefits needed for employer withdrawal liability purposes
- The present value of accumulated benefits (whether vested or not) for purposes such as assessing a plan's current funding status.

To complete an actuarial valuation, a plan actuary needs financial and participant data from the plan. The actuary must be provided detailed financial information regarding plan assets. The participant information required varies by type of participant as illustrated in the exhibit. The results of this valuation process are submitted annually to the Internal Revenue Service (IRS)—the federal agency that has the responsibility for monitoring whether a plan is properly funded.

It is quite common these days for a plan to have working retirees, which may require special handling by the actuary depending on plan rules for paying pensions when a retiree returns to perform work covered by the plan. There also may be a need for an actuary to perform special calculations for benefits awarded to participants' former spouses under qualified domestic relations orders (QDROs). All of this information is collected as of a single date, usually the first day of the plan year, called the *valuation date.*

Central to the calculations used in an actuarial valuation is the concept of *present value.* Assume a fund has an obligation *(liability)* to pay a plan participant $107 one year in the future. The amount of money needed today (the *present value*) is the amount that would earn enough interest to be worth $107 in one year. If the investment of plan funds is expected to yield a 7% return, the present value of this $107 obligation is $100; $100 invested for one year at 7% would accumulate to $107.

The calculations the actuary completes are actually much more complicated than this simple example because these additional assumptions must be considered:

- ***Withdrawal*** or ***turnover rates***—the probability (chance) that an active participant may terminate employment during a year

Exhibit

Participant Information Required for an Actuarial Valuation

	Active Participants	Inactive Participants*	Retirees
Date of birth	✔	✔	✔
Gender	✔	✔	✔
Date of employment	✔		
Earnings information (for plans with pay-related formulas)	✔		
Vesting credits	✔		
Accrued benefit	✔	✔	
Hours worked in the most recent year	✔		
Employer contributions required on participant's behalf	✔		
Amount of benefit being paid			✔
Form of benefit payment (e.g., life only, joint and survivor benefit, contingent annuitant, five-year certain benefit)			✔
Contingent annuitant's date of birth (if applicable)			✔
Contingent annuitant's gender (if applicable)			✔

*Persons who are eligible for, but not yet receiving, benefits.

- ***Disability rates***—the probability that an active participant may become disabled during a year
- ***Retirement rates***—the probability that an active participant may retire during a year
- ***Mortality rates***—the probability that a participant (active, terminated vested or retired) may die during a year
- ***Administrative expenses***—the estimated cost of operating the plan to be paid out during a year
- ***Benefit accrual during the year***—the amount of benefits earned during the year (and future years) by an active participant
- ***Rate of salary increase***—if the benefit formula is based on participant pay, an assumption regarding future compensation increases is required.

These actuarial assumptions are the foundation upon which the present value of a plan's current and future liabilities is determined. Under most accepted actuarial funding methods, an *actuarial accrued liability* is calculated representing the present value of benefits earned to a valuation date. This liability minus the actuarial value of assets on hand on the same date is the *unfunded actuarial accrued liability.* ERISA requires that this difference between plan liabilities and assets be spread out over a period of years *(amortized)* to ensure that the minimum contribution requirements for funding the unfunded liability are met.

Another aspect of actuarial funding methods is the asset valuation method. Depending upon the plan's investment policy and the types and characteristics of the plan's investments, a plan actuary may recommend determining the value of plan assets with a method other than market value. These alternative asset valuation methods reduce the size of asset value fluctuations from year to year. The plan actuary should advise trustees which actuarial funding methods to use for their particular pension plan. Knowing which method is used will help trustees fully understand the relationship between the plan contribution requirements and the contributions expected.

The actuarial assumptions and funding method develop the "expected" periodic costs of the plan. However, the true costs of the plan are based on the "actual" benefits earned. Differences between what is expected and what happens are the *actuarial gains* or *losses*. With most actuarial funding methods, these gains or losses are calculated annually and become a separate part of valuation results.

What Is the PPA Actuarial Certification?

PPA requires the plan actuary to annually submit an actuarial report that assigns a *zone status* reflecting the general health of the plan. The due date for submitting the PPA Actuarial Certification is no later than the 90th day of each plan year.

The zone status of a plan may be red (critical), orange (seriously endangered), yellow (endangered) or green (none of the above). If the plan is certified as *nongreen* for any year, then plan trustees must adopt either a Funding Improvement Plan (FIP) or a Rehabilitation Plan (RP) (depending on the plan's zone status). These will be discussed in more detail later in this chapter.

While additional measurements are used in some situations, zone status is generally based on two key measurements:

1. ***Funded percentage***—the actuarial value of plan assets at the beginning of the plan year divided by the present value of accumulated benefits on the same date
2. ***Funding standard account credit balance projection***—the amount (determined annually) by which historical employer contributions exceed a plan's minimum annual contribution requirements.

In general, a plan is in the green zone if (1) its funded percentage is at least 80% at the beginning of a plan year and (2) the plan is projected to have a positive credit balance at the end of the current year as well as the next six plan years. A plan that does not meet these requirements would be certified as yellow, orange or red, depending on the two key measurements and additional measurements.

A plan is certified as red if it fails any one of four tests, generally related to whether it is projected to have a funding deficiency within the next four years (five years for certain less funded or mature plans). A plan is certified as yellow if it is not red and either (1) the ratio of its assets to its liabilities is below 80% or (2) it is projected to have a funding deficiency within seven years. It is certified as orange if both of these conditions are true.

The actuarial certification is based on actuarial assumptions selected by the plan actuary. These assumptions must be the same as the actuarial assumptions selected for the annual actuarial valuation with one important exception—the *projected industry activity assumption*. When performing an actuarial valuation, a plan actuary is not required to make an assumption whether the number of contribution base units (e.g., hours worked) will go up, down or remain the same in years beyond the valuation year. The credit balance projection for the federal government, however, does require this projected industry activity assumption, which is based on information provided by the trustees, who are expected to "act reasonably and in good faith."

What Else Has Changed With the Passage of PPA?

PPA modified the minimum funding requirements under ERISA. For well-funded multiemployer defined benefit plans, the funding requirements were modified only slightly. But for underfunded plans, special rules were developed to improve the funded status of such plans in a short time period.

When the investment markets collapsed in 2008, complying with these special rules was so challenging that special legislative relief was passed twice. The Worker, Retiree, and Employer Recovery Act (WRERA) was passed in late 2008 followed by the Pension Relief Act (PRA) in 2010. Both laws were an attempt to ease the funding burden of underfunded multiemployer defined benefit plans. Without this relief, many plans would have found themselves unable to comply with the requirements of PPA.

PPA also added or changed certain participant notice requirements for defined benefit plans. The deadline for the annual funding notice provided to plan participants was moved to earlier in the year, and additional information is now required in the notice. New participant notices were established for nongreen plans as well as a requirement that all plans provide participants with periodic benefit statements. Finally, a new information report to contributing employers and participating unions was added.

What Are the Minimum Funding Requirements?

Under ERISA, as modified by PPA 2006 and PRA 2010, plan sponsors are required to meet annual minimum contribution requirements.

The Funding Standard Account

The minimum requirement is determined through a plan's *funding standard account* (FSA). The FSA is an historical accounting of a plan's funding requirements since the effective date of ERISA (usually 1976, for plans in effect prior to 1974).

The FSA operates much like a bank account with dollars added or subtracted at the end of each year. A positive *FSA credit balance* at the end of a year can be used to offset future minimum requirements. Of course, there is also the possibility that the account will have a *deficit* (negative balance) at the end of the year. If there is an FSA funding deficiency, a plan may have to pay certain excise taxes and be subjected to extra reporting requirements.

The actual credits and charges developed annually in the FSA are as follows:

Credits

- Prior-year FSA credit balance and interest
- Plan contributions and interest
- Amortization of actuarial gains
- Amortization of decreases in the unfunded actuarial accrued liability resulting from changes in actuarial assumptions, funding methods or plan provisions.

Charges

- Prior-year funding deficiency and interest
- *Normal cost* for the year (the value of the benefits it is anticipated active participants will earn in the next year)
- Amortization of the initial unfunded actuarial accrued liability, determined as of the date the FSA started
- Amortization of actuarial losses
- Amortization of increases in the unfunded actuarial accrued liability due to changes in actuarial assumptions, funding methods or plan provisions.

The difference between the credits and charges becomes the credit balance or funding deficiency.

Amortization

The amortization payments of the FSA are determined in a manner similar to mortgage payments, where a specific dollar amount is paid over a certain number of years with annual principal and interest payments, typically at the valuation interest rate. The specific periods for the amortization are as follows for multiemployer plans:

- **Initial unfunded or overfunded actuarial accrued liability:** 40 years for plans in existence before 2008, 15 years for plans coming into existence in 2008 or later
- **Actuarial gains and losses:** 20 years for amounts arising prior to 1980, 15 years for amounts arising during 1980 and later
- **Changes in actuarial funding methods:** 30 years if the change results in a credit, 40 years minus the number of years FSA is in effect if the change resulted in a charge prior to 1995, ten years for changes during 1995 and later that result in charges or credits
- **Changes in plan provisions:** 30 years for amendments adopted prior to 2008, 15 years for amendments adopted in 2008 or later years (except that amendments resulting in additional payouts that are expected to last less than 15 years are amortized over the expected payout period)
- **Changes in actuarial assumptions:** 30 years for changes made prior to 2008, 15 years for changes made in 2008 or later.

Under certain circumstances, IRS may grant an extension of specific amortization charges to lower a plan's minimum requirements.

Additional FSA Components

In addition to the basic charges and credits above, extra components of the FSA may be required, as follows:

- **Full-funding credit.** If a plan is well-funded, IRS allows a credit to the FSA where the annual minimum requirement for a plan becomes the amount necessary to fund fully current obligations. When the full-funding credit applies, the amortization bases are eliminated. In future years, only new amortization bases will be recognized.
- **Waived funding deficiency.** If the plan reported a funding deficiency for a prior year, IRS may have waived immediate payment of the deficit and allowed the deficiency to be amortized over 15 years as a charge to the FSA. No more than five waivers in any 15-year period can be received.
- **Shortfall charge.** Some multiemployer plans may periodically use a funding method known as the *shortfall method.* Simply described, the contribution requirement under the FSA becomes the expected contribution for the year using the prevailing contribution rate times expected reported units (hours, weeks, months, etc.). The difference between the actual FSA requirement and the expected contributions becomes an additional adjustment to the FSA.

What Special Rules Apply to an Underfunded Plan?

The additional requirements that apply to an underfunded pension plan depend on the actuarial certification made by the plan's actuary at the beginning of the plan year. If a plan is certified nongreen, federal law requires trustees to develop an action plan that gives the collective bargaining parties options to reduce plan liabilities, increase plan contributions or both to improve the funding condition of the plan within a set time frame. The severity of the actions required depends on the plan's zone status. There are significant penalties for trustees who fail to agree on a proposal within the time required by PPA.

Rehabilitation Plans

Trustees of a red zone plan must develop a *Rehabilitation Plan (RP)* that will bring their plan out of the red zone within ten years following adoption of the RP. This ten-year period is called the *rehabilitation period.* The actuary must be able to project that at some point during this ten-year rehabilitation period, the plan's FSA will not have a funding deficiency and that this lack of a deficiency will continue for at least ten years in a row. Under WRERA, trustees of a plan that was red for the first time in 2008 or 2009 had a one-time option to extend this ten-year period to 13 years.

Funding Improvement Plans

Trustees of a plan certified as yellow or orange must develop a *Funding Improvement Plan (FIP).* For a yellow zone plan, the FIP must be designed to improve the plan's funded status by one-third of the underfunded amount in the ten-year period following the adoption period *and* eliminate the funding deficiencies that are projected to occur in the ten-year period, if any. This ten-year period is called the *funding improvement period.* Consider a plan that is 73% funded when it is certified as yellow. The underfunded amount is 27% (100% − 73%). Trustees must create an FIP that will increase the funded percentage of the plan to at least 82% (73% + [27% × .33]) at the end of ten years. Under WRERA, the trustees of a plan that was yellow for the first time in 2008 or 2009 had the one-time option of extending this ten-year period to 13 years.

For an orange zone plan, the FIP must be designed to improve the funded percentage by 20% of the underfunded amount in the 15-year period following the adoption period (with an optional extension to 18 years under WRERA for a plan first certified as orange in 2008 or 2009). The 15-year period is also called a *funding improvement period.* For example, if a plan is 75% funded when it is certified as orange, the FIP must be designed to increase the funded percentage of the plan to no less than 80% (75% + [25% × .20]) at the end of 15 years.

The adoption period for RPs and FIPs is one or two plan years; it depends on when current bargaining agreements expire, as the bargaining parties must adopt one of the options presented by plan trustees. During the adoption period, the trustees are prohibited from accepting a collective bargaining agreement that reduces contribution rates or excludes employees. In addition, trustee ability to increase benefits is limited.

Employers participating in a plan that is certified as red will have a surcharge imposed on their required contributions from 60 days after the plan is certified until the time that they reach a new collective bargaining contract.

Trustees are required to monitor the progress of their plan in meeting the goals set forth in the RP or FIP and to make changes in the plan as necessary to reflect recent plan experience, so the plan will be restored to green status by the end of the RP or FIP.

What Happens if Contributions Exceed the Maximum Contribution Levels?

In general, employer contributions that exceed the maximum set by IRS in a given tax year cannot be deducted as a business expense when the employer files federal income tax forms. In addition, the excess contributions are subject to a 10% excise tax. In addition to meeting a plan's minimum contribution requirements, trustees must also give attention to this upper limit on contributions.*

A rule change in 2002 now allows employers to deduct fully contributions in a given year under special circumstances; the contributions must be less than the *unfunded current liability* of the plan. This liability is equal to the value of all accrued benefits of the plan, determined by using an interest rate that approximates current interest rate levels and a mortality table specified by IRS. In 2006, the limit was raised again to be based upon 140% of current liability.

In the current relatively low interest rate environment, contributions made by employers to almost all multiemployer plans will be fully deductible. However, if contributions are anticipated to exceed the maximum limitation, trustees must either decrease contributions or increase benefit eligibility and/or levels so the contribution requirements increase. This poses a dilemma for trustees, since contributions are governed under collective bargaining agreements. In addition, improving benefits generally means a contribution requirement increase, not only for the year in question, but for future years as well. A possible solution is to adopt

* The maximum limitation is the sum of the normal cost and expenses plus a ten-year amortization of the initial unfunded actuarial accrued liability and the bases described under the FSA. However, this limit may not be less than the FSA minimum requirement nor more than the amount necessary to fund fully current obligations.

certain types of improvements that do not automatically impact future years, such as a one-time lump-sum increase to retirees, sometimes referred to as a *13th check.* Depending on the timing of when the actuary notifies trustees of this situation, there may be other solutions, such as a temporary reduction in contributions, diverting the contributions to fund other participant benefits or temporarily parking excess contributions in an escrow fund.

What Happens if an Employer Withdraws From a Plan?

The Multiemployer Pension Plan Amendments Act of 1980 (MPPAA) imposes a liability on an employer that withdraws from a multiemployer pension plan. The amount of the liability that the withdrawing employer must pay is a portion of the plan's *unfunded vested benefits liability (UVBL).* A plan's UVBL equals the plan's vested accrued liabilities minus its assets. The actuarial assumptions and valuation methods used to calculate the UVBL for withdrawal liability may be different from those used for other purposes.

Plan trustees must select one of three statutory methods to allocate UVBL to each participating employer. In certain circumstances, the Pension Benefit Guaranty Corporation (PBGC) may approve an alternative allocation method. Plans in certain industries such as the construction industry are required to use a specific allocation method.

While the calculation of withdrawal liability can be complicated, the reason for assessing withdrawal liability is quite simple. When an employer withdraws from a plan, vested benefits for employees of this employer remain an obligation of the plan. If the liability for these employees is not fully funded, the remaining current and future employers would have to make up the difference.

PPA included several changes to previous law and regulations. One of the most important changes is that plan trustees may "fresh start" a plan's UVBL if the plan does not have one. Trustees may elect to make such a change for withdrawals occurring on or after January 1, 2007. Doing so simplifies the withdrawal liability calculation and eliminates certain inequities that previously existed, for example, the possibility that a withdrawing employer could incur a liability even if the plan as a whole had no UVBL at the end of the year prior to its withdrawal.

Another important change relates to the calculation of a withdrawing employer's share of the UVBL for a plan that is certified as red as defined in PPA. These plans must adopt a rehabilitation plan that includes surcharges on participating employers and may include benefit reductions applicable to past service. Any surcharges are disregarded in determining the assessment to a withdrawing employer, and any benefit reductions applicable to past service are disregarded in determining the UVBL of the plan.

One other recent development is that the Financial Accounting Standards Board (FASB) is expected to issue standards that require additional disclosure to end users (primarily investors and analysts) related to a participating employer's potential withdrawal liability due to participation in a multiemployer plan. In general, these standards are expected to take the form of footnote disclosures in the audited financial statements of contributing employers and likely will be limited to general information regarding employer participation in multiemployer plans.

Conclusion

The role of the actuary as an advisor to the trustees is crucial to the many complex decisions trustees must make. It is important that the actuary be able to fully communicate available options to trustees in a manner that allows the trustees to fulfill their fiduciary obligations.

Chapter 29

Pension Fund Mergers*

Barry S. Slevin

Multiemployer pension plans are increasingly considering fund mergers. The interest in combining funds is the result of a number of factors. This chapter will review some of the reasons mergers are contemplated and what trustees should consider before taking action.

Why Do Funds Merge?

Financial Strength

There are various reasons trustees explore fund mergers. A key reason is funding. In many cases, the combining of two funds will result in one fund that is stronger than its parts. Indeed, the Pension Protection Act of 2006 (PPA) refers to mergers as one way for multiemployer plans to address financial difficulties. Consider a fund that is financially in good health today but faces an uncertain future. Another fund has funding problems now but strong prospects for the future. A merger of the two funds would take advantage of one fund's healthy current funding status and the future prospects of the other. The fund created from these two funds would be better able to withstand both short- and long-term funding concerns.

Many funds are in declining industries. They face a declining number of active participants in combination with an aging population that places the financial future of these funds in doubt. For some of these funds, it may be possible to merge with a fund covering a different industry, even one that is growing. Just as investment diversification lowers risk of losses, participation from different industries could lower a merged fund's risk of decline.

Cost Efficiencies

Another reason for a merger is the cost savings that might result. Like most financial institutions, larger multiemployer funds benefit from economies of scale. Some of the costs of operating a multiemployer fund are *fixed*—they do not change when the number of participants goes up or down. The typically lower per participant cost of administering a large plan versus a small benefit plan offers proof that this is true. Generally, custodial and investment management fees are lower since these expenses are often based on the value of fund assets. A larger pool of assets yields lower overall investment fees. Administrative cost savings alone are probably not a sufficient reason to merge, but they are certainly an advantage of a merger.

Union Mergers

External factors may also create conditions that make a merger advantageous. For instance, the merger of unions may create opportunities for plan mergers. When unions merge, it may make sense to merge the plans that serve the workers represented by the union. It is increasingly common for international unions to merge, which presents opportunities for industry diversification; a single international union may cover more than one industry.

Trustee Quality

Retirements by trustees and difficulty replacing their expertise is another reason to consider a merger. Many plans have difficulty finding qualified trustees who are willing to serve.

*For a more detailed discussion of legal considerations and case law regarding mergers, visit www.ifebp.org/Handbook7.

A merger may be the best way to ensure a plan continues to have competent trustees.

Subsidization

It is not permissible for one fund to merge to subsidize another, or, to put it more bluntly, to bail out a fund in trouble. While some subsidization may be a consequence of a merger, it cannot be the purpose of the merger. The trustees of each fund must act solely and for the exclusive purpose of their own plan participants and beneficiaries. It would be a breach of fiduciary duty for a board of trustees of a "healthy" plan to merge to benefit a weaker plan and its participants. This is not to say, however, that any subsidization is prohibited. Combining two funds must make sense based on the profile of the resulting merged fund.

What Steps Are Involved in a Merger?

There is a set of tasks that must be performed when considering and implementing a merger. Not every step in the process must be followed by the next, as some tasks are completed at the same time. However, a well-organized merger involves making sure each task is performed.

Initial Exploration

Before anything else, there is a need to determine whether it is worth the time and expense to seriously explore a merger. Trustees must ask whether a merger makes sense.

Benefit design and funding. The first step is an investigation of the benefits provided and the funding status of the plans that might be merged. When analyzing the cost of each plan, all differences in plan provisions must be taken into account when making comparisons.

If the benefit designs are too different, a merger may not make sense (although there have been mergers in which the merged fund retained both benefit designs). If the difference in funding levels is too great, the plan that is more financially secure may not be interested in a merger despite other advantages of a merger.

The funding of the funds, both on a separate and merged basis, is the most important issue to consider. Plan actuaries should be involved early in the process and analyze this issue in depth. They should report to the boards of trustees the pros and cons of a merger. In the report, the actuary should examine the finances of the plans and the implications of a merger from a number of actuarial viewpoints including:

- The current funding status
- The long-term expected funding status
- The Employee Retirement Income Security Act of 1974 (ERISA) minimum funding requirements
- The present and future zone status enacted as part of the Pension Protection Act of 2006 (PPA)
- The impact on withdrawal liability.

Collective bargaining agreements. Another important issue to investigate early is the collective bargaining relationships and the specific language of the collective bargaining agreements. If a collective bargaining party is opposed to a merger, the language of the collective bargaining agreement may provide a means to block the merger. Indeed, an initial question to ask legal counsel is who has the power to merge--the collective bargaining parties or the trustees? Obviously, if the power to merge is with the collective bargaining parties, trustees can only investigate and make recommendations to the collective bargaining parties--the trustees cannot actually agree to a merger.

Governance. Governance issues can also hamper a merger. As a practical matter, current trustees may not want to give up control of plan administration. An early issue to resolve is who will serve on the board of trustees of the merged fund. Many plans deal with this issue by creating an expanded board of trustees, but there are pitfalls that come with a large board of trustees. Trustees must also come to an agreement early regarding the establishment of committees and delegating authority to committees. Policies of the merging funds should be reviewed as part of the due diligence process, and which policies will govern the merged fund should be discussed.

Providers. Another issue to address early is which providers will be involved in the merger and which providers will serve the merged fund. Some of the providers may already be serving both funds. When this is not the case, there can be a problem—especially if a provider losing a client is allowed to slow down or derail the merger process. Trustees have to analyze this issue at an early stage to ensure the process moves forward.

Tip for Trustees

During a merger, trustees of small funds sometimes discover that they do not have the bargaining power to negotiate changes in the way the merged fund will operate. If you are in this type of situation, keep in mind that well-considered suggestions may still be adopted if your ideas are good and consistent with the fiduciary responsibilities of the trustees participating in the process.

Merger Team and Timetable

Personal experience suggests moving a merger forward works best when trustees of the merging funds designate a team to do so. The team typically consists of at least one union and one employer trustee from each plan, as well as a designated administrative officer, legal counsel, accountant and actuary. Creation of a team also leads to accountability. Trustees getting reports on progress are assured that required actions are actually performed.

It also usually helps to agree on a timetable for considering the merger, including a proposed effective date and dates for specific actions to be taken beforehand. Of course, this timetable is for planning purposes only—it can be revised when needed or abandoned completely if it is later determined a merger doesn't make sense. Setting specific dates creates the incentive and accountability to make sure the process moves forward.

Due Diligence

If the initial exploration suggests a merger may make sense, the next step is a more extensive investigation of each plan by the other. All aspects of the plans should be reviewed so there are no surprises during the merger process. Thorough investigation also minimizes the likelihood of surprises after a merger.

This stage of investigation is the foundation to satisfying the trustees' obligation to act prudently, assuming the fiduciary responsibility provisions apply. The duty to act prudently requires fiduciaries to investigate all appropriate facts bearing on their decision, consider available alternative courses of action and consult with appropriate professionals as necessary to make a decision.

Once the boards of trustees have decided to pursue a merger, there should be no limit on the information exchanged—each plan must fully understand the implications of the merger. It is surprising what an investigation can reveal. Some of the issues uncovered during the due diligence process for a merger have included:

- No determination of tax qualification from IRS
- Failure to follow ERISA reporting and disclosure rules
- Insurance contracts constituting fund assets that are not worth the amount understood at the time of the initial merger discussions
- Funding status significantly different from what was originally represented due to different actuarial assumptions, data problems and the like
- Plan documents or amendments never adopted by the board of trustees
- Unsigned contracts with providers—including providers supposedly acting as investment managers without any signed agreement acknowledging they are a fiduciary, as required by ERISA to create investment manager status.

Issues must be identified so trustees can take corrective action and move forward with the merger.

Plan Design

One of the greatest challenges facing trustees—even trustees who have decided a merger should take place—is agreement on the plan benefits to be provided by the merged fund. The differences in benefits may be slight, or they may be so different that a merger seems unworkable. There is a variety of ways to deal with differences in benefit accruals.

The plans may be so different that trustees decided to keep the two sets of benefits intact in the merged plan. As long as all assets of a merged fund are available to pay all benefits, the fund is considered a single plan under ERISA. While the newly created fund with separate benefit programs can benefit from the merger, the fund does sacrifice some administrative simplicity that results from a unified, single plan of benefits. Over time, the plan may become more uniform if amendments are applied to both benefit programs to make them more similar.

Another way to deal with benefit differences is to lock in or *freeze* the benefits earned as of the date of the merger. Benefits prior to the merger date are based on the provisions of the prior plans while different provisions apply for the benefits that participants earn in the future. When participants retire, they would be paid one check that is the total of their benefits earned prior to the merger and their benefits earned after the merger.

Another complexity involves the benefit options available to participants. When combining plans, trustees have to decide whether to extend all benefit options previously provided under each plan to all participants or freeze them on the merger date as described for benefit accruals. With a freeze, there would be one set of benefit options for post-merger accruals. This approach avoids multiple options going forward, but the merged fund must still keep track of the separate benefit components earned before the merger.

Trustees face these difficult decisions because the law has an anticutback rule that prohibits plans from reducing benefits or eliminating benefit options for benefits that have accrued already. In 2006, PPA created exceptions to the anticutback rule for nonnormal retirement benefits provided by multiemployer plans in critical status, or the so-called *red* zone. Therefore, depending on the situation, plans in the red zone are now able to eliminate some benefits or benefit forms by following PPA procedures. For plans not in the red zone, the safest course is to assume benefits earned to date—as well as the benefit options and rules relating to those benefits—are preserved. Only benefits and options that will apply after the merger may be reduced or eliminated compared to the premerger benefits and options. Review specific features of the plan with legal counsel.

Zone Status

PPA created new funding requirements for multiemployer pension plans. It is beyond the scope of this chapter to review these rules, but it is important to consider PPA while considering and implementing a merger. For instance, plans in endangered or critical status (referred to as the *yellow* and *red* zones) are required to adopt long-term funding programs in a Funding Improvement Plan (FIP) and Rehabilitation Plan (RP) respectively. In considering a merger, the zone status of the merging plans—as well as the expected zone status of the merged plan must be analyzed. If the merged plan will be in the yellow or red zone, the trustees should discuss in advance the terms and schedules of the merged plan's FIP or RP. Upon expiration of the collective bargaining agreements associated with the merged plan, the bargaining parties will have to comply with one of the schedules in the merged plan's FIP or RP. For more information concerning the PPA funding requirements, read Chapters 27 and 28.

Withdrawal Liability

Another important issue is what withdrawal liability rules will govern the merged fund. There are a number of options under ERISA for implementing the withdrawal liability provisions, including what method to use to determine withdrawal liability and which *de minimis* rule will apply. Agreement must be reached on which withdrawal liability rules will apply after the merger.

The difference in the funded status of the two funds may lead to the conclusion that determining employer withdrawal liability based on the funding status of the merged fund would be unfair. This can take place, for example, when one fund has no unfunded vested benefits (and therefore, no withdrawal liability) while the other fund has unfunded vested benefits. In this situation, a special withdrawal liability rule may be established that keeps the two funds separate solely when determining withdrawal liability. While this approach is not specifically stated in ERISA, the Pension Benefit Guaranty Corporation (PBGC) has the authority to approve it.

Governance and Operations

Trustees must make numerous other decisions as well:

Board Composition. Determining who will be the trustees of the merged fund should occur before the merger takes place to avoid any surprises or disagreements after the merger.

Committees. Trustees need to decide whether existing committees will continue and the scope of their authority. In some cases, final decision-making authority is delegated to a committee. In other cases, a committee only has the power to make recommendations to the full board. Even if the merging plans did not have committees, committees may make sense with an expanded board of trustees for the merged fund.

Policies. Similarly, the trustees should review the policies governing plan operations. A well-run plan has at a minimum (1) an investment policy, (2) a delinquency policy and (3) a trustee expense policy.

Administration. Typically, trustees will have agreed preliminarily on which outside providers will be retained by the surviving fund. If either fund has in-house administration, difficult personnel issues may have to be addressed to take full advantage of the economies of scale resulting from a merger. A merged fund office may mean fewer personnel are needed. Trustees need to discuss with the administrative manager of the merged fund how to deal with these issues. If personnel have to be terminated, the trustees must decide how this will be accomplished. Consult with legal counsel to identify the fund obligations as an employer and decide what benefits will be provided to those who are terminated.

Tip for Trustees

Involve the administrative manager of each plan very early in the discussion and investigation of a merger. Trustees and other professionals sometimes do not appreciate the complications that can arise from combining plans maintained with different computer systems, different data and different communication practices. It is important to identify and address these differences.

Many of the issues involved in the merger will not affect participants. If the administrative issues are not dealt with appropriately, however, there is an increased chance disruption will occur during implementation of the merger and the potential for a loss of confidence in the plan by participants and contributing employers.

Investment management. The issue of providers is particularly knotty when it comes to investments. In consultation with an investment consultant, trustees have to craft an investment program for the surviving fund. A larger portfolio can yield lower investment management fees because of the increased asset value; however, these savings can only be realized if portfolios are combined. If there are multiple investment managers, trustees will have to review which managers have overlapping styles and which managers complement each other. Trustees must decide which firms will manage the assets of the surviving fund. If an investment manager ends up with a larger portfolio, this is an opportunity to renegotiate fees.

A related issue is whether to use transition managers to liquidate portfolios and reduce the costs of the transition. This also is addressed with the investment consultant.

What Should Be Part of the Merger Agreement?

The merger agreement formalizes the exchange of information that has taken place between the merging funds. The agreement should be a comprehensive record of what is taking place. All key documents that have been exchanged should be attached to the agreement as "exhibits."

The agreement should include representations made by each board to the other regarding the fund, the fund's status and compliance with law. The agreement should also document trustee decisions on merger issues such as those discussed in this chapter. Putting decisions in writing helps avoid any misunderstandings. Indeed, the process of drafting the agreement and negotiating the language typically helps uncover issues on which there may not be a complete understanding, so they can be resolved in advance. Documenting the merger process and decisions serves as a record of trustee prudence.

There are three major issues typically encountered in drafting a merger agreement. The first is the liability of trustees serving a fund going out of existence, and of former trustees who may resign as part of the merger process. How important indemnification and insurance issues are perceived is often an extension of any legal and regulatory problems found during the due diligence process. Even if the trustees are not aware of any problems, they will still want to have assurance they are protected from legal liability.

One solution is to have the surviving fund indemnify former trustees from liability. This is a helpful but limited first step, given ERISA prohibits funds from indemnifying trustees against fiduciary breach. A total solution typically involves making sure fiduciary insurance covers any claims that may be made. This can be accomplished by (1) adding former trustees to the fiduciary insurance of the surviving fund or (2) purchasing separate coverage, either a new policy or a continuation of the policy held by the fund going out of existence. The relative merits of options should be discussed with legal counsel and a fiduciary insurance broker.

A second critical issue is obtaining a determination of tax qualification for the merged fund. A common approach is to condition the merger on the surviving fund obtaining a determination of tax qualification from the Internal Revenue Service (IRS). The merger agreement should be specific as to who obtains the determination and what will occur in the unlikely event it is not obtained.

Third, the merger agreement should clearly specify who is responsible for filing the required governmental forms for the fund that is going out of existence. Unless there is a clear assignment of responsibilities, there is a risk the final Form 5500 and other required forms will not be filed.

What Happens at the Time of the Actual Merger?

Even after the merger agreement has been negotiated and signed, there is still work to be done. However, at this point, what needs to be accomplished is primarily mechanical. For example:

- A new trust agreement may have to be adopted—as well as new plan and withdrawal liability rules.
- A new summary plan description must be drafted and adopted.
- Assets are changed to the name of the surviving fund.
- All contracts are amended to ensure the contractual relationships are clear and in the name of the merged fund.
- Notifications are sent to employees, employers and providers to advise them of the merger and the impact of the merger on them.
- The fiduciary insurance carrier is notified.
- Finally, collective bargaining agreements may have to be amended to reflect the merged entity.

While fund administrative personnel and professionals should be taking these steps, it is important that trustees monitor the completion of these transitional tasks.

Conclusion

A merger of two multiemployer pension plans is a complicated undertaking. However, there are a number of advantages to merging, and therefore it may be in the best interests of participants and beneficiaries to do so. If the board of trustees assembles the right team and carefully investigates the merger and its implications through a methodical process, it can result in a smooth, beneficial merger that is to the benefit of everyone—trustees, participating employers and, most important, the participants and beneficiaries.

Chapter 30

Defined Contribution and Hybrid Plans Versus Defined Benefit Plans

Sheree Yoder

Prior to the passage of the Multiemployer Pension Plan Amendments Act (MPPAA) in 1980, there was little interest in defined contribution (DC) plans in the collective bargaining process. MPPAA amended the Employee Retirement Income Security Act of 1974 (ERISA) and imposed liability on employers for their unfunded vested benefit liabilities in a defined benefit (DB) plan if they stopped making contributions. The legislation made DC plans more attractive to employers, as these plans are designed to be fully funded and there is no guaranteed pension benefit. A contributing employer that wishes to withdraw from a plan has no liability beyond its previously required contributions.

Since 1980, there has been a significant growth in the number of multiemployer DC plans. Many companies have added DC plans to supplement DB plans. Some companies have discontinued pension and/or profit-sharing contributions or shifted to matching DC contributions. The result has been a transfer of a large amount of responsibility for retirement savings to plan participants.

How Are Defined Benefit and Defined Contribution Plans Different?

The most obvious difference between DB and DC plans is what is being "defined." A *defined benefit plan* determines the dollar benefit amount to be paid to plan participants and beneficiaries. The amount is guaranteed based on a preestablished formula that considers factors such as an employee's years of service, an employee's income while working and the anticipated market returns that trustees believe can be earned on plan assets over time.

All contributions to a DB plan are put into a common pool of assets. If the promised (accrued) benefits for all of a DB plan's participants is combined, the total may not equal the value of plan assets; the employer must make up any shortfalls. An employer whose employees are participating in a plan assumes the risk that plan assets may not be sufficient to pay the defined benefits (liabilities). Because market returns on investments vary greatly from year to year, an employer's contributions to a plan can also vary greatly from one year to the next.

In contrast to a DB plan, a *defined contribution plan* defines the contribution an employer or employee makes to a plan. Employees have individual accounts that contain only the contributions they make or their employers make on their behalf—and money earned as a result of investing these contributions. The actual balance for each participant is known at any time. As with a DB plan, market returns affect earnings on contributions, but this time it is the participating employee who assumes the risk if returns are not what is expected or desired. Participants will have lower benefits unless they or their employer increase the contributions to the individual accounts to make up for the lower returns. Exhibit 1 summarizes key differences between the plans.

What Are the Advantages and Disadvantages of the Two Types of Plans?

When compared to DC plans, the advantages of DB plans are:

- Employees know their benefit prior to retirement
- Inflation protection while participants are working

Exhibit 1

Defined Benefit versus Defined Contribution Plans

	Defined Benefit Plan	Defined Contribution Plan
Plan Contributions	Employers make contributions based on plan provisions and actuarial calculations.	Employers may contribute but it is often contingent on contributions by the plan participant. Individual participants generally have a choice as to whether they will contribute and how much within limits established by the federal government.
Plan Investments	Contributions for plan participants are commingled. Employers or plan trustees establish policies directing how funds will be managed.	Individual participants usually determine how funds will be invested—especially if the primary contributor is the participant.
Benefit Distribution	Plans typically have a structured process for how and when benefits will be distributed.	Individual participants decide how they will take their benefit distributions within plan and federal government constraints.
Benefit Amount	Participants receive an amount based on plan provisions, contributions and actuarial calculations.	The amount received by an individual participant depends on the amount contributed to the plan and investment returns. In some cases, constraints are established by the plan.

- A higher level of retirement income for long-term employees
- Investment expenses tend to be lower, given there is one fund versus many individual accounts with relatively low balances
- Benefit does not depend on employees' ability or willingness to contribute
- Contributions are automatic
- Employees are free from investment decisions; they do not need investment expertise and/or experience.

But DC plans also have advantages over DB plans. DC plans:

- Have a contribution amount that is easily defined
- Are easy for employees to understand
- Do not require long-term employment for an employee to receive a benefit
- May provide higher benefits for employees who do not work long term for any particular plan
- Have portable balances which allow participants to take contributions and earnings with them if they change jobs
- Are less complicated to administer
- Typically have lower administration costs.

Are Both Types of Plans Covered Under ERISA?

A plan sponsor has an obligation under ERISA to administer retirement plans in the sole interest of the plan participants and their beneficiaries. There is no distinction between DB and DC plans. Hence, trustees for either plan have these specific responsibilities among others:

- **Legal and compliance.** Plans must be operated in compliance with all applicable regulations and requirements issued by the Department of Labor and the Internal Revenue Service (IRS).
- **Custody.** A qualified financial institution should be hired to hold plan assets, account for plan assets, process transactions related to plan assets and provide financial asset reporting to the plan sponsor.
- **Plan investments.** Trustees either manage plan assets or choose investment options for the plan. The trustees must have internal expertise or hire a consultant or advisor who can provide these services.
- **Plan administration and recordkeeping.** Trustees and the administrators to whom they delegate authority have responsibility for managing contributions to, and distributions from, the plan and for

tracking each participant's benefit amount or balance. Typically, a qualified industry professional is hired to provide these services, in which case the trustees must oversee the individual or institution hired for this purpose.

- **Participant communication and education.** Plans are required to communicate to plan participants on a periodic basis regarding the balances in the plan, the plan's investments, their benefits within the plan, as well as general market and economic information. In plans where participants are required to direct their own investments, specific communication is required regarding their investment options.

What Are Some Examples of Defined Contribution Plan Options?

Money Purchase Plans

Like other DC plans, *money purchase plans* are impacted by market returns and individual participants can know at any time the balance in their individual plan account. The two features that distinguish money purchase plans from other DC plans are: (1) contributions are made by the employer, typically as a percentage of eligible compensation and (2) the investment of plan assets is often directed by the employer.

Profit-Sharing Plans

As the name suggests, *profit-sharing plans* are a specific type of DC plan that allows an employer to share business profit with employees. The employer has discretion as to how much profit is contributed to the plan, and this amount can be changed from year to year. A 401(k) feature that allows employees to defer salary on a pretax basis or make after-tax contributions may be added to the plan. The employer may direct investments, hire an investment manager to manage the assets of the accounts, or delegate investment decisions to the participants. Giving participants the responsibility for making investment choices is often the case when the plan includes a 401(k) feature.

401(k) Plans

401(k) plans are DC plans that allow employees to contribute part of their earnings on a pretax basis. Employer contributions are often made in the form of a matching contribution, typically a percentage of what is put into the account by the employee up to a maximum percentage of compensation. Contributions are not subject to federal tax withholding and are not reported as taxable income. The money is taxed when the participant withdraws money after retirement. If a participant withdraws any savings before he or she reaches the age of 59½ years, there is an early withdrawal penalty.

Both employee and employer contributions to 401(k) plans are subject to limits established by the IRS. Contributions are capped for individual employees at a specific dollar amount. Persons aged 50 or older are allowed higher limits called *catch-up contributions.* The dollar maximums are reviewed annually by the IRS to determine whether adjustments should be made. Current maximums may be found at www.irs.gov. A 401(k) plan may also have its own limitations on contributions.

Employee contributions to a 401(k) are always 100% *vested* (owned) by the employee. The percentage of the employer contribution to which an employee is entitled if the employee is terminated or changes employers is dictated by the plan's *vesting schedule.* The schedule specifies how much of an employer contribution is vested at different points of time in the worker's employment.

Investment options available to 401(k) plan participants are chosen by the employer or are designated by an investment advisor. Typically, the options consist of mutual funds, collective investment trusts, and in some cases, managed accounts.

With the delegation of investment decisions to participants, employers and plan trustees managing a DC plan have more responsibility concerning the selection and ongoing evaluation of the investment options that participants can choose. This responsibility may be handled by a qualified industry professional hired to advise trustees, but the trustees are still responsible for selection of the advisor or consultant.

Trustees also have increased responsibility for communicating with and educating plan participants concerning investment options and option changes, general principles of investing and asset allocation, and plan fees. In most cases, a service provider is used to handle these functions—particularly given the new requirements for fee disclosure to participants.

As stated previously, 401(k) plans allow participants to choose when they withdraw funds from their accounts. There are some special types of withdrawals, however, that may be governed by the plan or the IRS. Exhibit 2 summarizes these special situations.

Roth Contributions

Employees have the ability to make another type of contribution to a 401(k) plan: a *Roth contribution.* These contributions are made on an after-tax basis but neither the

Exhibit 2

401(k) Early Withdrawals

Loans	A plan may allow participants to borrow against their vested account balance within limits established by the IRS. Loans are paid back through payroll deduction on an after-tax basis. Assuming the employee repays the loan, the loan amount is not taxable to the employee at any time. However, should the employee default on the loan, the amount of the outstanding loan balance may be taxed as a plan distribution.
Early Withdrawals	A plan may allow participants to permanently withdraw dollars from their plans while they are still employed. Distributions taken by a participant prior to the age of 59½ are subject to a 10% early withdrawal penalty as well as normal income taxes.
Hardship Withdrawals	A plan may also have a hardship withdrawal provision that allows participants to withdraw their vested dollars. The IRS has identified specific situations when such a withdrawal is acceptable, and the plan must grant approval. Participants who take hardship withdrawals are not allowed to contribute to their plans for a period dictated by the plan document. The IRS requires a waiting period of at least six months. Like other early withdrawals, hardship withdrawals are subject to normal income taxes and the 10% early withdrawal penalty.
Death and Disability	Since employer contributions are typically 100% vested, participants can immediately take a distribution if they become disabled. In the event of the participant's death, his or her beneficiaries are eligible for the same benefits. Some plans require beneficiaries to take a distribution of the participant's assets within a particular time frame following the participant's death.

amount saved nor plan earnings are taxed when the participant withdraws money from the account (assuming certain requirements are met). Roth plans provide tax-free income when money is withdrawn. In contrast, traditional 401(k) plans "cost" less when a contribution is made because the participant's taxable income is reduced at the time of the contribution.

How Can a 401(k) Advisor Help Plan Trustees?

Trustees are tasked with varying degrees of responsibility relative to 401(k) plans. It is not uncommon for trustees to lack the time, tools and/or expertise to fulfill these responsibilities. A 401(k) consultant or advisor can fill this void. Consultants may provide a full range of services from plan design to investment advice for employees, or services may be more limited such as provider searches and investment consulting.

The most important task when considering professional assistance is to determine the specific needs that the consultant will address, and therefore, the role and responsibility of the consultant. Fees charged by the consultant should be appropriate for the service(s) being provided. Trustees of DC plans have an obligation to fully understand the fees being paid and services provided in return for those fees. Trustees may delegate responsibility for things such as choosing and evaluating investment options, but they still have a fiduciary responsibility for hiring a competent provider to perform these duties.

What Is a Hybrid Plan?

Hybrid plans combine features of DC and DB plans. Here are some examples of hybrids.

Cash Balance Plans

Cash balance plans are DB plans that look like DC plans. Plan participants have a hypothetical account balance, which is credited each year with contributions and interest. When participants become eligible to take a distribution, their balance is equal to the vested balance in their hypothetical account. The interest credited to these accounts is specified in the plan document—it may or may not match the actual return earned on the plan investments. Cash balance plans allow higher contribution rates than DC plans so they have the potential for faster accumulation of retirement savings.

Pension Equity Plans

Pension equity plans are DB plans that build cash throughout an employee's working life. They offer the guaranteed benefit of a DB plan, but the benefit is expressed as a current lump sum. This lump sum is portable, which means an employee can take it as a plan distribution when terminating employment—a feature similar to that of a DC plan.

Pension equity plans must make benefits available in the form of an annuity. In practice, however, the annuity requirement generally applies to employees nearing retirement. When an account balance is less than $5,000, employees may "cash out" and employers have no obligation to offer an annuity option. Easy access to lump-sum benefits can adversely impact workers who receive their benefits in cash and do not roll over the lump-sum benefit to an IRA or another qualified retirement plan. Lump-sum payments are taxed in the year the employee received payment. If the employee is under the age of 59½, there is an additional 10% tax penalty for early withdrawal.

Target-Benefit Plans

Target-benefit plans look like DB plans in that a target benefit is determined. Calculations are made based on actuarial assumptions to determine the size of the contribution required to meet the target benefit. However, this is where the similarities with DB plans end. Contributions are placed in individual accounts, and the same contribution is made each year. The benefit the participant receives at retirement is based on the actual contributions and the earnings on those contributions; this benefit amount may vary greatly from the target benefit. The employer has no responsibility to contribute additional dollars to ensure the target benefit is achieved. Because employee age is one of the factors that determine the contribution, target-benefit plans may have greater advantages for older employees in helping them achieve sufficient retirement savings.

Age-Weighted Profit-Sharing Plans

Age-weighted profit-sharing plans give employers a choice whether to make a contribution on behalf of employees, much like profit-sharing plans. One difference is that, like the plan's name implies, the IRS allows larger contributions for older participants. There are no required annual contributions by employers and no actuarial valuations. Contributions are segregated for each employee in the same way contributions are separated for DC plans.

A unique characteristic of age-weighted profit-sharing plans is that the contributions are allocated so the same benefit is purchased for each employee, regardless of age, and based on compounding interest calculations. The contribution is greater for older employees, but the benefit purchased is the same as for younger employees.

Floor Offset Plans

The objective of *floor offset plans* is to ensure employees receive a minimum benefit at retirement regardless of market returns on plan assets. A DC component serves as the primary retirement fund while a DB fund uses a benefit formula to establish the "floor" (minimum benefit) to be paid in retirement. If the DC benefits fall below the floor, the DB plan is used to make up any deficiency.

Conclusion

In order to maximize the benefits of any retirement plan for employees, it is advisable to consult with a retirement plan professional to determine what type of retirement plan is most appropriate in a specific situation. Although not included in this chapter, current contribution limits for all types of plans can be found on the IRS website (www.irs.gov). The U.S. Department of Labor website (www.dol.gov) also provides comprehensive information on all types of retirement plans and their associated features, benefits and requirements.

Chapter 31

Accounting and Auditing

Lawrence R. Beebe

Accounting and auditing are necessary parts of any employee benefit plan operation. A plan accountant (hereinafter referred to as the *internal accountant*) is responsible for:

- Designing and developing a plan's accounting system
- Collecting monies due to the plan and paying all monies owed by the plan
- Designing and implementing the plan's internal accounting control system to ensure accurate recording of all monies collected and paid
- Preparing the plan's financial statements in accordance with U.S. generally accepted accounting principles (GAAP) as explained in Chapter 32.

An independent certified public accountant (hereinafter referred to as the *external auditor*) is responsible for auditing the financial statements prepared by a plan. The external auditor conducts the audit in accordance with the U.S. generally accepted auditing standards (GAAS) and issues a report on the fairness of the statements. For a full explanation of GAAS, see the appendix to this chapter at www.ifebp.org/Handbook7. Fairness is explained in the Tip for Trustees on page 227 in this Chapter.

Of course, trustees have ultimate responsibility for their plan's financial statements, accounting systems and internal control systems.

What Is the Reason for the External Audit and the Other Documents Prepared and Filed for a Plan?

For a plan with more than 100 participants, ERISA requires an external audit at the beginning of each year. The audited financial statements must accompany the filing of the Form 5500 Annual Return/Report of Employee Benefit Plan. Form 5500 helps assure the federal government, plan participants and others that a plan is being managed according to ERISA and other government regulations. Form 5500 also ensures that participants and beneficiaries have sufficient information about their rights and benefits. The Department of Labor (DOL) and the Internal Revenue Service (IRS) share responsibility for enforcement of federal regulations; either can audit a plan's Form 5500.

While pension plans as well as health and welfare plans must file Form 5500 every year, joint apprenticeship and training plans can request a permanent exemption from filing the form. Health and welfare plans must also file the Form 990 Return of Organization Exempt from Tax. Besides providing financial information, Form 990 asks a series of questions concerning an organization's governance, management and disclosure. Some questions ask whether the organization has adopted certain governance policies. These are addressed in Chapter 36.

What Should Trustees Look For When Hiring an External Auditor?

An internal accountant normally has a bachelor's degree in accounting, while an external auditor must have an accounting degree and be licensed as a Certified Public Accountant (CPA). A CPA must pass a rigorous multipart exam. Passing the CPA exam, however, is just the first step in becoming an external auditor for employee benefit plans. The external auditor must also:

- Participate in continuing professional education required to maintain a CPA license
- Understand the laws that govern multiemployer plans, particularly the Taft-Hartley Act (see Chapter 2) and ERISA (see Chapters 4, 5 and 54)

- Keep up-to-date on the pronouncements issued by the Financial Accounting Standards Board (FASB), which establishes GAAP, and the Auditing Standards Board of the American Institute of Certified Public Accountants (AICPA), which issues GAAS requirements
- Understand collective bargaining agreements, unions and the industries in which plan participants work.

Recognizing that auditing employee benefit plans is a very specialized undertaking, AICPA has established the Employee Benefit Plan Audit Quality Center (EBPAQC) to aid CPA firms in performing benefit plan audits. Membership in EBPAQC is voluntary with members agreeing to meet certain auditing standards; most quality CPA firms that audit employee benefit plans are members.

All CPA firms that perform audits must have a peer review by another CPA firm every three years. In the other two years, these firms must conduct internal inspections on their own audit practice. CPA firms that are members of EBPAQC must have their peer review performed by another member of EBPAQC with employee benefit plan audits among those reviewed. Firms that perform benefit plan audits can also have their audit work reviewed by the Employee Benefits Security Administration (EBSA) of the Department of Labor (DOL).

When hiring an independent auditor, there are some specific questions to help assess the qualifications of candidates:

- Does the firm specialize in multiemployer plan audits?
- Does the firm stress continuity of staff on audit engagements?
- Does the firm educate its staff on how to perform employee benefit plan audits?
- Is the firm size appropriate given the size of the employee benefit plan?
- Is the firm a member of EBPAQC?
- Has the firm's audit opinion ever been rejected by DOL as the result of an audit?
- Does the firm have low turnover of its professional staff?

After hiring an external auditor, there are two more points to keep in mind. First, CPAs are experts in accounting and auditing. They should have an excellent understanding of internal control systems for plans, but CPAs are not actuaries, attorneys or administrators. Do not be surprised if an auditor refers questions to other professionals who are best qualified to provide answers. Secondly, a CPA is neither a part of a plan's management nor a fiduciary to the plan. The CPA is, however, a party in interest to a plan just like other professional advisors.

What Happens When There Is an External Audit of a Plan?

Planning

The first step in the external audit process is for the CPA to get an *engagement letter* signed by trustees (typically the cochair of the board) and the CPA firm. This letter states the responsibilities of both parties and states the fee for audit services.

The next step is for the auditor to plan the engagement. Adequately planning an audit is a generally accepted auditing standard. The steps in audit planning normally include, but are not limited to:

- Meeting with the board of trustees or an audit committee
- Identifying high-risk areas where most of the auditor's time will be spent. High-risk audit areas for benefit plans typically include investments, employer and employee contributions, benefits and claims, expenses, and participant data
- Determining which of the plan's internal control systems must be evaluated
- Making a preliminary determination of what constitutes a material error in the plan's financial statements
- Determining where plan fraud is likely to occur
- Preparing a planning document broadly outlining how the audit will be performed.

At the conclusion of the planning process, the auditor will draft an *audit program,* which is a list of the specific audit procedures to be performed. These procedures test, recalculate, observe and confirm the accounting transactions of the plan for the audit year.

The Audit

The next step in the process is the examination of plan procedures and documents; the independent auditor will:

- Study and evaluate the plan's internal control system
- Gather sufficient and appropriate audit evidence to conduct the audit.

The auditor will ask the plan trustees and administrator for a signed representation letter. Those who sign this letter state (1) they have primary responsibility for the financial statements of the plan and (2) to the best of their knowledge and belief, the financial statements are correct. The auditor also obtains a letter from the plan attorney (the *lawyer's letter*) dealing with any significant legal matters that arose or were settled during the plan year.

The Opinion

The auditor is now able to write the report and issue an opinion on the fairness of the plan's financial statements, which can be an unqualified opinion, a qualified opinion, a disclaimer of opinion or an adverse opinion. Form 5500 lists these four types of opinion; the preparer of the form checks a box stating which of the four opinions is attached.

What Do the Different Types of Opinions in a Financial Statement Mean?

The following describes each of the four types of audit opinion. The only types of opinion permitted by ERISA and acceptable to DOL are an unqualified opinion and the limited scope disclaimer.

Unqualified Opinion

Auditing standards allow an auditor to give an *unqualified opinion* only when all the following occur:

- The accounting principles selected by a client have general acceptance and are appropriate.
- The disclosures in the financial statements and footnotes are adequate.
- The data in the financial statements are reasonably summarized.
- The events and transactions during the period audited are accurately reflected in the financial statements.

The third paragraph of the opinion should say "present fairly." If these two words are there, without qualification or modification, the external auditor has rendered an unqualified opinion from the independent CPA. This is the highest level of assurance that an auditor can give. CPAs refer to it as a "clean" opinion.

Tip for Trustees

When reviewing audited financial statements for the plan, immediately turn to the report of the independent auditor to determine if the statements have an unqualified opinion. The third paragraph of the opinion should say "present fairly." If these two words are there, without qualification or modification, the external auditor has rendered an unqualified opinion from the independent certified public accountant. Why doesn't the CPA say the financial statements are accurate rather than saying "present fairly?" A CPA cannot say the statements are accurate unless all of the plan's transactions were audited. The cost to perform a test of all transactions would be too costly.

Qualified Opinion

An auditor gives a *qualified opinion* when his or her work was limited in some way. The auditor refers to this situation as a *scope limitation.* An example of a scope limitation is where a plan does not perform payroll audits on its contributing employers. As a result, the auditor cannot verify that all contributions due have been collected.

If an auditor gives a qualified opinion, the words "except for" will be in the third paragraph of the report. The wording of a qualified report might read:

> *The financial statements referred to above present fairly, in all material respects, except for employer contributions receivable and employer contributions which we were unable to verify because payroll audits were not performed on contributing employers.*

Disclaimer of Opinion

An external auditor gives a *disclaimer of opinion* in two sets of circumstances:

- The auditor is unable to gather sufficient audit evidence to give an opinion.
- The auditor is performing a limited scope engagement as permitted by ERISA.

When might an auditor be unable to give an opinion on a plan's financial statements? One situation occurs when an administrator has embezzled money from a plan, then covers up the theft by destroying all plan books and records. The auditor, in this case, would give a disclaimer of opinion stating an inability to give an opinion.

With respect to the second circumstance, ERISA allows a plan administrator to instruct an auditor not to audit investment information prepared and certified by a bank or an insurance company. The auditor still performs the other procedures required in a normal financial statement audit. Since investments are a material part of the plan's financial statements, the independent auditor gives a disclaimer of opinion on the overall financial statements and cites the ERISA exception as the reason for the disclaimer. This is the only circumstance in which DOL will accept a disclaimer of opinion as an acceptable audit report.

Adverse Opinion

An auditor gives an *adverse opinion* when he or she believes the overall financial statements unfairly present a plan's fi-

Tip for Trustees

Remember that financial statements must have either an unqualified opinion or an ERISA-approved limited scope opinion. Without one of these two opinions, DOL will reject the filing and require 90 days to "cure the deficiency." After 90 days, if the deficiency is not cured, trustees as a group will be fined $1,100 every day until the audit report with an acceptable opinion is filed. The plan cannot pay this fine—trustees must pay it using personal assets.

nancial position. It is more likely that an independent auditor will use the threat of an adverse opinion to ensure that a plan's financial statements are in accordance with GAAP. What scenario might cause a CPA to threaten an adverse opinion? Suppose a plan pays $100 million for securities early in a year and by the end of the year, the securities are only worth $70 million. The plan trustees instruct the plan's internal accountant to state the value of the securities at their original cost ($100 million) rather than at the fair market value of $70 million. Knowing GAAP requires securities be reported at their fair market value of $70 million, the external auditor threatens an adverse opinion saying the financial statements are not fairly presented. This threat is normally all that is required. The current value of the securities is corrected in the financial statements and the auditor can issue an unqualified opinion.

Where Is More Information Available on Plan Audits?

It is impossible to describe the entire audit process in this chapter. For further information on this subject, consult the AICPA's *Audit and Accounting Guide: Employee Benefit Plans,* which is updated and published annually. AICPA also publishes the annual *Employee Benefit Plans Industry Developments,* which alerts auditors to any recent accounting and auditing changes that would affect employee benefit plans.

Chapter 32

Reading and Understanding Employee Benefit Plan Financial Statements

David C. Lee and Patrick Stines

If an employee benefit plan has over 100 participants, Department of Labor (DOL) regulations require the inclusion of audited financial statements with a plan's annual Form 5500 filing. A primary objective of these statements is to provide trustees, plan participants and others the information needed to assess accurately a plan's ability to pay benefits. Understanding a plan's financial statements is an important fiduciary responsibility. A step-by-step reading of the documents will provide a much better understanding of a plan's financial health. Trustees will also be better able to make prudent decisions for their plan as well as the participants and beneficiaries served.

To strengthen a trustee's grasp of financial statements, this chapter provides an overview of the required financial statements and aims to make them more useful. While this chapter focuses on multiemployer plans, it is also applicable to single employer and other plan types.

Who Is Responsible for Preparing the Financial Statements?

Financial statements submitted with Form 5500 require an audit opinion by a certified public accountant (CPA). The audit must be performed according to generally accepted auditing standards (GAAS). When DOL regulations call for supplemental schedules, the Employee Retirement Income Security Act (ERISA) also requires the CPA to cover these schedules in the audit.

Ultimately, financial statements are the responsibility of plan management, even if an auditor assists in their preparation. The auditor is responsible for the audit report that provides an opinion whether the financial statements are free of material misstatements. The auditor does not guarantee the accuracy of the financial statements, but merely provides reasonable assurance that they are fairly stated.

What Must Be Included in Plan Financial Statements?

To give information about its resources and obligations, a plan is required to provide some or all of these five documents:

1. A statement of net assets available for benefits
2. A statement of changes in net assets available for benefits
3. A statement of benefit obligations
4. A statement of changes in benefit obligations
5. Notes to the financial statements.

It is important to keep in mind that "one size does *not* fit all" for benefit plans. There are different reporting requirements for defined benefit (DB) plans and defined contribution (DC) plans. Benefit obligations will not be listed in the statements of a DC plan such as a 401(k) plan or an annuity plan—the net assets available for benefits of a DC plan are equivalent to its benefit obligations. On the other hand, DB plans must present benefit obligations and the changes in those benefit obligations in financial statements in one of three ways. As a result, a DC plan will not have items 3 and 4 listed above.

DB plans must file all five documents but there is some flexibility in how they are filed. Documents 3 and 4 may be filed in one of three ways:

1. As separate statements
2. Combined with the other statements—the statement of benefit obligations (Item 3) and the statement of changes in benefit obligations (Item 4) are superimposed on the statement of net assets available

for benefits (Item 1) and the statement of changes in net assets available for benefits (Item 2), respectively.

3. Reported as a disclosure in the notes to the financial statements (Item 5).

What Is the Statement of Net Assets Available for Benefits?

A balance sheet is the corporate equivalent of the statement of net assets available for benefits. This statement shows the assets and liabilities of the plan. Some key items shown on this statement are:

- **Fair value of investments.** For a security that is traded, *fair value* means the quoted market price of the security. If a quoted market price is not readily available, an alternative method is used to establish the investment's worth; for example, real estate is valued through professional appraisal.
- **Contributions receivable.** Contributions due a plan are from employers and, if it is a contributory plan, from employees. For a DB plan, the statement may include a line for *withdrawal liability,* which is monies due from withdrawing employers for their share of unfunded benefit obligations.
- **Property assets.** This category includes property owned by a fund such as land, buildings, office furniture and equipment. It is important to understand how real estate is stated. It can be presented under property assets at a depreciated historical cost or under investments at appraised value. How it is reported depends on how it is used. If a plan has real estate used primarily to house plan operations and related entities such as other plans, it is presented as a property asset. If the purpose of the real estate is to generate rental income from unrelated third parties, it should be shown in the investment section described above.
- **Amounts due to and from related entities.** This item appears if there is an administrative expense-sharing arrangement among related plans or other entities. Trustees need to ensure that balances owed by or to the other entity are collected or paid in a timely fashion. It is a very good idea to have a written expense-sharing agreement in place and to update it periodically. Updates should be at least every three years, or more frequently if a major event occurs (e.g., an office relocation) that will change the expense allocation.
- **Amounts due to and from brokers for investment trades.** These are for trades a plan executes at year-end but are settled afterward.
- **Operating liabilities.** Accounts payable and accrued expenses are operating liabilities. Specific examples include rent, salaries and professional fees owed by the plan.
- **Net assets available for benefits.** This category is very important and deserves special attention. It presents a plan's total assets less total liabilities. This number, when compared with the benefit obligations, provides information on the funding status of a DB plan. In the case of a DC plan, the net assets balance equals the sum of the participants' account balances.

What Is a Statement of Changes in Net Assets Available for Benefits?

The statement of changes in net assets available for benefits includes a summary of a plan's financial activity–essentially, the plan's income and expenses for the fiscal year. This statement shows additions (income) to and deductions (expenses) from the net assets available for benefits. The corporate equivalent is the income statement. This statement also includes, among other things:

- **Net appreciation or depreciation.** This is the change in the fair value of investments reflecting both realized and unrealized gains and losses. A gain or loss in value is realized only when a security is sold. If the investment's market value changes and it is still owned by the plan, the gain or loss is unrealized.
- **Interest and dividends earned on investments**
- **Investment expenses.** These are investment costs such as fees paid to investment advisors, managers and custodians.
- **Employer (employee) contributions**
- **Benefits paid.** This item is always stated on a cash basis even though the statements may be on a modified cash or accrual basis of accounting.
- **Administrative expenses.** Salaries paid to plan personnel and office expenses are examples of administrative expenses.
- **Net increase or decrease in net assets,** or **total additions (income) less total deductions (expenses).** This is, in effect, the plan's bottom line, showing how well or poorly the plan has done financially.

What Is a Statement of a Plan's Obligations?

Health and Welfare Plans

A health and welfare plan statement would show some or all of the following benefit obligations:

- **Claims payable.** These are benefit claims that have been processed for payment but not paid at the end of the reporting period.
- **Claims incurred but not reported (IBNR).** These are injuries or illness that occurred before the end of the plan year but for which a claim has not yet been filed. In other words, these are the claims that do not exist at the end of the plan year. How can unknown claims be shown? Generally accepted accounting principles (GAAP) require these claims be estimated and reported. This amount can be combined with claims payable or reported as a separate total.
- **Accumulated eligibility credits (AEC).** This is an estimate of a plan's obligation to provide benefits to participants and dependents following the termination of the participant's employment. Where such coverage is provided, it is usually extended for a period of time—typically 30 to 90 days following termination, or a period where sufficient hours have not been worked to achieve full benefits. The length of time varies with the industry involved. Note that this is different from Consolidated Omnibus Budget Reconciliation Act (COBRA) coverage.
- **Postretirement obligations.** These promised benefits must be estimated and reported if a plan provides health and welfare benefits to retirees or their dependents. This can be a large amount—well in excess of a plan's net assets available for benefits. Unlike pension benefits, however, these benefits are not vested. They may be modified or even terminated, depending on the financial condition of a plan. Realize, however, that these are obligations of the plan and eventually must be resolved.

Since the last three items involve some degree of estimation, an actuary or benefit consultant usually provides the information needed for the statement.

Pension Plans

As mentioned above, DB plans do not include obligations for benefits in the statement of net assets available for benefits *(balance sheet)*. Often, these obligations will be presented in a separate statement. Sometimes they appear combined with information in another statement or in the footnotes to the statements. Multiemployer DB plans commonly present accumulated plan benefits in the footnotes. Regardless of how they are presented, a plan must show the various components of benefit obligations.

Measurement of accumulated DB plan benefits *(pension liabilities)* is also prepared by an actuary and presented as an annual actuarial valuation. Accumulated plan benefits should be reported in three categories: vested benefits of participants currently receiving benefits, other vested benefits and nonvested benefits.

> **Tip for Trustees**
>
> Review the footnotes before looking at the financial statements themselves. The footnotes provide background information that will help you review the financial statements.

What Is Disclosed in the Footnotes?

Readers of financial statements often make the mistake of skimming through footnote disclosures. Although the information is not as clear as the statements themselves, the footnotes provide supporting details that are important to getting the complete financial picture. Below are some of the significant disclosures often found in footnotes.

- **Description of the plan.** This footnote provides a brief description of plan features.
- **Summary of accounting policies.** This is a statement of significant accounting policies followed by the plan.
- **Related party transactions.** Both GAAP and ERISA require transactions involving related parties (referred to as *parties in interest* under ERISA) be reflected in footnotes to the financial statements. Parties in interest include fiduciaries or employees of a plan and the union(s) whose members are plan participants. Examples of related party transactions include expense-sharing arrangements among related plans and transactions with a contributing employer. Related party transactions in multiemployer plans are commonly scrutinized during DOL audits and need to be well-documented and supported.
- **Nonexempt (prohibited) transactions.** ERISA generally prohibits transactions between a plan and a party in interest. However, there are exemptions such as the provision of accounting and legal services. These *prohibited transactions* should be disclosed in the footnotes. Additionally, prohibited transactions must be disclosed in Part III (nonexempt transactions) of Schedule G of Form 5500. The attached auditor's report must state in the opinion whether the information reported on Schedule G is fairly stated.

- **Benefit obligations.** For DB pension and welfare plans, the footnotes must disclose additional information from the actuary's valuation. Remember, disclosure in the footnotes is one method for presenting the information related to benefit liabilities. The additional information that must be disclosed by one of the three methods includes:
  - The method and significant assumptions used in calculating the accumulated plan benefits of a pension plan, and the postretirement benefit obligations of a health and welfare plan
  - For a pension plan, whether minimum funding requirements were met.
- **Subsequent events.** This footnote states the plan has evaluated events occurring through the report date and, if applicable, discusses significant matters. Events occurring after the end of the fiscal year that may be disclosed are a decision to terminate or merge a plan, a large employer going out of business and a significant decrease in investment values.
- **Plan amendments.** GAAP requires the disclosure of significant plan amendments such as those pertaining to participants covered, vesting and benefit provisions.
- **Investments.** Individual investments that are equal to or greater than 5% of net assets available for benefits at the end of the plan year must be disclosed in the notes. This should not be confused with the ERISA requirement to list investments held at the end of the plan year on a supplemental schedule discussed later in this chapter. Additionally, the appreciation or depreciation in the fair value of investments must be disclosed by category of investment—common stock, corporate debt instruments, governmental securities and so forth.
- **Fair value.** GAAP fair value rules apply to the plan's investment portfolio. In recent years, accounting rules have significantly increased the amount of plan investment disclosure. Investments are now categorized as Levels I-III depending upon the method used to measure fair value. *Level I* is restricted to securities traded in an active market with quoted market (e.g., NYSE) prices. *Levels II-III* contain investments not traded in active markets that require other valuation measures (e.g., real estate appraisals and yield curves for bonds). Plans are now also required to report totals within each major asset category, market sector or other distinction (e.g., international equity, distressed debt hedge funds, high-yield corporate bonds). Generally speaking, the extent of plan disclosure varies with the sophistication of the portfolio. Fair value disclosures can be complex and require a collaborative effort among plan trustees and professional service providers.
- **Reconciliation between the financial statements and Form 5500.** Financial statements and Schedule H of Form 5500 report some information differently. For example, real estate held as an operating asset is reported at its depreciated historical cost in the financials, as required by GAAP. However, for Schedule H, fair market value is required. As a result, a building purchased for $50,000 might appear in the financials at a depreciated value of $40,000 and in Schedule H at today's market value of $200,000. Reconciliation is required to be included as a footnote disclosure in the financial statements.

Another example comes from health and welfare plans. The net assets balance shown in Schedule H is reduced by benefits payable and benefits incurred but not reported. These liabilities are not included in the statement of net assets available for benefits; this means the statement and the schedule will show different results. ERISA requires these differences be explained in the notes.

Additional items commonly presented in the footnotes include but are not limited to the following:

- **Plan funding policy**
- **Investment contracts with insurance companies**
- **Securities lending provisions**
- **Pension Protection Act of 2006 certifications and funding improvement or rehabilitation plans.**

What Schedules Are Required by ERISA?

In addition to what GAAP requires, ERISA requires the following supplemental schedules be included in the annual report whenever they apply:

- **Schedule of assets held for investment purposes and a listing of securities and other investments.** These are items such as real estate and participant loans held at the end of the year.
- **Schedule of reportable transactions.** Certain transactions over a 5% or greater threshold involving securities and individuals are reported here.
- **Schedule G of Form 5500**
  - **Part I—Schedule of Loans or Fixed Income Obligations in Default or Classified as Uncollectible**
  - **Part II—Schedule of Leases in Default or Classified as Uncollectible**
  - **Part III—Nonexempt Transactions.** All nonexempt (prohibited) transactions are reported, regardless of materiality.

Chapter 33

Internal Controls: An Overview

Michael A. Van Sertima

Trustees and plan professionals give a great deal of attention to benefit plan financial reports. Unless there has been fraud or a material error in a plan's financial statements, similar attention is rarely given to internal controls. Specific examples of internal control procedures are:

- Segregation of duties
- Proper authorization of transactions
- Safe custody of blank checks and signature stamps
- Timely reconciliation of all bank accounts
- Timely reconciliation of certain general ledger accounts to subsidiary records

What Are the Objectives of Internal Controls?

Internal controls are accounting policies and procedures that help a benefit plan reach its objectives. These controls help ensure (1) financial statements are reliable, (2) plan assets are safeguarded from misappropriation (e.g., misuse or theft), (3) operations are effective and efficient, and (4) there has been compliance with all applicable laws and regulations.

Reliability of Financial Reporting

Reliable financial data is critical to achieving plan objectives and fulfilling regulatory requirements. Trustees look at both financial and nonfinancial data to make sure plan operations and investments are consistent with plan policies. Good information is vital to making plan decisions (e.g., whether to outsource medical claims processing and how to invest new contributions). Regulatory filings such as Form 5500 require the inclusion of financial information stating plan income, expenses, assets and liabilities. Trustees want to be sure this financial data is fairly represented.

Safeguarding Assets

Trustees want safeguards that thwart the unauthorized use or theft of plan assets. Preventing and detecting the misappropriation of plan assets is probably the most well-known reason for having internal controls. Requiring two signatures on checks is one example of an internal control commonly used by many types of organizations. Policies that require trustee authorization of payroll increases, conference expenses, capital expenditures and the write-off of uncollectible receivables are other examples of controls. The plan should have controls in place to prevent the destruction or loss of plan records, as well as a means to recover documents if something occurs despite these controls.

The Effectiveness and Efficiency of Operations

When performing a financial statement audit, an auditor may notice something that could improve plan operations—this might be eliminating a job that is being duplicated or work that is not even needed. Perhaps information provided by a third party does not have to be collected by plan employees. Duplication of operations often occurs when a plan is growing in size. It is also common when there is a plan merger—especially if little or no attention has been given to combining or coordinating duties.

Suggestions for improving the effectiveness and efficiency of operations are usually included in a management letter from the plan auditor. A comprehensive review of operations can identify areas where streamlining and cost savings are possible. This review can be done internally by plan personnel or by an independent certified public accountant (CPA).

Compliance With Applicable Laws and Regulations

Internal controls also help prevent and detect noncompliance with the laws, rules and regulations governing plan operations. A plan should have written policies for the reimbursement of trustee expenses and the collection of delinquent contributions. If the plan shares any administrative expenses with another organization, there should be a written policy for this. If the plan provides health and welfare benefits, trustees will want to be sure it has the privacy protections required to comply with the Health Insurance Portability and Accountability Act (HIPAA). More information on HIPAA is found in Chapter 21. Of course, all policies should meet pertinent legal requirements and be followed as written.

Who Is Responsible for Internal Controls?

Trustees in partnership with plan administrators are responsible for developing, implementing and maintaining effective internal controls. Plan administrators are responsible for the day-to-day implementation and maintenance of the internal controls with respect to plan books, records and assets.

Trustees should show the same regard for internal controls that they expect from employees. Attitude and integrity filter down to employees. There is no better protection for a plan than a proactive and involved board of trustees.

Isn't the Plan Auditor Also Responsible for Internal Controls?

In short, no. The auditor's role is to understand plan internal controls in order to establish auditing procedures for plan financial statements. It is important to realize an auditor is not required to test internal controls in the course of performing a financial statement audit.

How can auditors determine whether financial statements are stated fairly if they do not test the internal controls? The answer is simple—auditors have other tools they can use.

It is nearly impossible to perform an effective audit of a relatively large employee benefit plan without performing some tests of a plan's internal controls. The complexity of the organization and the large number of transactions force the auditor to evaluate the processing of transactions through internal control testing. The auditor tests the effectiveness of the controls for assurance that the data used for the financial reports is reliable.

Many employee benefit plans are small and not very complex. From a cost perspective, it is usually not feasible for the auditor to review all of the plan's internal controls. This does not mean the auditor ignores the internal controls. An audit is substandard if the auditor does not understand a plan's controls. With this understanding, the auditor can determine what types of procedures to perform, choose the extent to which they are needed and when to perform them.

The Engagement Letter

An auditor's standard *engagement letter*—the contract between the auditor and the benefit plan for the performance of the audit—makes clear the responsibilities of the auditor and those of plan management. *Management* refers to a plan's board of trustees and any administrators who have been delegated responsibility. The letter for an audit of financial statements specifically states that management is responsible for:

- The establishment and maintenance of effective internal controls over financial reporting
- The design and implementation of programs and controls to prevent and detect fraud.

The standard engagement letter also states the auditor will obtain an understanding of the internal controls only as necessary to plan the financial statement audit. It goes on to say the audit is not designed to provide assurance on internal controls or to identify significant shortcomings in their design or operation.

The Management Letter

While only limited procedures concerning internal controls are performed as part of a financial statement audit, a benefit plan may still benefit from these procedures. If the auditor tests internal controls, he or she may uncover deficiencies in control design. The auditor may also identify deficiencies while obtaining an understanding of the plan's internal control. Even in a relatively small plan, it is possible these issues can be remedied in a cost-effective way.

Auditor findings of material weaknesses or significant deficiencies are communicated in writing to plan trustees. This correspondence is commonly referred to as a *management letter*. Findings that are neither material weaknesses nor significant deficiencies may be communicated orally.

Tip for Trustees

Material weakness and *significant deficiencies* are technical terms—ask an auditor to explain them.

It is important to note that these auditor communications, whether in writing or oral, are not comprehensive reports on a plan's internal controls. These communications bring attention to matters encountered while obtaining an understanding of, and in some cases testing, internal controls to plan the audit of the financial statements. A CPA must perform a special audit to provide an opinion on all of a plan's internal controls.

Is a Plan Responsible for the Internal Controls of Service Organizations?

Plans often outsource at least some transaction processing and recordkeeping to other organizations. A custodian bank frequently maintains the record of transactions for assets it has in its physical possession. A financial institution (e.g., a mutual fund company, a bank or an insurance company) that maintains individual account balances for a defined contribution retirement plan typically maintains the records for these individual accounts. Other examples of service organizations that maintain records are pharmacy benefit managers (PBMs), insurance companies providing administrative services only (ASO) for health claims processing, and dental claims processors. In some cases, third-party administrators (TPAs) handle administrative functions that may include plan bookkeeping.

If a plan uses one or more service organizations, the internal controls of these organizations are considered part of the plan's internal controls. When hiring a service organization (or anytime afterwards), ask the organization about the controls it has in place. The plan auditor must understand these additional controls for preparation of the plan's financial statement audit. To establish this understanding, the auditor should perform certain procedures, and then prepare a report. Trustees can ask for a copy of this report to get a better sense of how plan business is conducted by the service organization.

Many of the larger service organizations hire a CPA to perform a special audit on their internal controls. The CPA issues a report for this audit. It is normal for a plan's auditor to request this report because it provides useful information for planning and performing the audit. Again, trustees can ask to see this report, usually referred to as a SAS 70 report.

Are There Any Limitations on What We Can Expect From Internal Controls?

Regardless of how well a system of controls is designed and operates, there is no guarantee a plan will never experience a problem. Two of the primary reasons that fraud occurs are management override of internal controls and collusion. It is no coincidence that these are also the key limitations inherent in a system of internal controls:

1. **Management override.** A plan manager can pressure an employee to make improper accounting entries. This may be done to hide the misappropriation of assets, or to misrepresent the information reported in financial statements. Consider an administrator who wants to make a plan's financial status look better—the administrator might direct the cost of repairs and maintenance be recorded as additions to property to delay recognition of the expense.
2. **Collusion.** In small benefit plans, a bookkeeper performs many financial functions. The opportunity for fraud is great because there is little segregation of duties (discussed in the next section of this chapter). Collusion is not, however, limited to small organizations. In larger organizations, there are more likely to be layers of checking and crosschecking but collusion can still occur between two or more individuals. Some collusion is internal—involving only employees. In other cases, there is a conspiracy that includes internal and external parties; for example, an employee who works in partnership with a vendor can defraud a plan.

How Should a Plan Segregate Duties?

While a detailed discussion of the many internal control policies and procedures is outside the scope of this chapter, there is one control strategy that must be discussed—the *segregation of duties.* To the extent possible, one person should not be assigned a combination of duties that provide an opportunity to commit an error or fraud, and then conceal it.

Consider an employee who collects cash and checks, does banking and maintains accounting records. While this one person has custody of assets and maintains the records for the same assets, opportunity exists for this person to steal money then cover it up by falsifying the records. Whenever possible, the functions of and responsibility for (1) maintaining custody of assets, (2) executing a transaction and (3) recording a transaction should be assigned to different employees. This accomplishes the segregation of duties.

In smaller organizations, it is not always possible to have the degree of segregation just described. The procedures below—some that could also benefit larger plans—can still reduce the chance of problems.

- Be familiar with operations that increase the likelihood problems will be identified.

- Increase supervision of employees.
- Make sure accounting software leaves a trail of any bookkeeping entries that are changed or deleted. Once a transaction is recorded, it should only be removed or modified by posting another entry into the accounting records to reflect the deletion or change.
- Insist that monthly bank statements are reconciled in a timely manner. After preparation, a second employee or the plan administrator should independently review the bank reconciliations.
- Check that all bank correspondence, including bank statements, is being sent directly to the plan administrator or someone in a comparable position.
- Eliminate or minimize the use of signature stamps. If signature stamps are used, implement safeguards to prevent unauthorized use. Keep signature stamps securely locked with limited access.
- Make sure unused checks are stored in a safe or a locked file cabinet.
- Establish a rule that paid invoices be canceled so they are not used again to disburse cash.
- Make employee vacations mandatory. While one employee is on vacation, have another employee perform the duties of the absent employee.

This is not an exhaustive list—the plan's CPA should be able to help identify and implement additional procedures and policies.

What Are the Costs and Benefits of Internal Controls?

The costs and benefits of internal controls must always be considered. Every procedure put in place has a cost. It is important to keep in mind the desired goal with each procedure. There is no standard right decision. The specific circumstances along with the risk of errors or fraud must be carefully considered. Discussion with plan professionals will help trustees decide what controls are most appropriate for their plan.

What Else Is Important About Internal Controls?

Internal control policies and procedures are only as good as the people carrying them out. It is essential to hire a person with an accounting education or background as the plan's internal accountant.

Another important point is that internal controls become obsolete as time passes. For example, changes in technology are very likely to continue impacting how plans process data. These changes may require changes in an internal controls policy.

Controls may work perfectly 99% of the time, but there is the 1% of the time when they may fail. Continuous monitoring of an internal controls policy by administration and trustees is also essential to the effectiveness of controls.

Chapter 34

Increasing Income and Reducing Expenses

Lawrence R. Beebe

Trustees receive a great deal of information and advice on the best way to invest plan assets. It is unlikely trustees get similar support on how to increase their plan's income and reduce plan expenses. Just as trustees have a fiduciary responsibility to invest plan assets prudently, they have a fiduciary duty to manage plan income and expenses.

There is another very practical reason for giving attention to what money a plan brings in and spends. Suppose a benefit plan has $700,000 in total expenses each year. At a recent board meeting, trustees took steps to reduce these expenses by 1% (or $7,000). Now assume this is a permanent savings of $7,000 per year for the next 20 years. If the plan has an extra $7,000 to invest for each of the next 20 years—and is able to earn 7% compounded annually on these savings—the plan will have an extra $315,000!

Too often, trustees think about expense reduction only as how to be more economical. Attention to cost cutting may also be criticized for being a penny-pinching mentality. The wise trustee realizes that the savings achieved through improved plan operations are more dollars for plan participant benefits.

What Can We Do to Enhance Plan Income?

Trustees who "think outside the box" recognize that one of the best ways to control expenses is to increase plan income. Increasing revenue is frequently easier to accomplish than reducing expenses. For a multiemployer benefit plan, the primary sources of income are employer contributions and investment income. A board can take certain actions that will increase the income from these sources. There are also some circumstances where new sources of revenue can be created.

Tip for Trustees

Use the checklist in the appendix to this chapter to identify ways to enhance plan revenue and cut costs. Set aside time at one of your board meetings to discuss this list with key administrative staff and plan professionals. Adopt items on the checklist that will work for your plan.

Establish an aggressive collection policy. Is the plan doing all that it can to collect delinquent contributions from contributing employers? How many payroll audits does the plan conduct on an annual basis? What are the results of these audits? If the plan performs more payroll audits than it has in the past and continues to collect more revenue than it spends on these audits, trustees should continue to expand the payroll audit program. Spending more on attorneys and other methods of collection may also increase plan income (through increased collection of contributions) without a substantial extra cost. Taking action just once or twice may send a message to other employers that trustees take collection seriously, and they may be less likely to be delinquent in the future. (For more on payroll audits, see Chapter 35.)

Is it possible for a plan to spend too much on collection? Of course it is. Trustees must determine their particular comfort level (and the amount they are willing to spend) when pursuing delinquencies.

Establish a collection committee. If the plan does not already have one, trustees should establish a collection committee. This group normally consists of one management trustee, one labor trustee, the plan administrator, a plan employee responsible for collections, the plan collection attorney and the plan's payroll auditor. The committee should be responsible for monitoring the plan collection policy and making sure employer contributions are collected. Collection committee meetings should be held monthly or quarterly depending on the extent of delinquencies. A collection committee not only helps trustees collect contributions on a timely basis, it can also help reduce legal expenses for chasing outstanding contributions as they get older and older. (See Chapter 52 for more information on collection policies and procedures.)

Modify allocation of investments. A traditional asset allocation used by many plans is 60% equities (stocks) and 40% fixed income (bonds). In an effort to diversify plan investments and enhance yield, many boards of trustees now allocate a portion of plan funds to alternative investments. These "alternatives" include real estate, hedge funds, private equity, derivatives and commodities; they are chosen because they have a potentially greater return than stocks and bonds. Trustees of a plan moving in this direction should seek the advice of a trusted investment advisor and make careful decisions. With the enhanced return of alternative investments, there is also higher risk.

Provide services to others. Are there any other plans in the same locale or serving some of the same persons served by the plan that might benefit from the knowledge and skills of the plan employees? Trustees may want to consider contracting with another plan to provide some or all of its administrative services. Assuming existing personnel can accomplish the administrative workload, the income from providing the service will increase plan revenue.

What Can We Do to Reduce Plan Expenses?

It is very hard to generalize about cutting expenses for an employee benefit fund. Each fund is unique. There are few (if any) rules of thumb that apply to all funds. A discussion of some common ways that plans have been able to reduce or at least keep expenses in check follows. Some of the strategies suggested will require action on the part of the board of trustees. If trustees have delegated some plan responsibilities to an administrator, it is likely there are also some strategies that can be immediately implemented without board consent. Regardless of who has the authority to approve and implement these strategies, keep in mind that the board has the ultimate responsibility for making sure the plan is a cost-efficient operation.

Regularly assess operations. No matter how well a plan is operating, a periodic formal study of plan operations can be of great benefit in controlling costs. The assessment can be conducted internally, but an outsider may bring a different, more objective perspective. The purpose of an assessment should not be to reduce costs to the lowest possible level, but to ensure plan funds are being used effectively and efficiently. Some strategies for reducing administrative expenses can be done at any time:

- Use direct deposit benefit payments.
- Check prices paid for stationery, printing and supplies and consider competitive bidding.
- Consider bulk mail rates for large mailings.
- Control access to postage and expensive office supplies.
- Evaluate the current telephone service and investigate "package" deals.
- Do most photocopying at the machines that cost the least to operate.
- Consider replacing equipment rather than expensive maintenance contracts.
- Consider off-site storage.
- Cut the square footage for operations and consider subleasing the saved space.

Promote efficient computer operations. The typical individual administrator is not a technology expert. As a result, it is difficult for him or her to assess the efficiency of plan computer operations. The solution for such an administrator is to delegate authority for computer operations to someone he or she can trust. A person is needed who can (1) assess the overall productivity of the plan computer systems and (2) gauge whether plan personnel with computer responsibilities are performing at reasonable levels. Even with a trusted individual in charge, outsiders who can bring a fresh perspective to the situation should periodically evaluate computer operations.

Expand use of communication technology. E-mail, websites, voice mail and direct-dial extensions can be tremendous money savers for employee benefit plans. Many plans do not embrace these technologies, fearing they will not provide the personal touch demanded by members. With the proper controls, these communication technologies can enhance rather than hinder communication while saving time and money.

Renegotiate investment and custodial fees. Traditionally, these expenses are a percentage of the plan assets managed. Many plans are now negotiating fees based on an investment manager's performance compared to a predetermined benchmark. Underperforming managers receive only a fraction of the amount paid to managers that outperform their benchmarks. Trustees should compare plan costs with those of similar-sized plans. Do not be afraid to ask how the plan can get a better deal.

Monitor commission recapture. It is possible to reduce commission expenses on security purchases and sales by having plan transactions performed by a broker that returns a percentage of the commissions charged. This may appear to be a low-risk way of reducing expenses. Trustees should make sure, however, that the expenses after the recapture actually result in savings.

Securities lending. In a securities-lending program, plan securities are borrowed and collateral is pledged for the value of these securities. A plan's investment performance analyst should be able to tell trustees whether their plan's portfolio is appropriate for securities lending. Trustees should make sure the collateral pledged by a borrower is more than the value of the securities on loan and that cash and liquid securities used as collateral are not subject to market risk.

Control travel expenses. Many plans spend large amounts on travel. A clear, written trustee expense policy should state what is reimbursable and what documentation is required to receive reimbursement. Both board members and plan personnel should be required to follow this policy. One person, if possible, should approve all travel reimbursements and apply the standards uniformly. For large plans, use of a qualified travel planner may save a great deal on travel costs.

Adopt a disaster recovery program. While there is an obvious up-front cost of developing a disaster recovery program, the cost of an actual disaster will make the expense worth every penny. Without a plan, the potential loss could be enormous. A comprehensive recovery program takes into consideration computer files, hardware and software replacement, office space, paper documents, furniture and equipment, and temporary or permanent replacement of key personnel. A plan may never use the program in place, but trustees must consider whether it is prudent not having a program.

Merge operations. Done successfully, merging with another plan can eliminate duplicate procedures and yield savings through economies of scale.

Audit benefit eligibility and claims. With rising health care spending, payers of health care benefits are anxious to hold down costs. Health care services providers are equally anxious to increase their revenues. Some health care providers use techniques called *revenue enhancements* to increase revenues. Trustees might refer to these revenue enhancements as "ripoffs." Another technique that can be used by plans is to perform a dependent audit. This audit "tests" the eligibility of dependents to ensure that only legitimate persons are being covered

Find new ways to manage benefit costs. With escalating health care costs, it is impossible for a plan to provide for everything. How can a plan get the most for its money when providing benefits? Trustees should consider eliminating costly benefits that help relatively few participants such as experimental treatments or aggressive treatment for those who are terminally ill. There may be more cost-effective uses for this money such as preventive strategies that reduce serious health conditions for other participants later on. A lower copayment might be used as a financial incentive to encourage participants to use a generic versus brand-name drug that yields cost savings to the plan.

Does Cost Reduction Always Work?

When trying to save money, trustees often cut spending in the wrong places. The following are a few areas that are typically not good choices for reductions.

Fewer payroll compliance audits. A payroll audit verifies a plan is collecting all employer contributions to which it is entitled. These audits also help ensure employers have reported all workers who are entitled to plan benefits. A well-run payroll compliance program can collect more dollars owed than the program costs. When there is no compliance audit, there is also the risk that a plan's CPA may qualify the opinion on the plan's audited financial statements, leading to a Department of Labor rejection of the Form 5500.

Education for trustees and plan personnel. Educating trustees and employees costs money, but well-educated individuals are more likely to introduce innovations that keep a plan running smoothly and efficiently. In the long term, a plan with an appropriate education program should have fewer problems and be less costly to run than plans that have not invested in education.

No aggressive collection policy. Collecting dollars owed by contributing employers is another one of a trustee's fiduciary duties. This does not mean the plan must throw money away trying to collect money in situations where trustees know collection will be impossible. It also does not mean trustees cannot be compassionate in working out a payment program for employers with financial problems. A well-run, consistent collection program will not be less expensive, but the increased collections achieved should more than offset any increased expenses.

Hiring professionals with the lowest bid. If trustees consistently follow this policy, they will not have competent professionals in the long term. They risk hiring professionals who will not do what they should to keep the plan out of trouble. One plan had a policy of hiring plan professionals, including the plan auditor, based only on the lowest submitted bid. The plan had a $700,000 embezzlement that occurred and remained undetected for many years. The trustees would have saved a great deal of money had they originally hired a competent professional auditor.

What Is the Future for Cost Control?

Trustees will have to constantly reevaluate and challenge existing methods of operation. The goal will continue to be finding ways to help plans operate with maximum efficiency and economy. To be successful, trustees will have to accept change as inevitable and seek out new ways to control costs. Here are a few areas that are likely to face rapid change, and where the challenges to controlling costs will be the greatest.

Claims. If the government scales back on health care subsidies, more cost pressures could be placed on the private sector. The cost of medical coverage will continue to increase at a much faster rate than inflation. Perceptive trustees will recognize this and adopt strategies to ensure that health care claims processing is cost-efficient, while still providing the participant with quality health care. Plans will stress claims audits, claims adjudication, evaluations of benefits provided and other strategies to hold costs to an affordable level.

Technology. Technology will continue to be one of the greatest challenges facing plans in the 21st century. How can a plan afford to keep up with technology? It is essential to have a written technology plan and then follow it as much as possible. Trustees should budget technology expenditures, adopt replacement policies for hardware and software, train personnel in technology use, outsource tasks that the plan cannot accomplish in-house and have a system in place to measure savings compared to costs incurred. The high cost of technology requires trustees to be constantly vigilant. Costs will be incurred; trustees should make sure benefits are achieved.

Maximize trustee effectiveness. The number of board meetings a plan has ranges from two a year to as many as one every month. For large boards, these meetings can be expensive and time-consuming. Some boards are assigning authority for many administrative tasks (including management of the investment advisors) to a smaller committee with two or three trustees representing labor and the same number representing management. The smaller committee meets more frequently than the full board and does most of the detail work. The full board can spend its time on major policy decisions. This approach is efficient and reduces costs.

Utilize the plan professionals properly. Who should manage a benefit plan, the trustees or plan professionals? As obvious as the answer to this question should be, trustees in many plans abdicate their responsibilities to plan professionals. Trustees who do this open themselves to criticism for not doing their jobs. In addition, plan professionals charge much more to run the plan. Trustees are responsible for controlling plan operations.

Streamline plan operations. With all of the complexities inherent in an employee benefit plan, trustees should strive to simplify whenever possible. The fair question to ask any plan professional is, "What can we do simpler and cheaper?" The results might be pleasantly surprising.

Control investment costs. What is the plan purchasing with its investment fees? How much of the investment expense dollar is being spent for execution, management and research? Is it paying for unnecessary information or services? Trustees will be asking many questions in this area in the near future. Plans spend a great deal of money in this area and deserve some accountability.

Consider a merger. As the plan is currently structured, is it providing the best possible benefits for participants? The answer to this question may be *no,* and the solution may be to merge that plan with another to reduce costs and provide more participant benefits.

Checklist of Potential Income Enhancememts and Expense Savings

Our Plan Should Consider:	Yes	No	N/A	Reference
A. GENERAL				
1. An overall study of plan operations	☐	☐	☐	________
2. A more aggressive collection policy	☐	☐	☐	________
3. More compliance audits	☐	☐	☐	________
4. An improved cash management program to enhance income	☐	☐	☐	________
5. Improved use of communication technology	☐	☐	☐	________
6. A study of computer operations	☐	☐	☐	________
7. A new education program for trustees	☐	☐	☐	________
8. A new education program for staff	☐	☐	☐	________
9. Adopting a commission recapture program	☐	☐	☐	________
10. Adoption of a travel expense policy	☐	☐	☐	________
11. Bidding for professional fees	☐	☐	☐	________
12. Adoption of a disaster recovery program	☐	☐	☐	________
13. Renegotiation of investment advisory fees	☐	☐	☐	________
14. Renegotiation of custodial fees	☐	☐	☐	________
15. Providing awards or bonuses for cash suggestions	☐	☐	☐	________
16. Going paperless	☐	☐	☐	________
17. Consolidating operations of multiple plans	☐	☐	☐	________
18. Outsourcing claims adjudication and payment	☐	☐	☐	________
19. Other				
______________________________	☐	☐	☐	________
______________________________	☐	☐	☐	________
______________________________	☐	☐	☐	________
B. PENSION PLANS				
1. Death scans for retirees	☐	☐	☐	________
2. Determining benefits as a percentage of contributions received	☐	☐	☐	________
3. Other				
______________________________	☐	☐	☐	________
______________________________	☐	☐	☐	________
______________________________	☐	☐	☐	________

Our Plan Should Consider:	Yes	No	N/A	Reference
C. HEALTH AND WELFARE PLANS				
1. Creating panels of physicians	☐	☐	☐	________
2. Increasing the copay for brand-name drugs	☐	☐	☐	________
3. Negotiation of hospital bills	☐	☐	☐	________
4. Software scans for claims abuse	☐	☐	☐	________
5. Internal or external claims audits	☐	☐	☐	________
6. Using a nurse in claims review	☐	☐	☐	________
7. Using a dental consultant	☐	☐	☐	________
8. Requiring preauthorization	☐	☐	☐	________
9. Second opinions	☐	☐	☐	________
10. Claims fraud-prevention programs	☐	☐	☐	________
11. Other				
______________________	☐	☐	☐	________
______________________	☐	☐	☐	________
______________________	☐	☐	☐	________
D. APPRENTICE FUNDS				
1. Cosponsorship of training	☐	☐	☐	________
2. Swap teaching	☐	☐	☐	________
3. Obtaining grants to offset expenses	☐	☐	☐	________
4. Other				
______________________	☐	☐	☐	________
______________________	☐	☐	☐	________
______________________	☐	☐	☐	________
E. LEGAL SERVICES FUNDS				
1. Expanded panel of attorneys	☐	☐	☐	________
2. Other				
______________________	☐	☐	☐	________
______________________	☐	☐	☐	________
______________________	☐	☐	☐	________

Our Plan Should Consider:	Yes	No	N/A	Reference
F. ADMINISTRATIVE				
1. Quotes for stationery and supplies	☐	☐	☐	__________
2. Bulk mailing	☐	☐	☐	__________
3. Subleasing excess space	☐	☐	☐	__________
4. Compression of office space	☐	☐	☐	__________
5. Sharing of desk space	☐	☐	☐	__________
6. Limiting access to supplies	☐	☐	☐	__________
7. Controlling telephone usage	☐	☐	☐	__________
8. Using cheaper machines for photocopies	☐	☐	☐	__________
9. Direct deposit of payments	☐	☐	☐	__________
10. Equipment replacement vs. repair	☐	☐	☐	__________
11. Other				
______________________________	☐	☐	☐	__________
______________________________	☐	☐	☐	__________
______________________________	☐	☐	☐	__________

Chapter 35

Payroll Auditing

Lawrence R. Beebe

A *payroll audit* is primarily an examination of a contributing employer's records to determine whether the employer has submitted payments to a benefit plan as required by the collective bargaining agreement (CBA). The auditor looks for under- and overpayments from intentional or unintentional reporting errors regarding workers' hours worked or paid. If the employer paid less than what was required, there is a *deficiency.* Sometimes, an employer does not submit the required reports and/or payments. This is a *delinquency.*

Payroll auditing, done properly, can be a source of revenue for a multiemployer benefit plan. The plan should constantly monitor the revenue generated by payroll audits and compare it to the expenses of conducting the audits. If the revenue increases from year to year, then the plan should probably conduct more audits. If the cost of audits increases faster than the revenue generated from year to year, then fewer audits should be performed. Constant monitoring by trustees is essential.

Is There a Difference Between Payroll and Compliance Audits?

The simple answer is "no." Some multiemployer benefit plans refer to *payroll audits* as *compliance audits.* Why? Two reasons are usually given. First, payroll audit suggests an auditor is looking only at payroll records. To be thorough, an auditor must also look at an employer's cash receipt and disbursement records, the general ledger and personnel records. The auditor might also look at an employer's financial statements and income tax returns. Access to more than payroll records is essential to an auditor who is trying to judge whether the *remittance* (payment) reports accurately represent the hours worked by or wages paid to employees covered by the CBA.

A second reason for using *compliance audit* is that employers seem to be less offended by it. A payroll audit has a negative connotation to some—like an IRS audit! Compliance, on the other hand, suggests adherence to plan rules. Is this just smoke and mirrors? Perhaps. In the future, "compliance audit" may replace "payroll audit." For now, let's just use the term *payroll audit.*

What Employer Records Are Produced for a Payroll Audit?

The agreement and declaration of trust should be as inclusive as possible in stating the records that the contributing employer should produce for a payroll auditor. Employer records that should be required as part of the payroll audit process are:

- Payroll records including detail on hours worked and paid (weekly or monthly)
- Individual employee earnings records (quarterly or yearly)
- Federal 941 Quarterly Payroll Tax Returns
- Annual employee earnings reports (Forms W-2, W-3, 1099 and 1096)

Tip for Trustees

Check that your plan has a written agreement, declaration of trust or other document that allows a plan auditor to access the employer records needed to complete a payroll audit.

- Copies of monthly remittance reports to all fringe benefit funds to which the employer contributes
- Cash disbursements records
- All pertinent personnel information, such as a hire and termination list
- General ledger
- Records of payments made for leased employees
- Corporate or personal income tax returns.

Why Are Payroll Audits Needed?

One of the fiduciary duties of a trustee is to collect delinquent contributions. In the case of *Central States Pension Fund v. Central Transport, Inc.*, 472 U.S. 559 (1985), the court rejected the argument that the responsibility for collecting contributions was that of the union, the Department of Labor (DOL) or the beneficiaries. The Employee Retirement Income Security Act of 1974 (ERISA) gives this responsibility to trustees, and if trustees do not make what is considered a reasonable effort to collect contributions, they can be held personally liable. Payroll audits provide assurance that all employer contributions have been submitted to a plan.

Another reason for payroll audits concerns a plan's audited financial statements. Auditors of employee benefit plans must follow rules established by the accounting profession including the generally accepted auditing standards (GAAS). An auditor who does not follow GAAS when conducting an audit could have civil and criminal liability. The auditor could also lose his or her license and/or be sanctioned by the American Institute of Certified Public Accountants (AICPA). One of the ten GAAS requires certified public accountants (CPAs) who examine benefit plan financial statements to gather sufficient information to support the opinion given on the statements. As part of the process, an auditor must verify plan income including employer contributions. In a multiemployer plan audit it is difficult, if not impossible, to gather enough information regarding the completeness of employer contributions without doing payroll audits.

AICPA has published *Audits of Employee Benefit Plans*—a guide that interprets GAAS and should be adhered to by CPAs. The guide states that auditors should compare employer contribution reports with participant payroll records to gather participant data. The guide does not use the term *payroll audit,* but the requirement is clear. The guide suggests several alternatives to payroll audits, but all of these alternatives have complications and risks.

What happens if an auditor is not able to gather the necessary participant data? The result is that the auditor will not be able to give an unqualified opinion on the plan's financial statements. Instead, the auditor will have to give a qualified opinion or disclaimer of opinion. This can have disastrous consequences for a plan.

DOL and the Internal Revenue Service require plans with more than 100 participants to attach an independent auditor's report of plan financial statements to the Form 5500. DOL will not accept the auditor's report with a qualified opinion that indicates there is no payroll audit program. When a Form 5500 filing is rejected, DOL treats the filing as if it were a nonfiling. DOL can assess penalties of up to $1,100 per day for failing to file timely and complete reports.[1]

In addition to meeting trustees' fiduciary duty, here are five more reasons for conducting payroll audits:

1. **Checking suspicious contributions.** Local union officials may complain to trustees that an employer is not properly reporting all employees covered by the CBA. Perhaps after annual statements are sent to participants, the plan administrator receives complaints from participants about the information in the statements. A payroll audit will help the plan determine whether employers are fulfilling the terms of the CBA—more specifically, whether there are any unreported employees or other reporting issues. Do keep in mind, however, that a payroll audit may not be successful in finding problems if the employer hides employees or wages by paying cash.
2. **Keeping employers honest.** We want to believe that all employers pay their contributions to employee trust funds because they are genuinely concerned about the welfare of their workers. For most employers, this is true. For others, the only factor that keeps them honest is fear they will be caught and penalized. A payroll audit program puts the less-than-honorable

Tip for Trustees

Make sure the plan you represent has a detailed written collection policy. This policy should include the policies and procedures for auditing contributions made by contributing employers. Chapter 52 on Collection Litigation identifies items that should be in a written policy.

Trustee Questions

It is common for trustees to have questions for auditors concerning payroll audits. Here are answers to some of the questions frequently asked:

1. **Why does an audit take so much time?**
   A proper payroll audit takes time. The time doing the fieldwork at the employer's office may be only a day or even half a day. Once the payroll auditor leaves the field, he or she spends a great deal of time investigating the records. The auditor must determine whether all employees were reported and their employment information is correct. If there are unreported hours, these hours must be summarized and totaled by type of error. In addition, the audit report must be written.

   There are many reasons why fieldwork takes longer than usual. The employer was in a remote location. The employer was not prepared and kept the auditor waiting. The employer's records were not in good order or organized in a way that makes auditing difficult. Many audit findings require the auditor to look at 100% of the records.

2. **How much should a payroll audit cost the plan?**
   The cost of the payroll audit depends on the answers to many questions. Just a few of these questions are:
   - *Who is performing the audit? Is it an internal audit staff or a CPA firm?*
   - *Will the auditors examine all hours paid or will they use a sampling approach?*
   - *How large is the employer being audited?*
   - *Do the employer's covered employees represent a small or a large percentage of the workforce?*
   - *Will the auditor find a small or large number of errors?*
   - *Will the employer have all records available and displayed in a logical sequence when the audit starts?*
   - *Does the auditor have to measure hours paid, hours worked or some other unit of measurement?*
   - *Are hours paid weekly summarized by the month, by the quarter or annually?*

3. **Why don't we audit every employer every three years?**
   A plan should annually measure the amount of funds collected as a result of payroll audits relative to the cost of the audits. The goal is to collect more money performing payroll audits than the payroll audit program costs. Many successful payroll audit programs identify deficiencies that represent a multiple of the cost of the program. The amount of the multiple depends on such factors as the employer's industry and how rapidly delinquencies can be identified and collected.

   The ideal time to audit the average employer may be every three years—or it could be four, five or six years. Each plan is different. How often a plan audits an employer depends on plan policy and the plan's history with the employer.

4. **Should we have payroll auditors perform a 100% examination or should we instruct the auditor to sample the employer's payroll, isolate errors by type and then do 100% examination on those error types?**
   Some plans prefer the 100% audit. The major advantage of the 100% examination is that almost (if not) all errors will be identified. The major disadvantage of this method is the cost. A 100% examination is extremely time-consuming. It works best when a plan has an internal payroll audit staff. Experience suggests that the majority of plans that do payroll audits do not perform a 100% examination.

5. **Why can't the employer send us all the records to do a payroll audit in the auditor's office?**
   Most payroll audits have to be done in the employer's office. The sheer volume of records reviewed compels the auditor to visit the employer.

   One other reason for doing the audit on site is that the payroll auditor can observe how the employer operates. The auditor quickly discovers how cooperative the employer will be, and almost as quickly determines whether deficiencies are likely to be found in the audit.

employer on notice that trustees are serious about collection. If Employer X is audited and penalized for nonreporting, Employer Y may pay what he owes to avoid the same penalties. Payroll auditing is preventive medicine.

3. **Helping new employers.** New employers often do not understand the reporting requirements set forth by the CBA. Many funds audit new employers after six or nine months of reporting. The audit provides an opportunity to help the employer properly report.
4. **Determining liability upon termination.** Employers that cease to be covered by a CBA also present a problem. Employers may stop their contributions before the CBA expires. A payroll audit on terminating employers ensures that remittances are sent through the termination date of the CBA.
5. **Documenting for collection.** When an employer experiences financial difficulty, benefit payments often slow or stop completely. If an employer fails to make contributions, the matter may have to be referred to legal counsel. A payroll audit supports the legal action the plan's attorney will take to enforce payment.

What Kinds of Problems Do Payroll Audits Identify?

Some problems are common and easily found:

- Clerical errors
- Failure to report:
  - New and/or terminated employees
  - Paid overtime hours
  - Paid sick pay and bonus hours
  - Apprentices
  - Covered nonunion employees
  - Subcontracted or leased employees
  - The fifth week of a month.
- Employees whose work changes from noncovered to covered status
- Capping reported hours incorrectly.

Other deficiencies are unusual and difficult to identify:

- Disguising hours paid as materials or other expenses
- Using an alter ego company
- Failure to report a covered group
- A double set of books
- Payments off the books
- Payments for owners, relatives and other noncovered employees.

For a full description of these deficiencies, see the separate article posted at www.ifebp.org/Handbook7.

Employer Questions

Payroll audits generate many questions. The following are questions (and *answers*) often asked by employers.

1. **I only want to give you payroll records for collectively bargained employees. I don't want to give you records for office staff or officers of the company. Why is this a problem?**
   The Supreme Court has ruled that an employer must produce payroll records of all employees for the payroll auditor.[2] The payroll auditor does not have an interest in the payroll records of noncollectively bargained employees. However, the auditor must look at all records to judge who the collectively bargained employees are.
   On occasion, an employer asks an auditor to sign a statement that the wages of noncollectively bargained employees will not be revealed to the benefit plan. Under normal circumstances, the auditor will agree to this. If an employer objects to showing individual salaries for officers and office employees, the payroll auditor may give the employer permission to blank out individual salaries and leave the total so overall payroll can be verified.

2. **Why should I have to pay on nonunion employees? They cannot get benefits.**
   A nonunion employee can receive benefits. A plan cannot discriminate in favor of a participant just because that participant is a union member. If a person's job is covered by a collective bargaining agreement (CBA), the employer must pay on that individual. Once the individual earns enough credits, he or she gets the benefits.

3. **Our state is a right-to-work state. Why should I pay on those who choose not to join the union?**
   Employees in a right-to-work state have the right to decide whether to join the union. Whether they join the union or not has nothing to do with their benefits. If they are performing work covered by the CBA, contributions must be made on their behalf.

4. **Why should I pay on temporary employees or summer help? They will never receive a pension.**
   Defined benefit plans recognize that not all employees will receive enough credit to earn a pension. In determining the pension benefits for participants, the actuary considers contributions for these workers even though they (the workers) will never be paid benefits.

5. **Why should I let you see my cash disbursements journal? That is a private record.**
The agreement and declaration of trust—signed by the employer—state the plan may conduct a payroll audit and identify the records the payroll auditor is entitled to examine during the audit. Normally this includes reference to payroll records and cash disbursement journals. Some plans even include the general ledger and the income tax returns.

6. **Why did the union select me for an audit?**
The union has nothing to do with who is selected for a payroll audit. The plan determines who is audited. There are many different reasons an employer is chosen for a payroll audit. The employer may have been chosen at random—participating employers had an equal chance of being selected for audit. The decision to audit may also be the result of complaints filed by a participant or something a plan employee noticed while processing reports submitted with contributions. Some plans audit all employers on a four-year cycle and the employer's number just came up. Typically, the auditor has nothing to do with the selection process and can honestly respond that he or she does not know why the employer was selected.

7. **Why are you auditing me? I'm sure you don't audit the employer trustees.**
For most plans, the answer to this question is that the plan has a payroll audit program that requires all employers—including companies owned by employer trustees—to be audited every three or four years. Employer trustees often insist their companies be audited first to avoid any hint of favoritism or special treatment.

The purpose of a payroll audit is not to harass an employer. It is performed to ensure the employer is reporting correctly and to determine that all covered employees receive the benefits to which they are entitled.

8. **Why have you written down the hours paid for that employee? It says on his payroll record that he is a shop employee, and shop employees are not covered.**
It is usually easy to identify shop employees (and other noncovered employees) because their hourly pay rate is lower and/or different from the wage rates of covered employees. When the rate of the shop worker is near the wage rates of covered workers, the auditor writes down the hours paid and does further research to make sure the individual is not a covered employee.

9. **Even though I own this business, I spend a majority of my time working with the tools of the trade. Can't I be a covered employee?**
There are certain circumstances where owner/employees can be treated as covered employees. Plans have specific rules that must be followed to allow owners to participate. The owner/employee normally must sign an agreement to be placed in this category.

10. **Why should I pay for coverage on my son?**
Unless the son has an ownership interest in the company, he must be treated the same as any other covered employee.

11. **I have been overpaying for years. Why can't I get a refund for the entire overpayment?**
Many employee benefit plans specify that when an employer has overpaid contributions, the employer can receive a refund of no more than one year's overpayment to the plan. ERISA states that the plan can limit credit for overpayments to one year.

12. **Why do I have to pay on probationary employees?**
Probation to join the union or for seniority may differ from the probationary period before a person becomes a plan participant.

The CBA or participation agreement normally indicates whether contributions are due from the first day of employment or there is a probationary period (e.g., 30 days or 60 days) before contributions are required. The CBA determines the hours reported for probationary employees.

13. **How long will the audit take?**
The payroll auditor should tell the employer whether the audit is budgeted for a half day, a full day or multiple days. The auditor should also explain that the actual time depends on factors such as the volume and auditability of records examined. As the audit progresses, the auditor may provide a status update with a revised estimated completion time.

14. The local union's plan audited us last year. Why is the national plan auditing us this year?
In an ideal world, all of an employer's payroll audits would be at the same time. Often it is difficult to coordinate audits. The hours examined by each plan may also be different; this means the plans are looking at different records. When an employer has workers in more than one local, the local that audited last year may not be affiliated with the national benefit plan.

15. I am too busy to sit with the auditor all day. Do I have to?
No. If the records are set aside for the audit, the employer (or his representative) often needs to spend very little time with the auditor. The employer usually spends time only at the very beginning to explain the records. The employer should then be available to answer questions as the job progresses and at the conclusion for an exit interview. The actual time spent with a payroll auditor is usually less than one hour.

16. The local union could not provide any people when I needed them. Why should I contribute for persons I hired without the local's help?
The employer's reporting obligation is for all persons covered by the CBA regardless of how they were hired. The employer may have a legitimate complaint for the union to address, but it does not affect the plan's reporting requirements.

17. Why do I have to pay for vacation hours when an employee terminates?
The CBA normally requires the employer to report all hours "paid" to covered employees. Vacation hours are reported regardless of when they were paid.

18. I am a construction contractor. Why do I have to report on an employee if the person worked only two weeks?
In the construction industry, employees change jobs frequently. An employee may work only two weeks for a particular employer but may have worked for other employers on a full-time basis. Proper reporting by each employer ensures the worker gets the credit necessary to earn plan benefits.

Endnotes

1. ERISA §502(c)(2).
2. *Central States Southeast and Southwest Area Pension Fund v. Central Transport, Inc.*, 472 U.S. 559 (1985),

Chapter 36

Plan Policies and Documentation Requirements

Lawrence R. Beebe

There was a time when employee benefit plans were plans with few (if any) written policies and procedures. The world has changed and the operation of benefit plans has had to change with it. Today, written policies dictate how most business organizations operate. Reading this chapter will introduce trustees to (1) the key policy statements used by employee benefit plans, (2) the content of these policies and (3) the benefits of having these policies.

To help trustees analyze the adequacy of their plan's policies, this chapter provides checklists of common provisions for various employee benefit plan policies. To see policies created by other organizations, visit www.ifebp.org/sampledocuments; this International Foundation web page offers sample policy statements shared by Foundation members. These checklists and sample policy statements are a starting point. Trustees should ask their plan attorney and other plan professionals to help them develop policies that best fit a plan's unique circumstances. No two employee benefit plans are the same. A policy that works well for one plan might have to be different for another plan. Trustees have a responsibility to establish these policies and make sure they are appropriate for their plan.

How a plan operates changes over time. Trustees shouldn't assume that once a policy is in place, the work is finished. Changes will continue to occur. It is also a trustee responsibility to examine all plan policies periodically to make sure they are still relevant. New situations may warrant new policies. Trustees and plan administrators must be vigilant if policy statements are to remain consistent with plan operations.

What Are the Advantages of Plan Policies?

Occasionally, a plan trustee might say, "We operated for years without written policies and it never hurt us." Another trustee might say, "Written policies place too many restrictions on us." Are these valid arguments? Here are five fundamental reasons a plan should have written policies for its operations:

1. **Compliance.** Written policies are evidence a plan is in compliance (or tried to comply) with government regulations issued by the U.S. Department of Labor (DOL), the Internal Revenue Service and other agencies. During investigations, government regulators tend to be more tolerant when a plan has tried to follow the rules and has documentation that reflects the effort to comply.
2. **Consistency.** The operation of a plan requires an enormous number of decisions. Without plan policies, there is the chance that plan decision makers will not be consistent in the actions they take. Trustees probably realize it can be difficult remembering why a decision was made from one meeting to the next. Written policies help them remember and reduce the risk they will be accused of not being consistent. When an administrator makes a decision such as whether a claim will be covered or the amount of benefit to be paid, plan participants expect to be treated fairly—in other words, their claims are treated exactly the same as every other participant's claims. Written policies help ensure this happens.

3. **Liability.** Plan policies are legal documents that help trustees and plan employees avoid legal liability. Participants sometimes sue a plan when a benefit decision is not in their favor. Legal suits can also result for a variety of other reasons. When these cases go to court, judges look to plan documents including plan policies. Judges often base their decision on whether a decision followed plan documents and policies.
4. **Transparency.** Plan managers may understand how a plan operates, but others associated with the plan (e.g., participants, plan professionals, plan employees and vendors) may not. Written plan policies are available for all to see and use.
5. **Assurance.** Documentation has become a way of life. Everyone expects a well-run organization to have policies in place. Written policies assure plan participants and other stakeholders that a plan is in good hands—decisions have been carefully thought through and trustees are making an effort to do what is best for the plan and plan participants.

What Policies Does a Plan Need?

Plan policies guide trustees, plan employees, plan professionals and others associated with a plan in how the plan operates and conducts its business. A well-run employee benefit plan should have these written policies:

- Investment policy
- Conflict-of-interest policy
- Whistle-blower policy
- Records retention and destruction policy
- Disaster recovery plan
- Collection policy
- Educational and expense reimbursement policy
- Shared expense policy or agreement.

What Should Be in an Investment Policy?

The Employee Retirement Income Security Act (ERISA) dictates that trustees discharge their duties in the same way as a "prudent person." When making investment decisions, diversifying assets to minimize the risk of large losses is an essential element in meeting the fiduciary standard of prudence. (For more information on the diversification of assets, see Chapter 37.) A DOL bulletin says trustees can demonstrate compliance with the diversification requirement by adopting a written investment policy that documents investment decisions.

An *investment policy* provides trustees and plan investment managers with guidelines to be followed when making investment decisions. An investment policy normally includes:

- **Investment objectives.** The primary investment objective of most employee benefit plans is to achieve the rate of return assumed by the plan's actuary. Another objective is usually a statement concerning the degree of risk that trustees are willing to take to meet a plan's investment objectives.
- **Permissible and nonpermissible asset classes.** Some plans, such as health and welfare plans, do not accumulate significant assets; they are limited to short-term investments. Trustees of plans with significant assets may have a conservative outlook and restrict investments to stocks and bonds. Plan trustees who are open to more risk are more likely to allow alternative investments (e.g., real estate, hedge funds, limited partnerships and private equities). This section of an investment policy also describes plan participation, if any, in securities lending and a commission recapture program.
- **Diversification objectives.** It is important to keep diversification objectives up to date. If investment categories are changed, policy objectives also should be changed.
- **Ranges for each investment type.** Based on the board of trustees' risk tolerance and recognizing that diversification is essential, trustees establish upper and lower ranges for the percentage of assets held (1) in each investment type, (2) by the entire fund and (3) by each investment manager.
- **Benchmarks.** A plan should specify the benchmarks that will be used to assess performance for each of the plan's investment types and performance managers. There are many benchmarks available. (More information on investment benchmarks and assessing performance is provided in Chapter 48.)
- **Expected rate of return.** Once ranges for investment types and benchmarks for these investments have been established, a calculation of expected rate of return for the fund should be somewhat automatic.
- **Criteria for evaluating investment managers.** It is important for each investment manager to understand how his or her performance will be assessed. A common consideration is whether a manager met his or her performance benchmarks. Some plans look at other factors during the evaluation process. These standards should be detailed in the investment pol-

icy. (See Chapter 42 for more on evaluating a manager's performance.)

- **Review of investment performance.** This section spells out the procedures and how frequently a plan's investment managers and consultants are evaluated.
- **Proxy voting.** Who will vote the proxies? The investment policy should designate who will vote the proxies for plan investments and state the criteria to be used when deciding how to vote.

Chapter 47 provides additional discussion regarding investment policy statements.

What Are the Benefits of Having an Investment Policy?

A properly prepared written investment policy provides:

- **Legal protection.** The policy shows DOL and other regulators that trustees take seriously their responsibility to invest plan assets prudently.
- **Improved communication.** A great deal of interaction is required between plan personnel and investment professionals to draft a policy. Once a policy has been established, trustees must maintain the same level of communication so that the guidelines are mutually understood.
- **Written guidelines.** The investment policy details acceptable practices to be followed by managers. It can also be used as the guide for measuring the performance of the fund manager(s).

What Is Included in a Conflict-of-Interest Policy?

Trustees have a duty under ERISA to act in the best interest of plan participants and beneficiaries. ERISA also lists "prohibited transactions" that trustees and other plan fiduciaries are not allowed to do. Many plans have a *conflict-of-interest policy* (sometimes referred to as a *fraud policy*) to help ensure fiduciaries and others act within these constraints. The contents of an effective conflict-of-interest policy include:

- **Standards of conduct.** An overall statement sets forth standards to be followed. It describes the conduct expected of trustees, plan employees, plan professionals and vendors when conducting plan business. Areas of concern that trustees will want to address are:
  - Potential conflicts of interest
  - Outside activities, employment and directorships
  - Relationships with contributing employers and suppliers
  - Gifts, entertainment and favors from contributing employers and service providers
  - Prohibitions against kickbacks and commissions.
- **A definition of *fraud*.** In the employee benefit world, *fraud* is a deception committed or lie told for the purpose of (1) stealing an asset or (2) causing a person to act on the lie or deception. Theft of an asset is relatively easy to understand. The second outcome is not as easy to grasp. An example of this type of fraud is when a trustee or administrator provides misleading information that results in a plan purchasing a particular investment or using a specific vendor.
- **Notification.** People are sometimes reluctant to come forward when they suspect fraud. If a plan's policy details exactly who to contact to report fraud and outlines the reporting procedures, a person with suspicions is much more likely to come forward.
- **Consequences.** Sanctions and/or any other consequences of conflicts and committing a fraud should be clearly stated.

What Are the Benefits of a Conflict-of-Interest Policy?

Well-run organizations have conflict-of-interest policies. Trustees want to provide notice to everyone that their plan is well-run. Many plans have everyone associated with a plan sign an acknowledgment that they have read, understand and will abide by the plan's conflict-of-interest policy. Other benefits of such a policy follow:

- **Due diligence.** A conflict-of-interest policy tells the plan administrator, employees, professionals, vendors, participants and others associated with a plan that the board of trustees takes its responsibilities seriously. A written policy provides evidence that trustees are committed to avoiding conflicts of interest and fraud, and that they expect the same of everyone else. Having the policy in writing also provides a valuable formal reminder of everyone's responsibility to avoid inappropriate situations.
- **Awareness.** Too often persons associated with benefit plans think they do not have to worry about conflicts of interest or fraud. Evidence suggests otherwise. For example, it is estimated 10% or more of health care claims are fraudulent. A conflict-of-interest policy creates an awareness that potential conflicts and other unacceptable behaviors can occur. It tells everyone to be attentive to potential trouble. A healthy skepticism is a plus.

- **Deterrent.** The existence of a policy and making sure everyone knows it exists can help reduce the chance a plan will experience a conflict or fraud. To put it another way, a conflict-of-interest policy helps keep people honest.
- **Early detection.** If a problem occurs despite trustees' best efforts to avoid it, a conflict-of-interest policy may still help minimize the size of a plan's loss. In addition to creating awareness that a problem may occur, a conflict-of-interest policy encourages persons to report their suspicions of problems and provides the reporting procedure they should follow. Early detection is essential in minimizing fraud when it occurs.
- **Clear consequences.** If a violation of the policy occurs, persons cannot plead ignorance—especially if they signed an acknowledgment they have read the policy and received a written copy.

See Chapter 47 for a more detailed discussion of investment objectives and policy statements.

Do Plans Need a Whistle-Blower Policy?

A *whistle-blower policy* protects people who inform the public or someone in authority about possible illegal activities or dishonest acts that have occurred within a plan. Persons who find or suspect fraudulent activities within their organization are often reluctant to come forward. They may fear they will lose their job or be subjected to other retaliation if they expose what they know. A whistle-blower policy protects these *whistle-blowers* from retaliation and, when possible, their identity.

Whistle-blower policies were not common until recently. In 2002, the U.S. Congress passed the Sarbanes-Oxley Act. While this law applies primarily to publically traded companies, it does have two provisions that apply to all organizations including employee benefit plans. Sarbanes-Oxley imposes criminal penalties when there is retaliation against those who report illegal activities within their organization. The act also imposes criminal penalties for intentionally destroying, concealing, falsifying or altering documents related to a federal investigation. As a result of the enactment of Sarbanes-Oxley, all organizations should have a whistle-blower policy and records retention policy.

What Are Recommendations for a Whistle-Blower Policy?

The policy should contain provisions regarding:

- **Policy objectives.** Detail how the policy operates and the actions the organization will take to maintain confidentiality and prevent retaliation.
- **Reporting responsibility.** Trustees and employees should be required to report (1) questionable or improper accounting matters, (2) illegal practices and (3) any violations of the plan's conflict-of-interest policy.
- **Authority.** Detail who in the organization is responsible for implementing provisions of the whistle-blower policy when a matter is brought to his or her attention.
- **Reporting concerns.** Specify the actions that a person should take in filing a complaint as well as the actions required of those persons who receive the complaint.
- **Confidentiality.** To the extent possible, an assurance of confidentiality should be included for the person filing the complaint.

What Needs to Be Addressed in a Records Retention and Destruction Policy?

A written records retention and destruction policy (1) ensures that plan documents are maintained and disposed of in a logical, rational and orderly manner; (2) limits the chance that plan documents are accidentally destroyed; and (3) can help if a plan is faced with a federal investigation. To achieve these goals, a records retention and destruction policy normally contains:

- A statement detailing the purpose of the policy
- A statement as to what records are covered by the policy. Covered records normally include personnel records, accounting records, information necessary for government filings, legal documents, minutes, policies, resolutions, plan documents, e-mails and electronic records.
- A schedule showing how long each record will be kept
- Indication of how and when documents should be destroyed
- Details on backup procedures, archiving requirements and checkups on the reliability of the system
- Procedures requiring that document destruction cease if a federal investigation takes place.

A good records retention and destruction policy incorporates legal and regulatory requirements. For a health and welfare plan that files Form 990, one of the questions on the form is whether the plan has a written records retention and destruction policy. ERISA has some very specific records retention requirements for all benefit plans:

- Any organization that files a Form 5500 ". . . must maintain sufficient records to verify, explain or clarify the basic information and data in the report for a period of not less than six years."
- Plans must maintain sufficient records to determine the benefits due to participants and participant beneficiaries. Service and compensation records must be kept back to a participant's date of hire.

Most plans now use electronic media for recordkeeping. ERISA has some additional standards for these recordkeeping systems:

- The system must have reasonable controls to ensure the integrity, accuracy, authenticity and reliability of the records kept in electronic form.
- The records must be maintained in reasonable order, in a safe and accessible place, and in a manner that may be readily inspected or examined.
- The records must be readily convertible into legible and readable paper copy.
- The system should not be subject to any agreement or restriction that would compromise or limit the plan's ability to comply with any ERISA reporting or disclosure requirement.
- Adequate records management practices must be established and implemented. These practices should be formalized and incorporated into records retention procedures and include specific procedures for:
  - Labeling electronically maintained or retained records
  - Providing a secure storage environment
  - Creating backup electronic copies
  - Selecting an off-site storage location
  - Quality assurance evidenced by regular evaluation of the system including periodic checks of electronically maintained or retained records
  - Retaining paper copies of records that cannot be clearly, accurately or completely transferred to an electronic recordkeeping system.

What Should Be Included in a Disaster Recovery Plan?

Employee benefit plans have been slow to adopt disaster recovery plans. It is common to think of disasters only as environmental events such as fire, floods, wind and earthquakes. The reality is that disasters can come in many other forms such as:

- Loss of information when stored computer data becomes corrupted, destroyed or inaccessible
- Computer applications become disabled and cannot be restored.
- Networks are disabled or inaccessible.
- Terrorist activity prevents access to the workplace for a prolonged period of time.

The primary challenge to establishing a disaster recovery plan is that solutions for many of the problems caused by disasters are complex and costly. Consequently, many organizations are paralyzed and postpone dealing with the issue. This is not a prudent option.

Most disaster recovery plans concentrate on replacement of (1) the workplace and (2) computer hardware, software and storage. Another critical concern must be the people in the organization and their safety. Many organizations in New Orleans had adequate backups for their premises and computers when Hurricane Katrina arrived but it never occurred to them that 50% or more of their employees would flee the area and never return. How do trustees plan for that?

In preparing a disaster recovery plan, address these issues:

- What is considered a disaster, who will respond and how (with what tools, strategies, etc.)
- Meeting compliance obligations. For example, the Health Insurance Portability and Accountability Act (HIPAA) requires health and welfare plans to adopt a contingency plan to respond to an emergency or other events that may damage or destroy systems containing electronically protected health information. HIPAA emphasizes the proper backup and recovery of data.
- How all plan records will be safeguarded against the risk of loss or destruction
- Instructions for all persons involved in planning and executing the disaster procedures are available in an easy-to-use and accessible format. Periodic updating of these instructions to keep them current should be a requirement.
- Regularly testing processes and procedures to ensure everyone knows how to implement the plan when the time comes. One of the heroes of September 11, 2001 was the head of security for a major brokerage firm. He made his firm practice an evacuation drill over and over. Unfortunately, he died in the disaster making sure that all of his people were out of the building safely. Many of the survivors in his firm attribute his insistence on testing the program for saving many lives.
- An identification of the priorities for responding to the disaster and restoring plan operations. Obviously, the safety of employees and other persons comes first followed by plan business processes and related information technology systems. Which processes

and systems are mission critical must be determined. For example, it may be decided that benefit administration is the most important system and should be restored first.
- Recovery objectives such as how long after an event it should take to get mission-critical systems running again and how functional those systems will be when they are operational
- An identification of how to address all possible risks to plan computer data.

What Should Be Included in a Collection Policy?

See Chapter 52 on Collection Litigation for a list of items that should be included in a written collection policy for multiemployer benefit plans.

What Should Be Included in an Educational and Expense Reimbursement Policy?

Because the education of plan trustees, administrators and employees is essential to a well-managed organization, plans typically cover the costs of some educational programs. In addition, funds must be used at times to provide reimbursement to trustees and employees for other expenses they have incurred. A plan's educational and expense reimbursement policy should contain:

- A description of education programs the plan will support and a limit on how many can be attended per year
- The preapproval process required of an individual attending a program
- A description of how advances for programs should be handled
- Limits on transportation costs, lodging, meals and other allowed expenses. The policy should also list expenses that will not be reimbursed.
- A statement that reimbursement for educational programs is dependent on submitting proof of attendance such as an attendance report and a certificate of attendance (if one is issued)
- A requirement that a travel expense report must be completed after each program with attached receipts for all expenditures over $25
- The approval process required for a travel expense form before payment is made
- A list of all other types of expenses that are covered under this policy
- A statement that reimbursable expenses include only direct, reasonable expenses that are properly and actually incurred
- A statement that no expense will be reimbursed that is reimbursable by another party
- A statement of how per diem (by the day) is calculated and what per diem expenses cover if they are allowed for employee expenses. Per diem allowances should not be used for the expenses of plan trustees.

What Should Be Included in a Shared Expense Agreement?

If a multiemployer plan shares services, supplies and/or facilities with another multiemployer plan, a multiemployer association, an affiliated employer, employee organization or union, a shared expense policy or agreement is needed. This document should include:

- What expenses are shared
  - Salaries, fringe benefits and payroll taxes
  - Administrative expenses, computers, furniture, equipment, supplies and telephone
  - Rent, office space and utilities
- Other expenses. Other expenses may or may not be shared such as professional fees, computer software and trustee expenses. To the extent these expenses are shared, they must also be allocated.
- Methods for allocating expenses. Salaries and fringe benefits are normally split based on the amount of time each employee works for each organization. Other allocations are based on the percentage of office space or actual usage by each organization (e.g., number of copies, boxes of paper). The method of allocation for each expense should be the one that is the most logical allocation for that expense.
- Payment terms
- Duration of the agreement
- Conditions that necessitate amendment or termination
- Identification of those records to be maintained to support the allocation
- A statement that no plan can pay more than its fair share of expenses.

Get It in Writing

A fund's operation involves many processes. Without adequate documentation, legal liability might follow. But even when no liability hazard follows, these policies stand as a template for effective plan administration.

Chapter 37

Investment Fundamentals*

One of a benefit plan trustee's most important responsibilities is making decisions concerning the investment of plan funds. Trustees have a responsibility to make decisions that are in the best interests of their plan and plan participants. To ensure their plan is able to provide the benefits promised today and in the future, trustees must do all they can to understand the factors that are key to investment success. The purpose of this chapter is to (1) introduce the basics that are critical to investment decision making and (2) provide a framework for understanding the more in-depth investment chapters that follow. This chapter introduces:

- The types of investments available to benefit plans
- Key investment concepts such as risk, return, diversity and active management
- The role of mutual and commingled funds used by plans and plan participants to diversify their investment portfolios.

What Asset Classes Are Available for Benefit Plan Investment?

The universe of assets that a benefit plan can choose from is quite large. Choices are generally divided into different types called *asset classes.* Specific asset classes include equities, fixed income, real estate, etc. Multiemployer funds typically have substantial investments in two asset classes referred to as *traditional investments:* fixed income and public equity securities. Real estate is a third investment option that is now common among benefit plan trusts. Money can also be invested in a wide range of other options collectively referred to as *alternative investments.* Exhibit 1 provides a quick introduction to some well-known assets. These categories are further explained in the chapters that follow. Understanding investment basics is the first step in deciding what asset types are most appropriate for a benefit plan portfolio.

What Investment Basics Must Be Kept in Mind?

While there are certainly many other investment concepts that are helpful to understand, these are some of the most important.

Risk and Return

Some investments offer higher returns than others: Higher returns come with higher risks. *Return* is the amount of income a plan receives from its investments; it is the money earned as interest on bonds, dividends on stocks, rent on real estate, etc. If a plan sells an asset for more than the asset's purchase price, the plan receives another type of income, a *capital gain.* Of course, there is always the chance an asset will be worth less when it is sold. A plan then has a *capital loss.*

Risk represents the uncertainty whether an investment will be able to hold its value, pay the income anticipated and provide protection against *inflation* (increases in the prices for goods and services). Exhibit 2 explains these and other risks that can negatively impact the return.

---

*Portions of this chapter are drawn from previous content on investing written by Eugene B. Burroughs for the 6th Edition of the *Trustee Handbook: A Practical Guide to Labor-Management Employee Benefit Plans* that was edited by Marc Gertner and published by the International Foundation of Employee Benefit Plans in 2006.

Exhibit 1

Investment Options

Fixed Income	When most people think of fixed income assets, they think of *bonds*—debt securities (IOUs) issued by governments, government agencies and corporations. In exchange for the money they borrow, bond issuers promise investors interest payments or another return. (Chapter 39)
Public Equity	Investments in publicly traded companies are referred to as *public equity*. Equity shares in a company are more popularly called *stocks*, which are sold via markets referred to as *stock exchanges*. When the price of a stock increases above its purchase price, there is *capital appreciation*. Stockholders (owners) can also benefit from stock *dividends*—corporate earnings paid out to investors. (Chapter 40)
Real Estate	A multitude of properties including shopping centers, office buildings, hotels and residential spaces are referred to as *real estate*. Real estate can produce returns in two ways: (1) *income* such as rent and money earned on agricultural products grown on land, and (2) *appreciation* which is an increase in the value of property over time. (Chapters 41 and 42)
Private Equity	*Private equity* refers to money invested in companies that are not publicly traded; this includes money used to buy out publicly traded companies in order to make them private companies. (Chapter 43)
Hedge Funds	The term *hedge fund* is a generic term for different investment options intended to "hedge out" market risk and produce returns independent of overall market performance. Each hedge fund poses a unique set of risks and opportunities. (Chapter 43)

Exhibit 2

Types of Investment Risk

Business risk—the uncertainty whether a company will have enough cash to meet its financial obligations

Credit risk (also called *default risk*)—the chance a borrower will not make payments as promised

Currency risk—when an investment is made across national borders, a change in the value of one nation's money relative to the other nation's money may impact the value of an investment. Some or all of the return a U.S. investor receives on investments in another country may be canceled out if the value of the other nation's currency increases in value relative to the U.S. dollar.

Inflation risk—the uncertainty that the purchasing power of assets will be preserved. Inflation risk is of particular concern in making it possible for pension plan beneficiaries to maintain the same level of living throughout their retirement years. Even a "modest" level of inflation, say 3% over many years, can reduce the purchasing power of a retirement benefit payment significantly.

Interest rate risk—the possibility that changes in interest rates will negatively affect the values of securities and opportunities for reinvestment. When interest rates go up, the market value of assets producing a fixed stream of return (e.g., bonds) declines.

Liquidity risk—how difficult it will be to convert an asset to cash without a significant loss of its value. Most stocks and fixed income securities are very liquid, which means the assets can be sold relatively easily and quickly if a plan needs cash to provide benefits or cover other expenses. Real estate, private equity and hedge funds are not as liquid and may take substantial time to sell. If the market for the asset is down at the time the asset is sold, the plan could experience an investment loss.

Management risk—the possibility that an investment professional's decisions to buy and sell will negatively affect a portfolio's value. There is no guarantee that a manager will provide the return trustees might expect to achieve.

Market risk—the chance an investment's value will decline as the result of a major economic event that affects all assets in the market. Think about stocks and bonds; both are sensitive to broad economic events. When the economy is doing well, the return on these securities also tends to be good. On the other hand, when the economy is not doing very well, the opposite can occur.

Exhibit 3

Risk and Return on Select Investment Vehicles

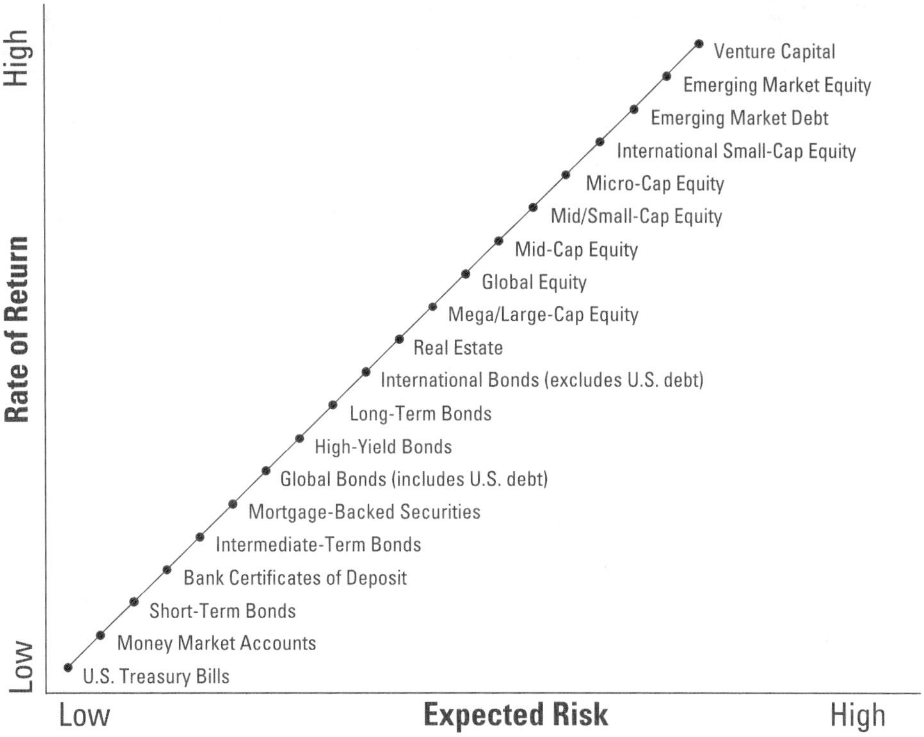

Assets that have higher levels of risk must have greater expected returns to make up for the greater risk. Exhibit 3 shows the overall relationship between risk and return for many of the investment options discussed in later chapters. As risk increases, so does the expected rate of return.

Note that for many of the assets identified in Exhibit 3 there are subcategories; for example, there are large-, mid-, small- and microcap equities representing different size companies in the U.S. There is also a subgroup for international equities. Bonds have classifications such as as short-, intermediate- and long-term as well as high-yield, There are variations in risk and return within asset categories influenced by the unique features of these asset subcategories.

For now it is sufficient to understand that larger cap stocks tend to have less risk and more return than smaller cap stocks. When U.S. corporate stock is compared to the stock of corporations of the same size in other nations, the U.S. equity tends to have less risk and return. Longer term bonds tend to have more risk and return than shorter term bonds. U.S. Treasury bills and other government securities are considered to be almost risk-free because they are guaranteed by the federal government; as a result, they have a relatively low return and return compared to corporate bonds as well as all other investment options.

It is essential to understand that in the short-term, the return on various assets and asset subcategories does not look as neat as Exhibit 3 might suggest. Looking at the historical return on investment options, there is substantial variation. Exhibit 4, which shows the historical return on U.S. assets for the twenty-year period spanning 1991-2010, illustrates the variance in annual returns that has occurred. The return on stocks varies more than the return on bonds, with small-cap equities having greater fluctuations than large-cap equities. Long-term corporate bond returns vary more than long-term government bonds which vary more than short-term bonds (U.S. Treasury Bills).

Over the very long-term—way back to the 1920s—the average annual return on U.S. stocks has been 9% but this figure in one year has been as much as 18% higher or lower. For the same period, bonds have averaged 6% with a range of 12% on either side of the average. The variability in the return on stocks has been 50% greater than on bonds, but the return on stock has also been about 50% higher than bonds—evidence of the long-term relationship been investment risk and return illustrated by Exhibit 3.

Time Horizon

Next on the list of important concepts is *time horizon,* how much time a plan has to achieve its objectives. A benefit plan providing health benefits typically has a short-time horizon with most contributions being used the same year they are received. There is little time to make up poor returns. As a result, health and welfare plan trustees must limit most investing to assets with lower risk (variability) and their resulting lower returns.

In contrast, pension plans promise benefits far into the future and have a long investment time horizon. This means trustees can purchase assets for a plan and hold on to them for many years before they are sold. More time makes it possible to take more risk with plan funds; trustees can invest in assets with more market risk knowing the longer time horizon provides more time for fluctuating returns to average out. If these investments do not do well some years, there is still time for recovery. Good years can make up for the bad years. Exhibit 5 illustrates how time can smooth out some of the variation of returns for the assets in which multiemployer plans most commonly invest. The longer these assets are held, the more likely their returns will average out to a *normalized* or "normal" return.

Diversification

Diversification, mixing assets to reduce risk, is another essential investment concept. Imagine a plan has just enough money to buy Portfolio A (100 shares of Stock X) or Portfolio B (one share of 100 different stocks, including one share of Stock X). Since Portfolio A is fully invested in Stock X, Portfolio A will do poorly if Stock X does poorly. On the other hand, Portfolio B is diversified and has 99 shares of other stocks that have the potential to make up for the poor returns on Stock X. There is no guarantee that all 100 stocks in Portfolio B will do well, but it is very unlikely that all 100 will do poorly. Think of diversification as the old saying—don't put all of your eggs (money) in one basket (asset).

Assets do not always react to events such as economic downturns in the same way. While some assets have returns that move in the same direction, others move in the opposite direction. The return on some assets moves a great deal while others move only a little bit. If two stocks go up and down in price the same amount at the same time and this pattern continues over time, the two assets have a *correlation coefficient* of +1.0. A correlation coefficient is one of the most important ways to measure diversification. A score of 1.0 indicates perfect correlation between two assets and no diversification. A plan would get the same risk and return from owning either stock.

If the two assets move the same amount but in the opposite direction, they have a -1.0 correlation. Investing in both of these two stocks would add substantial diversification to a plan's investment portfolio. A correlation coefficient of zero means the ups and downs of the returns are random.

The key to diversification is to find assets that do not move in the same direction in the same amount at the same time. A diversified portfolio has a variety of assets (e.g., stocks, bonds, real estate) with a mix of risks and returns. Portfolios must also be diversified within categories of assets, for example, holding stocks that represent a mix of industries such as technology, health care, financial and industrial.

Over long investment periods, the two major asset classes (i.e., stocks and bonds) have a positive correlation. The level of correlation, however, is low enough to provide a substantial reduction in risk. Real estate tends to be less correlated to stocks than bonds. Treasury bills tend to have a correlation close to zero with stocks, which means any correlation is random. For shorter investment periods, the correlation between these asset types can vary greatly. Trustees must examine the risks, returns and correlations across each major asset type as well as the asset subcategories.

Tip for Trustees

A long time horizon can be friend or foe. The advantage is that there is time to allow good returns to make up for periods of bad returns. With the longer time horizon, however, it is tempting to hold on to a poor investment thinking it will eventually do better and it may not. Even with a long investment period, investors face choices. Will the investments that are doing poorly turn around, or is it time to get rid of them?

Active vs. Passive Management

Until relatively recently, most benefit plans used only an *active management* approach to investment; an investment manager is given broad discretion to buy and sell within guidelines established by plan trustees. The guidelines usually specify the type of assets that managers can purchase, the amount of risk they are allowed to take and the benchmark upon which returns will be compared. Their objective is to "beat" market returns for similar assets.

Exhibit 4

Historical U.S. Investment Returns, 1991-2010

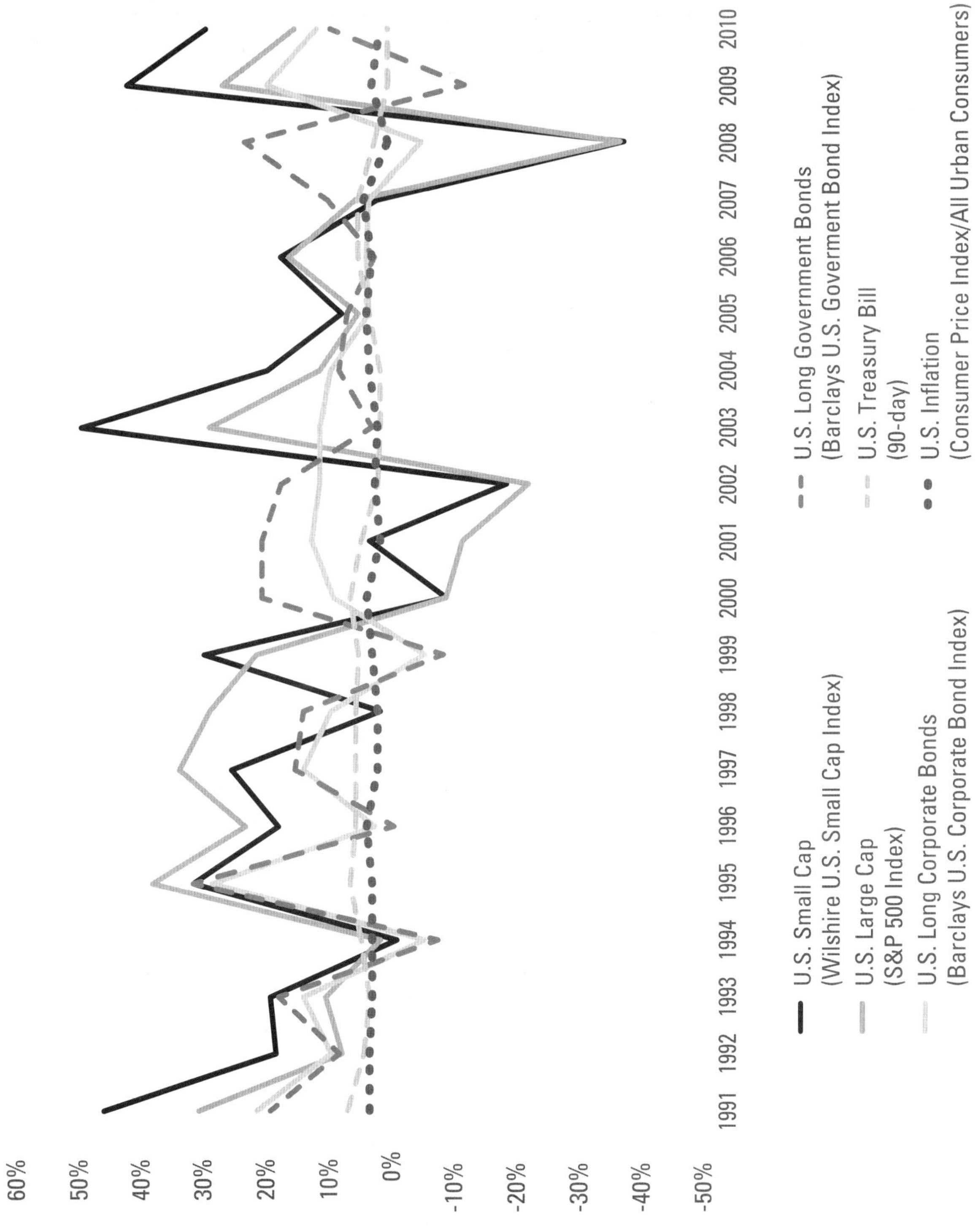

Source: Wilshire Associates.

Active management can be very profitable when it is successful, but keep in mind that not all managers outperform the market. Active management has an element of management risk and should be used when trustees have confidence that a manager's skills are among the best. The manager risk combined with higher management fees and trading costs has led some trustees to have part or all of their assets passively managed.

The introduction of index funds has offered this alternative to active investing. *Index funds* are mutual funds or variations thereof that contain assets mirroring a designated market index (e.g., S&P 500, Russell 2000). Exhibit 6 identifies some of the most widely used indexes.

Instead of trying to outdo the return on a market or segment of a market, *passive management* seeks to match the average return and risk of a market or index by attempting to mirror its make up. It is essentially a buy-and-hold investment strategy with zero management risk but full-market risk. A market portfolio must accept all of the interim negative returns on the way to the sought-after long-term returns. Because this approach matches an index, the fees are lower with no additional resources needed to make "active" judgments. There is also less trading expense.

There are also management options that fall somewhere between the active and passive strategies A *passive/active strategy* uses both strategies in a portfolio. Some assets are chosen for active management while others are passively managed. A *passive-plus* approach uses index funds for the core portion of a portfolio while active managers are used selectively in an attempt to add value above the core returns.

What Is a Commingled Account?

Not all plans have the resources or expertise to hire full-time staff to manage investments as separate accounts. Many external investment managers require a large amount of money before they are willing to accept the responsibility for overseeing investments in separate accounts. One solution to this dilemma is the use of commingled funds for some or all of a plan's investments.

In a *commingled account* (or *"fund"*), the assets of a plan are combined with the assets of other investors. The manager of the commingled account buys and sells assets as directed by a legal document that states how the money will be invested. Instead of holding any specific assets, the plan holds units in the commingled account. Essentially, the units are prorated shares of the commingled account's investments. Most people have some familiarity with mutual funds, one type of commingled account. Other types of commingled accounts include a(n):

- Insurance company separate account
- Group trust
- Limited partnership
- Real estate investment trust (REIT).

REITs, the last account type listed, pool funds to purchase and manage real estate assets and/or mortgage loans. For more information regarding REITs and investing in real estate, read Chapters 41 and 42.

The major advantage of a commingled fund is that small investors can access some of the best investment management at a reasonable cost. The biggest negative is that having plan assets mixed with the assets of others lim-

Exhibit 5

Return on Assets (Stocks, Long-Term Bonds and Real Estate) Over Time

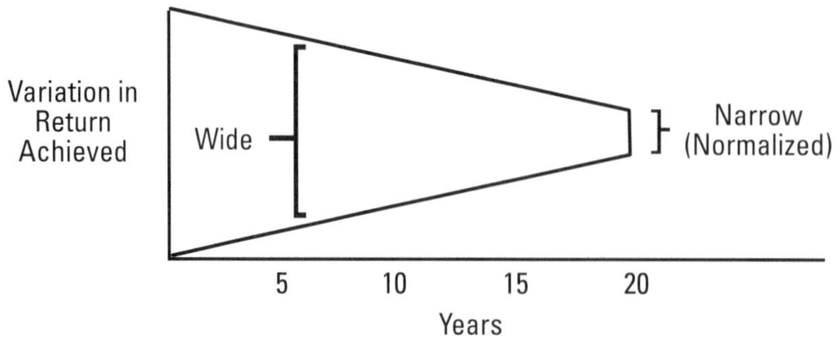

Source: Eugene B. Burroughs. "Investment Fundamentals," *Trustee Handbook: A Practical Guide to Labor-Management Employee Benefit Plans,* Sixth Edition. (International Foundation of Employee Benefit Plans, 2006): 284.

Exhibit 6

Some Widely Used Market Indexes

Asset Class	Representative Benchmark	Description
Public equity		
U.S. equity	S&P 500 Index	500 blue-chip, mostly large-cap U.S. stocks
	Russell 2000 Index	2,000 small-cap U.S. stocks
	Russell 3000 Index	Largest 3,000 U.S. stocks by market cap (Large, mid and small)
Non-U.S. equity	MSCI World ex U.S. Index	Approximately 85% of the market cap of 22 developed-market equity markets, excluding the U.S.
Developed-market equity	MSCI EAFE Index	Same as above but excluding Canada
Emerging-market equity	MSCI Emerging Markets Index	Approximately 85% of the market cap of 22 emerging-market equity markets
Global equity	MSCI All Country World Index	Combined developed- and emerging-market equity indexes (including the U.S.)
Fixed income		
Core fixed income	Barclays Capital Aggregate Bond Index	Investment-grade, government-sponsored, corporate, mortgaged-backed bonds and other asset-backed securities, issued in U.S. dollars
High Yield	Merrill Lynch U.S. High-Yield Cash Pay Index	Debt securities issued by corporations rated lower than investment grade by one or more of the major rating agencies
Emerging-market debt	J.P. Morgan Emerging Markets Bond Index Global	Dollar-denominated debt securities issued by emerging-market countries
	J.P. Morgan Government Bond Index—Emerging Markets	Local-currency-denominated debt securities issued by emerging-market countries
Global sovereign debt	Citigroup World Government Bond Index	Sovereign bonds issued by 23 developed countries (all investment grade)
TIPS	Barclays Capital U.S. TIPS Index	All inflation-linked bonds issued by the U.S. Treasury
Alternative investments		
Real estate	FTSE EPRA/NAREIT Developed Index	All real estate investment trust (REIT) securities issued in developed markets in North America, Europe and Asia
	NCREIF Property Index	A noninvestable index that tracks unlevered returns on more than 6,000 U.S. properties held by institutional investors in the office, retail, industrial and apartment sectors
Private equity	Cambridge Associates U.S. Venture Capital Index	A noninvestable index based on return data compiled on funds representing more than three-quarters of the total dollars raised by venture capital managers since 1981
	Cambridge Associates Buyout Index	A noninvestable index based on return data compiled on funds representing more than two-thirds of the total dollars raised by leveraged buyout, subordinated debt and special situations managers since 1986
Absolute return	HFRX Global Hedge Fund	A noninvestable non-value-weighted index of liquid, transparent hedge fund separate accounts engineered to achieve representative performance of a larger universe of hedge fund strategies
	HFRI Fund of Funds Composite Index	A noninvestable equally weighted index of more than 800 hedge funds of funds.

Notes: HFR+ Hedge Fund research; NCREIF = National Council of Real Estate Investment Fiduciaries; MSCI = Morgan Stanley Capital International: TIPS + Treasury Inflation-Protected Securities. All indices are market-capitalization weighted unless indicated otherwise.

Source: Jeffery V. Bailey, Jesse L. Phillips and Thomas M. Richards. *A Primer for Investment Trustees.* (The Research Foundation of CFA Institute, 2011): 60.

Exhibit 7

Commingled Funds

	Open-End Funds	Closed-End Funds
"Window" to invest	Opened quarterly	Open only during the subscription period (six to 12 months)
Portfolio disclosure	Investors can "kick the tires," if desired.	"Blind pool" strategy but not returns
Value of units	Appraisal process	Cost of assets
Diversification	Broad, across geographic property type and "time"	More specialized and targeted • stage of development • type of properties • geographic concentration
Liquidity	Withdrawals at discretion of investor, within portfolio limitations	Liquidation at discretion of manager, over long period (up to 12 years)

Source: Eugene B. Burroughs. *Investment Policy Guidebook for Trustees* (International Foundation of Employee Benefit Plans, 2005): 194.

its plan trustees' ability to customize the investments to a plan's unique interests.

Open-End Funds

Commingled accounts are either open- or closed-end funds. At least theoretically, *open-end* funds are always "open" to new investment capital (money). Investment earnings are normally reinvested in the account. The value of shares held by an investor is the combination of the appraised fair market value of the assets in the account and the earnings kept *(retained)* in the account. To realize a profit on the increased value of a fund, investors must sell *(redeem)* their shares. Most funds report their value on a quarterly basis.

The advantage of an open-end structure is that it can provide some liquidity for an asset that is relatively illiquid. Many employee benefit plans have been hesitant to invest in real estate because it is *illiquid*—it can be difficult to sell property quickly without the risk of substantial loss in value. REITs make it possible for a plan to invest in real estate. Before investing in a commingled fund, an important question to ask is whether redemption of shares is guaranteed. The money for redemption comes from the commingled fund. If there is enough cash available in the fund, the shares can be redeemed. If not, an investor may have to wait until there is sufficient cash available to do so.

Because open-end funds reinvest earnings, they continue to buy assets using the same investment strategy through both the ups and downs of a market. As a result, they tend to reflect what is happening in the market. Assume a plan has invested in a REIT. When the real estate market is doing well, the REIT should also do well; when the market is down, investors can expect also to see a downturn in the REIT. There is also the potential for dilution when many new contributions come into a fund. A successful fund can get so big that its manager has trouble finding good new investments.

Closed-End Funds

A *closed-end* commingled fund is structured for one-time investment at the time the fund is established and then "closed" to new investors. This type of fund is said to be a *blind pool* because there are no assets in the fund prior to its creation. Assets are bought after the fund is formed. The price of shares in a closed-fund is based on the cost of the fund's assets rather than the asset's appraised values. Most closed-end funds operate for a specific term such as ten years; the earnings and proceeds from the sale of the assets are then distributed back to the investors.

Closed-end funds can target their investment strategies much more precisely than open-end funds because they do not have to reinvest earnings or new capital. They have the ability to identify a specific opportunity in a particular phase of a market cycle and hold that position free from the dilution that would occur by investing in other phases of a market cycle. For these reasons, the closed-end structure is more adaptable to timing investments than an open-ended structure.

On the downside, closed-end funds do not have liquidity as a prime objective, though some funds do offer some form of redemption mechanism. Closed-end funds are based on the premise that some assets such as real estate are long-term investments. Because these structures are typically smaller than those that are open ended, closed-end funds also tend to offer less asset diversity. Exhibit 7 summarizes the characteristics of open- and closed-end commingled funds.

What Are Mutual Funds?

Mutual funds are pools of assets belonging to many shareholders. They invest in stocks, bonds, REITs and other publicly traded securities. Smaller retirement plans often use mutual funds, although not exclusively, to achieve investment objectives and meet the diversification requirements of the Employee Retirement Income Security Act of 1974 (ERISA). Like commingled funds, there are open-end and closed-end options. There are also load and no-load mutual funds to choose from.

Open-End Versus Closed-End Mutual Funds

Open-end mutual funds buy and sell investor shares on an ongoing basis. The shares are sold at the net asset value (NAV) plus sales fees (if any). Computed daily, NAV is the total market value of the securities held by the mutual fund divided by the total number of shares of the fund held by shareholders. For example, a fund valued at $100,000,000 and having 20,000,000 outstanding shares would have a net asset value of $5 ($100,000,000 ÷ 20,000,000 shares) on that day. The major advantage of investing in an open-end mutual fund versus a closed-end fund is the liquidity—being able to buy and sell at almost any time.

With a closed-end mutual fund, NAV is not calculated continuously. The fund is established with money provided by investors and, from that point on, no new shares are created. Shares of mutual funds with a closed structure are frequently bought and sold via an auction such as an over-the-counter (OTC) market. Shares of these funds may be transferred from one investor to another, but the price may not be equal to the net asset value of the fund at the time of the sale. Let's say the NAV is $20 one day. The third-party buyer of the shares may pay more or less than $20 depending on factors that are influencing the stock, bond or other asset markets in general.

Since investors cannot depend on being able to sell shares of a closed-end fund for an amount at least equal to the shares' NAV, a disadvantage of close-end funds is poor liquidity. The advantage of these funds is that they cannot be diluted with new cash that requires the creation of new shares. There is also no chance an unexpected large withdrawal will force an untimely sale of some of the fund's assets. Both the fund manager and shareholders have some comfort that investment objectives will not be compromised by an unanticipated change.

Load vs. No-Load Mutual Funds

Many open-end mutual funds charge a sales fee. To purchase shares of one of these *load funds,* an investor pays the NAV and a sales charge. There is no sales charge on *no-load funds.* Keep in mind, however, that the fee for a large purchase that a plan might make to establish a position in a fund is likely to be substantially less than what an individual investor might have to pay. The fee charged by a load fund declines as the size of the purchase goes up. For new capital contributions, the load also may be reduced via cumulative purchase privileges.

Advantages and Disadvantages

Mutual funds offer plan sponsors diversification, flexibility, liquidity, a means of specialization, cost efficiencies and, in certain instances, superior performance. In addition, the mutual fund industry is regulated by the Investment Company Act of 1940, which states a mutual fund must set forth clearly in its prospectus (updated annually and whenever necessary): (1) its investment objectives, (2) a report of its holdings, (3) its performance and (4) frequency of dividend distribution. Performance information is updated and reported quarterly.

Diversification. When investors purchase shares in a mutual fund, they are investing in a broad range of industries and/or companies. The degree of diversification within a fund generally varies between 25 and 200 companies, depending on investment philosophy and style. Since a variety of mutual funds is available, it is possible to use different funds to achieve diverse objectives; for example, a bond fund for income, a stock fund for growth in value and a money market account for cash liquidity. *Balanced mutual funds* combine stocks, bonds and sometimes a money market component into one portfolio to provide current income and long-term growth. The mix in the fund tends to be relatively fixed, typically 60% stocks and 40% bonds.

Specialization. Mutual funds may also specialize in a particular type of asset or market sector. For example, funds are available that only invest in stock from specific sizes of companies. Others emphasize a specific type of return such as income or capital growth. Funds also exist that invest in selected stock market sectors, such as technology, health care, utilities, energy, precious metals and minerals. Bond funds are available that focus on different types of public and private debt. There are funds comprised only of U.S. assets, non-U.S. assets or a combination of both. Funds are also available for other geographic regions in the world such as Asia, Latin America or emerging nations.

Flexibility. Since most mutual funds can be bought and sold quickly at their NAV, shifts in a fund from one type of asset to another can be done quickly. Additionally, new fund contributions can be invested within a day's time. Thirdly, in contrast to the delays associated with severing ties with a poorly performing independent investment manager, a mutual fund can be liquidated and reinvested elsewhere within 24 hours.

Cost efficiencies. Economies of scale are another benefit of mutual funds. As just one of many shareholders, investors are able to take advantage of reduced transaction costs that may result when large quantities of assets are bought and sold by the mutual fund. In addition, there is no need for investors to employ custodial and portfolio recordkeeping services; the mutual funds provide these services.

Mutual funds are particularly beneficial to small benefit plans; they make it possible to create the kind of multimanager investment program once available only to large plans. Smaller plans can hire an investment advisory firm to make decisions regarding asset allocation as well as specific mutual fund investments. Alternatively, small plans can invest using a mutual fund management company that offers different types of mutual funds that fit the plan's investment objectives. In the first case, the advisory firm should be willing to assume responsibility for asset allocation adjustments, both as a function of market outlook and plan tolerance for risk and reward. In the second scenario, plan trustees and/or a plan administrator would be responsible for asset readjustments over time.

Investing in mutual finds, like all other investing, also has potential disadvantages. Among these disadvantages is the absence of individual account servicing. Usually, there is no direct relationship between benefit plan personnel and the mutual fund manager. An independent mutual fund investment counseling firm can serve to bridge this gap.

How Do Trustees Make Sure an Investment Plan Is Successful?

Most trustees have a full-time job and limited experience making investment decisions—particularly decisions of the magnitude required for a multiemployer investment plan. While trustees are responsible for the overall success of their plan's investment program, they do not have to make a decision concerning every stock or bond that is bought or sold. The job of the trustee is to establish guidelines and a team of experts to help ensure investments are prudent. For plans that have been around for a while, much of this work should already be done; the job of current trustees is to (1) monitor that investment policies are being followed, and (2) make sure updates and changes are made as needed.

Establish Objectives and an Investment Policy Statement

The establishment of appropriate investment objectives and policies may be the single most important factor to a plan's investment success. *Investment objectives* are what trustees want to accomplish by investing a benefit plan's funds over time. *Investment policies* help guarantee these results are achieved.

Investment objectives and policies make up a plan's *investment policy statement.* This document is where asset allocation guidelines for the plan should be stated. *Asset allocation* is the mix of stocks, bonds and other assets that trustees determine should be held in their plan's investment portfolio; it is the framework used to ensure investments are diversified across asset types. Asset allocation is also the combination of assets that trustees believe will maximize returns relative to the risk they are willing to take with plan investments.

An investment policy statement establishes the benchmarks by which investment returns of individual assets, total assets and the investment manager accounts will be judged. *Benchmarks* are the reference points for comparing returns, risks and success on other objectives.

Any transactions or investments that are prohibited—at least without prior discussion or approval— also should be included in the investment policy statement. For a more complete discussion of investment objectives and the investment policy statement, read Chapter 47.

Seek the Help of Professionals

Trustees delegate to other individuals and organizations the responsibility for carrying out specific investment policy directives. These "others" may include any or all of the following: investment staff, investment managers, investment consultants and custodian banks.

Investment staff employed by a plan may be responsible for monitoring the diversification of plan assets, overseeing investment managers and preparing regular investment reports for trustees to review. Some larger plans have persons on staff who invest some or all plan assets. Hiring and retaining staff qualified to manage investments, however, is costly so outsourcing management duties is a common practice.

Investment managers, whether on staff *(internal management)* or provided by an outside organization *(external management),* decide which plan assets to buy and sell. While there are advantages to both approaches, external management is the most common model used for multiemployer funds today. Chapter 46 discusses the duties, selection and evaluation of investment managers.

Investment consultants can provide advice on issues such as investment policy, selecting and monitoring investment managers, and evaluating a plan's overall investment performance. The extent to which a fund uses consultants and the precise services provided varies from plan to plan. Some plans rely substantially on consultants while others use them for very limited and specific functions. Chapter 45 addresses the role of investment consultants and offers guidance on selecting and monitoring their performance.

Custodian banks are the institutions responsible for the safekeeping of publicly traded plan assets. In addition, a custodian bank keeps records and prepares reports for trustees and staff concerning investment transactions and holdings. It is also the bank that provides information for the various audits a plan undergoes each year.

Monitor Investment Activity and Results

Each quarter, investment professionals (i.e., fund managers and consultants) should provide trustees with performance reports along with an interpretation of the data in the reports. In addition to information on the plan portfolio as a whole, data should be provided concerning:

- Individual assets in a plan portfolio
- Major asset components (i.e., stocks, bonds, cash equivalents and alternative investments)
- Portfolios of the individual investment managers.

This report should include results for the current quarter as well as the year's prior quarters. Annual returns for previous years, if available, are essential for analyzing annual return patterns. It makes no sense to look at one outstanding year of results that hides two or three years of poor performance.

Cumulative return (sometimes called *compound returns*) must also be evaluated. This measure reflects fund investment returns spanning one, three, five, ten or more years. It shows what investments earned over multiple years so trustees can gauge their progress toward meeting longer term investment objectives.

An investment consultant, manager or custodian can provide trustees with measures of risk for most asset types. The terms used will sound very technical, but they address very commonsense issues:

- How diversified is the investment portfolio? Does it rely on just a few sectors or securities to earn a return?
- How volatile are the assets? Do prices or returns bounce around a great deal? Perhaps more than expected?
- What are the risks in different economic conditions?

It is the responsibility of trustees to review these reports in a timely manner, examining the risks and returns for each investment product and manager. Trustees should look for potential problems and trends that merit watching. Problems to watch for include a mix of assets that moves outside allocation targets, underperforming managers and risks that are inappropriate. It is critical to document management performance over time, as this is frequently the basis for retaining or terminating managers.

Active managers are usually expected to be in the top half of managers in their peer group, and frequently expected to beat an index, as well. While results are measured quarterly, the judgment to retain or terminate a manager is a longer term proposition (usually multiyear), unless circumstances require more immediate action.

When monitoring the performance of an investment manager, trustees must also take into consideration changes that may influence future returns on investment. If a manager's firm loses key decision makers or team members, is sold or merged, or loses a major account, this should trigger concern and merits attention. Here are a few other warning signs:

- Deviation from an investment manager's normal style
- Trading activity higher than normal
- Significant changes in risk measurements
- Fast growth in certain assets, new accounts or new products.

For an in-depth discussion of performance measurement, read Chapter 48.

Conclusion

The world of investing as well as multiemployer benefit plans is constantly changing. It is essential that trustees seek out new ideas and strategies by participating in conferences and other education programs available through organizations such as the International Foundation. A plan's investment consultant and legal counsel should also be keeping trustees informed of changes—providing the education that leads to wise investment choices.

Chapter 38

Fiduciary Responsibility in the Investment of ERISA Plan Assets

*Rory Judd Albert**

Previous chapters have addressed the general fiduciary responsibilities of trustees and others relating to the establishment, operation and administration of an employee benefit plan subject to the Employee Retirement Income Security Act of 1974 (ERISA). These duties are to:

- Act solely in the interest of plan participants and beneficiaries
- Act prudently
- Diversify plan assets
- Act in accordance with plan documents.[1]

All of these duties also apply to fiduciary decisions regarding the investment of the assets of an employee benefit plan. Every decision made by fiduciaries that affects plan assets must be the result of a diligent prudent investigation that has taken into account every reasonable consideration. An intentional or even unintended failure to do so can trigger ERISA enforcement and penalty provisions. Penalties can be quite severe given the potential enormity of investment losses.

This chapter explores the factors and processes involved when fiduciaries make investment decisions. Among the most critical decisions are those establishing a benefit plan investment policy and objectives. This chapter also addresses other investment issues faced by fiduciaries including asset diversification, proxy voting and social/economically targeted investments.

How Does Prudence Apply to the Investment of Plan Assets?

ERISA provides that plan fiduciaries must discharge their duties "with the care, skill, prudence, and diligence, under the circumstances then prevailing, that a prudent man acting in a like capacity and familiar with such matters would use in the conduct of an enterprise of a like character and with like aims." The courts generally have held that ERISA's prudence standard "is not that of a prudent layperson but rather that of a prudent fiduciary with experience dealing with a similar enterprise."[2]

The legislative history accompanying ERISA indicates that the expertise required of a plan fiduciary varies with the size and scope of the benefit plan. Thus, individuals managing large plans with enormous assets are required to exercise a more professional approach to investment management than individuals administering small plans with limited portfolios.

A hallmark of prudence under ERISA is whether a fiduciary conducted a thorough and complete investigation before taking an investment action.[3] Fiduciary responsibility, however, does not end when an investment option has been chosen. Fiduciaries also are expected to monitor investments with reasonable diligence and, if necessary, dispose of improper investments.[4]

Two tests are used to determine whether fiduciaries

*Mr. Albert wishes to gratefully acknowledge the invaluable assistance received from Pamela A. Onufer and Nicole Stein in the preparation of this chapter.

have met the prudence standard as applied to investments: one test is procedural, the second is substantive. *Procedural prudence* focuses on the process used when selecting a particular investment. The concern is not necessarily how well an investment performs but, instead, the steps fiduciaries have taken to reach and implement an investment decision.[5] *Substantive prudence*, on the other hand, focuses on the actual merits of the fiduciary's decision at the time an investment decision is made. In practical terms, this means a fiduciary must consider the following when making investment decisions:

- The investment fits within the context of the plan's overall portfolio.
- The design of the portfolio, including the investment, is reasonable for the purposes of the plan.
- The risk of loss and opportunity for gain (or other returns) must be favorable, relative to alternative investments.
- The investment fits into the diversification scheme of the portfolio.
- The investment does not affect adversely the liquidity and current return of the entire portfolio relative to anticipated cash flow requirements of the plan.
- The investment takes into consideration the projected return of the portfolio relative to the funding objectives of the plan.[6]

As long as there is no conflict of interest that would impair the fiduciary's judgment, a fiduciary who considers these factors (substantive prudence) and does so using proper procedures (procedural prudence) will satisfy the prudence requirement in most cases.[7]

Prudent Investment Strategies and Decisions

Given ERISA has been in place for nearly four decades, and there are trillions of dollars committed to ERISA plan investments, it is interesting that there have been relatively few court cases focused on whether an investment was prudent. However, in the cases addressing this subject, the fiduciary's failure to live up to his duties is easily identified.[8] For example, one court found that an investment manager's decision to invest one-third of a welfare plan portfolio in highly volatile inverse floaters was a violation of ERISA's prudence standard.[9]

Courts have developed general standards for determining whether a fiduciary acted prudently when designing investment strategies and making investment decisions. Essentially, the proper test is whether the fiduciary:

- Used proper methods to investigate, evaluate and structure the investment
- Acted in a manner that was the same as others who have a capacity and familiarity with such matters
- Exercised independent judgment when making investment decisions.[10]

Fiduciaries must be able to establish that when they made their investment decisions, they:

- Conducted an impartial, arm's length study of the advantages and disadvantages of the particular transaction
- Used acceptable standards in retaining qualified experts and consultants[11]
- Relied on complete and up-to-date information.

Finally, fiduciary investment decisions must be made in accordance with plan documents, to the extent these documents are consistent with ERISA. Investment decisions that are not permitted by the plan are flatly prohibited by ERISA—even if an argument could be made that the investments were prudent.

Establishing an Investment Policy and Objectives

The first step in the prudent investment of plan assets is establishing prudent investment objectives and strategies. Broad issues that must be considered include:

- The nature of the plan
- The purpose of the plan and the employer's aim in offering the plan (taking into account the age, income levels and investment needs of participants)
- The plan's funding characteristics and funding provisions
- The size of the plan
- The plan's liquidity requirements (e.g., a health and welfare fund will generally need more liquidity than a defined benefit pension plan)
- Acceptable risk-to-return ratios.

In addition, the following specific factors—among others—should be considered with respect to the plan assets:

- Whether the particular investment or investment course of action is reasonable, as part of the portfolio, to further the purposes of the plan—taking into consideration the potential risk of loss and opportunity for gain (or other return)
- The composition of the portfolio with regard to diversification
- The liquidity and current return of the portfolio relative to the anticipated cash flow needs of the plan
- The projected return of the portfolio relative to the plan's funding objectives.[12]

After weighing the above considerations, fiduciaries should prepare a written statement that (1) describes the plan's investment objectives and (2) provides guidelines and general instructions for various types of investment management decisions. The investment guidelines may include restrictions, for instance, on:

- The types of investments (e.g., no foreign securities or venture capital issues)
- Asset allocation requirements (e.g., limiting plan investments in equities to a specific percentage of the portfolio)
- Minimum bond quality grades (e.g., no more than a certain percentage of the total fixed income portfolio should be invested in bonds rated less than "A")
- Proxy voting decisions (e.g., criteria regarding the support of or opposition to recurring issues, such as proposals to create classified board of directors, approval of stock incentive plans).

Although ERISA does not specifically require plan fiduciaries to prepare an investment policy statement, the Department of Labor (DOL) takes the position that issuing a policy statement is inherent in the named fiduciary's authority to appoint investment managers.[13] DOL believes that an investment policy statement (1) helps ensure investments are made in a prudent and rational manner and (2) furthers the purposes of the plan and its funding.[14] Federal court decisions support this view.[15] Such statements need to take into account factors such as the plan's funding policy and its liquidity needs as well as issues of prudence, diversification and other fiduciary requirements.

The investment policy statement becomes the overall game plan from which all investment strategies evolve. The statement fosters a mutual understanding among all participants in the process. Lines of responsibility are carefully drawn, permitting appropriate accountability and adjustments in the review, reevaluation and modification process.

Communication of the Plan's Investment Objectives

Courts recognize that not all plan fiduciaries can be experts in every phase of an employee benefit plan's investments, administration, etc. Therefore, fiduciaries have a duty to seek the advice of independent experts when their own ability is insufficient.[16] For a more detailed discussion concerning the retention of investment consultants and managers, see Chapters 46 and 47, respectively.

The policy statement for a plan is the steppingstone for the individual policy statements provided to plan investment managers. The individualized statement includes:

- Background information on the plan and its investments
- Future funding and cash flow projections
- Investment objectives
- Policies related to the voting of proxies
- Portfolio guidelines
- Report requirements
- Review, evaluation and modification methods.

Plan fiduciaries responsible for the investment of plan assets, or their authorized representatives, should identify beforehand an investment style for the plan assets to be committed to each investment manager. Once an investment style has been selected, the fiduciary responsible for appointing the manager should establish a clear understanding with the manager as to:

- The rate of return sought
- The level of acceptable risk tolerance and diversification latitude
- The scope of the manager's discretion to acquire and maintain particular types of assets and to determine the amounts of each type of asset
- The time frame for measuring performance
- The procedures to be used in monitoring and evaluating the performance of the manager
- A clearly defined list of investment restrictions concerning, for example:
  - Private equity investments
  - Hedge fund investments
  - Bond quality grades
  - Uncovered options
  - Short sales
  - Futures contracts
  - Restricted stock or private placements (with the possible exception of Section 144A securities)
  - Margin transactions (or any other borrowing of money)
  - Volatile *derivative* instruments.

The list of investment types is not an exhaustive list. Depending on the particular characteristics of a plan, its portfolio and other circumstances, some (or all) of these investments may be appropriate.

Except where properly delegated to an investment manager, authority over investment decisions remains with plan fiduciaries.[17] Accordingly, the advice of experts should set forth adequately the benefits and risks of a particular transaction in a form that is comprehensible. The experts should provide sufficient analysis and grounds for making informed decisions.

What Does Asset Diversity Mean Under ERISA?

In general, *diversification* is the strategy of including a variety of securities in a portfolio. ERISA does not tell plan fiduciaries how to diversify a plan portfolio. In fact, there is recognition that diversification "depends upon the facts and circumstances surrounding each plan and investment."[18] Still, the history of ERISA suggests fiduciaries should consider each of these factors:

- The purpose of the plan
- The amount of plan assets
- Financial and industrial conditions
- The type of investment, whether mortgages, bonds or shares, or stock or otherwise
- Distribution as to geographic location
- Distribution as to industries
- The dates of maturity of the investment and loan maturity.[19]

ERISA requires the diversification of a plan's investment portfolio to minimize the risk of large losses—unless there are circumstances where it is clearly prudent not to diversify. The theory behind the diversification requirement is that potential losses in one area of a plan portfolio will be offset by gains in another area.[20] Moreover, even where such a loss is not offset, its impact is limited to a relatively small portion of the plan.[21]

Case law makes it clear that both individual investments and the asset allocation of a plan's entire investment portfolio are evaluated for diversification.[22] If it is shown in court that plan fiduciaries failed to diversify plan investments, the fiduciaries must prove the prudence of their failure to diversify.[23] In addition, fiduciaries must demonstrate their plan was not exposed to any significant risk of large losses as a result of the failure to diversify.[24]

Employer-Related Investments

ERISA Section 407(a) specifically addresses diversification as it applies to real property leased to an employer and securities issued by the employer. Such real property (called *qualifying employer real property*) is a permissible investment only if, among other things, the real estate is geographically dispersed.[29] Employer securities eligible for plan investment (called *qualifying employer securities*) must be either stock that meets certain diversified ownership criteria or debt obligations that are *marketable obligations* meeting certain diversified holding requirements.[30]

Mutual Funds and Insurance Contracts

Congress also recognized that many plan fiduciaries would invest plan assets largely or totally in pooled investment vehicles such as mutual funds. The diversification requirement is met if the underlying assets of the pooled investment vehicle are diversified.[31] Similarly, a plan may invest all of its assets in insurance contracts as long as the insurance company's investments are diversified.[32]

Decisions From the Courts

Diversification Depends on the Facts and Circumstances

Court cases bear testimony that diversification of benefit plan assets is literally a "facts and circumstances" test. Consider one case in which a court found that concentrating 36% of plan assets in one type of investment was a violation of ERISA, while another court found no fiduciary breach in another case where one parcel of undeveloped real estate represented 63% of the plan's assets.[25] In a third case, no breach was found though three investments represented 90% of the plan's assets.[26]

In a district court case, plan participants charged that a trustee breached his fiduciary duty by increasing the use of margin debt coupled with a decrease in diversification of the plan assets. The court found that the trustee had clearly invested the assets of the plan aggressively, but that he had invested prudently to maximize profits.[27] The court further found that, although plan assets were not diversified to minimize the risk of all large losses, under the circumstances the trustee was clearly not imprudent in his aggressive investment strategy because he invested in 20 different stocks.[28]

What Are the Fiduciary Responsibilities for Proxy Voting?

Shareholders of companies are given the right to vote on certain corporate issues. The voting procedure is referred to as the *voting of proxies* or *proxy voting*. Trustees are advised to include proxy voting policy in their plan's statement of investment policy to help ensure proxy voting decisions are consistent with other aspects of investment policy. In addition, if a plan has many investment managers, a written proxy voting policy may prevent investment managers from taking conflicting positions on a given issue.

DOL takes the position that the fiduciary act of managing plan assets includes proxy voting for shares of stock owned by a plan.[33] If trustees delegate authority for the acquisition or disposal of plan assets to an investment manager, generally the authority to vote proxies is delegated to the manager as well. This holds true unless the plan document permits trustees or other fiduciaries to vote proxies and the investment management agreement expressly bars the investment manager from voting proxies.

Fiduciaries should carefully review plan documents and investment management agreements to ensure that they are not precluded from delegating voting authority to an investment manager. Fiduciaries must also negotiate investment management agreements with specific language delegating to the investment manager the fiduciary duty to vote proxies or specific language retaining the fiduciary duty to vote proxies.

Reservation of Voting Rights

DOL Interpretive Bulletin 08-2 (Oct. 17, 2008) clarifies that when delegating investment management authority to an investment manager, trustees may reserve the right to direct a trustee to vote proxies for specified shares of stocks. If a plan has procedures for allocating fiduciary responsibilities among named fiduciaries, the right of proxy voting may also be reserved for a named fiduciary.[34]

When a named fiduciary reserves the right to vote employer securities (e.g., in an Employee Stock Ownership Plan (ESOP)) and such right is not passed through to plan participants and beneficiaries (provided that pass-through voting is not legally required),[35] fiduciaries should exercise extensive caution in voting to avoid prohibited transactions under Section 406(b) of ERISA and conflicts of interest.

Delegation of Voting Authority

If trustees have appointed an investment manager and have not reserved the right to vote proxies, the investment manager has a fiduciary duty to (1) confirm that it has received the proper number of proxies, (2) vote the proxies and (3) maintain accurate records as to the voting of proxies including the rationale for the vote.[36] Plan fiduciaries may not decide how to vote the proxies being managed and are relieved of liability for the improper exercise of proxies by plan investment managers.

If voting authority is delegated to an investment manager, the manager should be provided specific procedures for voting proxies. These instructions should separate voting into established categories (i.e., routine matters, nonroutine matters, corporate governance matters and social issues).

When proxy voting is delegated, trustees retain the responsibility for monitoring both proxy voting procedures and voting. Fiduciaries should establish procedures for monitoring and reviewing proxy voting activity. In this regard, they should consider establishing an internal proxy monitoring or corporate governance committee or retaining an outside evaluator to help with this task.

Regardless of who votes proxies, Bulletin 08-2 prohibits the consideration of noneconomic motives when voting. DOL states only that "[v]otes shall only be cast in accordance with a plan's economic interests."[37]

Tip for Trustees

Trustees should be wary of creating portfolios with the following characteristics:

- Disproportionately heavy investments in a security of a single issuer
- Securities dependent upon the success of a single enterprise
- Securities dependent upon conditions in one locality
- Stock of corporations engaged in one industry
- Mortgages concentrated in one geographic allocation
- Mortgages on one particular class of property.

Can Fiduciaries Consider Other Factors Such as Social Policy When Making Investment Decisions?

The primary objective of a pension plan is to provide employee retirement income security. To accomplish this, plan assets must be invested in a manner that satisfies ERISA requirements of loyalty, prudence and diversification. The question that this section seeks to answer is whether there is room, within these fiduciary obligations, for a fiduciary to engage in socially responsible or economically targeted investing.

Socially Responsible Investing

Socially responsible investing is an investment strategy that considers an investor's financial needs as well as the impact of the investment on society. Typically, these investments are analyzed based on financial/economic factors. Noneconomic or societal factors are secondary considerations.[38]

Examples of socially responsible investments range from community projects (such as low-income housing or below-market interest rate mortgages) to investments in environmentally sound products. Socially responsible investments may be designed to spur local economies, increase the use of union labor and provide jobs to certain groups. A socially responsible investment strategy may also be the decision not to invest; for example, refusing to purchase the stock of a company:

- Doing business in a country that supports political (or other) policies with which plan fiduciaries do not agree
- That manufactures products harmful to human health (e.g., cigarettes) or the environment (e.g., certain sectors of the chemical industry).

There are no ERISA provisions or DOL regulations that specifically address whether plan fiduciaries may make investment decisions based on social policy concerns. There are, however, opinion letters, commentaries and a DOL interpretive bulletin that indicate fiduciaries may not implement an investment policy that has social underpinnings—unless they first satisfy ERISA general fiduciary obligations (i.e., the sole benefit of participants, prudence and diversification).[39] Any such "extra" benefits offered by an investment may be pivotal in a decision only if the investment is expected to provide an investment return equal to alternative investments with similar risks.[40]

Regarding union campaigns and goals, DOL issued Advisory Opinion Letter No. 08-05A, to explain that "the use, or threat of use, of pension plan assets or plan management to achieve a particular collective bargaining objective…subordinates the interests of participants and beneficiaries in their retirement income…"

Contrary to opinions just noted that suggest socially responsible investing may be allowed if economic benefit is the primary consideration, comments made by senior staff members of DOL and the Pension Benefit Guaranty Corporation (PBGC) indicate that these individuals are not convinced that socially responsible investing is consistent with ERISA obligations to invest plan assets for the exclusive benefit of plan participants.

Given there is little judicial or solid administrative guidance regarding socially responsible investing, fiduciaries should proceed very cautiously in pursuing such a strategy. While socially responsible investing may not be a per se violation of ERISA's fiduciary obligations, it appears that socially responsible investing—like economically targeted investments (discussed below)—may only be a viable option in extremely limited circumstances.

Economically Targeted Investments

Economically targeted investments (ETIs) are broadly defined as investments selected for the economic benefit they provide separate from their investment return to an employee benefit plan. ETIs provide "extra" benefits such as the creation of jobs or affordable housing to certain targeted groups (e.g., union members, plan participants, communities in which the plan operates).

In June 1994, DOL released an interpretive bulletin to eliminate a misperception that plan investments in ETIs are incompatible with ERISA fiduciary obligations.[41] DOL released a second bulletin in 2008 clarifying that while investing in ETIs is not incompatible, the circumstances under which a plan may do so are extremely limited. In this second bulletin, DOL makes it clear that fiduciaries can select an ETI over another investment alternative only after they have first determined the ETI and alternative investments are "truly equal with respect to the economic impact on the plan." [42] This economic analysis must take into account the level of diversification, degree of liquidity and the potential risk/return of the ETI versus the alternatives serving a similar role in a plan portfolio.

In the 2008 bulletin, DOL cautioned that any fiduciary who considers factors outside of a plan's economic interests and selects an ETI should maintain a written account of the economic analysis that concluded the ETI and alternatives considered were of equal economic value. In the DOL view, without this written account, plan fiduciaries "will rarely be able to demonstrate compliance with ERISA." This language sends a clear and strong message that DOL is very skeptical of the validity of such investments.

Conclusion

The investment of plan assets is one of the (if not the) most important duties assumed by plan fiduciaries. While the objective of this chapter has been to set forth the key legal—and practical—considerations associated with this vital responsibility, fiduciaries are well served if they remember just two pieces of advice from this chapter.

1. Act prudently, and be sure to be cautious and diligent every step of the way when investing plan assets.
2. Seek professional advice whenever appropriate. Trained experts are available to assist fiduciaries from the initial step of designing investment objectives to selecting an investment manager and then to monitoring investment performance.

Adherence to these guiding principles will help ensure fiduciaries meet their obligations under ERISA when it comes to plan investments while avoiding (what can be) Draconian penalties.

Endnotes

1. Part 4 of Title I of ERISA, where Section 404(a)(1).
2. *Whitfield v. Cohen*, 682 F.Supp. 188, 194 (S.D.N.Y. 1988) (quoting 29 U.S.C. §1104(a)(1)(B)).
3. *Harley v. Minn. Mining & Mfg. Co.*, 42 F.Supp. 2d 898, 906 (D.Minn.

1999) ("Under this standard, a fiduciary is obligated to undertake an independent investigation of the merits of an investment and to use appropriate, prudent methods in conducting the investigation."), cert. denied, 537 U.S. 1106 (2003); *Fink v. Nat'l Sav. & Trust Co.*, 772 F.2d 951, 957 (D.C. Cir. 1985).

4. *Keach v. U.S. Trust Co., N.A.*, 313 F.Supp. 2d 818, 871 (C.D.Ill. 2004), aff'd by 419 F.3d 626 (7th Cir. 2005); *Hunt v. Magnell*, 758 F.Supp. 1292 (D.Minn. 1991); *Harley v. Minn. Mining & Mfg. Co.*, 42 F.Supp. 2d 898, 906 (D.Minn. 1999) ("Once the investment is made, a fiduciary has an ongoing duty to monitor investments with reasonable diligence and remove plan assets from an investment that is improper."), cert. denied, 537 U.S. 1106 (2003).
5. *Cal. Ironworkers Field Pension Trust v. Loomis Sayles & Co.*, 259 F.3d 1036, 1043 (9th Cir. 2001).
6. 29 C.F.R. §2550.404a-1(b).
7. *Chao v. Trust Fund Advisors*, 2004 U.S. Dist. LEXIS 4026, 4034 (D.D.C. 2004) (citing *Katsaros v. Cody*, 744 F.2d 270, 279 (2d Cir.), cert. denied, 469 U.S. 1072 (1984)).
8. See, e.g., In re Unisys Sav. Plan Litig., 74 F.3d 420 (3d Cir.), cert. denied, 117 S.Ct. 56 (1996) (it is a breach of the prudence standard if a plan administrator, without conducting an independent investigation, passively accepts a consultant's positive appraisal of a debt investment in a corporation that subsequently becomes bankrupt); *Int'l Brotherhood of Electrical Workers, Local 90 v. Nat'l Elec. Contractors Assoc.*, 2008 WL 918481 (Mar. 31, 2008) (defendant breached fiduciary duty by failing to appoint and monitor plan trustees); *Meyer v. Berkshire Life Ins. Co.*, 250 F.Supp. 2d 544 (D.Md. 2003) (violation of fiduciary duty of prudence demonstrated by insurance investor's choice of conservative investments without regard to plan's risk preference, frequent transfer of funds and inability to identify reasons for investment selections); *White v. Martin*, 286 F.Supp. 2d 1029, 1039 (D.Minn. 2003) (loss occurring over two years to plan with significant investment in one company by managing trustee, the employer's wife, was not indicative of fiduciary breach because of lack of proof that the investments "were improper, imprudent, or represented an unduly large portion of the Plan's assets"); *Harley v. Minn. Mining & Mfg. Co.*, 42 F.Supp. 2d 898 (D.Minn. 1999) (summary judgment precluded based on genuine issues of material fact as to whether employer conducted sufficient investigation or undertook reasonably prudent efforts to monitor investments), cert. denied, 537 U.S. 1106 (2003); *Liss v. Smith*, 991 F.Supp. 278 (S.D.N.Y. 1998) (trustees demonstrated no deliberation or investigation as to the safety of an investment and breached the prudence standard when it approved the purchase of collateralized mortgage obligations constituting over 25% of plan assets on the day following receipt of broker's recommendation); *Board of Trustees of the Local 295 v. Callan Assocs., Inc.*, 1998 U.S. Dist. LEXIS 8196 (S.D.N.Y. 1998) (investment consultant did not breach the prudence standard in deciding to transition assets in cash rather than in kind to a new investment manager, even though the pension fund sustained over $1.15 million in losses from an unexpected shift in interest rates), aff'd, 175 F.3d 1007 (2d Cir. 1999); *Reich v. Hall Holding Co.*, Inc., 990 F.Supp. 955 (N.D. Ohio 1998) (ESOP plan administrators breached the prudence standard by relying on a stock valuation based on ownership of 100% of the company and, as a result, paying more than adequate consideration for their minority stake), aff'd sub nom., *Chao v. Hall Holding Co.*, Inc., 285 F.3d 415 (6th Cir. 2002), cert. denied, 537 U.S. 1168 (2003); In re Bicostal Corp., 191 B.R. 238, 244 (asset manager's "lackadaisical approach" in her use of plan assets to finance a real estate developer's purchase of property was "nothing short of gross negligence" where plan's actuary, accountant, counsel and professional investor advised against the investment); *GIW Indus., Inc. v. Trevor, Stewart, Burton & Jacobsen, Inc.*, 895 F.2d 729 (11th Cir. 1990), aff'g, 10 EBC 2290 (S.D.Ga. 1989) (investment manager held imprudent where he failed to conduct appropriate investigation of plan's cash flow needs and failed to diversify investments resulting in plan's loss of $537,000 upon liquidation of investments in order to meet cash flow needs); *Katsaros v. Cody*, 744 F.2d 270, 279 (2d Cir.), cert. denied, 469 U.S. 1072 (1984) (trustees breached prudence standard in connection with $2 million loan to bank, where they considered only information presented by interested parties who sought loan, and failed to conduct an independent investigation); *Donovan v. Mazzola*, 2 EBC 2115 (N.D.Cal. 1981), aff'd, 716 F.2d 1226 (9th Cir. 1983), cert. denied, 464 U.S. 1040 (1984); *Marshall v. Glass/Metal Assoc. and Glaziers and Glassworks Pension Plan*, 507 F.Supp. 378, 383 (D.Hawaii 1980). Compare *Metzler v. Graham*, 112 F.3d 207 (5th Cir. 1997); *Etter v. Pearse Construction Co., Inc.*, 963 F.2d 1005 (7th Cir. 1992); *Reich v. King*, 867 F.Supp. 341 (D.Md. 1994); *Jones v. O'Higgins*, 11 EBC 1660 (N.D.N.Y. 1989). In these cases, a plan potentially in violation of Section 404 on nondiversification grounds was found not to violate ERISA because under the particular facts and circumstances the investment decisions had been prudently made. See also *DeBruyne v. Equitable Life Assurance Soc'y*, 920 F.2d 457 (7th Cir. 1990), aff'g, 720 F.Supp. 1342 (N.D.Ill. 1989) (investment manager did not act imprudently despite fact that fund lost 18% in 1987 stock market crash).
9. *Cal. Ironworkers Field Pension Trust v. Loomis Sayles & Co.*, 259 F.3d 1036 (9th Cir. 2001).
10. *Jones v. O'Higgins*, 11 EBC 1660, 1667 (N.D.N.Y. 1989), citing, inter alia, *Katsaros v. Cody*, 744 F.2d 270, 279 (2d Cir.), cert. denied, 469 U.S. 1072 (1984).
11. Depending on the jurisdiction in which the plan operates, a fiduciary's investigative conduct may even have to satisfy prevailing industry standards. Compare *Jones v. O'Higgins*, 11 EBC 1660, 1668 (N.D.N.Y. 1989) (To find the defendant liable, this court would have to be provided with evidence that the defendant acted imprudently within the standards of the investment industry), with *GIW Indus., Inc. v. Trevor, Stewart, Burton & Jacobsen, Inc.*, 10 EBC 2290, 2304 n.23 (S.D.Ga. 1989) (While investment management industry custom and practice enter into an evaluation of prudence, the particular obligations of a fiduciary under ERISA are not controlled by the investment management industry but by statute), aff'd, 895 F.2d 729 (11th Cir. 1990).
12. 29 C.F.R. §2550.404a-1(b).
13. DOL Interpretive Bulletin 94-2 (July 29, 1994); ERISA §402(c)(3).
14. DOL Interpretive Bulletin 08-2 (Oct. 17, 2008). See also ERISA §402(c)(3).
15. *White v. Martin*, 286 F.Supp. 2d 1029, 1033 (D.Minn. 2003) (recognizing the benefits of creating a statement of investment policy, but refusing to find mandatory statement of investment policy); but see *Liss v. Smith*, 991 F.Supp. 278, 296 (S.D.N.Y. 1998) (The maintenance by an employee benefit plan of a statement of investment policy designed to further the purposes of the plan and its funding policy is consistent with the fiduciary obligations set forth in ERISA.).
16. *King v. Guynn*, 1992 U.S. Dist. LEXIS 21582 at *35 (E.D.Va. 1992). (ERISA encourages fiduciaries to seek the advice of qualified experts in order to satisfy this procedural standard of prudence.) See also *Katsaros v. Cody*, 744 F.2d 270, 279 (2d Cir.), cert. denied, 469 U.S. 1072 (1984) (trustees breached ERISA's prudence standard in connection with $2 million loan to bank, where trustees considered only information presented by bank holding company president who sought loan, and failed to conduct an independent investigation); *Donovan v. Tricario*, 5 EBC 2057, 2064 (S.D.Fla. 1984), affi'd sub nom. *Brock v. Tricario*, 768 F.2d 1351 (11th Cir. 1985) (fiduciaries violated prudent man standard in connection with plan's purchase of individual whole life insurance, without initiating competitive bids, and without obtaining expert advice on the prudency of whole life benefits, causing the plan to incur investment costs 300% to 400% greater than that of group insurance); *Dimond v. Retirement Plan for Employees of Michael Baker Corp. & Affiliates*, 582 F.Supp. 892 (W.D.Pa. 1983) (failure to seek independent advice, and reliance on a mere belief that investment is "wise," constitutes breach of "prudent man" duty).
17. See, e.g., *Liss v. Smith*, 991 F.Supp. 278 (S.D.N.Y. 1998) (trustees are obligated to seek independent advice where it is essential, but ultimate decision-making authority and responsibility for investments rest with the trustees); *Donovan v. Tricario*, 5 EBC (BNA) 2057, 2064 (S.D.Fla. 1984), aff'd sub nom., *Brock v. Tricario*, 768 F.2d 1351 (11th Cir. 1985) ([M]ere retention of an expert cannot be permitted to protect defendants against claims of failure to discharge their own fiduciary responsibilities. Expert advice must be con-

sidered as carefully as any other information that the trustees have available to them when making decisions to commit plan assets.).

18. *Marshall v. Glass/Metal Assoc. & Glaziers & Glassworks Pension Plan*, 507 F.Supp. 378, 383 (D.Hawaii 1980).
19. H.R. Rep. No. 93-1280 (1974), reprinted in 1974 U.S.C.C.A.N. 5038, at 5084-5085.
20. See *Donovan v. Guaranty Nat'l Bank*, 4 EBC 1686, 1688 (S.D.W.Va. 1983).
21. Ibid.
22. See *Brock v. Citizens Bank of Clovis*, 1985 WL 71535 (D.N.M. 1986), aff'd, 841 F.2d 344 (10th Cir.), cert. denied, *Citizens Bank of Clovis v. McLaughlin*, 488 U.S. 829 (1988).
23. *Olsen v. Hegarty*, 180 F.Supp. 2d 552, 566-67 (D.N.J. 2001); *Jones v. O'Higgins*, 11 EBC 1660, 1665 (N.D.N.Y. 1989).
24. *Jones v. O'Higgins*, 11 EBC 1660, 1665 (N.D.N.Y. 1989).
25. See *Marshall v. Teamster Local 282 Pension Trust Fund*, 458 F.Supp. 986 (E.D.N.Y. 1978).
26. See *Jones v. O'Higgins*, 11 EBC 1660 (N.D.N.Y. 1989) (no breach where 90% of plan assets invested in only three investments).
27. *Simons v. Barnette*, 2003 U.S. Dist. LEXIS 25008, at *1 (M.D.Fla. 2003); see also *Lanka v. O'Higgins*, 810 F.Supp. 379 (N.D.N.Y. 1992).
28. *Simons v. Barnette*, 2003 U.S. Dist. LEXIS 25008, at *1 (M.D.Fla. 2003).
29. See 29 U.S.C. §1107(d)(4)(A); *Pearland Investment Co. v. Commissioner*, 14 EBC 1928, 1930 (U.S. Tax Ct. 1991).
30. See 29 U.S.C. §1107(d)(5).
31. H.R. Rep. No. 93-1280, 93rd Cong., 2nd Session at 304-305 (1974).
32. DOL Adv. Op. Ltr. No. 79A-75.
33. DOL Letter to Helmuth Fandl, Chairman of Retirement Board of Avon Products, Inc. (Feb. 23, 1988).
34. DOL has also stated that the decision to tender shares of stock in a tender offer is a fiduciary act. However, there is not an automatic requirement that fiduciaries must accept a tender offer when the offer represents a premium over the prevailing market price.
35. See, e.g., "Labor Department Guidance on Voting Provisions in Collectively Bargained Employee Stock Ownership Plans," 22 Pen. & Ben. Rep. (BNA) 2249, 2250-51 (Sept. 28, 1995). The Labor Department addressed a directed trustee's role where an ESOP plan granted plan participants the authority to direct the trustee regarding the tendering of stock or proxy voting of stock allocated to their own accounts. As such, the participants were fiduciaries for the limited purpose of giving such directions. The letter states that the trustee can satisfy §403(a)(1) and assure itself that a participant's instructions are proper and not contrary to ERISA and the plan if it follows procedures to ensure that the eligible individual account plan's provisions are fairly implemented; the directing participant has not been subject to coercion or undue pressure in its decision; necessary information was provided to the participant; and that clearly false information or misleading information is not distributed to the participant, or that any false or misleading information that may have been distributed by other parties is corrected. Id. at 2250. Furthermore, DOL stated that the fact that the named fiduciary-participant issues such a direction with respect to a tender offer or proxy vote related to stock in its individual account "does not diminish the trustee's duty to diligently investigate and evaluate the merits of the course of action required by the plan document to determine that the instructions are consistent with titles I and IV [of ERISA]."
36. See DOL Letter to Robert A. G. Monks, Institutional Shareholders Services, Inc. (Jan. 23, 1990).
37. DOL Interpretive Bulletin 08-2 (Oct. 17, 2008). See also DOL Adv. Op. Ltr. 2007-07A.
38. Socially responsible investing should be distinguished from social investing. *Social investing* has been defined as investing where the principal impetus is not to maximize investment returns to benefit plan participants or their beneficiaries, but to further some other "social" policy or goal. Social investing results in a per se violation of ERISA fiduciary duties.
39. ERISA Advisory Opinion Letter No. 98-04A (May 28, 1998), issued to the Calvert Group Ltd., dealt with investment in socially responsible funds. Citing DOL Reg. §2509.94-1 (which has been superseded by DOL Reg. §2509.08-1), DOL stated that it "has expressed the view that the fiduciary standards of sections 403 and 404 do not preclude consideration of collateral benefits, such as those offered by a 'socially-responsible' fund, in a fiduciary's evaluation of a particular investment opportunity."
40. ERISA Adv. Op. Ltr. No. 98-04A (May 28, 1998).
41. DOL Interpretive Bulletin 94-1; DOL Reg. §2509.94-1.
42. DOL Interpretive Bulletin 08-1; DOL Reg. §2509.08-1.

Chapter 39

Fixed Income Assets

Russell J. Walker

According to data compiled by the Bank for International Settlements (www.bis.org), the value of the worldwide fixed income market was nearly $90 trillion as of June 30, 2010. Of this amount, U.S. bonds comprised $31.8 trillion, while non-U.S. bonds from developed nations comprised another $46.6 trillion and emerging-market debt totaled $10.8 trillion. Clearly, fixed income assets are an investment opportunity for multiemployer benefit plans.

Why Invest in Fixed Income?

Fixed income assets are an attractive investment option because they provide a steady cash flow essential to making benefit payments to plan participants. Fixed income securities also have lower price volatility than equities (i.e., stocks). In exchange for the steady income and lower risk, however, fixed income assets also have lower potential for asset growth. Fixed income securities also help diversify a fund portfolio—a variety of assets held in an investment portfolio may yield lower total risk than the individual asset categories because each asset type behaves differently during market cycles.

What is a Fixed Income Asset?

Fixed income encompasses a broad class of investment vehicles representing money that has been borrowed and will be paid back over time. The issuing entity can be a government or quasi-governmental agency, a municipality or a corporation. The owner *(holder)* of a fixed income asset essentially loans money to the borrower *(issuer)* who promises to return the money at some future date.

The cash generated by fixed income assets consists of a combination of periodic interest payments (sometimes known as *coupon payments*) paid by the borrower and/or the repayment of the borrowed money itself (the *principal*) on the promised ending date of the loan (the *maturity date*).

The *principal amount* of the asset, also known as *par value* or *face value,* represents the amount borrowed that will be repaid by the maturity date. Bond prices are quoted in dollar amounts equaling a percent of par; for example, a bond with a face value of $100 priced at 105% of par is quoted at $105.00. Some fixed income instruments, known as *zero-coupon securities,* are purchased at less than face value and appreciate over time without paying coupons. Other instruments have coupons for which the rate moves in relation to a benchmark interest rate *(floating-rate bonds),* or for which the rate resets in fixed increments on a specific schedule *(step-rate bonds),* or a combination of fixed and floating rates *(mixed-rate bonds).*

Fixed income investments fall into two categories: *cash equivalents* and *longer term bond investments. Maturity,* the stated time the borrower has to repay a debt, is what separates these two forms of investment.

Cash Equivalents

Fixed income assets that mature in less than one year are typically considered *cash equivalents.* These liquid holdings convert to cash easily with extremely low risk. Investors accept the lower returns on these investments in exchange for the high liquidity. Cash equivalent securities typically yield a rate of return slightly higher than the current rate of inflation. Over time, cash equivalents exhibit a positive correlation with the rate of inflation; in other words, the return on cash rises and falls with inflation.

When managing a benefit trust fund, it is vital to put contributions and other cash income to work as soon as possible to achieve asset growth or to generate a steady income. On the other hand, there is a need to have some cash available for short-term needs. Cash equivalents provide easy access to money but have a small return with relatively low volatility; this return is still better than the return on money that has not been invested.

Custodial banks or trust companies normally provide a pooled common trust investment vehicle for institutional investors known as a *short-term investment fund (STIF)*. The funds of multiple investors are used to purchase short-term fixed income securities. The market value of these funds does not fluctuate with interest rates or bond market events. STIFs generally provide a monthly income at a rate reflecting current short-term interest rates. *Money market funds* offered by mutual fund companies are an additional vehicle for cash equivalents; these pooled funds are similar to STIFs and are commonly the least-risky investment option in 401(k) and other defined contribution retirement plans.

Some of the more common types of cash equivalent investment vehicles found in institutional portfolios alongside STIFs are identified below.

- **U.S. Treasury Bills** are non-interest-paying securities issued by the U.S. Treasury to finance the national debt in the short term. "T-Bills" are priced and traded at a discount to their face value until a stated maturity date. At that time, the full face value is paid to the holder.
- **Federal agency discount notes** are non-interest-paying discount bonds issued by government agencies or government-sponsored corporations for short-term financing needs. Most commonly, these notes are issued by the Federal National Mortgage Association (FNMA or Fannie Mae) to fund secondary-market mortgage operations, the Federal Home Loan Banks system to support credit operations in the savings and loan industry, and the Federal Farm Credit Banks Funding Corporation to fund ongoing credit needs.
- **Certificates of deposit**, or **CDs**, are interest-paying instruments issued by banks or thrifts and represent money on deposit. CDs are issued with specific maturity dates. They may be *nonnegotiable* (the principal cannot be withdrawn prior to the stated maturity date without penalty) or *negotiable* (the depositor may sell the CD in the open market prior to the maturity date). CDs are insured by the Federal Deposit Insurance Corporation (FDIC) up to the legal limit for deposits (currently $250,000).
- **Commercial paper** refers to short-term unsecured notes issued by corporations in the open market for short-term borrowing needs. *Unsecured* notes are backed by the full faith and credit of the issuer, but not by specific assets.
- **Repurchase agreements**, or **Repos**, are short-term collateralized loans. The issuer sells a security to the buyer with a specific commitment to buy the security back on a specific future date at a specified price. The reverse agreement, or **reverse repo**, in which a dealer agrees to buy a security with a commitment to sell it back at a future date, is a frequent tool to cover short positions in a portfolio.

Longer Term U.S. Options

Bond investments can be categorized by issuer type:

- Debt issued by the federal government and its agencies (or, in the case of non-U.S. debt, the sovereign government of the nation in question)
- Debt issued by corporations
- Debt issued by municipal governments and affiliated agencies (e.g., cities, counties, school districts, states, redevelopment agencies, and public airports and harbors)

Federal government debt, backed by the full faith and credit of the U.S. government, often acts as a safe harbor for investors in times of extreme volatility in the public equity markets. U.S. Treasury debt represents the direct borrowing of the U.S. government and receives the highest safety ratings from the various credit rating agencies that judge creditworthiness, described later in this chapter.

The U.S. Treasury began issuing inflation-protected bonds in 1997 alongside standard Treasury debt securities. The U.S. *Treasury Inflation Protected Securities (TIPS)* protect investors from inflation by offering cash payments with a constant *real rate of return*—the rate of return after the rate of inflation has been subtracted. TIPS accomplish this by periodically adjusting the bond's principal upward when there is an increase in the consumer inflation rate. The interest paid a bondholder is calculated using the increased value of the bond. This ensures the return on the bond remains the same as what was promised at purchase.

Fixed income securities issued by corporations can be issued as (1) *secured notes*, in which the property of the corporation serves as *collateral* (a guaranty) for the underlying loans, or (2) *unsecured notes* (or *debentures*) backed by the promise of the business to repay the note but not backed by any corporate property. The relative creditworthiness of the issuing company is also factored into the cost of borrowing *(return)* on the notes. *Convertible bonds* issued by corporations carry a special right to be exchanged for a specific amount of the firm's common stock, usually expressed in shares per $1,000 par value held.

Another type of high-yield fixed income security found in an increasing number of institutional portfolios is the *bank loan.* Instead of issuing bonds, many corporations are borrowing directly from banks. Bank loans are normally taken out by companies with lower credit ratings; they can be issued on a secured or unsecured basis. The lower credit quality translates into a higher interest rate. These bank loans can be bought and sold in the secondary market

Municipal debt can be categorized by what is being funded by the borrowed monies. *General obligation bonds* raise funds for the overall operation of the issuing municipality and are backed by its full faith, credit and taxing powers. *Revenue bonds* serve to fund specific projects and/or municipal agencies (toll road authorities, hospitals, transit companies, etc.) and are backed by the economic activity generated by the issuing authorities.

The majority of municipal bonds are exempt from federal income taxes. In addition, the coupons and resultant yield on municipal bonds are markedly lower than those of comparable taxable debt such as U.S. Treasury bonds under normal market conditions. For these reasons, "munis" are of little interest to tax-exempt institutional investors such as pension funds. Indeed, individual investors, commercial banks, mutual funds, and property and casualty insurance companies dominate the municipal bond market; all benefit from the tax-exempt income and capital gains on their assets. Institutional investors, however, can and do cross over into the municipal bond markets to take advantage of high yields when the opportunity comes up.

Bonds can be subdivided further by the presence or absence of a "call" or "put" option that establishes whether the principal can be paid before the bond's maturity date. Some bonds are issued with a *call option*—the issuer has the right (but not the obligation) to retire the debt, fully or partially, before the maturity date. This typically occurs when interest rates fall and the issuer wants to refinance the debt to take advantage of lower borrowing costs. Many bonds also carry *put options*—the holder has the right to sell the bonds back to the issuer at par (face value) on predefined put dates. This primarily appeals to an investor if interest rates rise and depress the bond's price. The bondholder can retire the bond at full face value to lock in a profit.

Mortgage-backed securities (MBS) make up a large portion of the U.S. bond market. These vehicles are backed by pools of consumer mortgages so their cash flows reflect the payment schedules of mortgages. On a monthly basis, the investor receives a payment based on the outstanding principal of the mortgage—a pro-rata share of the actual principal retired that month—and any prepaid principal within the mortgage pool. Mortgages can be prepaid at any time, either through the normal buying and selling of residential real estate or through loan-refinancing activities. Refinancing introduces a special type of reinvestment risk to MBS bondholders—*prepayment risk* is the chance that the mortgages will be repaid before the expected payment period and that the investor will not be able to find another investment that provides a similar return for these prepaid dollars. This risk is offset by interest rates higher than the rates against which mortgages are benchmarked (ten-year U.S. Treasury yields are a common benchmark rate) as well as guarantees of a regular cash flow payment offered by the MBS-issuing entity.

Liquid MBSs are structured and guaranteed by federal agencies such as the Government National Mortgage Association ("Ginnie Mae") as well as government-chartered corporations such as the Federal National Mortgage Association ("Fannie Mae") and the Federal Home Loan Mortgage Corporation ("Freddie Mac"). Despite the turmoil of the mortgage markets starting in 2007 and the placing of both Fannie Mae and Freddie Mac into Federal Housing Finance Agency conservatorship, these agencies still help provide vital liquidity in the home loan market through mortgage securitization.

Collateralized mortgage obligations (CMOs) are a class of fixed income instruments created from mortgage-backed securities. CMOs were a response to investor interest in the high credit quality and attractive market yields offered by MBS, but CMOs address the prepayment risk of MBSs. A CMO deal redistributes the cash flows generated by the underlying MBS into groups of varying cash flow schedules, coupons and principal repayment. The safest groups often behave like short- to intermediate-term plain-vanilla bonds; riskier ones can offer price and performance volatility on a par with speculative-grade high-yield bonds.

Commercial mortgage-backed securities (CMBS) are backed by pools of loans financing the purchase of income-producing properties such as office buildings, multifamily residences, shopping centers, industrial properties and hospitals. The credit risk associated with a CMBS depends in great part on the economic health of the underlying property; the income generated by the venture provides the cash flow to CMBS investors.

Asset-backed securities (ABS) are similar to MBS in that they are pools of consumer debt. ABS can be backed by auto loans, revolving credit accounts, home-equity loans or home-equity lines of credit. The loan payments are pooled and passed through to ABS bondholders by the issuer. The credit rating of a given ABS will depend on the issuer, the nature of the loans and the creditworthiness of the pool of borrowers.

Non-U.S. Options

Institutional investors also have many opportunities to invest in fixed income securities issued by non-U.S. organizations. Some foreign entities issue bonds designed specifically for trade in the U.S. and hence *denominated* (valued) in U.S. dollars. Currency movements do not factor into the accounting or analysis of these bonds. Their risk is comparable to U.S.-issued debt. The non-dollar-denominated global bond markets offer vast investment opportunities. Thanks to technological advances in the marketplace, issues such as currency exchange, trade settlement and asset custody need not prevent investment outside the U.S.

On the other hand, investing in bonds denominated in foreign currencies requires analysis of the interest rates in the foreign countries from which the bonds were issued *as well as* the current and future prospects of the bonds' currencies. Investment in the bonds of a market in which interest rates are falling will result in price appreciation on a local-currency basis. If the currency strengthens relative to the U.S. dollar, the increased value of the bonds will be even greater when converted to dollars. Global bond portfolio management strikes a balance between using a given market exposure as an interest-rate play and using it as a currency play.

Until recently, global bond portfolios focused primarily on the local-currency debt of nations and their agencies. However, the global credit market—the local-market corporate and other nongovernment debt securities—has rapidly developed in the last twenty years or so. Credit analysis of global corporate debt has become more readily available to investors. Global multinational corporations, including many major U.S. companies, now issue debt in multiple currencies worldwide to take advantage of borrowing opportunities wherever they occur, further expanding opportunities for fixed income investing globally.

Emerging-market debt is an important sector of the non-U.S. bond market that consists of securities issued by entities located in emerging nations. Although these countries do have active domestic bond markets, most foreign investors hold emerging-market fixed income as external debt, issued outside the country under foreign-market jurisdiction. These are high-risk securities overall, comparable to U.S. high-yield fixed income assets.

Institutional plans have historically shown a strong home-market bias toward fixed income investment. Allocation to non-U.S. dollar-denominated debt is uniformly low across plan categories and sponsor types. Much of this bias is traced to early difficulties obtaining information on these markets. In past periods, there was also resistance to investing in a market where return forecasts could not overcome currency volatility. These concerns have lessened to a large degree over time, but emerging-market debt in portfolios remains low.

What is the Return on Fixed Income Assets and How Is It Measured?

Yield is the interest or income on a fixed income investment, in other words, the investment return. Yield can be expressed in different forms:

- ***Coupon yield***—the interest rate stated on a bond
- ***Current yield***—the dollar amount of interest paid for a year divided by the current price of the bond
- ***Yield to maturity***—the estimated rate of return an investor receives if a bond is held to maturity
- ***Yield-to-call***—the interest rate received until a bond is "called" back by the lender

Bonds that have a "call" provision afford the issuer the option to retire the debt early. They are referred to as *callable bonds.*

In addition to yield, it is helpful to understand another measurement used by bond managers. *Duration* summarizes in a single number what happens to a bond's price when interest rates fall 1.00% (referred to as *100 basis points).* Duration takes into consideration the amount of the coupon, how frequently a bondholder will be paid, and the price of the bond. For example, a ten-year U.S. Treasury security with an effective duration of seven years (years being the unit of measure for duration) should see a price increase of roughly 7% if short-term rates drop 1%. Callable bonds will have shorter durations than noncallable bonds with the same stated maturity date. Floating-rate bonds will also have short durations compared to fixed-rate paper of the same maturity.

What Risks Are Associated With These Securities?

Liquidity Risk

All other things being equal, investors expect a *liquidity premium* on longer term assets. In other words, the longer money is tied up, the higher the expected return on the investment. Longer term fixed income investments typically have a higher return than short-term investments.

Interest Rate Risk

Nothing has more immediate impact on the value of a bond than changes in interest rates. The chance that changes in interest rates will adversely affect the values of securities and opportunities for reinvestment is *interest rate risk.* Among the factors that influence interest rates are:

- **Inflation**—higher prices on consumer goods and services cause interest rates to rise.
- **Federal Reserve policy**—increases in the interest rates charged to banks that borrow money and other actions that reduce the availability of credit push other interest rates up, particularly short-term rates.
- **Federal debt**—increases in U.S. government borrowing require more bonds, which causes interest rates to increase, especially rates on long-term bonds.
- **Credit supply and demand**—interest rates also rise when a lot of people want to borrow and there isn't enough money for everyone who wants a loan.

Most bond prices move in the opposite direction to interest rates. If rates rise, most bond prices fall. If rates go down, bond prices go up. In general, longer term bonds react more to changes in interest rates than shorter term bonds.

Credit Risk

Since fixed income instruments represent borrowed money, the most basic type of risk is the borrower's ability to repay the loan, referred to as *credit risk.* If a borrower fails to repay a loan, the debt passes into *default.* While serious, a default does not always result in a complete loss of the holder's investment. Distressed borrowers are frequently able to renegotiate the terms of their loans following a default event; bondholders typically assume a loss of the periodic coupon payments and/or some principal for defaulted bonds, but complete loss of the original investment is relatively uncommon.

Credit risk also factors into a bond's expected return. Investors expect a reward for the extra risk they assume. Bond investors often refer to the increase in return from holding a non-Treasury bond as its *spread.* Think of the spread as the additional interest paid compared to that of a Treasury security with the same maturity. The higher the credit risk, the higher the spread. Treasury securities are considered to have little or no credit risk because they are backed by the U.S. government.

As noted, credit quality is a key factor driving the relationship between a given bond's yield and that of Treasury securities of a similar time to maturity, known as its *yield spread.* As interest rates rise and fall, bond prices normally fall; this is accompanied by an increase in the bond's yield.

Exhibit 1

U.S. Credit Rating Companies and Their Bond Ratings

CREDIT LEVEL	Moody's	S&P	Fitch
Investment Grade			
Highest; no default risk	Aaa	AAA	AAA
Very high grade	Aa1	AA+	AA+
	Aa2	AA	AA
	Aa3	AA-	AA-
Upper medium grade	A1	A+	A+
	A2	A	A
	A3	A-	A-
Lower medium grade	Baa1	BBB+	BBB+
	Baa2	BBB	BBB
	Baa3	BBB-	BBB-
Speculative Grade			
Low grade	Ba1	BB+	BB+
	Ba2	BB	BB
	Ba3	BB-	BB-
Highly speculative	B1	B+	B+
	B2	B	B
	B3	B-	B-
Very Risky			
In poor standing	Caa	CCC+	CCC+
		CCC	CCC
Default very likely	Ca	CC	CC
Default imminent	C	C	C
Income bond, not paying interest			CI
In Default			
	D	D	DDD
			DD
			D
No Rating Assigned	NR	NR	NR

Yield spreads can indicate investment opportunities as well as highlight pricing pressure on portfolio holdings.

Individual debt securities as well as the entities issuing fixed income securities are assigned a *credit rating* that indicates their credit risk. There are three nationally recognized companies that provide credit ratings in the United States: Moody's Investors Service, Standard & Poor's Corporation (S&P), and Fitch Ratings. Exhibit 1 shows bond ratings from highest to lowest. While there are slight variations among the three rating organizations, an "A" rating generally indicates minimal risk while those with a "C" are very risky.

Trust fund and other institutional investors typically make a clear distinction in asset allocation between *investment-grade bonds* and *speculative-grade holdings* (including "very risky" and "in default" instruments). Speculative-grade holdings are also known as *high-yield fixed income bonds* or *junk bonds*. An issuer whose bond receives a speculative grade has a much higher borrowing cost than a comparable investment-grade issuer does. The market factors the higher debt-servicing costs on speculative-grade bonds into increased price volatility, which in lower quality issuance can have price volatility similar to equities. To control the risk, fund investment guidelines normally establish a maximum that can be invested in these high-yield securities, either a percentage of fixed income assets or total plan assets. Individual investment managers of a fund may also be given limits on the credit quality within which they are allowed to select holdings; for example, no bonds below Caa may be purchased, or no non-rated bonds may be purchased.

The importance of credit risk extends beyond bonds to mortgage-backed securities, asset-backed securities and other structured debt products. Historically, structured debt products have been considered low-risk investments because they pool debts: The default of any one borrower in these securities does not have the same impact as when a bond is issued by just one borrower. Recent events, however, have changed thinking on how safe these products are.

Today, a clear distinction must be drawn between structured debt containing *prime debt* (high-quality consumer loans) and that consisting of *subprime debt* (lower quality consumer loans). Subprime debt has a much higher default rate than prime debt.

The bursting of the U.S. real estate market bubble that began in the latter half of the 2000s decade has led to increased consumer loan delinquencies and defaults; this has put considerable price pressure on structured debt products and resulted in periods of sharply higher yields for these instruments. Credit risk analysis in this sector is more important than ever.

What Strategies Are Appropriate for Managing Fixed Income Securities?

There are several approaches to the management of fixed income portfolios. A few key strategies are described here.

Indexation

Fixed income assets can be managed on an indexed basis. The indexed portfolio matches the investment and risk characteristics of a predefined market index such as Barclays U.S. Aggregate Index**.** Index funds are a low-cost way to invest in a given asset class, especially in *efficient markets* such as U.S. large-company public equity or investment-grade U.S. fixed income. In efficient markets, investors have equal, essentially open access to the exchanges where the assets are traded, as well as equal access to all information used to price the assets. In these markets, opportunities to achieve returns in excess of the broad market itself are limited, making indexing the most cost-effective means of investing the assets. The investor is not seeking return greater than the benchmark. Instead, the goal is to *track* (match) the benchmark. See Chapter 37, Exhibit 4 for a chart showing some commonly used indexes.

Active Management

An actively managed fixed income portfolio tries to exceed the returns of a benchmark or index. Naturally, to achieve returns greater than a given benchmark, the manager must assume greater risk. Active managers may favor bottom-up investment decisions, or security selection, within their investable universe. Security selection involves the analysis and trading of individual bonds; investors may seek out unique opportunities for high long-term yield or short-term gains in instruments that seem to be mispriced in the market. Alternatively, managers may utilize *top-down portfolio construction* techniques, focusing on individual risk factors such as duration or economic sector exposure management to derive incremental return. If the manager feels that a given risk factor will markedly outperform or underperform other risk factors, he or she can increase or decrease the exposure to that factor relative to the benchmark. For example, if long-duration bonds are expected to be the strongest performers, a top-down manager will increase the total duration of his or her portfolio to take advantage of that expectation. Many managers utilize some combination of top-down and bottom-up approaches. There are many types of approaches to investment and management of the fixed income portfolio, some of which are:

- **Core management.** These portfolios seek to outperform a benchmark representing the broad investment-grade bond market. There is diversification across market sectors and credit qualities as found in the benchmark. The assets are often expected to have benchmarklike duration. They are sometimes supplemented by permissible *derivative securities* (securities whose price movements are derived from those of other securities or economic indicators such as inflation or U.S. stock volatility).

- **Core-plus management.** These portfolios tactically invest in asset classes that lie outside an investment-grade market benchmark, while maintaining an overall structure similar to the benchmark. Such assets can include non-U.S. dollar bonds, emerging-market debt and high-yield fixed income securities.
- **Investment-grade corporate fixed income strategies.** These portfolios have a concentration in non-government debt, focusing on the paper of high-credit quality corporations. In periods of low Treasury yields, these strategies become popular because they offer higher overall portfolio yield than the core, core-plus or government paper strategies.
- **High-yield corporate fixed income strategies.** These portfolios primarily invest in speculative-grade corporate fixed income securities. Interest rate risk factors tend to be secondary to credit risk as drivers of performance in high-yield bond portfolios. Bottom-up security selection is a more common investment process in high-yield portfolio management, with credit analysis assuming a key role in uncovering investment opportunities and managing risk.

Regardless of investment style, a fixed income manager should be able to articulate clearly the investment philosophy and process underlying portfolio construction and maintenance. He or she should be able to detail the sources of portfolio risk and return, be they top-down market factors such as duration, bond quality or sector exposure, or bottom-up security selection via credit analysis and comparisons, and to quantify incremental return earned against the market benchmark.

Portfolio Immunization and Dedication

It is possible to use fixed income securities to either match the duration, that is, the interest rate risk, of the pension benefit liability *(immunization)* or to match the cash flows of the fund obligations themselves *(dedication)*. Careful coordination between the plan's actuary, fixed income investment manager and trustees is required to understand and assess the appropriateness of these techniques.

Portfolio immunization involves the analysis of the projected schedule of a pension plan's benefit payments (the projected plan liability) as if the plan were a bond. The duration (interest rate sensitivity) of the plan's liability is calculated, and then fixed income assets are selected and structured so that the portfolio's duration matches the liability's duration, thereby reducing the asset pool's interest rate risk compared to that of the liability. A fund can immunize a fixed income program by combining bonds with derivative securities (briefly defined above)) to extend the overall duration of the total portfolio; in this situation one frequently employs instruments such as futures contracts and interest rate swaps. Plan sponsors may choose to immunize their fixed income program by allocating individual asset assignments to long-duration strategies; the aggregate duration of the individual portfolios can be extended to match the duration of the plan liability. Alternatively, a derivatives overlay approach may be used, in which a separate portfolio of derivative securities is maintained against the entire fixed income program in order to extend the duration of the aggregated assets. Immunization focuses on minimizing or eliminating any interest rate volatility mismatch between the plan's assets and projected liability. Many fixed income management firms currently offer *liability-directed investment* (LDI) strategies that utilize immunization principles and techniques to *defease* (offset) long-term plan liabilities.

The second approach, portfolio dedication, matches fixed income investments to the projected cash flows of a pension plan. Credit risk and overall interest rate risk are less important than matching the plan's cash flow. A dedicated bond portfolio is constructed most efficiently via a pool of zero-coupon Treasury securities with *laddered* maturity dates (i.e., bonds maturing at regular intervals, typically annually or up to every three months) approximately matching the cash stream schedule of the liability or spending policy.

Chapter 40

Investing in Public Equity

Terry A. Dennison

When a plan invests in the stock of a company, it is buying part of the company. Each equity share a plan holds represents one unit of ownership in a company. Most publicly traded companies issue hundreds of millions of shares. The value of each share can be a few dollars or hundreds of dollars. For an investment portfolio, equities offer higher potential return but carry higher risk than bonds.

What Are the Returns for Investing in Equities?

When a plan invests in equities, there are two types of returns: dividends and capital appreciation. *Dividends* represent a portion of a company's profit and are usually paid quarterly. To attract investors to their stocks, companies often try to maintain or increase dividend payments over time. Keep in mind, however, that the payment of dividends is optional, and a company may decide to reduce or even stop paying dividends during difficult economic times. The relationship between the dividends paid by a corporation in one year and the corporation's stock price is called *yield.*

Corporate profits not paid as dividends are *retained earnings.* This money is reinvested in the business to support further growth. It is not unusual for a rapidly growing company to retain all or nearly all of its profits. A more mature company is more likely to pay out a larger portion of earnings as dividends.

Capital appreciation, the second source of shareholder return, is the increase in the dollar value of a company. When you see a stock price going up, you are seeing capital appreciation. The increase in price reflects earnings that may result in bigger dividends and/or company growth. A higher stock price may also indicate investors are willing to pay more per share because they believe the current price does not fully reflect the future growth potential of the company. Since perceptions of a company's future vary among investors and across time, returns from capital appreciation are more uncertain and variable than returns from dividends. Of course, equity capital can also decrease in value.

Are There Different Types of Equities?

Equities can be categorized as common stock or preferred stock. Investors who own shares of *common stock* are usually given the right to vote on important company issues. Typically, *stockholders* (share owners) vote once a year on issues submitted by the management of the company. This voting process is via *proxy*—a legal document that shareholders use authorizing a specific vote on their behalf at a corporate meeting. If a fund owns individual stocks, it should have a proxy voting process as part of its investment policy statement. For more on proxies and these statements, read Chapters 38 and 47.

In addition to common stock, there is *preferred stock*—a hybrid between bonds and common stock. Preferred stock pays a dividend like common stock but the dividend is a fixed dollar amount per share. Preferred stock dividends are paid only after company debt (e.g., bonds, loans) has been paid. Likewise, common stock dividends cannot be paid unless all preferred stock dividends have been paid. Some preferred stocks, called *convertible preferred stocks,* can be converted to a fixed number of common stock shares if the shareholder opts to do so.

Equities, particularly common stocks, can be bought

for companies around the world. Stocks of companies based in other nations are often priced in the currency of the other country, not U.S. dollars. An *American depositary receipt (ADR)* allows a U.S. investor to purchase the stock of these non-U.S. companies in U.S. dollars on U.S. markets *(exchanges)*. Each ADR represents a set number of foreign shares held by a trustee bank in the United States that issued the ADR. Use of the ADR and the related *global depositary receipt (GDR)* make it possible for U.S. investors to purchase foreign equities free of concerns for sending stock certificates back and forth to other countries, as well as dealing with foreign currencies.

There are many different types of common stocks and multiple ways of classifying them.

Size

One important way to classify stocks is by *market capitalization* or *"market cap,"* which refers to the total market value of a company's stock owned by shareholders. Market capitalization is the *size* of a corporation. Below are approximate market cap classifications:

Mega-Cap	Above $50 billion
Large-Cap	Between $10 billion and $50 billion
Mid-Cap	Between $2 billion and $10 billion
Small-Cap	Between $500 million and $2 billion
Micro-Cap	Less than $500 million.

Mega- and large-cap stocks represent the largest and most established corporations; the size of these companies makes it unlikely they will grow rapidly. The advantage of these larger caps is that they can weather difficult economic times.

Small- and micro-cap companies are typically younger and are capable of growing more rapidly. However, there is a trade-off; smaller caps are more fragile and likely to suffer in tough economic times. Many of the smallest micro-cap stocks are so small that they may not be appropriate for a fund portfolio. These stocks may only have market capitalizations in the several hundred thousand dollar range.

Between the large- and small-cap stocks are the mid-caps that have some characteristics of each of the other cap sizes. They have the greater stability of large-caps and some of the growth potential of small-caps.

Investment products such as mutual funds and exchange-traded funds (ETFs) are available offering a variety of stocks that are just one cap size. Other products offer stocks that span several caps. Examples are a mid- and small-cap vehicle called a *SMID product* and an *all-cap product* that includes a broader range (but generally not micro-caps).

Exhibit 1

Stock Valuation

Valuation is critical to investment management decisions. Often market valuations rise to unreasonably high levels that cannot be justified by any likely level of future growth. These situations are often called *bubbles*. An example is the "dot com" bubble in the late 1990s.

- *Price/earnings (P/E)*—share price relative to a stock's earnings
- *Price/sales (P/S)*—share price relative to company revenue (sales)
- *Price/book value (P/B)*—the share price relative to the company's assets minus its liabilities
- *Cash flow per share*—the company's cash on the balance sheet per share rather than earnings per share
- *Growth in cash flow per share*—growth in cash value per share indicates a company's revenue (sales) is being translated to cash on the balance sheet.

Valuation

Valuation is a measure of a stock's "value" in terms of its dollar price per dollar of earnings rather than its dollar price per share. This relationship is the *price/earnings ratio (P/E)*—sometimes called a "P/E multiple" or just "multiple."

$$\text{Price/earnings ratio} = \frac{\text{Price per share}}{\text{Earnings per share}}$$

Price per share is the current market price of one share of a company's stock. *Earnings per share* refers to a stock's current or estimated future earnings per share. A company stock with earnings of $5/share that is selling for $50/share (P/E = $50/$5 = 10×) has a PE valuation less than a stock with earnings of $1/share that is selling for $20/share (P/E = $20/$1 = 20×). The price/earnings ratios make it possible for investors to compare the cost of a dollar of earnings between two stocks with different prices. Generally, the market is willing to pay a higher multiple or P/E ratio for companies with rapidly growing earnings per share.

Exhibit 1 provides a brief summary of other methods used to assess stock valuation in addition to the P/E ratio.

Style

Stocks fit on a continuum with value stocks on one side and growth stocks on the other. While one group of investment managers invests in value stocks, another focuses on growth stocks. Both types of managers believe their way is the "right" way to invest.

Managers who invest in growth stocks are willing to pay higher P/Es because they believe earnings are likely to grow rapidly. With increased earnings reflected by the P/E, the company has money to invest to create new products, enhance efficiency and seek new markets. Growth companies also have a glamour factor—they often lead in technology or social trends. Be aware, however, that growth stocks can also be a disappointment; the projected earnings may not occur. The result will be a drop in both a stock's price and P/E ratio.

The earnings of *value stocks* may not be growing as fast as growth stocks, but they are inexpensive in terms of the P/E ratio. Value stocks are typically older, slow-growing but profitable companies in unglamorous businesses. They often pay a sizable dividend. The argument for value is that if you pay a cheap price for a stream of earnings, only a little improvement may yield a significant increase in the stock's market price.

It is important to understand that any one stock can move from growth to value or the reverse along the style continuum depending on events and circumstances. A product failure can derail a growth stock and push it into the value category, while new management can raise expectations that it will begin to grow more rapidly.

Most investment products are size- and style-specific, but some contain a range of sizes and styles. Most invest-

Exhibit 2

Types of Stocks

"Blue Chips"—stocks of well-known, established companies with a strong financial position.

Core—stocks in the middle zone between value and growth.

Cyclical Stocks—stocks of companies that are very sensitive to the business cycle. They do well when the economy is doing well. But when there is an economic decline, they also tend to decline.

Deep Value—extremely cheap stocks (very low P/E). Often a very distressed company for which any sign of a turnaround will be rewarded.

Defensive—stocks of companies that do well in difficult economic times.

Growth—stocks of companies that are rapidly growing, often benefitting from new technologies or trends that the market believes will be more valuable in the future. The expected returns from growth stocks are primarily from capital appreciation with little or no return from dividends. Growth stocks generally deliver their greatest appreciation in periods of rising markets where the market psychology is positive.

Growth at a Reasonable Price—stocks with slightly elevated P/E ratios with good but not spectacular growth prospects.

Income—stocks that pay high dividends are often mature companies that have limited growth potential, such as utilities. Income stocks tend to be less volatile as they provide a dividend return in addition to any price appreciation.

Interest-Rate Sensitive—stocks of companies whose profits are strongly impacted by changes in the level of interest rates. For example, financial services stocks such as banks tend to do better in periods of rising interest rates since they can raise the interest rates they charge borrowers faster than the rates they pay depositors. On the other hand, homebuilders are negatively impacted by rising interest rates because it is more difficult for people to purchase and finance a home.

Momentum—selecting stocks that have recently seen their prices rise. While prices may continue to rise further, they may increase beyond a reasonable valuation and later adjust downward.

Relative Value—stocks cheaper than the market or cheaper than competitors in the same sector or industry.

Traditional Growth—rapidly growing stocks with the potential to increase their growth rate to more than what the P/E would indicate.

Traditional Value—cheap stocks in out-of-favor industries. In addition, companies whose earnings fall short of analyst expectations or that suffer modest misfortune.

ment teams specialize in either growth or value because they strongly believe their way is the right way to invest. Many substyles exist on the growth-value continuum; many stock types in Exhibit 2 are examples of these substyles.

Geography

Another way of classifying equities is geographic. From the perspective of the investor there is often considered to be a home market and a nonhome market. For an investor in the U.S, these markets would be U.S. equities and non-U.S equities. There are also groupings of nations such as nations in western Europe or Asia, mature countries except for the U.S., and emerging markets. *Emerging markets* include companies based in nations with social and business activity that are in the process of rapid growth and industrialization.

Investing outside the U.S. is very common today. Many investors consider non-U.S. equities to (1) enhance returns and (2) reduce risk through diversification. Equity returns are influenced by a nation's economic health including its economic growth. When the U.S. economy slows down or goes into a recession, it has a negative impact on corporate profits and, as a result, on equity returns. When the U.S. economy is doing well, stocks tend to do better in terms of return. Holding equities from other nations where market conditions are different from those in the United States helps reduce the total volatility of a plan's investment portfolio. Many businesses outside the United States, particularly those in the developing world, also have more potential for growth and higher returns than those in the mature U.S. economy.

When investing in securities that are priced in currencies other than the U.S. dollar, there is a currency risk—a chance that the value of another nation's money will negatively affect the value of the investment. This risk must be considered when making an investment decision. There are currency-hedging strategies that investment advisors can recommend that can reduce or eliminate the impact of currency on investment return.

The emerging trend among investors is to view investments more globally rather than home/nonhome markets or even regional markets. As the business has globalized, it is increasingly difficult to differentiate clearly between U.S. and non-U.S. companies. A significant portion of a typical U.S. company's revenue and profits come from outside the United States. Many U.S. companies have operations around the world that serve a global customer base.

Sector

Sectors are specific industries, such as technology, health, communications, finance, natural resources, utilities and energy. Investment managers typically allocate stocks to most if not all sectors. It is important to recognize that stocks in a sector have a tendency to move together since the same factors that affect the industry (e.g., interest rates, regulations and global competition) will affect all companies in that industry. Examples of sectors where stocks tend to move together are:

- Technology—driven by innovation and cultural trends
- Health care—impacted by regulation and population trends
- Energy—driven by cost and availability of energy, particularly oil
- Materials—driven by economic activity, particularly by demands of rapidly industrializing economies.

Managers may put a larger proportion of assets in specific sectors to take advantage of current trends, but an overconcentration in any one sector creates additional portfolio volatility.

What Options Does a Plan Have When Investing in Equities?

While most equities are simply common stock, there are many ways to invest in these equities. Choices have evolved to provide investor convenience or economic advantages; each has its pluses and minuses. (An) investment manager(s) can generally select whichever vehicle(s) best address(es) plan needs and policy objectives.

Mutual Funds

Mutual funds are portfolios of securities offered by many investment management firms. For a low initial investment, almost any investor can buy shares. Mutual fund fees can be a relatively high, fixed percentage of a fund's assets. Large investors such as benefit plans, however, are often able to invest for a lower fee than individuals. The investment objectives and guidelines of a mutual fund are contained in a prospectus and apply to all investments. The mutual fund's *net asset value (NAV)* reflects the market price of all assets held by the mutual fund. It is calculated daily and serves as the price for buying and selling shares for that particular day. To protect investors, the U.S. Securities and Exchange Commission (SEC) tightly regulates mutual funds. For more information on mutual funds, including their advantages and disadvantages, read Chapter 37.

Commingled Funds

Similar to mutual funds, commingled funds are also collective investment vehicles with multiple investor owners.

Assets of a commingled fund are held by a trust company with the value of units calculated daily. These funds can be restricted to tax-exempt employee benefit funds. Some are further restricted to ERISA-qualified plans. Minimum investments are often $1 million or more. Generally, fees for commingled funds are lower than for mutual funds. The investment objectives and guidelines are available in an *offering memorandum* and apply to all investors. While efforts are made to reduce the impact, a large transaction by another investor may negatively affect an investment. Regulation is much lighter than for mutual funds and generally is the responsibility of banking regulators. More information on commingled funds is provided in Chapter 37.

Separate Accounts

Separate accounts are "accounts" with assets owned by only one investor. The assets are managed according to the investment objectives and guidelines negotiated between the investor and the investment manager. Fees are negotiated and depend on the size of the assets in the *pool* (the account). Minimum investment requirements for this type of account can be significant. The SEC, however, regulates the investment manager.

Exchange-Traded Funds (ETFs)

ETFs have grown rapidly in the past several years. ETFs began as low-cost substitutes for index mutual funds but there are now around 1,000 ETFs available with active, passive and other investment management strategies. (ETFs trade like stocks and are, in fact, a basket of stocks.) They trade throughout the day but, unlike mutual funds and commingled funds, the prices change continuously. How an ETF is regulated depends on its legal structure. The manager or bank sponsor is usually regulated by the SEC and/or banking regulators.

How Is the Performance of Equities Measured?

When evaluating the performance of an equity (or any other portfolio of assets), a "yard stick" is required for comparison. The yard stick is a *benchmark* that represents the performance of the investment asset(s). The benchmark is usually a market index matching the specific type of assets and management style.

A *market index* is a measure developed to track the performance of a specific segment of the equity market. Often the index consists of all or most of the stocks in that segment. The number of stock shares in the index is usually weighted by market capitalization; the largest stocks have the highest weights in the index while smaller stocks have less weight. An example of a market index is the Standard and Poor's (S&P) 500 Stock Index, which is a capitalization-weighted index of the 500 largest stocks in the U.S. market. There are indexes for virtually every major size and style category as well as U.S. and non-U.S. markets. Market indexes are used as benchmarks for assessing the performance of investment managers as well as the assets in a plan's portfolio.

What Does It Mean to Have an Active or Passive Fund?

Passive Funds

An investment portfolio can be constructed to match the performance of a market index—these portfolios are referred to as *index* (or *passive*) *funds.* An index fund usually holds every security in the market index with index weights. Index funds can provide the performance of market index at a very low cost. The reason index funds are also referred to as *passive funds* is because there is not a lot of buying and selling of fund assets. Changes in holdings tend to be long term and automatic based on changes in the index.

Active Funds

In contrast to an index fund, an *active fund* uses a variety of techniques and strategies that typically requires more frequent market trading. Investment managers try to outperform the return on a market index. Of course, higher expected returns have higher levels of expected risk. More return than the market with the same or less market risk is even better. Unfortunately, it is very unlikely that any investment strategy can consistently do this. More information on active and passive management, including a chart of some of the most popular market indexes is located in Chapter 37.

Among active managers, there are a number of different investment approaches. Most managers invest based on one of two general philosophies: (1) fundamental or (2) quantitative. Some managers combine elements of both of these approaches.

Fundamental managers do intensive analysis of a company, its competitors and its business prospects. They frequently build detailed forecasts on the financial aspects of the company. They interview company management. They attempt, within the limits of disclosure rules, to assess the company's future business and financial prospects. They are looking for sources of value in the company that others have not found. Fundamental investment managers try to take advantage of forecasts. Delving as deeply as they do into companies and developing personal relationships with company management can result in a manager "falling in love with their stocks" and refusing to recognize they made a mistake.

Quantitative managers generally do not do company-level research. Instead, they thoroughly research financial and market information to identify factors or patterns that have been profitable in the past. Quantitative managers often build models that guide their investment decisions. While quantitative managers are seemingly immune to some of the emotional issues of fundamental managers, they can miss signals that a company analyst would readily see but are not visible in the financial statements.

How Is an Equity Portfolio Built?

There are three key approaches to choosing equities for a portfolio: (1) style (growth vs. value), (2) size (large-, mid- and small-cap) and (3) fundamental vs. quantitative analysis. When the equity market moves—sometimes rapidly through its cycles—any one of these three approaches to investing may suddenly be in favor. There are also periods where one approach seems to be in favor for a very long time.

Just as it is a good idea to diversify the stocks in a plan portfolio, it is also wise to diversify in terms of style, size and approach or strategy. At any given time, some investment managers will be doing well while others are underperforming. A mix of approaches forces investors to give up the circumstances when one choice does extremely well but avoids the occasions when the same choice does very badly.

What Do Investment Managers Mean When They Talk About Alpha and Beta?

Alpha is the difference between the risk-adjusted return from a stock (or portfolio of stocks) and a market index used as an investment benchmark. Alpha is the true measure of value added (or lost) from active management, hence it is also called the *active return*. Frequently, the risk adjustment is ignored and alpha is considered simply the difference in return.

Beta refers to the return on a stock (or portfolio of stocks) that can be attributed to the return of the market. If a portfolio has a historic beta of 1.5 and the market is up 10%, the expected beta return of the portfolio is 15%. The difference between the beta return and the portfolio's actual return is alpha—the return that can be attributed to the manager.

When considering the contribution of an active manager, it is important to compare these two returns. For example, if the market is up 20% and the fund portfolio is up 18%, the active manager provided a return that is 2% less than what would have been earned using a market index fund. In contrast, if the market index is down 10% and the fund portfolio's value is down just 7%, the manager enhanced the fund's stock performance 3% by losing less value.

Beta has a more common use to assess how much an individual stock's price will change given a change in a market index. Let's say a stock has a beta of 1.0. For every change in the market, the stock moves the same percentage amount. If the market is up 5%, the stock will also be up about 5%. If the market is down 10%, the stock will be down around 10%.

A beta greater than 1.0 indicates that the stock will move greater than the market moves, both up and down. If a stock has a beta of 1.5 and the market is up 10%, the stock will be up around 15%. A beta of less than 1.0 indicates that the stock will move less than the market moves, both up and down. If a stock has a beta of 0.8 and the market is down 20%, the stock will be down about 16%.

Conclusion

Being an effective trustee concerning investment matters requires study and knowledge of terms. Concerning equities, this chapter will significantly improve a trustee's knowledge and command of terms.

Chapter 41

Real Estate Investments

Scott Krouse, Dan Krivinskas, Roman Nemtsov and Mark Bartmann

Over the last several decades, real estate investment has become a widely accepted investment for employee benefit plans and other institutional investors, taking its place beside stocks, bonds and cash. The real estate market is vast, with the size of the global commercial real estate market alone totaling $23.9 trillion in 2010.[1] Given the size and diversity of the market, opportunities exist for investors to target specific types of real estate such as hotels; office buildings; industrial warehouses; apartment buildings; and undeveloped land, timber and agricultural properties. Investment in real estate can also be concentrated in specific geographic regions. Approaches to real estate investing range from the direct purchase of individual properties to private commingled real estate funds made up of a number of individual properties to publicly traded real estate investment trusts (REITs) that can be comprised of hundreds of properties.

Investment in real estate produces returns in two ways: (1) income and (2) appreciation. The majority of the return from real estate comes from *income*—cash flow produced by the property. This income is primarily rent from tenants using the property or money earned from agricultural products grown on the property. *Appreciation* is the increase in the value of real estate over time due to higher demand for the property, inflation or income growth.

Why Is Real Estate an Attractive Investment?

Real estate has certain characteristics that make it an attractive asset to hold in a diversified investment portfolio.

Scarcity

Real estate is tangible; it consists of land, wood, metal, bricks and mortar. For this reason, there is a limited supply available to meet the demand of those who wish to purchase it. Real estate also cannot be created as easily as many financial assets (e.g., U.S. dollars) that are—at least in theory—available in an unlimited supply.

Low Correlation

Real estate typically has a *low correlation* to traditional asset classes such as stocks: Real estate tends to "zig" when other assets "zag," which helps smooth out the returns for a diversified portfolio. This low correlation is beneficial when an investor is trying to avoid return volatility. In a diversified portfolio, it helps investors achieve a higher overall risk-adjusted return.

Inflationary Hedge

Real estate also acts as an *inflationary hedge* within a portfolio. Leases expire and are renewed regularly over time at prevailing market prices so rent increases typically track inflation. In contrast, most fixed income investments (e.g., bonds) pay a preset coupon payment until maturity, which leaves bond income vulnerable to a decline in real return over time due to increases in inflation.

Liability Matching

By its nature, real estate is a long-term investment. Real estate is relatively *illiquid;* its sale takes more time to sell than stocks and bonds. Unlike the sale of these traditional asset classes, the sale of real estate also involves high transaction costs. As a result, real estate functions extremely well in an employee benefit plan where it can match a plan's long-term liabilities.

What Mechanisms Are Available for Investing in Real Estate?

Real estate investments typically fit into two broad categories: public and private. Generally, *public real estate* is property that is relatively easy to buy and sell on an exchange, much like stocks are bought and sold on a stock exchange and bonds are bought and sold in a bond market. *Private real estate* does not have a central exchange where buyers are ready to purchase property at any given time.

Private Real Estate

There are many ways to invest in private real estate; these options include:

- ***Direct investment*** involves the purchase of a specific property. It might be an office building, a shopping center, an apartment building, a commercial warehouse or a hotel. With direct investments, the investor holds a title of ownership for the property. This form of ownership is not the preferred method for an institutional investor because it is less liquid than most other real estate investment options and it offers little asset diversification for an investment portfolio. Since the investor owns and controls the property, the investor has operational, management, insurance and liability concerns. Anyone who has ever owned a home is familiar with the private real estate market and direct investment in real estate. Institutional investors invest in properties that are larger and usually more costly.
- ***Commingled funds*** pool money from several investors into funds that invest in multiple real estate properties. These funds can be diversified or focus on a particular type of property (e.g., office) or geography (e.g., Southeast United States). Commingled funds vary in the terms and length of their investment commitments. For instance, *open-ended funds* offer an investor the ability to request and get back investment funds, typically within 90-120 days. If real estate property is not selling well, the waiting period may be longer, sometimes much longer, with investors waiting in line (a *queue*) to exit the fund. *Closed-ended funds* require investors to commit capital for long periods (typically seven to ten years) without the ability to redeem capital. (Chapter 37 provides more information on commingled funds.)
- ***Separate accounts*** are a hybrid of direct investment and commingled fund approaches. They are typically best suited for large investors with significant real estate holdings ($500 million or more).

Public Real Estate

Public real estate is primarily REITs and REOCs:

- ***Real estate investment trusts (REITs)*** pool funds to purchase and manage real estate assets and/or mortgage loans. Shares of public REITs sell on major exchanges much like stocks on a stock exchange. Investments can be made directly in a REIT or through a mutual fund that specializes in REITs. Earnings from a REIT are distributed proportionately to owners of the REIT. The emphasis is on providing owners a cash flow.
- ***Real estate operating companies (REOCs)*** are similar to REITS in that they pool funds and invest in real estate that has shares trading on an exchange. While a REIT distributes earnings to its owners, a REOC reinvests its earnings emphasizing appreciation versus income. REOCs are more flexible than REITs in terms of what types of real estate investments they can make. An operating company is a REOC if—
  - At least 50% of its assets (valued at cost) are invested in real estate that is managed or developed.
  - The company has the right to substantially participate directly in the management or development of the eligible real estate.
  - The entity engages directly in real estate management or development.[2]

* * *

Not all REOCs and REITs are public. For example, some commingled funds are structured as private REITs that do not trade on an exchange. There also some large global real estate companies (particularly developers) set up as *nonpublic REOCs* taxed at the corporate level. These REOCs are not forced to distribute all of their income like public REOCs. The investor owns a real estate-related corporation, but not necessarily assets such as office buildings, hotels or apartments.

What Risks Are Associated With Investments in Real Estate?

As with any asset class, investments in real estate present certain risks for plan fiduciaries that should be closely analyzed and monitored to minimize risk. Different real estate assets have different types and levels of risk.

Liquidity

Assets vary greatly in their *liquidity,* in other words, how quickly and easily they can be sold without a significant loss in value. When compared to other assets, real estate is relatively illiquid with high liquidity risk. The lack of a central market means the owner of private real estate may have to wait a long time for a buyer who is willing and able to buy. Many homeowners have become all too familiar with this difficulty when the housing bubble burst in 2008. Plan trustees should only commit *capital* (dollars) to real estate investments that can be "locked up" for an extended period. For most commingled real estate fund investments, capital is "locked up" for a period of six to ten years.

Though public real estate shares are traded daily on an exchange, they still have a liquidity risk. Private real estate shares are subject to rapid fluctuations in value. There is no guarantee a favorable price will be available when shares must be sold.

Lack of Standardization

Unlike a stock representing a share of ownership in a company, or a bond representing debt paid back with interest, each real estate asset is unique. Each property is in a different location. Buildings have different sizes, designs, building materials and contractors. Substantial differences exist in age. Some buildings are subjected to more wear and tear than others are. Management and maintenance from one property to another also varies. The result of this lack of standardization is that real estate values vary considerably. With real estate investments, it is essential that trustees (1) gather this information for the properties under consideration and analyze how these factors impact the properties' values, or (2) use external managers who possess this knowledge and will act in the best interests of the benefit plan. This is particularly the case for direct investments.

Geographic and Political Risk

Like many assets, supply and demand affect the value of real estate. Imbalances in supply and demand can occur in geographic areas due to economic conditions or demographic shifts. Consider Detroit, where the loss of manufacturing jobs between 2005 and 2010 led to a population loss and significant declines in overall real estate values; whereas an increase in public sector jobs drove real estate prices up in the Washington, DC area. With such local variances, it is imperative to consider geography. It may be appropriate to avoid investing in markets likely to decline in the future. At minimum, investments in real estate should be well diversified with respect to location.

When investing in real estate internationally, attention must be given to property rights and private ownership, which can vary widely from one country to another. Stories have been heard of governments (e.g., China) telling foreign real estate investors that parcels of property that they thought they had purchased do not belong to them: The investors are given a different piece of land to carry out development. Additionally, certain nations (e.g., Venezuela, Cuba) have at times nationalized all private property, essentially wiping out the entire value of an investment. Foreign real estate investment should be undertaken only with local expertise and the ability to navigate local politics.

Cash Flow Risk

Different types of real estate investments offer varying levels of current cash flow. For example, the investment return on raw unimproved land comes solely from price appreciation or the potential to develop the land into an income-producing asset in the future. Other real estate investments, such as fully leased office buildings, provide a much larger amount of current income. The more the overall investment return potential is weighted toward price appreciation versus current cash flow, the greater the risk tends to be.

Which Real Estate Investments Have the Most Risk?

Institutional investors classify real estate into three broad categories reflecting the level of risk: core, value-added and opportunistic as detailed in Exhibit 1.

- ***Core real estate*** is primarily existing office, retail, residential, industrial and hotel properties that are fully leased. This category generally has lower price volatility and lower likely overall return potential; return is more likely to be in the form of income versus price appreciation.
- ***Value-added real estate*** includes the same properties plus some additions such as self-storage facilities. Buildings associated with these properties tend to be a somewhat lower quality. Redevelopment, releasing or reposition of the properties is required to maximize investment return relative to risk. Value-added real estate has moderate levels of price volatility with both income and appreciation components in its overall expected return.
- ***Opportunistic real estate*** crosses all types of property including niche sectors such as health care facilities and senior housing. These properties are those most likely to have lower quality buildings that require extensive redevelopment or land needing development. They have the greatest fluctuations in price but the most return potential. Return is primarily (although not exclusively) price appreciation.

Exhibit 1

Relative Real Estate Investment Risk and Return

	Core	Value-Added	Opportunistic
Property Types	Primarily the five major property types (office, retail, residential, industrial and hotel)	Five major property types plus some selective additional property types (e.g., self-storage)	All property types include niche sectors (e.g., health care facilities, senior housing)
Property Class	Class A	Typically lower quality buildings, but can be converted to Class A	Typically lower quality buildings, but can be converted to Class A. Sometimes ground-up development
Life Cycle	Existing, fully leased and stabilized	Existing, but requires redevelopment, releasing and/or repositioning	Development and/or existing properties that require extensive redevelopment, releasing
Fund Structure	Typically open ended	Both open ended and close ended	Typically closed ended
Holding Period	Buy and hold	Three to seven years depending on the position of the current market cycle	Implement strategy and sell
Markets	Typically primary markets	Both primary and secondary markets	Primary/secondary markets and domestic/international
Income and Appreciation	Greater than 75% of return is income.	Contains both income and appreciation components	Mostly appreciation
Leverage	Up to 40% loan-to-value (LTV)	Up to 65% LTV	Often greater than 65% LTV
Diversification	Fully diversified	Limited diversification	Diversification often not a high consideration in the investment process
Liquidity	Relatively high (subject to potential entry and redemption queues)	Moderate to low depending on structure	Low
Fee Structure	Based on assets under management plus some sort of incentive fee	Based on committed capital, plus incentive fee. May include other fees (e.g., acquisition, disposition)	Based on committed capital, plus incentive fee. May include other fees (e.g., acquisition, disposition)

As with other investment options, real estate choices with higher risk also have the potential for higher return. Exhibit 2 shows how core real estate investments that have less risk also yield a lower return relative to the other two categories. At the other extreme with the most risk and potential for the greatest return are opportunistic investments. Value-added properties fall in between.

Exhibit 2

Real Estate Investment Categories

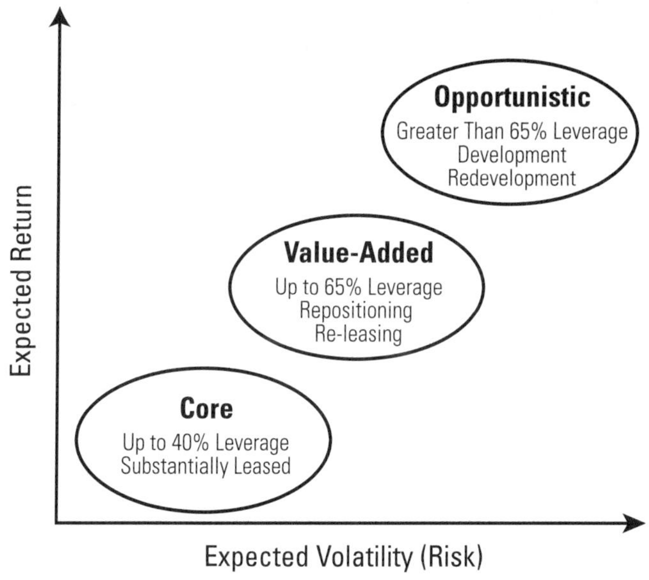

What Factors Must Be Considered When Investing in Private Real Estate?

Valuation

Because they require an appraisal, it is more difficult to measure private real estate returns than REITs, equities and fixed income investments that have daily pricing on their respective exchanges. The three main approaches to valuing private real estate can lead to different outcomes.

1. ***Replacement cost approach*** values a building by determining how much it would cost to construct the same building today.
2. ***Comparative sales approach*** determines value through a comparison of similar and recent building sales, the approach used when a home is valued for approval of a mortgage.
3. ***Discounted cash flow approach,*** also referred to as the *income approach,* calculates the net present value of the income expected from a particular building.

Each of these methodologies has its pros and cons. A property appraisal for institutional investment purpose should be a weighted blend of all three methods.

Liquidity

As stated previously, investment in private real estate funds cannot be entered into or liquidated as quickly as REITs, stocks and bonds. In 2008 and 2009, for example, many core open-ended funds had *redemption queues* that forced investors to wait a long time before they could withdraw funds. In 2011, many core open-ended funds have swung in the other direction and have *entry queues* that have resulted in a three- to 18-month waiting period to invest.

Fees

Private real estate investment options usually are more expensive from a fee perspective than investment in public real estate. However, private real estate vehicles range from core to opportunistic, with a wide range of strategies and fee structures that may merit the increased cost.

Leverage

Leverage—the use of borrowed money to make a purchase—can greatly affect the return on a real estate investment. Because real estate is a tangible asset that can be used as collateral to secure a loan, real estate investors have traditionally used a high degree of leverage. Such loans are made on a *nonrecourse basis*—investor risk is limited to the investment in the property.

Leverage can provide many benefits to an investor, but it can also have serious consequences. Leverage amplifies investment gains and losses. For example, if the return on the total purchase price of a property increases by 1%, the return on equity (if the investor put 50% as a down payment) is 1.5%. The inverse also holds true; leverage may create skewed capital losses. In addition, aggressive borrowing can force an investor to sell real estate assets as values decline, which is the worst time to do so.

Leverage can change a rather conservative investment into a riskier one by increasing the operating breakeven point of a building. A building purchased with cash may be able to break even with a lower occupancy level than a financed property that must generate extra cash for debt payments. The higher the required occupancy rate and loan payments, the greater the risk of a negative cash flow.

Investors should also pay close attention to the financing period used to purchase real estate. Assume an investor purchases a building with a loan that comes due in three years. There is the possibility that in three years, the markets will have changed and banks have less interest in refinancing the loan. An otherwise solid real estate asset could be foreclosed because financing is not available on reasonable terms. The debt term on real estate should always closely match or exceed the expected holding period of the property.

Management

Trustees with the support of their investment advisors should investigate the team involved in the selection and management of any real estate programs.

- How long has the team been operating?
- Who are the key principals of the firm and what are their reputations?
- What is the team's track record in terms of risk and return?
- What is the manager's philosophy on use of leverage?
- From whom do they purchase real estate assets and to whom do they sell?
- What are the management fees?
- Are manager interests aligned with investors' interests?
- During past periods of distress in the real estate market, did the manager deal fairly with lenders, investors and others?

Conclusion

Trustees should always view real estate as a long-term asset used to diversify a portfolio. It should not be a trading asset or a "bet" on the future direction of real estate values. Trustees considering any investment in real estate should give careful consideration of risks before getting involved in a venture.

Endnotes

1. *A Bird's Eye View of Global Real Estate Markets: 2011 Update*, March 2011. Prudential Real Estate Investors.
2. DOL Reg. §2510.3-101(e).

Chapter 42

Legal Considerations of Real Estate Investment

*Neal S. Schelberg**

Chapter 38 contains a comprehensive review of the legal requirements for the investment of plan assets under the Employee Retirement Income Security Act of 1974 (ERISA). In the investment area, ERISA primarily focuses on the process that plan fiduciaries must follow in deciding whether and where to invest plan assets. This same process must be followed in making real estate investments. Given the unique characteristics of some real estate investments, satisfaction of the fiduciary responsibilities under ERISA may require additional steps and considerations. These extra concerns are addressed in this chapter. How multiemployer plans can assist plan participants and beneficiaries in the purchase of their own real estate is also discussed.

What Proportion of Plan Assets Should Be Invested in Real Estate?

Once plan fiduciaries decide to proceed with a real estate investment program, they must determine what percentage of plan assets will be invested. ERISA dictates that plan fiduciaries consider a plan's financial, actuarial and investment needs. Fiduciaries should also consider the nature and characteristics of their plan, such as whether the plan provides pension or welfare benefits and, if a pension plan, whether it is a defined benefit or defined contribution plan. While there is no "one-size-fits-all" response to this question, most investment consultants recommend between 5% and 20% of a plan's assets be committed to real estate, with the majority targeting 10%.[1]

What Plan Policies Are Needed When Investing in Real Estate?

Before actually committing plan assets to real estate investments, plan fiduciaries should establish prudent written investment objectives and strategies that take into account the particular features of this asset class. These guidelines should be part of the investment policy statement.

If the Department of Labor (DOL) challenges a benefit plan's investment program, it generally does so under Section 404 of ERISA (fiduciary duties), Section 406 of ERISA (prohibited transactions), or both. DOL's primary concern is the process plan fiduciaries undertake when making investment decisions. To avoid (or minimize the potential for) Sections 404 and 406 violations, plan fiduciaries should have clear standards and guidelines with respect to:

- The percentage of plan assets that will be invested in real estate
- The types of real estate investments that will be made (debt or equity)
- Location and economic diversification
- Length and terms of leases that will be necessary to ensure an adequate return on investments
- Type and diversity of tenants
- Borrower or tenant creditworthiness
- The methodology and frequency for valuing real estate assets
- The standards for selection and retention of investment managers

*The author wishes to acknowledge the invaluable assistance of his colleagues, Pamela Onufer, Esq. and Thelma Ofori, Esq., in preparing this chapter.

- The standards for evaluating performance of the plan's investment managers and the investments under the manager's control
- The level of fiduciary responsibility for the investments that will be retained and/or delegated by the plan fiduciaries.[2]

What Should Be Considered When Selecting and Evaluating a Real Estate Investment Manager?

Chapter 46 contains an extensive general discussion on the selection of investment managers that applies equally to managers of real estate. Fiduciaries should select a manager specializing in the particular type of real estate investment being considered. Guidelines, benchmarks and procedures for evaluating the performance of the investment manager should be established in consultation with the manager. An investment consultant may also be helpful during this process. The performance of the real estate investment manager should be reviewed by plan fiduciaries in such manner as may be reasonably expected to ensure the performance complies with the needs and terms of the plan, the plan's investment guidelines and legal standards.[3]

Who Has Fiduciary Responsibility for Real Estate Held by Another Entity?

As a general rule, any type of property to which a plan holds legal title is a plan asset. It is not uncommon, however, for a plan to invest in another entity that holds the title to real estate and other assets. Real estate investment trusts (REITs) and real estate operating companies (REOCs) that pool funds from multiple investors to purchase and manage real estate assets and/or mortgage loans are just two scenarios where plans invest in this manner. For further discussion on these and other mechanisms for investing in real estate, read Chapter 41.

Generally, if a plan's equity interest in another entity is a privately offered security or an equity interest that is not issued by an investment company registered under the Investment Advisers Act of 1940, the plan's investment in that entity is subject to look-through rules. The plan's equity in the other entity and the undivided interest in the underlying assets of the entity are considered plan assets. Any person with authority or control over the management of the underlying assets, as well as any person providing investment advice for a fee concerning these underlying assets, is considered a plan fiduciary subject to all of the responsibilities and liabilities prescribed by ERISA.[4]

A plan's investment in another entity is exempt from these look-through rules when:

- The investment is in an *operating company* (i.e., an entity that is primarily engaged in the production or sale of goods or services other than the investment of capital), a venture capital operating company (VCOC) or an REOC. (In a real estate context, these operating companies are primarily REOCs).
- The equity participation in the entity by all invested benefit plans subject to ERISA or Section 4975 of the Internal Revenue Code (IRC) is not significant. Equity interest by plans is considered *not significant* when they hold less than 25% of the value of each class of equity interest in the entity.

When an equity investment is exempt from the look-through rules, only the investment in the entity, not the underlying assets owned by the entity, is treated as a plan asset subject to ERISA fiduciary obligation and prohibited transaction provisions.[5] This means plan trustees have fiduciary responsibility for selecting the investment in the entity, but the manager of the entity is not an ERISA fiduciary and does not have fiduciary obligations under ERISA in connection with the operation and management of the entity.

Are There Special Fiduciary Concerns for Real Estate Investments?

The general duties and obligations of ERISA fiduciaries are discussed in Chapters 5 and 38; these apply equally to real estate investments. Some of these fiduciary duties have specific application to real estate investments.

Exclusive Benefit Rule

Some investments such as economically targeted investments (ETIs) have benefits apart from their investment return to the employee benefit plan. For instance, an ETI might include a pension plan's financing of low-income housing or below-market interest rate mortgages; or it might be an investment in a local construction project designed to create jobs and increase the use of unionized labor. The latter would be intended to directly benefit plan participants through increased employer contributions into the trust fund.

When plan fiduciaries make an investment decision, a crucial test is whether the decision is made primarily for the benefit of the plan and its participants. In the context of real estate investments, the exclusive benefit rule prevents trustees from engaging in investments that are designed primarily to further socially desirable or economically targeted goals (e.g., job creation, community development). This is not to say that ETIs are per se unlawful under ERISA. ETIs are a viable investment option, but only in extremely limited circumstances. Fiduciaries faced with two real estate investment options that are truly equal—taking into account the quantitative and qualitative economic impact on the plan (including the level of diversification, degree of liquidity and the potential risk/return)—can select the ETI. Nevertheless, recent DOL guidance on ETIs serves to discourage their use by plan fiduciaries.[6]

Prudent Man Rule

Under ERISA, fiduciaries are required to discharge their duties with the care, skill and diligence of a prudent person. Real estate may require additional steps to comply with this requirement. For example, before extending a loan to finance the development of commercial real estate, a fiduciary's due diligence should include, among other things, an examination of the:

- Borrower's financial capability and track record
- Market for the project to be financed by the loan
- Economic feasibility of the project
- Value and liquidity of the collateral for the loan
- Existence and availability of other financing as a source of repayment for the loan
- Terms and length of the loan.

Another example is the decision to invest plan assets in raw (unimproved) land or commercial real estate. Fiduciaries should obtain a valuation or appraisal by a qualified real estate appraiser or otherwise ascertain its value before approving the investment. Fiduciaries should also investigate local legal requirements such as zoning and land use restrictions, before proceeding with the investment; these factors could impact the marketability and value of the investment. Plan fiduciaries should also consider using a qualified professional asset manager (QPAM) to assist in the purchase.[7] In fact, some plan documents require the use of a QPAM before making such an investment.

Diversification

ERISA requires the diversification of plan investments to minimize risks. There are two chief risks associated with equity real estate investments The first is that economic forces may depress property values and affect resale value. The second risk is that a property being developed for residential or commercial purposes may fail to produce an acceptable income stream.

As to debt investments in real estate such as mortgages, courts have recognized four risks:[8]

- ***Default risk***—the risk that payments on a property loan will not be made or that foreclosure will occur
- ***Interest rate risk***—the risk that the lender's cost of funds will approach or exceed the interest rate charged to the borrower
- ***Inflation risk***—the risk that the real rate of return on a mortgage will not be realized because of unanticipated inflation
- ***Liquidity risk***—the risk that a plan would have to sell the loans below face value and experience a financial loss.

Investments in real estate loans have been challenged as an ERISA violation using "textbook type theories that appear far removed from the actual realities of [the] mortgages. . . ".[9] However, courts have recently rejected these theories, and instead have required specific facts demonstrating the above enumerated risks outweighed the potential rewards in making the loan.[10]

For ERISA diversification purposes, plans can be divided into three categories. Some plans have asset allocations that satisfy the diversification requirement. With these plans, it is important to recognize that because the plan's investments are diversified, it does not ensure that the plan's investments also comply with the other ERISA requirements in Sections 404 and 406.

Plans of the second group are not diversified on their face, but circumstances are such that nondiversification is clearly prudent. In instances where courts have found prudence in the absence of diversification, a common theme emerges. The trustees:

- Were experienced in real estate and knew both the local market and its development potential
- Often visited the site personally and inquired about current and future development or use of adjacent and nearby land
- Discussed the investment with their plan's actuary, counsel, auditor and sometimes even plan participants
- Gave due consideration to independent appraisals.

When acting as a lender, the trustees considered the:

- Payment histories of their borrowers
- The loan-to-value ratios of the loans
- The practices of other local lenders.

It is also noteworthy that the plan fiduciaries always considered several other properties before committing to the investment.

Finally, there are plans that are not diversified and, under the circumstances, such nondiversification is not prudent. These plans violate ERISA's diversification requirement.

Plan Documents

The final aspect of ERISA's fiduciary duty requirements is to act in accordance with the documents governing the plan. This requirement seems obvious, but if overlooked, it can cause problems. Before investing in real estate, for example, plan fiduciaries should ensure the plan's trust agreement and other documents authorizes such investments.[11] If not, plan trustees may wish to consider making appropriate amendments to the plan documents. In the course of making such amendments, the plan fiduciaries should also review (and revise where necessary) the plan's investment guidelines to determine whether they are clearly authorized to make the real estate investment being considered.

Do the Same Prohibited Transaction Rules Apply?

Buttressing ERISA's fiduciary provisions are the prohibited transaction rules.[12] These rules prohibit persons with close relationships to an employee benefit plan from benefitting from such relationships. They also bar fiduciaries from engaging in transactions involving conflicts of interest and self-dealing. Before investing in real estate (as with any other investment), plan fiduciaries should develop a checklist of the parties involved in the investment to determine if there are any "parties in interest" that are involved in the proposed investment. If there is such a person or organization, the plan cannot proceed with the transaction unless there is an exemption from the prohibited transaction rules.

Below is a general discussion of the statutory and administrative prohibited transaction class exemptions typically used by plans to engage in real estate transactions. For any exemption to apply, all conditions of the exemption must be satisfied. Accordingly, plan fiduciaries should ensure that all of the conditions for the exemption are satisfied before moving forward with the investment.

Leasing of Necessary Office Space by a Party in Interest to the Plan

A common and extremely useful exemption applies when plans lease office space from a party in interest (including a fiduciary). Under Section 408(b)(2), such a lease is not prohibited if (1) the contract or other arrangement is reasonable, (2) the office space is necessary for the establishment or operation of the plan and (3) no more than reasonable compensation is paid for the office space.

In determining whether an arrangement is reasonable and to prevent a plan from becoming locked into an arrangement that has become disadvantageous, DOL regulations provide that the employee benefit plan must have the right to terminate an arrangement with reasonably short notice under the circumstances.[13] The termination must be allowed without penalty, even if there is a long-term lease involved. Reasonable compensation to the lessor of the office space for loss upon early termination is not considered a penalty. For instance, a lease with an early termination fee that covers reasonable expenses connected with the vacancy and reletting of the office space is not a penalty. On the other hand, a provision requiring payment in excess of the actual loss is not considered reasonable compensation. *Reasonable compensation* generally means compensation that is reasonable under the facts and circumstances of each case.[14]

It is important to note that Section 408(b)(2) provides relief only from the prohibitions in Section 406(a) of ERISA, and not the conflict-of-interest and self-dealing prohibitions in Section 406(b) of ERISA.[15] This means a fiduciary to an employee benefit plan cannot cause a plan to enter into a lease arrangement for office space and receive compensation from the plan because this would violate the self-dealing provisions contained in Section 406(b) of ERISA. Instead, in order for a fiduciary and plan to rely on the exemption contained in Section 408(b)(2) when entering into the lease for office space, the lease arrangement would have to be negotiated and approved on behalf of the plan by another fiduciary that is independent of and unrelated to the fiduciary.

Leasing Office Space by a Plan to a Party in Interest

In the case of collectively bargained multiemployer plans, two prohibited transaction class exemptions, PTCE 76-1[16] and PTCE 77-10[17], provide relief in connection with the provision of office space by a multiemployer plan to certain parties in interest including affiliated unions and related plans. Specifically, PTCE 76-1 provides relief from the prohibited transaction under ERISA Section 406(a) for the leasing of office space by the multiemployer plan to a participating employee organization, participating employer (provided such office space constitutes "qualifying employer real property" under ERISA), participating employer association or another multiemployer plan. PTCE 77-10 provides relief from ERISA Section 406(b)(2) for the leasing of office space by a multiemployer plan to a participating employee organization, participating employer (regardless of whether such office space constitutes "qualifying employer real property" under the act), participating employer association or another multiemployer plan.

Qualifying Employer Real Property (QERP)

Employer real property is defined as real property (and related personal property) which is leased to an employer of employees covered by a plan, or to an affiliate of such employer. In general, *qualifying employer real property* (QERP) is defined as parcels of employer real property that (1) are geographically dispersed, (2) are suitable for multiple uses, (3) may be leased to an employer, and (4) whose acquisition and retention comply with the fiduciary provisions of ERISA, other than the diversification requirements. ERISA's prohibited transaction rules place limits on a plan's acquisition of QERP.

ERISA Section 407 generally prohibits a plan from acquiring or holding QERP if the total fair market value of the QERP exceeds 10% of the total fair market value of plan assets at the time of acquisition. However, an eligible individual account plan (e.g., a profit-sharing, stock bonus, thrift or savings plan or employee stock ownership plan (ESOP)) may acquire or hold more than 10% of the value of plan assets in QERP without violating ERISA's diversification requirements. In addition, if a plan does acquire QERP, under ERISA Section 408(e); the plan's acquisition, lease or sale of the QERP must be for "adequate consideration" and no commission may be charged. In a typical transaction, a plan either purchases unencumbered real property (i.e., real property that is free from competing claims, liens or anything else that would hinder its transfer) from the employer at a price not exceeding fair market value, or the plan receives the real property from the employer as a contribution to the plan.[18] The plan may then lease the property back to the employer. The plan must receive rental income that provides the plan with no less than adequate consideration for the lease.

Construction Mortgage Loans

The prohibited transaction rules must also be considered when a plan is acting as a lender for a contributing employer's construction loan. This may occur, for example, to generate work for local contractors who also are contributing employers to the plan. The result is the creation of jobs for members of the bargaining unit, who also are plan participants.[19] Such loans result in the extension of credit between a plan and a party in interest (the contributing employer) and a transfer of plan assets to a party in interest—neither of which is permitted under the prohibited transaction rules unless there is an applicable exemption.

PTCE 76-1 provides an exemption for construction mortgage loans if certain conditions are satisfied, including:

- The loan must be a construction loan.
- The decision to make the loan must be made on behalf of the plan by a bank, insurance company, or savings and loan association.
- Neither the plan, the participating employer to whom the loan is made, nor the employee organization that has members covered by the plan has the power to exercise a controlling influence over the management or policies of the bank, insurance company, or savings and loan association.
- The bank, insurance company, or savings and loan association commonly makes construction loans on similar terms and conditions from its own funds.
- The construction loan satisfies the qualifications established by the bank, insurance company, or savings and loan association for making such loan from its own funds.
- Before the loan is made, the participating employer to whom the loan is made and the plan have received a written commitment running to both the plan as construction lender and such employer for permanent financing from a person other than the plan to enable full repayment of such loan upon completion of construction.
- The total amount of investments (including loans) of the plan in such participating employer does not exceed 10% of the fair market value of the plan's assets.
- The total amount of investments of the plan in loans to all participating employers does not exceed 35% of the fair market value of the plan's assets.

Qualified Professional Asset Managers (QPAMs)

PTCE 84-14[20] allows fiduciaries to segregate and place a portion of plan assets under the exclusive management and control of a sophisticated investment manager called a *QPAM.* Because of its scope, this is one of the most widely used prohibited transaction class exemptions. The exemption permits the QPAM to enter into nearly any type of transaction on behalf of the plan with almost any party in interest to the plan.

Not every financial institution or financial advisor can serve as a QPAM. The QPAM must be a bank, savings and loan association, insurance company or an investment advisor registered under the Investment Advisers Act of 1940 that meets certain financial standards. The QPAM must also acknowledge in writing that it is a plan fiduciary.

In addition, the exemption requires various other conditions to be satisfied. These conditions include (but are not limited to) the following:

- The QPAM must be independent of the parties in interest involved in the transaction. This means that the party in interest to the transaction cannot be the QPAM or any person related to the QPAM. In addition, the exemption cannot be used to exempt a transaction between any party in interest (or its affiliate) that has the authority to appoint or terminate the QPAM as a manager of the plan assets involved in the transaction, or to negotiate the terms of the QPAM's management agreement (including renewals and modifications) with respect to the plan assets involved in the transaction.
- The terms of the transaction must be negotiated on behalf of the plan by the QPAM (or under its direction in certain circumstances).
- The transaction must be at least as favorable to the plan as the terms generally available in an arm's length transaction between unrelated parties.
- To ensure no client (e.g., employer or plan) can unduly influence the QPAM, the plan assets under the management of the QPAM, when combined with the assets of other plans established or maintained by the same employer (or affiliate thereof) and managed by the QPAM, may not represent more than 20% of the total client assets managed by the QPAM at the time of the transaction.
- Neither the QPAM (or any affiliate thereof) nor any owner (direct or indirect) of a 5% or more interest in the QPAM has been convicted or released from prison for certain crimes within the ten years preceding the transaction.

Importantly, the exemption cannot be used for a transaction described in PTCE 2006-16[21] (relating to securities lending arrangements); PTCE 83-1[22] (relating to acquisitions by plans of interests in mortgage pools); or PTCE 88-59[23] (relating to certain mortgage financing arrangements).

In-House Asset Managers (INHAMs)

PTCE 96-23 is an exemption regarding the use of in-house asset managers (INHAMs).[24] It allows plans to enter into transactions with a party in interest provided certain conditions are met, including (but not limited to):

- The person or entity is a party in interest solely as the result of providing services to the plan, and does not have discretionary authority or control over the investment of the plan assets involved in the transaction and does not render investment advice with respect to those assets.
- The party in interest is neither the INHAM nor a party related to the INHAM and the terms of the transaction are negotiated on behalf of the plan by, or under the authority or general direction of, the INHAM.
- The transaction is not part of an agreement, arrangement or understanding designed to benefit a party in interest.
- The INHAM (or property manager) acts in accordance with written guidelines established and administered by the INHAM and makes the decision to enter into the transaction on behalf of the plan. Notwithstanding the foregoing, a transaction involving an amount of $5 million or more (which transaction has been negotiated by the INHAM) will not fail to satisfy this condition solely because the plan sponsor or its designee retains the right to veto or approve the transaction.
- The transaction is not described in PTCE 81-6[25] (relating to securities lending arrangements); PTCE 83-1[26] (relating to acquisitions by plans of interests in mortgage pools); or PTCE 88-59[27] (relating to certain mortgage financing arrangements).
- At the time the transaction is entered into, and at the time of any subsequent renewal or modification requiring the INHAM's consent, the terms of the transaction are at least as favorable to the plan as they would be in an arm's length transaction between unrelated parties.
- On an annual basis, an independent auditor with appropriate technical training or experience and proficiency with ERISA's fiduciary responsibility provisions must test the INHAM's practices against its written policies and procedures as well as the objective requirements of the exemption.

In addition to the general exemption described above, PTCE 96-23 also provides two specific exemptions with respect to real estate. The first provides that office or commercial space owned by a plan and managed by an INHAM may be leased to an employer (any of whose employees are covered by the plan or an affiliate); this is not considered a prohibited transaction as long as certain requirements of the general exemption are met *and* the following additional conditions are satisfied:

- The plan acquires the office or commercial space subject to an existing lease with the employer (or its affiliate) as a result of a foreclosure on a mortgage or deed of trust.
- The INHAM exercises discretionary authority in deciding on behalf of the plan to foreclose on the mortgage or deed of trust.

- Certain conditions tied to the duration or renewal of the lease are met.
- The amount of space covered by the lease does not exceed 15% of the rentable space of the office building or commercial center.

The second special exemption allows a plan to lease residential space to a party in interest if, in addition to certain requirements of the general exemption, the following conditions are met:

- The party in interest is an employee of an employer (any of whose employees are covered by the plan or an affiliate).
- The employee does not have discretionary authority or control with respect to the investment of the assets involved in the lease transaction and does not render investment advice with respect to those assets.
- The employee is neither an officer, director nor 10% shareholder of the employer or an affiliate of such employer.
- The terms of the transaction are not less favorable to the plan than the terms afforded by the plan to other, unrelated lessees in comparable arm's length transactions.
- The amount of space covered by the lease does not exceed 5% of the property's rentable space.
- The aggregate space leased to all employees of the employer (or an affiliate) cannot exceed 10% of such rentable space.

Mortgage Pools

PTCE 83-1[28] permits plans to invest in pass-through certificates when a pool sponsor, trustee or insurer is a party in interest to the investing plan. Generally, the plan cannot pay more than fair market value for the certificates, and the rights evidenced by the certificates cannot be subordinated to the rights of other certificate holders. In addition, the certificates must be backed by single-family, residential mortgage loans.

Residential Mortgage Financing Arrangements

PTCE 88-59[29] exempts various types of residential mortgage financing transactions in which plans may participate if certain conditions are satisfied. Under the exemption, plans are permitted to issue mortgage commitments to purchasers of residential dwelling units and receive a fee in exchange for such issuance.

REITS

Under PTCE 2004-7[30], individual account plans sponsored by real estate investment trusts (REITs) or their affiliates can acquire, hold and sell certain publicly traded shares of beneficial interest in an REIT that is structured under state law as a business trust (trust REIT).As noted above, Section 407(a) of ERISA states that a plan may not acquire or hold an employer security that does not constitute a "qualifying employer security." Prior to PTCE 2004-7, it was not clear whether shares issued by trust REITs constituted "qualifying employer securities" under Section 407(d)(5) of ERISA. PTCE 2004-7 specifically allows individual account plans sponsored by REITs to acquire, hold and sell such shares if certain conditions are satisfied (e.g., the participant must have discretionary authority to direct the trustee to sell shares purchased by his account no less frequently than monthly). PTCE 2004-7 also describes the conditions for retroactive relief for transactions occurring up to six years prior to the date of the final exemption.[31]

Individual Exemptions. Where a transaction does not fall within the requirements of a statutory or administrative prohibited transaction exemption, plan fiduciaries may seek an individual administrative exemption from DOL. An individual exemption applies only to (and can only be relied upon by) the specific parties in interest named or otherwise defined in the exemption granted by DOL. It would also apply only to the transaction specified in the exemption granted by DOL. DOL has issued various individual exemptions involving real estate issues; these exemptions have typically required the involvement of an independent fiduciary to oversee the initial and ongoing phases of the transaction.[32]

Conflicts of Interest. Section 406(b) of ERISA prohibits plan fiduciaries from acting in a conflict-of-interest position or where there is the potential for self-dealing. As with ERISA's exclusive benefit rule, under the Section 406(b) prohibited transaction provisions, a fiduciary cannot have dual loyalties. Some potential real estate investments, particularly those involving employment-generating investment programs, raise questions under the conflict-of-interest and self-dealing provisions of Section 406(b). Because the facts in each of these cases are unique, DOL has not issued prohibited transaction class exemptions but rather has dealt with these issues on a case-by-case basis.

Specific steps can be taken to minimize the possibility of violating the conflict-of-interest and self-dealing prohibited transactions. For example, if a fiduciary (i.e., a trustee) has an interest in an employer involved in a construction project that is to be financed by a loan from the plan, or if the plan is considering participation in the loan, the fiduciary should:

- Avoid any participation in the discussion and consideration of the proposed loan (and consider physically absenting himself from the room during these discussions).
- Abstain from voting on whether to make the loan.
- State in the minutes that the fiduciary has not discussed the proposed loan with any other trustee, has not participated in plan deliberations relating to the loan, and has not attempted to exert any influence on any trustee regarding the loan.

How Can Benefit Plans Assist Participants in the Purchase of Real Estate?

Mortgage Loan Programs

ERISA permits benefit plans to make loans to participants and their beneficiaries.[33] Such loans must:

- Be offered to all participants and beneficiaries on a reasonably equivalent basis
- Not be available to highly compensated employees under terms that are more favorable than those offered to non-highly compensated employees
- Be made in accordance with the terms of the plan
- Be adequately secured.

Of course, in addition to these requirements, the general fiduciary duties of prudence and loyalty under ERISA must be met.

Taft-Hartley Housing Trust Funds

In a 1990 amendment to the Labor-Management Relations Act of 1947 (LMRA), Congress authorized the establishment of a new type of employee benefit trust fund to aid employees and their families in purchasing homes.[34] Taft-Hartley housing trust funds can accept employer contributions for the explicit purpose of providing participants with financial assistance for employee housing. The plan document establishing the housing trust should specify the type(s) of financial assistance (i.e., benefit) that may be provided under the trust. While "financial assistance" is not defined in LMRA, legislative history suggests that it was intended to be limited to assistance in the form of mortgage collateral, lower closing costs, interest rates and down payments, etc.[35] The legislative history also suggests that this assistance was not intended to include the direct sale of property by a housing trust to an employee, or the housing trust acting as lender and extending mortgage loans to plan participants.[36]

Housing assistance benefits provided under housing trusts are considered welfare benefits under ERISA. Thus, the trustees of such trusts are plan fiduciaries and subject to ERISA's fiduciary duties and prohibited transaction rules. In applying these duties and rules to housing trusts, it is important to remember the financial assistance is the *benefit* provided under the trust. The payment of that benefit to the employees does not involve the housing trust's investment in real estate. ERISA's fiduciary rules apply somewhat differently in the context of a provision of a benefit as opposed to a decision concerning the safeguarding and investment of plan assets.[37] As a result, neither the diversification requirements of Section 404 of ERISA,[38] nor the prohibited transaction restrictions of Section 406 of ERISA, are applicable to the provision of the benefit. For example, assume that a housing trust is established for union members located in one particular geographic location (e.g., New York) and the financial assistance offered was a grant in the amount of closing costs associated with the purchase of a union member's primary residence. DOL would not likely assert that the fiduciaries of the housing trust violated their fiduciary duty to diversify assets even though all of the grants were made in the same geographic location. Also, DOL would likely not argue that the granting by the plan of closing costs violated Section 406(a)(1)(D) of ERISA, which prohibits the transfer of plan assets to parties in interest (including employees of contributing employers).

Like other multiemployer benefit plans, housing trusts must follow terms established in the collective bargaining agreement. In addition, the rules under the Taft-Hartley Act governing the administration of trust funds such as those jointly administered by employer and employee representatives, must all be followed.

Conclusion

Investments in real estate may play an important role in an employee benefit plan's overall investment portfolio. However, given the unique characteristics of this asset class, the investment decision must be approached carefully and scrutinized thoroughly to determine whether it is an appropriate investment vehicle for the plan. Most plan fiduciaries will lack the specialized knowledge and experience to invest in many real estate investments. To satisfy ERISA fiduciary requirements, plan fiduciaries should seriously consider retaining a professional advisor with specific expertise in the contemplated real estate investment.

Endnotes

1. See Bruce J. Korter, "Why Invest in Real Estate Today?" *Employee Benefits Journal,* at 16 (March 1997) (citing *The Handbook of Real Estate Portfolio Management,* (Joseph L. Pagliari Jr. ed., 1995))., at 16.
2. See Stanley L. Iezman, *Complying with ERISA: A Primer for Pension Plan Trustees,* Real Est. Rev., at 18, 18-19 (Spring 1997).
3. DOL Interpretive Bulletin 75-5 (June 25, 1975), codified in 29 CFR §2509.75-8 (1975). *See Whitfield v. Cohen,* 682 F.Supp. 188, 196 (S.D.N.Y. 1988) ("fiduciary must ascertain within a reasonable time whether an agent to whom he has delegated a trust power is properly carrying out his responsibilities").
4. DOL Reg. §2510.3-101(a)(2).
5. DOL Reg. §2510.3-101(c)(1) and (f)(1).
6. DOL Interpretive Bulletin 08-01, 73 Fed. Reg. 61,734, codified in 29 CFR §2509.08-1 (2008).
7. See the discussion relating to QPAMs in footnote 48 and the accompanying text, *infra.*
8. See, e.g., *Metzler v. Graham,* 112 F.3d 207, 211 n.8 (5th Cir. 1997); *Brock v. Citizens Bank of Clovis,* No. Civ. 83-1054 BB, 1985 WL 71535, at *4 (D.N.M. Dec. 20, 1985).
9. *Reich v. King,* 867 F.Supp. 341, 345 (D.Md. 1994).
10. *Id.* at 344.
11. See Morton P. Fisher, Jr., et al., *ERISA Pitfalls in Real Estate Transactions Involving Pension Funds,* 17 Real Prop. Prob. & Tr. J. 595, 603 (1982).
12. Section 4975 of the Internal Revenue Code contains prohibited transaction provisions analogous to the ERISA requirements that are applicable to certain qualified pension plans, IRAs, individual retirement annuities and other plans.
13. 29 CFR §2550.408b-2(c).
14. 29 CFR §2550.408b-2(d); 29 C.F.R. §2550.408c-2.
15. 29 CFR §2550.408b-2(a).
16. 1976-1 C.B. 357 (Jan. 1976).
17. 1977-10 C.B. 435 (July 1977).
18. See DOL Interpretive Bulletin 94-3, 59 Fed. Reg. 66,735 (Dec. 28, 1994), codified in 29 CFR §2509.94-3 (1994) (setting forth DOL's view that in-kind contributions (i.e., any property other than cash) that reduce an employer's contribution obligation to the plan constitute prohibited transactions under Section 4975(c)(1)(A) of the Internal Revenue Code and Section 406(a)(1)(A) of ERISA. Although the Supreme Court in *Comm'r v. Keystone Consol. Indus., Inc.,* 508 U.S. 152 (1993) held only that an employer's contribution of unencumbered real property to a tax-qualified defined benefit pension plan in satisfaction of the employer's funding obligation is a "sale or exchange" prohibited by Section 4975(c)(1)(A) of the Code, the Interpretive Bulletin is broader than *Keystone,* applying equally with respect to in-kind contributions to plans other than defined benefit pension plans and in-kind contributions that are in excess of the statutory minimum funding obligations of Section 302 of ERISA and Section 412 of the Code. Finally, the Interpretive Bulletin reaffirms DOL's position that the decision to accept a contribution is a fiduciary decision subject to Section 404 of ERISA.
19. See, Union Labor Life Ins. Co.'s (ULLICO) Mortgage Separate Account "J for Jobs" program. J for Jobs is an open-ended commingled mortgage account consisting of the pension investments of over 170 Taft-Hartley pension plans. They utilize those pension assets to provide developers financing for commercial real estate projects, with the stipulation that all work must be 100% union built. *See also* Jayne Elizabeth Zanglein, *High Performance Investing: Harnessing the Power of Pension Funds to Promote Economic Growth and Workplace Integrity,* 11 Lab. Law. 59, 70 (1995).
20. 49 Fed. Reg. 9,494 (March 13, 1984).
21. 71 Fed. Reg. 210 (October 31, 2006).
22. 53 Fed. Reg. 24,811 (June 30, 1988).
23. 48 Fed. Reg. 895 (January 7, 1983).
24. 61 Fed. Reg. 15,975 (Apr. 10, 1996).
25. 46 Fed. Reg. 7,527 (Jan. 23, 1981).
26. 48 Fed. Reg. 895 (Jan. 7, 1983).
27. 53 Fed. Reg. 24,811 (June 30, 1988).
28. 48 Fed. Reg. 895.
29. 53 Fed. Reg. 24,811 (June 30, 1988).
30. 69 Fed. Reg. 23,220 (April 28, 2004).
31. This exemption is generally similar to an individual exemption that was previously granted by DOL. See Crown American, PTE 97-64 (FR 66690 (Dec. 19, 1997)).
32. See 1977-10 C.B. 435 (July 1977). In several other prohibited transaction exemptions, DOL has permitted plans to sell illiquid real estate holdings to interested parties in order to acquire plan assets that were more amenable to individual investment decision making on a self-directed basis. For example, in PTCE 96-13, DOL authorized a proposed cash sale of improved real property by the plan to the sponsoring employer's sole shareholder, who also served as plan administrator. The plan intended to invest the proceeds in marketable securities, which would facilitate the establishment of participant-directed individual plan accounts.
33. *See* ERISA §408(b)(1); Internal Revenue Code §4975(d)(1) .
34. *See* Pub. L. No. 101-273 (1990), reprinted in, 1 U.S. Code Cong. & Admin. News, 1990, at 104 Stat. 138 (West 1990).
35. H.R. Rep. No. 101-441 (1990), reprinted in, 4 U.S. Code Cong. & Admin. News, 1990, at 143, 145 (West 1990).
36. *Ibid.*
37. *Ibid.*
38. Notably, the diversification requirement is not implicated in the case of a Taft-Hartley housing trust. In the language of the legislative history of the 1990 amendments to LMRA, the diversification requirement of Part 4 (of the Title I fiduciary provisions of ERISA) is a requirement concerning the investment of plan assets and is not applicable to the mere payout of plan benefits. Nothing (in the bill) would require plans to provide a housing benefit in the form of a plan investment. Thus, in administering such benefits, a fiduciary would not necessarily be concerned with the diversification requirement relating to the investment of plan assets. *Id.*

Chapter 43

Alternative Investments

Ted Disabato

Alternative investments have received increasing attention from benefit plan trustees. This trend has accelerated in the last decade because traditional equity and fixed income assets have not met investor expectations for risk *or* return. Increasingly, trustees have asked, "Isn't there something besides stocks that can provide a reasonable return, yet reduce risk?"

At the same time, investment firms have been creative in developing new investment vehicles that give investors (including plan trustees) increased flexibility to respond to changing markets. There is a growing mystique that the managers of alternative investments represent "special people making special investments" or "smart money" that investors cannot ignore.

This chapter cuts through the hype and explores the basics of alternative investments. Since derivatives often play an important part in an alternative investment portfolio, especially hedge funds and managed futures funds, an introduction to derivatives is also provided. Key areas of fiduciary oversight for trustees and their advisors who invest in these vehicles will be highlighted as well.

What Are Alternative Investments?

Alternative investments generally fall into one of these categories:

- Hedge funds
- Private equity and debt
- Infrastructure
- Managed futures
- Commodities
- Natural resources, timber and land.

These investments are designed to behave differently from traditional asset classes (primarily publicly traded stocks and bonds). Though they are not always successful in doing so, alternative investments generally seek to provide returns that do not depend on the performance of traditional stock and bond markets.

The definition of an *alternative investment* has evolved over time. Not too long ago, real estate was considered an

Exhibit 1

Average Alternative Allocations

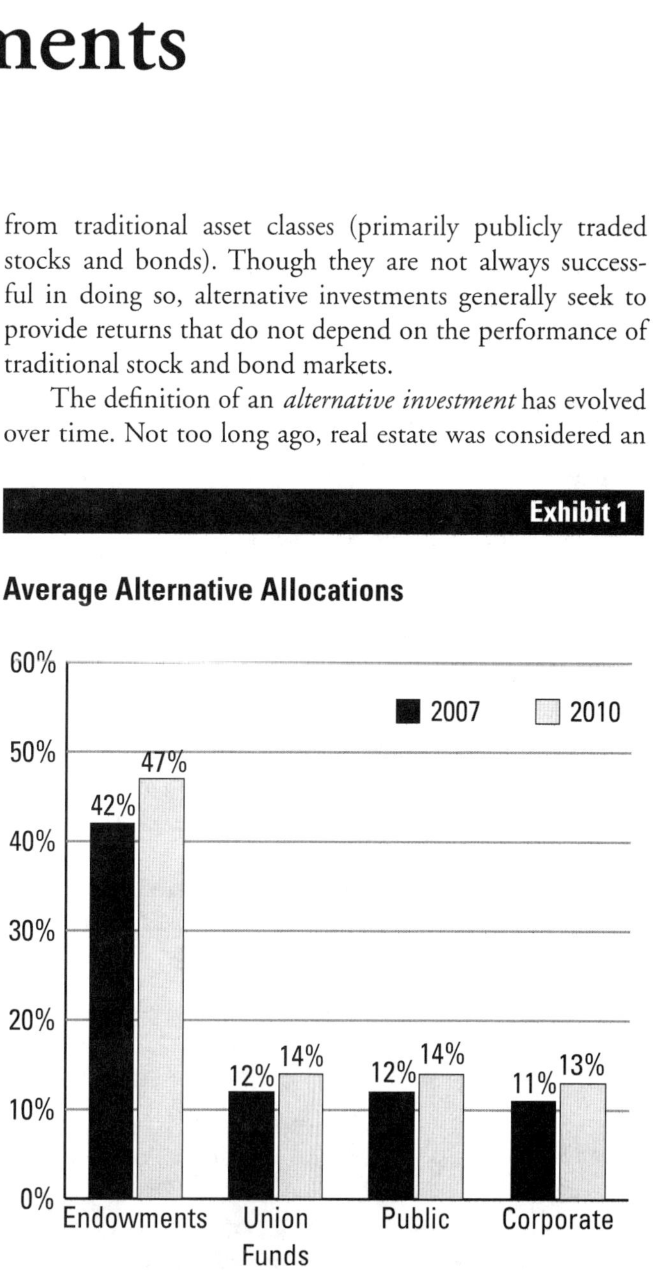

Source: 2007 and 2010 survey results from JP Morgan, Merrill Lynch, NACUBO and Commonfund.

alternative investment. But real estate has now become such a common part of investment portfolios that many advisors consider it part of a traditional investment portfolio.

As Exhibit 1 illustrates, alternative investments are a growing component of institutional portfolios in the United States. In 2010, alternative investments on average accounted for approximately 14% of union trust fund assets—up from 12% in 2007.

What Are the Pros and Cons of Alternative Investments?

Diversification

The primary reason to invest in alternative assets is that they have a low correlation to traditional stock and bond portfolios. *Low correlation* means there is a tendency for return on alternative investments to move in a different direction from traditional investments, which helps diversify a plan portfolio. The low correlation may be due to the characteristics of the alternative investments (like the physical nature of commodities), lower liquidity and barriers to entry in certain markets, or the hedging activities of alternative investment managers.

To understand the power of this diversification, consider the three investment portfolios in Exhibit 2.

Look at what happens when you combine two portfolios with low correlations. Over three years, Portfolio A (perhaps a traditional stock fund) has a risk of 9.8% and return of 8.2%. Portfolio B (perhaps a hedge fund) has a risk and return similar to those of Portfolio A at 8.5% and 8.0% respectively. However, a combined portfolio (A + B) provides lower risk of 1.1% and a higher return of 8.5%. It may seem like a parlor trick to produce a return that is higher than either portfolio by itself, but that is the advantage of low correlation in a variable market.

Exhibit 2

Combining Portfolios With Low Correlation

	Portfolios		
	A	B	A + B
Year 1 Return	-4.0%	20.0%	8.0%
Year 2 Return	10.0%	5.0%	7.5%
Year 3 Return	20.0%	0.0%	10.0%
Total Return	8.2%	8.0%	8.5%
*Risk**	*9.8%*	*8.5%*	*1.1%*

* As measured by standard deviation.

Target Returns

Since risk and return are related, reducing portfolio volatility tends to produce lower returns. Therefore, many alternative investment portfolios apply leverage to increase returns. For example, a manager might borrow one dollar for every dollar of client assets—this is termed *one times (1X) leverage* or *100% leverage.* This leveraged portfolio has the potential to double the return for investors. Of course, this leverage may also double the losses if there is a decline in value.

Managers often state the target return for the fund or portfolio they manage in terms of a risk-free rate (like T-bills or LIBOR) plus a fixed percentage to emphasize the "absolute return" characteristic of these. A typical benchmark for an alternative investment such as a hedge fund might be T-bills plus 5%.

Complex Investment Structure

Alternative investment funds are more complex than other investment vehicles. Investing in alternative investments often involves a legal structure called a *limited partnership* (LP). Like mutual funds and commingled investment trusts (CITs), LPs combine the assets of various investors, but LPs have less regulatory oversight and more restrictions on how assets are contributed and withdrawn.

In an LP, a general partner (GP) raises capital (or a "commitment" to contribute capital) and manages the assets of the partnership. The capital may be contributed on a regular basis, as is the case with most hedge funds, or it may be "called" by the GP over several years, as is the case with most private equity funds after the GP finds the assets in which the partnership will invest.

Alternative investments often use a limited partnership structure governed by a private placement memorandum (PPM). This arrangement allows greater flexibility with fewer regulatory restrictions. It is also suited to investments that might have low liquidity or can only be purchased with some effort in a nonpublic transaction.

Side Letters

Side letters can be a useful tool for trustees who would like to customize the terms of an LP agreement. The documents that govern commingled funds, like prospectuses and PPMs, generally cannot be modified by investors or limited partners. But GPs will often sign side letters that will expand or customize certain terms of a PPM. Before executing the documents, trustees should ask their advisors if it is appropriate to execute a side-letter agreement with the GP.

Limited Liquidity

Low liquidity is an added risk when investing in alternative investments as they may require long holding periods and can only be transferred or liquidated before the end of the specified period with considerable effort. For example, an investment in a timber partnership might require eight to ten years before the trees mature and yield a profit. The same is true for private equity funds, which can only be liquidated over time after buyers are found for the companies held in the partnership.

Alternative investment managers may seek to accommodate the illiquid nature of some securities by establishing a *side pocket* to hold illiquid or hard-to-value assets. This will ensure that these particular assets will not affect the liquidity or return of the main fund.

Valuation

The value of an LP is often based on an appraisal that is formally reported on an IRS Form K-1 delivered to investors after a considerable time delay. The value reported to investors may not fluctuate as much as publicly traded market prices, which can be good for investors; but the appraisal process may also understate the variability of the partnership. Trustees may have to use other methods to assess the risk of these investments. A plan auditor may also classify these assets as Level 3 on the FAS 157 (Fair Value Measurements) section of an audit report; this does not indicate a problem, just the need for closer attention since the valuation is based on factors that are "unobservable" in a public market.

Unrelated Business Taxable Income

Under certain circumstances, IRS may consider income produced by alternative investments to be unrelated business taxable income (UBTI), which requires tax payments and filings, even for a tax-exempt employee benefit fund. Investors often avoid this complication by investing in the offshore "sleeve" of a fund, domiciled in a place like the Cayman Islands.

Transparency

Alternative investments may also be more risky because there is less transparency regarding the assets held. Investors in LPs may receive a statement of their interest in the partnership, but they may not have access to the custodial statements of the fund. The investors must rely on the partnership auditor, servicing agent and custodian to provide the true value of their accounts.

Fees and Expenses

Fees for alternative investments are typically higher and often include a share of the profits. It has become standard in the alternative investment industry for GPs to be compensated by both a percent of the assets and a percent of the profits. In the past, a typical arrangement was two and 20, meaning that the fees were 2% of the assets and 20% of the profits. Recently, investor pressure has been pushing down management fees to where the average incentive fee for funds launched in 2009 was closer to 18%.[1] Investors should also be prepared to pay this management fee on the total amount of the "committed capital" rather than just the amount deposited in the fund. This generally applies to funds like private equity and infrastructure, which require the GP to seek out investments and call capital from investors over a period of time.

One positive characteristic for investors is the fact that the realized and unrealized "profits" upon which the incentive fee is based are often calculated after the investor receives a *preferred return* of something like 8%. In addition, managers typically will agree to offset future profits by past losses—the incentive fee is only paid when fund profits hit a new *high-water mark.* A high-water mark represents the highest value reached by the investment, and it means that the manager will receive incentive compensation only when the investment makes up past losses (if any). Such a promise is often called a *loss carry forward provision.*

Incentive fees are intended to align the interests of the manager and the investor. But there is some controversy regarding whether this is accomplished; some suggest fees encourage managers to take excessive risks.

* * *

All of these issues may lead trustees to believe that alternative investments are not worth the effort. But the diversification benefit and the superior return of alternative investments are significant motivators for funds that can accommodate the constraints. The key for trustees is that alternative investments require much greater due diligence than most traditional investment portfolios.

What Is a Hedge Fund?

The term *hedge fund* is used to describe a broad range of private investment vehicles that are intended to "hedge out" market risk and produce returns independent of overall market performance. Hedge funds seek to invest in a manner that neutralizes overall market movements. Hedge fund managers typically achieve this goal by buying "going long" assets they expect will increase in price and selling "going short or shorting" assets they expect to decline in price.

A *short* position is created when an investor sells a security that they do not own. This may seem like a strange concept, but the only way to make money on a security that is falling in value is to "borrow" the security from someone else, allow the security to fall in value, buy it back in the market at a lower price and return it to the person from whom it was borrowed. Many custodians have a business of securities lending that facilitates the borrowing of securities among investors. Securities lending is also part of many margin accounts at brokerage firms. Hedge fund managers often have both long and short portfolios in the same fund, since this makes the performance of their fund more dependent on security selection and less dependent on whether the market goes up or down.

The first hedge fund was started by Alfred Winslow Jones in 1949, but it was not until the 1990s that these funds gained wide acceptance. In 2010, there were more than 12,000 unique hedge funds (approximately 70% from outside of the United States), with assets of approximately $2 trillion.[2] However, only about half of all hedge funds manage more than $25 million.

Many of the early hedge funds specialized in just one strategy, and most often that was the long/short equity approach started by Jones. However, a lack of diversification and proper risk controls caused many of the early funds to stop trading during the difficult stock market of 1973 to 1974. During the 1990s, the number of hedge funds surged again along with the stock market. Cash flow hit a peak in 2007 as investors sought to avoid the volatility of the stock market.

Hedge Fund Regulations

Unlike mutual funds and other investment vehicles intended for use by a wide range of investors, hedge funds and their managers are often not registered by the Securities and Exchange Commission (SEC). Private investment funds are typically exempt from registration with SEC due to exceptions in the definition of *securities* and *investment companies*.[3] However, this area of the law is changing, and hedge funds are expected to come under greater regulatory oversight.

Fund of Funds

The operational and risk characteristics of hedge funds require diversification among various hedge funds, but many attractive managers impose investment minimums of $5 million and higher. This means investors must commit $50 to $75 million to achieve an adequately diversified portfolio. For investors unable or unwilling to commit this much capital, the answer is to invest in a *fund of hedge funds,* essentially a mutual fund that invests in multiple hedge funds. A fund of funds typically invests in 20 to 50 individual hedge funds providing immediate diversification. The typical minimum for these funds is $1 million to $5 million.

A fund of funds also offers investors the manager access and focused due diligence that is suited to the complex nature of hedge fund investments. On the down side, these worthwhile services come with another layer of fees (including incentive fees) that further reduces the effective return of the investment.

The first fund of funds was created in 1969, but the sector did not experience significant growth until the late 1990s and early 2000s. By 2010, there were more than 3,000 funds of funds, with assets of more than $500 billion.

ERISA Assets and the 25% Rule

Trustees should also be aware that many hedge funds avoid the designation of holding ERISA plan assets by limiting the total investment by ERISA plans to less than 25% of plan assets. An employee benefit plan can still invest in a hedge fund that is not designated as holding ERISA plan assets, but the manager's standard of care is less stringent.

What Investment Strategies Are Used by Hedge Funds?

Hedge fund strategies can be difficult to categorize, but it is possible to separate the major strategies into three groups: (1) relative-value strategies, (2) event-driven strategies and (3) opportunistic strategies.

Relative-Value Strategies

Relative-value strategies attempt to generate returns by taking advantage of pricing differences between related securities. Because the manager is not making a directional bet on a market, these strategies tend to have lower volatility. Taking advantage of price difference for identical or similar securities sold in different forms or on different markets is referred to as *arbitrage*.

Convertible Arbitrage. Bonds and preferred stock that can be exchanged for shares of common stock are referred to as *convertible securities*. The objective of this strategy is to try to profit by buying or selling convertibles and offsetting market risk by taking the opposite position in the underlying company's stock.

Fixed Income Arbitrage. Managers in these strategies are trying to profit from pricing differences within and across global fixed income markets. For example, they may try to make simultaneous trades in two markets (e.g., securities and their corresponding futures contracts) to profit from a price difference. *Spreads,* the difference in prices in the two markets, tend to be very small; therefore, managers tend to use large amounts of *leverage* (borrowed money), which can make this a risky strategy.

Equity Market Neutral. In this strategy, managers try to profit from price differences among world equity markets, or the relative attractiveness of one market sector versus another. For example, a manager may have no opinion on the direction of semiconductor stocks, but may believe Intel stock is overpriced relative to IBM, so the manager will buy IBM and sell short Intel.

Index/Basis Arbitrage and ***Volatility Arbitrage.*** These investment strategies that seek to exploit the differences in price movements between markets for the same securities.

Event-Driven Strategies

Event-driven strategies attempt to profit from the impact of extraordinary events on specific securities. These events include mergers, takeovers, spin-offs, bankruptcies, restructurings and similar situations. The success of this strategy is based on a manager's ability to analyze and understand the legal decisions and the negotiating dynamics associated with these events.

Merger Arbitrage (also known as ***Risk Arbitrage***). Managers in this strategy buy the stock of a company that is the target of a merger or takeover. Often companies will trade just below the takeover price, and investors can profit when the merger is actually completed at the announced price; additional gains are possible if the price has to be raised to complete the transaction. In a variant of this strategy, a manager might buy the target company and short the acquiring company, or buy other companies in the same sector that might be put "in play."

Distressed Securities. These managers invest in the debt or equity of companies that are experiencing financial difficulties, or may actually be in bankruptcy. Distressed securities may receive limited coverage from Wall Street analysts, allowing skilled managers to identify good values. Many distressed security funds are long only.

Trade Claims. A strategy of financing and purchasing small trade claims (goods owed) at a discount, often arising from large bankruptcy proceedings. For example, a small supplier might have a claim against a chain store in bankruptcy, and the manager buys the claim at a discount hoping to collect the amount due.

Special Situations. Strategies pursued by "activist" investors seeking to influence the management strategies or business practices of target companies.

Opportunistic Strategies

Opportunistic managers take bets on the direction of specific markets or securities. Therefore, opportunistic strategies will have more market exposure and greater volatility than either relative-value or event-driven strategies.

Global Macrofunds. Macrofunds have significant flexibility in their investment style. They often have a base strategy in one market and look to couple this with a few large directional bets in other markets where they see opportunity. These directional bets can take place in just about any market from precious metals to currencies. Many of the largest and well-known alternative investment funds, such as those run by Soros Fund Management, are global macrofunds.

Short and Short-Bias Funds. Short sellers are trying to generate returns from declining stock prices. They may also generate a small portion of their return by investing the cash proceeds of the short sale. Security selection is the key in whether a manager succeeds with this strategy.

Emerging Markets. These strategies focus on equity and fixed income securities of emerging market countries (as opposed to developed markets). These strategies are typically long biased due to restrictions on short-selling securities in many emerging market countries.

Long/Short Equity (also known as ***Equity Hedge***). Managers using this strategy have both long and short positions in securities but typically have a long bias. The magnitude of this bias significantly impacts the volatility of this strategy. Managers in this classification can operate in any type of market, including regional and/or industry/sector specific.

What Are Private Equity and Debt Investments?

Private equity funds invest in companies that are not traded on public stock exchanges. In 2010 the industry raised about $86 billion in 336 funds, which brought the total value of private equity to approximately $1.2 trillion in the United States and $2.6 trillion worldwide.[4] The most common private equity investment strategies follow.

Leveraged Buyouts (LBOs)—the purchase of companies using a significant amount of borrowed money (bonds or loans). In a classic example, the management of a company (or a division of a larger firm) combines an investment from a private equity fund with a bank loan to buy the company and "go private." Often, the assets of the company being purchased are used as collateral to secure the loans in addition to the assets of the organization making the purchase. The purpose of leveraged buyouts is to buy without having to commit a lot of capital, with the debt portion of an LBO being 60% to 90% of the transaction price.[7]

Companies suitable for an LBO are typically mature businesses with stable cash flow sufficient to service new debt. The private equity firm expects the company management to improve operations, pay down the debt and sell the company for a profit. Some observers have criticized this type of investment since the added debt requires the company to cut expenses, which often means cutting jobs.

Growth Capital—seeking to maximize the value of company assets over the long term. The growth capital strategy tries to achieve *capital appreciation* by providing money to established companies to expand or restructure their operations. In particular, the private equity investor may be financing changes expected to expand significantly a company's value. The private equity fund may also become actively involved in the company to help manage the change.

Distressed Investment—buying financial instruments (e.g., stocks, bank debt, corporate bonds or trade claims) of a company that is near or going through bankruptcy. As a result of the financial difficulties, these securities are available at a substantial reduction in value. Sometime the strategy is *loan to own* or *distressed to own* when the intent is to gain control of the business.

Venture Capital—money provided to relatively young companies for the launch, early development or significant expansion of the business. Usually, the GPs of venture capital funds are actively engaged with the companies in their fund; often they take a seat on the board of directors and have regular interaction with the management team. Many famous technology companies, like Microsoft, Intel and Facebook, were initially funded by venture capital.

Venture capital is typically divided between early- and late-stage venture investments. The risks and potential payoffs vary significantly based on the development and the potential of the company. This is a high-risk/high-reward endeavor with many companies producing no significant return offset by a few investments with a very large return.

Venture capital investments are typically illiquid and hard to value until the companies begin to mature, which may take five to eight years. The companies may also require additional investments until they begin to generate a profit. The additional "rounds" of capital and extended development period mean that venture capital investing requires a long-term commitment.

Private Debt—a variety of strategies that provide senior and mezzanine financing to private companies that are too small to access the public debt market or that do not have enough collateral for a bank loan. *Mezzanine financing* gives the investor the right to convert to an equity (ownership) interest in the company if the loan is not paid back on time and in full. Mezzanine debt typically is given lower payback priority than *senior financing* from banks and venture capital companies. Such financing also occurs very quickly with little due diligence on the part of the lender and little or no collateral on the part of the borrower. Given the risk, lenders typically seek a return of 20-30%.

Investing in private equity has a different dynamic than investing in a traditional public stock portfolio. Private equity funds establish a fund-raising schedule that typically lasts 12 to 18 months. During this time, the fund opens, raises commitments to provide capital from clients and then closes. Investors must be willing to meet the time line established or wait until the manager opens a new fund, typically in two years.

After collecting the binding commitments from clients, which typically amounts to several hundred million dollars (during the peak years, large private equity firms raised multibillion dollar funds), the GP issues a "capital call" and the limited partners then transfer the requested capital into the fund.

Private equity investors should assume it will take several years for a GP to call all of the capital committed to the fund. In fact, GPs often return capital to investors (from the sale of companies held in the portfolio) before all of the capital is called. Therefore, investors often commit to a dollar value above the target to achieve a specific target allocation to private equity.

The J-Curve Effect and Private Equity Performance

Private equity funds are also somewhat unique in the way they produce returns to investors. In the initial years, a fund will typically have more expenses than income and capital gains. Expenses are the same as if the fund were fully invested (e.g., management fees are billed on total committed capital) and it may take several years for the appraised value of the portfolio companies to increase in value. The return looks like the letter *J*, with falling values in the first few years offset by increasing returns in the later years.

It may not seem fair that private equity managers charge based on committed capital even before it is invested in the fund. But remember the private equity concept is that the GP is currently working to find all of the investments in the fund.

The time line of capital contributions also impacts the manner in which the performance of a private equity fund is measured. The standard method of calculating performance in a traditional stock and bond portfolio is called a *time-weighted rate of return* (TWR) because the client chooses the time to make the investment and the TWR process takes into account the timing of cash flows into the portfolio. In a private equity fund, however, the GP controls when investments are made. As a result, the standard in the industry for determining performance is to calculate an *internal rate of return* (IRR) that recognizes the timing of the GP capital calls.

Studies from the University of Chicago and MIT seem to indicate that the return on the median private equity fund (net of fees) is roughly comparable or even slightly below the S&P 500 Index.[5] But there is considerable variation among private equity funds.

Perhaps the most important finding from the studies of private equity performance is that top-performing GPs tend to repeat their strong performance. That means investors can look at the performance of a specific GP's Fund I and Fund II and predict that the performance of Fund III will be above avaerge. This "persistence of performance" is not often found in traditional investment portfolios; for example, a specific mutual fund might perform well in the past but poorly in the future. However, strong relative performance in private equity funds tends to hold (on average) in future years. This also means the top-performing private equity funds are in great demand and may limit access to new investors.

The performance study also found an inverse relationship between performance and the amount of fund-raising during a vintage year. In other words, the years with the largest fund-raising tended to be the vintage years that produced lower returns. Since private equity fund-raising was below average in 2009 and 2010, it may allow these vintage years to outperform in the future.

Exhibit 3

Private Equity Performance

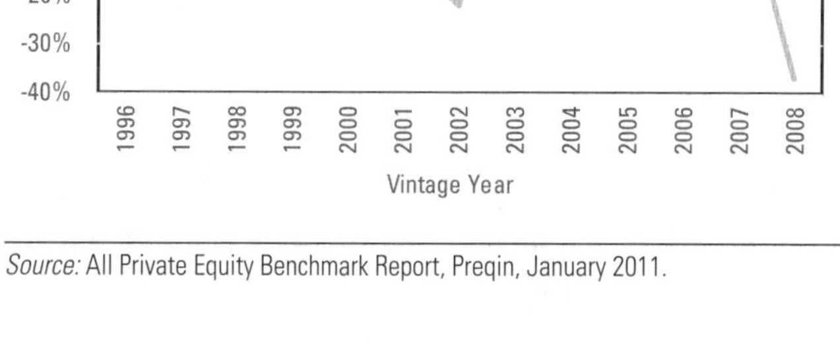

Source: All Private Equity Benchmark Report, Preqin, January 2011.

What Are Infrastructure Investments?

Infrastructure refers to several types of physical assets, facilities and systems that are critical to the functioning of local economies. It includes the transportation (toll roads, bridges, tunnels, airports, seaports, railroads), energy (pipelines, storage facilities), utilities (power generation, fuels, water systems), communication (cell towers, networks) and social (schools, hospitals, prisons, other public buildings) assets. They are long-lived, real assets that are costly and time-consuming to replace and typically generate relatively stable cash flows that increase with inflation.

Infrastructure investments possess an attractive characteristic—they have a high barrier to entry due to capital requirements and government regulations. With monopoly like assets, regulated returns, and explicit or implicit inflation pass-through, investments in infrastructure can provide stable returns, an inflation hedge and diversification to a portfolio. There are three primary methods to gain exposure in infrastructure:

1. **Direct investment**—typically requires significant amounts of capital for a single purchase. Since infrastructure assets are often highly regulated, direct investments carry high regulatory risk.
2. **Private partnerships**—invest directly in infrastructure assets on behalf of investors. They offer a more diversified portfolio with smaller capital requirements per investor.
3. **Listed infrastructure fund**—comprised of publicly traded stocks whose business is directly related to infrastructure assets. The liquidity and exchange trade are their advantages.

What Are Commodity, Natural Resource, Timber and Land Investments?

Investors have four primary methods to gain exposure to commodities:

1. **Commodity index funds**—one of the easiest methods to gain broad commodity exposure is to invest in a fund that uses commodity futures to track commodity index performance. Two popular indexes are the Dow Jones Commodity Index and the S&P Goldman Sachs Commodity Index.
2. **Actively managed commodity funds**—use futures, common stocks, exchange-traded funds and other securities to gain commodity exposure.
3. **Buying the stocks of commodity producers**—an indirect method to gain commodity exposure. The returns may be impacted by company-specific factors beyond the change in commodity prices.
4. **Owning physical commodities**—involves storage, transportation and insurance that is not practical for most investors.

Natural resource investments include direct investment in companies and properties involved in harvesting or extracting products from the earth. The funds can be grouped into three main categories:

1. **Extraction**—primarily oil and gas production and mineral mining. Oil and gas funds include both upstream and midstream activities, with mining focused on mineral and metals production.
2. **Harvesting**—generates return from agricultural production, typically farmland and timber. Characteristics are similar to real estate, but more sensitive to commodity prices.
3. **Renewable energy**—creates returns from activities related to alternative energy such as solar, biofuels and wind.

Rising global demand for natural resources is a key return driver. Most natural resource funds are positively correlated to commodity prices and have low correlations to other asset classes. They can also provide a hedge against inflation.

What Are Managed Futures Accounts?

The futures markets were originally created to manage prices in agricultural commodities, like corn or cotton. Without the futures markets, the price of corn, for example, might plummet at harvest time, when supply outstrips demand. Today, futures markets have expanded to encompass both commodity and financial markets, and the primary objective is to match "hedgers" (like farmers and airlines [jet fuel]) with "speculators" such as the specialized futures managers called *commodity trading advisors* (CTAs). Because the futures markets are not primarily focused on capital formation (like the traditional stock and bond markets), they are regulated by the Commodities Futures Trading Commission (CFTC), rather than the Securities and Exchange Commission (SEC).

Managed futures portfolios are often confused with long commodity investment portfolios. Although the two are related, managed futures accounts are not the same as investing in commodities, and typically managed futures portfolios might hold more Treasury bond futures than corn futures. In addition, the return on managed futures accounts is derived more from risk intermediation between hedgers and speculators than the fact that a specific commodity price might rise over time. Unlike the shares of a growing company that can rise and create value over time, there is no "inherent return" or growth in a commodity; in fact, people tend to use less of a commodity as its price rises.

Futures markets are also needed to allow investment in physical commodities, some of which are perishable. Investing in common stock is based on a paper document that is easily traded between investors; but investing in oil, for example, is difficult unless you happen to own an oil well or a tank farm. The futures markets have been developed to accommodate this process.

Managed futures portfolios are rarely long only and are very actively managed with high turnover. The investment strategies can typically be classified by the trading approach, either systematic or discretionary. Systematic trading typically uses a rule-based trading model, based on past prices, that is designed to identify and follow price trends. Trend following, which is the primary approach for many CTAs, does not attempt to predict the beginning and ending of a trend, but uses quantitative tools to identify whether a trend is in place and when to enter and exit a trend. Managers often focus on short-term, medium-term or long-term trends.

Managed futures have a long history outside the mainstream. They attracted significant attention in the 1980s, but interest fell with the decline in inflation. Recently, managed futures have gained more attention from institutional investors, since managed futures returns are not dependent on the economic growth or the level of interest rates. Managed futures also have low correlations to many other asset classes.

What Is a Derivative?

Derivatives often play an important part in an alternative investment portfolio, especially hedge funds and managed futures funds. Though derivatives are sometimes complex and hard to understand, it is helpful to have a basic knowledge of what they are and how they work.

A *derivative* is a financial contract that promises a future payment or the receipt of money that depends on an underlying asset or other factor. The value of derivatives may be based on:

- **Tradable assets,** for example, stocks, bonds, commodities, residential mortgages, commercial real estate, loans; or
- **Nontradable items** such as a stock market index, currency exchange rate, interest rate, unemployment rate or even weather conditions.

Derivatives are broadly categorized by:

- The relationship between the underlying asset and the derivative (e.g., forward, option, swap)
- The type of underlying asset (e.g., equity derivatives, foreign exchange derivatives, interest rate derivatives, commodity derivatives or credit derivatives)
- The market in which they trade (e.g., exchange traded or over the counter)
- Their payoff.

Derivatives can be used to *speculate,* which is basically betting on what is going to happen to the underlying assets (or items). In contrast, they can be used like insurance to protect against investment portfolio losses. Using derivatives to avoid or reduce investment losses is called *hedging.*

In the Berkshire Hathaway 2002 annual report, Warren Buffet famously called derivatives "financial weapons of mass destruction." He was referring primarily to the systemwide risk that can be created by dealers in derivatives markets, a risk that became obvious during the credit crisis of 2008. Another well-known example was the problem caused by Long-Term Capital Management (LTCM). In 1998, due to excess borrowing amplified through derivative investments, LTCM caused financial stress so severe that the Federal Reserve felt it might destabilize the entire financial system.

The market for derivatives is estimated to be more than $600 trillion in 2011; for comparison, the total value of publicly traded U.S. equities is less than $20 trillion.[6] This lower figure refers to the *notional value* or *total dollar value* of the underlying assets represented by these derivative contracts. But in most cases only a small portion of that value, about $15 trillion, is real money changing hands. This is still a very big market and one that trustees need to understand.

Although the scale and complexity of the market may be scary, derivatives and the alternative investment vehicles that hold them can still be a prudent investment for a responsible trustee; these investment choices just require careful monitoring and prudent limits on exposure. Trustees should also understand that unless derivatives are backed by securities such as stocks or bonds, their value will also depend on the creditworthiness of the other parties (the *counterparties*) in these contracts.

Exhibit 4

Options

	CALL	PUT
BUYER	The **right,** but not the obligation, **to buy**	The **right,** but not the obligation, **to sell**
SELLER	Potential **obligation to sell**	Potential **obligation to buy**

The International Swaps and Derivatives Association (ISDA) has worked to make over-the-counter (OTC) derivatives markets more safe and efficient. The association developed the ISDA Master Agreement (and a range of other documentation that is available on their website) that has helped to reduce the credit and legal risk of derivative contracts.

The most common derivatives are options, futures and swaps.

Options

An *option* is a contract between two parties to trade an asset at a future date at a set price. The option buyer has the right, but no obligation, to fulfill this contract. The seller of the option contract, however, does have the obligation to fulfill the contract if the buyer chooses to go through with the transaction. Therefore, trustees should be especially careful when an investment manager sells or "writes" options for a plan.

An option to buy something is called a *call option* (or just a *call)* while an option to sell an asset is called a *put option* (or just a *put).* Generally, investors purchase a call if they expect the price of an asset to rise and a put if they expect the price to drop. The option market gives investors the ability to hedge price movements; an investor can pay a small premium to place a bet on the movement of an asset's price.

The price at which the buyer and seller (or *writer*) of an option agree to trade is called the *strike price* or *exercise price.* Most options have a relatively short expiration date, on the order of several months. Long-term options are called LEAPS®. If the option is not *exercised* (which is the term used to describe the buyer's decision to fulfill the option contract) by the expiration date, it typically becomes worthless for the buyer.

The right to buy or sell something at a set price in the future is valuable, so the buyer of an option typically pays a premium that takes into consideration: (1) how much the future strike price differs from the current price, (2) the time until the contract expires and (3) the volatility of the asset.

Options can be bought on many different assets, but the biggest markets are in stocks, bonds, currencies and the futures on these assets. Most options are created in a standardized form and traded on an options exchange.

One relatively low risk option strategy is *covered-call writing.* In this strategy, an investment manager sells (writes) a call on a stock that is held in the portfolio. The investor receives the premium for selling the call and is obligated to deliver the stock only if the stock's price rises above the strike price. In a low-growth environment, this premium can increase returns or cushion a decline in stock prices.

Futures and Forwards

Futures are another instrument used by alternative investment managers, especially managed futures or CTAs. A *futures contract* is a promise by two parties to exchange a predetermined quantity and quality of an asset for a set price at a future date. Some futures contracts settle in cash and others must be settled in the actual physical transfer of the asset being traded.

The futures markets began as a way for buyers and sellers of agricultural commodities (e.g., corn, wheat, cattle, sugar) to transact business and to even out market price fluctuations. Imagine if farmers waited until harvest season when everyone else is selling, the price might be very low or perhaps very high depending on the success of the growing season. This is a risk that neither the buyer nor the farmer might want to take.

Unlike the option contracts described above, both the buyer and seller of a futures contract must fulfill the contract on the future delivery date. The buyer of the contract is said to be *"long" the asset,* while the seller of the contract is said to be *"short" the asset.* In many cases, the underlying asset may not be a traditional agricultural commodity; *financial futures* cover stock indexes, interest rates or currencies.

A futures contract may cost nothing to enter, but the exchange requires both parties to put up *margin;* an initial amount of cash as *collateral* (a pledge of specific property to secure the contract). The exchange will then add to *(credit)* or take from *(debit)* this *margin account* as necessary based on the daily profit or loss of the contract. The use of a margin minimizes the risk that either the buyer or the seller of the futures contract will fail to follow through on the contract.

A closely related contract often used in currency markets is called a *forward contract.* A forward is similar to a futures contract in that it specifies the exchange of goods for a specified price at a specified future date. But forwards are typically traded over-the-counter, are not standardized and typically do not require the same margin required by an exchange.

There are two specialized words that are used to describe the difference between the *spot* (current) and future price in a futures contract. When the future price is higher than the spot price, the market is said to be in *contango,* and when the future price is lower than the spot price, the market is said to be in *backwardation.*

Swaps

A *swap* is a contract in which two parties agree to exchange certain benefits (often cash flows) of two related financial instruments. The swap agreement defines the dates when the cash flows are to be paid and the way they are calculated. Trustees should have an understanding of the swaps market since it is by far the largest investment market in the world, making up more than $400 trillion of the total derivatives market discussed earlier.

Swaps can be used to hedge certain risks or to speculate on changes in underlying factors. The primary types of swaps, in order of size, are interest rate swaps, credit default swaps (CDS), commodity swaps and equity swaps.

Interest rate swaps. One of the most common or "plain-vanilla" swaps is the exchange of a floating interest rate for a fixed interest rate. A company might issue floating rate debt to take advantage of lower interest rates and to reduce its market risk, while a bank may be willing to swap a fixed rate for a floating rate because it can more easily hedge the risk and will receive a fee for taking that risk.

Credit default swaps. Another important derivative for trustees to understand is a *credit default swap* (CDS) because it is often used to hedge risk in a traditional fixed income portfolio. The buyer of the CDS makes a series of payments (referred to as a *spread*) to the seller of the CDS and in return receives a payout if the bond or loan defaults.

Buying CDS has been compared to buying insurance because the buyer pays a premium and receives a settlement if the default occurs. However, unlike a typical insurance contract, the buyer can receive a payout on an asset they do not own. For example, when auto parts supplier Delphi filed for bankruptcy in 2005, the firm had $2 billion of senior debt outstanding, but the outstanding CDS had a notional value of $28 billion[7]; so more investors were using CDS to speculate on the demise of Delphi rather than hedging the risk of their bonds.

Total return swaps (TRS). Although TRS are used in many markets, it is worthwhile for trustees to understand these swaps in the context of the equity market since they are often used by hedge funds as an alternative to equity exposure. A TRS is an agreement where one party pays the total return of an asset for a series of periodic payments.

Hedge funds use TRS to obtain leverage on an asset; they receive the return of the asset, typically from a bank, without having to lay out the entire cost of the asset, and therefore obtaining leverage. TRS are also common in many structured finance transactions such as collateralized debt obligations (CDOs).

Conclusion

Alternative investments have many characteristics that can help diversify the risks and returns for investment portfolios. But alternative investments also involve complex investment structures and other risks that need to be carefully considered before you invest; some of the key differences between alternative and traditional investments are summarized in Exhibit 5.

Exhibit 5

Alternative Versus Traditional Investments

Alternative	Traditional
Long and short	Long
Use leverage	No leverage
Low correlation	Tracks benchmark
Absolute return objective	Relative return objective
Performance-based fee	Asset-based fee
Less regulated	More regulated
Manager controls exit.	Client controls exit.

Endnotes

1. Hedge Fund Research, Inc. March 2010.
2. Sizing the 2010 Hedge Fund Universe: A PerTrac Study, April 2011 and Deutsche Bank Ninth Annual Alternative Investment Survey, March 2011.
3. See *Goldstein v. SEC,* 451 F.3d 873 (D.C. Cir. 2006).
4. Dow Jones LP Source, January 2011.
5. Kaplan and Schoar, *Journal of Finance,* August 2005, based on pre-2000 vintage-year funds reported to Venture Economics. Higher returns have been reported by Cambridge Associates and Burgiss Private IQ.
6. Bank for International Settlements, Semiannual OTC Derivatives Markets Statistics, December 2010.
7. ISDA Credit Derivative Symposium, Fordham University, September 29, 2006.

Chapter 44

Insurance and Annuity Products

*Rory Judd Albert**

Benefit plans typically purchase annuity contracts from an insurance company that guarantee the payment of benefits to participants under one of two circumstances: (1) a plan is being terminated or (2) participants are retiring or separating from service with accrued vested benefits from an ongoing plan. Such contracts are commonly known as *benefit distribution annuities.* Plan fiduciaries may also purchase annuities as a plan investment.

When an annuity is purchased to cover a participant's pension benefits, liability for the benefits promised by the plan is transferred to the insurance company selling the annuity. Indeed, the Department of Labor (DOL), the Internal Revenue Service and the Pension Benefit Guaranty Corporation (PBGC) all agree that if the benefit rights of an individual are fully guaranteed by an insurance company, this individual is no longer a plan participant.[1]

The selection of an annuity provider for an employee benefit plan must be made in a prudent manner consistent with the general fiduciary and investment principles discussed in Chapters 5 and 38). As with the selection of any other type of investment vehicle, it is the fiduciary's process in selecting and purchasing annuities—rather than the ultimate result of the fiduciary's decision—that determines whether ERISA prudence requirements have been met.

Another type of insurance product purchased by employee benefit plans and discussed in this chapter is a guaranteed investment contract (GIC). As with the selection of an annuity provider, the purchase of a GIC must also comply with fiduciary obligations under ERISA.

Why Is Selection of an Annuity Provider So Important?

The highly publicized problems of some insurance companies to satisfy their annuity liabilities because of their investment in high-risk debt securities (i.e., junk bonds), troubled real estate loans or a combination of both have substantial implications for pension plans, their sponsors, fiduciaries and participants.[2]

PBGC has taken the position (in connection with a terminated plan) that once a plan sponsor has purchased benefit distribution annuities, the plan sponsor has satisfied its ERISA obligations even if the insurance company is later unable to pay the benefits it has guaranteed through the annuity contract. In a May 1991 opinion letter, PBGC detailed this position in connection with annuity contracts issued by Executive Life. When the insurance company was given a court order to pay only 70% of the amounts owed under retirement annuity policies, PBGC stated the plan sponsor had no liability for the difference.[3]

PBGC also takes the position that if the insurance company is unable to satisfy its annuity contract commitments, PBGC will not pay such benefits. This position is directly contrary to an earlier PBGC position; in 1981 PBGC advised that it generally would guarantee these retirement benefits if an insurance company is unable to pay the benefit under the annuity.

On the other hand, if plan fiduciaries are not prudent in selecting an annuity provider, fiduciaries may be liable. DOL has brought numerous lawsuits against employers whose plans purchased annuities on the grounds that the

*Mr. Albert wishes to gratefully acknowledge the invaluable assistance received from Pamela A. Onufer and Nicole Stein in the preparation of this chapter.

plan fiduciaries failed to follow adequate procedures designed to select the safest available annuity provider.[4]

The Pension Annuitants Protection Act of 1994 amends ERISA and clarifies that former participants or beneficiaries may seek relief if a fiduciary breach has occurred involving the purchase of insurance contracts in connection with their termination as plan participants or beneficiaries.[5] In addition, a DOL Interpretive Bulletin states that a termination is not a valid standard termination under Title IV of ERISA unless the plan administrator selects an insurer in accordance with the fiduciary standards of Title I of ERISA.[6]

What Is Considered the Prudent Selection of an Annuity Provider?

According to DOL, ERISA requires plan fiduciaries to conduct an "objective, thorough and analytical search" to identify and select annuity providers. In conducting this search, fiduciaries must evaluate factors that relate to the provider's claim-paying ability and creditworthiness, including:

- The quality and diversification of the provider's investment portfolio
- The size of the insurer relative to the proposed contract
- The level of the insurer's capital and surplus
- The lines of business of the provider and other indications of the insurer's exposure to liability
- The structure of the annuity contract and guaranties supporting the annuities, such as the use of separate accounts
- The availability of additional protection through state guaranty associations and the extent of the guaranties.

DOL cases make it clear that considering an insurer's financial strength is not enough to satisfy fiduciary duties under ERISA. Recent DOL opinions signal more specifically that it is not acceptable for fiduciaries to rely on rating services rather than independently evaluating an insurance company's financial solvency—even if the company's rating is high.

Unless fiduciaries possess the expertise to evaluate these factors, fiduciaries must obtain the advice of a qualified, independent expert. An amendment to Interpretive Bulletin 95-1 clarifies that an expert is not required in all cases; determining whether an expert is needed is on a case-by-case basis.[7] As an added enforcement measure when single employer plans are terminated, PBGC has announced proposed rules stating that part of its standard termination audit program will be the auditing of insurer selections for compliance with these fiduciary standards.[8]

Safe Harbor for Defined Contribution Plans

In 2008, DOL issued a directive that only defined benefit plans must find the "safest annuity available." At the same time, DOL created a safe harbor for the selection of annuity providers and contracts for benefit distributions from individual account plans.[9] The safe harbor for individual accounts requires that fiduciaries:

- Engage in an objective, thorough and analytical search for the purposes of identifying and selecting providers from which to purchase annuities
- Appropriately consider information sufficient to assess the ability of the annuity provider to make all future payments under the annuity contract
- Appropriately consider the cost (including fees and commissions) of the annuity contract in relation to the benefits and administrative services to be provided under such contract
- Appropriately conclude that, at the time of the selection, the annuity provider is financially able to make all future payments under the annuity contract and the cost of the contract is reasonable in relation to the benefits and services provided under the contract
- If necessary, consult with an expert or experts for purposes of compliance with these conditions.

What Is a Guaranteed Investment Contract (GIC)?

One of the investment vehicles often chosen by plan fiduciaries and offered to participants as an investment option is a contract issued by an insurance company (GIC) or a bank (BIC) that "guarantees" the return of principal and pays a fixed rate of interest.

What Factors Should Be Considered When Selecting a GIC?

In choosing GICs as an investment option, plan fiduciaries should consider several important points. First is that while "guaranteed" is a prominent part of their name, GICs are not guaranteed by either the federal (or any state) government or by plan fiduciaries. The security of a GIC depends entirely on the financial stability of the issuer. If the issuer fails, the investor (i.e., the plan, or plan participants and beneficiaries) may not receive the stated interest rate promised and may even lose part or all of the original investment.

The next factor to consider is that GICs, like other investments, have investment risks that affect whether participants receive the benefits they are promised. One risk is that the investments underlying GICs—typically private placement bonds, mortgages and real estate—are linked to the real estate industry. Over a long period of time, the fixed income return on GICs may not compare with the return obtained from equity investments (e.g., stocks).

Finally, many GICs impose penalties for early withdrawal. If there is a mass layoff or division shutdown, a plan or plan participant may need to make an early withdrawal. It is essential, therefore, to review GIC provisions and clarify what will trigger penalties. Participants considering GICs as an investment option must be advised as to the situations in which they will bear a penalty.

Be aware that the insurance company issuing the GIC may be a plan fiduciary. Under ERISA, a person or organization that exercises authority or control over a plan or its assets is a fiduciary. Since the insurance contract is a plan asset, exercising discretionary authority over the contract makes the insurer a fiduciary.[10]

Guidelines for Fiduciaries

In reaction to the relatively recent financial difficulties in the insurance industry, plan fiduciaries might be considering substituting other fixed income investment options (i.e., government bonds, high-quality corporate debt vehicles, money market funds, etc.) for GICs. Rather than eliminate GICs entirely, however, plan fiduciaries should:

- Evaluate and adjust, if necessary, the plan performance goals and strategies
- Investigate methods to enhance the security and performance of GICs
- Engage in the prudent selection of GICs by soliciting and comparing several bids
- Implement guidelines to ensure the prudent selection of GIC issuers
- Beware of replacing the default risk associated with GICs with an increased market risk
- Consider making shorter term commitments and diversifying investments among various insurance carriers
- Review contracts and other documentation on a periodic basis.

In selecting an issuer, plan fiduciaries should also consider the factors set forth in the discussion relating to the selection of an investment manager provided in Chapter 46.

Communicating the Nature of GICs to Plan Participants

When GICs are offered as an investment option to plan participants, plan fiduciaries should review all plan communications and materials to ensure there is an adequate and accurate description of the plan's GICs and other investment options. In doing so, fiduciaries should seriously consider eliminating the term "guaranteed" to avoid any suggestion that rates or the return of principal are guaranteed by the insurer, the plan or other plan fiduciaries. Terms such as "fixed income fund" or "stable value fund" should be used instead.

Because no rate is guaranteed, when projecting annual rates for a GIC, plan fiduciaries should communicate to participants (1) the current rate of return, (2) historical rates of return and (3) the rates of other accounts with similar liquidity. This will provide plan participants a basis for comparison.

Information should be made available to plan participants regarding the quality of the GIC offered. For example, participants should be advised, among other things, as to:

- The number of issuers represented in the portfolio
- The percentage of the portfolio that is held by any single issuer
- The average maturity of all contracts in the portfolio
- The quality standards used to determine whether an issuer may be included in the portfolio.

Plan participants should be made aware, in clear and concise terms, of the action that will be taken in the event that the issuer defaults on its obligations or otherwise fails.

Plan fiduciaries should also clarify the alternatives to GICs that are offered by the plan. Such clarification should include an explanation as to how and when transfers may be made from a GIC to another vehicle, as well as a description of any risks associated with such a transfer. Plan investment guidelines may have to be revised to permit other high-quality, stable value investments, in addition to GICs, that are consistent with the plan objectives.

Finally, and perhaps most importantly, plan fiduciaries should consider retaining outside investment experts to assist plan participants in understanding the relative security of their GIC portfolio, notwithstanding the events in the insurance industry.

What Fiduciary Duties Apply to the Purchase of GICs?

As with all investment decisions, fiduciaries purchasing GICs are subject to the fiduciary obligations imposed under ERISA. Not surprisingly, the test of prudence with respect to a GIC is whether trustees appropriately investigated and structured the investment at the time the investment was made.[11] According to DOL, it would not be prudent to choose a GIC that provides less return than other investments with comparable risk. Similarly, it would not be prudent to choose a GIC that involves greater risk but offered a similar return.[12] In deciding whether to invest in a GIC and which insurer to use, fiduciaries must:

- Investigate the options
- Assess the prudence of their decisions
- Adequately investigate the soundness and stability of the insurance company.[13]

By way of example, investment in a GIC that has a single maturity date, rather than staggered dates, may be a breach of fiduciary duty if the investment does not address a plan's cash flow needs. One court held that it was a breach of prudence and diversification duties to invest 70% of plan assets in long-term bonds with the same maturity dates; the bonds had to be sold at a loss in order to cover benefit distributions.[14]

Do Fiduciaries Have Any Other Responsibilities With Respect to Insurance Products?

Where plans have investments in insurance companies that are known to be experiencing economic difficulties, fiduciaries must (1) take action to understand all facts relating to the troubled investment (including the nature of the plan's investment and the plan's contractual rights and obligations) and (2) rigorously evaluate and monitor the investment as well as the regulatory developments governing the insurance company and the particular investment.

Endnotes

1. See PBGC Adv. Op. Ltr. No. 91-1 1991 PBGC LEXIS 3 (Jan. 14, 1991); 29 CFR §2510.3-3(d)(2)(ii).
2. Among these companies are Executive Life Company of California, Executive Life Company of New York, Mutual Benefit Life in New Jersey and, most recently, Confederation Life.
3. See PBGC Adv. Op. Ltr. No. 914 1991 PBGC LEXIS 4 (May 3, 1991).
4. See *Martin v. BMC Industries, Inc.*, 19 Pens. Rep. 630 (D.Minn. 1992); *Martin v. Geosource Inc.*, 18 Pens. Rep. 2012 (S.D.Texas 1991); *Martin v. AFG Industries, Inc.*, 18 Pens. Rep. 1242 (N.D.Texas 1991) (fiduciaries failed to implement a meaningful bid process or meaningful analysis of Executive Life's creditworthiness or claims paying ability); *Martin v. Magnetek*, 18 Pens. Rep. 991 (E.D.Wis. 1991); and *Martin v. Pacific Lumber Co.*, 18 Pens. Rep. 991 (N.D.Cal. 1991). The complaints in these cases charge that it is insufficient for a plan fiduciary to rely on the rating services, all of which initially rated Executive Life very highly, rather than independently evaluating the solvency of a company offering a pension plan. See also *Martin v. StrouseAdler* (D.Conn. 1991) (complaint alleges that the fiduciaries violated ERISA's exclusive purpose and fiduciary duty provisions by causing the plan to purchase annuities from Presidential Life Insurance Company to fund benefits upon plan termination when the plan had sufficient assets to purchase annuities from a more secure insurance carrier).
5. Pension Annuitants Protection Act of 1994, Pub L. No. 103-401 (Oct. 22, 1994).
6. DOL Interpretive Bulletin 95-1 (Mar. 6, 1995).
7. Amendment to Interpretive Bulletin No. 95-1, 73 *Fed. Reg.* 58,447 (Oct. 7, 2008).
8. See 62 *Fed. Reg.* 60424, Final Rule of PBGC for termination of single employer plans (amending termination regulation to extend deadlines, to otherwise simplify the termination process, and to ensure that plan participants receive information on state guaranty coverage of annuities).
9. 73 *Fed. Reg.* 58,447 (Oct. 7, 2008).
10. See *Chicago Bd. Options Exchange, Inc. v. Conn. Gen. Life Ins. Co.*, 713 F.2d 254, 260 (7th Cir. 1983) (insurer was a fiduciary because it had power to amend contract). See also *Harris Trust & Sav. Bank v. John Hancock Mut. Life Ins. Co.*, 114 S.Ct. 517 (1993), affirmed in part and reversed in part, 302 F.3d 18 (2d Cir. 2002) ("To the extent that [the insurer] engages in the discretionary management of assets attributable to that phase of the contract which provides no guarantee of benefit payments or fixed rates of return, it seems to us that [the insurer] should be subject to fiduciary responsibility.") (insurance company was not a fiduciary in regard to guaranteed group annuity contract where it did not exercise any discretionary authority or control over the management or disposition of the policy itself; however, fiduciary duties were implicated with respect to portion of plan assets that were not guaranteed). But see *Mack Boring & Parts v. Meeker Sharkey Moffitt*, 930 F.2d 267 (3d Cir. 1991) (appellee insurer was not an ERISA fiduciary by virtue of ERISA's guaranteed benefit policy exception under §1101(b)(2) because the account at issue was a general account insurance contract in which the issuing insurance company guaranteed to the plan participants a fixed amount of benefits, payable at a clearly stated time, without variable, and therefore not subject to plan asset treatment).
11. In re Unisys Savings Plan Litig., 74 F.3d 420, 435 (3d Cir.), cert. denied, 117 S.Ct. 56 (1996) (fiduciaries were obligated to impart to plaintiffs material information within their knowledge that was sufficient to apprise plaintiffs of the risks associated with the GIC investments at issue).
12. DOL Adv. Op. Ltr. (WSB) No. DL0014 (Mar. 4, 1985).
13. See *Whitfield v. Tomasso*, 682 F.Supp. 1287 (E.D.N.Y. 1988) (trustees breached fiduciary duties of prudence and diversification by investing substantial amount of plan assets in questionable insurance company; trustees did not investigate financial soundness of company, did not review ratings and did not consult an expert).
14. See *GIW Indus., Inc. v. Trevor, Stewart, Burton & Jacobsen, Inc.*, 895 F.2d 729 (11th Cir. 1990), aff'g, 10 EBC 2290 (S.D.Ga. 1989); cf. In re Unisys Savings Plan Litig., 74 F.3d 420, 435 (3d Cir.), cert. denied, 117 S.Ct. 56 (1996).

Chapter 45

The Role of the Investment Consultant

Julian M. Regan

Investment consultants provide a valuable service to multiemployer benefit plans and fiduciaries. Consultants should be trusted, independent advisors that:

- Help develop a plan's investment policy statement
- Deliver guidance concerning a plan's asset allocation strategy
- Recommend investment managers and a management structure to help implement asset allocation strategy
- Oversee plan investment performance in line with established objectives and risk tolerances
- Assist in oversight of investment administration
- Recommend corrective action as appropriate
- Monitor markets and the economy.

While some consulting firms service all kinds of institutions including multiemployer, public and corporate plans, others specialize in one or more of these client groups. Most firms have the ability to consult on defined benefit, defined contribution, and health and welfare plans. Others possess specific expertise in one or more of these areas. Some consulting firms focus exclusively on a particular type of asset such as hedge funds, private equity or real estate.

From an organizational perspective, consulting firms may be distinguished from one another by whether they operate independently or are part of a larger firm that includes other business lines. A number of firms that provide actuarial or brokerage services also provide investment consulting.

What Should Trustees Expect From an Investment Consultant?

Most plans use a consulting firm on an ongoing basis for guidance with investment policy development, asset allocation, investment manager selection, performance evaluation and investment education. With such a broad-based relationship, the investment consultant is a key advisor to plan trustees and administrators. A plan may also have a shorter term relationship—hiring a consulting firm for a specific function. For example, a consulting firm might assist with management of one asset category such as hedge funds, provide advice on asset allocation or prepare performance reports. Due to resource considerations, selecting a consultant for a specialty role is more common among larger plans.

A number of consulting firms also provide specialty capabilities such as custodian bank reviews, proxy voting services, defined contribution service provider fee analysis and other assessments. Exhibit 1 describes in more detail services that are generally offered by investment consultants.

What Is the Process for Selecting an Investment Consultant?

When trustees select a consulting firm, they are choosing an individual as well as a firm. A good starting point in the process is to define the duties for the investment consultant to perform. As stated earlier, the duties of the consultant may be very general in nature or they may serve a very specific function.

Minimum qualifications need to be established for the firms to be considered. These criteria should be broad enough to include a range of capable firms but specific enough to avoid evaluating unqualified firms. Minimum qualifications might address:

- The number of years the firm has been in business
- The firm's status as an SEC registered investment advisor

Exhibit 1

Investment Consultant Services

Service	Capabilities and Resources
Investment objectives and policy development	• Performance benchmarks and risk guidelines • Asset allocation targets, thresholds and return objectives • Roles, responsibilities and reporting requirements of fiduciaries
Asset allocation	• Asset/liability studies • Capital market assumptions (risk, return, etc.) • Asset class correlations • Liquidity/cash flow analysis
Investment manager selection	• Investment manager databases • Interviews of potential managers with trustees • Quantitative screens and qualitative analysis • Due diligence questionnaires and on-site meetings
Performance reporting	• Annualized, quarterly and inception-to-date returns • Performance benchmarks and risk characteristics • Universe comparison services, organizational changes
Investment education	• Meetings with subject matter experts • Presentations and seminars • Updates on investment and regulatory developments • Research on investment strategies or asset classes

- The number of years of investment experience of the proposed primary consultant.

Beyond setting objectives and minimum qualifications, trustees must establish criteria to evaluate the candidates, including:

- The history, stability and commitment of the firm as measured by ownership, years in the business and client base
- The firm's business strategy and the distinguishing characteristics of its service
- Availability of resources in key areas such as research and performance reporting
- Experience and skill sets of the proposed consulting team
- The proposed consultants' work load and availability to appear at trustee meetings
- Availability of support staff and backup personnel
- Independence and freedom from potential conflicts of interest
- Strength of operational controls and of the firm's internal compliance program
- Reputation and service quality as evidenced by client references
- Locations of offices and backup/disaster recovery capabilities
- Fees and costs encompassing all foreseeable assignments.

Two of the most important characteristics expected of an investment consultant are independence and objectivity. Questions to ask candidate firms are whether they (1) receive revenue from any investment management organizations, (2) have other conflicts of interest that should be disclosed and (3) have internal compliance policies designed to ensure independence and objectivity. Other essential questions to ask during the selection process are provided in the appendix—a questionnaire developed by Bernard M. Baum, counsel to a large number of pension plans.

What Are the Primary Services of an Investment Consultant?

Investment Objectives and Policy Development

An investment policy statement is the primary governance document for a plan's investment program. As such, all decisions, contracts, monitoring actions and reports should tie back to it. As shown in Exhibit 2, trustees and administrators, assisted by an investment consultant, are responsible for development and implementation of plan investment policy. While investment managers may be responsible for tactical implementation of portions of a policy, they may not have a broad view of the whole plan and the many factors that influence it. Trustees, administrators and an investment consultant are in the best position to manage the overall investment program.

A good investment consultant must understand a plan's funded status, future liabilities and cash flow needs as well as demographics. The plan's consultant can then advise on alternatives for meeting the plan's absolute and relative return objectives. The *absolute return objective* is the return required to meet the plan's benefit obligations, actuarial assumptions and other factors. The *relative return objective* is a return that meets or exceeds a benchmark representing the plan's mix of investment assets.

Consultants have the responsibility to educate plan decision makers on the risks associated with investment options. This will help trustees establish the plan's risk tolerance, which is then documented in the investment policy statement. A discussion of correlation between asset classes will help trustees understand how a combination of asset types with different patterns of return and risk can reduce risk (volatility) and increase potential return.

The consultant will help trustees decide which strategies are appropriate to achieve plan investment objectives and whether to seek out the assistance of an investment manager or managers. More specifically, a consultant can help trustees decide:

- Whether to employ active investment strategies in an effort to exceed index performance benchmarks or passive strategies to meet benchmark results
- The number of investment managers to utilize and strategies for each asset class
- Whether to use generalist managers, specialty managers or both.

The role of the consultant is to help trustees make these decisions—outlining the benefits, risks and costs associated with each alternative. Consultants can also help trustees implement decisions.

Asset Allocation

A plan's asset allocation strategy is a major element of a plan's investment policy. Research studies indicate that asset allocation determines a substantial portion of a portfolio's long-term performance. Other investment decisions such as whether to manage assets in an active or passive strategy, the number and categories of managers utilized and security selection are important, but have less effect on a portfolio's return.

Asset allocation is an investment strategy that is aimed at achieving an appropriate balance between risk and return based on a plan's goals, risk tolerance and time horizon. It is implemented by diversifying assets across various asset classes. These classes range from traditional equities (stocks) and fixed income (bonds), to alternatives such as real estate, private equity and hedge funds.

Once trustees establish target allocations for each asset class, a consultant can stress test different asset mixes to help determine the best approach for achieving fund objectives. Trustees will want to focus on risks associated with the most volatile asset classes, such as equities, and on the least liquid asset classes. No single asset mix is appropriate for all plans.

An investment consultant will also prepare the periodic investment reviews needed to determine whether the asset allocation strategies are achieving the plan's long-term benefit obligations. Information that is part of this process includes the plan's:

- Investment objectives, risk tolerances, liquidity needs and history
- Asset class returns, risk and correlations on a historical and forward-looking basis
- Funded status, liability structure and demographics.

Investment Manager Selection and Evaluation

Investment consulting organizations typically have a department responsible for investment manager search and evaluation. The persons in this unit:

- Collect detailed information on hundreds of investment management firms
- Verify these firms' investment results and characteristics
- Conduct due diligence interviews and site visits to assess the firms' management capabilities and risk controls.

Exhibit 2

Sample Structure of Investment Roles*

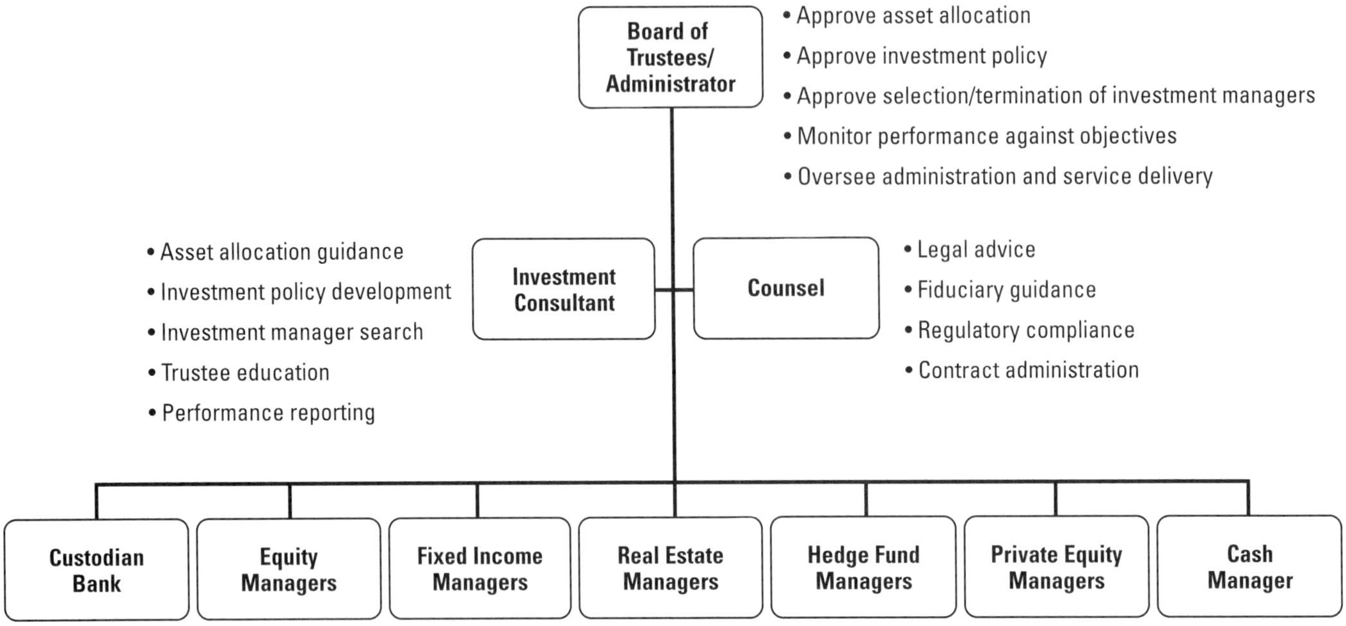

*Chart does not include other consultants, such as an auditor and actuary.

This department within a consulting firm can provide the information needed to identify the best candidates. This department can help narrow the list of firms to be interviewed. It can also help with the interview process, selecting managers, checking references, negotiating fees, etc. It is also the people in this department who are usually responsible for gathering information on new investment strategies that trustees may want to consider as the plan's investment program and markets evolve.

A consultant's independence from conflicts of interest is particularly important when considering investment management firms. In some cases, a manager may subscribe to performance-ranking services offered by the consultant. Another scenario is the possibility that the consultant is partially owned by an investment firm. Relationships do not preclude the consultant from providing independent advice. The consultant should proactively communicate to everyone involved that a relationship exists. Those with fiduciary responsibility for the selection of a manager must document this fact and reach conclusions as to who is the most appropriate management choice.

Performance Measurement and Evaluation

Trustees need reports that will help assess how well the investment managers are meeting the criteria established when they were hired. Performance measurement and evaluation services should be an integral part of the ongoing relationship with the consultant. Reports provide an objective, independent evaluation of a plan's overall investment performance and risk. These reports typically include:

- Updates on the market environment in which investment results were achieved
- The market value of asset class holdings relative to the asset allocation targets
- Returns over multiple periods relative to a benchmark index and peer groups
- Risk characteristics (e.g., duration for a bond manager) relative to guidelines
- Information on cash flows into and out of the trust fund
- Estimated fees and costs associated with the investment strategies.

To prepare these reports, a consulting firm will collect asset and transaction data from the plan's custodian bank and investment manager(s), edit the data, account for all securities and calculate rates of return. This is a detail-oriented, time-consuming operation that requires rigorous quality control. The firm calculates returns based on data provided by the plan's custodian bank rather than data available from the investment manager. A representative of the consulting firm then compares the firm's results to those calculated by the investment manager, and reconciles any differences.

The performance report spotlights where further analysis or corrective action may be needed. The consulting firm will also provide information to assess each manager, including any material changes in management, regulatory status or strategy.

If a plan uses any active management strategies, it is likely there will be occasions when a manager does not achieve the established objectives. Trustees may determine that some reasons for a manager's underperformance are acceptable. In other situations, the reasons may be unacceptable and require corrective action. The decision to replace an underperforming manager should be based on objective analysis using appropriate time periods and criteria.

How Can a Consultant Help With Proxy Voting?

Corporate governance can be influenced through proxy voting and is an area of increasing focus for benefit plans. This is especially true in the wake of recent financial crises and studies that link best governance practices to improved returns for long-term shareholders. The U.S. Department of Labor has made it clear that voting via the proxy ballots associated with common stocks owned by the plan is a fiduciary act.

A small number of investment consulting firms now offer a proxy voting service to institutional investors. While responsibility for researching issues and voting proxies may be delegated to a plan's investment managers or other registered investment advisor, the investment consultant is likely to be in a better position than managers to research and vote the proxies based on a plan's versus others' interests. Using a consultant also helps ensure that proxy ballots for companies held by more than one manager are voted uniformly.

How Can a Consultant Help With Custodian Bank Monitoring?

Custodian banks are responsible for the safekeeping of plan assets, pricing securities, collecting dividend and interest payments, settling trades, investing idle cash within each investment manager's account and providing audited accounting reports. To a large degree, these activities occur in the background. As a result, it can be challenging to determine whether a custodian is performing appropriately. Although this is a service not offered by all consultant firms, consultants are in a position to monitor a custodian and determine whether the custodian has the necessary expertise and resources.

Conclusion

Investment consultants perform a critical role assisting institutional investors develop, implement and oversee investment programs. Increasingly, such investors are using investment consultants. As of 2008, 85% of institutional investors reported utilizing an investment consultant. Knowledgeable investment consultants with an understanding of individual benefit plan needs are well-positioned to help fiduciaries meet the challenges created by recent changes in the economy, financial markets and regulatory environment. It is essential that plan trustees seek consultants that are well-qualified, independent and objective.

SAMPLE PENSION INVESTMENT CONSULTANT QUESTIONNAIRE

Name of Respondent: ______________________________

Title: ______________________________

Address: ______________________________

Telephone: ______________________________

I. ORGANIZATION

A. GENERAL

1. When was your firm founded?
2. What is the present ownership of your organization? Please be specific.
3. Has your firm merged with, been acquired by, or acquired another organization within the past three years?
4. Does your firm or any affiliate of your firm provide trust, investment management or securities brokerage services? If yes, please explain.

B. PENSION INVESTMENT CONSULTING

1. When did your firm begin providing investment consulting?
2. What were the revenues attributable to your investment consulting practice during your last fiscal year?
3. What percentage of your organization's revenues was attributable to the investment consulting practice?
4. What has been the compound growth rate in investment consulting revenues during the past three fiscal years?
5. Besides consulting, what other investment-related services do you provide to pension clients?
6. Does your firm provide investment-related services to investment managers? If yes, please describe them and detail any revenues.

The remainder of this questionnaire applies to your firm's investment consulting practice unless otherwise indicated.

II. STAFFING

1. What is the total size of your staff?
   How many of these are consultants?
2. Please attach biographical information on your five most senior consultants.
3. Please list all consultants who have left your staff during the past three years. Include their reasons for leaving and present employer (if known).
4. Based on what you know at this point, what consultant(s) would you expect to assign to the client's relationship? Please provide biographical information below.

III. CLIENTS

1. Please provide on an attachment a representative list of your investment consulting clients.
   Please list your Taft-Hartley clients and the size of the portfolios you manage for them.
2. How many clients pay you an agreed-upon retainer fee?
   Are you willing to accept nonretainer clients for specific assignments?
3. Of your retainer clients, how many are in each of the following categories?
   Taft-Hartley __________
   Corporate __________
   Public Funds __________
   Foundation and Endowment __________
   Other __________
4. Please list clients that have terminated your firm's services during the past three years. Indicate their reasons for terminating your services.
5. Please provide five references below. To the extent you have them, include Taft-Hartley clients for whom you provide performance measurement/evaluation services. Please indicate contact name, address and telephone number.

IV. SERVICES

A. GENERAL

1. Please indicate with an "X" which of the services listed below your firm provides.
   Investment policy development __________
   Asset mix modeling __________
   Asset/liability modeling __________
   Investment manager selection __________
   Domestic equity __________
   Domestic fixed income __________
   International equity __________
   International fixed income __________
   Alternative investments (e.g., real estate) __________
   Other: ______________________________ __________
   ______________________________ __________
   Insurance contract selection/negotiation __________
   Performance measurement/evaluation __________
   Analysis of trading __________
   Proxy voting __________

Please respond to the following questions regarding specific services.

B. ASSET ALLOCATION/INVESTMENT POLICY DEVELOPMENT

1. Describe briefly the processes and tools your firm uses to help clients develop investment policies and objectives.
   To what extent do you use models or quantitative techniques? Please describe them.
2. Does your firm assist clients in making shorter term tactical asset allocation decisions? If yes, please describe the process you use.

C. MANAGER SELECTION

1. How many investment managers are in your manager database?
   Please indicate how many are in the following categories:

U.S. equity	__________
U.S. fixed income	__________
Non-U.S. equity	__________
Non-U.S. fixed income	__________
Real estate equity	__________
Hedge funds	__________
Private equity	__________
Other alternatives	__________

2. What process do you use to evaluate investment managers? Do you conduct on-site visits? Please explain.
3. Do you classify equity managers by style? If yes, please indicate the style categories you use.
   What process do you use to determine a manager's style?
4. How do you verify the validity of a manager's performance records?

D. PERFORMANCE MEASUREMENT AND EVALUATION

1. How frequently do you produce performance evaluation reports for your clients?
   How frequently do you meet with your performance evaluation clients?
2. Do you purchase universe data or do you maintain your own? If purchased, from whom?
   Please specify the universes you have available.
   Do you maintain a separate universe of Taft-Hartley funds?
3. Besides your performance universes, what other databases do you use in your performance evaluation and analysis?
4. Describe the types of analysis included in a typical performance evaluation report. Please enclose a sample performance report.
5. To what extent can your performance reports be customized to meet a particular client's needs? Please explain.
6. What do you believe sets your performance evaluation services apart from the competition?

V. FEES

1. How are your fees normally determined?
2. To the extent your firm has agreed-upon retainer fees, what services are typically covered by the retainer?
3. Does your firm offer an all-inclusive retainer?
4. What is the range of the annual retainer fees currently being paid by your clients?
5. Do you accept "soft-dollar" payments? Please explain.
6. Please estimate your annual fee for providing performance evaluation consulting to our plan. You may use the following assumptions:

Defined Benefit Plan	($00,000,000.00)
Defined Contribution Plan	($00,000,000.00)
The portfolios include:	Number and Categories of Managers
	Quarterly Reports
	Quarterly Meetings

7. Please estimate additional fees, if any, for:

Selecting investment manager(s)	__________
Developing/reevaluating investment policies	__________

VI. LEGAL

1. Is your firm registered as an investment advisor with the Securities and Exchange Commission?
2. Does your firm consider itself to be a fiduciary in its role as pension investment consultant?
3. Has your firm or a principal of your firm ever been investigated by SEC or another regulatory agency? If yes, please explain.
4. Has your firm or a principal of your firm ever been charged by SEC or any other regulatory agency of any violation of applicable law? If yes, please explain.
5. Do you have any clients or associations that could present a conflict of interest and preclude you from representing this fund? If yes, please explain.
6. At the present time, does your firm have any lawsuits pending against it concerning the performance of investment consulting services for any client? If yes, please explain.

Source: Bernard M. Baum, Of Counsel, Baum, Sigman, Auerbach & Neuman, Ltd., Chicago, Illinois.

Chapter 46

Selecting an Investment Manager

Julian M. Regan

Benefit plan investment managers that manage benefit plan assets are diverse in their structure and size. They include divisions of banks, insurance companies and large financial services companies as well as smaller independent firms. Investment managers may specialize in traditional asset classes, such as stocks or bonds, or they may specialize in alternative investments such as real estate equity, private equity or funds of hedge funds.

Some firms provide investment management services across multiple asset classes and strategies, while others are dedicated to a few strategies or even a single strategy. As a matter of practice, most plans contract with multiple investment managers for different capabilities within different asset classes.

Depending on the amount of plan assets, investment managers may propose managing investments through a separate account established specifically for a plan, mutual funds or commingled vehicles. Within traditional asset classes, investment managers may specialize in active management focused on outperforming a specific benchmark or on passive management designed to match a benchmark.

Larger firms typically offer products across a number of asset classes, while smaller firms may offer investment management within a limited number of strategies.

Who Regulates Investment Managers?

The U.S. Securities and Exchange Commission (SEC) is the principal regulator of investment managers and companies in the United States. The major laws that govern investment companies and advisors are the Investment Company Act of 1940 and the Investment Advisers Act of 1940. Additional laws include the Securities Act of 1933 and the Securities Exchange Act of 1934. Investment manager activities are also governed by the Financial Industry Regulatory Authority (FINRA), the U.S. Department of Labor (DOL), the Internal Revenue Service (IRS), other federal agencies and statutes (e.g., anti-money-laundering statutes) plus various state regulatory agencies. The Dodd–Frank Wall Street Reform and Consumer Protection Act further impacted the regulatory framework for certain types of investment management. As of this writing, authorities were in the process of developing regulations under this act.

What Roles and Responsibilities Do Trustees Have When Selecting Investment Managers?

Benefit plan trustees have a fiduciary duty to choose fund managers based on the best interests of plan participants and beneficiaries. Further, trustees are required to select and monitor managers in a manner that is prudent and consistent with a plan's written investment policy statement. Fiduciary responsibilities are spelled out by the Employee Retirement Income Security Act of 1974 (ERISA) and other federal and state laws, as well as by other rules and regulations governing multiemployer, corporate and public retirement plans.

Trustees of a benefit plan may delegate investment-related decisions to a subset of the board by forming a standing investment committee. In addition, trustees often delegate authority for investment-related decisions and tasks to an executive staff, administrator and/or investment consultant. The plan's investment policy statement, contracts and other governance documents should spell out how this delegation works.

When trustees contract with an investment manager, they are delegating authority for the management of certain assets of the plan among allowable asset classes. The investment manager is generally responsible for the selection and sale of individual securities within the allowable asset class. Managers are also responsible for diversifying the portfolio in a manner that minimizes risk and is consistent with the plan's investment policy statement.

Trustees must have a high degree of trust in any managers employed as well as confidence in their abilities to meet the objectives set for them. However, trust is never a substitute for verifying the capabilities of a manager prior to and during the relationship. Therefore, many plans employ an independent investment consultant to assist in selecting managers and monitoring their results. Typically, the investment consultant also assists trustees in setting the plan asset allocation and writing the investment policy statement.

How Can an Investment Consultant Help in the Selection Process?

When selecting an investment manager, a consultant can help trustees:

- Identify investment management firms that are most likely to meet plan's needs
- Screen prospective investment managers to result in a manageable number
- Provide tools and reports that will help trustees compare different managers
- Provide independently verified data on each manager's historical performance and risk
- Assess costs, capabilities, regulatory compliance and organizational history.

Like trustees, investment consultants have a fiduciary duty to the plan within the scope of the services they provide. For more information on investment consultants, including how to select one, read Chapter 45.

What Is the Process for Selecting an Investment Manager?

A plan's investment policy statement and other plan policies provide a broad framework for selecting an investment manager. The process includes the following steps:

- **Investment manager screen.** A consultant or plan employee conducts an initial search for a manageable number of candidates who meet preestablished criteria.
- **Request for Proposal (RFP).** The consultant or plan employee may issue an RFP or questionnaire requesting specific information from each candidate. This information typically includes background on the organization, the firm's investment philosophy and process, portfolio characteristics and performance, risk management, key and related personnel, fees, similar clients, regulatory and legal issues, etc.
- **Written summary of candidates.** Based on the responses to the RFP, questionnaire or other due diligence process, the consultant or plan employee prepares a summary for trustees and other plan decision makers.
- **Selection of finalists.** Typically, trustees and administrators, with the assistance of a consultant, select a smaller group of finalists from the original, larger group of candidates.
- **Finalist interviews.** Assisted by the consultant and/or staff and other advisors, trustees and administrators typically conduct interviews of the finalist firms, although under certain arrangements they may delegate this task.
- **Reference checks/site visits.** Staff or the consultant may conduct reference checks and, possibly, on-site visits. This step may precede the finalist interview process.
- **Selection and contract negotiations.** Once trustees have made a decision, the plan's legal counsel begins contract negotiations with the selected firm.

What Factors Should Be Considered When Selecting an Investment Manager?

Once trustees have the necessary information about each potential manager, it is time to evaluate the candidates and their products against preestablished selection criteria. Examination typically includes these characteristics:

- Experience as evidenced by years in business, clients and client assets under management
- Stability of management as evidenced by the tenure of the portfolio management team
- Experience managing assets using the investment strategy or strategies being considered
- Historical performance as measured by returns and risks compared to a benchmark and the candidate's peers
- Adherence to the specified style and strategy through market cycles
- Conformity to standards such as the Global Investment Performance Standards (GIPS)
- Capability in managing market risk, operations
- Adherence to fiduciary duty
- Competitiveness of fees
- Insurance coverage in place at the firm.

Tip for Trustees

Selecting an investment manager is integral in meeting a plan's investment objectives. Keep these points in mind when carrying out this task on behalf of plan participants and beneficiaries:

- Selecting investment managers is dependent on sound decision making regarding the plan's asset allocation structure, investment manager structure and investment policy.
- Given the complexity, number of investment managers, and qualitative and quantitative criteria to be tracked, it is critical to take a systematic approach to selecting managers.
- Document every step in the investment manager selection process and termination process, if the latter applies.
- Investment manager's past performance and adherence to risk controls are selection criteria, but historical returns do not guarantee future results and should be used as just one of many inputs into the selection decision.
- Assess investment managers' performance over time periods such as market cycles in reaching conclusions about their capabilities.
- Fees are important selection criteria. They will vary depending on the investment strategy being considered.
- Given the level of trust that must be placed in investment managers, it is critical to get independent, verifiable reporting on manager performance and risk.

How Are Investment Management Services Monitored and Evaluated?

Performance Measurement

In addition to the preestablished performance and risk criteria provided a manager as part of the contract process, independent information is needed to assess how well the manager is meeting a plan's investment guidelines. This information includes:

- Quarterly performance reviews and risk reports with a comparison against a benchmark or peer group representing investment strategies or approaches provided by the plan's investment consultant and/or internal staff
- Asset valuations provided by the custodian bank that serves as the plan's book of record
- Audits and control testing performed by the plan's auditor
- Periodic reviews of investment manager regulatory filings such as Form SEC ADV Part I and Part II
- Updates on market and regulatory developments affecting the manager's strategy
- Periodic meetings held with the investment manager to discuss performance and risk.

A plan's investment policy statement typically spells out the investment manager's responsibility to provide reports.

Consideration of Corrective Action

If a plan has retained active investment managers, they are expected to beat the return on a certain benchmark and to outperform their peers over certain time periods. The investment policy statement will document the manager's benchmark and peer group along with periods for assessing their performance. In some cases, an active investment manager may fail to achieve the benchmark assigned. Depending on the circumstances, this outcome may or may not be viewed as acceptable. For those situations that are not explainable or where underperformance has occurred over a market cycle, trustees will want to strongly consider taking corrective action. This may include placing the manager under a heightened monitoring process or terminating the manager and replacing them. In all cases, the steps taken should tie back to the language in the investment policy statement.

In considering corrective action, trustees should perform an objective and careful analysis of the manager's long-term performance, risk and adherence to fund guidelines. This type of analysis is typically facilitated by the investment consultant. Beyond risk-adjusted performance there are other reasons for a plan to terminate an investment manager. These may include the trustees' decision to adopt a new asset allocation policy or developments at the investment management firm unrelated to performance, such as the departure of key investment personnel. As is always the case, trustees should consider these developments in the context of participants' best interest and the provisions of the investment policy statement.

Chapter 47

Investment Objectives and Policy Statements

Sandy Lincoln

The establishment of appropriate investment objectives and policies may be the single most important factor to a plan's investment success. *Investment objectives* are the desired results for investing a benefit plan's assets over time. *Investment policies* are the key means to help achieve these results. For most plans, the establishment of investment objectives and policies has already been done and, hopefully, they are well documented. Nevertheless, it is important to revisit these issues on a regular basis.

Why Are Investment Objectives and Policy Statements Needed?

Investment objectives and policies are keys to securing benefits for plan beneficiaries. They provide guidelines for the decisions trustees and others make concerning the investment of plan funds. It is not uncommon for many people and organizations to make fund investment decisions. Clear roles and responsibilities as well as lines of authority are invaluable. They assure accountability for the decision made. Having this information in writing helps provide legal protection, improves communication and instructs investment managers.

- **For legal protection.** If a fund is subjected to a compliance audit by the Department of Labor, chances are the investigating officer will begin by asking, "May I see a copy of your investment policy statement?" It is comforting be able to respond by pulling a document out of a file that states the basis upon which fiduciaries have made decisions. ERISA requires that "care, skill, prudence and diligence" be applied in the investment decision process; it is presumptuous to think this can be accomplished without clear written directives.

Tip for Trustees

Ask to review a copy of your plan's investment objectives. They are probably part of your plan's investment policy statement. Investment objectives are your desired results—not guaranteed results!

- **For improving communication.** Reaching agreement on a policy statement requires substantial communication among the trustees and professional advisors involved. The understanding that develops among participants combined with an improved flow of information provides the basis for implementation as well as future evaluation and changes.
- **For instructing investment managers.** A written statement provides investment managers with important background information concerning the fund, including the fund's goals, objectives and any unique requirements. The statement helps ensure actions of managers are consistent with plan needs.

What Are Appropriate Investment Objectives for a Benefit Plan?

Objectives that are common for the investment of pension funds are to:

- **Earn a return that meets or exceeds the plan's actuarial interest rate.** The most essential item objective is what rate of return to seek on investments over the long term. The financial condition of the plan reflected in the plan's actuarial interest rate will influence the return chosen. Of course, the higher the return, the more risk. The higher the desired return, the more risk that is required. Generally, stocks offer more return than bonds. Stocks also involve more variation and uncertainty, in other words, more risk.

- **Earn returns above inflation.** Earning a return higher than inflation over a long period helps provide assurance that plan assets will keep pace with and, hopefully, stay ahead of inflation. Inflation moves up and down significantly over time. A return greater than inflation over the long term is key to maintaining both the purchasing power of a plan and plan participants' benefits. The return earned in excess of inflation is called the *real return.* If a plan's trustees and actuary expect long-term inflation to be 2%, the plan needs a return of 5% to achieve a real return of 3%. Sometimes, the real return is easy to meet or beat, other times it can be a challenge.
- **Earn returns that rank in the top half (or better) compared to others.** Comparing a fund to other funds with a similar investment profile is helpful to judge the performance of an investment plan. Trustees establish *relative performance objectives* that compare the investment performance of their plan to other plans with similar asset allocations (similar levels invested in stocks, bonds, real estate, etc.). Data on other plans' investments is usually provided by a plan's investment consultant or custodian. When a plan earns a -6% return, it is important to know if other funds during the same period earned a higher or lower return. Trustees frequently adopt a relative performance objective that their plan's investments will rank in the top half of funds with a similar asset allocation over multiple time periods.
- **Earn returns that meet or exceed returns of a blended index.** In addition to comparing a plan's investment returns with similar funds, it is common to compare a plan's returns with those generated from a blend of index returns. A *blended index* is created by a plan's investment consultant or custodian and is made up of different indexes weighted to reflect the percentage of assets held in the plan's investment portfolio. As a simple example, assume a plan is invested 50% in the stocks of larger U.S. companies and 50% in a mix of traditional U.S. government and corporate bonds. A comparison may be made with the return of a blended index that is 50% from the Standard and Poor's 500 Index (an index of 500 larger U.S. companies) and 50% from Barclays Aggregate Bond Index (a widely accepted index for U.S. government and corporate bonds). Indexes are available across and within a wide spectrum of asset types, including common stocks, bonds, real estate, alternatives, etc., so a blended index can similarly span a variety of assets. Exhibit 6 in Chapter 37 provides a sampling of the many indexes that can be used for comparisons.

Occasionally, there may be additional investment objectives such as to improve or maintain the funded status of the plan (ratio of assets to projected liabilities) or to have sufficient income or liquidity to make benefit payments, etc. These do not lend themselves to index or other fund performance comparisons, but they may merit mention in a plan's investment objectives or policies.

Every benefit plan has investment objectives that are unique to its individual circumstances. Nevertheless, it is possible to generalize about the objectives for three broad types of benefit plans: health and welfare plans, defined benefit plans and defined contribution plans. Exhibit 1 examines these three plans and the influence of specific factors including liquidity, liability matching, market risk and financial risk.

In the case of welfare plans, access to cash (liquidity) is essential as most income received is spent. When reserves exist, the primary emphasis is preservation so funds are available when needed to pay benefits.

In contrast, the liquidity needs of defined benefit (DB) pension plans are much less because of the extended period between receipts of employer contributions and benefit payments. Trustees are generally in a position to commit assets to long-term investments. Exhibit 1 suggests investments appropriate for shorter and long-term time horizons, including the trade-offs that occur with each.

For defined contribution (DC) pension plans, trustees do not have responsibility for the actual allocation of assets. Instead, trustees are charged with providing employees a variety of investment options—primarily mutual funds

Tip for Trustees

Besides using an index to compare the results of investing plan assets, indexes are also *investable*—a plan can invest in a portfolio of assets identical to the index. The result is a return that is the same as the index. Sometimes, but not always, the returns on an index outperform investment managers or advisors who try to do better than that index.

Exhibit 1

Needs of Different Benefit Plans

Need	Health and Welfare	Defined Benefit	Defined Contribution
Liquidity	High priority due to potential for adverse claims experience	Minimum required, unless it is a matured plan	Uncertain benefit payout demands require liquid reserves
Match liabilities with maturing assets	Potentially shortened payment schedule requires liquidity	Deemed desirable to protect surplus—some matching is desirable	There are no surplus/deficit constraints
Control market risk	Highly desirable to provide redemption, if needed, at little or no loss of principal	Largely a decision of trustees, since they are "responsible" for any shortfall	Participants/beneficiaries bear the risk; they generally opt for limited fluctuations in their accounts
Control financial (credit) risk	Highly desirable to forgo return from credit risk exposure to preserve principal value	Prudence generally requires high-quality portfolio with limited risk of payment default by a borrower	Participants/beneficiaries generally opt for very high quality portfolios to assure principal protection

Source: Eugene B. Burroughs. *"Developing Investment Policy,"* Trustees Handbook: A Practical Guide to Labor-Management Employee Benefit Plans (International Foundation of Employee Benefit Plans, 2006): 303.

and/or similar investment vehicles—that allow participants to create and manage their retirement assets in a manner that is consistent with their individual circumstances and needs.

What Is Involved in Establishing an Investment Policy?

First, trustees must assess their plan from several different points of view; this involves bringing together the professionals who advise them on investment, actuarial, legal, accounting and administrative matters. These professionals will assist trustees with gathering and documenting information on these issues among others:

- The history of the plan
- The current and projected condition of the plan
- Plan provisions
- Key actuarial information including demographics
- The actuarial funding method and interest rate used
- Plan investment history and performance
- Legal issues
- Administrative details and operation.

The more trustees know, the better equipped they are to design and implement an appropriate investment plan. A briefing concerning this information and a followup discussion with a plan's professional advisors provide trustees the foundation upon which investment objectives can be formed that suit the plan and its circumstances.

Asset Allocation

The key component of an investment policy is *asset allocation,* determining what percent of a plan's money will be invested in different asset types. The choices made should produce the combination that provides the best chance of meeting the plan's investment objectives at an acceptable level of risk. How much will be invested in stocks and what kinds of stocks? How much will be invested in bonds and what types of bonds? What about real estate, alternative investments, etc.?

If plan trustees have modest expectations for returns, then the investment allocation should reflect this. If objectives for a plan are more aggressive, the policies will need to reflect the additional risk necessary to achieve the higher return.

Choosing the assets that are the most appropriate investments for a plan involves examining the risks and returns of asset classes over the short, intermediate and long term. While there is no guarantee that what has happened in the past will happen in the future, history is a useful guide when assessing the risks, returns and appropriateness of different asset types. Trustees can see the pattern of returns over one- and multiyear periods (three, five, ten years and beyond). For a few asset classes there is a history of over 80 years that can be examined. Exhibit 4 in Chapter 37 provides a 20-year overview of annual returns for some of the broadest asset categories: large- and small-company stocks, long-term corporate bonds and U.S. government bonds, and Treasury Bills compared to inflation.

Trustees in partnership with their investment consultant should look at what happens to return and risk with different asset combinations in their plan's investment portfolio. For example, trustees might look at a portfolio that is invested 20% in large-cap growth stocks, 15% in large-company value stocks, 10% in small-company growth stocks, 10% international stocks, 20% U.S. corporate bonds, 15% U.S government bonds and 10% real estate. This portfolio could be one of many hypothetical combinations that trustees study to see which mix of assets best achieves the fund's investment objectives over one- and multiyear periods.

This process is not all about numbers. Some very important other factors come into play as well. There is typically a debate on issues like these:

- How much risk should be taken?
- What is the time horizon for riskier assets?
- What are the liquidity needs of the fund?
- How many different types of investments should be included in the plan's portfolio?
- Are some assets just too risky despite their attractive returns?
- Are trustees willing to spend the time required to oversee the investment of complicated, hard-to-understand assets?

Once trustees have determined what percentage of their fund will be allocated to each asset class, called the *target allocation,* the next step is to set a permitted range around each target. Over time, the prices of assets move up and down. The percentage of a plan portfolio that trustees desire for each type of asset does not just stay neatly on target. Perhaps trustees decide to hold 20% in large-company growth stocks, but how much above or below this 20% target can the value of these stocks move before trustees need to review the portfolio and possibly take action to return the proportion back to 20%? In this example, trustees might decide a range of 15% to 25% is acceptable. A range for an asset type should not be so large that a plan takes on more or less risk than desired. On the other hand, it should not be so tight that it forces frequent changes.

Components of an Investment Policy Statement

An investment policy statement for a benefit plan typically includes this type of information:

- Annual meeting schedule for the investment committee
- Investment objectives
- Asset allocation
- Cash flow requirements
- Rebalancing guidelines
- Policy prohibitions
- Investment management structure
- Performance measures
- Process for appointing, reviewing and terminating managers
- Voting of proxies.

It may also reference and include:

- Background information on the plan
- Identification of fiduciaries and custodians
- Lines of authority and delegation.

Rebalancing Guidelines

As the values of individual assets change, some securities may need to be sold and others purchased, a process referred to as *rebalancing.* Generally, trustees examine the allocations for a plan's total portfolio as well as for each asset class and each manager on a quarterly basis. If an asset type or a manager hits the maximum or minimum, the trustees, investment consultant and investment manager discuss the cause(s) and decide what action to take, if any. One of the most frequent and major reasons that assets move outside a range is simply that the assets are doing very well or very poorly.

There are occasions when an event may trigger the need for a full or partial rebalancing between the dates in a predetermined schedule:

- A significant cash inflow or outflow
- Reaching a predetermined limit on the amount of money invested in a specific asset type
- A dramatic change in the outlook for a specific investment or asset type.

Policy Prohibitions

Selecting the appropriate mix of assets and target ranges is probably the most important factor in the success of the investment plan, but there are other issues that should also be addressed. An investment policy statement is where trustees state what investments are *not* allowed. For example, trustees might forbid the use of certain hedge fund strategies or the purchase of "junk" bonds. Prohibitions are largely subjective but it is important to discuss with legal counsel and others on what investments might be unacceptable.

Investment Manager Structure

For highly marketable assets (e.g., stocks and bonds), trustees make decisions as to how many investment managers their plan will have for each asset type and how the assets will be managed (active, passive or a combination for each asset type). It is important to create a structure that is straightforward and understandable and can be administered with relative ease between the trustees and the investment consultant. Larger plans frequently require a more complex or at least a larger structure. Some trustees provide guidelines on this structure as part of their plan's investment policy statement. (Chapters 37 and 46 provides an explanation of active and other management styles that trustees may want to consider for their plan.)

For less marketable investments like real estate, private equity and hedge funds, the structural complexities relate to what legal form to choose and how many strategies to employ. These too need to be examined in partnership with the investment consultant.

Performance Measures

The policy statement communicates trustee expectations for each asset type and asset manager, what benchmark(s) will be used to judge success, how often results will be measured (usually quarterly, at least for marketable securities) and the time horizon over which returns will be judged.

It is important to use the right benchmark(s) to compare risks and returns across a variety of investment classes. For example, if an investment manager specializes in small, growth companies, their benchmark should reflect the same approach, not a benchmark for the overall stock market. Chapter 48 discusses performance expectations in detail.

Proxy Voting

Shareholders of public companies are permitted to vote on certain issues that influence corporate behavior and the long-term value of the company. For example, shareholders may be given the opportunity to vote out managers who are mishandling the company, demand that top executives are paid based on the company's performance, or prevent a merger that is ill-advised. *Proxy voting* is the system that allows shareholders to take part in these important decisions without attending a company's annual meeting. Through their *proxy*, shareholders grant voting authority and give voting instructions to others, usually corporate managers, to vote their shares on these issues.

Trustees should include a proxy voting policy in their plan's investment policy statement to help ensure proxy voting decisions are consistent with other aspects of investment policy. Trustees that delegate the responsibility for buying and selling stocks to an investment manager usually delegate the authority to vote proxies to the manager as well. A written proxy voting policy may prevent investment managers from taking positions conflicting with those of the plan and plan trustees.

Conclusion

Investment objectives and policy are the heart and soul of a good investment program. Trustees are well served to pay attention on an ongoing basis to these fundamentals.

Chapter 48

The Basics of Performance Measurement

Sandy Lincoln

A critical duty for trustees is to monitor a fund's investment performance. This function is essential to evaluate if fund investment objectives are achieved. Investment returns and risks must be assessed regularly and over multiple time periods. There are three major steps to the performance measurement process: (1) measure returns and risks, (2) compare risks and returns over time, and (3) interpret these findings.

How Are Returns Measured?

The *total return* on an investment asset equals the income (e.g., dividends, interest, rents) on the asset plus or minus the change in the asset's market value (price) over the measurement period. A comprehensive assessment of fund returns measures returns for a fund's (1) total assets; (2) major asset components (i.e., stocks, bonds, cash equivalents and alternative investments); and (3) individual investment managers or advisors.

There is an industry standard for calculating returns called the *time-weighted rate of return* that eliminates the effect of fund additions and withdrawals that are beyond the control of a manager—for example, the deposit of a significant benefit contribution or payout. This approach allows equitable means to compare returns across funds or managers. This is the method consultants and custodians use when reporting returns.

Investments such as stocks and bonds are bought and sold daily on public stock exchanges and bond markets, providing up-to-date prices for calculating an investment return. Such is not the case, however, for most alternative investments such as private equity, some forms of real estate and selected hedge funds. For these investments, a different measurement approach is frequently needed. A property appraisal may help determine the value of an investment in real estate. Private equity investments may be valued at their purchase price until they are sold, or otherwise revalued. This means it may be some time before there is a recorded gain or loss. Some hedge funds may also require specialized measurement techniques.

How Is Risk Measured?

Trustees quickly realize that there is a relationship between return and risk. Higher returns involve higher risk, while lower returns should have lower risk over time. It is a trustee's responsibility to monitor the risk taken to achieve a fund's return objectives.

An investment consultant, manager or custodian can provide trustees with measures of risk for most types of assets. The terms used will sound very technical but they address very commonsense issues:

- How diversified is the investment portfolio? Does it rely on just a few sectors or securities to earn a return?
- How volatile are the assets? Do prices or returns bounce around a great deal? Perhaps more than expected?
- What are the risks in different economic conditions, etc.?

What Time Periods Should Be Used to Measure Investment Performance?

Investment professionals (i.e., fund managers and consultants) should provide trustees with performance data each quarter. This report should include results for the current quarter as well as the year's prior quarters. Annual returns for prior periods, if available, are essential to analyze patterns of returns.

Cumulative return (sometimes called *compound returns*) must also be evaluated. This measure reflects fund investment returns spanning one, three, five, ten or more years. It shows what investments earned over multiple years so trustees can gauge their progress toward meeting longer term investment objectives.

For certain assets, the return in favorable or unfavorable market conditions may also be included.

What Indicates a Good Return?

Just as it is critical to measure returns for a fund's total assets, major asset categories and each investment manager, it is also vital to compare returns and risks. A fund's investment consultant or custodian bank can provide "benchmark" figures to help determine whether a fund's returns are better or worse compared to others pursuing a similar approach or strategy. Benchmarks come from two sources: (1) index comparisons, and (2) databases of investment managers and funds. It is quite common for institutional investors to use benchmarks from both sources.

Indexes

An *index* is a group of securities tracked collectively for their return and risk. The securities that make up an index may represent a market or some portion of a market. There are indexes that track specific types of assets (e.g., stocks or bonds), indexes that focus on assets in specific countries (e.g., U.S., Europe, non-U.S.) and even specific management styles (e.g., small, medium or large caps; growth or value). Indexes are available for almost all categories of assets, including certain alternative investments. Most indexes used to compare investment performance are also available as investment options. For more discussion of indexes, see Chapter 37.

Databases

The databases that consultants and custodians maintain for comparisons are massive. They include performance data from hundreds or even thousands of funds and fund managers. Databases also contain historical information allowing comparisons with past returns. Using a database makes it possible to view a range of returns—from the best to worst, and the midpoint. A fund's current and historical performance levels are viewed next to these results. Investment professionals serving a fund should be able to provide this information in an easy-to-interpret graphic format.

In addition to comparing performance for specific funds or fund managers, databases can be broken down by investment approach. For example, a fund may hire a manager to invest in stocks of small and faster growing companies (called *small cap growth style investing*); the fund can use databases to compare the manager's returns to the returns of hundreds of other managers who are also using a small cap growth investment strategy. Fund trustees are able to compare not only apples to apples, but Jonathan Apples to Jonathan Apples. Customized database breakdowns can be provided for a variety of equity and bond styles in both U.S and non-U.S markets.

* * *

At the broadest level, trustees need to know how their fund's entire investment portfolio performed, summing up stock, bond, real estate and alternatives into a *total fund return.* An index can also be constructed to compare this return with that of other funds. Databases come in handy here too. A fund that is 50% U.S. stocks, 10% international stocks, 30% U.S. fixed income assets and 10% real estate can be compared with funds that are similar in type and asset allocation. A fair and objective evaluation of total fund return requires a comparison of performance with other funds that have similar asset allocation. Likewise, assessment of a manager requires a comparison with other managers using a similar style.

Comparisons are a bit more difficult with alternative investment categories. The availability of an index or investment managers with similar approaches is often limited. Trustees have to be cautious when making comparisons where the holdings are less conventional and frequently not publicly traded.

Are There Other Important Comparisons?

If a fund has an objective for a specific rate of return, this is another area for comparison. Some plans establish a return higher than inflation as a long-term investment objective. The rate of return that exceeds inflation is the *real rate of return.* This strategy helps a benefit plan ensure that the purchasing power of the plan and its plan participants is not diminished by price increases over time.

How does this work? Assume trustees are seeking a return of 3% over annual inflation, and inflation is 2%. A return is 5% (3% plus 2% inflation) is needed to meet the trustees' investment objective. Now, suppose other funds with similar investments and strategies earn 8% on average.

This presents a dilemma. Trustees have met their fund's long-term objective but their fund underperformed another very appropriate benchmark.

The ease in reaching a benchmark can vary greatly from one period to another. If the inflation rate is very low and stock market returns are high, meeting a real rate of return objective may be easy. However, this is not always what happens! This partially explains why comparisons to other funds and/or indexes play a role in judging overall results.

How Are Results Interpreted?

The final step in performance measurement is looking at returns, risks and comparisons to (1) decide whether a fund's policies and objectives are met, (2) identify any problems that exist and (3) pinpoint trends that merit watching. Problems to watch for include a mix of assets that moves outside allocation targets, underperforming managers and risks that are inappropriate.

Interpretation is not all in the numbers. When evaluating the performance of an investment manager, you must also take into consideration changes that may influence future returns on investment. If a manager's firm loses key decision makers or team members, is sold or merged, or loses a major account, this should trigger concern and merits attention. Here are a few other warning signs:

- Deviation from an investment manager's normal style
- Trading activity higher than normal
- Significant changes in risk measurements
- Fast growth in certain assets, new accounts or new products.

Conclusion

There is an art and a science to evaluating investment results. Taking appropriate action is frequently a judgment call. There are many useful tools and measurements to assist along the way but common sense is still a big, big help.

Chapter 49

Plan Administration Functions and Options

William J. Einhorn

The history of multiemployer benefit plans as we know them today is relatively short—a little more than 60 years. During this period, these plans have evolved from common law trusts to highly complex and federally regulated entities. A myriad of laws and regulations have followed the passage of the momentous Employee Retirement Income Security Act of 1974 (ERISA). Some of the legislation approved by Congress includes:

- The Tax Equity and Fiscal Responsibility Act of 1982 (TEFRA)
- The Deficit Reduction Act of 1984 (DEFRA)
- The Retirement Equity Act of 1984 (REA)
- The Tax Reform Act of 1986 (TRA '86)
- The Consolidated Omnibus Budget Reconciliation Act of 1985 (COBRA)
- The Omnibus Reconciliation Acts (OBRA '85, '86, '87 and '89) and more recently,
- The Economic Growth and Tax Relief Reconciliation Act of 2001 (EGTRRA).

These reconciliation bills have resulted in almost annual changes to the Internal Revenue Code with a significant impact on employee benefit plans.

Along the way, a variety of other laws profoundly affected benefit plans. Consider the following legislation:

- Health Insurance Portability and Accountability Act of 1996 (HIPAA) and the subsequent Privacy and Security Regulations
- Newborns' and Mothers' Health Protection Act of 1996
- The Small Business Job Protection Act of 1996
- The Women's Health and Cancer Rights Act of 1998
- The Medicare Prescription Drug, Improvement and Modernization Act of 2003
- The Veterans Benefits Improvement Act of 2004 (modifying and amending portions of the Uniformed Services Employment and Reemployment Rights Act of 1994 (USERRA))
- The Pension Protection Act of 2006 (PPA '06)
- Mental Health Parity and Addiction Equity Act of 2008 which replaced and expanded the Mental Health Parity Act of 1996
- The Health Information Technology for Economic and Clinical Health Act (HITECH) of 2009 (amending and expanding HIPAA)
- The Patient Protection and Affordable Care Act of 2010 (PPACA).

This bombardment of significant changes has placed increasing responsibility on persons entrusted with multiemployer plan administration.

Trustees, administrative managers and those involved in the collective bargaining process find much of their work is adapting administrative methods and internal plan rules in response to the ever-changing federal laws and regulations, workplace realities, and the "give-and-take" that is integral to collective bargaining. Administrators are required to work closely with plan attorneys, accountants and actuaries to implement this myriad of changes.

In recent years, there has been a tsunami of change. The Pension Protection Act of 2006 was the most sweeping pension legislation since ERISA—establishing new funding standards; additional notifications, certification and reporting requirements; and many other significant adjustments. The HITECH amendments to the HIPAA privacy regulations encourage rapid adoption of electronic health record (EHR) systems among providers. Of course, there is also ACA and its amendments (known collectively as the Affordable Care Act (ACA)), and the regulations that will follow. The transformation of the nation's health care system begun in 2010 will not be fully implemented until 2018; along the way, multiemployer plan trustees and administrators will face a multitude of decisions and more change.

Trustees of early multiemployer benefit plans quickly recognized that, even though they have fiduciary responsibility for plan administration, they could not personally handle the numerous administrative tasks involved. Actually, it was never intended that trustees would individually or collectively possess the time, specialized skills and experience required for effective plan administration. The Taft-Hartley Act of 1947 allows trustees to employ third parties to handle the everyday activities of a plan. It has always seemed logical for trustees to delegate administrative responsibilities to professionals as appropriate. This trustee reliance on others stimulated the emergence of professional benefit plan administrators.

Administrative managers provide services covering a broad range of plan operations such as general management, finance, personnel administration, recordkeeping, benefit claims, data processing, collection, investments, insurance and customer service. Managers deal with other plan professionals, trustees, participants, beneficiaries, outside vendors and government agencies among others. Exhibit 1 provides a brief summary of the responsibilities trustees commonly delegate to a plan administrator (or in some cases, administrators). This chapter provides an overview of the functions typically fulfilled by a plan administrator.

Today's administrative managers include rank-and-file union members as well as persons who have worked their way up from clerical positions to benefit plan administrators. At the other end of the spectrum are professionals who are certified public accountants (CPAs) and those who have a master's degree in business administration (M.B.A.). Others include lawyers, economists and computer experts.

Obviously, those employed to administer a plan must be chosen with care. The delegation of responsibility must be specifically authorized in the legal documents that establish a plan and comply with federal and state regulations. Trustees maintain the fiduciary responsibility to constantly monitor these administrators to ensure their actions (1) are in accordance with their contractual obligations, (2) comply with plan policies and (3) are in the sole, exclusive and best interests of plan participants.

Proper delegation of administrative tasks by trustees generally requires that independent third parties be employed for this purpose. In accordance with the spirit of the Taft-Hartley Act, courts have generally held that fund operations must be kept completely separate from union and management operations.[1]

Exhibit 1

Plan Administrative Functions

ERISA Section 404 requires that a plan be administered "in accordance with the documents and instruments governing the plan." These functions usually include, but are not limited to:

- Establish an office with the personnel to perform plan operations
- Collect contributions and other income
- Determine benefit eligibility and process claims
- Track and prepare reports regarding plan assets, income and expenses
- Retain and maintain plan data and records
- Secure plan records and assets
- Comply with the laws and regulations of the federal and state governments
- Coordinate activities of plan professionals
- Communicate with plan participants, trustees, plan professionals, participating local unions and employers.

Establishing policies concerning these functions and the prudent selection of an administrative manager for their implementation remains the responsibility of a plan's board of trustees.

What Options Are Available for Plan Administration?

One of the first decisions of a newly established plan is to determine how it should be administered. In other words, where will the "back office" be located and who will run it? Most plans are self-administered with a salaried administrator and full- or part-time support personnel. There are, however, a significant number of plans that contract with external administrators. A small number of plans use banks or insurance companies for administration.

Salaried vs. Third-Party Administrators

Salaried administrators are employed on a full-time basis to handle the day-to-day operations at a plan's permanent office(s). These administrators are focused only on operations of a single plan or small group of related plans. *Contract administrators,* sometimes referred to as *third-party administrators (TPAs),* administer a number of unrelated plans to achieve a more cost-efficient operation; these plans may be a mix of multiemployer and single employer plans. TPAs can spread the fixed costs for office and operational expenses (e.g., salaries, data/claims processing and communication) among the multiple plans they serve. They have become one of the fastest growing elements in employee benefit plan administration, particularly with respect to health and welfare plans.

Trustees must decide which administrative approach best fits their plan, taking into consideration their plan's unique requirements and circumstances. Full-time salaried administrators are responsible only to the trustees and participants of the particular plan or small group of plans that hired them. This can provide a continuity of operations and avoid conflicts that might arise when a contract administrator is responsible for multiple plans. Self-administered plan offices may also be smaller and deliver more personal, local service than a large outside TPA. A final advantage of self-administration is that there is no need to build in a profit margin for the third party.

On the other hand, TPAs may be able to provide a level of expertise, training and capabilities that exceeds that of a salaried administrative office; this is especially true for small plans. A TPA may be better able to handle customer call peaks and offer 24/7 service. The loss of a staff person at a large TPA may not be as disruptive as the loss of a person in a small self-administered office. Another advantage concerns trustees' liability. The errors and omissions, and professional liability insurance of an external contract administrator can be a reassuring, bonus protection for trustees.

Combined Arrangements

Combination or hybrid arrangements offer additional options for plan administration. One approach is for several plans from one industry or related industries to join together for their administration. For example, building trade funds with collective bargaining agreements spread over a large geographical area might create and be administered by a nonprofit corporation yielding economies of scale similar to those of a TPA. The plans are able to offer a central location for industry workers to get benefit support. The advantages of self-administration on a relatively local level with some direct contact and no profit margin are retained.

Another hybrid arrangement has emerged using a combination of contract and third-party administration. This approach is particularly common among health and welfare plans that are partially self-funded. Consider a plan that provides medical benefits through an insurance company but "carves out" and self-funds mental health benefits. Plan personnel directly pay mental health claims while the insurance company is responsible for other health claims. Similarly, pension plans may be self-funded with the exception of death benefits so beneficiaries are able to take full advantage of the federal income tax exclusion for life insurance benefits. The pension plan handles all aspects connected with retirement benefits, but the insurance company is responsible for the death benefit program.

Claims Payment Only Services

Some health and welfare plans are self-administered with full-time personnel handling all aspects of administration *except* the processing of benefit claims. A specialized TPA handles these claims. (Frequently, the TPA also offers stop-loss insurance to provide a maximum limit on the claims liability of the self-insured fund.)

When health and welfare plans provide benefits on a fully insured basis or use an insurance company only to pay claims, the structure is the same as when a plan engages a TPA for claims-payment-only services. The plan pays the insurance premiums to the carrier, which, in turn, provides claims services. The insurer's people and data processing equipment have fixed costs that are spread among a number of customer plans. Many TPAs and insurance companies offer assistance with controlling health care costs in addition to processing health care claims.

Administrative Services Only

An important innovation in plan administration that has become commonplace is the *administrative-services-only (ASO)* arrangement for noninsured health and welfare plans. ASO contracts are written on a case-by-case basis for the benefits a plan provides. Such contracts include services such as claims processing, payment and control; management reports; tabulation of data for governmental reports; actuarial and underwriting services; and assistance in preparing plan booklets.

Under a typical ASO arrangement, the insurance company pays claims using its checking account or the checking account of the plan. If the company uses its own checking account to pay claims, it bills the plan for reimbursement. The plan pays the insurer a fee for administration established by the contract. A variation of the ASO procedure is called a *minimum premium insurance arrangement;* the insurance carrier sets up a special trust fund where the plan's insurance payment for participants is deposited. The insurer uses this fund to pay claims. If claims exceed the amount in the special fund, the remaining claims are paid directly by the insurer.

Historically, insurance companies have not focused on the contributions and eligibility recordkeeping associated with the administration of benefit plans. More recently, however, some carriers have branched out to provide a wide variety of administrative and investment services for health, welfare and pension plans.

A small number of banks also provide benefit plan services. Plans have always used banks to safeguard records and assets, and provide investment services. Now, some banks:

- Receive and record employer contributions and other income
- Do general reporting and accounting
- Process claims and make claim payments
- Prepare governmental reports.

Banks performing these services are more likely to do so for pension plans than health and welfare plans. Like insurance companies with ASO contracts, banks may enter into arrangements to provide only specific services such as handling receipts and recordkeeping and/or claims processing and payment.

Managed Care Organizations

Since the latter part of the 1990s, managed care organizations (MCOs) have offered contract services for multiemployer health benefit plans. These organizations negotiate contracts with medical, dental and prescription drug providers; pay claims; collect and analyze data; and offer a variety of programs to help reduce a plan's claim costs. Many MCOs (e.g., HMOs and PPOs) also provide health care services.

What Are the Specifics of a Plan's Administrative Functions?

Whether administrators are salaried or contract, their job is to run the day-to-day operations of their plan(s) as directed by plan trustees. An administrator's specific duties depend on a multitude of factors that include, among others, the purpose of the plan; how benefits are provided; and the number of contributing employers, participating employees and beneficiaries. Much depends on what trustees expect from an administrative manager and the capabilities of the administrator. In some cases, the administrator prepares and maintains board minutes and agendas. Frequently, the administrator is asked to prepare, produce and distribute plan booklets. Some plans own buildings with space rented to other parties and it is the administrator who manages the property. What follows is an overview of functions commonly provided by a plan administrator.

Office Operations

Administrative managers mobilize the physical and human resources needed to operate a plan. Typical activities include:

- Evaluate the adequacy of office facilities in terms of space and participant accessibility over the short and longer term
- Assess present and future personnel needs and prepare job descriptions
- Recruit, hire and retain qualified individuals and entities to perform work for the plan
- Allocate floor space, equipment and staff to facilitate an efficient workflow
- Formulate personnel policies regarding work conditions, compensation and benefits
- Conduct performance reviews and recommend professional development/training opportunities for plan employees
- Procure and maintain the office equipment, furniture, fixtures, etc. required to operate effectively and in a manner that conveys the desired image to the participants, beneficiaries, unions and employers served
- Maintain an inventory of plan property
- Oversee insurance, bonding and fiduciary coverage needed to protect plan assets, employees and trustees.

This mobilization of plan resources involves a massive amount of effort and countless decisions regarding office facilities and equipment, personnel, recordkeeping, security measures, and so forth. Trustees sometimes look on these decisions casually—as if they were made and implemented with little effort. The reality is much to the contrary. In addition, it is these activities that ultimately determine the quality of service provided plan stakeholders (e.g., participants, beneficiaries and contributing employers).

Obviously, administrative managers do not make all of these decisions alone, nor do they always have the broadest range of possible choices. It is reasonable to assume trustees will be involved in some decisions—especially when trust fund dollars are involved. In some instances, an outside consultant is retained to evaluate and make recommendations regarding personnel, equipment, space requirements or other aspects of administration. Given it is the administrative manager's responsibility to get the job done with the resources available, it is obviously also the manager's duty to keep trustees informed as to what resources are necessary to carry out a plan's day-to-day work.

Collection of Contributions

The primary source of revenue for the majority of multiemployer benefit plans is employer contributions. The amount an employer contributes is generally set forth in the collective bargaining agreement and expressed as a fixed amount per hour, percentage of payroll, or flat weekly/monthly amount per employee. There are some situations when the contribution amount is based on the employees' pay for each shift, production unit, etc. These contributions are essential to the payment of benefits and administrative expenses. As a result, efficient collection processes are fundamental to the successful operation of multiemployer plans. Specific administrative responsibilities associated with the collection of contributions are:

- Accept, process and account for employer contributions
- Confirm the accuracy of employer contributions and credits to individual employee accounts. If directed by trustees, audit employer payroll records.
- Provide trustees with regular contribution reports
- Carry out the established procedures for handling delinquent and incomplete accounts
- Handle employee self-payments (including COBRA administration).

Every plan must have an accounting and reporting system to make certain contributions are received in full and in a timely fashion. Reporting is usually done on a weekly or monthly basis. Proper credit for payment must be given to each employer as well as the individual employees participating in the benefit plan. Most plans provide employers with remittance forms and specific instructions for making contributions. In recent years, it is more commonplace for forms to be sent out and returned electronically with the employer transferring contributions from its bank account to a plan bank account.

Although the forms vary from plan to plan, they generally include a list of employees, Social Security numbers and the unit (e.g., hours) upon which contributions are based. When contributions for more than one employee benefit plan are part of the same collective bargaining agreement, they are often handled by one benefit office with one remittance form covering contributions for all of the plans. For example, one form might be sent to one office for welfare, pension and apprenticeship training plans.

When a plan provides an employer a form with plan participants listed, the employer is asked to (1) add employees who were not employed the previous month and (2) delete those who were terminated. Most health benefit plans ask the employer to furnish the date of, and reason for, termination to facilitate proper administration under the COBRA continuation program required under federal law.

Upon receipt of the employer's completed form and payment, the plan's personnel check the accuracy of the information and the contribution, then update the records for the employer and the individual employees. If a payment has not been received, the administrator normally reports the delinquency to plan trustees and legal counsel, who must follow plan procedures to collect the late payment. (Chapter 52 discusses collection policies and litigation.) Trust plans generally have criteria that establish when an employer is considered delinquent. An employer may be considered delinquent if they:

- Fail to submit a report or payment on the due date
- Submit a report without payment or with a check that does not clear the bank
- Submit a report and payment, but do not include all employees, hours or contributions required by the collective bargaining agreement.

Frequently, administrators are also responsible for communicating delinquencies to the labor and management associations associated with the collective bargaining agreement.

To ensure proper administration of contributions, most plans establish a payroll audit process. (Chapter 35 discusses this process.) Some plans require a report direct from employees as to the name of their employer and time worked on a weekly or monthly basis; this information can be compared to the information provided by employers. Other plans ask shop stewards or the union to report the hours worked by employees. Still other plans provide reports to the individual employees on a monthly or quarterly basis so employees can independently verify the information submitted by their employers. The Internet offers a new means for verification—a web site with the information accessible to employees "24 hours per day/7 days per week."

There are occasions where individual employees make payments directly to a plan. For example, an employee may be able to make payments to continue benefits during a layoff, when the person is disabled or upon termination. When certain COBRA "qualifying events" occur, the federal government requires plans to accept employee payments that temporarily continue the employee's health insurance coverage.

When self-payments are made, a reporting system is needed to make sure the timing of payments is correct and appropriate credit is given to individual employee accounts. A procedure is needed to notify employees when payments are overdue and grace periods are about to expire. For health benefits, the notification procedures must comply with the very specific COBRA notice requirements.

Determine Eligibility and Process Claims

The primary purpose of a multiemployer plan is to provide benefits to those persons who meet plan eligibility rules. A plan administrator is responsible for the development and maintenance of the system tracking which employees have met these rules and are eligible to receive benefits. The precise information gathered, the form in which it is maintained and how it is made available varies greatly depending on the type of plan and plan resources. For health and welfare plans, the typical database indicates each employee's:

- Name
- Birth date
- Contact information (e.g., address, phone number, e-mail)
- Employer
- Union affiliation
- Total credits toward eligibility
- Date of initial eligibility
- Current eligibility status
- Benefit coverage
- Marital status
- Dependents eligible for coverage (including each dependent's name, relationship to participant and birth date)
- Social Security and other identification number(s).

The system should be set up to accommodate the rules of the plan and signal situations that might lead to a loss of benefits such as an employee's failure to meet minimum work requirements, disability or a failure to make self-payments. The system should support compliance with federal regulations, for example, signaling when a loss of coverage requires individuals be notified of their rights to continue coverage under COBRA. HIPAA requires plans to furnish certificates showing when a person was covered by the plan and limits the waiting period till a plan's coverage begins. Hence, dates should be kept for when each person's:

- Waiting period for coverage began
- Coverage began
- Coverage ended.

It may be desirable (and in some cases, essential) to obtain the Social Security number for each employee's spouse and child. In 2011, the federal government mandated quarterly reporting of eligible participants in a health plan who are over the age of 45 to the Centers for Medicaid and Medicare Services (CMS) to allow the agency to more effectively enforce Medicare secondary payer provisions.

As with health and welfare records, defined benefit pension data systems should be structured to signal points when a participant's eligibility might be suspended, terminated or lost. These danger points often include a break in service, failure to file a claim, an appeal within a specified time frame, or a return to work in a craft or industry after retirement. ERISA and subsequent regulations have specific requirements with respect to breaks in service and, under certain circumstances, reemployment after retirement.

An employee's pension eligibility is usually based upon the history accumulated in a plan's database. When an employee claims additional credits, it may be necessary for the administrative office to obtain additional information from:

- Past employers
- The Social Security Administration
- The union
- Other funds concerning reciprocal credits
- Other sources that can provide background relating to an employee's work history.

Individual eligibility records for employees in defined contribution (DC) benefit plans and annuity plans are similar to those for defined benefit (DB) pension plans. In lieu of work records, however, benefits are based upon actual employer and/or employee contributions to each employee's account. The total amount credited to the account combined with investment returns on the account less any administrative or management fees are the basis for determining the participant's retirement amount or lump-sum payment upon termination of employment.

Restrictions and legal assignments pertaining to benefits are also maintained in a participant database. For example, survivor options and qualified domestic relations orders (QDROs) are needed for pension plan participants. Life insurance and other death benefits require designation of beneficiaries. Identification of an employee's dependents who are college students may be needed to determine health plan eligibility. Health plans also need the employment status of family members if there is a coordination of benefits (COB) procedure. Qualified medical child support orders (QMCSOs) requiring enrollment of dependents in a plan also needs to be noted.

Chapter 51 is devoted to a discussion of claims processing.

Financial Accounts

In addition to maintaining data concerning employer contributions and employee benefit status/claims, an administrator oversees the general financial accounts of a plan. For trustees to determine the status of a plan at any particular time, it is essential that financial statements be available. Financial reports are also important for government compliance. Some of the information that should be readily available includes:

- The status of employer contributions—the amount and age of any delinquencies as well as any efforts to collect
- The cash flow needed to meet current benefit claims and operating expenditures
- The dollars available for investment purposes and the amount of assets allocated for short- and long-term investments
- The performance of the investment portfolio in terms of return including capital gains or losses
- The fees and expenses paid to professional advisors for services rendered
- Plan liabilities such as insurance premiums payable, benefits payable, liability for claims processed but unpaid, general liabilities, and liability for future eligibility of participants.

Interim, unaudited financial statements may be prepared by an administrative manager based upon the records maintained by plan personnel. An annual report is prepared by an independent CPA (and, frequently, periodic interim reports). The audited financial statement is part of a plan's annual report furnished to the Department of Labor and the Internal Revenue Service. The results of the annual report must be "available for inspection by interested persons at the principal office of the trust fund and at such other place as may be designated in such written agreement."[2]

As with employer and employee contributions, investment returns must be received on time, accounted for and monitored. Plan assets must also be tracked. The administrative manager's responsibility includes verification of earnings received and reported by the plan's custodian or investment manager if either of these entities accept investment income on behalf of the plan. Administrators also maintain a record of the assets their plan holds by type (e.g., stocks, bonds, mortgages). Depending on the type of investment, accounting is also needed on market values, dividends and interest received, brokerage costs, proxy voting and so forth.

Many plans maintain their own records as a cross-check on the periodic reports of custodians and investment managers. Others rely on the annual audit by a certified public accountant to verify the accuracy of income and physical existence of documents of ownership.

Retention and Maintenance of Records

What records are maintained by a benefit plan and how long they are kept varies with the type of plan and its idiosyncrasies. The administrative manager usually works with a certified public accountant (CPA) and trustees to initially design a recordkeeping system. With the guidance of plan accountants, the manager is then responsible for following the procedures established and, when appropriate, suggesting improvements. While some adjustments to a recordkeeping system make day-to-day operations more efficient or provide additional information that is of value in plan decision making, other changes are required to comply with the latest government rules.

Financial records must be kept in accordance with generally accepted accounting principles tailored for Taft-Hartley multiemployer benefit plans. The annual audit of these records by an independent public accountant assures plan stakeholders (e.g., trustees, employers and participants) that records are being properly recorded and maintained and that the financial condition of the plan as reported is accurate. After the annual audit, the independent auditor should furnish a letter with comments and recommendations concerning maintenance of the plan records.

Records Retention. Every plan should have a records retention policy that specifies how long specific types of records should be maintained. The administrative manager is responsible for seeing the policy is followed.

- Government reports and annual financial statements should be kept permanently as they may be required at any time for government review or inspection by others in accordance with federal law.
- Given the long-term nature of defined benefit pension plans, data for determining eligibility and benefit payments must be kept throughout the working career of an employee.
- In contrast, retention of health records for a period of six years may be sufficient.

The availability of low-cost, high-speed scanning equipment in recent years has reduced the arduous nature of record retention that plan personnel faced in the past. The new technology allows for the easy filing and retrieval of records and the mass destruction of boxes of paper documents taking up office space.

Electronic Data Systems. The boxes are disappearing, but the technological innovations in recordkeeping have placed new responsibilities on the shoulders of plan administrators; a critical job is establishing and maintaining sophisticated computer data systems. Computer systems vary with the type of benefits provided by a plan, the number of plan participants and a plan's resources. Some plans use in-house equipment. Internal or external experts may help maintain and upgrade the system in response to changes in technology, plan operations and government standards. Other plans use hardware and software maintained at a location separate from the plan office. With an external system, plan personnel access the system remotely. Hardware and software updates, enhancements and improvements are made by the service provider. In this fashion, the plan has the use of the "latest and greatest" technology.

The successful design, implementation and ongoing operation of an electronic data system requires much thought and planning. Careful, up-front design avoids costly surprises during setup, provides ready access to the data needed for the plan's daily operations, and permits future expansion.

A plan administrator monitors the effectiveness of the computer system(s) being used and reports to trustees when equipment and software updates are needed. When a major change in a system is being considered, a consultant is normally asked to submit recommendations for the plan. With the input of the administrative manager, trustees generally make the final decision as to what actions will be taken. Plan personnel (including the administrator) may work with consultants or service providers to make sure the system produces the end results desired. The outside "experts" may also train employees how to use the system.

Security and Internal Controls

Plans have always needed policies and procedures to minimize the chance (and impact) of hazards such as fire, flood and theft. Plan administrators have a responsibility for ensuring the safety of plan records and other property. The emergence of electronic data storage and sharing of plan information has added new security dimensions to be addressed such as unauthorized access, data tampering and data theft. Among an administrator's activities concerning plan security and internal controls are:

- Give valuable property and important documents to a custodian for safekeeping or store them in a safe deposit vault at an outside location with access limited to authorized persons.
- Arrange for the frequent and routine backup of electronic data at a separate location where it can be retrieved in case of an equipment failure, natural disaster or other unanticipated event.
- Whenever possible, spread financial functions over several individuals and departments to avoid monetary theft and fraud. Some plans (especially larger ones) have a system of checks and balances to monitor and control all aspects of operation. In smaller plans with fewer employees, it may not be as necessary or practical to set up internal controls for all operations.
- Formulate and enforce privacy and security policies regarding access to records by staff, trustees, participants and others in accordance with HIPAA and other applicable laws and regulations.

With respect to the final item, handling *protected health information* or PHI as detailed in HIPAA guidelines is a critical concern for health and welfare plans. The civil and criminal fines, as well as potential private lawsuits, could yield significant liability for a plan that is not in compliance.

Compliance

For the most part, it is a plan's administrative office that ensures required government documents (Forms 5500, 990, PBGC-1, etc.) have been prepared and filed with the appropriate government agency. Copies of these filings are kept along with proof of filing in case any questions arise.

As described in Chapters 21 and 54, federal law requires plans to provide certain notices and plan documents to participants. For example, the federal government requires pension and welfare benefit plans to provide plan participants:

- A ***summary plan description (SPD)*** describing the provisions and features of a plan within 90 days after a participant is covered by a plan
- A ***summary of material modifications*** when a significant change is made to a plan
- A ***summary annual report*** containing financial statements and other information concerning the plan's most recent year's activities.

ERISA requires defined benefit plans to give participants and other stakeholders an annual funding notice with miscellaneous information regarding the plan, including a statement of the plan's funding status.

At least once a year, all pension plans must also provide participants and beneficiaries individualized information regarding their retirement benefits. This type of report usually indicates pension credits a worker has been credited to date and the amount of vested benefits. For an annuity plan, the report typically states the total amount contributed to an individual's account and the value of benefits that could be obtained from the present accumulated contributions. This statement must be provided quarterly to participants and beneficiaries who have the right to direct the investments in their plan.

Health plans must provide an annual notice concerning a woman's right to reconstructive surgery with a mas-

Key Indicators of Plan Operations

Given the complexity of today's benefit plans, it is of the utmost importance that trustees "keep their finger on the pulse" of a plan's funding and operations. An in-depth analysis by trustees of each and every aspect of a plan is impractical and even more likely, impossible. It is reasonable, however, for a plan administrator to provide trustees with *key indicators* summarizing operations. These indicators will help trustees quickly analyze which areas are doing well and those that may need more attention or action. The indicators for any type of plan can be formatted on one, easy-to-read page for efficient and effective review.

Health Plans

- Aggregate income and expense
- Per employee per month (PEPM) trend
- PEPM income and expenses compared to budget, compared to previous period
- Average enrollment
- Average contributory hours by participant
- Average contract size (i.e., member/dependent ratios)
- Medical
  - Admits/1,000; bed days/1,000
  - Average length of stay
  - Average cost per admission
  - Benefit costs by place/type of service
  - Participant share of allowed expense
- Dental
  - Aggregate costs
  - PEPM costs per type of service
  - Benefit costs by type of service
  - Participant share of allowed expense
- Prescription drug
  - PEPM script utilization
  - Generic fill rate
  - Average fund cost per script
  - Participant cost share percentage
- Investments
  - Holdings
  - Performance vs. benchmarks
  - Valuation
- Administrative expenses

Defined Benefit Plans

- Aggregate income and expense
- Average contributory hours by participant
- Active/inactive ratio
- Administrative expenses
- Rolling 12 averages of contributory hours
- Changes in pension rolls
- Retiree payouts (benefit options), aggregate numbers and payments
- Investments
  - Holdings
  - Performance vs. benchmarks
  - Valuation
- Administrative expenses

Defined Contribution Plans

- Aggregate income and expense
- Average contributory hours by participant
- Active/inactive ratio
- Administrative expenses
- Rolling 12 averages of contributory hours
- Plan investments by category
- Open accounts, number and value ranges
- Retiree payouts and rollovers

---

tectomy under the Women's Health and Cancer Rights Act. When persons are first covered by a health plan, they must be advised of their rights under COBRA. Other notices are required when certain "qualifying events" occur such as a dependent reaching the maximum age for coverage and an employee's termination. HIPAA requires all employees be notified of special enrollment rights when they can first enroll in a health plan. Another notice is required concerning an employee's prior participation in a plan when they lose coverage.

Federal law also imposes requirements on parties that process employee benefit claims. If a plan handles its own claims processing, the administrative office must have procedures to comply with the regulations and implement these procedures. Should a participant's claim be denied, the individual must be told the reason for the denial with a reference to the plan document. The participant must also be advised how to appeal the decision.

Communication

Administrators are often expected to be a plan's "point person" for communication with participants, service providers, contributing employers, employer associations and labor organizations affiliated with a plan. Administrators become conduits for information of importance to trustees and other plan stakeholders.

Plan trustees typically delegate their fiduciary responsibility for the preparation and dissemination of participant information to an administrative manager. A substantial amount of the communication with participants falls under the categories of customer service (e.g., benefit details and claims processing) and government compliance—both discussed previously. But communication is also required to support trustee objectives for a plan; for example, educating participants how they can help keep health care plan costs under control.

Administrators also gather information from participants and others that is shared with trustees. Administrators seek information regarding benefit trends, service providers, technological advances and so forth. Similarly, administrators directly and indirectly collect participants' comments, inquiries and complaints. When appropriate, this information is relayed to trustees. All of this knowledge and understanding is beneficial in making plan decisions and providing the highest quality service to plan members.

The relationship among administrators, trustees and other plan members is the subject of Chapter 50. For practical advice concerning the establishing of communication objectives for a plan and communication techniques, see Chapters 55 and 56.

Which Administrative Activities Are Most Commonly Fulfilled In-House?

Functions usually assumed by benefit plans include:

- A database for contributing employers and participating employees
- General accounting and recordkeeping
- Individual recordkeeping for employer contributions and delinquencies
- Determination of employee eligibility and credits applicable to each participant
- Arranging for reporting forms for employer contributions (there may be substantial savings in administrative costs if the contributions of more than one fund are reported and paid jointly)
- Collection efforts by plan personnel
- Determination of amounts available for investment and transfer to investment resources
- Record retention
- Reports to trustees and outside professionals
- Communication with employees, employers and unions.

What Activities Are Most Likely to Be Performed Externally?

Plan functions that are most frequently transferred to an outside source are:

- **Meeting minutes.** Preparation of trustees meeting minutes by legal counsel and their distribution to trustees and professionals.
- **Data processing and storage.** For many plans, sophisticated computerization of participant data, eligibility, claims payments and so forth is the responsibility of a service bureau rather than office staff.
- **Communication.** The preparation of announcements, summary plan descriptions, newsletters and other reporting and disclosure documents is assigned by some plans to outside communication specialists and insurance companies. These external providers may even arrange for distribution to plan participants.
- **Claims processing and payment.** Some health and welfare plans use an insurance company for processing and paying claims to participants. The company may be liable for claims or may handle claims in an administrative-services-only (ASO) capacity. Other third-party administrators are also used to pay claims.
- **Health cost containment.** Many insured plans use the services of their insurance carrier to arrange for preapproval of medical services, utilization review, case management, second surgical opinions, service provider audits and other cost-management strategies. Self-administered funds incur substantial expenses to arrange similar services. A plan that chooses to take on these activities will incur substantially increased costs for personnel, telephone, printing, etc.
- **Compliance.** Plans use different methods in handling the reporting and disclosure requirements of COBRA and other federal laws, state insurance conversion laws, certification notices required by HIPAA, self-pay arrangements and related required communications. Specialized third-party administrators and insurance companies may be engaged to provide these services.

- **Pension checks.** Many pension plans arrange for a bank custodian, insurance company or other servicing organization to issue and process pension checks. Others directly issue checks to participants and beneficiaries. Issuing checks is accompanied by a substantial amount of tax reporting that may be outsourced as well.
- **Investments records.** Many plans do not keep accounting records for investments. Instead, they accept the reports of custodians and investment advisors. Other plans maintain a complex records system to monitor assets and investment income and to compare the performance of various investment managers.

Conclusion

As has been described in this chapter, multiemployer plan administration is not as simple and straightforward as one might initially believe. Collective bargaining, changes in trades and industries, technological advances, participant expectations and the dictates of an ever-growing body of federal law and regulation have all contributed to the evolution of today's plan office into a complex, multifaceted business operation.

Endnotes

1. This principle was expressly recognized on a number of occasions by the U.S. Supreme Court, beginning with its decision in *NLRB v. Amax Coal Company.*
2. ERISA §§103(b) and 302(c)(5).

Chapter 50

The Administrative Manager's Relationship With Plan Stakeholders

William J. Einhorn

The previous chapter outlines the major functions of plan administration. A central role of the administrative manager is to serve as an agent of the plan and plan trustees dealing with participants, employers, service providers and collective bargaining entities. The administrator's relationship with these plan stakeholders is the subject of this chapter.

What Is an Administrator's Relationship With Trustees?

The relationship between a plan administrator and trustees differs with each plan—influenced by plan needs and trustees' preferences. In some plans, administrators are active participates in almost all elements of plan operations and partner with trustees on many decisions. In others, trustees take a more direct administrative role, and the administrator's job is limited to a few functions following trustee directives.

The Decision Process

When trustees make a decision, the process followed involves these steps:

- Identify the issue or problem
- Accumulate information concerning the matter
- Develop alternative solutions
- Assess the pros and cons of the alternatives
- Select the best solution
- Implement the solution.

An administrator may participate in all of these phases except the choice of the final solution.

Identify the problem. Involved in day-to-day operations, administrators are often most aware of problems and issues faced by a plan. As a consequence, administrative managers are the persons most likely to identify and understand which matters require board attention. Administrators are almost always responsible for reporting to trustees how economic, legislative or regulatory changes will impact a plan. If a change requires adjustments in policy or operations, the administrator brings it to the attention of the trustees at the next board meeting or through other communicating as appropriate.

Submitting a concise and clearly written explanation of an issue can avoid wasted time and effort by trustees and others. The administrator should indicate to the board of trustees the relative importance of the issue, for example:

- Is the problem experienced by many participants or one that applies to only a small number of employees?
- Does the problem consume a lot of staff time and other plan resources or is it just a minor irritation?

Accumulate information. Administrators have access to information from plan records, experience and the actual details of the matters trustees must discuss. By accumulating such information and presenting it to trustees in an efficient form, the administrator plays a vital role helping trustees make fully informed decisions. Administrators also suggest outside parties that trustees may want to talk with for further input.

Develop and evaluate alternatives. The vital element in the resolution of any problem is to identify potential solutions. The degree to which an administrative manager is involved in the development and evaluation of alternatives generally varies with the nature of the issue. If a problem is primarily an administrative one, the administrative manager usually develops the options. If the problem concerns plan policy, financial stability, government requirements, investment changes or other major considerations, it is more likely the administrator will seek the input of plan professionals in advance to provide alternatives to the trustees.

In many instances, the board of trustees expects a recommendation from the administrator. On policy issues, some administrators are expected to take an aggressive position while others are expected to remain neutral. In the latter case, the administrator presents the issue and alternatives, along with input from outside professionals, especially information from legal counsel if there are legal issues involved.

Implement. Once trustees make a decision, administrators are responsible for implementation. Administrators may also be the eyes and ears of the trustees providing feedback on how implementation is proceeding and the impact.

Trustee Meetings

In addition to the day-to-day contact that may occur between plan administrators and trustees, there is the formal relationship that occurs at board of trustees meetings. The frequency of meetings depends upon trust agreement requirements, the nature of the plan and its operations, and circumstances that may require special meetings.

Plan administrators generally arrange the dates, sites and amenities for trustee board meetings. After consulting with plan staff, trustees, legal counsel and other plan professionals, administrative managers typically prepare the meeting agenda—sending it out with the meeting notice and preliminary information trustees should review prior to the meeting. The exhibit presents a list of items found on a typical plan agenda.

Gathering the information and preparing the reports that trustees use to make decisions is also a common duty of plan managers. Among the reports needed are:

- Summary of employer contributions
- Summary of investment results
- Budget for internal operations and administrative expenses
- Approval of expenditures
- Interim financial statements and cash projections
- Listing of delinquent employers
- Recommendation for matters to be submitted to legal counsel
- Summary of claims paid
- Claim trends
- Proposed capital costs
- Changes in personnel.

Administrators may also be charged with coordinating and participating in special committee meetings; some boards have committees or subcommittees that do background work on behalf of the entire board.

Administrative managers usually maintain the minutes of trustees meetings, either by directly writing the minutes or holding the permanent minutes that are written by legal counsel or the secretary of the board of trustees. In some instances, administrators prepare a draft of minutes that is forwarded to counsel for final review. In any event, the administrative manager must review the final minutes to be sure they are an accurate record of the meeting.

Exhibit

Meeting Agenda Items

- Review and approve minutes of the prior meeting
- Review plan finances, including the independent accountant's report (when available)
- Review employer collections and delinquencies
- Review reports of committees of the board
- Review reports and recommendations of legal counsel and other professionals
- Administrative manager's report and recommendations
- Consider items raised in the administrative manager's report not previously covered
- Review any special matters and issues that arise
- Consider unfinished business
- Claim appeals or committee reports on appeals
- Review benefit applications, if not covered in the administrative manager's report
- Establish the date and location of the next meeting of the board and/or committees

What Is an Administrator's Relationship With Service Providers?

Besides plan administrators, trustees rely on attorneys, investment consultants, investment managers, benefit consultants, certified public accountants (CPAs), computer consultants, insurance brokers and others for advice. Defined benefit plans need actuaries to help predict future benefit liabilities, while defined contribution plans may employ preretirement planning counselors to help participants with self-directed investment options. In recent years, health benefit plans have used a cadre of third-party service providers in efforts to contain claim expenditures.

It is plan administrators who:

- Assist trustees in the selection of plan professionals
- Identify matters that should be referred to these consultants
- Coordinate consultant activities to avoid duplication and needless expenditures
- Furnish plan information that consultants need to fulfill their obligations
- Partner with consultants to prepare reports submitted to trustees
- Provide trustees with comments and recommendations concerning reports.

It is not unusual for administrators to review reports of plan professionals and offer preliminary feedback for adjustments that improve the value of the report before distribution to the trustees. For some plans, administrators also participate in the evaluation of plan professionals and other third-party vendors.

When a health and welfare plan includes alternative service delivery systems such as health maintenance organizations (HMOs), individual practitioner associations (IPAs), preferred provider organizations (PPOs), exclusive provider organizations (EPOs), physician hospital organizations (PHOs), closed panels and so forth, the plan administrator also deals with these providers, sometimes serving as an intermediary with plan participants.

Legal Counsel

Virtually every jointly managed multiemployer benefit plan engages legal counsel. During a plan's inception, attorneys help develop the legal documents and assist in the application to the Internal Revenue Service (IRS) for status as a tax-exempt qualified entity. Attorneys collaborate with administrative managers, benefit plan consultants and actuaries to formulate plan rules and regulations, plan documents governing benefits and participant rights, summary plan descriptions and announcement materials.

After a plan is established, legal counsel is usually engaged on an ongoing basis. A law firm may also handle collection of contribution delinquencies and other routine legal matters. Some plans use one legal firm for general counsel and another for collection. Coordination between counsel and the administrative manager is essential in these efforts.

Fiduciary advice. For every plan, trustees rely on general counsel to interpret laws and regulations governing plan policies and operation. These attorneys provide advice relating to the fulfillment of fiduciary obligations and the legal consequences of trustee actions (or inaction in certain circumstances). Frequently, general counsel informs trustees of legal and regulatory changes that impact plan policy and operations. If changes to a trust agreement or other formal plan document are required, these attorneys may prepare the amendments.

Plan documents. The role of legal counsel with respect to plan documents varies with the style of the trustees, administrator and attorney. A plan may delegate to an attorney the sole responsibility for preparation and periodic review of governing documents, written policies, contracts and minutes of meetings. In addition, the attorney may prepare the actual wording of notices for plan participants and employers, summary plan descriptions, summary annual reports, reports to the government, investment guidelines and administrative policy. For another plan, the attorney may retain primary responsibility for these documents but confer with a benefit consultant and administrator. In still another arrangement, legal counsel may have primary responsibility for drafting and maintaining plan documents and work with the administrator to develop operating policy. Minutes, summary plan descriptions and other notices might be prepared by the administrator then reviewed by counsel.

Trustee meetings. Typically, a plan's general counsel attends trustees meetings. This attorney may initiate original reports and information submitted directly to the board of trustees or respond to requests for specific information, opinions and recommendations as requested. Much of general counsel's work develops at trustees meetings as problems emerge during discussion.

Government inquiries. General counsel represents the plan, its administrators and trustees with IRS and the U.S. Department of Labor (DOL). When a question or issue is raised by a government agency, plan administrators usually refer the matter to counsel to research and develop a formal reply on behalf of the board.

Contracts and routine legal issues. While the administrative manager may have the day-to-day contact with plan professionals and vendors, it is general counsel who is involved with the development of a plan's contracts with insurance companies, professionals and other providers of plan goods and services. In addition, counsel may help with routine matters such as space and equipment leases; employment, mortgage and real estate contracts; and investment documents.

Litigation. When a legal dispute arises concerning a participant's benefit eligibility or claims, the administrator refers the matter to plan counsel. In fact, some plans require counsel to attend initial claim review/appeal meetings in an effort to avoid full-blown litigation. These attorneys may be asked to prepare a memorandum to support their legal opinion or the finding of the trustees. Any time an administrator identifies a problem with a substantial chance of litigation, the matter should be turned over to legal counsel as soon as possible.

Collection. A plan's administrative manager and/or board of trustees determine which delinquent employer accounts are forwarded to legal counsel for collection. Once the attorney has information concerning the amount owed by a delinquent employer, the attorney begins collection procedures. When some (or all) of the amount owed is received, the manager notifies counsel to modify (or drop) the legal action.

Reciprocal agreements. Attorneys are also involved in the arrangement of reciprocal agreements with other benefit plans. These agreements vary considerably and are often complicated, but they are essential to protecting the service credits of plan participants who work under more than one collective bargaining agreement in an industry. With input from the administrator and trustees, legal counsel proposes an agreement and/or negotiates with the counsel for other plans.

The relationship between a plan's administrative manager and attorney is generally close. The administrator often implements counsel recommendations. A harmonious relationship with mutual respect is beneficial to both parties and the plan; the result is an efficient and effective partnership.

The board of trustees determines the compensation for legal counsel, which is commonly an annual retainer to cover specific legal services detailed in the legal engagement agreement. A provision may exist for additional compensation in the event of litigation or collection efforts.

Administrative managers often participate in the selection of legal counsel. When a board of trustees is contemplating a change, it may ask the administrative manager to prepare a list of available, experienced attorneys with a background in jointly managed employee benefit plans. The manager may then be authorized to contact select attorneys from the list, request proposals, make arrangements, help interview and participate in the final selection process.

Similarly, counsel may be involved in the recruitment and selection of the administrator and other professionals. If the position of contract administrator is open, counsel may take part in recruiting and interviewing applicants. When a salaried administrator is sought, counsel may have a lesser role with the board of trustees (or a subcommittee of the board) more directly involved in the recruitment and interviews. In either case, legal counsel generally prepares the final contract of employment with the administrator selected.

Benefit Consultants/Actuaries

With the exception of a relatively small number of plans that use an insurance company for providing benefits and related counsel services, virtually all plans engage benefit plan consultants. The Employee Retirement Income Security Act of 1974 (ERISA) requires defined benefit (DB) pension plans to engage an enrolled actuary to prepare an annual actuarial valuation. In addition, these actuaries submit information on the cost of proposed and mandated benefit changes and may certify individual pension applications. Pension actuaries and consultants fill the same role for pension funds as employee benefit consultants do for other funds. Frequently, the actuary and benefit consultant are from the same consulting firm.

Advice and formal reports. Benefit consultants provide information to trustees on policy issues and costs affecting benefits, prepare written documents to meet reporting and disclosure requirements, and help develop and execute administrative procedures. They assist with everyday problems such as claim appeals, eligibility rules, and reporting and disclosure requirements. Benefit consultants have expertise concerning:

- Funding methods
- Plan design alternatives
- Plan administration and rules
- Benefit cost controls
- Claim-processing procedures and controls
- The impact of legislation, regulations, court decisions, changes in accounting rules, public policy, etc.

They furnish reports annually or as needed concerning:

- Projected comparisons of contribution income to benefit claims and operating expenses
- Costs of maintaining, changing or improving benefits
- Review of eligibility rules and self-payment programs
- Legal and technical developments, such as continuing health insurance coverage under the Consolidated Omnibus Budget Reconciliation Act (COBRA)
- Recommendations for establishing financial reserves with respect to claims (reserves for incurred and unreported claims, liability for received and unpaid claims, liability for continued eligibility established under trustee rules, etc.)
- Reserves that might be required for postretirement health care and death benefits

- Review of insurance contracts, rates, administrative charges and renewal actions
- Reasonableness of claim and premium reserves established by insurance carriers
- Changes in policy to an administrative-services-only (ASO) or minimum premium type of funding
- Changes to self-insurance
- Expansion of programs to better manage participant health care
- Establishment of annual self-pay and COBRA premium rates
- Reasonableness and appropriateness of reciprocity agreements.

Benefit consultants serve a vital role apprising administrators and trustees of the latest technology and changes that may affect plan participant benefits. With their knowledge of how benefit programs operate and the "players" in the benefits field, these consultants are able to offer valuable advice to trustees trying to deliver significant, yet cost-effective, benefits. Consultants can present the options available while the administrative managers provide insight on the particular needs of their plan and plan participants.

Insurance. Benefit consultants usually prepare bid specifications issued to insurance companies. They also obtain and review the responses from these carriers, summarize the responses, and issue a report to trustees comparing the bidders' proposals. In some instances, consultants recommend one of the bidders in the report. Benefit consultants are also involved in implementing the arrangements with new insurance carriers and help finalize any administrative procedures that may need to occur with the change.

Health service contracts. Responding to escalating health care costs, many health and welfare plans now contract with health care service providers and cost-management consultants. Benefit consultants are often involved in the negotiation of contracts with these entities as well as those that assist a plan with claims administration.

Administration. Trustees often look to benefit consultants for help reviewing/evaluating administrative procedures and arrangements. They may ask a consultant to develop specifications for a change in administrative managers. The consultant might also provide a recommendation whether to use a contract or salaried administrator. Most consultants attend a number of trustee meetings during the year: They always attend the meeting when the board reviews their annual report.

Plan materials. For most plans, the consultant has full or shared responsibility for drafting plan documents, announcements, notices and summary plan descriptions subject to review by counsel and the administrator.

Withdrawal liability. The pension actuary works with the pension plan manager to determine the liability of employers that withdraw from a plan. Determining withdrawal liability must be done in accordance with the Multiemployer Pension Plan Amendments Act of 1980 (MPPAA).

* * *

The administrative manager has a vital role in ensuring the benefit consultant and actuary are able to accomplish their designated tasks; these consultants depend on the manager to furnish the data needed to prepare their reports and to respond to specific trustee inquiries. Information used by consultants and actuaries spans a wide spectrum that includes:

- The number of participants
- Participant demographics (e.g., age, gender)
- Service credits and eligibility status
- Pension vesting status
- Health and pension benefit payments by type and amount
- Employee turnover
- Mortality statistics
- Total hours of employment
- Claims by type of procedure and classification of participant, etc.

In many instances, administrators provide data in a digital format. Supplied this way, both the time to complete the valuation and the chance of transmission errors are reduced. The accuracy and completeness of the data influence the efficiency and quality of the actuarial work. Absent good data, the value of a report is diluted.

Benefit consultants/actuaries work exclusively and closely with plan administrators. Administrators and consultants have frequent, verbal and personal contact on everyday problems relating to claims, eligibility and routine administrative matters.

In some pension plans, managers obtain pension applications from prospective retirees, review the applications in detail and submit the files to the actuary for certification before approval by the board of trustees. This procedure reduces the possibility of an error and helps assure trustees of the propriety of pension approvals. For other pension plans, this application process may be handled exclusively by administrative managers and staff subject to an annual audit by the actuary preparing the plan valuation.

Besides compiling data for benefit consultants/actuaries, administrators serve as the conduit for communication between the consultants and plan trustees. Administrators review and distribute the reports produced; coordinate the exchange of information between the consultants and the independent CPA as needed for the mutual preparation of government reports; and collect consultant information needed by legal counsel to reply to governmental requests. This accumulation of input from and to these various professionals is coordinated by the administrator.

Independent Auditors

Independent auditors not only provide the external examination of a plan's financial records to meet the requirements of the federal government, they also serve as essential advisors to plan trustees and administrators. The communication and coordination between an administrative manager and auditor are extensive and continual in their mutual effort to ensure proper recordkeeping and the safeguarding of plan resources.

Administrators coordinate the preparation of preliminary financial statements and the supporting data that auditors need for the examination. Generally, independent auditors request outside verification of specific aspects of the financial statements. Plan managers arrange for the preparation of the requests and identify the firms that will receive the requests. Responses to these verification requests are sent directly to the CPA firm.

Administrative managers make available copies of all of a plan's board minutes and governmental reports for the year and other documentation requested by the auditor for the exam. These other documents provide information regarding eligibility, claims payments and experience, insurance contracts, premium reports, etc., reflecting and supporting the plan's financial records.

Investment Advisors

Benefit plans use a wide variety of investment advisors. Virtually all plans engage a professional investment consultant to help trustees understand investments, develop investment guidelines and goals, and gain the highest possible return on a prudent basis. Investment managers are often given discretionary authority to make investments and are expected to meet the investment objectives given them by the trustees. In some plans, multiple investment managers are engaged, particularly with larger funds.

Investment consultants or an evaluation firm help trustees monitor each investment manager's performance and adherence to guidelines on a regular or ad hoc basis. Investment consultants also help trustees on matters such as the periodic review of investment policy guidelines, asset allocation and searches for investment managers.

Regardless of the type of plan, its size or method of administration, plan administrators almost always serve as the coordinator between the board of trustees and these investment advisors. The relationships and communication with the investment consultants, managers and ancillary firms (e.g., brokers, custodians) are constant and ongoing. Administrative managers receive daily reports of investment changes and are responsible—to an extent—for making certain managers follow guidelines established by the trustees.

Administrators maintain the investment records, monitor the receipt of interest and dividends, and watch for errors that could result in a loss of investment income. In addition, administrative managers coordinate contact and reports from all those involved in the investment process.

Administrative managers work with plan investment consultants, investment managers and auditors to develop a short-term cash management program meeting benefit payout needs and to allocate amounts for long-term investment. When specific cash needs arise, the administrator notifies the investment manager to liquidate investments.

Some benefit plans (usually pension plans) make mortgage or other large loans directly to specific borrowers. In these situations, the administrative manager works with legal counsel to develop and execute contracts and other documents such as service agreements with mortgage service companies, mortgage commitment letters, purchase lease agreements and mortgage participation agreements.

If trustees do not delegate authority for loans to an outside party, administrators also become involved in the communication, collections and accounting for the loans. Administrators handle all the duties normally handled by a mortgage servicing company or custodian. They are responsible for recording and following up on payments; communicating with borrowers; and furnishing information to the trustees on defaults, arrears, unpaid taxes, inadequate insurance, lack of maintenance and so forth.

Banks

Normally, administrators represent boards of trustees in relations with banks and their trust departments. This could include:

- Establishing a lockbox arrangement to receive employer contributions and direct bank deposits
- Receiving and sending wire fund transfers
- Maintaining checking and savings accounts with banks, including arrangements to replenish $0 balance accounts as needed to cover expenditures as authorized by the administrator

- Implementing "positive pay" features and other procedures to prevent check fraud
- Short-term investments and cash management.

Administrators may coordinate arrangements between investment managers and banks to provide the necessary funds for investment, as well as to handle interest, dividends and other income from investments owned by the plan.

Administrative managers participate in the designation of depository banks and maintain relationships with employees of these institutions. Because bank representatives rarely attend trustees meetings, they depend upon the administrator to handle their recommendations and reports. Administrative managers forward instructions from trustees directly to the bank; receive, review and record bank reports on a regular basis; and verify the action and propriety of bank transactions.

Health Care Professionals and Providers

Many health and welfare plans employ medical and dental consultants to assist in plan design, as well as claim processing. The coordination between trustees and these persons is usually handled exclusively by administrative managers and other plan personnel. Trustees expect this cadre of consultants to assure them that:

- Claim dollars are being spent appropriately.
- Plan participants have access to quality care.
- Medical services and the fees charged for them are appropriate.

Provider contracts. Many plans now give participants choices: a traditional fee-for-service plan, an HMO, a PPO, an exclusive provider organization, a closed panel of medical/dental groups, IPAs, as well as specific hospitals and other medical providers that have negotiated special arrangements with the plan. Working with the benefit consultant and legal counsel in many instances, the administrative manager spends considerable time and effort finalizing such arrangements, preparing and delivering information to facilitate participant choices, and monitoring the charges and care provided by these many providers.

Pharmacy plan design. With the popularity of drug card plans, plan administrators now work with pharmacy service firms and have duties related to:

- Eligibility, cost and quality controls
- Types of prescription drugs to be covered
- Identification and utilization of participating pharmacies
- Recommendations for plan design, changes and modifications in response to ever-changing technologies and pharmaceutical advances.

The administrator furnishes the names of eligible participants to the card service firm. This company disseminates the information to participating pharmacies, arranges for identification cards, receives and processes claims, etc.

Second opinions. Many health and welfare plans have mandatory or voluntary second surgical opinion programs that are used for certain types of elective surgery. Plan personnel arrange for the appointments and confirmation reports prepared by board-certified specialists.

When a claim is for disability, the administrative manager usually works with a medical consultant to determine whether the applicant meets plan requirements. Often, the administrative manager arranges for these medical examinations.

Claim decisions. Health care consultants help establish parameters for reasonable care and charges based on their personal experience and public data. They help administrators and other personnel determine whether complex and/or innovative medical procedures are covered by plan provisions, whether the procedures are appropriate and necessary, and whether the fees for the procedures are reasonable and customary.

Administrative managers submit specific claims to the consultants for review or establish a procedure for automatically forwarding particular types of claims. The response from the consultant and/or communication with participants and health providers help determine whether to pay a claim and the amount of payment. In addition, managers may arrange for consultants to do a random review of claims paid to test the accuracy of claim processing.

Claim appeals. A health care service provider occasionally characterizes a claim appeal by a participant as "urgent." This action triggers a relatively short period for a plan to conduct a claim review. The responsibility for arranging expedited reviews typically falls on administrative managers. In addition, with the advent of the Patient Protection and Affordable Care Act (ACA), independent health care professionals play a pivotal role in the claims review and appeal process, as the law requires different reviewers to review a claim at different levels of appeal.

Fraud and unusual claims. When there is concern that fraud exists or a patient claim seems unreasonable, an administrator may ask a consultant to obtain medical and hospital records for a detailed review of the claim. This may involve requesting x-rays and results of diagnostic tests, and even arranging for the examination of the patient by the medical or dental consultant.

Health Care Cost-Containment Consultants

As health care costs have escalated, trustees have instituted a variety of cost-management procedures. Many plans contract with utilization review firms to monitor the appropriateness of hospital and other health care. These organizations may also review the propriety of provider charges.

Other significant innovations include the development of case management and disease management. *Case management* is concerned with major or large claims. Trustees contract with case management firms to:

- Intervene
- Review the proposed method, type and sequence of treatment
- Ascertain that the most cost-effective procedures are utilized.

Disease management focuses on participants with chronic conditions that, if left unchecked, will develop into more serious and costly medical problems. Disease management firms are engaged to:

- Identify patients with chronic conditions such as asthma, diabetes, congestive heart failure, hypertension, HIV/AIDS and hepatitis C infection
- Contact patients to determine their current medical status and lifestyle
- Provide patients with advice and educational material for recommended lifestyle changes
- Provide guidance for treatment options with these patients' physicians
- Follow up and work closely with treating physicians to maximize favorable outcomes and to avoid escalation of the medical problem to a chronic condition.

With both case management and disease management, administrative managers identify prospective patients and arrange for the transmittal of information to the service providers.

Insurance Brokers

Some plans utilize insurance brokers to obtain insurance services relating to health care and death benefits, guaranteed investment contracts or general pension services. In addition, brokers help plans obtain insurance for the normal risks and hazards of operating a benefits office such as general property and liability insurance, workers' compensation, fidelity bonds and fiduciary liability coverage. Administrators serve as the coordinating link between trustees and insurance brokers.

For health and welfare plans that self-finance benefits, stop-loss insurance covers large and catastrophic claims. A plan may work through an insurance broker and/or risk manager to acquire this coverage. Frequently, a benefit plan consultant assists the administrator in this activity.

Other Service Providers

Plans require many vendors to provide the facilities, services and supplies necessary to conduct plan business. Invariably, an administrator handles such arrangements. Administrators gather information on needed products and services and, when appropriate, submit proposals to trustees with comments and recommendations. These "other" service providers span the spectrum from real estate agents for office facilities, to consultants for computer hardware and software upgrades, to firms providing payroll and interim auditing services.

Administrators relay information to and from these parties, coordinate their activities, and comment upon and expand their reports and recommendations. It requires a major effort on the part of an administrative manager to integrate the work products of all these individuals and firms into the information provided trustees for subsequent review, consideration and action.

What Is an Administrator's Relationship With Plan Participants?

The main contact between plan participants and a plan is the administrative manager and staff.

How benefit information is communicated and how participants and their families are treated have much to do with participant attitudes toward a plan and plan trustees. Effective communication can create goodwill and has the potential to reduce the number of inquiries, complaints and appeals that must be handled by plan administrators and trustees. Of course, communication is also essential to government compliance as discussed in Chapters, 54, 55 and 56. Below is a sampling of the types of information that must be properly and adequately communicated to participants, dependents and beneficiaries in general:

- Benefit structures
- The extent and limits of coverage
- Qualification requirements
- Notices concerning eligibility and rights
- Financial disclosures
- Danger areas that might adversely affect receipt of benefits
- Changes in benefits that result from collective bargaining, government regulation, etc.
- Financial disclosures.

As much as possible, information must meet legal requirements yet be in language the participants can easily understand. The means of communication may be print materials (e.g., plan booklets, brochures or letters); the posting of content via the Internet; audiovisual media; group events; or individual contact by phone, e-mail or in person. In one-on-one communication, plan personnel are frequently asked to address personal questions and issues concerning:

- Eligibility status
- Potential loss of eligibility
- Dependent coverage
- Application for benefits and the submission of claims
- The effect of new legislation that affects existing coverage
- Tax aspects of benefits.

In recent years, communication responsibilities of plan administrators have greatly expanded. For health plans, a key strategy for containing costs has been communication that encourages a sense of consumerism among plan participants. The ultimate goal is to help participants become value-conscious purchasers of health care. The availability of participant-directed 401(k) retirement plans gives participants more choice with respect to how their retirement funds will be invested but also places new demands on plans and plan administrators to provide the education and support participants need to make these choices. For example, participants must be furnished:

- Details on the types of investment choices available
- Current account balances and investment returns
- Details as to the available investments and choices
- Instruction concerning loan and other withdrawal features of these plans
- Advice, education programs and other support to help participants make decisions regarding investment strategies and asset allocation.

Administrators and other plan personnel may also have a new layer of communication duties (and recordkeeping) concerning participant account balances, loans, withdrawals, transfers among investment options, etc. Some plans have instituted voice technology and Internet capabilities so plan participants may obtain their current account balances on a daily, weekly or monthly basis.

In addition to "pushing" information out to participants, a primary role of plan administrators is to collect and distill feedback from participants. Participants' comments, inquiries and complaints made to administrators and plan personnel over the phone, via e-mail, at a meeting, etc. can provide crucial input for plan decisions made by an administrator and trustees. Such contact can bring to light unforeseen problems that can be remedied once known.

Communication Partnerships

Benefit plans often partner with employers, employer associations and unions to provide plan information to participants regarding:

- New benefit options and programs
- Changes in benefits
- Toll-free telephone numbers, websites and other sources of participant information and assistance
- Procedures for making self-payments
- Tips for retirement planning and controlling health costs.

Employers distribute plan materials in the form of payroll stuffers and brochures with employee paychecks. Plans also provide posters and notices that employers and unions post at worksites, union meeting halls, hiring halls, etc. to ensure maximum exposure.

Frequently, unions and employer associations publish newsletters, newspapers or other periodicals for distribution to plan participants and/or contributing employers. Plans use these materials to make announcements and provide benefit updates.

What Is an Administrator's Relationship With Employers and Employer Associations?

The amount of time administrators spend interacting with employers is usually less than the time devoted to participants and beneficiaries. Nevertheless, the quality of this interaction can influence the administrative work load and the ease of providing benefits. Communication with employers may be oral or written, and can relate to any of the following:

- Contribution rates, effective dates and procedures for making payments
- Obtaining signatures of new employers to become parties to the trust document
- Continuation of the employers' obligation to contribute after the expiration of an agreement and during periods of negotiations
- Verification of contributions
- Contribution delinquencies
- Withdrawal liability
- Payroll reports
- Payroll audit arrangements
- Contractual requirements
- Information concerning individual participants and their families

- Contact information
  - Employment status (e.g., new, terminated, disabled employees, on leave of absence)
  - Benefit eligibility
  - Claims status
  - Self-pay arrangements
  - Continuation of health coverage under COBRA
- Notices required by the Health Insurance Portability and Accountability Act of 1996 (HIPAA), COBRA, etc.
- Reporting and disclosure under ERISA and the Pension Protection Act of 2006
- Requests for plan booklets, claim forms, retirement applications, reporting forms, etc.

Often an employer's human resources department acts as a go-between, ombudsman or advocate on behalf of plan participants. Participants seek the aid of someone on their employer's staff to obtain answers when they do not understand a plan provision or a claim determination. Before HIPAA, the flow of communication was relatively open and simple. Because some of this information is now protected health information (PHI), signed authorizations must be obtained from the participant before the information can be discussed with anyone other than the participant. Plans have had to establish policies and procedures for the receipt of a participant's claim information from an employer. An inquiry may be logged with the plan, but the answer is given only to the plan participant.

At the request of trustees, plan administrators also communicate with employer associations. The issue may be that an employer's contributions are delinquent and the plan hopes the association will help expedite payment. Contact may be made to determine whether an employer has withdrawn from the industry in a particular geographic area served by the plan. When there is industrywide bargaining, the administrative manager may have extensive communication with representatives of the employer association.

What Is an Administrator's Relationship With Unions?

Because eligibility for benefit plans often stems from a union rather than the benefit plan, it is not unusual for union members to look to their union, its offices and staff for information concerning benefit programs and rules. Both the union and the benefit plan may be liable if a representative of the union provides unauthorized, incomplete or inaccurate information that causes a participant or beneficiary to do something that is to the participant's disadvantage. Many unions instruct their representatives and office staff not to furnish benefit plan information. They are told to refer the individual participants and beneficiaries to the plan office to ensure the accuracy of the information provided. Trustees of several plans have gone so far as to put disclaimers at the beginning of plan booklets that advise relying on advice from anyone other than a plan administrator is at the participant's risk.

Day-to-day communication between plans and their local unions often concerns:

- Names of employers that are parties to the collective bargaining agreement
- The effective date an employer becomes party to an agreement
- Changes in contribution rates for individual employers
- Changes in agreements that may affect the liability or contributions for particular types of employees
- Collection efforts by unions with respect to delinquencies and whether liquidated damages or employer bonds are to be obtained
- Collection efforts for pension withdrawal liability
- Names and addresses of new union members/plan participants
- Identity of employees who have obtained employment in the jurisdiction of other benefit funds with which there may be a reciprocity agreement
- Results of payroll audits
- Meeting the requirements of COBRA, the Family and Medical Leave Act, HIPAA, the Medicare Secondary Payer Act and now, the Patient Protection and Affordable Care Act of 2010 as amended (ACA).

Contribution Collections

As a party to the collective bargaining agreement, the union has an obligation to enforce the agreement's terms with respect to contribution delinquencies. In a typical case, plan trustees with the advice of legal counsel develop a policy and procedure that involves the union in collecting late contributions and imposing sanctions on the delinquent employer. The plan and union should have a procedure for transmitting information regarding employer contributions, variances, payroll audit discoveries, delinquencies, legal actions and collections.

Information for Negotiations

An area to be handled with great care, and with advice from counsel, is furnishing information to collective bargaining parties during the negotiation process. A plan's administrator may be asked to estimate the cost implications for plan improvements or eligibility rule changes that may be subject to collective bargaining negotiations. Such information must be furnished to all parties involved in the negotiations, with the release authorized by the plan's board of trustees.

An issue related to the provision of information to negotiators is the delicate question of who must pay for such studies and data retrievals: Compilation can be expensive and time consuming. Most plans have a policy for the distribution of reports and studies. There must be a balance of interest between information that a union, association or employer would like to have and the primary purpose of the trust, providing benefits to participants and their dependents.

Conclusion

Administrative managers and support personnel are a central hub in the exchange of ideas and data among plan stakeholders—participants, contributing employers, affiliated local unions, plan professionals, vendors, etc. The administrative manager cannot be complacent and assume communication between the plan and these parties is adequate "because it's always been done that way." If a process is not already in place, a plan's administrator and trustees should consider creating a formal or informal procedure for feedback. The approach might be a major survey of plan participants or something as simple as regular meetings with representatives of the union and employers to discuss problems being encountered between stakeholders and the plan's administrative personnel. In this way, there is ongoing attention to the improvement of plan operations.

Chapter 51

Claims Processing and Control

William J. Einhorn

Multiemployer plans provide benefits under the terms established by plan trustees. Processing claims involves the determination of whether a person is eligible and the amount payable under these terms—and the payment of claims deemed appropriate. How claims are paid depends on the type of the plan (welfare, pension, vacation, etc.) and how the plan is administered.

How Are Pension Benefits Processed?

The responsibility for determining an applicant's eligibility for pension benefits is almost always given to a pension plan's administrative office. The plan administrator also accumulates the data necessary to determine the level of benefits owed a participant.

Self-Financed Defined Benefit Pension Plans

In a self-financed situation, plan personnel:

- Prepare and distribute application forms and information detailing pension benefit options
- Review completed applications submitted by participants
- Determine participant eligibility and the level of benefits—subject to the review and approval of the trustees
- Issue the pension certificate and arrange for the monthly payment of benefit checks directly from the pension fund
- Comply with government procedures for the tax reporting of payments made.

Once benefit payments begin, an entirely separate set of data must be maintained by plan personnel or a designated third party for the plan's annual actuarial valuation.

Annuity Plans

If a plan uses an insurance company to handle pension claims, the carrier checks with the plan concerning the participant's eligibility and reviews the data accumulated by the plan to establish the dollar amount of the annuity account and periodic (most often monthly) pension payments. Otherwise, the processing of annuity benefits is much the same as for a defined benefit or defined contribution plan.

Defined Contribution Plans

A similar procedure is followed for defined contribution (DC) plans. The primary difference is that the basis for benefits paid to retirees and beneficiaries is the amount in the DC account versus any amount guaranteed by the plan. There is no need for the annual actuarial valuation.

What Processing Is Needed for Vacation Fund Payouts?

Some vacation funds require participants to apply for benefits from the fund with approval of employers to avoid a mass number of employees taking vacation at the same time. Other plans automatically make regular payments according to the terms stated in the trust or collective bargaining agreement; the vacation money is paid uniformly on designated dates.

How Are Health and Welfare Claims Processed?

Certification of eligibility is normally a function of a plan's administrative office. Determining who is eligible for benefits is facilitated by clear and reasonable rules that have been communicated to participants in a manner that is easy to comprehend. When third parties handle claims processing, plans periodically transmit data to these external entities as to who is currently eligible for plan benefits.

Trustees, in general, have considerable authority to formulate eligibility requirements and decide questions of eligibility. Nevertheless, there have been cases where the courts and arbitrators have decided trustees (1) exceeded their authority as specified in a trust agreement, (2) adopted unreasonable eligibility rules or (3) applied reasonable eligibility requirements in a discriminatory or capricious manner. In addition to determining whether participants and their dependents are eligible for plan benefits, the processing of health and welfare claims consists of verifying and paying claims, the preparation and analysis of claims reports, and compliance with federal and state requirements. Exhibit 1 identifies specific tasks considered part of health and welfare claims processing.

Insured Plans

When benefits are provided in part or in full by an insurance company, the insurance carrier or the benefit plan may verify claims and issue claim payments. If the carrier makes the payments, plan personnel certify eligibility in advance but may retrospectively review claims to make certain benefits are not being paid to ineligible persons, and are in accordance with plan terms and conditions.

When plan personnel pay claims—whether using checks from a plan account or drafts on an insurance carrier's account—an internal audit should be performed to assure the accuracy and propriety of payments. If an insurance account is involved, an external post audit may be performed by the insurance carrier, as well as by the plan accountant, for further verification.

Self-Financed Plans

Personnel of self-financed plans often handle all phases of claims processing, from certification of eligibility to payment of claims. In some instances, self-financed plans certify eligibility but a third party handles claims. This approach is similar to that used when a plan uses insurance to provide benefits, but the claims processor is an independent third-party administrator (TPA), an insurance carrier operating on an administrative-services-only (ASO) basis or a preferred provider organization (PPO).

When an outside party is involved in claims processing, both an internal and external audit should be completed. The plan must establish internal control standards and procedures to guard against external fraud and abuse, so a public accountant should verify claim payments as part of a periodic review.

Exhibit 1

Health and Welfare Claims Processing

- Determine whether participants and their dependents are enrolled in the plan
- When a claim is filed—
  - Verify it is a type of claim covered by the plan
  - Check whether the person is eligible for benefits on the date the claim occurred
  - Determine the amount of the claim payment to be made by the plan
  - Pay the participant or health care provider
- Issue benefit statements with an explanation of payments made and/or denied
- Monitor claims to ascertain—
  - Treatments are appropriate and necessary for medical conditions indicated
  - Charges are reasonable, usual and customary for such treatments and conditions
- Prepare claim experience reports for review by trustees
- Prepare annual reports required by government
- Comply with HIPAA privacy and security regulations with regard to the personal health information (PHI) of plan participants

Eligibility and Claim Denials

Plan trustees bear the ultimate responsibility for deciding whether a participant is eligible for benefits and the extent to which a claim is covered. It is trustees who hear and rule on any appeals regarding eligibility and claims. Exhibit 2 summarizes the federal regulations pertaining to claims processing and appeals.

How Can Claims Processing Support Cost Containment?

The upsurge in health care costs in recent years is shining a bright light on the importance of claims control and other cost-containment efforts. Such activities are essential to maintaining the financial solvency of health and welfare benefit programs.

A vital prerequisite to cost containment is accumulating and analyzing data that points to the causes of increasing costs. With the right data, it is possible to identify what is contributing to the cost increases and to seek less-costly solutions. The data must be accurate, complete, timely and understandable.

Exhibit 2

Federal Regulation of Claims Processing

The processing of employee benefit claims must comply with ERISA and U.S. Department of Labor regulations. Any plan or third party responsible for claims processing must have policies and procedures in place to comply with these rules. The purpose of the rules is to (1) ensure timely claims processing and (2) make certain claim denials are given a "full and fair review."

Timely Processing

Federal regulations stipulate a claim must be replied to or paid within 90 days after a plan receives a claim. An extension is allowed if the claimant is given written notice. In no event may the extension exceed a second 90-day period.

Claim Denials

When a claim is denied, Section 503 of ERISA requires the claimant be provided a written notice that:

- States the specific reason for the denial
- Specifies the plan provisions on which the denial was based
- Describes any additional material or information necessary to complete the claim
- Explains why any additional information is needed
- Details the steps to be taken if the claimant wants to request a claim review.

The law also requires that the notice be prepared in a manner that can be understood by the claimant.

Appeals

Plans must have procedures in place that give claimants (and their authorized representatives) a "reasonable opportunity for a full and fair review" of a denied claim.

The appeal procedures must permit claimants to submit a written request for a review and the right to examine documents pertinent to the claim being appealed.

The claim review may be conducted by a named plan fiduciary or person designated by plan fiduciaries. Responsibility for reviews may also be assigned to an insurance company, managed care organization or similar organization. Trustees of insured plans and those that employ a third-party organization subject to state insurance laws may elect to retain the responsibility for claims review versus delegating this function to the insurance company.

Appeal procedures may limit the period in which claimants may file requests for review. The time limit must be reasonable relative to the nature of the benefit and other circumstances. At minimum, claimants must be given 60 days to request a review measured from the date the claimant receives written notification of denial.

Reviews and decisions must be prompt. The U.S. Department of Labor differentiates pre- and postservice claim appeals. Preservice appeals are further categorized as urgent and nonurgent. Postservice reviews and decisions ordinarily must occur within 60 days after a plan receives a review request. If special circumstances exist, an extension is allowed but the decision must be rendered as soon as possible—no later than 120 days after the initial request for review.

Prior to the passage of the Patient Protection and Affordable Care Act of 2010 (ACA), a 72-hour time limit applied for plan responses to urgent appeals. At the time this chapter was written, interim rules were in place that expand claimant protections for plans that are not grandfathered under ACA. These protections include additional standards for internal appeals and offer participants an external appeals process. One of the new standards is a reduction in the time limit for urgent internal claims to 24 hours.

At a minimum, trustees and consultants considering cost-containment strategies need:

- Summary claim reports by type of claim, including the deductible and coinsurance costs incurred by plan participants
- Reports on savings gained through of coordination benefits and subrogation recoveries
- Claims-lag studies that measure the time between the date of the medical treatment and the date payment is made to help determine the cash reserves required by the plan
- Analysis of benefits paid by type (e.g., hospitaliza-

tion, outpatient ambulatory surgery, inpatient surgery, medical, dental, diagnostic, x-ray and prescription drug)
- Analysis of claims by major classification of illness using a standard type of medical coding such as "major diagnostic category"
- Analysis of medical and dental claims reflecting the average payments for specific procedures
- Comparison of hospital average length of stay and cost of average confinement among other hospital costs and utilization trends
- Calculation of "per employee per month" (PEPM) data to adequately plan for plan contribution rates.

Much of this data can be compared with the experience of others in an industry or region, as well as national statistics. These numbers are useful in predicting future costs relative to future income. Knowledge of costs and current utilization patterns is extremely helpful in negotiating fees and discounts with a preferred provider organization (PPO).

Facts and figures are imperative when trying to identify which cost-management strategies to implement and assessing their effectiveness once they are in place. Claims data is useful when:

- Identifying services with high utilization and excessive costs that might be targeted for reduction through—
  - Participant information and education
  - Wellness programs (e.g., nutrition counseling, weight control, smoking cessation, stress management, physical fitness)
  - Adjustments in cost sharing (i.e., coinsurance, deductibles, inside benefit limits)
  - Changes in scheduled coverages (e.g., examinations covered more or less frequently)
  - Utilization review, disease management and similar programs.
- Considering funding and administrative changes such as a switch to self-financing or a third-party administrator to reduce costs
- Considering expanding plan design beyond traditional fee-for-service plans to alternatives such as health maintenance organizations (HMOs) and preferred provider organizations (PPOs)
- Attempting to assess the savings achieved through tighter coordination of benefits or increased subrogation efforts.

Chapters 16 and 17 examine these and other cost-management strategies being adopted by health benefit plans.

Data collection is a natural by-product of claims processing. Therefore, the burden of collecting, comparing and analyzing health claims data usually falls on the plan administrator, assisted by plan consultants. If a third party such as a TPA or insurance carrier has responsibility for processing claims, it is likely they will be collecting data as well. In some cases the third-party data will be sufficient to meet plan needs, but not always. Many plans maintain their own databank of claims to supplement reports received from these third parties.

What Is the Purpose of a Claims Audit?

Auditing the records of health providers is a way to avoid unnecessary claim payments. A claims audit may involve a visit to a hospital and/or doctor's office to review medical records to assess whether services were necessary, properly administered and properly billed. This is an opportunity to determine whether fees were consistent with the rates established with the provider and/or at reasonable and customary levels.

Plan administrators should also implement controls to prevent abuse and excessive claim payments. Items to watch for with medical claims are:

- Unnecessary medical services rendered (e.g., x-rays and lab tests)
- Longer than necessary hospital confinements
- Submission of a claim for covered care when in reality the care was not covered (e.g., cosmetic surgery).

For disability claims, look for:

- Returns to work or other employment while receiving disability benefits from the plan
- Longer absences from work than medically necessary.

Many plans use a precertification method by which an independent party determines the need for medical/dental services. A utilization review organization monitors hospital admissions and length of stay. Third parties can also be used to determine when a disabled person is able to return to work.

How Does Coordination of Benefits Work?

Many plans and plan insurance contracts have *coordination of benefits* (COB) provisions to prevent a situation in which someone receives payment greater than the actual cost of the health care. This can occur when a person is covered by two health plans, for example, when an employee's spouse is covered by the employee's plan as well as a plan provided by the employer of the spouse.

Primary and Secondary Carriers

When a COB provision is in effect, one plan is named

the *primary carrier* responsible for the claim. The other carrier, called the *secondary carrier,* only pays for charges it covers that are in excess of the amounts paid by the primary carrier. There are various methods for determining which provider is the primary and secondary provider. To promote uniformity and avoid processing delays, the National Association of Insurance Commissioners (NAIC) has established COB rules for health care plans. It is at the discretion of each state whether group health plans must follow these guidelines.

NAIC rules provide that when a plan participant (i.e., employee, retiree) is also covered as a dependent on another plan, the primary carrier is the participant's plan. It is the participant's plan that would pay the participant's medical expenses. Expenses that exceed the coverage provided by this plan would be the responsibility of the secondary carrier within its coverage limits.

On the other hand, if a plan covers a participant's spouse and the spouse has coverage through another plan as a result of his or her own employment, that spouse's plan is the primary carrier for the spouse. The participant's plan is the secondary carrier and has only partial liability, if any, for the care of the spouse.

When duplicate coverage exists for a child through parental coverage, the NAIC's "birthday rule" is used. The plan of the parent with the earlier birthday (month and day) during the calendar year is the child's primary carrier. The other parent's plan is the secondary carrier.

There are some important exceptions to these rules. Even if a state decides to adopt these rules, self-financed ERISA plans are not bound by them. Another exception applies to Medicare recipients; Medicare is always the secondary carrier for dependent coverage and the primary carrier for persons other than a dependent (e.g., employee, retiree).

Participant Disclosure

Federal criminal statues can be interpreted to require participants to disclose other insurance or health benefits when a benefit plan has a COB provision. More specifically, 18 U.S.C. §1027 makes it a federal crime to make a false statement or knowingly conceal any fact needed to verify, explain, clarify or check for the accuracy and completeness of any report or document required to be kept as part of the records of any welfare benefit plan. This statute was used to prosecute a plan participant whose failure to disclose COB information resulted in a plan paying out more in benefits than it would have if the COB information had been disclosed.

To encourage the disclosure of COB information, many plans have incorporated within their plan design a "COB savings bank." Under such an arrangement, COB savings are credited to a participant and may be used during the remainder of the plan year to cover otherwise uncovered medical expenses. Typically, the savings are not carried forward after the plan year.

What Is Subrogation?

Subrogation can be described as a plan "standing in the shoes" of a participant with the right to recover claim payments from a third party responsible for causing the condition requiring medical treatment. Who is this third party? It could be the driver of a car who caused a collision and injured the plan participant, or perhaps, a property owner whose negligence caused a participant to slip and fall requiring medical care. In both of these situations, an insurance company that provides liability coverage to the third party may also be involved.

When there is potential third-party liability, plans typically require the injured participant to sign a subrogation/reimbursement agreement as a condition of providing benefits. If the participant receives money from the third party or the third party's insurer for medical expenses paid by the plan, the participant must reimburse the plan for these expenses.

A successful subrogation recovery program requires specific procedures be in place to:

- Identify claims representing potential subrogation
- Gather information from participants and/or their attorneys regarding the particulars of the accident/incident
- Secure signed subrogation/reimbursement agreements from participants
- Update and communicate the extent of the plan's subrogation lien to participants and/or plan legal counsel
- Track notice and collection efforts
- Flag claims and eligibility in the event a participant refuses to honor the subrogation/reimbursement agreement.

See Chapter 24 for a more complete discussion of subrogation.

What Fraud Risks Are Associated With Claims?

Preventing and identifying fraud is another duty assigned to a plan's administrator and/or benefit claims payer. While fraudulent claims do not appear to be as prevalent as other

Exhibit 3

Opportunities for Fraud

Benefit Disbursements

Pension funds

- Deceased pensioners
- Phony pensioners
- Manipulation of pension calculation

Health and welfare funds

- Unbundling and up-coding of services
- Sweetheart deals with network providers
- General kickbacks
  - Monetary
  - Things of value
- Fictitious services
  - Physician
  - Service provider
- Nontransmittal of appropriate rebates and discounts
- Claims
  - Fictitious claims by service providers
    - » Billing for services not rendered
    - » Upgrade in services provided
    - » Performance of unnecessary services
    - » Referral kickbacks from providers
  - Fictitious claims by participants
    - » Claims for invalid dependents
    - » Phony out-of-pocket expenses
    - » Duplicate claims
    - » Abuse
- Duplicate coverage

Apprenticeship funds

- Fund buying tools for personal use
- Service to homes of officers
- Payment to fictitious instructors

Annuity funds

- Registration fees never turned in
- Fictitious annuitants
- Theft of unclaimed annuity benefits
- Interception of annuity checks

Legal services funds

- Service provider bills for incorrect case type
- Improper continuation of case
- Billings in excess of plan limitation
- Inflated hours or fictitious casework

Employer Contributions

- Alter egos
- Omission of covered employees
- Omission of covered pay types
- Omission of covered wages
- Improper inclusion of owners/relatives
- Delinquency
- Deficiency
- Diversion of employer contributions

Administrative Expenses

- Inflated professional fees
- Fictitious employees
- Unreasonable allocation of shared expenses
- Inflated purchase prices
- Fictitious payments for goods and services
- Inflated travel expenses
- Kickbacks
- Inflated payroll tax deposits
- Personal use of computer equipment
- Inflated salaries
- Personal expenses paid by fund
- Diversion of rental and other income

Investments

- Unauthorized transfer from investment accounts
- Diversion of investment income
- Investments with no substance
- Kickbacks
- Self-dealing investment transactions

Source: Weaver, Susan P. "Fraud in a Financial Statement Audit," *Benefits & Compensation Digest*, v 42, n 4 (International Foundation of Employee Benefit Plans, April 2005).

abuses, they do occur. Fraud against employee benefit plans can be committed by participants, service providers and others. Numerous opportunities exist including:

- Theft of claimant or provider identify
- Fake or inaccurate billing for supplies or services provided
- False statements regarding the cause of illness or injury
- Failure to advise the plan that other coverage exists.

Susan P. Weaver, a member of an independent auditing firm specializing in employee benefit plan audits has detailed the many ways fraud might be committed against a multiemployer plan. Her list is provided as Exhibit 3. Clearly, there are any number of ways fraud might be perpetrated upon a benefit plan. Administrative procedures must be put in place to minimize the risk of such fraudulent acts.

It is possible to submit fraudulent claims without a participant's knowledge, especially when claims are sent directly to a plan for payment by a health provider. In such cases, participants may not be aware someone has assumed their identity and obtained free health care or an unscrupulous provider has submitted claims for services never rendered. These scenarios illustrate why it is so critical for participants to review their benefit statements. Urging participants to do so is one tactic for combating fraud.

In other situations, participants know fraud is occurring. They may be helping an ineligible participant or a nonparticipant obtain medical care paid by the plan. Claims may be submitted with the signature of a fictitious provider or the forged signature of a bona fide provider. A more common fraud is entering false information on claim forms or leaving questions unanswered about other group health insurance. This information must be obtained during claims processing.

With disability claims, participants or employers may make fraudulent statements about the cause of illness or injury, and indicate there is no liability under workers' compensation insurance. Participants must be educated that false answers and omissions constitute fraud—and false claims reduce the money available for legitimate claims.

Chapter 52

Collection Litigation

Travis J. Ketterman

A benefit trust fund consists of employer contributions and the investment income generated from these contributions. If an employer fails to make proper and timely contributions, the financial stability of the fund may be put in jeopardy. Every benefit plan should have written collection policies and procedures that encourage prompt payment and resolution of collection issues. Trustees have a fiduciary duty to ensure that these policies and procedures are implemented, monitored and enforced.

This chapter outlines the key elements a plan should have in its written collection guidelines along with an introduction to legal options a plan has when faced with a delinquent contribution. This information is drawn from a more thorough discussion of the collection process provided in the author's book *Collecting Employer Contributions: The ERISA Litigation Guide* also published by the International Foundation. The book includes samples of many of the documents that an attorney uses in a collection case.[1]

What Should Be Included in a Written Collections Statement?

The U.S. Department of Labor (DOL) requires funds to make "systematic, reasonable and diligent collection efforts." To meet these requirements, DOL recommends written collection policies and procedures with these provisions:

- Regular reviews of employer contributions to the trust fund
- A plan for regular payroll audits
- Automatic charges for liquidated damages, interest and plan expenses that result from collecting delinquent contributions
- Employer questionnaires that can be used to gather key information
- Surety bonds to guarantee contribution payments
- Placing contributions in escrow accounts if the contributions are received prior to being due
- Instituting legal action to collect the delinquent contributions.

The written guidelines should also establish a(n):

- Time frame for monitoring and collecting delinquent contributions
- Time frame for referring the delinquency to the plan's attorney for legal action
- Committee to monitor delinquent contributions
- Audit policy
- Policy regarding mistaken contributions
- Requirements for written reports for each regularly scheduled trustees' meeting regarding the monitoring and collection of delinquent contributions.

All persons who work on fund collections should know these policies and procedures.

What Legal Grounds Do Funds Have for Collecting Delinquent Contributions?

Employers contributing to multiemployer benefit plans are often part of a collective bargaining agreement. The terms of the agreement and the plan dictate the amount and manner in which an employer must make payments. The Employee Retirement Income Security Act of 1974 (ERISA) not only requires trustees to pursue collection of delinquent contributions, it includes provisions that help plans pursue collection through the federal court system.

Delinquent contribution cases generally fall into two categories of federal lawsuits:

- In the first category, an employer fails to submit monthly reports and/or contributions. The goal of the lawsuit is to get the reports and contributions that are missing. For the purposes of this chapter, these lawsuits will be referred to as *report cases.*
- In the second category of lawsuits, plans want to conduct an audit of an employer to check that the employer paid the proper contribution amount. These lawsuits will be referred to as *audit cases.*

Often, a case is more complicated than the fact that an employer failed to pay contributions. Benefit plans must sometimes pursue related companies that employers use to escape a collective bargaining agreement. Courts use alter ego, single employer and successor employer analysis to determine whether an employer has shifted work to a non-union firm the employer owns. There are also situations where individuals must be pursued as well as a business for delinquent contributions. The legal term for this strategy is to *pierce the corporate veil.*

Alter Ego Analysis

A corporation's *alter ego* is a separate business created to commit fraud or to provide a shield from liability. There are specific facts a judge explores to determine whether an alter ego exists:

- A substantially identical business purpose
- Common employees
- Common operation
- Common equipment
- Common customers
- Joint supervision
- Shared financial control
- Common financial institutions
- The same office location
- Common job sites
- Common professional services (legal and accounting)
- The same federal tax identification number
- Exchange of equipment or business for less than fair market value
- Undercapitalization
- Common management
- Common ownership.

Of these facts, federal courts routinely emphasize as the most important: common employees, common ownership and common management or control of labor relations. In addition, a federal court will not find an alter ego relationship exists without some proof of an unlawful motive on the part of the corporation. In other words, a plan must demonstrate that the employer intended to avoid its collective bargaining obligations using an alter ego company.

Single Employer Analysis

In contrast to alter ego analysis, *single employer analysis* is an effort to determine whether two businesses are actually one employer. This approach to a lawsuit is sometimes more attractive to plans than the alter ego approach. To determine whether there is one employer, courts generally consider:

- The interrelation of operations
- Common management
- Common ownership
- Centralized control of labor relations and personnel.

Successor Liability Analysis

Successor liability applies when:

- There is substantial continuity in the operation of business
- The successor had notice of the claim against the predecessor.

Pierce the Corporate Veil

In addition to proving one employer was functioning as multiple businesses, a plan may pursue individuals under a *pierce the corporate veil* theory. Only employers are obligated to make benefit plan contributions under ERISA. Generally, officers and owners of a corporation are not considered employers; as a result, they are not liable for benefit contributions. Federal courts, however, will "pierce the corporate veil" to hold officers or owners liable for contributions if these persons are liable for other corporate debt under state law. To establish whether to pierce the corporate veil, courts consider:

- The respect paid by the shareholders themselves to the separate corporate identity
- Any fraudulent intent of the individual defendants
- The degree of injustice that would result from recognizing the corporate identity.

Is There Any Way to Avoid Going to Court?

Trustees make the decision whether to (1) file a lawsuit immediately or (2) try to resolve the situation out of court first. Never underestimate the power of a law firm's letterhead to spur an employer to take collection actions more seriously. Unless trustees are absolutely convinced all efforts to resolve the dispute without a lawsuit have been exhausted, the minimal time and money involved in having an attorney send a formal demand letter are worth the investment.

In the letter, the attorney should encourage a confidential meeting that includes a plan representative, the employer and the attorneys representing both sides (*parties*). The employer can be given assurances that the statements in the meeting will not be used in later court proceedings.

Such a meeting should occur only after trustees and/or administrators have some idea of how much is owed—typically determined through contribution reports or an audit. If the employer has not permitted an audit, the initial discussion will be limited to whether the employer will produce the desired records without a lawsuit.

How Does a Plan File a Lawsuit?

The formal document filed with the court to start a lawsuit is a *complaint.* A good complaint identifies the parties involved in the lawsuit, the relevant facts leading to the case and the laws that support the complaint. Federal rules require three specific elements be included in a complaint. If a plan is filing a collections case, these would be short and simple statements that:

1. Support the plan has filed in the correct court
2. Show the plan is entitled to employer contributions (typically because of a collective bargaining agreement) and that the employer has failed to do so
3. Tell the court what the plan wants the court to do.

The plan's attorney will prepare this document and submit it to the court.

What Else Happens in Court?

Once the complaint is filed, the plan legal counsel and those persons representing the employer meet to discuss the claim as well as the information both parties need for a trial. They may discuss the possibility of settlement—99% of all civil cases settle before they go to trial. More information on settlement is provided later in this chapter.

While settlement is a very likely outcome, the plan attorney should still aggressively pursue the case. In the rare exception that the case goes to trial, the plan will want to have an attorney who takes advantage of all opportunities to gather information that strengthens the case when it gets to court. The old proverb that "knowledge is power" is true in court. The process in which the attorneys representing the plan and the employer share information is *discovery.* A variety of legal tools help "discover" the relevant facts of a case. Four important ones are discussed here.

Depositions

During a *deposition,* an attorney questions an individual or organization named in the legal suit. Persons representing both sides of the dispute as well as their attorneys are usually present. A court reporter prepares a *transcript* of the meeting—a record of the questions and answers during the deposition that can be used at later stages in the case. A judge is not present for depositions, but may be consulted in rare cases.

Depositions give attorneys an opportunity to test the strength of a case; more specifically, testing the ability of witnesses (and any document the witnesses provide) to tell the story leading to the lawsuit. Depositions are almost a dress rehearsal for the trial. They lock witnesses into their version of what happened.

Interrogatories

Interrogatories are written questions from one party that must be answered in writing by another party in the case. Interrogatories are enormously useful as a discovery tool. Interrogatories in a case seeking reports should ask the following information concerning bargaining unit employees:

- Name, address and title of employees who performed bargaining unit work during the period the reports are missing
- Number of hours worked by each employee during the period the reports are missing
- Wages earned by the employees during the period reports are missing
- Whether federal and state income tax was withheld from the employees during the period the reports are missing
- Whether dues payments were withheld from the employees during the period the reports are missing.

When a plan has an audit report showing discrepancies, the interrogatories help identify:

- Objections to the audit findings
- Whether the discrepancies are accurate and, if not accurate, why
- All documents, if any, which support the audit report
- All individuals and entities who reviewed the audit report
- Any individual or entity that assisted in preparing or providing a response to the audit report.

Responses to interrogatories help narrow the issues in the dispute. They are not filed with the court, but they may be used in a later stage of the legal process.

Requests to Produce Documents

A plan may request documents, materials or other "tangible things" as part of discovery. This tool is essential in audit cases. The plan requests the employer's books and records needed to undertake or complete an audit. Like interrogatories, a request for documents may only be made of persons or organizations named in the lawsuit. However, documents from individuals or businesses that are not parties (known as *third parties*) may be obtained by a *subpoena*—a court order to testify in court or provide documents. Requests for documents should be as specific as possible. Simply asking for "all relevant documents" is not enough.

Responding parties must turn over documents in their possession, custody or control. This extends to any document a party has the legal right to obtain on demand. There is one potential obstacle in this process, the party requesting a document must prove the responding party has control over the documents. The responding party must respond in writing to the request for documents within 30 days. The party asking for the documents may examine and copy them.

In some audit cases, a plan's auditor may have reviewed the bulk of the requested books and records, and the employer is only objecting to a limited number of specific documents. There are other occasions when an employer refuses to allow the auditing of books and records. In these situations, the plan should seek the following documents, along with any additional records specifically requested by the auditors, be given direct to the auditors:

- Employer's quarterly tax returns, IRS Form No. 941
- State Unemployment Compensation Form U.C. No. 3
- Payroll journal, cash disbursement journal, cash receipts journal, payroll subsidiaries
- General ledger
- Invoices of subcontractors and suppliers
- Time and job record cards
- Listing or schedule of subcontractors
- Check stubs and canceled checks
- W-2 wage statements and all other payroll records
- Any other contribution reports involving employees filed with other trust funds
- IRS Forms 1099 and 1096
- Workers' compensation policies including any workers' compensation audit reports
- Construction loan data
- Waivers of lien
- Federal income tax returns
- Transmittal of Income and Tax Statements, IRS Form W-3.

Requests for Admissions

A request for admission is another valuable tool—too often it is not used to its full advantage. A *request for admission* is a "request" from one party to another in a case to agree (admit) or disagree (deny) that a statement is true. For example, a plan will usually ask an employer to admit that an attached collective bargaining agreement or monthly contribution report is a genuine and true document. Through an admission, a fact becomes undisputed and does not require further proof later in a case. Eliminating issues where there is agreement may save money and it will certainly save time.

Any request not denied in writing within 30 days after the service to the opposing party is considered admitted. This rule is so important it bears repeating: if a party fails to deny a "fact" in the proper manner, the request is admitted regardless of whether the "fact" is true. The failure to respond and the introduction of such a fact may end the litigation—again saving time and possibly money.

What Is a Settlement Conference?

A settlement conference is an ideal opportunity to resolve a case or narrow the issues in dispute. During a *settlement conference*, a plan representative is physically present in the same room as an employer representative. This often leads to a frank and productive conversation.

Sometimes, especially early in the process, a settlement conference is a meeting of the parties without legal counsel. However, lawyers can be brought into the conference via telephone if settlement is reached. The attorneys confirm the settlement details and draft the settlement agreement.

In preparation for a conference, both the plan representative and legal counsel should be familiar with:

- The collective bargaining agreement signed by the employer
- The basis for the claim of delinquent contributions
- Information provided by the employees or the union connected with the dispute
- Information obtained through discovery.

Plan representatives and legal counsel should also make a realistic assessment of the following factors:

- Ability to collect a judgment
- Risk of the employer filing bankruptcy
- Weaknesses of the plan's case
- Cost of continued litigation
- Time needed to continue litigation and the effect of the delay on the participants and the plan.

If a federal judge is going to be part of the settlement conference, the judge may require the parties to exchange a settlement demand and offer before the meeting. The judge will also require the parties to exchange a brief description of the strengths and weaknesses in the case. All of this information is usually shared with the judge prior to the conference.

During a settlement conference conducted by a judge, the judge typically orders that a person with full authority to settle the case be physically present. The reason for this requirement is obvious: a settlement might occur during the conference.

Mediation

Settlement conferences may involve a mediation process. In *facilitative mediation,* a judge or other neutral person tries to help the two sides in the case reach a resolution or settlement. The mediator may make suggestions, ask questions and clarify points only to assist the parties in trying to come to some kind of agreement. The mediator does not make a decision who wins or loses.

An alternative process, *evaluative mediation,* the mediator does make decisions on the value of the arguments presented and suggests a settlement. In some cases, evaluative mediation only happens after facilitative mediation does not yield a settlement. Judges–especially those who will continue to be involved in the litigation if the case is not settled–are reluctant to engage in evaluative mediation. Generally, federal judges use a facilitative approach.

The Settlement Process

If a judge is present, a settlement conference usually starts with plan legal counsel making an informal opening statement reviewing the case from the plan's point of view. The attorney also states the terms the plan proposed for settlement. The employer's attorney is then given an opportunity to make a similar statement reviewing the employer's position including the rationale for the employer's offer.

Depending on the civility of the parties and the judge's personal preferences, the parties may continue to discuss settlement face-to-face. Another approach is for the judge to move the parties into different rooms and discuss settlement with each party separately. If the parties are separated, the judge uses "shuttle diplomacy" until (1) the parties reach an agreement, (2) there is no chance of agreement or (3) the judge decides a face-to-face meeting may be more productive.

Settlement conferences are confidential. Under the Federal Rules of Evidence, statements made during a settlement conference are usually inadmissible at trial. Many times, if a settlement is reached, the judge will have the agreement placed in the court's records. The settlement agreement must still be put in writing and signed by both parties.

What Should Be Included in a Settlement Agreement?

A settlement agreement should include the following provisions:

- Description of the dispute (e.g., audit or basic monthly reporting requirements)
- Time period of the dispute (e.g., the audit period or the period of reports without contributions)
- Amount of payment by the employer to the plan
- Timing of the payment (lump sum or installment plan)
- Release of liability to the employer
- Dismissal of the lawsuit
- Statement that both parties are receiving something of value by settling the case (the legal term is *consideration*)
- Statement that the signing individuals are authorized to represent the plan and the employer
- Statement that the settlement agreement constitutes the entire agreement between the parties
- Statement that the settlement agreement may only be modified by a written document signed by the parties
- Statement that the parties either consulted with legal counsel or had the opportunity to consult with legal counsel prior to entering into the settlement agreement
- Statement that the parties did not rely on representations by an adverse party other than the statements in the settlement agreement
- Statement that the parties may sign separate copies of the settlement agreement
- Statement that fax signatures are as acceptable as original signatures.

Can a Plan Settle for Less Than the Full Amount Owed or Accept Installment Payments?

Given the financial realities of the business world, there are times when a plan may have to:

- Allow an employer to make installment payments for delinquent contributions and expenses owed
- Allow an employer to pay less than the full amount of contributions and expenses owed (in either a lump sum or installment payments)

- Cease collection efforts against an employer whose contributions are determined to be uncollectible.

Accepting less than what is owed or an installment plan may be considered a prohibited transaction under ERISA. Trustees can avoid this if the agreement:

- Follows "reasonable, diligent and systematic efforts" to collect all amounts owed in a lump sum basis
- Is in writing
- Is "reasonable under the circumstances based on the likelihood of collecting such contributions or approximate expenses" if the plan continued its collection efforts
- Is based on the "exclusive purpose of facilitating the collection" of contributions.

A plan must satisfy all of these criteria before it settles a collection dispute with an employer.

What Happens If a Plan Cannot Settle?

In the absence of settlement, a plan will need a federal judge to determine whether the employer owes the delinquent contributions. The two main vehicles for getting a determination are summary judgment and a trial on the merits.

Summary Judgment

A motion for *summary judgment* is an excellent tool when there is an agreement between the two parties on the facts of the case but a legal issue is in dispute. Let's say both parties agree on this fact: the employer sent a letter on a specific date stating a collective bargaining agreement was being terminated. However, one party disagrees whether the letter was sufficient from a legal standpoint to terminate the agreement. Since there is agreement that the fact is correct but a legal issue exists, summary judgment is proper.

In another situation, a plan may seek to divide liability and damages. For example, the plan files a motion on whether an employer should be responsible for the contributions of certain subcontractors. The parties agree the subcontractor is liable for the contributions. If the case is not settled, both parties go to trial but the case is limited to the amount owed.

A summary judgment motion must be in writing. The parties submit statements of material facts and legal briefs supporting their positions. The judge issues a written decision. If the summary judgment covers liability and damages, the award of a summary judgment may end the case at the trial court level.

The advantages of a motion for summary judgment are:

- If successful, the case may be resolved more quickly than would be possible with a trial before the judge.
- The motion forces the opposing attorneys to reveal their best legal arguments and evidence.
- A partial motion for summary judgment may narrow the issues for trial.
- A motion for summary judgment (or the threat of one) may force the employer into settlement.
- The documents used in the summary judgment motion (e.g., the statement of facts) may be used during the trial documents.

There are also disadvantages:

- The motion may actually delay the trial and the resolution of the case.
- Depending on the judge's schedule, it may be more efficient to simply try the case than prepare the motion for summary judgment.
- The motion may be expensive to draft and compile;
- The motion may alert the employer to any weaknesses in the case.
- A denial of the motion for summary judgment may embolden the employer to try the case rather than settle.

Trial

Anyone who has watched any courtroom TV shows is familiar with trial procedures. Trials of employer contribution collection cases are held before a federal judge, not a jury, and are called *bench trials.* In court, the plan must establish the following elements to win a case:

- The plan is a multiemployer fringe benefit plan under ERISA.
- The employer is bound to a collective bargaining agreement (or other contract).
- Through the contract, the employer is bound to make fringe benefit contributions to the plan.
- The employer failed to make all of the required contributions.

To establish the elements, the following witnesses typically speak on behalf of a plan:

- Plan representative
- Union representative (if contract is disputed)
- Employees who worked for the defendant employer (if the performance of bargaining unit work is disputed)
- Auditor
- Employer owners, officers and management (called as adverse witnesses).

Remedies

ERISA requires the following types of damages to be awarded to multiemployer plans:

- Unpaid contributions
- Interest on the unpaid contributions
- An amount equal to the greater of (1) interest on the unpaid contributions or (2) liquidated damages provided for under the plan in an amount not in excess of 20%
- Reasonable attorney fees and costs as determined by the court
- Such other legal and equitable relief as the court deems appropriate.

If the Plan Wins, How Does It Get the Money?

Although obtaining a court judgment is a worthwhile endeavor, a plan is only truly successful if the employer actually pays money owed. Making payment is called *satisfying the judgment.* Plans have various options and procedures to collect money after obtaining a judgment from a federal court. These options are the enforcement procedures of the state in which the federal court is located. Say a plan wins its case in the U.S. District Court for the Northern District of Illinois (in Chicago), the plan can use the laws of the state of Illinois to collect the judgment. How a judgment is collected depends on the state in which the federal court is located. The most common options are introduced below. The plan's legal counsel can provide more information as to their appropriateness and how to proceed.

Court Orders for Examinations

In most states, a plan is able to get a court order forcing the delinquent employer to answer questions about the employer's assets. The employer may be required to answer these questions under oath with a court reporter present. An employer that refuses to participate may be held in contempt of court.

If a plan is able to get information on the assets a specific bank is holding for the employer, it is possible to "freeze" these assets so they cannot be withdrawn. In fact, under many state laws, the bank can freeze assets in an amount greater than the judgment. In Illinois, a bank may freeze an amount equal to double the amount of the judgment. A court order is then requested directing the bank to pay the frozen money to the trust fund on behalf of the employer.

A court may also order others that owe money to the employer to pay the money owed to the plan to satisfy judgment. In the construction industry, this group includes owners, developers, general contractors and other subcontractors. These parties are forbidden from paying money to the employer without a court order.

Bankruptcy

In the usual case involving bankruptcy, an employer halts collection efforts by filing for bankruptcy protection under Chapter 7 (the employer ceases doing business) or Chapter 11 (the employer stays in business under a plan of reorganization). If this occurs, a plan should file a proof of claim and determine which amounts it is owed, if any, may be entitled to priority payment status in the bankruptcy.

The Bankruptcy Code also provides a mechanism that is of special value to plans in collecting on the judgment. Three creditors with claims against an employer may be able to force an employer into involuntary bankruptcy under either Chapter 7 or 11. A single creditor cannot do this, but benefit plan trust funds generally consist of three or more independent funds that the court will consider three or more separate creditors.

Bonds

A bond required by the collective bargaining agreement *(surety bond)* sometimes covers an employer's debts to a trust fund. A bond may also have been required for the employer to work under a governmental contract or by others such as owners or developers *(performance bond).* These surety and performance bonds may be another source of recovery for the trust funds.

Liens

Liens ranging from mechanic liens to judgment liens are one more avenue for collection. The rules governing liens vary from state to state and are extremely specific. Short time frames to file are common. A plan's legal counsel can explain what is available in specific geographical jurisdictions.

Conclusion

Making sure that all the monies for which collection is possible are in fact deposited in a benefit plan trust fund represents a key element of a trustee's responsibility. Working closely with legal counsel on these matters and requiring support from the plan administrator helps a plan's balance sheet and expands trustee understanding of the collection process.

Endnote

1. T. Ketterman. *Collecting Employer Contributions: The ERISA Litigation Guide.* International Foundation of Employee Benefit Plans. 2009.

Chapter 53

Measuring and Evaluating Plan Administration

William J. Einhorn

Few employee benefit subjects have created as much controversy as attempts to quantify and compare the costs of administrative services for multiemployer benefit programs. Just as important as the efficient administration of a plan is how well a plan is serving participants. Evaluating quality is just as challenging as quantitative assessments. Nevertheless, it is important for trustees to continually monitor the efficiencies of their plan office.

What Are the Challenges to Evaluating Administrative Costs?

There is so much variety from plan to plan that it is nearly impossible to compare administrative costs without a detailed investigation of each plan. Some of the factors that cause difficulties when comparing costs are the type of plan, who handles plan administration, whether administrative costs can be shared with other plans, the size and scope of a plan, geography, and the demographics used to analyze costs.

Plan Type

Health and welfare plan administrators must deal with the day-to-day eligibility of participants and their families as well as the payment of a large number of claims each year. The result is higher operating expenses than those experienced by a pension plan that accumulates dollars over a long period and pays claims only when a participant retires, dies or terminates.

Administrative Functions

Functions assumed by administrative offices vary tremendously from plan to plan. Some plans use third parties for many services. A welfare plan, for example, might be fully insured, with the insurance carrier providing participants with claim forms, receiving claim requests and paying claims. The only function of the benefit plan is notifying the insurer who is eligible for benefits. Obviously, this plan would have far lower expenses than a similar plan of exactly the same size that processed and paid its own claims. The latter plan would need a much larger staff and office space.

Some plans employ their own collection agents and payroll auditors, rather than using the services of outside attorneys and payroll service firms. While some plans handle their own data processing, others use consultants and external services. Some trustees ask their administrative office to handle virtually all phases of administration—all minutes, reports and studies are prepared by the administrative manager after consultation with outside professionals. This can result in lower costs than if outside professionals and consultants directly handled such functions.

Shared Administration

In industries such as construction, unions often negotiate with an employer association and/or group of employers for participation in multiple benefit plans; for example, health and welfare, pension, training, vacation and holiday, scholarship, legal services and even day care. Multiple plans created by the same collective bargaining agreement are often able to share administrative personnel and offices. Efficiencies are created that are not possible for a plan that must operate on its own. The jointly administered plans are likely to have expenses far lower than those of a solo plan.

Plan Size, Scope and Geography

Due to economies of scale, plans with a large number of

participants and employers may have far lower per capita costs than smaller plans. Some plans cover large geographical areas and have many offices while other plans are small with one office and limited staff. Variances also exist in the cost of services, rentals, personnel and operating expenses from one locale to another.

Demographics

When drilling down into a plan's per capita cost figures and ratios, there are also different perspectives as to who should be included in these statistics. Should only active, fully eligible employees be examined, or should employees for whom contributions are made but who are not eligible also be included? Should adjustments be made if there are different contribution rates and benefits for certain groups of employees?

For many older plans, the ratio of active to retired employees is decreasing. With little or no contributions being made to the plans for these retirees, the costs of administration are spread among a declining number of active employees. At the same time, these plans are experiencing higher per capita benefit costs because they are serving retirees and relatively older active participants. This problem is particularly acute for health plans.

What Approaches Are Used to Evaluate Administrative Costs?

The methods used to assess administrative costs along with their limitations are illustrated in a comparison of the annual operating income and expenses for two hypothetical health and welfare plans (Exhibits 1 and 2). For both plans, it is assumed:

2,500	Active, eligible participants
500	Retired, eligible participants
500	Average number of employees reported who do not meet eligibility rules, including 100 that are subject to reciprocity transfers

Employer contribution rates—

Two-thirds of hours at $2.00

One-third of hours at $1.50

Exhibit 1 reflects the annual income and expenses for Plan A. This plan obtains insurance coverage through an insurance company with the insurer handling all phases of benefit processing from the issuance of benefit booklets to claims investigation and payment. The $6 million premium paid to the insurance carrier represents the plan's total benefit costs. The premium represents 83.9% of employer and employee contributions. Taking investment income into consideration, this premium represents approximately 75.9% of total income.

Excluding plan professional and trustee expenses, administrative costs for Plan A are $600,000, representing 8.4% of employer and employee contributions and 7.6% of total income. The cost for plan professionals, trustee liability insurance and trustee meetings/educational expenses is approximately $80,000, adding another 1.1% of contributions or 1% of total income to Plan A's total expenses. Total administrative expenses were 9.5% of employer contributions or 8.6% of total income. This is a highly efficient operation.

The Percentile Method

When compared to a self-insured plan, it is reasonable to expect insured Plan A to operate much more efficiently; Plan A does not have the substantial administration expenses of a self-insured plan. The administrative expenses for participant booklets and claims processing are part of the premium that Plan A pays its insurer.

Using a percentage of costs is the most likely way to distort the overall expenses of a plan. A percentage of employer contributions is not meaningful unless the same relative amount of employer contributions were constant in all plans being compared. Collective bargaining determines the amount of employer contribution for a plan, not any action taken by the trustees directly. For example, in Exhibit 1, employer contributions for Plan A were $7,150,000; if employer contributions had been doubled as a result of collective bargaining, would this really mean administrative costs decreased by 50%? Clearly, they did not. Thus, the percentile method is hardly a measure of the efficiency of a plan.

Per Capita Measures

A more accurate measure is per capita costs. In Exhibit 1, per capita costs for Plan A are calculated using three different participant counts:

1. Eligible employees for whom contributions are made (2,500)
2. Average number of active and retired employees who are eligible for benefits (3,000)
3. Average number of active and retired eligible employees and the average number of reported employees who never become eligible because they do not meet the eligibility standards or are subject to reciprocity transfer (3,500).

Exhibit 1

Plan A (Benefits Are Fully Insured; Insurance Carrier Processes Claims)

			Percentage of Contribution Income	Percentage of Total Income	Per Capita (Annual) Active (2,500)	Per Capita (Annual) Act./Retired (3,000)	Per Capita (Annual) All (3,500)
Income							
Employer and employee contributions (3,900,000 hours)							
2/3 (2,600,000 × $2)	$5,200,000						
1/3 (1,300,000 × $1.50)	$1,950,000						
Total Contribution Income		$7,150,000	100.0%	90.4%	$2,860	$2,383	$2,043
Investment income							
($10 million portfolio @ 8%)	$ 800,000						
Less investment advisor and custodian expense	$ 60,000						
	$ 740,000						
Unrealized investment income	$ 20,000	$ 760,000		9.6%	$ 304	$ 253	$ 217
Total Income		$7,910,000		100.0%	$3,164	$2,637	$2,260
Benefit payments							
Insurance premiums for benefits	$6,000,000						
Self-insured benefits	$ 0						
Stop-loss insurance premiums	$ 0						
Total Benefit Cost		$6,000,000	83.9%	75.9%	$2,400	$2,000	$1,714
Administrative costs							
Direct costs (personnel, fringes, office, data processing, etc.)	$600,000						
Claims processing expenses	$ 0						
Cost-containment expenses	$ 0						
Total Direct Administrative Costs		$ 600,000	8.4%	7.6%	$ 240	$ 200	$ 171
Plan professionals	$ 60,000						
Trustees' liability insurance	$ 10,000						
Trustees' meeting and educational expenses	$ 10,000						
Total Other Expenses		$ 80,000	1.1%	1.0%	$ 32	$ 27	$ 23
Total Expenses		$ 680,000	9.5%	8.6%	$ 272	$ 227	$ 194
Total Benefits and Administrative Expenses		$6,680,000	93.4%	84.5%	$2,672	$2,227	$1,909
Surplus (Deficit)		$1,230,000		15.5%			

Exhibit 2

Plan B (Self-Insured Plan Processing Claims Directly)

			Percentage of Contribution Income	Percentage of Total Income	Per Capita (Annual) Active (2,500)	Per Capita (Annual) Act./Retired (3,000)	Per Capita (Annual) All (3,500)
Income							
Employer and employee contributions (3,900,000 hours)							
2/3 (2,600,000 × $2)	$5,200,000						
1/3 (1,300,000 × $1.50)	$1,950,000						
Total Contribution Income		$7,150,000	100.0%	90.4%	$2,860	$2,383	$2,043
Investment income							
($10 million portfolio @ 8%)	$ 800,000						
Less investment advisor and custodian expense	$ 60,000						
	$ 740,000						
Unrealized investment income	$ 20,000	$ 760,000		9.6%	$ 304	$ 253	$ 217
Total Income		$7,910,000		100.0%	$3,164	$2,637	$2,260
Benefit payments							
Insurance premiums for benefits	$ 0						
Self-insured benefits	$5,400,000						
Stop-loss insurance premiums	$ 100,000						
Total Benefit Cost		$5,500,000	76.9%	69.5%	$2,200	$1,833	$1,571
Administrative costs							
Direct costs (personnel, fringes, office, data processing, etc.)	$650,000						
Claims processing expense	$150,000						
Cost-containment expenses	$ 80,000						
Total direct administrative costs		$880,000	12.3%	11.1%	$ 352	$ 293	$ 251
Plan professionals	$ 80,000						
Trustees' liability insurance	$ 20,000						
Trustees' meeting and educational expenses	$ 10,000						
Total Other Expenses		$ 110,000	1.5%	1.4%	$ 44	$ 37	$ 31
Total Expenses		$ 990,000	13.8%	12.5%	$ 396	$ 330	$ 283
Total Benefits and Administrative Expenses		$6,490,000	90.8%	82.0%	$2,596	$2,163	$1,854
Surplus (Deficit)		$1,420,000		18.0%			

What is the proper per capita amount to use? All three are used regularly in determining per capita costs.

Spreading all expenses among active eligible employees is the most consistent way to compare costs, but what if retired employees are provided with benefits and make self-payments? Shouldn't some part of costs be allocated to the retirees as in the second method? The third method includes all employees for whom contributions are received, even those who never become insured. Is it fair to spread administrative costs among this last group of employees who will never receive benefits?

A more objective method for calculating per capita cost is to place a value on every plan function, then apply these actual costs to each category of employees. While theoretically sound, it hardly seems practical to do this in a way that is consistent across the nation. The bottom line: There is an ongoing problem of how to measure per capita costs and make comparisons among plans.

Exhibit 2 presents a second plan that is exactly the same as Plan A with one exception—Plan B is self-insured and self-administered. Plan B provides all benefits directly to plan participants and purchases stop-loss coverage for catastrophic claims. Looking at the operating costs of Plan B compared to Plan A, Plan B's total expenses appear higher; $990,000 compared to $680,000 for Plan A because Plan B has:

- Direct administrative costs that are $50,000 more than those of Plan A. The difference represents the additional cost of printing, supplies, claim checks, recordkeeping, telephone calls and correspondence relating to Plan B's claims processing.
- A claims-processing cost of $150,000, which represents the labor and other costs of direct processing of claims such as data processing, recordkeeping, correspondence and postage
- A cost-containment expenditure of $80,000 for second surgical opinion arrangements, utilization review, predetermination of claims, use of medical and dental consultants, audit of health provider bills and other cost-management efforts
- A $20,000 difference in legal, accounting and consulting fees required for self-insurance
- A doubling in the cost of trustee liability and bonding insurance from $10,000 to $20,000 because of the higher hazards faced by a plan processing its own claims and hiring more employees.

The overall difference for self-insured Plan B is $310,000 in administrative costs.

The per capita costs are also considerably higher for Plan B than for Plan A:

1. Based on the average number of active, insured, eligible employees, the per capita cost for Plan A is $272 and $396 for Plan B.
2. Based upon active and retired employees, the per capita cost is $227 for Plan A compared to $330 for Plan B.
3. Based upon employees reported to the plan, active and retired and those not eligible, the per capita cost is $194 for Plan A compared to $283 for Plan B.

These are substantial differences in costs, but is Plan A more efficient than Plan B? Exhibit 3 provides some insight in answering this question.

Plan B's benefit payments totaled $5,500,000 ($5,400,000 in claim payments plus the $100,000 premium for stop-loss and specific excess insurance), about

Exhibit 3

Plan A Versus Plan B Per Capita Costs

	Plan A	Plan A Adjusted for Insurance Carrier Admin. Expenses	Plan B
Benefit costs	$6,000,000	$5,500,000	$5,500,000
Administrative costs	$ 680,000	$1,180,000	$ 990,000
Percentage of contribution income	9.5%	16.5%	13.8%
Percentage of total income	8.6%	14.9%	12.5%
Per capita cost for 2,500 actives	$ 272	$ 472	$ 396

$500,000 less than the $6,000,000 insurance premium Plan A paid its insurance carrier as its total benefit costs. But remember, the insurance company for Plan A functioned as an administrator providing participant materials and processing claims. The cost of these activities was part of the insurance premium paid by Plan A.

If Plan A and Plan B have the same participants filing the same claims, the $500,000 difference in benefit costs represents administrative expenses for Plan A. Shifting the $500,000 from benefit costs to administrative costs increases Plan A's administrative costs to $1,180,000 ($680,000 plus $500,000) and changes the landscape. While the self-insured Plan B's administrative increase of $310,000 was a substantial increase, it is more than offset by the $500,000 reduction in benefit costs as a result of the elimination of the insurance carrier's administrative expenses and retention. The net effect is an increased plan gain for the year of $190,000.

On a per capita basis, Plan B is also the more efficient plan. As a result of the switch from insurance to self-financing, benefit costs decreased from 84% to 77% and administrative costs increased from 9.5% to 13.8% of total contributions; yet the exact result was quite different. The plan improved its efficiency and effectiveness, even though its per capita costs went up.

A caveat is that this is a hypothetical situation; not every plan benefits as greatly from changing to self-insurance. The purpose of these illustrations is not necessarily to show the advantages of self-insurance compared to insured arrangements, but merely to show the challenges when comparing the operations of health and welfare plans.

What Can Small Plans Do to Address High Administrative Costs?

Plans with a relatively small number of participants are frequently faced with a large portion of income being used to cover administrative expenses. Regardless of whether a plan services 500 or 5,000 participants, it still needs office space, accounting services, legal counsel, an auditor, etc. These costs are spread over a small number of persons causing higher per capita operating costs than those of larger plans. Trustees of a small plan may decide that the higher costs are acceptable in meeting plan objectives but, nevertheless, there should be constant scrutiny to make sure every effort is made to keep administration as economical as possible. In some instances, smaller plans have merged with other plans so costs are spread over a larger number of participants. Other small plans have been able to survive by participating in an administrative arrangement involving multiple plans.

How Is the Quality of a Plan Assessed?

Quality of service is just as important as the cost-effectiveness of a plan—but it is also extremely difficult to measure. Perhaps the most effective method for evaluating the quality of internal operations is a peer review from time to time by a team comprised of the plan administrator, benefit consultant and certified public accountant (and possibly, an attorney). For larger plans with sufficient resources to do so and under special circumstances for other plans, it may be beneficial to engage an objective external consultant. A person or firm with extensive knowledge and experience concerning employee benefit administration would be a good choice for such an evaluation.

Claim payment procedures should be carefully scrutinized each year by an independent certified public accountant and the benefit consultant to make sure claims are being paid expeditiously after careful review. The procedures should balance the need of participants to receive benefits promptly with safeguarding the financial interests of the plan.

Periodic evaluations of contract and/or salaried administrators should also be conducted by a committee of trustees or the entire board. These evaluations must take into consideration the ever-changing nature and structure of employee benefit plans, and the need for administrators and staff to adjust to these changes.

Trustees are expected to establish the highest possible standards of service for their plan. Likewise, administrators should strive for excellence in the services they provide. Trustees should make certain they reaffirm this mission to administrators and plan personnel on a regular basis, taking every possible step to ascertain standards are being met. Participants, beneficiaries, employers and unions have a right to expect the highest level of service.

Conclusion

Over the years, attempts to establish quantitative measurements that allow comparisons of benefit plans have been unsuccessful. It is still incumbent upon plan trustees and administrators to make certain a plan is operating on the most efficient and cost-effective basis in the best interest of participants. The best way to evaluate a plan is to review plan procedures, costs and the quality of service. Periodic review by the board of trustees or a committee of trustees with the assistance of various professionals is essential. Exhibit 4 offers a starting place when identifying assessment criteria. Though it may be difficult to compare one plan to another, it is not difficult to determine whether a plan is fulfilling its mission in an efficient and cost-effective manner.

Plan Administration Checklist

Recordkeeping

- Plan-governing documents (trust agreement, plan of benefits, SPDs, collective bargaining agreements, etc.) maintained and readily available
- Service provider agreements in writing, maintained and available
- Financial records in good order
- Accounting controls in place
  - Adequate and appropriate internal controls in place to reduce risk of fraud in collections, eligibility determinations, benefit approvals and payments?
  - Adequate and appropriate accounting for and tracking of investments?
- Trustee policies and directives followed
  - Delinquency/collection policy
  - Record retention policy
  - Travel reimbursement/ educational policy
  - Investment policy statement

Claim Processing and Records

- Timely
- Accurate
- Appeals handled in accordance with mandated procedures
- Claims experience available for ongoing analysis
  - Data processing/database sufficient for plan needs
  - Individuals' records adequately maintained
  - Compliant with HIPAA/HITECH privacy and security regulations
- Cost controls in place to prevent unnecessary benefit expenditures
  - Utilization review
  - Large-case management
  - Disease management
  - Coordination of benefits
  - Subrogation
  - Antifraud procedures and controls

Trustees Meetings

- Materials to be covered at the meeting sent out in advance, when possible
- Meetings effectively organized
- Reliable, timely and comprehensive reports provided by plan administration

Coordination With Plan Professionals

- Administrator understands and can relate content of reports of plan professionals.
- Flow of information between administrative office and plan professionals is smooth and efficient.
- Plan professionals get the information they need to perform the services for which they were engaged.

Communication With Plan Participants

- SPDs up to date
- Notices/announcements/program materials disseminated and available
- Helpful, effective, accurate and courteous service rendered by plan office
- Benefit statements/information provided to participants readily understandable

Communication With Union/Employers

- Plan rules clearly explained
- Helpful, effective, accurate and courteous service rendered by plan office
- Appropriate assistance given by plan office in area of collective bargaining
- Notice(s) of delinquencies given by plan office to all appropriate parties

Governmental Reporting and Compliance

- Annual tax returns accurate and timely filed
- Summary annual reports (SARs) published when required
- Required notices published (e.g., WHCRA annual notice)
- Compliance with COBRA, FMLA, HIPAA, USERRA, etc.
- Appeals handled within time frames dictated by federal regulations

Plan Office

- Appropriate location to service parties in interest, especially participants
- Properly equipped to fulfill scope of needed operations

Staffing

- Smooth and efficient workflow
- Personnel practices and policies clearly defined and followed
- Economical and efficient
- HIPAA/HITECH trained

Security

- Compliance with HIPAA/HITECH security
- Insurance and bonding in place
- Internal control of assets, records and other property sufficient

Administrative Costs

- Costs periodically reviewed
- Reasonable, given established norms

Chapter 54

Reporting and Disclosure Under ERISA*

Lonie A. Hassel

The Employee Retirement Income Security Act of 1974 (ERISA) requires plan administrators to provide certain types of information to plan participants and others. Some disclosure requirements are clearly spelled out in ERISA, such as the duty to provide summary plan descriptions. Other requirements are more general. In addition, the courts have found that ERISA's fiduciary duty of sole interest requires certain disclosures that are not expressly stated in ERISA.

Compliance with disclosure requirements ensures that plan participants and beneficiaries have the information they need to obtain the benefits they are entitled to receive. Failure to comply with these requirements not only can shortchange participants, but it also can put plan fiduciaries at risk for breach of fiduciary duty and monetary penalties.

This chapter serves as a guide to identifying information that must be provided and determining whether disclosure should be made even if not expressly required by ERISA. In addition, the chapter discusses the risks of miscommunication and inadvertent vesting of retiree welfare benefits.

What Disclosures Are Required for Multiemployer Pension and Welfare Benefit Plans?

Summary Plan Description

A *summary plan description (SPD)* is a written statement in plain language that describes the provisions and features of a benefit plan. It includes information concerning who is eligible for benefits, coverage, employee rights and appeal procedures. Department of Labor (DOL) regulations prescribe the specific information that must be included in the SPD.[1]

The SPD and all changes to the SPD must be provided within 90 days after a participant becomes covered by a plan or a beneficiary begins receiving benefits.[2] If no changes have been made to a plan, each plan participant must be provided a copy of the SPD every ten years. If changes have been made, a copy must be provided to each participant every five years.[3]

Summary of Material Modifications

Changes to the SPD must be described in a *summary of material modifications (SMM).* Plan administrators must distribute an SMM to each plan participant and to each beneficiary receiving benefits within 210 days after the end of a plan year in which any material modification is adopted. Like the SPD, the SMM must be written in plain language.[4]

Summary Annual Report

A *summary annual report (SAR)* contains financial statements and other information necessary to fairly summarize the most recent plan year activities. For plans other than defined benefit pension plans, the plan administrator must distribute a summary annual report to each participant within nine months after the end of a plan year. Beneficiaries receiving benefits under a plan other than a defined benefit pension or welfare plan, must also receive this report within nine months.[5]

---

* This chapter does not address disclosures required under the Internal Revenue Code, Health Insurance Portability and Accountability Act security provisions, or Patient Protection and Affordable Care Act provisions effective after 2010.

Are There Any Other Disclosures Required of Pension Plans?

Benefit Statement

Plan administrators must issue a benefit statement at least once each quarter to each participant in individual account plans (e.g., 401(k) plans) that permit participants to direct their investments. If the individual account plan does not permit participants to direct their investments, the notice is required at least once each year.

Plan administrators of defined benefit plans are required to provide a pension benefit statement at least once every three years to each participant with a nonforfeitable accrued benefit. Alternatively, a plan administrator may fulfill this requirement by notifying participants once a year that a benefit statement is available. This notice must include instructions on how the participant or beneficiary can obtain a copy of the benefit statement. The notice may be written, electronic or in any other form that is reasonably accessible to plan participants.[6]

A benefit statement must be written so the average plan participant can understand it. The benefit statement must be based on the latest available information and include:

- The total amount of benefits accrued by participant
- Any nonforfeitable pension benefits that have accrued, or the earliest date on which benefits will become nonforfeitable. To meet this requirement, a plan administrator must, at least annually, either (1) update the information provided in the pension benefit statement or (2) provide a separate statement with the information a plan participant or beneficiary needs to determine his or her nonforfeitable vested benefits
- An explanation of any exception to the general contribution or accrued benefit requirements permitted under Section 401(l) of the Internal Revenue Code (where applicable) and an explanation of any other benefit plan that affects the accrued benefit under this plan.

A court may assess personal liability on individual fiduciaries of up to $110 per day for each day a plan fails to provide benefit statements as required.[7]

Annual Funding Notice

ERISA also requires that plan administrators of defined benefit pension plans provide an annual funding notice to:

- Pension Benefit Guaranty Corporation (PBGC)
- Each plan participant and beneficiary
- Each labor organization representing the participants and beneficiaries
- Each employer with an obligation to contribute to the plan.

The funding notice must be issued within 120 days after the end of the plan year and contain the following information:

- Plan name
- Address and phone number of the plan administrator
- Plan's principal administrative officer
- Plan sponsor's employee identification number (EIN)
- Plan number
- Statement as to whether the plan's funded percentage for the plan year and for the preceding two plan years is at least 100%. If the funded percentage is less than 100%, the actual percentage must be given.
- Value of the plan's assets and liabilities for the plan year as of the last day of the plan year, and for the preceding two plan years
- Number of participants who are—
  - Retired or separated from service and are receiving benefits
  - Retired or separated and entitled to future benefits
  - Active participants under the plan.
- Funding policy of the plan
- Asset allocation of investments under the plan as of the end of the plan year—expressed as percentages of total assets
- Whether the plan was in critical or endangered status (as defined by ERISA Section 305) and, if so, a description of how a person may obtain—
  - A copy of the plan's funding improvement or rehabilitation plan adopted under ERISA Section 305
  - The actuarial and financial data that demonstrate any action taken by the plan toward fiscal improvement.
- A summary of any funding improvement, rehabilitation plan or modification adopted under Section 305 during the plan year
- An explanation of any plan amendment, scheduled benefit increase or reduction, or other event taking effect in the plan year that will have a material effect on plan liabilities or assets for the year, and a projection to the end of the plan year of the effect on plan liabilities
- A summary of the rules governing plan reorganization or insolvency, including the limitations on benefit payments
- A general description of the benefits under the plan which are eligible to be guaranteed by PBGC along with an explanation of the limitations on the guarantee and the circumstances under which the limitations apply

- A statement that a person may request a copy of the plan's annual report through the DOL website, or an intranet website maintained by the plan sponsor, or by the plan administrator on behalf of the plan sponsor
- A statement that the plan administrator will, upon request, provide to any labor organization representing plan participants and beneficiaries and any employer that has an obligation to contribute to the plan, a copy of the annual report and any additional information which the plan administrator elects to include (to the extent consistent with regulations).[8]

The Department of Labor (DOL) has provided a model notice for this purpose, which is available at www.dol.gov/ebsa/regs/fab2009-1.html.

A court may assess a fine against the plan administrator of up to $110 per day for each day a plan fails to provide annual funding notices as required.[9]

Endangered or Critical Status Notice

ERISA and the Internal Revenue Code (IRC) have established "endangered" and "critical" status for multiemployer defined benefit pension plans based on the plan's funded level and whether they have or are expected to have a funding deficiency. Sponsors of plans certified to be in endangered or critical status must notify participants, beneficiaries, the bargaining parties, PBGC and DOL within 30 days after certification. See Chapters 27 and 28 for an explanation of plan funding status.

Notice of Significant Reduction in Future Benefit Accruals

Plan administrators must provide written notice to participants, alternate payees and unions representing participants before the effective date of a plan amendment that significantly reduces future benefit accruals.[10] Generally, the notice must be provided 15 days in advance. In the event of an egregious failure to comply with the notice requirement, participants may receive the greater of the benefits they would have been entitled to receive with and without the amendment.

Contribution Information

ERISA requires administrators of defined benefit pension plans to provide a contributions report to each union and each employer obligated to make plan contributions.[11] This report is due within 30 days after the due date of the plan's Form 5500 and must contain:

- A description of the contribution schedules and benefit formulas under the plan as well as any modifications to the schedules and formulas made during the plan year
- The number of employers obligated to contribute to the plan
- A list of employers that contributed more than 5% of the total contributions to the plan during the plan year
- The number of plan participants for whom no contributions were made by an employer for the plan year and for each of the two preceding plan years
- Whether the plan was in critical or endangered status (as defined by ERISA Section 305) for the plan year
- If the plan was in critical or endangered status, the report must include—
  - A list of actions taken by the plan to improve its funding status
  - A statement describing how someone may obtain (1) a copy of the plan's funding improvement or rehabilitation plan, and (2) the actuarial and financial data that demonstrate any action taken by the plan toward fiscal improvement.
- The number of employers that withdrew from the plan during the preceding plan year and the aggregate amount of withdrawal liability assessed, or estimated to be assessed, against the withdrawn employers, as reported on the annual report for the plan year
- If the multiemployer plan merged with another plan or assets and liabilities have been transferred to another plan, the actuarial valuation of the assets and liabilities of each affected plan during the year preceding the effective date of the merger or transfer
- A statement whether the plan sought or received an amortization extension or used the shortfall funding method for the plan year
- A notification that the union and contributing employers have a right to a copy of the Form 5500, SPD, and SMM, upon written request—limited to one copy of each within any 12-month period and subject to reasonable charges for furnishing the documents.

What Disclosures Must Be Made Upon Request?

Plan Documents

Upon written request of a participant or beneficiary, ERISA requires plan administrators to furnish a copy of:

- The latest updated plan description and SPD
- The latest Form 5500
- The annual report
- Any terminal report
- The bargaining agreement

- The trust agreement
- Contracts and any other instruments under which the plan is established or operated.[12]

The plan administrator may charge a reasonable copying fee, which may not exceed $0.25 per page, for the requested documents.

Determining documents that must be provided. While the requirement to furnish certain documents is plainly stated, the extent to which "other instruments under which the plan is established or operated" is not as clear. At the extreme, this could include virtually every plan document. Fortunately for our forests, courts have interpreted this requirement narrowly. It is still difficult, however, to discern a consistent disclosure standard from court opinions. For example, some courts have found that this provision requires a plan administrator to supply a copy of the plan's actuarial report, procedure for calculating benefits, and plan funding and investment policies. Others have found that this provision does not require disclosure of the actuarial report, IRS determination letter, bonding policy, physician compensation agreements, participant lists and certain trustee meeting minutes. Given the lack of consistent guidance from the courts, it may be necessary to consult with legal counsel when a participant or beneficiary submits a written request for a document that is not expressly required to be provided under Section 104(b)(4) of ERISA.

Consequences of failure to timely provide requested documents. A court has the discretion to assess personal liability against a plan administrator who fails to provide requested documents within 30 days after receiving a written request from a plan participant or beneficiary. The fine is up to $110 per day for each day following the date of the failure.[13] In deciding whether and how much liability to assess, the court considers factors such as the plan administrator's bad faith or intentional conduct, the length of the delay, the number of requests made, the documents withheld, and any prejudice to the participant or beneficiary.

Pension Benefit Statement

In addition to providing pension benefit statements to active employees (described above), plan administrators must provide a pension benefit statement once within any 12-month period in response to a written request from:

- A participant or beneficiary in a defined benefit plan
- A beneficiary for an individual account (for example, a 401(k) plan) who does not receive benefit statements automatically.

Defined Benefit Plan Information

Section 101(k) of ERISA requires administrators of multiemployer defined benefit pension plans to provide certain documents in response to a written request from:

- A plan participant
- A plan beneficiary receiving benefits under the plan
- Any labor organization representing participants under the plan
- Any employer that is a party to a collective bargaining agreement pursuant to which the plan is maintained
- Any employer that may be subject to withdrawal liability.

The documents that may be requested under Section 101(k) are:

- Any periodic actuarial report (including any sensitivity testing)
- Any quarterly, semiannual or annual financial report that was prepared for the plan by—
  - An investment manager (without regard to whether the investment advisor is a fiduciary)
  - An advisor
  - Any other fiduciary.
- A copy of any application filed with the Secretary of the Treasury requesting an amortization extension.

These documents must be provided within 30 days after the plan receives the request. Documents may be provided in writing, electronically or in any form that is reasonably accessible to the person making the request. Requesting parties are entitled to one copy of each document within a 12-month period.

The same ERISA section recognizes that some information should not be disclosed:

- Any information that the plan administrator reasonably determines to be individually identifiable information regarding any—
  - Participant
  - Beneficiary
  - Employee
  - Fiduciary
  - Contributing employer.
- Any information that the plan administrator reasonably determines to be proprietary information regarding—
  - The plan
  - Any contributing employer
  - A plan service provider.

The plan administrator must tell the requesting party if any information is withheld from the disclosed material because the information is individually identifiable or proprietary.

The Secretary of Labor may assess a penalty of up to $1,100 per day for failure to comply with the requirement to provide the requested documents.[14]

Withdrawal Liability Estimate

Upon receipt of a written request, administrators of a multiemployer defined benefit pension plan must give a contributing employer an estimated withdrawal liability and an explanation of how the estimate was determined. The estimate and explanation must be provided within 180 days after the plan receives the request. If the plan uses the "direct attribution method" (which is rare) or an "alternative method" for determining withdrawal liability, regulations may give the plan a longer time to respond. The form and manner in which the information must be provided is specified in regulations issued by the Secretary of Labor. The Secretary of Labor may assess a penalty of up to $1,100 per day for failure to comply with the requirement to provide a withdrawal liability estimate.[15]

What Kinds of Miscommunication Can Happen and How Can Miscommunication Be Avoided?

Material Misrepresentations

The Supreme Court has found that it is a breach of duty for plan fiduciaries to knowingly and significantly mislead plan participants.[16] Other courts similarly have found fiduciary disclosure duties beyond the express disclosure requirements in ERISA. Fiduciaries must answer questions forthrightly, and may be found liable for *material misrepresentations.* A misrepresentation is material if there is a substantial likelihood that the communication would mislead a reasonable employee in making an adequately informed decision. For example, a fiduciary's repeated statements that retiree benefits would continue—even though the plan sponsor had reserved the right to terminate retiree benefits—has been found to be a breach of fiduciary duty.

Information Not Requested

A fiduciary may also have a duty to provide a participant with information that was not requested if the fiduciary knows the participant does not have the information he or she needs. Consider a participant with a terminal illness who asks a general question about his or her benefits. In that case, assume also that the plan administrator knows a particular benefit option could maximize the benefit amounts payable to the participant and participant beneficiaries under the plan. The administrator has a fiduciary duty to provide information on this option even though it was not requested.

Tip for Trustees

Union representatives and employer sponsors are sometimes a source of benefit plan information for multiemployer plan participants. Often, plan participants do not distinguish between a union and the plan. To avoid misunderstandings and to help ensure that participants receive accurate information, participants should be told to submit questions about plan benefits to plan representatives, *not* union representatives.

Mistakes

Often, day-to-day communications with participants and beneficiaries regarding benefits are performed by plan employees or contractors hired to provide this service. Whether these individuals are fiduciaries depends on their discretionary authority in the administration of the plan. Plan employees whose responsibility is to answer telephone questions concerning the plan are generally not fiduciaries—in general, their communications with participants and beneficiaries should not give rise to a fiduciary breach. Nonetheless, it is important that plan employees receive regular information and training concerning plan rules and policies so that they will provide accurate information.

What happens if a fiduciary makes a mistake? Fiduciaries can and do make mistakes. As long as the mistakes are honest and not made willfully or in bad faith—generally, they should not constitute a fiduciary breach.[17]

Promises of Benefits for Life

Unlike pension benefits, ERISA does require that retiree health benefits and other welfare benefits be vested. In light of this distinction, the United States Supreme Court has concluded that welfare plans may be modified or terminated at any time.[18] On the other hand, ERISA does not prohibit vesting of welfare benefits. Welfare benefits can become vested if there has been a promise that the benefits will not be changed or reduced. To determine whether these benefits are vested, courts look at statements made in prior collective bargaining agreements, plan documents, SPDs and other related documents.[19]

There are no special words that turn welfare benefits into vested benefits. The courts look for language in the plan document, SPD, or collective bargaining agreement that indicates an intent to provide benefits throughout retirement. A written statement that benefits "will be continued for the rest of your life" has been found to promise benefits for the lives of participants.[20] So too has contract language saying a plan "will provide insurance benefits [to retirees] equal to the active group."[21] In another contract, a statement that retired employees "after completion of twenty years of full-time permanent service and at least age 55 will be insured" was similarly determined by a court to be promise of benefits for life.[22]

In many legal cases concerning promises about benefits for life, the courts focus on the presence or absence of language in the plan documents that specifically reserves an employer's power to amend, modify or terminate plan benefits. Such *reservation-of-rights clauses* are often treated as evidence that the employer neither intended nor communicated any intention to vest retiree benefits.[23] The presence of a reservation-of-rights clause, however, does not automatically mean benefits are not vested. In one court decision, the judge stated that the facts of each case must be considered and the determination of benefits must be based on the language of the particular plan.[24]

To avoid inadvertently vesting costly welfare benefits, review the SPD, plan document and notices provided to participants. Plan representatives should search for any promises of lifetime benefits or unqualified promises to continue benefits.

Endnotes

1. DOL Regs. 29 C.F.R. §2520.102-3.
2. ERISA §104(b).
3. ERISA §104(b).
4. ERISA §104(b).
5. DOL Regs. 29 C.F.R. §2520.104b-10.
6. ERISA §105(a).
7. ERISA §502(c)(1)(A).
8. ERISA §101(f) .
9. ERISA §502(c)(1)(A).
10. ERISA §204(h).
11. ERISA §104(d).
12. ERISA §104(b)(4).
13. ERISA §502(c)(1).
14. ERISA §502(c)(4).
15. ERISA §502(c)(4).
16. *Varity Corporation v. Howe*, 516 U.S. 489, 506 (1996).
17. E.g., *Frahm v. Equitable Life Assurance Society of the United States*, 137 F.3d 955, 960 (7th Cir. 1998), *cert. denied*, 525 U.S. 817 (1998); *Burke v. Latrobe Steel Co.*, 775 F.2d 88, 91 (3d Cir. 1985).
18. E.g., *Curtiss-Wright Corp. v. Schoonejongen*, 514 U.S. 73, 78 (1995).
19. E.g., *U.A.W. v. Skinner Engine Co.*, 188 F.3d 130, 139 (3d Cir. 1999) (retiree welfare benefits may vest "under a collective bargaining agreement, SPD, or other plan document"); *United Food & Commercial Workers Int'l Union Local 150-A v. Dubuque Packing Co.*, 756 F.2d 66, 70 (8th Cir. 1985) (despite plant closing and termination of collective bargaining agreement, retiree health and welfare benefits had vested because there were "many indications in the agreements and course of dealing that the parties intended the right to benefits would vest upon retirement"); *United Steelworkers of America v. Connors Steel Co.*, 855 F.2d 1499, 1505 (11th Cir. 1988) (employer obligated to provide retiree benefits under an expired collective bargaining agreement); *Jensen v. SIPCO, Inc.*, 38 F.3d 945, 949-52 (8th Cir. 1994) (retiree health benefits are vested under the terms of SPDs).
20. *Helwig v. Kelsey-Hayes Co.*, 93 F.3d 243, 248 (6th Cir. 1996).
21. *International Union, UAW v. Yard-Man, Inc.*, 716 F.2d 1476, 1480 (6th Cir. 1983).
22. *Devlin v. Empire Blue Cross & Blue Shield*, 274 F.3d 76, 79 (2d Cir. 2001), *cert. denied*, 123 S.Ct. 1015 (2003).
23. E.g., *In re Unisys Corp. Retiree Med. Benefit Litig.*, 58 F.3d 896, 904 (3d Cir. 1996); *Sprague v. General Motors Corp.*, 133 F.3d 388, 400 (6th Cir. 1998) (en banc); *Chiles v. Certain Corp.*, 95 F.3d 1505, 1511-13 (10th Cir. 1996); *Alday v. Container Corp. of America*, 906 F.2d 660, 663 (11th Cir. 1990).
24. *In re Unisys Corp.*, 58 F.3d at 904 n.11.

Chapter 55

Communication Objectives and Principles

Claude L. Kordus

Plan trustees must make sure overall objectives are met, operations meet legal standards and finances are sound. Given these and their many other responsibilities, trustees often give another plan activity a low priority—communicating with plan participants, beneficiaries, contributing employers and the community.

The federal government requires extensive reporting and disclosure to participants, beneficiaries and government. Under the Employee Retirement Income Security Act of 1974 (ERISA), trustees are typically the ones responsible for compliance with these requirements. Plan communication is looked upon as complying with reporting and disclosure regulations. Compliance, however, does not equate to communication effectiveness. In addition, communication is an opportunity to improve participant satisfaction with a plan and a means to fulfill other goals of union and management.

Ronald J. Lind, president of a United Food and Commercial Workers local and a trustee of several pension and health plans, states that while "[e]very trust fund communicates with its participants.... [f]rom telephone contact to benefit summaries to newsletters.... [o]ften, the communication process has not been evaluated in years."[1]

The material in this chapter and the one that follows views plan communication from two vantage points. This first chapter provides an overview of communication principles. Its purpose is to help trustees think through communication objectives for their plan and how these objectives might be accomplished. The next chapter offers insight into specific techniques that yield successful communication. Also, it provides a basis for trustees to judge the effectiveness of communication efforts by administrators, benefits consultants and communication consultants. This material can help trustees improve their personal communication skills while serving as plan trustee as well as when on the job.

What Is Communication?

Usually communication is thought of in terms of publishing and distributing materials that describe a benefit plan. In reality, communication is much more.

Listening

This is the most neglected aspect of communication, whether on benefits or any other subject. Effectively conveying a message requires an understanding of the recipient. What do participants know? What do participants know that isn't true? What do participants want to know or need to know? How do participants want to receive information? Specifics on effective listening appear in the next chapter.

Describing

Telling participants what benefits the plan provides and explaining how the plan works is basic.

Reporting

The money handled by trustees belongs to plan participants; as a result, the importance of reporting stands high. There are two kinds of reports: (1) reports on the financial status of the plan, its size, its growth, its investments, its performance in providing benefits, etc. and (2) reports of the individual member's status in the plan, credits that have been built up for him or her, and what the participant is entitled to and when.

Why Should Trustees Be Concerned About Communication?

There are at least three compelling reasons why trustees should give serious attention to plan communication.

To Meet Legal Requirements

As stated previously, the federal government requires plans to provide certain types of information to plan participants and others. In summary, plan participants must be provided:[2]

- Summary plan description (SPD)
- Updated summary plan descriptions
- Description of material changes (SMM)
- Summaries of the latest annual reports (SAR)
- Statement of participant rights
- Claim denial information
- Notice of any forfeitable right
- Upon written request, bargaining agreements, trust agreements, contracts or other plan documents under which a plan is established or operated.

Materials that must be distributed to participants and beneficiaries must be:

- Sent by first-class mail, or
- Delivered by "methods likely to result in full distribution."

Making materials generally available—in the cafeteria, personnel office or an employee work area, for example—is typically not acceptable. Some information must be available for viewing or be provided upon request. Participants must be informed where they can examine or how they can request these copies.

Federal requirements with respect to reporting and disclosure are covered in detail in Chapter 54.

To Meet the Needs of Participants

The value of a plan to participants greatly depends on the peace of mind it provides them. Participants must know what benefits they have, under what circumstances they or their families can receive these benefits, how to apply for benefits, and whom to contact if they are experiencing any difficulties in receiving the benefits they have been promised.

To meet the needs of participants, plan communication must appeal to a variety of participant groups. Many groups may exist within one plan:

- Long-term participants
- New participants
- Retirees
- Spouses and domestic partners
- Children and other eligible dependents.

There may also be diversity in terms of:

- Age
- Gender
- Race, ethnicity and national origin
- Education
- Language.

Lind says: *"If 10% or more of your participants speak a language other than English, it's time to consider communicating in that language. While many of your participants may be bilingual, on the important and often-confusing issue of health or pension benefits they may be more comfortable with communications that are… [provided] in their native language."*[3]

To Meet the Needs of Trustees

Trustees themselves gain from improved communication. A plan that is adequately communicated—one in which participants have a good idea of what the plan will do and what it won't do—will operate more smoothly than one that is poorly communicated. There will be fewer disappointments, fewer complaints, fewer appeals and fewer opportunities for litigation.

What Communication Objectives Should a Plan Have?

The establishment of communication objectives for a benefit plan and a clear understanding of these objectives make the implementation of a communication program much easier for all involved—trustees, administrators and communication consultants. More importantly, clear objectives can lead to a more effective communication program that increases participant satisfaction concerning plan benefits.

Following are sample objectives for trustees to consider that can be modified to fit the specific needs of their plan:

- To meet the communication requirements set forth in federal disclosure laws, tax regulations and state insurance statutes
- To give participants sufficient information so they can, with relative ease, understand plan rights and benefits
- To promote benefits to participants as a desirable element of their employment
- To prevent unnecessary claims and overutilization of services
- To provide participants and their families a sense of security

- To inform participants how to claim benefits
- To involve spouses in information and decision processes
- To tell the plan's story.

The more specific trustees can be about what they want to accomplish with their communication program, the more effective the program is likely to be. Lind says "… it's important to be as specific as possible about… *quantifiable* goals. Receiving fewer calls about the new prescription drug copayments or driving more participants to generics are examples of quantifiable goals."[4]

What Techniques Are Available to Carry Out the Communication Function?

Listening

There are many techniques available for appraising the knowledge and attitudes of plan participants; these include:

- Interviews
- Focus groups
- Questionnaires—administered by mail, e-mail or in person
- Analysis of inquiries that come to the plan office
- Discussions and questions at union meetings
- Discussions and questions at benefit education events.

Describing and Reporting

Oral. Oral communication ranges from a phone conversation with individual participants regarding their specific benefits issues to a meeting with a roomful of participants providing information on what is included in their benefit package. This is a highly desirable technique, since the communicator can achieve immediate feedback on whether the message is being received and understood. The communicator can then adapt to the audience.

The use of visual or audiovisual aids such as these can enhance face-to-face communication:

- Flip charts
- PowerPoint slides
- Videotapes
- Webcasts.

Some large funds have used video to a very good effect. Group presentations may be supported by written materials.

Written. Plans have traditionally depended on print materials for communications; for example:

- Booklets and brochures
- Letters
- Bulletins and newsletters
- Reports
- Personal benefit statements.

The Internet now offers new ways to communicate via the written word with an ever-expanding list of options that includes tweets, blogs, chat rooms, e-mail and Web pages.

What Is Effective Communication?

It is not easy to communicate in terms that people can understand, that will hold their interest and that are also technically correct. But the results are worth the effort. Effective communication is also:

Understandable

Benefits communication is always a compromise. Attorneys often are most comfortable when text is that of a legal document. The public relations person may advocate a comic book description. It is between these two views that trustees have to take a stand.

The following two examples illustrate the difference between information that is understandable and material that is so technical it is difficult for participants to grasp. The text is from actual benefit statements telling participants that their major medical maximum is automatically reinstated.

Effective

> The maximum total benefit amount payable for each person covered by the plan is $500,000. If the person uses part of this amount, up to $100,000 will be automatically reinstated each year. If the covered person can prove good health (insurability), all of the maximum will be reinstated.

Ineffective

> Whenever benefits of $100,000 or more have become payable to an Insured Person under the Out-of-Hospital Major Medical Expense section, the full $500,000 Lifetime benefit may be reinstated by such person furnishing, at his own expense, evidence of insurability satisfactory to the insurance company.
>
> If such satisfactory evidence of insurability is furnished, the full lifetime benefit will be reinstated as of the date that the insurance company gives written approval of the evidence submitted. If benefits have become payable to an Insured Person under the Out-of-Hospital Major Medical Expense section and the full Lifetime benefit has not been

reinstated to such person at the end of any calendar year in accordance with the preceding paragraph, an automatic reinstatement of a portion of benefits shall be applicable. This automatic reinstatement, which will not require submission of evidence of insurability, will be equal to the lesser of $50,000 and the entire portion of the Lifetime benefit which has not previously been reinstated, and shall become effective as of the first day of the next following calendar year.

All insurance under the Out-of-Hospital Major Medical Expense section will terminate as to an Insured Person on the date the $500,000 Lifetime benefit is paid or becomes payable for all losses for all injuries and sicknesses covered by the Out-of-Hospital Major Medical section, subject to the reinstatement provision stated above.[5]

Accurate

It is not necessary—or even desirable—for every piece of communication to tell the whole story, but it is important that the information provided be accurate as far as it goes. In a number of court cases, plan sponsors have been required to live up to the language of their communication material.

Some plans have given participants a benefits booklet versus a copy of the benefit plan. Despite the fact these booklets had the typical hedge language (e.g., "In case of conflict with the plan, the plan will govern."), the courts have concluded plan participants should be able to rely on the booklet—the material supplied to them.

Redundant

It is human to assume that once something is said, the job is done. Yet a basic principle of effective communication is redundancy—repetition of the message. This is precisely the approach used in advertising.

Trustees cannot assume participants receive information the first time it is communicated. Even if it was received, there is no guarantee it was understood. And, even if understood, it may not be remembered. There is also the fact that benefit plan participants are constantly changing—some persons are hired, others retire and still others leave the trade. Even participants who stay in a plan for a long time need constant communication, since their interest in benefits and benefit features changes as they age and experience changes in family circumstances.

As evidence of the importance of repetition in communication, consider what has been learned in the business world. Authors of a soon-to-be published paper in the Harvard Business School publication *Working Knowledge* delve into why many managers tend to send the same message, over and over, via multiple media to team members. At first blush, this strategy may sound like nagging or a waste of time. But as it turns out, asking multiple times gets results. Managers who are deliberately redundant as communicators move their projects forward more quickly and smoothly than those who are not.[6]

Are There Any Other Challenges That Must Be Considered During the Communication Process?

The following points are based on comments by Hideya Kumata, a professor of communications at Michigan State University made during an International Foundation preconference session titled *Communication Dynamics for Employee Plans.*[7]

Selective Perception and Interpretation

One of the first challenges faced when communicating benefit plan information is "selective perception." Though the entire message may be right in front of them, people often choose to read only those bits and pieces that interest them. People starting out with the same information don't necessarily end up with the same conclusion. Different people can take the same facts and do almost anything they want to do with them. A lot of information people receive is subject to interpretation. People will get a pension benefits brochure, for instance, and they will say to themselves, "Well, it says that, but it really means something else." This is a quirk of human nature that must simply be dealt with.

The "Believe—Then See" Problem

There's an old saying: "Seeing is believing." Applied to benefit plan communications, one might assume that if plan participants are given the facts, they will realize a change has to be made and accept it. Unfortunately, it doesn't always work this way!

The saying should read in the reverse: "First we believe, then we see." Keep this in mind—especially when those receiving a message have deep personal involvement. People who don't particularly care one way or the other about an issue are much more likely to be rational and reach sensible conclusions. When people have interest in an issue—something other than reasoning and logic sets in.

Plan participants are interested in what their plan is doing for them—and they believe their views concerning plan benefits are right. It is human nature to look for things to support one's beliefs. This information is not necessarily complete but it proves their views are the right views. They try to fit reality into what they believe is true versus the other way around. Very often the challenge when communicating is not so much getting out information, it is how to present a message that conveys the reality of the situation and changes beliefs. Surveys or focus groups conducted prior to implementation of a communication program are essential to identifying what participants think, believe and value.

Message Competition

Another major obstacle is "message competition." Given the number of messages bombarding people everyday—it is easy to experience information "overload." In addition, benefit plan messages compete with other messages that are more professional and more attractive. These competing messages have more pizzazz. As a result, the most important messages are not always the ones chosen by participants to get attention.

Compounding the competition issue is "delayed reception." Even when receivers realize a message is important, they may feel they can postpone giving it attention until sometime in the future. Print brochures provide a case in point. What is stated in a brochure is important and the recipients recognize it is important. But many will say to themselves: "I have the brochure so I can read it when I need to." The brochure ends up forgotten in a desk drawer. To counteract these hurdles, messages must be as interesting and attractive as possible.

The Absent Audience

Many trustees realize that the people who attend meetings are also the ones who read plan brochures and keep informed in other ways. These are the people who are already interested, and they are also the ones who probably need additional messages the least. The other participants are the "absent audience" who probably need the information the most. Unless a message is very exciting, it will probably be bypassed by this group. Unfortunately, this is often the majority of plan participants.

It is not that people have any negative feelings about plan benefits; they are simply disinterested or distracted by other responsibilities. Getting plan information isn't high on their priority list. New communication strategies that make information available at the point in time when people need the information and face-to-face networks are helpful in overcoming this challenge.

* * *

In addition to the communication challenges identified by Kumata, there are some others that may have to be overcome:

- Limited resources
- Limited access to participants
- Communication material loaded with the jargon of the benefits field
- Dependence on written materials with little opportunity for face-to-face, one-on-one interaction
- New technology participants cannot navigate
- Lack of connection with opinion leaders
- Lack of trust.

There is no one-size-fits-all solution to addressing these obstacles, but keeping them in mind while developing a communications program may yield creative solutions that can minimize their impact.

Who Can Help Trustees Better Communicate With Participants?

Plans generally employ experts in areas such as law and actuarial science. They also contract with skilled administrators. Effective communication requires similar specialized expertise for planning and implementation.

Potential sources of help are administrators, benefit and communication consultants, audiovisual producers, public relations and advertising people, editors and printers. In getting the story of a plan out to plan participants, it may also be possible to enlist the aid of supervisors and job stewards.

Conclusion

Some may think that communication, beyond government requirements, is low on the list of trustee priorities. However, for participants and their families, plan information is extremely important when one of life's hazards strikes. From this perspective, communicating clearly and thoroughly should be a high priority among trustees.

The next time a new benefit is adopted or an old one changed, stop and consider the varied techniques and media available to communicate the message. Communication is not a one-time task; it requires more than a half-hearted paraphrasing of a plan document. Even a modest outlay of time, effort and money can enhance the large investment made in a benefit and can pay dividends through better understanding and acceptance.

While there are no standards for establishing a communication budget for benefit plans, there needs to be an annual appraisal of participant needs and the cost/benefit ratio for meeting these needs. Communication needs to be planned and budgeted as a part of the regular business of the benefit plan—an essential part of operations. There will be peaks and valleys in communication activity related to the needs at a given point in time, but it should not be allowed to end.

Endnotes

1. Robert J. Lind, "Communicating With Plan Participants—A Fresh Perspective," *Benefits and Compensation Digest,* November 2006, p. 42.
2. Kathleen Kennedy-Luczak, J.D., Melanie King, J.D., Linda Panszczyk, J.D., CEBS, and Tulay Turan, J.D., 2010 U.S. *Master Employee Benefits Guide*, Chicago: Wolters Kluwer, c. 2010, p. 197.
3. Lind, p. 43.
4. Lind, p. 43.
5. These kinds of coverage limitations are no longer allowed under the Patient Protection and Affordable Care Act as amended (ACA), but this illustration of poor writing, taken from an earlier version of this *Handbook*, remains valid.
6. Kim Girard, "It's Not Nagging: Why Persistent, Redundant Communication Works," *Working Knowledge*, a Harvard Business School website, April 18, 2011.
7. Hideya Kumata. *Communication Dynamics for Employee Benefit Plans.* (Brookfield, WI: International Foundation of Employee Benefit Plans, 1978).

Chapter 56

Communication Techniques

Claude L. Kordus

The intent of the previous chapter was to help trustees think through the objectives for their benefit plan's communication programs and how to accomplish these objectives. The next step is execution; otherwise, all the time spent planning is a wasted. This chapter focuses on the "how-tos" for both oral and written communication efforts.

Why should trustees be interested in plan communications? Isn't this the job of the administrator, benefit consultant or a communication consultant? Yes, but———

- Trustees must make decisions on what communication strategies to use and acceptable costs.
- Trustees must judge the effectiveness of the communication.
- Trustees might do some communication themselves.
- Trustees may wish to improve their own communication skills to become better trustees, more effective participants in their union or employment, and more influential contributors to their community.

For many people, being an effective communicator means being able to speak and write well. While this chapter will address both of these important skills, it will also explore a third dimension that is often overlooked but that is just as essential—the ability to listen effectively. In many situations, listening is more important that the other communication skills.

People Skills Are Mainly Communication Skills

Before jumping into the practicalities of communication, it is important to emphasize that the foundation of communication—whether oral, written or listening—is people skills. Researchers as well as educators suggest three personal characteristics provide the underpinning for all communication. These three traits are genuineness, respect and empathy.[1]

Genuineness. Successful leaders are genuine, which forms the basis for trust. Persons who are genuine are transparent—they allow everyone to know what they are thinking and feeling, and how their moral compass is working. When people are working together, the process is much smoother when each person is genuine in communications and actions.

One might think that being genuine when making a speech is not very important, but it is. Studies have shown that people communicate who they are when making a speech. Their words, their voice tone, their facial expressions, their gestures—all send signals that people pick up. Many of the same nonverbal signals are also important when listening to someone else who is speaking.

Respect. The second key trait that fosters effective communication is respect. This characteristic can also be labeled as *care* or *acceptance*. Unfortunately, many people don't grasp its importance in creating a positive organizational culture. Showing respect, caring for others, being kind, acting humbly—all of these can move an organization forward much more quickly than a concern for efficiency, task correctness and personal achievement. Think about the plan administration office and how positive comments can improve relationships with participants or staff and improve morale.

Noted psychotherapist Karl Menninger talks of this quality as a person's "patience, his fairness, his consistency, his rationality, his kindliness, in short—his real love."[2]

Theologians use the word "agape" to describe this quality. *Agape* is "concern for the well-being of others."[3] In the world of work, people who are respectful of others generally receive the same treatment back. Ralph Waldo Emerson said it well, "The only way to have a friend is to be one."

Fortune Magazine conducts a survey of employees to determine the "100 Best Companies to Work for in America." In 1999, Synovus Financial Corporation achieved the number one position on this list. CEO James Blanchard talked about the culture of respect that caused his company to succeed financially as well as humanely:

> *The secret, the clue, the common thread is simply how you treat folks. It's how you treat your fellow man, and how you treat your team members and how you treat your customers, your regulators, your general public, your audiences, your communities. How you value the worth of an individual, how you bring the human factor into real importance and not just a statement you make in your annual report.*[4]

Empathy. The final trait, empathy, is the most difficult of the three qualities to achieve. Genuineness and respect are behavioral. Empathy comes from deep psychological habits, attitudes and beliefs. It involves more heart, more feelings and more intuition. Empathy is not feeling for someone but feeling *with* someone. In his book *Caring*, Milton Mayerhoff notes:

> *To care for another person, I must be able to understand him and his world as if I were inside it. I must be able to see, as it were, with his eyes what his world is like…and how he sees himself.*[5]

It is important to point out that empathy is also dependent on one of the principal communication skills—the ability to listen to others.

Shifting feelings about one's self and others is no small task. A friend, mentor or coach can be useful for this task. For example, ask a friend how one came across when the friend wished to talk about a serious personal issue.

* * *

Genuineness, respect and empathy demand constant attention. In *Stanford Business*, a magazine for the Stanford University Graduate School of Business alumni, Garth Saloner (dean of the school) observed:

> *…[T]he ability to work effectively with and through people is one of the most important determinants of success in any organization. Self-awareness, knowledge of the impact of one's style on others, and skill at interpersonal interactions are at least as important a part of the leader's skill set as is training in the more traditional business disciplines.*[6]

For those who are visually oriented, Exhibit 1 offers a model of communication and how it depends on these three qualities. The three traits overlap as individuals participate in their family, the workplace, among friends and within their community.

Exhibit 1

Communication Effectiveness

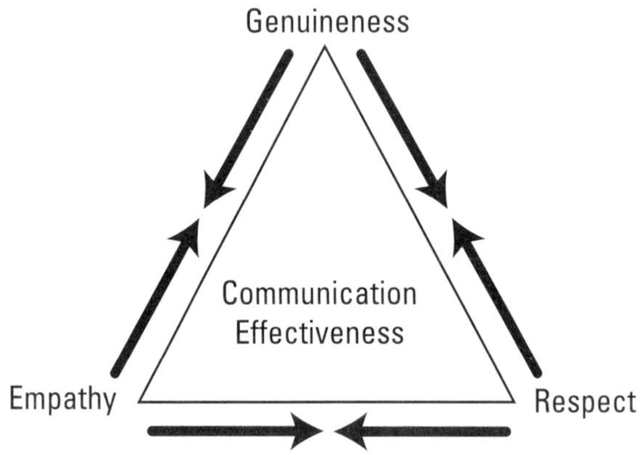

How Can People Listen Better?

Unfortunately, people are rarely good listeners—and they have no idea what they are missing! Consider these facts regarding people's listening skills:

- Most people in the United States talk at a rate of about 125 words per minute, but they are able to listen at a rate three to four times faster. As a result, people are easily distracted when listening.[7]
- The average listener forgets 33% to 50% within eight hours and 75% after two months.[8] Why don't people take notes?

Listening affects the management and operation of benefit plans in no small way. Imagine plan representatives trying to address the questions and concerns of participants without being good listeners. And how can trustees identify solutions to problems and make wise

Exhibit 2

Barriers to Listening and Their Antidotes

Barriers	Antidotes
Knowing the Answer	
• Makes quick judgment • Interrupts • Argues before speaker lays out case	• Keep an open, receptive mind • Wait three seconds after a speaker is finished to reply • Make a commitment to search for new ideas
Trying to Be Helpful	
• Thinks about how to solve problem • Tries to rescue speaker • Doesn't respect speaker	• Give attention as an act of respect • Schedule a separate meeting for giving advice • Recognize the speaker has probably already thought of the same solution
Treating Discussion as Competition	
• Challenges every point • Views agreement as sign of weakness	• Affirm points of agreement • Provide positive feedback • Be specific when there is a valid disagreement
Ulterior Motives	
• Tries to impress or influence rather than listen • Uses extra listening time to think about the next move	• Regularly recognize personal motives • Work on being open to all • Reduce the number of secrets
Misplaced Trust in the Precision of Words	
• Assumes that words that are clear to one person are clear to another • Personal beliefs or experiences connected to a word trigger emotional response or misunderstanding.	• Ask the speaker questions that clarify what is meant • Try to get into the other person's shoes and analyze what the speaker is feeling

Source: Adapted from *Eight Barriers to Effective Listening* by Michael Webb, March 2006. www.sklatch.net/thoughtlets/listen.html.

decisions without listening to fellow trustees, plan personnel, professional advisors and participants? Listening leads to better interaction with plan personnel and to better trustee meetings.

It can be argued, the listener bears more responsibility than the speaker for the quality of communication. Listening better requires individuals to self-examine what they may be doing that hinders their ability to hear what others are saying. Some common barriers and their antidotes are provided in Exhibit 2.

Body Language

To encourage a speaker to relax and be more forthcoming, the use of appropriate body language is part of being an effective listener. A person with a blank stare slouching in a chair can create a chilling effect for a person attempting to communicate. A listener communicates interest and concern for the speaker in these ways:

- **Leaning forward** tells the speaker that the listener is paying attention and is thoroughly connected to the speaker and the speaker's message.

- **Keeping arms uncrossed** tells the speaker the conversation is desired and of interest. In contrast, crossed arms telegraph a lack of interest.
- **Making eye contact** with the speaker also demonstrates interest and concern. Nothing is more insulting and more disrespectful than looking about the room, or worse, looking at one's watch. Making eye contact does not mean staring at the speaker—just looking somewhere near the speaker's face.
- **Making sounds and facial responses.** The listener can smile, nod, say "uh huh," "I understand," "that's interesting" and the like—all show the listener is absorbed.
- **Touching the person.** A tap on the hand or arm, or similar noninvasive touching, communicates warmth and empathy. (Yes, men can hug.) [9]

The literature on body language is vast; it describes many more body language movements than can be covered here.

What Are Some Tips for Public Speaking?

Trustees, administrators and advisors often are asked to make comments or a presentation concerning the activities and status of a benefit plan. The audience might be plan participants, participant families, contributing employers, government officials or attendees at an International Foundation event. These public speaking activities contribute to the overall effectiveness of a jointly managed plan.

Some people fear public speaking more than death. Undoubtedly, many see talking in front of others as a problem rather than a solution, a threat rather than an opportunity. What many people don't understand is that (1) addressing one's fears requires a great deal of self-examination that can deflate one's ego and (2) being a good speaker is a long road with a lot of less-than-satisfactory attempts on the way.

There are hundreds of texts, manuals and how-to books on public speaking, but many miss some of the most important principles and techniques. The importance of being genuine, respectful and empathetic as just discussed is a good example of what is overlooked—few materials on public speaking emphasize the importance of a speaker's character. Getting to the essentials of what makes a good speaker can also be difficult. This chapter covers only a small number of the most important themes on the topic.

Connect With the Listener

A good place to begin is the model presented previously: Be genuine and open, respectful and caring, and empathetic with listeners. Speakers who fail to show these qualities through words, gestures, facial expressions, tone of voice and attitude are in trouble. Quick ways for speakers to get an audience to tune out are:

- Talk a lot about themselves
- Forget eye contact
- Frown
- Read an entire speech
- Use ironic, bitter humor.

When asked to make a presentation to a group of people that are unknown, the person who does not have time to research the group should decline the invitation. Speakers who have not researched their audience too often find themselves talking about a topic the audience does not care about, or taking a position contrary to the audience's beliefs. The person extending the invitation should be asked:[10]

- What is the meeting theme?
- What are the expectations of those who extended the invitation as well as those in the audience? What needs to be done to meet these expectations?
- Who and how many people will attend?
- What do the attendees have in common?
- How is the presentation relevant to the attendees?
- How might the information help the attendees?
- What does the audience know about the topic?
- What do attendees know about the presenter?
- Is it a friendly, neutral or hostile audience?
- Do the attendees get along? Do they laugh easily?
- Will decision makers be in the room? Will they be there for part of or the entire presentation? What might cause these persons to miss it or leave before the event is over?
- Are there other important persons who will be in the room? What are their names, titles, roles and responsibilities?
- What are the starting and ending times for the meeting?
- What agenda items come before and after the presentation?
- What is the seating arrangement ? If appropriate, can it be changed?
- What is the expected attire? Is it formal, business, business casual or casual? Be sure to find out as much as possible—business casual can mean different things to different groups. Casual to some is slacks, jackets and ties.

Set the Tone

Precisely what is *tone?* Is it speaker characteristics such as being genuine, respectful and empathetic as already discussed?

Is it the choice of words used? A combination of all of this or something else? One expert has suggested tone has two dimensions controlled by the words the speaker uses:

- **Positive** (The office will remain open until 7 p.m.) versus **Negative** (The office will close at 7 p.m.)
- **Informal** with pronouns (i.e., I, you, she, he, it, we, you, they) and contractions (e.g., don't, can't, won't) versus **Formal** with no pronouns and contractions.[11]

Tell Stories

Telling a story that is appropriate to the theme of a speech can be powerful. Stories work particularly well in the introduction and conclusion of a speech; they work because everyone enjoys stories, especially if they follow some rules. The story should:

- Be relevant to the main point of the speech
- Told with conviction
- Be short (long stories can be deadly)
- Include some humor
- Be personal (while this is not necessary, it is helpful).

As an example, picture a legislator who believes that the new federal medical system is wrong for the country telling this story:

> *Before our Constitution in the 1780s, the United States was floundering in debt. One day during this period, Benjamin Franklin entertained Dr. Benjamin Rush and Thomas Jefferson. The conversation turned to determining what was the oldest profession. Dr. Rush, a physician, said the oldest profession was his. "After all, it was a surgical operation that made Eve out of Adam's rib." But Jefferson, who built Monticello, said, "No, it was the architect. Surely it was an architect who brought the world out of chaos." Then Franklin replied "You're both wrong. It's the politician. After all, who do you think created the chaos?"*[12]

The story is relevant, certainly told with conviction and short, and incorporates humor.

Observe the Rule of Three

What is the rule of three? How do you use it in speeches? Trios, triplets and triads abound in Western culture in many disciplines. Exhibit 3 offers examples of some memorable triads. Why does the rule of three work? Experts are not sure. A triad does give a sense of completeness, closure—besides that, it's magic. The examples from history show how effective a triad can be in a speech.

Exhibit 3

Notable Triads

Nursery Rhymes

- *Three Little Pigs*
- *Goldilocks and the Three Bears*

Christianity

- Father, Son and Holy Spirit
- Three Wise Men with their gold, frankincense and myrrh

Movies and Books

- *The Good, the Bad and the Ugly*
- *Sex, Lies and Videotape*

Politics and Government

- U.S. branches of government: Executive, Judicial and Legislative
- U.S. Declaration of Independence: "Life, liberty and the pursuit of happiness"
- The abundance of three-colored flags

Mottos

- Fire safety motto: *Stop, Drop and Roll*
- Olympic motto: *Faster, Higher, Stronger*
- Real estate: *Location, Location, Location*

History

- Shakespeare's Julius Caesar: *"Friends, Romans, Countrymen. Lend me your ears."*
- Abraham Lincoln's Gettysburg Address: *"We can not dedicate—we can not consecrate—we can not hallow—this ground."* and *"Government of the people, by the people, for the people"*
- General MacArthur, West Point Address, 1962: *"Duty, Honor, Country"* [repeated several times in the speech]
- Barack Obama, Inaugural Speech: *"[W]e must pick ourselves up, dust ourselves off, and begin again the work of remaking America."*

Source: Examples from ***Six Minutes: Speaking and Presentation Skills*** (sixminutes.dlugan.com), an exceptional website for speech-making ideas and examples.

Ten More Speechmaking Tips

These tips are drawn from a blog by Dan Pallotta for the *Harvard Business Review's* blog network:

1. **Know your goal.** When the speech is over, what do you want the audience to do? Be inspired? Be informed? Be convinced? Be persuaded to act? And what specific act?
2. **Memorize your speech.** This advice goes against a lot of common advice. Reading a speech is a good way to put people to sleep. Even using notes reduces audience contact. Once a speaker has the words right, he or she can concentrate on other elements of an excellent speech performance: eye contact, verbal variety, appropriate gestures and the like.
3. **Practice the transition.** To eliminate the "ahs," the speaker should stamp transitions on his or her brain: words like "if," "when," "now we turn to," "as another advantage" and "start by."
4. **Don't fear silence.** Give the audience time for reflection. Audiences are used to speakers filling every second with sound. The audience will appreciate it.
5. **Distrust PowerPoint.** *Do not use it for a script*—otherwise the presentation will be dominated by what is on the screen.
6. **Give something of yourself.** Getting personal—even in short spurts—lets the audience experience what the speaker is feeling.
7. **Be yourself.** Do not try to copy outstanding speakers or famous figures like John F. Kennedy or Martin Luther King Jr. Speakers must be their honest selves. Show sincere interest in the audience. Use high energy, but not high bombast.
8. **Don't speak in abstractions.** People are sick of "paradigms" and "tectonic shifts."
9. **Make eye contact.** Don't think of this behavior as a tactic, but as a way of connecting with the audience.
10. **Be the person you want the audience to believe you are.** On this subject, Pallotta comments, "When you allow yourself to feel the humanity of your audience, you have succeeded in taking the focus off yourself. This is the place from which change is made. From here you can move mountains."[13]

We return to genuineness, respect and empathy noted at the beginning of this chapter.

What Are Some Tips for Written Communication?

A great deal of the communication with plan participants is written—a letter, a brochure, a booklet or perhaps text posted on a Web page. While oral communication is often a better approach, it is often not possible given the time and talent available, and the cost. Then, there is the reality that the federal government mandates a lot of written communication. Some practical tips follow on creating written materials for participants; much of this advice applies anytime a person must provide written information.

1. **Be receiver-oriented.** The focus must be on the attitudes, feelings, interests and background of the persons who will be receive the written material. In practice, this means the developer must ask, "How can I best respond to the needs and wants of the recipients?"
2. **Keep it short.** Make sure the written message is worthy of the targeted audience's attention and that the audience will be able to get the message with minimum effort. Keeping text short and to the point is extremely important.
3. **Check the readability.** There are a couple of easy ways to check the readability of your material. A very simple way is to take a random sample of the text and analyze it:
   a. **Paragraphs** that consistently exceed ten lines reduce readability. Keep in mind these are averages.
   b. **Sentences** should average 20 to 25 words per sentence.
   c. **Multisyllabic words** (there's a good example) immediately raise the difficulty level of the message. For the average audience—average education, average interest in the subject—words of more than one syllable should not exceed 30% of the total. Put another way, about 70% of the words in the copy should have only one syllable.

These three guides are easy to remember as the 10-20-30% rules: ten lines per paragraph, 20 words per sentence and no more than 30% multisyllable words.* Naturally, some sentences and some paragraphs will run longer. And some will be shorter. If everything were always the same, the result would be boring. The idea is to abide by the rules overall. Paragraphs that are always longer than ten lines look forbidding to a reader.

The Challenges to Good Writing

In a world in which benefit plans and trustees are increasingly willing to invest in a wide array of new technologies to communicate with participants and their families, the fundamental principles of written communication are too

*A similar 10-20-30 guideline exists for PowerPoint: ten slides for each presentation, 20 minutes speaking time, 30-point font or greater. These guidelines come from Guy Kawasaki, author and venture capitalist.

Benefit Booklets

Benefit plans widely use booklets as a communication tool. The following advice on developing effective benefit booklets is adapted from an article by Howard L. Peck, a former partner of Hewitt Associates. This material appeared in the 3rd edition of the *Trustee Handbook.*

* * *

Consider the benefit booklet. It isn't very big. Usually about five by seven inches—and skinny. It isn't very attractive, ordinarily. A few pages of dull prose. But it is entrusted with a big job, telling millions of participants about private welfare and pension plans.

True, other media are used, ranging from the pay envelope stuffer to the Internet. In fact, communication efforts that rely on any one medium or technique are likely to fall short. Keep in mind that booklets have limitations and they should be viewed as only one element in a program.

What is the role of the booklet? How well does it fill its role? What are reasonable objectives for a booklet? How can they be attained?

Role

What is unique about the booklet? What does it do that other media do not do?

- The booklet is generally a reasonably complete statement of the key provisions and features of a benefit plan. It differs from many other communication devices, which may deal with only one aspect.
- The booklet has a degree of permanence. It is typically intended to be kept and used as a reference.
- The booklet provides tangible evidence to participants that their benefit plan exists and the coverage they are being provided.
- The booklet is the summary plan description as required by ERISA.
- Because of these various roles, the booklet takes on an "official" status not generally accorded to other communication forms.

Objectives

Obviously, the booklet is intended to explain the plan to the employee. But trustees need to think about what else they want their plan's communication program to accomplish. Here are some possibilities:

- To inform participants and create a degree of understanding and acceptance of the plan or program as a whole.
- To provide participants a convenient reference source. The booklet should give a clear explanation of the key provisions of the plan or program—including enough details so that participants can find answers to the questions they are most likely to ask.
- To create a favorable impression of the plan or program. The booklet symbolically represents the plan. Its character may communicate volumes about how the plan's importance is viewed.
- To instill recognition of the value of the plan or program and its importance as a form of compensation. As benefits absorb an increasing part of the payroll dollar, many believe that it becomes more and more important to emphasize the scope of benefits and their substantial value as a form of pay.
- To create an understanding of the economics of insured benefits, and of the participant's responsibility to use benefits intelligently without abusing them. Few participants—particularly those in larger groups—realize the cost of benefits for the entire group is the sum of the claims paid, the cost of administration and a reasonable profit for an insurance company. Some participants believe they are justified in collecting as much as possible because a company pays their claims. By presenting facts in a clear and straightforward way, a booklet can help encourage actions that are more informed.
- To inform participant families about the benefits. One of the reasons that booklets often are mailed to the home rather than distributed at work is because plans value keeping the family informed. Spouses and children often have a more immediate interest in a benefit program than a participant does. Benefits that cover dependents—as well as benefits such as retirement income and life insurance—directly affect the welfare of other household members.

(continued on next page)

Character

Once objectives are established, it is time to decide the character of the booklet. Consider one other vital factor—the nature of the targeted audience members. What are their reading and language skills? What is their interest in the subject? Are individuals in the group relatively the same or very different?

The booklet may range from a comic book to formal text. Consider page size, page count and shape (it doesn't have to be the same as all the rest), font type, ink colors, the kind and color of paper, the nature and arrangement of illustrations (None? Humorous? Realistic? Charts?).

Text

Good copy is not easy to come by. It must be accurate, interesting and readable. Start with the recognition that everything may be a compromise. The lawyers will be quick to say that nothing less than the legalese of the plan document or contract can be completely accurate. So try to be factual and precise—but in a language that can be understood by the participant and participant's family.

- Don't think people with a limited ability to understand English or to read are the only problem. Another issue is whether participants will take the trouble to understand. Someone once said, "You must write not only so that you can be understood, but also that you cannot be misunderstood."
- When it seems the booklet is simple and clear, go back and simplify some more.
- Don't "write down." Nothing is more irritating to a reader than a condescending air. On the other hand, do not be afraid of simplicity. Highly skilled readers appreciate simple language—and the rest need it.
- Remember too that this is an age of "lookers" (TV, picture magazines, computers), not readers. Use illustrations to support information, not just to fill a space at the bottom of the page.
- Recognize there are varying levels of interest in a subject. If writing about a pension plan, for example, do not expect younger employees to show the same interest as those approaching retirement. Consider organizing the material so that each group can find what it wants quickly *and* easily.

All of these considerations show a need for regular interaction between trustees and communication specialists.

The "Package"

In most multiemployer benefit plan situations, each benefit is represented by a different booklet—different in size, shape, design and theme. Some plan sponsors have seen the wisdom of adopting a package concept in which a uniform design and theme is developed for the entire benefit program. Some use a series of booklets in a ring binder. Others use a loose-leaf format. Others have individual booklets housed in a jacket or box. In each case, benefits are presented as a unified, integrated program. The package can be kept up to date by revising small units.

NOTE: For those seeking similar information about newsletters, please review the following articles published in the International Foundation *Benefits and Compensation Digest:*

- "Newsletters for Employees and Plan Participants," May 2007
- "The Power of Print: A Printed Newsletter Can Still Be the Best Choice," July 2007.

frequently overlooked. Part of the problem is a misconception that simple, plain language means "dumbing down" the content. When done correctly, the content is the same. The objective of plain language is to reduce the effort required on the part of the reader—increasing the likelihood the participant or beneficiary will (1) actually read what has been offered and (2) understand it.

For communication that is the exact opposite of plain language (e.g., complex sentences, legalese and jargon), a relatively dependable source is a plan attorney. Plan trustees and administrators have a responsibility to make sure plan communications (1) comply with government regulations and (2) do not place their plans at risk of a legal dispute. It is often forgotten that many government regulations are an effort to make sure plan participants and beneficiaries are fully informed. Developing and revising written plan materials is a delicate balancing act that must consider both the letter and the intent of the law.

Another reason plans have been slow to embrace plain language is the lack of expertise to put it into practice. Writing simply and directly may *look* easy, but it takes skill, hard work and a commitment to doing it right. Only the best writers can cut through legal and technical language and make it easy to grasp. Good writers also have the ability to choose helpful examples that support the points being made and select graphics that make the text more appealing. All of this must be done while taking into account literacy level, interests and existing knowledge of the target audience.

Assessing a plan's written communications requires honesty about whether the content is appropriate for the recipient. If in doubt, written materials should be tested on a sample of the targeted group. Communications that are read—and understood—without difficulty represent money well spent. The result is more informed participants and participant families that are also more satisfied with their benefit plan.

Conclusion

Knowing what to communicate and how to communicate represent major components of effective communication, but who the communicator is as a human being stands equal to the what and how.

Endnotes

1. Robert Bolton, *People Skills: How to Assert Yourself, Listen to Others, and Resolve Conflicts.*
2. Bolton, 236.
3. Bolton, 263.
4. Steven M.R. Covey. *The Speed of Trust.* (New York: Free Press, 2006): 152
5. Bolton, 272.
6. Garth Saloner, Dean of the Stanford University Graduate School of Business in the alumni magazine. *Stanford Business.*
7. Nichols and Stevens, 6, 7.
8. Nichols and Stevens, 13, 14.
9. Matthew McKay, Ph.D., Martha Davis, Ph.D., and Patrick Fanning, *How to Communicate.* Second Edition (New York: Barnes & Noble Books, c. 1995) 183, 184.
10. Adapted from Timothy J. Koegel's *The Exceptional Presenter.* (Greenleaf Book Group Press) May 1, 2007.
11. Brandon Royal, *The Little Red Writing Book* (New York: Metro Books, 2009) 84.
12. James C. Humes. *Speak Like Churchill, Stand Like Lincoln: 21 Powerful Secrets of History's Greatest Speakers* (New York: Three Rivers Press, c. 2002) 74.
13. Dan Pallotta. Delivering the Speech of Your Life. Blog posted March 4, 2011. blogs.hbr.org/pallotta/2011/03/delivering-the-speech-of-your.html.

Acronyms and Abbreviations*

Entries are alphabetized as if they were single words. Ampersands, commas, slashes and spaces are ignored in alphabetization. Letters combined with numbers appear before letters combined with letters. If an entry has more than one definition, those definitions appear in alphabetical order within the entry.

AAA (1) American Academy of Actuaries
(2) American Accounting Association
(3) American Arbitration Association

AAC (1) actual acquisition cost
(2) affirmative action clause
(3) affirmative action committee

AAHP American Association of Health Plans

AAP affirmative action program

AAPPO American Association of Preferred Provider Organizations

AARP American Association of Retired Persons

ABA (1) American Bankers Association
(2) American Bar Association

ABCP asset-backed commercial paper

ABO accumulated benefit obligation

ABP (1) account balance pension
(2) average benefit percentage

ABS asset-backed securities

ACA Affordable Care Act (amended version of the Patient Protection and Affordable Care Act of 2010)

ACO accountable care organization

ACP (1) actual contribution percentage
(2) average contribution percentage

ACR (1) accelerated cost recovery
(2) accounts receivable
(3) actual contribution ratio
(4) adjusted community rating
(5) average cost ratio

AcSB Accounting Standards Board

AD&D accidental death and dismemberment

ADA (1) American Dental Association
(2) American Diabetes Association
(3) Americans with Disabilities Act

ADB accidental death benefit

ADEA Age Discrimination in Employment Act

ADL activities of daily living

ADP actual deferral percentage

*Many of the acronyms and abbreviations listed are drawn from the *Benefits and Compensation Glossary* (International Foundation of Employee Benefit Plans, 2010)

ADR (1) actual deferral ratio
(2) adverse drug reaction
(3) alternative dispute resolution
(4) American Depositary Receipt

ADS (1) alternative delivery system
(2) American Depositary Share

AEC accumulated eligibility credits

AFFE acquired fund fees and expenses

AHRQ Agency for Healthcare and Research Quality

AICPA American Institute of Certified Public Accountants

ALOS average length of stay

AMB accrual monthly benefit

AMEX American Stock Exchange

APB Accounting Principles Board

APBO (1) actuarial present value of accumulated benefits
(2) actuarial present value of future benefits

APPWP Association of Private Pension and Welfare Plans

APR annual percentage rate

APRSC Administrative Policy Regarding Self-Correction

APV actuarial present value

APY annual percentage yield

AR accounts receivable

ASA (1) Associate of the Society of Actuaries
(2) Fellow of the Society of Actuaries

ASB Actuarial Standards Board

ASC administrative services contract

ASO (1) administrative services only
(2) administrative services organization

ASOP Actuarial Standards of Practice

ASPA American Society of Pension Actuaries

ASTD American Society for Training and Development

AVA actuarial value of assets

BCBSA Blue Cross and Blue Shield Association

BIC bank investment contract

BIS break in service

BLS Bureau of Labor Statistics

BMI body mass index

BP or bp basis point

CA chartered accountant

CAP Closing Agreement Program

CAPM capital asset pricing model

CAPP cash account pension plan

CAT computerized axial tomography

CBA (1) collective bargaining agreement
(2) cost/benefit analysis

CBOE Chicago Board Options Exchange

CBP cash balance plan

CBU contribution base unit

CD certificate of deposit

CDC (1) Centers for Disease Control and Prevention
(2) Community Development Corporation

CDHC consumer-driven health care

CDHP (1) consumer-directed health plan
(2) consumer-driven health plan

CDO collateralized debt obligations

CDS credit default swap

CEA cost-effectiveness analysis

CEO chief executive officer

CFA Chartered Financial Analyst

CFO chief financial officer

CFR Code of Federal Regulations

CFTC Commodities Futures Trading Commission

ChFA Chartered Financial Analyst

ChFC Chartered Financial Consultant

CHIP Children's Health Insurance Program

CHIPRA Children's Health Insurance Program Reauthorization Act of 2009

CI critical illness

CIMA Certified Investment Management Analyst

CIPM Certificate in Investment Performance Measurement

CLO collateralized loan obligations

CLU Chartered Life Underwriter

CM case management

CMA cost-minimization analysis

CMBS commercial mortgage-backed securities

CMO collateralized mortgage obligation

CMS Centers for Medicare and Medicaid Services

CMV current market value

COB coordination of benefits

COBRA Consolidated Omnibus Budget Reconciliation Act of 1985

COI certificate of insurance

COLA (1) cost-of-living adjustment
(2) cost-of-living allowance

CON certificate of need

CP commercial paper

CPA Certified Public Accountant

CPC Certified Pension Consultant

CPCU Chartered Property Casualty Underwriter

CPI Consumer Price Index

CPR customary, prevailing and reasonable

CRPC Chartered Retirement Planning Counselor

CRPS Chartered Retirement Plans Specialist

CS credited service

CSO (1) chief security officer
(2) claims services only

CTA commodity trading advisor

CV convertible

D&O director and officer

d/b/a doing business as

DALYs disability adjusted life years

DB defined benefit

DBP defined benefit plan

DC (1) deferred compensation
(2) defined contribution
(3) Doctor of Chiropractic

DCI duplicate coverage inquiry

DCP defined contribution plan

DFVCP Delinquent Filer Voluntary Compliance Program

DHHS Department of Health and Human Services

DHMO dental health maintenance organization

DI (1) disability income
(2) disability insurance

DJIA Dow Jones Industrial Average

DO (1) Doctor of Optometry
(2) Doctor of Osteopathy

DOB date of birth

DOL Department of Labor

DOT (1) Department of Transportation
(2) Dictionary of Occupational Titles

DPO dental plan organization

DPSP deferred profit-sharing plan

DRG diagnosis related grouping

DRIP dividend reinvestment plan

DRO domestic relations order

DROP deferred retirement option plan

DSM disease state management

DSO dental service organization

DTC Depository Trust Company

DUE drug use evaluation

DUM drug utilization management

DUR drug utilization review

E&O	errors and omissions
EA	Enrolled Actuary
EAC	estimated acquisition cost
EACA	eligible automatic contribution arrangement
EBIS	EMPLOYEE BENEFITS INFOSOURCE™
EBRI	Employee Benefit Research Institute
EBPAQC	Employee Benefit Plan Audit Quality Center
EBSA	Employee Benefits Security Administration (formerly Pension and Welfare Benefits Administration)
ECA	eligible automatic contribution arrangement
ED	(Department of) Education
EDGAR	Electronic Data Gathering, Analysis, and Retrieval system
EDI	electronic data interchange
EDP	electronic data processing
EEO	equal employment opportunity
EEOC	Equal Employment Opportunity Commission
EFAST	ERISA Filing Acceptance System
EGTRRA	Economic Growth and Tax Relief Reconciliation Act of 2001
EIN	Employer Identification Number
ELOS	estimated length of stay
EOB	explanation of benefits
EOE	equal opportunity employer
EPA	(1) Environmental Protection Agency (2) Equal Pay Act of 1963
EPCRS	Employee Plans Compliance Resolution System
EPEO	employee plans and exempt organizations
ePHI	electronic protected health information
EPO	exclusive provider organization
EPR	electronic patient record
EPS	earnings per share
EPSP	employee profit-sharing plan
ERIC	ERISA Industry Committee
ERIP	early retirement incentive programs
ERISA	Employee Retirement Income Security Act of 1974
ERPA	Enrolled Retirement Plan Agent
ERR	expected rate of return
ESS	employee self-service
ETA	Employment and Training Administration
ETF	exchange-traded fund
ETI	economically targeted investing
EWL	employer withdrawal liability
FAF	Financial Accounting Foundation
FAMC	Federal Agricultural Mortgage Corporation (Farmer Mac)
FAQ	frequently asked questions
FAS	Financial Accounting Standard
FASB	Financial Accounting Standards Board
FDIC	Federal Deposit Insurance Corporation
FFS	fee for service
FHA	Federal Housing Administration
FHLB	Federal Home Loan Bank
FHLBB	Federal Home Loan Bank Board
FHLMC	Federal Home Loan Mortgage Corporation (Freddie Mac)
FI	fiscal intermediary
FINRA	Financial Industry Regulatory Authority
FIP	Funding Improvement Plan
FLMI	Fellow, Life Management Institute
FLSA	Fair Labor Standards Act
FMLA	Family and Medical Leave Act of 1993
FMV	fair market value
FNMA	Federal National Mortgage Association (Fannie Mae)

FOIA	Freedom of Information Act
FS	financial statement
FSA	(1) Fellow of the Society of Actuaries (2) flexible spending account (3) flexible spending arrangement (4) funding standard account
FSPA	Fellow, Society of Pension Actuaries
FTE	full-time equivalent
FY	fiscal year
FYB	fiscal year budget
GAAP	Generally Accepted Accounting Principles
GAAS	Generally Accepted Auditing Standards
GAO	Government Accountability Office
GASB	Governmental Accounting Standards Board
GATT	General Agreement on Tariffs and Trade
GBA	Group Benefits Associate
GDP	gross domestic product
GDR	Global Depositary Receipt
GDS	Global Depositary Share
GIC	guaranteed investment contract
GINA	Genetic Information Nondiscrimination Act of 2008
GLS	group legal services
GLSO	group legal services organization
GNMA	Government National Mortgage Association (Ginnie Mae)
GNP	gross national product
GO	general obligation
GP	general partner
HCA	health care account
HCE	highly compensated employee
HCFA	Health Care Financing Administration
HCO	health care organization
HCPCS	HCFA Common Procedural Coding System
HCSA	health care spending account
HDHP	high-deductible health plan
HEART	Heroes Earnings Assistance and Relief Tax Act of 2008
HEDIS®	Healthcare Effectiveness Data and Information Set
HERO	Heroes Earned Retirement Opportunities Act
HHC	home health care
HHS	(Department of) Health and Human Services
HI	(1) health insurance (2) hospital insurance
HIAA	Health Insurance Association of America
HIP	health incentive plan
HIPAA	Health Insurance Portability and Accountability Act of 1996
HIPC	(1) health insurance purchasing coalition (2) health insurance purchasing cooperative
HITECH	Health Information Technology for Economic and Clinical Health Act
HMO	health maintenance organization
HPA	Hospital-Physician Alliance
HPO	hospital-physician organization
HPPC	health plan purchasing cooperative
HR	human resources
HRA	(1) health reimbursement arrangement (2) health risk assessment
HSA	health savings account
HUD	(Department of) Housing and Urban Development
IB	interpretive bulletin
IBNR	incurred but not reported
ICD-10	International Classification of Diseases and Related Health Problems
ICF	intermediate care facility
ICM	individual case management

ICU	intensive care unit
IDM	integrated disability management
IDN	integrated delivery network
IDR	International Depositary Receipt
IDS	integrated delivery system
IFEBP	International Foundation of Employee Benefit Plans
IHM	integrated health management
ILP	independent living program
IME	independent medical examination
INHM	in-house asset manager
IO	investment only
IP	(1) inpatient (2) integrated provider
IPA	(1) independent practice association (2) individual practice association (3) independent physician association
IPO	initial public offering
IRA	individual retirement account
IRB	Internal Revenue Bulletin
IRC	Internal Revenue Code
IRR	internal rate of return
IRS	Internal Revenue Service
ISE	International Securities Exchange
IUC	incurred but unreported claims
IVR	interactive voice response (system)
J&S	joint and survivor (annuity)
JATC	Joint Apprenticeship and Training Committee
JCAHO	Joint Commission on Accreditation of Healthcare Organizations
JCWAA	Job Creation and Workers Assistance Act of 2002
JOBS	Job Opportunities and Basic Skills Training
JSOA	joint and survivor option annuity
JV	joint venture
KMS	knowledge management system
KSOP	401(k) employee stock option plan
LBO	leveraged buyout
LDI	liability directed investment
LIF	life income fund
LLC	limited liability corporation
LMRA	Labor-Management Relations Act of 1947 (Taft-Hartley Act)
LMRDA	Labor-Management Reporting and Disclosure Act of 1959 (Landrum-Griffin Act)
LMS	learning management system
LOS	length of stay
LP	limited partnership
LTC	long-term care
LTD	long-term disability
LTV	loan-to-value
M&A	mergers and acquisitions
MAAC	maximum allowable actual charge
MAC	maximum allowable cost
MBS	mortgage-backed security
MC	managed care
MCCA	Medicare Catastrophic Coverage Act
MCM	medical case management
MCO	managed care organization
MCP	managed care plan
MD	Doctor of Medicine
MDC	major diagnostic categories
MEPP	multi-employer pension plan
MET	multiple employer trust
MEWA	multiple employer welfare arrangement
MFB	maximum family benefit
MGIC	Mortgage Guaranty Insurance Corporation

MH/CD mental health/chemical dependency

MH/SA mental health/substance Abuse

MHPA Mental Health Parity Act

MHPAEA Mental Health Parity and Addiction Equity Act of 2011

MIS management information system

MIT modern investment theory

MLR (1) medical loss ratio
(2) multiple location risk

MMA Medicare Prescription Drug, Improvement, and Modernization Act of 2003

MNC (1) multinational company
(2) multinational corporation

MOB maintenance of benefits

MPP minimum premium plan

MPPAA Multiemployer Pension Plan Amendments Act of 1980

MPT modern portfolio theory

MSA medical savings account

MSO management services organization

MSP Medicare secondary payer

MSPA Member, Society of Pension Actuaries

MTM medication therapy management

NA not applicable

NABP National Association of Boards of Pharmacy

NAIC National Association of Insurance Commissioners

NASDAQ National Association of Securities Dealers Automatic Quotation System

NAV net asset value

NCCI National Council on Compensation Insurance

NCD negotiable certificate of deposit

NCPDP National Council on Prescription Drug Programs

NCQA National Committee for Quality Assurance

NFA National Futures Association

NHCAA National Health Care Anti-Fraud Association

NHCE non-highly compensated employee

NHIC National Health Information Center

NLRA National Labor Relations Act of 1935 (Wagner Act)

NLRB National Labor Relations Board

NMB National Mediation Board

NMHPA Newborns' and Mothers' Health Protection Act of 1996

NP nurse practitioner

NPI national provider identifier

NPO nonprofit organization

NPV net present value

NRA normal retirement age

NRD normal retirement date

NSF not sufficient funds

NYSE New York Stock Exchange

OASDHI Old-Age, Survivors, Disability, and Health Insurance

OB-GYN obstetrics and gynecology

OBRA Omnibus Budget Reconciliation Act

OCC (1) Office of the Comptroller of Currency
(2) Options Clearing Corporation

OJT on-the-job training

OLMS Office of Labor-Management Standards

OMO open market operations

OOA out of area

OOP out of pocket

OP outpatient

OPEB other postemployment benefits

OSHA (1) Occupational Safety and Health Act
(2) Occupational Safety and Health Administration

OT occupational therapy

OTC over the counter

OWBPA Older Workers Benefit Protection Act of 1990

OWCP Office of Workers' Compensation Programs

P&L profit and loss statement

P&T pharmacy and therapeutics

P/B price to book

P/E price/earnings

PA (1) pension adjustment
(2) performance appraisal
(3) physician's assistant

PADRO plan-approved domestic relations order

PAR pension adjustment reversal

PARCA Patient Access to Responsible Health Care Act of 1997

PAT preadmission testing

PAYG pay as you go

PBGC Pension Benefit Guaranty Corporation

PBM (1) pharmacy benefits management
(2) pharmacy benefits manager

PBO projected benefit obligation

PBSA Pension Benefits Standards Act

PCMA Pharmaceutical Care Management Association

PCN (1) primary care network
(2) primary care nurse

PCP primary care physician

PDA Pregnancy Discrimination Act of 1978

PDP prescription drug plan

PEBES Personal Earnings and Benefit Estimate Statement

PEP pension equity plan

PEPPRA Public Employee Pension Plan Reporting and Accountability Act

PFEA Pension Funding Equity Act of 2004

PFS Personal Financial Specialist

PHI protected health information

PHO physician-hospital organization

PHR (1) personal health record
(2) Professional in Human Resources

PIA primary insurance amount

PIN personal identification number

PLR private letter ruling

PMPM per member per month

POP premium-only plan

POS point of service

PPA Pension Protection Act

PPACA Patent Protection and Affordable Care Act of 2010 (first version of 2010 health care reform)

PPD permanent partial disability

PPM private placement memorandum

PPO preferred provider organization

PRA Pension Relief Act of 2010

PRD pro-rata distribution

PRI Principles for Responsible Investment

PSAO pharmacy services administrative organization

PSPA past service pension adjustment

PT (1) physical therapy
(2) prohibited transaction

PTCE prohibited transaction class exemption

PTD permanent and total disability

PTE prohibited transaction exemption

PTO paid time off

PWBA Pension and Welfare Benefits Administration (former name for Employee Benefits Security Administration)

QA (1) quality assessment
(2) quality assurance

QACA qualified automatic contribution arrangement

QALY quality adjusted life year

QBU qualified business unit

QC (1) quality control
(2) quarters of coverage

QDRO qualified domestic relations order

QERP qualifying employer real property

QJSA qualified joint-and-survivor annuity

QKA Qualified 401(k) Administrator

QMAC qualified matching contributions

QMB qualified Medicare beneficiary

QMCSO qualified medical child support order

QOSA qualified optional survivor annuity

QPA Qualified Pension Administrator

QPAM Qualified Professional Asset Manager

QPFC Qualified Plan Financial Consultant

QPSA qualified preretirement survivor annuity

R&C reasonable and customary

R/W returned to work

RAN revenue anticipation note

RBP reference-based pricing

RBD required beginning date

RDS retiree drug subsidy

REA Retirement Equity Act of 1984

REIT real estate investment trust

REMIC real estate mortgage investment conduits

REOC real estate operating company

RESPA Real Estate Settlement Procedures Act of 1974

RFI request for information

RFP (1) Registered Financial Planner
(2) request for proposal

RIA registered investment adviser

RICO Racketeer Influenced Corrupt Organizations Act of 1971

RIPA Retirement Income Policy Act of 1985

RLR retired lives reserves

RMA retiree medical account

RMBS reverse mortgage-backed securities

RMD required minimum distribution

ROE return on equity

ROI (1) release of information
(2) return on investment

ROR rate of return

RP (1) Rehabilitation Plan
(2) repurchase agreement

RPA (1) Retirement Protection Act of 1994
(2) Retirement Plans Associate

RPh Registered Pharmacist

RRB real return bond

RSI (1) repetitive strain injury
(2) repetitive stress injury

RTC residential treatment center

RTK right to know

S&P Standard & Poor's

S/HMO social/health maintenance organization

SAR (1) stock appreciation right
(2) summary annual report

SAVER Savings Are Vital to Everyone's Retirement Act of 1997

SBJPA Small Business Job Protection Act of 1996

SCHIP State Children's Health Insurance Program

SCP Self-Correction Program

SDI state disability insurance

SEC Securities and Exchange Commission

SEPPAA Single Employer Pension Plan Amendments Act of 1986

SFAS Statement of Financial Accounting Standards

SHOP Small Business Health Options Program

SIPC Securities Investor Protection Corporation

SLMA Student Loan Marketing Association (Sallie Mae)

SMA separately managed account

SMI (1) serious mental illness
(2) supplementary medical insurance

SMM summary of material modifications

SNF skilled nursing facility

SNP special needs plan

SOP standard operating procedure

SOX Sarbanes-Oxley Act of 2002

SPD summary plan description

SPDA single premium deferred annuity

SRI socially responsible investing

SSA (1) Social Security Act of 1935
(2) Social Security Administration

SSDI Social Security Disability Insurance

SSI Supplemental Security Income

SSN Social Security Number

SSOP second surgical opinion program

SSRA Social Security retirement age

STD (1) sexually transmitted disease
(2) short-term disability

STIF short-term investment fund

TAMRA Technical and Miscellaneous Revenue Act of 1988

TDB temporary disability benefits

TDD/TTY telecommunications device for the deaf/teletypewriter

TDI temporary disability insurance

TEFRA Tax Equity and Fiscal Responsibility Act

TI terminal illness

TIN Individual Taxpayer Identification Number

TIPRA Tax Increase Prevention and Reconciliation Act of 2005

TIPS Treasury inflation-protected securities

TMWX Wilshire 5000 Total Market Index

TPA third-party administrator

TRA (1) Tax Reform Acts 1984, 1986
(2) Taxpayer Relief Act of 1997

TRS total return swap

TSA tax-sheltered annuity

U&C usual and customary

UAAL unfunded actuarial accrued liability

UBTI unrelated business taxable income

UCR usual, customary and reasonable

UI unemployment insurance

UIT unit investment trust

UM utilization management

UPIA Uniform Prudent Investors Act

UPIN unique physician identifier number

UPP uniform pension plan

UR utilization review

URAC Utilization Review Accreditation Commission

URO utilization review organization

U.S.C. United States Code

USERRA Uniformed Services Employment and Reemployment Rights Act of 1994

UVB unfunded vested benefits

UVBL unfunded vested benefits liability

UVL unfunded vested liability

VA (Department of) Veterans Affairs

VBHM value-based health management

VBO vested benefit obligation

VCP Voluntary Correction Program

VCR (1) variable coupon renewable note
(2) Voluntary Compliance Resolution Program

VEBA voluntary employees' beneficiary association

VFCP Voluntary Fiduciary Compliance Program

VIPPS Verified Internet Pharmacy Provider Sites™

W-2 Wage and Tax Statement

WC workers' compensation

WFTRA Working Families Tax Relief Act of 2004

WHCRA Women's Health and Cancer Rights Act of 1998

WHEA Women's Health Equity Act of 1990

WPPDA Welfare and Pension Plans Disclosure Act

WRERA Worker, Retiree, and Employer Recovery Act of 2008

XRA expected retirement age

YBE year's basic exemption

YMPE year's maximum pensionable earnings

YTM yield to maturity

YRT yearly renewable term

YTD year to date

YTM yield to maturity

Index

B

C

D

E

F

G

H

I

J

L

M

N

O

P

T

U

V

W

Y

Z